WOOD TECHNOLOGY

WOOD TECHNOLOGY

G. E. BAKER
University of Missouri, Columbia

L. DAYLE YEAGER
East Texas State University, Commerce

HOWARD W. SAMS & CO., INC.
INDIANAPOLIS

To:

Judy and Betty Jayne for their support, help, and sufferance.

FIRST EDITION

Second Printing—1976

International Standard Book Number: 0-672-20917-9
Library of Congress Catalog Card Number: 72-83817

Contents

Section I

WOOD — A VITAL INDUSTRY

Section II

DESIGN OF WOOD PRODUCTS

Section III

SAFETY IN WOODWORKING

Section IV

BASIC TOOL PROCESSES

Section V

ASSEMBLY AND FINISHING

Section VI

LATHEWORK

Section VII

MASS PRODUCTION

Section VIII

WOOD IN THE WORLD OF CONSTRUCTION

Section IX

UPHOLSTERY

Acknowledgments

The authors wish to recognize Dr. Niel Edmunds for his assistance in preparing portions of the section on mass production and Mr. Eldred Adams for his assistance in preparing portions of the unit on laminations.

The authors also recognize the following firms for their generous contributions and assistance. Without their technical help and aid with illustrations, this text would have been impossible.

Adjustable Clamp Company

Aluminum Company of America

American Forest Institute

Arco Chemical Company

Black & Decker Mfg. Co., The

Boice Crane, A Division of
Wilton Corp.

Brett-Guard Division, The Foredom
Electric Company, Inc.

California Redwood Association

Conwed Corporation

Deft

DeVilbiss Company, The

duPont de Nemours, E. S. & Co., Inc.

Fine Hardwoods Association

Ford Motor Company

Frank Paxton Lumber Co.

General Motors Corporation

Idaco Engineering & Equipment Co.

Irwin Auger Bit Company, The

Kingsberry Homes, Boise Cascade
Corporation

Lindal Cedar Homes, Inc.

Lyon Metal Products, Inc

Masonite Corporation

Minwax Company, Inc.

Moore Dry Kiln Company

Monsanto Company

Murphy-Miller, Inc.

NASA (National Aeronautics and
Space Administration)

National Gypsum Association

National Homes Corporation

Nicholson File Company

Oliver Machinery Company

Onsrud Machine Works, Inc.

Paslode, Signode Corporation

Potlatch Forests, Inc.

Powermatic, Houdaille Industries, Inc.

Proctor Products Company

Republic Steel Corporation

Rockwell Manufacturing Company,
Power Tool Division

Rolscreen Company, Pelle

Sellstrom Manufacturing Company

Seng Company, The

Stanley Works, The

Starrett Company, The L. S.

Thomasville Furniture Industries, Inc.

Timber Structures, Inc.

United States Plywood Corporation

Western Wood Products Association

Westinghouse Electric Corporation

Weyerhauser Company

Preface

The intent of this textbook is to bridge the gap between traditional industrial education wood programs and the new innovations developing in the field. The authors intend this book to be the first comprehensive textbook that permits the study of woodworking, construction, and manufacturing from a single textbook. In addition to these concepts, the authors have attempted to incorporate the newest industrial developments in wood technology that are adaptable to the school shop. Particular emphasis has been placed upon the use of power hand tools, with less stress on the operation of specialized production tools.

Potential career education materials have been provided in the first section, which explores the various processes in the broad spectrum of wood-using industries. In addition, the authors feel this textbook is unique in providing insights and learning activities in environmental factors relating to wood technology. Furthermore, the design is approached from a functional standpoint that attempts to provide reasons for the design factors, rather than the rote memory process of both functional and aesthetic design.

The authors, who have taught woodworking at various levels from junior high school through college and who have worked in the woods industries, have attempted to provide solutions to the problems in wood programs today that they have experienced as practitioners. They hope that in doing so the textbook will be used by teachers, and written by teachers.

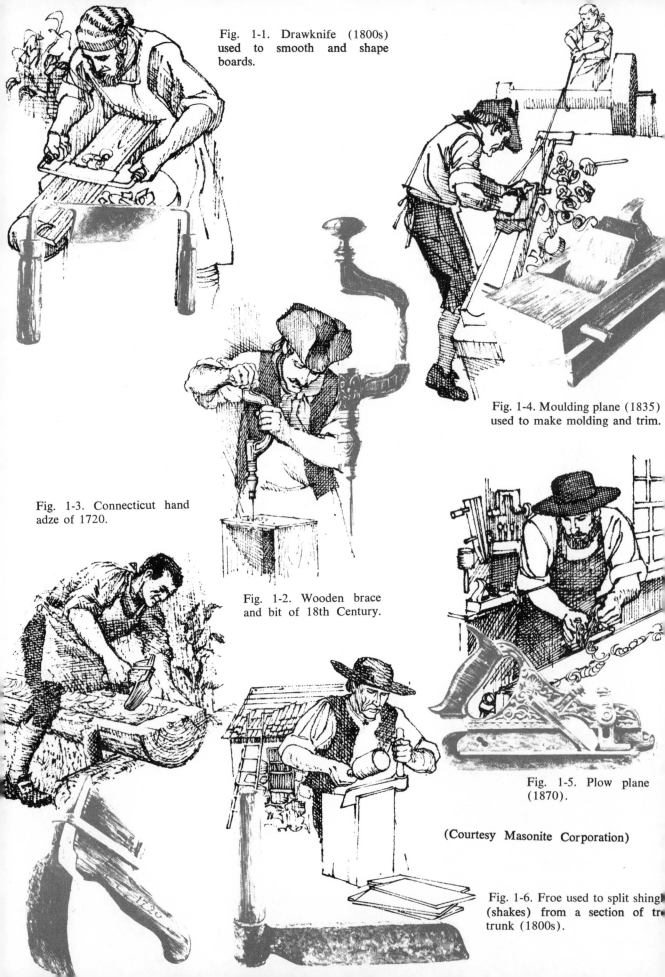

Fig. 1-1. Drawknife (1800s) used to smooth and shape boards.

Fig. 1-4. Moulding plane (1835) used to make molding and trim.

Fig. 1-3. Connecticut hand adze of 1720.

Fig. 1-2. Wooden brace and bit of 18th Century.

Fig. 1-5. Plow plane (1870).

(Courtesy Masonite Corporation)

Fig. 1-6. Froe used to split shingles (shakes) from a section of tree trunk (1800s).

Wood—A Vital Industry

Unit 1– The Importance and Development of the Wood Industries

Wood was perhaps the earliest plastic or shapable material that man could work or fashion into useful objects. Thousands of years ago, man used tools made of wood to kill animals for his food, wooden frames with flinted cutting edges to cut his grain, and pieces of wood to form the framework of his dwelling. As his knowledge and technology increased, the importance of wood to man increased.

Only a few centuries ago, the metal tools available to man were quite limited. Man made his ships, his machines, and his tools of wood. Wood was relatively easy to shape with the tools and technology available only a few years ago, while metal was both expensive and difficult to shape and form. Some of the early wooden tools available to man are shown in Figs. 1-1 through 1-6. Tools like these began to be replaced by metal tools around 1900—really not many years ago. In fact, wooden tools like those shown in Figs. 1-1 through 1-6 can be purchased in Europe and many other nations today.

Wood in Early America

In the early days of the English colonies, wood was extremely important. In 1600, England was a mighty sea power under Queen Elizabeth I. Only a few years previously, England had defeated the mighty Spanish Armada to become the greatest sea power in the world—all in ships made of wood. England, however, did not have the straight trees in its forests needed to make the masts for her ships.

The first permanent English colony was founded in Jamestown, Virginia in 1607. Captain John Smith was one of the leaders of the colony. During the second and third years of operation of the colony, the Board of Governors, who lived in England, directed Captain Smith either to find gold in Virginia or to find some method of paying the expenses of the colony. Captain Smith could not find gold; but he found a valuable commodity in another form. Virginia had many tall trees. From the vast pine forests of Virginia, also came the products from the trees—turpentine, tar, and pitch. All these products were vital to England, whose might and wealth depended on her wooden ships. Lumbering became the first profitable export industry in North America.

The extent of the availability of trees in the New World was so impressive that an early law in the colonies required the

British Navy to mark all the trees suitable for the masts of ships. These trees were considered the property of the King of England and could not be cut down by the colonists, except at the direction of the British Navy. Needless to say, this was not a popular law in the colonies. One colony in particular, Pennsylvania, was founded on the strength of its vast forests. The name Pennsylvania was derived from two sources: (1) The colony was founded by Sir William Penn, a prime minister of England; and (2) The word "sylvan" is the Latin word for forest. Thus, the word "Pennsylvania" literally means Penn's forests.

During the early years of the United States as an independent nation, both Presidents Washington and Jefferson were concerned so vitally about one of the nation's greatest natural resources— its forests—that they urged conservation practices in harvesting our forests. Both presidents attempted to warn the early Americans of the dangers of soil erosion and of clearing the land completely.

Most Americans thought the forests were so large that it would be impossible to run out of trees. As in the early days of the colonies along the eastern coast, the people of early America supported themselves largely by trade and by their forest resources. During the eighteen hundreds, America expanded westward to the Pacific Ocean. Theodore Roosevelt became president in 1901 and by this time Americans had literally lumbered their way across the nation. Most of the early lumbering was done without regard to conservation practices—only for profit. Since Theodore Roosevelt was an ardent conservationist and outdoorsman, he made great efforts to begin conservation of our forests. He appointed Gifford Pinchot the first Chief Forester of the United

States. Conservation then became a reality. Pinchot felt the need to protect, restore, and perpetuate the forests of the United States by planting forests which could be harvested, seeded, and grown and harvested again, in much the same manner that a farmer harvests, seeds, and grows and harvests his wheat. This was the birth of our modern lumbering industries.

The Need for Conservation

In the early days, the workmen merely cut down all the trees and hauled them away. This was extremely detrimental to conservation of the land, since the trees break up the rainfall as it falls on the land. The force of the raindrops falling from the sky is broken by the leaves and branches of the trees. The humus, which consists of soil, decomposing leaves, and vegetable material, soaks up the water from the rain or melting snow. Then the humus permits the water to seep slowly into the ground. Thus, the water does not run off—it is absorbed. The absorbed water seeps deeply into the earth and provides ground moisture and water for the mountain springs and streams.

When the forests are eliminated, the raindrops fall upon the ground with full force and the soil is packed. The soil becomes hardened and the rainfall runs off, rather than being absorbed. Many tons of soil are carried away by the water that runs off the surface to fill the rivers and streams at flood proportions. Thus, an area which previously has been green and bountiful can be changed into an ugly gash on which only a slight quantity of animal or vegetable material can exist.

A growing tree uses large quantities of water. A hardwood tree, such a birch or a maple, can throw off into the atmosphere as much as eight or nine hundred gallons of water through its leaves in a single summer day. All this water has been absorbed by the tiny root tips below ground; then it moves from the root system into the tips, branches, and leaves. The water is thrown off into the air during the process of photosynthesis. This process is utilized by the tree to form new cellulose or wood cells from the minerals and water, using the energy from sunlight. Large forest areas are considered essential to regulate and to provide adequate rainfall, since large quantities of water are thrown off by the trees. When large areas of trees or forests are removed, the annual rainfall suffers.

Tree Growth

All trees are grown by essentially the same basic process (Fig. 1-7). Tree growth begins, as in most plants, with a seed. The seeds are dormant during the winter. When spring arrives and the earth becomes warm and moist, the seed bursts open and a tiny shoot pushes downward through the soil. This is the root, and it anchors the young tree shoot in place. After the root begins to absorb water and soil nutrients, a slender green stem begins to grow upward. New cells form at the ends of the slender stem to form new twig links. The seedling grows into a sapling, which is a small tree; then the sapling grows into a tree. With sufficient water, minerals, and sunlight, the tree continues to grow taller and larger in diameter each year. The cells at the ends of the roots and the twigs increase the length of the tree. The cells at the tips of the top of the tree increase the height of the tree. Once a cell in a tree has been formed, it retains that location or position in the tree. The trunk does not stretch upward as the tree grows; therefore, a nail driven into a tree trunk at a given

Saplings

Fig. 1-7. Growth cycle of a tree from seed to maturity. (Courtesy St. Regis Paper Company)

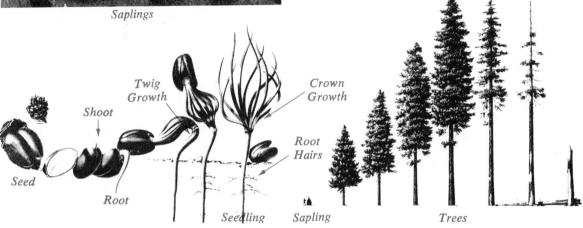

Seed · Shoot · Root · Twig Growth · Seedling · Crown Growth · Root Hairs · Sapling · Trees

spot remains in that spot until the tree falls. The nail does not increase or decrease in height on the trunk of the tree.

In a tree trunk, only a small portion is active, or alive. The living parts are the root tips, leaves, buds and flowers, and the thin layer of cells called the *cambium*. The cambium layer does all the work; it brings the moisture and the nutrients from the roots upward to the new tips and leaves. As the tree grows, the older cambium cells become inactive in the winter, lose their moisture, and become part of the sapwood.

The cambium is the layer of cells in which the growth occurs. The cambium cells thicken and divide to form new growth on both the inner (or sapwood) and bark sides of the cambium layer. The sapwood is softer than the heartwood, since it contains more moisture.

A cross section of a typical tree trunk is diagrammed in Fig. 1-8. The heartwood is the rigid portion of the tree; it provides strength and support. This lifeless core, or heartwood, is the principle source of lumber and pulp from the tree. The cambium and bark supply the chemicals, wood distillates, and, to some extent, fuel. The cambium layer is only a few cells deep; the cells formed on the outer side of the layer form new bark, and the older

cells are no longer active as the cambium becomes moist sapwood which, in turn, becomes heartwood. The cambium is the portion which absorbs and transmits moisture from the roots to the tops; it forms a new growth ring each spring as the tree begins to grow. These growth rings, sometimes known as annular rings, permit the tree to be dated. Archaeologists often use the annular rings to date building sites; this often can be done accurately within a 5-year period. The Indian ruins and cliff dwellings in the Southwest, such as Mesa Verde (Fig. 1-9), have been dated quite accurately by this technique.

The oldest tree known is a small, gnarled bristle-cone pine in eastern California. This tree is known to be more than four thousand years old. Scientists have determined its age by boring a small hole into the center, removing the core formed by the boring tool, and then counting and examining the rings. The giant sequoia or redwood trees in California also are known to be very, very old. Some of these trees are more than one thousand years old.

Harvesting Trees

The three processes of harvesting trees are: (1) Clear cutting; (2) Selective cut-

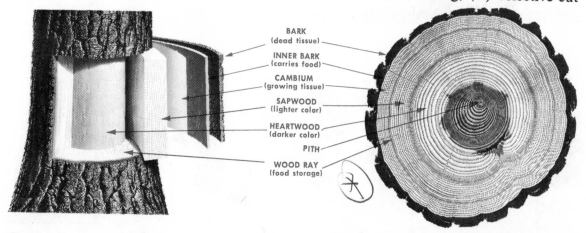

BARK
(dead tissue)

INNER BARK
(carries food)

CAMBIUM
(growing tissue)

SAPWOOD
(lighter color)

HEARTWOOD
(darker color)

PITH

WOOD RAY
(food storage)

Fig. 1-8. Cutaway view (left) and cross section (right) of tree trunk. (Courtesy St. Regis Paper Company)

Fig. 1-9. Indian cliff dwellings at Mesa Verde, Colorado dated archaeologically by growth patterns in the wood used in construction of the dwellings.

Fig. 1-10. On the large tree farms, timber is managed as a crop for a perpetual supply of wood. The harvesting methods are based on the growth habits of the Douglas fir tree. Since the seedlings do not thrive in the deep shade of older and larger trees, a logging system called forest area selection is used. Selected blocks or strips of timber are cut and intermittent islands of trees are left unharvested to serve as a seed source. Thus, forests are replaced faster than they are harvested. (Courtesy Weyerhaeuser Company)

ting; and (3) Seed-tree cutting. All three of these methods are utilized to obtain maximum yield without devastating the forests.

Clear Cutting

Clear cutting is practiced when all the trees in an area are cut down. In other words, the land is cleared entirely of the trees. In modern practices, these tracts of land generally are small, including only about one hundred acres. By alternating a cleared area with the tree growth areas, soil conservation is maintained (Fig. 1-10).

Selective Cutting

Selective cutting is used principally to harvest trees that grow well in the shade of other trees. These trees include the ponderosa pine, spruce, and some hardwood trees such as walnut, oak, and maple. In selective cutting, a lumberman proceeds through the forest, marking the trees for cutting with a bright-colored paint (Fig. 1-11). The lumber crews then cut only the marked trees, being careful to spare the other trees; then they remove the selected trees from the forested areas.

Seed-Tree Cutting

Seed-tree cutting is a variation of clear cutting. Normally, it is done in the South-

Fig. 1-11. A skilled forester marks a pine tree for harvesting on a tree farm in Eastern Oregon for selective cutting. The tree farms are managed to produce an orderly harvest of mature timber in balance with growth, economic demands, and community stability. (Courtesy Weyerhaeuser Company)

ern forests; four or five trees are left on each acre of ground cleared. These large seed trees then "reseed" the area that has been harvested. A southern pine can reseed a large area merely by means of the wind distributing the seeds around the standing tree.

Lumbering Today

The modern major lumbering industries do not harvest the trees—they grow them. Vast tracts of land are used in a continuous process of growing and harvesting trees. The major differences between a tree farm and other types of farms lie in the size of the farm and the length of time required to grow a new crop of trees. To grow a crop of trees for harvest can require twenty-five to one hundred fifty years. During this time, great care is required for the growing trees. This is necessary during the growth periods, for the same reasons that it is necessary for a farmer to tend his field crops during their growing period. The modern lumber industry selects the sites, plants the trees, tends and cares for them, and harvests them at the proper time.

In the early lumbering industries, men cut down the trees with axes or crosscut handsaws. The men who worked on the logging crews were called "lumberjacks." The legendary lumberjack, Paul Bunyan, and his great ox are the basis of many "tall tales" about various deeds of great strength and ability. The early lumberjacks cut the trees with hand axes and hauled the lumber to civilization or to the rivers, using teams of oxen. Paul Bunyan's ox, Blue Babe, was nearly as famous as the lengendary lumberman himself.

Lumber camps often were located along the banks of the rivers; then the cut trees or logs could be pushed into the river and floated cheaply in huge log rafts downstream to cities and towns where they were cut into lumber at the sawmills. The sawmills cut the best of the lumber and discarded the remainder. Huge mountains of sawdust, wood chips, and scrap pieces of wood were burned only because there was no other use for them.

Today, the modern lumbering industries are still using the rivers for logging (Figs. 1-12 and 1-13). However, they are using trucks to haul the logs (Fig. 1-14); motorized chain saws (Figs. 1-15 and 1-16) to cut down the trees; airplanes to fight the forest fires; tree pullers to fell the trees (Fig. 1-17); and helicopters to seed the new forest lands (Fig. 1-18). Various methods are used to replant seedlings (Figs. 1-19 through 1-21). Balloons also are used to haul the trees. They permit the remote areas to be reached without cutting roads, thereby saving both time and expense in making the roads and in saving trees which would have been ruined or cut in building the roads.

Fig. 1-12. Manpower is the first tactic employed by loggers to move snagged logs back into the current to continue their journey downstream. Most logs reach their destination without incident, but some logs become snagged on sandbars, islands, or along the river bank, requiring coaxing to resume their 90-mile trip. (Courtesy Potlatch Forests, Inc.)

Fig. 1-13. Transporting logs by barge. (Courtesy Potlatch Forests, Inc.)

Fig. 1-14. On this tree farm in western Washington, the logs are pulled by cable to a portable steel tower. Trucks transport the logs to a sawmill. (Courtesy Weyerhaeuser Company)

Fig. 1-15. Winter logging in the Clearwater mountains of Idaho. (Courtesy Potlatch Forests, Inc.)

Fig. 1-16. A good faller can drop a 220-foot fir tree exactly where he wants it to fall—where it will not break or damage other trees. Here, the logger's chain saw bites out an undercut wedge to direct the tree's fall. (Courtesy Weyerhaeuser Company)

Fig. 1-17. This Omark Model C-10 tree harvester is used by the Northwest Paper Company on northern Minnesota pulpwood tree farms. Depending on conditions, in 60 seconds it can fall, limb, top, buck, and stack an entire tree, using only one operator. (Courtesy Potlatch Forests, Inc.)

Fig. 1-18. This aerial-seeding helicopter hovers in midair while preparing to drop millions of Douglas fir seeds at the Weyerhaeuser Company's 500,000-acre St. Helen's Tree Farm in western Washington. The helicopters insure adequate and quick reforestation of harvested forest land. A one-mile square area receives more than 25 million seeds. (Courtesy Weyerhaeuser Company)

Fig. 1-19. Seven hundred Norway pine seedlings per hour can be replanted with this planting machine. (Courtesy Potlatch Forests, Inc.)

Fig. 1-20. Experiments are made continually to discover new methods of replanting. Here, the seedlings are grown for six weeks in sheltered plastic tubes before planting. (Courtesy Potlatch Forests, Inc.)

Fig. 1-21. The seedling is planted in its tiny soil-filled tube, which permits ease of handling during planting. (Courtesy Potlatch Forests, Inc.)

Fig. 1-22. The head sawyer is a key man in the production of quality wood products. He must know how to cut each log to obtain the most value from it. The logs are sawed into huge rough slices; then they are moved through the mill for further cutting and shaping. (Courtesy Weyerhaeuser Company)

Using the Whole Tree

The modern lumbering industries saw the wood into desirable pieces, as in the old days. Many different processes, such as the large band saw used to cut the logs in Fig. 1-22, are used in sawing. In addition, the products previously considered to be "waste" now are saved and utilized for many different products. The entire tree is utilized, where only a portion of the tree was used previously. As shown in Fig. 1-23, the bark of the tree can be used for fuel, the cambium and sapwood layers of the tree are used for veneers, and the heart of the tree can be used for lumber, timber, pulp, or chemicals. The chemicals derived from wood also comprise many of the chemicals used in making plastics.

In the past, man was extremely wasteful when he had more forests than he could cut. He used the heartwood of the tree for lumber and pulp for paper; he used the sap and juices for chemicals, such as turpentine and pitch or tar; and he used the fruits and berries for food products. However, since our forests have become increasingly more precious in recent years, man has turned to research to find methods of utilizing all the parts of the tree.

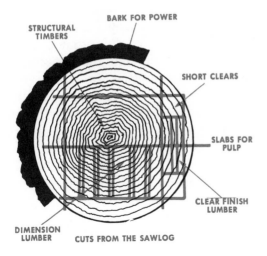

BARK FOR POWER

STRUCTURAL
TIMBERS

SHORT CLEARS

SLABS FOR
PULP

CLEAR FINISH
LUMBER

DIMENSION
LUMBER   CUTS FROM THE SAWLOG

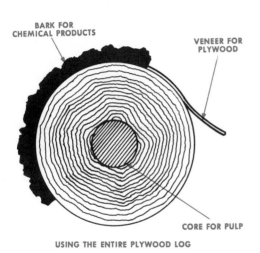

BARK FOR
CHEMICAL PRODUCTS

VENEER FOR
PLYWOOD

CORE FOR PULP

USING THE ENTIRE PLYWOOD LOG

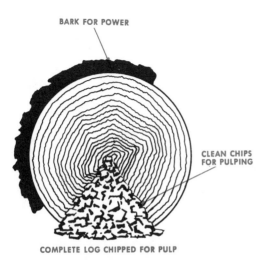

BARK FOR POWER

CLEAN CHIPS
FOR PULPING

COMPLETE LOG CHIPPED FOR PULP

Fig. 1-23. Typical products from a tree log.

Wood Products

The trees can be used for wood and fuels; the bark can be used for insulation, drugs, adhesives, and chemicals in tanning hides. The leaves and needles are used for various oils, such as pine oil and cedar oil, and even the sawdust from cutting the lumber is used. Hardboard and particle board are products of the chips formed during the lumber cutting processes; these products previously were burned or dumped. Now, the chips are used in producing additional usable construction materials.

The sawdust is used in producing plastics, paint, custodial supplies, and composition flooring, such as tiles and linoleum; also, it is used in filters, insulation, and many other products which require the basic wood chemicals. Other wood products include chemicals, cardboard, and various other items. Wood products are used in paper for reading and writing, and in the heavier papers and felts for roofing, decking, and waterproofing. The oils and spirits used for medicines are derived from the needles and leaves of trees. Explosives, gardening and soil conditioners, fertilizers, and countless other uses are devised from wood and wood products.

Even some of our food comes from forest products. The long-known maple syrup is a wood product. Other food products include sugar, fruit, berries, and nuts. A person on a reducing diet might use diet pills to reduce his appetite; these pills might be only wood filler which expands in the stomach to prevent hunger.

The limbs, trimmings, and all parts of the trees are now utilized. This has increased greatly the productive output of our forests. In the past, when only the lumber was the primary product, only 35 to 40 percent of the tree was considered useful. Today, through research and careful study of our forests and their products, man successfully can use 70 to 80 percent of the wood products.

It is evident that there are many uses of wood, other than for the wood itself. Many products made from wood and trees are vital to the industrial development and standard of living of man. As Captain John Smith found in the early Jamestown colony, great wealth lies in the products of the forests.

Many uses of forest products are indicated in the diagrams in Fig. 1-24. A modern industrial plant in Oklahoma, for example, produces insulation board, sheathing, and several other wood-fiber products from wood chips. The process requires large quantities of water. In former years, the process used the water and then permitted it to run off to pollute rivers and streams. Now, the plant reprocesses this water to produce useful elements for chemicals, salvaging many of the particles which formerly polluted the water.

Another industrial plant in Arkansas, in the Southern Forest, formerly burned the bark for fuel, and the process produced large quantities of dense, black smoke. Now, the material formerly used for fuel is fed into a carbonizing unit and made into charcoal for the charcoal briquets used in charcoal grills for cooking. The other waste products formerly burned with the bark are now placed in a special burning unit in which the remainder of the dense black smoke is recycled and used for fuel, resulting in approximately a 50-percent increase in efficiency, along with a large decrease in pollution.

This does not mean that pollution has been conquered entirely. Nearly all the forest industries are concerned with conservation and pollution, and they spend vast sums of money to overcome these problems. However, man must continue to seek ways and means of improving his industrial plants and factories with respect to efficiency, utilization of materials, and reduction of pollution.

Fig. 1-24. Forest products and their uses. (Courtesy American Forest Institute)

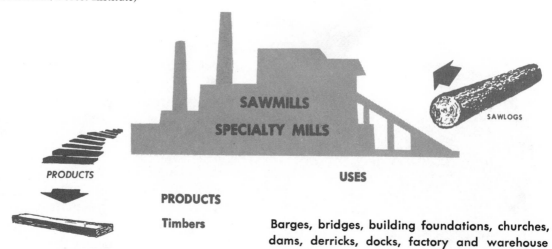

PRODUCTS

Timbers

Barges, bridges, building foundations, churches, dams, derricks, docks, factory and warehouse buildings, mine timbers, schools, ships, stringers, trailers, trucks, tugs

Construction Lumber

Beams, boards, boat hulls and parts, dimension of all kinds, factory flooring, form lumber, heavy framing, joists, light framing, planks, posts, rafters, sheathing, sills, studs, subfloors, walls.

Finished Lumber

Baseboard, battens, casing, ceiling, flooring, lath, paneling, pickets, scaffolding, ship decking, siding, stepping

Remanufactured Lumber

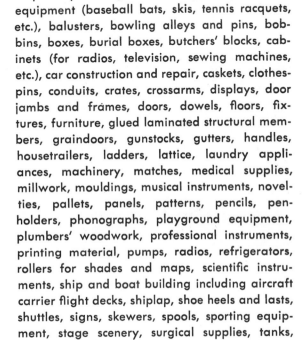

Airplane parts, agricultural implements, athletic equipment (baseball bats, skis, tennis racquets, etc.), balusters, bowling alleys and pins, bobbins, boxes, burial boxes, butchers' blocks, cabinets (for radios, television, sewing machines, etc.), car construction and repair, caskets, clothespins, conduits, crates, crossarms, displays, door jambs and frames, doors, dowels, floors, fixtures, furniture, glued laminated structural members, graindoors, gunstocks, gutters, handles, housetrailers, ladders, lattice, laundry appliances, machinery, matches, medical supplies, millwork, mouldings, musical instruments, novelties, pallets, panels, patterns, pencils, penholders, phonographs, playground equipment, plumbers' woodwork, professional instruments, printing material, pumps, radios, refrigerators, rollers for shades and maps, scientific instruments, ship and boat building including aircraft carrier flight decks, shiplap, shoe heels and lasts, shuttles, signs, skewers, spools, sporting equipment, stage scenery, surgical supplies, tanks, toothpicks, toys, trim, trunks, valises, vehicles, venetian blinds, wedges, window frames, wood pipe, wooden shoes, woodenware

Ties

Railroad cross ties, mine ties, switch ties

Cooperage (Staves)

Barrels, buckets, cooling towers, kegs, pipes, silos, tanks, tubs

Miscellaneous

Acid washers, benches, corncribs, dunnage, elevators, fence pickets, grain bins, insulator pins, planks, reels, shingles, stakes, trestles, tunnel and mine props, wood chips for making wood pulp, wood turnings (for buttons, jewelry, etc.)

Residues

Fuel, planer shavings for compressed fuel logs and briquettes, poultry litter and raw material for hardboard, particle board and other bark, pulp and sawdust products (such as sawdust soil conditioner)

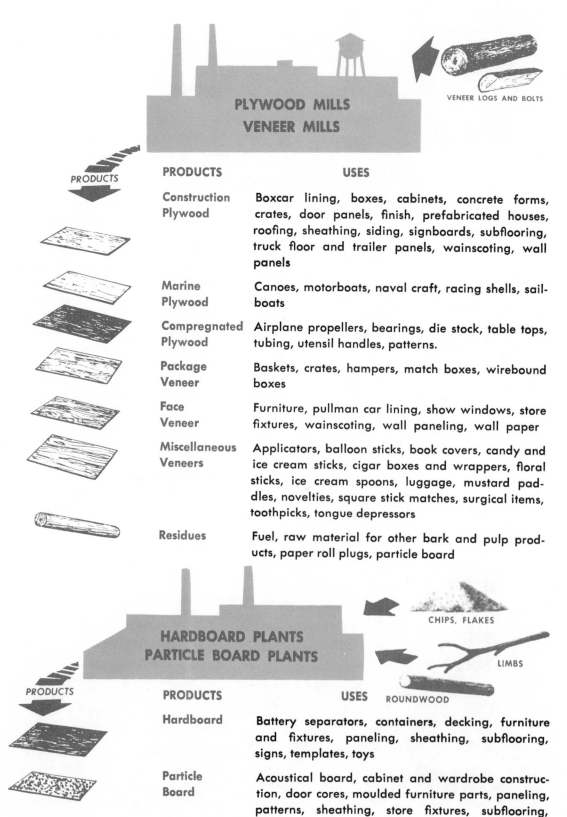

PLYWOOD MILLS
VENEER MILLS

VENEER LOGS AND BOLTS

PRODUCTS

PRODUCTS	USES
Construction Plywood	Boxcar lining, boxes, cabinets, concrete forms, crates, door panels, finish, prefabricated houses, roofing, sheathing, siding, signboards, subflooring, truck floor and trailer panels, wainscoting, wall panels
Marine Plywood	Canoes, motorboats, naval craft, racing shells, sailboats
Compregnated Plywood	Airplane propellers, bearings, die stock, table tops, tubing, utensil handles, patterns.
Package Veneer	Baskets, crates, hampers, match boxes, wirebound boxes
Face Veneer	Furniture, pullman car lining, show windows, store fixtures, wainscoting, wall paneling, wall paper
Miscellaneous Veneers	Applicators, balloon sticks, book covers, candy and ice cream sticks, cigar boxes and wrappers, floral sticks, ice cream spoons, luggage, mustard paddles, novelties, square stick matches, surgical items, toothpicks, tongue depressors
Residues	Fuel, raw material for other bark and pulp products, paper roll plugs, particle board

HARDBOARD PLANTS
PARTICLE BOARD PLANTS

CHIPS, FLAKES

LIMBS

PRODUCTS

PRODUCTS	USES	ROUNDWOOD
Hardboard	Battery separators, containers, decking, furniture and fixtures, paneling, sheathing, subflooring, signs, templates, toys	
Particle Board	Acoustical board, cabinet and wardrobe construction, door cores, moulded furniture parts, paneling, patterns, sheathing, store fixtures, subflooring, window displays	

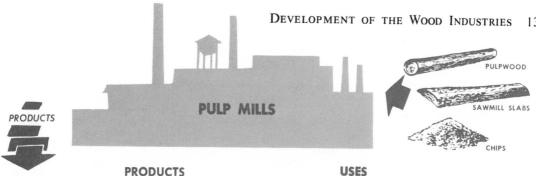

PRODUCTS	USES

Sulphite Pulp

Paper and paperboard for bags, blotters, printing papers, boxes, bristol board, envelopes, folding box-board, fruit wrappers, greaseproof packaging, insulation, labels, paper napkins, patent coated boards, photo processing paper, sanitary tissues, stationery, stencils, tag board, wall paper, waterproof packaging, wrapping

Dissolving pulps for cellophane, explosives, lacquers, plastics, photo film, rayon

Sulphate Pulp

Paper and paperboard for bags, printing papers, bond paper, boxes, bristol board, chart paper, coating raw stock, condenser tissues, corrugated box-board, envelopes, food containers, folding boxboard, insulation, ledger paper, liner board, offset paper, onion-skin, parchment, sheathing paper, stationery, tag stock, towels, twisted cord and rope, waxed paper

Soda Pulp

Paper and paperboard for blotters, printing papers, bristol board, corrugated paper, filters, insulating and wall boards, labels, liners for coated boards, stationery, testliners

Semi-Chemical Pulp

Corrugated paper, egg cartons, insulating board, test liners, wall board, printing papers, glassine paper

Groundwood Pulp

Absorbent papers, bags, boards, building and insulating papers, newsprint, printing papers, wall board, wood cement boards and blocks, wrapping paper, writing papers

Residues
(Liquor containing left-over cellulose and lignin not used in paper manufacture)

Sulphite liquors used in making adhesives, building briquettes, core binder, cymene, dyes, emulsifiers, ethyl alcohol, fatty acids, feeding yeast, fertilizers, fuel briquettes, lineoleum cement, mordants, paint and varnish remover, plastics, road binder, tannins, vanillin

Sulphate liquors used in making acetic acid, acetone, dimethyl-sulphide, fatty acids, furfural, methyl alcohol, oxalic acid, pine oil, rosin soap, rosin acids, tall oil, turpentine, ore flotation, pharmaceutical chemicals

Soda liquors used in making acetic acid, acetone, calcium carbonate, methyl alcohol, oxalic acid, plastics

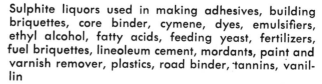

WOOD DISTILLATION PLANTS

BOLTS
· LIMBS
STUMPS
EDGINGS

HARDWOOD DISTILLATION PRODUCTS

PRODUCTS	USES
Acetic Acid	Acetate solvents, cellulose acetate for rayon, photo film, lacquers, and plastics; coagulant for latex, perfumes, and textile dyeing; manufacturing inorganic acetates, white lead pigments
Acetone	Acetylene, explosives (cordite), solvent
Charcoal	Activated carbon, black powder explosives, chemical manufacture, fuel, livestock and poultry foods, manufacturing charcoal iron, medicines, metacase hardening compounds, producer gas, water purification
Methanol	Antifreeze, dry-cleaning agents, formaldehyde, manufacturing chemical compounds, paints, pyroxylins, shellac, textile finishing agents, varnishes
Pitch	Insulation in electric transformers, rubber filler
Tar Oil	Flotation oils, gasoline (inhibitor oil), paints and stains, preservatives, solvent oils, wood creosote

SOFTWOOD DISTILLATION PRODUCTS

PRODUCTS	USES
Cedar Oils	Furniture polish
Charcoal	Activated carbon, black powder explosives, chemical manufacture, fuel, livestock and poultry foods, manufacturing charcoal iron, medicines, metacase hardening compounds, water filtration
Creosote Oils	Cattle and sheep dips, disinfectants, medicines
Dipentene	Solvent for reclaiming old rubber
Lacquer Solvent	Lacquers, paints, varnish
Pine Oil	Disinfectants, fabric dyeing, flotation oil, paints
Pine Tar	Coating and binding materials, disinfectants, manufacturing cordage, medicines, oakum, soaps

Rosin	Paper sizing, varnish, soap, greases, waterproofing, linoleum
Tar Oil Solvents	Disinfectants, flotation oils, paints, soaps, stains
Wood Turpentine	Paint and varnish manufacture, synthetic camphor for celluloid manufacture

Growing repeated timber crops is the main purpose of a Tree Farm. From trees the forest industries make thousands of things, like lumber and paper, that enrich our lives.

Tree farming also means good streams for fishing; water for home and industry; wooded areas for recreation; food and homes for wildlife; jobs for millions of workers in the woods and mills.

Through the American Tree Farm System, operated by the wood-using industries, people are encouraged to grow timber as a crop on taxpaying lands. This is tree farming. It means wood for today and tomorrow.

On this chart are shown many products of a Tree Farm and how they move from the forest to you through various forest industry plants; how, in some cases, one plant's leftovers become another's raw material.

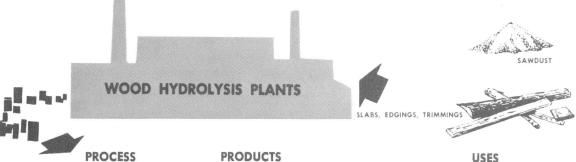

WOOD HYDROLYSIS PLANTS

SAWDUST

SLABS, EDGINGS, TRIMMINGS

PROCESS	PRODUCTS	USES
WOOD HYDROLYSIS	**Acetic Acid**	Textile manufacture, white lead pigment, cellulose acetate, perfume
	Baking Yeast	Bakery products
	Butadiene	Synthetic rubber
	Carbonic Acid	Industrial chemicals
	Ethyl Alcohol	Solvents
	Animal Food	Cattle feed, chicken feed
	Furfural	Resins, plastics
	Glycerine	Medicines, industrial chemicals
	Lignin Powder	Plastics and laminates
	Sugars	Stock feed, ethanol

WOOD CONDENSATION	Furfural	Resins, plastics
	Soil Conditioner	To make soils more porous
ALKALINE FUSION	Oxalic Acid	Bleaching, industrial chemicals
	Pyrogallol	Stains
	Resins	Plastics

MISCELLANEOUS PRODUCTS

PRODUCTS	USES
Poles, Posts, Pilings 	Antennae, arbors, bridges, channel markers, dams, docks, pole frame buildings, fence posts, flag poles, foundations, guard rails, jetties, levees, revetments, sign posts, tank traps, telephone poles, weirs, wharves
Fuelwood	Fireplace, stove, steam boilers
Sap and Gum 	Balsam, birch beer, butternut syrup, gumthus, heptane, larch (Venetian turp.), maple sugar, mesquite gum, rosin, spruce gum, storax, turpentine
Bark	Adhesives, birch (flavoring) oil, cascara (drug), clothing (wood wool), drilling mud dispersants (oil industry), dye (osage orange and black oak), insulating wool, slippery elm (drug), soil building, tannins (hemlock, chestnut and tanbark oak.)
Edible Fruits 	Butternuts, chinquapins, hickory nuts, pawpaws, pecans, pinon nuts, serviceberries, walnuts, wild plums
Needles	Pine and cedar needle oil
Sawdust	Absorbent for explosives, artificial leather, artificial wood, body for paint, butcher shops, camouflage, clay products, composition flooring, curing concrete, filler for linoleum, filter for oil and gas, fireworks, glues, hand soaps, ice storage, insulating, insulating brick, livestock bedding, meat smoking, mild abrasives for cleaners, moth deterrent, nursery mulch, packing, plastics, soil conditioners, and wood flour for billiard balls, bowling balls, explosives, moulded products
Roofing Felts 	Roll roofing, shingles
Christmas Trees	Ornamentals

Questions

1. List several reasons why wood was an important natural resource in the English colonies of America?
2. Who was appointed the first Chief Forester of the United States?
3. When were the first steps made toward conservation of our forests?
4. Why are trees important to soil conservation?
5. In what part of the tree does the growth occur?
6. How do the "hardwood" and "cambium" differ?
7. What methods of cutting are used to harvest trees?
8. What is the principal use of the wood in a tree?
9. How is the wood used to produce other products?

Unit 2 – Forests and Trees

Eight major forest areas are found in the United States; some of these areas produce only one or two types of trees, while other forest areas produce many types of trees. The locations of these forests can be found in Fig. 2-1.

Forest Regions of the United States

The eight major forest regions of the United States are the Alaskan Forest, Hawaiian Forest, West Coast Forest, Western Forest, Central Hardwood Forest, Tropical Forest, Northern Forest, and Southern Forest. These forests are part of America's most vital resources, since most of this nation's timber and wood products are derived from approximately thirty-five types of trees found in the eight major forest areas. The most frequently used woods and their sources are listed in Table 2-1.

West Coast Forest

The West Coast Forest produces approximately one-third of the United States needs in lumber. It produces approximately one-fifth the pulpwood used to make paper, and nearly all the fir plywood produced in the United States. The forest is located along the western slopes of the Rocky Mountains in Washington, Oregon, and northern California. Some of these areas receive more than one hundred inches of rain each year, most of which is brought in by breezes blowing inward from the Pacific Ocean. The trees included in these forests are the giant redwoods, spruce, and Douglas fir. The West Coast Forest contains approximately three-fourths of the Douglas fir timber in the United States. Douglas fir is

used for construction work and for very long beams and rafters; its most important uses are in plywood, pulp paper, and telephone poles. The less-numerous types of trees include the spruce, various pines, and various species of cedars and other firs.

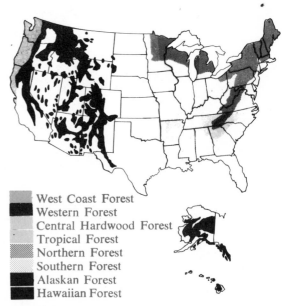

West Coast Forest
Western Forest
Central Hardwood Forest
Tropical Forest
Northern Forest
Southern Forest
Alaskan Forest
Hawaiian Forest

Fig. 2-1. Major forest areas of the United States.

Western Forest

The Western Forest rambles over approximately twelve states and produces about 20 percent of the lumber used in the United States. The area has less rainfall and is less prolific in its production of timber than the West Coast Forest. The Western Forest extends from Canada to Mexico, and its width stretches from the middle of the Rocky Mountains to the eastern slopes of the Rocky Mountains. The most predominant species of trees are the ponderosa, Idaho, and sugar pines. Some Douglas fir and white fir are included; also included are some cedars,

Table 2-1. Wood Properties

WOOD SPECIES	COLOR (heartwood)	WORKABILITY (hand tools)	HARDNESS	STRENGTH	COST
Hardwoods					
Ash, white	off-white	hard	hard	high	medium
Balsa	cream white	easy	soft	low	medium
Basswood	cream white	easy	soft	low	medium
Beech	light brown	hard	hard	high	medium
Birch	light brown	hard	hard	high	high
Cherry	medium reddish-brown	hard	hard	high	high
Gum, red	reddish-brown	medium	medium	medium	medium to high
Gum, black (tupelo)	yellow-brown	medium	medium	medium	medium
Limba (Korina*)	pale gold	medium	medium	medium	high
Mahogany, Honduras	reddish-brown	easy	medium	medium	high
Mahogany, Philippine	medium red	easy	medium	medium	medium-high
Maple, hard	reddish-cream	hard	hard	high	medium-high
Maple, soft (southern)	reddish-brown	medium	medium	medium	medium-low
Oak, red (average)	flesh brown	hard	hard	high	medium
Oak, white (average)	gray-brown	hard	hard	high	medium-high
Padouk (red narra)	red to orange	hard	hard	high	medium-high
Pecan	dark red-brown	hard	hard	high	medium-high
Poplar, yellow	light to dark yellow	easy	soft	low	medium
Walnut, black	dark brown	hard	hard	high	high
Willow, black	medium brown	easy	soft	medium	low
Softwoods					
Cedar, Tennessee Red	red	medium	medium	medium	medium
Cypress	yellow to red-brown	medium	soft	medium	medium-high
Fir, Douglas	light orange-brown	medium	soft	medium	medium
Pine (average)	cream to orange or brown	easy	soft	low	medium
Redwood	deep red-brown	easy	soft	medium	medium
Spruce (average)	white	easy	soft	low	medium

spruce, and larch trees. The main hardwood trees are the aspen and the cottonwood, which are not used extensively for lumber.

Central Hardwood Forest

The Central Hardwood Forest is the largest of the forests in area, but it yields only about 5 percent of the nation's lumber and about 10 percent of its pulpwood. The forest is composed principally of hardwood trees, such as walnut, maple, birch, hickory, oak, ash, poplar, and the various elms, along with some conifers. The conifers include white pine, short-leaf pine, and red cedar. Most of the hardwoods used for furniture and veneers are from these forests.

Southern Forest

The Southern Forest supplies about 30 percent of the lumber for the United States and about 60 percent of the pulpwood. This forest covers most of the South, extending from Virginia on the Atlantic seaboard to eastern Texas in the center of the continent. The soil in this area is predominantly sandy soil and supports a form of pine tree often called "hard pine." The hard pines include the short-leaf, longleaf, and yellow pines. Other trees in this forest include cypress, black gum or tupelo, and several species of oak, cedar, willow, ash, and pecan. Although yellow pine is used to some extent in making plywood, the total pine plywood output is only a small portion of the plywood market.

Northern Forest

The Northern Forest produces approximately 10 percent of the lumber in the United States and approximately 20 percent of its pulpwood. The Northern Forest extends from northeastern Maine on the East Coast through the Middle West to Minnesota and northern Wisconsin. It extends as far south as northern Georgia and Tennessee. The principle trees in the Northern Forest are the jack pine, Norway pine, spruce, fir, maple, birch, and beech trees.

Tropical Forest

The Tropical Forest is of little commercial value in the United States. It includes the southern tip of Florida and the southern tip of Texas. The leading lumber species of these forest areas are the mahogany and mangrove trees. However, no appreciable quantities of these trees are harvested.

Alaskan Forest

The Alaskan Forest is similar to the West Coast Forest. However, about nine-tenths of the timber is western hemlock and sitka spruce; this wood is harvested primarily for pulp, rather than for lumber. The interior forest of Alaska contains few trees suitable for large-scale hardwood lumbering.

Hawaiian Forest

The Hawaiian Forest consists of two subdivisions—wet and dry. In the wet forest, the tropical trees are peculiar to the climate, including the tree fern, euca-

lyptus, and others. They are used chiefly for furniture, some lumber, and carvings. The dry forest is of little commercial value and consists of trees like the monkeypod, wiliwili, and others. The forests are considered to be of little commercial significance.

Types of Trees

Several types of trees are used commercially. An indication and comparison of the major types of lumber and commercial trees can be made in Table 2-1. Since there are more than one thousand species of trees in the United States alone, all the species of trees cannot be included; nor are all these species considered to be of significant commercial value. When the early colonists arrived in this country, they began to use the trees for various purposes. Furniture was made from the trees which provided lumber with durability, ease of working, and natural beauty. Trees which provided a sturdy wood were preferred to trees which provided woods that rotted or decomposed easily. Building was done with trees which were easy to form and shape and were available in sufficient lengths and sizes.

Some of the more commonly used woods in school shops include ash, birch, cherry, red gum, Honduras and Philippine mahogany, hard and soft maple, red and white oak, walnut, and willow. The common softwoods used include cedar, fir, redwood, and several variations of pine. Woods used commercially include basswood, hickory, tupelo (black gum), fir, and spruce.

Hardwoods and Softwoods

Many people are often confused about the classifications of wood. Wood is generally divided into two broad categories:

(1) Hardwoods and (2) Softwoods. These categories are misleading, since these two broad classifications are not truly indicative of the actual hardness or softness of the wood. The classifications indicate only whether the tree loses or retains its leaves during winter. The trees which shed their leaves in winter are placed in the hardwood category and are known as *deciduous* trees. The trees which do not shed their leaves are in the softwood category and are known as the evergreens or *coniferous* trees. The deciduous trees include ash, cherry, walnut, hickory, magnolia, mahogany, etc. The conifers include the cedars, pines, firs, and spruces.

Although the general classification of hardwoods and softwoods indicates whether they are evergreen or deciduous, the terms "hardwood" and "softwood" are misleading. Some of the softwoods are harder than some of the hardwoods. For example, balsa is a very soft, porous wood used—because it is a lightweight wood— for modelmaking and for fishing floats; but it is classified a hardwood, since it is a deciduous tree. The hardwoods also are porous in cell structure. The porous cell structure is referred to as "open-grain"; however, not all the hardwoods are open-grain woods. The open grain structure is not always large enough to determine with the naked eye. The more common open-grain woods are walnut, oak, and mahogany. The cells in these woods are large and quite noticeable. Although maple and cherry are open-grain hardwoods, their cell structure is so small they are virtually closed-grain woods.

Under a microscope, the cell structure of a hardwood is open-ended (Fig. 2-2A). The cell structure of the softwoods is closed (Fig. 2-2B). The fibers of a softwood are long, and they are not open.

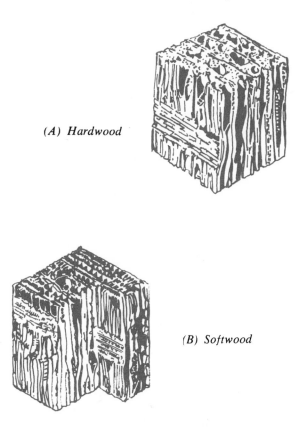

(A) Hardwood

(B) Softwood

Fig. 2-2. Enlarged cell structures.(Courtesy Forest Products Laboratory)

There are no empty or open cell areas in the wood. Note, however, the open spaces in the cell structure of the hardwoods (see Fig. 2-2A). In Fig. 2-3, note that the open cell spaces are larger and more numerous in the summer phase of the annular ring than in the winter or spring phase of the wood. The wood ceases its growth during the winter; thus, the layer becomes quite hard and dense, making the annular ring readily noticeable in most woods. The size and shape of the cell structure varies in the various woods. These variations produce certain effects in the woods which serve both to identify the wood and to provide a portion of its inherent natural beauty.

The pith, or center portion of the tree, contains lines which extend toward the

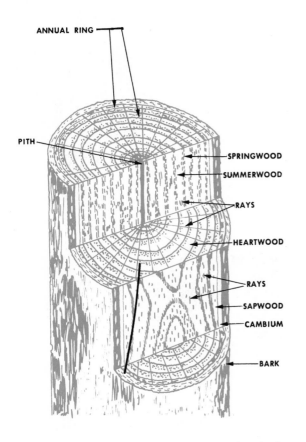

Fig. 2-3. Cutaway view (top) and sectional view (bottom) of a log. (Courtesy Frank Paxton Lumber Company)

outside areas of the tree. These lines are *medullary rays,* or simply rays. The medullary rays help the tree to conduct food into the heartwood for storage and for movement. These rays are not found in all trees, but they are quite noticeable in some trees. The trees with the most noticeable ray effects are the oak, beech, and sycamore. Although the rays add 'beauty to some woods, the larger the rays, the more they seem to cause shrinking and checking, or cracking, of the lumber.

The cell structure of a wood determines its building characteristics. Nails hold better in the soft-textured woods, such as pine, redwood, cypress, mahogany, and basswood. When a nail is forced into the wood, the wood is pushed aside; then it expands backward around the nail to hold it. Thus, the hole seems to fill after it is made. Paint normally adheres to the wood quite well, since the material in the paint is absorbed into the pores of the wood.

The air spaces and the hollow cellular structure provide the wood with excellent insulator characteristics. Wood can pro-

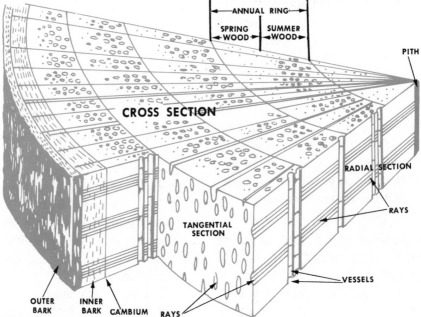

vide insulation against heat, sound, vibration, and cold. It is an excellent flooring material for shops and businesses in which machinery is used, since it does not transmit the vibrations. It is preferred for gymnasium floors, since its natural resiliency reduces fatigue. A few inches of solid wood aid in keeping out stifling heat or bitter cold. Many of the vacation homes (Fig. 2-4) and chalets from the European Alps (Fig. 2-5) are built with solid-wood walls approximately three inches in thickness.

Fig. 2-5. Swiss chalets featuring solid-wood walls.

Fig. 2-4. Vacation home. (Courtesy Lindal Cedar Homes)

Questions

1. How many forest regions are found in the United States?
2. Which forest produces most of the hardwood lumber?
3. Which forest produces most of the fir, spruce, and plywood?
4. Which forest produces most of the pulpwood?
5. What is pulpwood?
6. What factors determine whether a tree is a "hardwood" or a "softwood"?
7. What is an "annular" ring?
8. Why is wood an excellent insulator?

Unit 3 – Cutting, Seasoning, and Grading Lumber

Before lumber can be used, the logs must be debarked or "peeled" and prepared for sawing (Fig. 3-1). After peeling, the logs are then cut into lumber, veneer, or timber. When first cut, the lumber is very rough from the coarse teeth of the saws. Then it is seasoned and finished into smooth pieces of lumber.

Fig. 3-1. Bark is blasted from the logs by jets of water under 1500 pounds pressure. Removing the bark by this method permits recovery of the slabs and edgings for conversion to chips for pulp and other wood products. (Courtesy Weyerhaeuser Company)

Drying and Curing Lumber

Both the hardwoods and the softwoods normally are cured before they are sold on the market. The curing process is called *seasoning,* which permits the wood to shrink and lose its moisture content before it is used. This loss of moisture reduces warping, checking or cracking, and twisting of the boards.

The naturally seasoned wood requires considerable time to dry and can reduce the moisture content only to approxi- mately fifteen percent. This moisture content is suitable for some purposes, such as construction lumber, but it is not suitable for most of the hardwoods, which must have a lower moisture content to minimize warping, cracking, and shrinking. The moisture content of most hardwoods should be approximately seven or eight percent. A *kiln* is necessary to reduce the moisture content of the hardwoods to this percentage.

When the lumber is dry, it is then surfaced and shaped as desired for lumber, timber, etc. Two methods of drying are used: (1) Stacking the lumber in open piles or *ricks* (Fig. 3-2) and (2) Drying the lumber in a large oven or kiln (Fig. 3-3). Nearly all the lumber in use today is kiln-dried (Fig. 3-3A). There are two major types of kilns—the compartment kiln and the progressive kiln. The compartment kiln (Fig. 3-3B) is merely a large oven; the lumber enters the kiln and is dried, remaining in the same location until it is seasoned as desired. The progressive kiln (Fig. 3-3C) is a longer oven in which the lumber is stacked on small trollies which enter from one end and are moved slowly through the kiln. When the

Fig. 3-2. Lumber drying in open-air ricks. (Courtesy Potlatch Forests, Inc.)

(A) Moving ricked lumber to kilns for further drying. (Courtesy Potlatch Forests, Inc.)

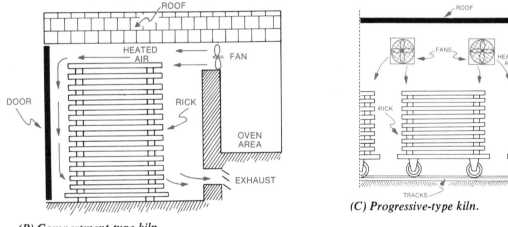

(B) Compartment-type kiln.

(C) Progressive-type kiln.

Fig. 3-3. Nearly all lumber is kiln-dried.

lumber is dry, the trollies are removed from the opposite end of the kiln. This is similar to an assembly line. The general construction of a dry kiln can be seen in Fig. 3-3. The progressive and compartment types of kilns are similar in construction.

Before it is dried, the lumber is cut to a general dimension, leaving a rough surface. After the lumber is dried, it is surfaced and straightened. The lumber shrinks 5 to 10 percent during the seasoning process. Some checking and crack-ing occurs, especially in the hardwoods with medullary rays. Some softwoods are surfaced before seasoning and permitted to shrink to the correct size.

Surfaced lumber is smaller in dimension than the rough-cut lumber, but it requires fewer finishing operations. Most of the softwoods, such as cedar, fir, and pine, are nearly always surfaced before use. The standard rough and surfaced thicknesses of the common types of boards available in most lumber yards can be found in Table 3-1.

Table 3-1. Standard Lumber Sizes

These are typical grade stamps now used to identify seasoned, unseasoned, or specially dried lumber.

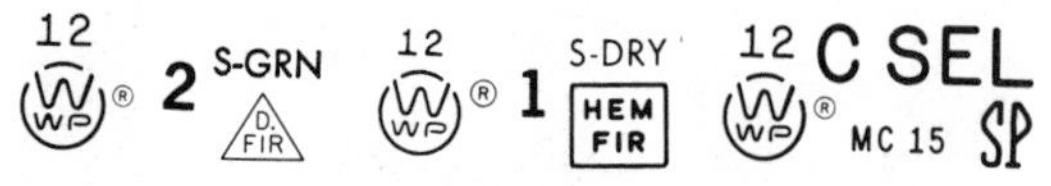
12
WP ® 2 S-GRN
D. FIR
12
WP ® 1 S-DRY
HEM FIR
12 C SEL
WP ®
MC 15 SP

(Moisture content exceeds 19%)	(Moisture content 19% or less)	(Specially dried to 15% or less moisture content)

New Grade Designations: apply to dimension lumber of all species. WWPA rules incorporate the National Dimension Rules, as follows:

Category	Grades	Sizes
Light Framing	Construction, Standard, Utility, Economy	2" to 4" thick 2" to 4" wide
Studs	Stud, Economy	2" to 4" thick 2" to 4" wide
Structural Light Framing	Select Structural No. 1, No. 2, No. 3, Economy	2" to 4" thick 2" to 4" wide
Appearance Framing	Appearance	2" to 4" thick 6" and wider
Structural Joists and Planks	Select Structural No. 1, No. 2, No. 3, Economy	2" to 4" thick 2" and wider
*Decking	Selected Decking Commercial Decking	2" to 4" thick 4" and wider
*Beams and Stringers Posts and Timbers	Select Structural No. 1, No. 2, No. 3	5" and thicker 5" and wider

*Not included in National Dimension Rules.

Old and New Sizes of Dimensional Lumber and Board Lumber

PRODUCT CLASS (Nominal Size)		OLD SIZES (Dry or Unseasoned)	NEW SIZES	
			Unseasoned	Dry
DIMENSION LUMBER	2 x 4	1 5/8 x 3 5/8	1 9/16 x 3 9/16	1 1/2 x 3 1/2
	2 x 6	1 5/8 x 5 1/2	1 9/16 x 5 5/8	1 1/2 x 5 1/2
	2 x 8	1 5/8 x 7 1/2	1 9/16 x 7 1/2	1 1/2 x 7 1/4
	2 x 10	1 5/8 x 9 1/2	1 9/16 x 9 1/2	1 1/2 x 9 1/4
	2 x 12	1 5/8 x 11 1/2	1 9/16 x 11 1/2	1 1/2 x 11 1/4
BOARD LUMBER	1 x 4	25/32 x 3 5/8	25/32 x 3 9/16	3/4 x 3 1/2
	1 x 6	25/32 x 5 1/2	25/32 x 5 5/8	3/4 x 5 1/2
	1 x 8	25/32 x 7 1/2	25/32 x 7 1/2	3/4 x 7 1/4
	1 x 10	25/32 x 9 1/2	25/32 x 9 1/2	3/4 x 9 1/4
	1 x 12	25/32 x 11 1/2	25/32 x 11 1/2	3/4 x 11 1/4

These new sizes get 8% more usable lumber from every harvested tree!

Standard Surfaced Thicknesses

Rough Thickness	S2S Hardwoods	S2S Pine
3/8"	1/4"	5/16"
1/2"	3/8"	3/8"
5/8"	7/16"	7/16"
1"	25/32"	25/32"
1 1/4"	1 1/16"	1 5/32"
1 1/2"	1 5/16"	1 13/32"
2"	1 3/4"	1 13/16"
2 1/2"	2 1/4"	2 3/8"
3"	2 3/4"	2 3/4"
4"	3 5/8"	3 5/8"

Methods of Sawing Lumber

Two principal methods of cutting trees into lumber are used. These are (1) Plain-sawing (Fig. 3-4), and (2) Quartersawing (Fig. 3-5). The plain-sawing method provides some advantages, whereas the quartersawing method provides other distinct advantages. Note in the quartersawed lumber that the annular rings are perpendicular to the face of the lumber (see Fig. 3-5). In the plain-sawed lumber, the annular rings are at only a slight angle to the face of the lumber (see Fig. 3-4).

The advantages of the plain-sawed lumber are:

1. More lumber from the tree.
2. Cheaper and easier to cut.
3. Easier to season and dry.

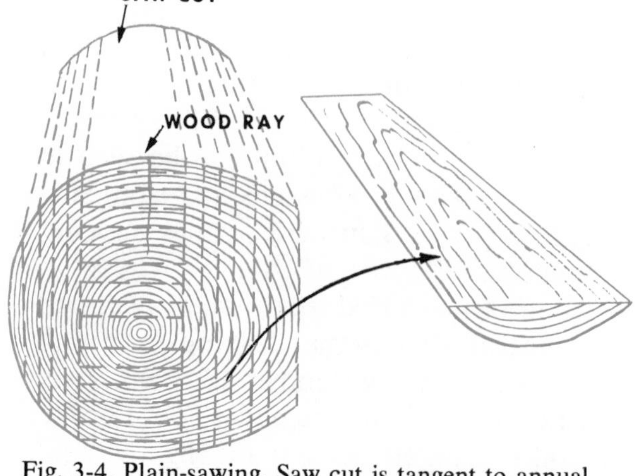
SAW CUT
WOOD RAY

Fig. 3-4. Plain-sawing. Saw cut is tangent to annual rings. (Courtesy Frank Paxton Lumber Company)

The advantages of quartersawing are:

1. The wood does not wind, or twist, or cup as easily.
2. Less warping and shrinking.
3. The wood is less susceptible to wear, since the hard annular rings are exposed and protect the softer portion of the summer growth. Quartersawed wood is especially desirable for flooring or decking.
4. Less checks and surface blemishes during seasoning.

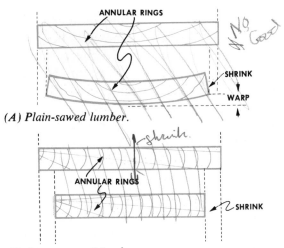

(A) Plain-sawed lumber.

(B) Quartersawed lumber.

Fig. 3-6. Shrink and warp of lumber.

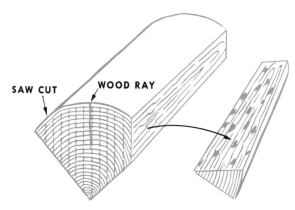

Fig. 3-5. Quartersawing. Annual rings are perpendicular to the face of the lumber. (Courtesy Frank Paxton Lumber Company)

The differences in shrinking, warping, and checking in quartersawed and plain-sawed lumber are demonstrated in Fig. 3-6. The direction of the annular rings is important to determine the direction of shrinkage; thus the two types of sawing can be used to fit specific needs in lumber.

Softwood Lumber

Softwoods are graded in accordance with the appearance of the entire piece of wood or board. Uniform standards have been established for uniform grading in thickness, widths, and lengths and in grade or appearance. The grades commonly recognized by most lumbering associations are: (1) *Yard* lumber; (2) Factory or *shop* lumber; and (3) *Timbers* for structural purposes.

Yard Lumber

Yard lumber for softwoods is divided further into subclassifications. These are the *Selects* and *Commons*, each with subclasses, and *Dimension* lumber. The Select, or Finish lumber, as it is sometimes called, is graded A, B, C, and D. The Select grades of lumber are used for construction where the board or lumber will be visible. This includes the framing of windows and doors, window parts, and decoration and trim pieces. The lumber is clear, or free of knots and blemishes; the grain is straight and is not twisted.

"Select" lumber is more expensive than the other grades, since it has no defects. In addition, the lumber mills are required to hire inspectors and graders to sort the lumber into the proper grades. Generally, the lower the grade, the less the price of the lumber.

The Common grades are divided into five groups and are numbered, rather than lettered, to aid in distinguishing them from the Select or Finish grades. Grades No. 1, 2, and 3 are the most common grades. Grades No. 4 and 5 are sometimes used. The No. 1 Common lumber is free from structural defects with no loose knots to affect the physical characteristics of the board. The No. 2 Common boards can have noticeable knots and can lack uniformity in the grain. However, these factors should not affect the strength of the board. The No. 3 Common lumber is obviously knotted, can have loose or open knotholes, and can be visibly warped; it is generally considered to be sound for structural use. The Common grades are used for sheathing, subflooring, decking, and construction purposes. Normally, the Common grades are used for pieces that will not be seen, such as rafters, wall framing, floor joists, and other construction braces (Table 3-2).

Factory or Shop Lumber

Factory or Shop lumber normally is thicker than 1 inch and is utilized for special construction, including window sashes, door pieces, and the guides, legs, and bracing of some furniture. The lumber can be clear, or it can have minor defects. However, it is normally a good grade of lumber which is adapted to production in large quantities.

Timbers

Timbers are used almost entirely for structural purposes. They can be rounded for poles, such as telephone poles, or they can be sawed to shape. When sawed, they are 4 inches in thickness or larger; and they are referred to as "timber," rather than lumber. They can be either surfaced or rough, depending on the intended use. If they are to serve as exposed beams or supports, timbers normally are finished or surfaced; but when they are used for structural supports which will not be seen, they normally are used rough. This is true merely because it is more expensive to

Table 3-2. Uses of Grades of Softwood Lumber

Category	Grades
Selects	B & Better—1 & 2 Clear
	C Select
	D Select
Finish	Superior
	Prime
	E
Paneling	Clear (any select or finish grade).
	No. 2 Common selected for knotty paneling.
	No. 3 Common selected for knotty paneling.
Siding (Bevel and Bungalow)	Superior
	Prime
Boards	No. 1 Common
	No. 2 Common
Sheathing and Form Lumber	No. 3 Common
	No. 4 Common
	No. 5 Common

surface the lumber; and surfacing is not done where it is not needed.

Sizing Softwood Lumber

After drying and grading, most of the softwoods are surfaced in a planing mill and then cut into standard sizes (Fig. 3-7). The standard thicknesses are shown in Table 3-1. Lumber can be purchased either rough (RGH) or dressed. If one side of the lumber is requested to be surfaced, it is "surfaced one side," which is indicated by the abbreviation S1S. Thus, S2S lumber has been surfaced on two sides. Most standard softwood lumber has been surfaced four sides (S4S), and it has been cut and planed or surfaced to standard dimension. The softwoods are standard in both widths and thicknesses. The standard 1-inch pine stock is actually only approximately ¾-inch in thickness, and is sometimes referred to as "three-quarter" stock. Two-inch stock is actually 1½ inches in thickness. Four-inch widths and thicknesses are actually 3½ inches, and 6-inch widths are actually 5½ inches in width. Boards which are 8-, 10-, and 12-inch widths lose ½ inch in surfacing.

Fig. 3-7. Two-by-fours are sawed to standard lengths on a trimmer. (Courtesy Potlatch Forests, Inc.)

The softwoods normally are cut in increments of 1 inch in thickness and 2 inches in width. The rough lumber is cut exactly on the inch dimensions; but when it is seasoned and surfaced, the widths and thicknesses naturally are less. Standard widths and thicknesses for the planed or dressed lumber have been adopted for construction purposes and for ease in building.

Standard Sizes

The standard lengths of softwood lumber range from 8 to 20 feet in intervals of 2 feet. A piece of lumber might be designated a 2″ x 4″ x 10′. This means that the lumber is 2 inches in thickness by 4 inches in width by 10 feet in length.

Standardized Sizes Aid Construction

Since most softwood lumber, timber, and plywoods are used in constructing homes and buildings, standardizing the sizes aids in more efficient planning, assembly, and finishing (Fig. 3-8). Insulation can be mass-produced to the correct thickness in a plant hundreds of miles

from the building site to fit between the walls perfectly; the correct size hardware mountings can be purchased from different contractors; plumbing fixtures can be purchased to fit; along with dozens of other devices used in constructing a building. Standardized sizes merely make

Fig. 3-8. Moving and storing lumber cut to standard sizes. (Courtesy Weyerhaeuser Company)

it possible for carpenters, electricians, architects, contractors, plumbers, concrete finishers, and the many other construction workers to work together in construction.

Sizing and Grading Hardwoods

Hardwood lumber is graded on the amount of usable lumber on the board that is free from blemishes. The three major classifications of hardwood are: (1) Firsts and Seconds (FAS); (2) Selects; and (3) Common grades.

Firsts and Seconds

The Firsts and Seconds (FAS) originally were two grades; but generally, they are now considered to be in the same category. This grade of lumber must be clear and free of blemishes on one face; the other face must be sound, which means that it cannot have any holes or defects in the second face. The boards are sawed to standard thicknesses (see Table 3-1), and are cut from the log to obtain the most usable lumber. Most FAS lumber is 6 inches in width, or wider, and 8 feet in length, or longer. Exceptions are principally in walnut lumber, which is becoming increasingly scarce and expensive.

Select Grades

The Select grades of hardwood lumber indicate that the boards are more narrow and that the reverse face can contain open knotholes or defects. Select grades are generally 4 inches in width, and wider, with a minimum length of 6 feet.

Common Grades

The Common grades, sometimes called "thrift" grades, are less exacting. Both sides can contain knots, knotholes, and defects. The boards can be very narrow, but they should be at least 3 inches wide.

The boards are not necessarily the same width over the entire length, and can include sapwood pieces near the bark, which reduces the width of the board considerably. However, these grades of hardwood can be used by careful or selective cutting. These grades are less expensive and are commonly used by hobbyists, schools, and home craftsmen, where waste and maximum usage for production work are not the major considerations.

Hardwood lumber is cut in standard thicknesses, but there are no standard widths or lengths. The thicknesses normally are in ¼-inch increments when rough-sawed from the logs. Boards can be purchased that are 1½ inches in thickness; these are called "six-quarter" stock. Lumber surfaced on both faces has become more popular; but when surfaced, it is usually surfaced to a standard thickness different from that of the softwoods (see Table 3-1). Since hardwood lumber is not standard in width or length, it is usually purchased in Random Widths and Lengths (RWL).

Purchasing Lumber

In purchasing lumber, it is necessary to state the specifications clearly. These specifications include the type of wood, thickness, grade, finish—rough or surfaced, and the amount of lumber requested. An example of a common lumber order for a softwood board is:

1MBF, 2″ x 4″ x 10′, No. 2 pine
where,

1M means 1000 (1M)
BF indicates board feet (BF),
2″ x 4″ x 10′ indicates the size of the boards,
No. 2 is the grade of yard lumber, and pine is the type of wood.

No remarks are required for surfacing, since softwood lumber normally is surfaced.

For a hardwood board, a common lumber order is:

1MBF, 1″, FAS, walnut, KD, RWL, S2S
where,

> 1MBF indicates 1000 (1M) board feet (BF),
> 1″ is the thickness of the boards,
> FAS is First And Second grade,
> walnut is the type of wood,
> KD is kiln-dried,
> RWL is random (R) widths (W) and lengths (L), and
> S2S is surfaced (S) two (2) sides (S).

In ordering the hardwoods, it is common not to include the RWL listing, since the hardwood is sold in random widths and lengths, unless specified otherwise. When specified otherwise, an additional charge is usually made. In addition, hardwood normally is sold in the rough (RGH) condition. When surfaced a small additional charge is made.

Abbreviations used to indicate the number of board feet include the letters *C* and *M*. These are the Roman numerals for 100 and 1000, respectively. They are used in shipping, and lumber prices are based on the cost per 1000 (M) board feet.

Questions

1. What is meant by seasoning of lumber?
2. What is a kiln?
3. What is the chief difference between plain-sawing and quartersawing?
4. List the advantages of quartersawed lumber.
5. List the advantages of plain-sawed lumber.
6. What is meant by Dimension lumber?
7. Why are the standard dimensions in lumber important?
8. What is the difference in size between lumber and timber?
9. What is meant by FAS?
10. How is the number of board feet in a board calculated?

Unit 4 – Veneer and Plywood

Veneers were known to the Pharaohs of Egypt more than four thousand years ago. Veneering is merely a process of placing a thin, beautiful piece of wood over a wood of lesser quality or beauty. The Egyptians, who had very little wood suitable for furniture, used the precious woods obtained from other lands sparingly. They made their furniture from one type of wood; then covered it with a thin layer of the more attractive wood. Nearly every civilization has done this. In the past, the veneering process has not always been successful, since satisfactory glues and adhesives were lacking and man did not have the technical ability to produce the thin veneer slices.

Most of the wood used in building construction has been solid wood, since it was so easy to obtain. Today, this is no longer true. Increasing technology and decreasing natural resources have caused man to utilize the tree more efficiently, in many instances, by making the entire tree into plywood. Plywood is made by gluing together successive layers of thin veneer slices to form a thicker piece of wood. The successive layers, or *crossbands,* are placed at right angles to avoid any weakness in the plywood resulting from grain direction. The woods used in manufacturing common plywood are not the costly cabinet woods; they are mostly fir and pine. Plywood is used extensively for building construction, concrete forms, and surfaces to be painted.

Wood for Veneers

The woods used for veneers, sometimes called *cabinet woods,* are obtained from all over the world. The cabinet woods are veneered by making thin slices of an attractive wood and gluing them to a core of less desirable wood. The expensive cabinet plywoods usually are called *hardwood veneers* to distinguish them from the common plywoods made from pine and fir. The practice of veneering extends the beauty man can obtain from a small quantity of lumber and still retain certain structural advantages. Veneer can be made in very wide sheets, and since the layers of wood are alternated in grain direction, there is little or no warping, twisting, or checking. Thus, both waste and distortion are reduced. Another advantage in using the hardwood veneers is the reduction in assembly time required for the various products. Wide pieces of material are cut easily in a single piece, instead of gluing together several narrow pieces of solid wood and then cutting the desired piece from the glued-together stock. The basic construction of veneers and plywoods is diagrammed in Fig. 4-1.

The face veneers are normally $\frac{1}{20}$ inch in thickness for commercial use (softwoods) and $\frac{1}{28}$ inch in thickness for face veneers of the more expensive and more exotic cabinet woods. The thickness can vary from 0.01 inch to much thicker pieces. The plywood and cabinet veneers are made from odd-numbered layers (three, five, seven) placed with the grain directions at right angles to each other; thus the layers reinforce each other. A lumber-core construction is often used for furniture; a solid-hardwood core is used with thin crossbands and faces. On a weight basis, veneer or plywood is extremely strong and is considered stronger than steel when compared pound for pound. For example, a plywood floor weighing 100 pounds can support more weight with less sag than 100 pounds of steel sheet used on the same area.

The more widely used cabinet veneers include the Philippine and Honduras mahoganies, rosewood, walnut, red gum, maple, birch, pecan, and ash. In all, there are more than ninety thousand woods to choose from around the world. The improved use and development of adhesives and technical processes, in conjunction with the increasing scarcity of the prime cabinet woods, have made the use of veneers more efficient and more economical. When a solid-hardwood core is used (Fig. 4-1B), the core wood is generally from a less valuable wood or a lesser grade of the same wood. The thin veneer is then applied over the core to provide a solid-wood appearance.

Veneers are not new in furniture manufacturing; they are only more common. High-quality furniture has always included the veneered pieces. The furniture bearing the great names in cabinetmaking, such as Duncan Phyfe, Thomas Chippendale, the Hepplewhites, and others, has always featured the veneers. The veneers, however, now are used more extensively than in former years. The trends in furniture manufacturing today include the increasing use of veneers; the increasing use of laminated plastics, such as for countertops; and the increasing combination of wood and veneers with other materials, such as plastics, molded-wood fibers, particle boards, metal, and cloth. Fiber-glass techniques also have extended the range and variety of the furniture available today. Fiber-glass materials are used to form the free-flowing shapes not possible with the common woodworking methods. These shapes can be combined with the natural beauty of the woods for contrast and enhancement. Fiber glass is strong,

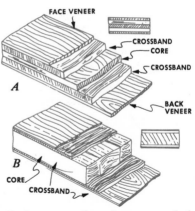

Fig. 4-1. Basic construction of veneers and plywood. Five-ply, veneer core (A) and five-ply, lumber core (B).

resilient, and easily worked; and it is quickly becoming a major furniture material.

Cutting Plywood

Both veneers and plywoods can be cut on essentially the same machinery by the same processes. The veneers can be cut with either a knife or a saw. They can be sliced, cut flat, rotated, or partially rotated to produce a veneer piece. The best logs for veneers are free from knots, cracks, and other defects. These logs are sent to a mill where they are made into face cuts to be used on the outside surfaces for maximum beauty and appearance.

Logs of pine and fir are chosen for strength and sturdiness, as opposed to appearance, and they are used for common plywood. Hardwood logs with minor defects also are used for making the lumber cores of hardwood veneers. Plywood is constructed from soft woods in commercial plywood plants. It is used for subflooring, various construction uses, forms or molds for concrete, roof decking, and paneling of walls to which additional material, such as shingles or even paint, are to be applied.

Softwood plywood is cut predominately in only one fashion. The straight trunkwood logs, called peeler logs, are debarked, stored in a pond or damp area, and steamed or conditioned to soften the wood. After conditioning, the peeler log, which has been cut to an exact length, is placed in a large lathe (Fig. 4-2); then

Fig. 4-2. This huge lathe makes a long, continuous sheet of veneer by "unpeeling" log sections specially selected for plywood production. Then the veneers are cut to prescribed sizes and bonded together to produce strong, lightweight plywood. (Courtesy Weyerhaeuser Company)

the log is rotated against a sharp knife, with the wood peeling off in a thin continuous slice (Fig. 4-3). After the slices are cut from the log, they are sized (cut to proper size for making laminated boards), glued (Fig. 4-4), and laminated together. The lamination process is performed in machines which apply pressure and heat to squeeze and dry the glue quickly. After the plywood pieces are formed, they are again sawed and trimmed to size and inspected for shipment (Fig. 4-5).

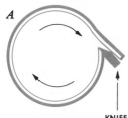

Fig. 4-3. Basic principle of rotary cutting. The log is mounted centrally in the lathe and turned against a razor-sharp knife blade (A), like unwinding a roll of paper. Since this cut follows the annular growth ring of the log, a bold variegated grain marking results (B). (Courtesy U.S. Plywood Corporation.)

Fig. 4-4. Spreading glue on sheets of veneer before "sandwiching" them into panels. (Courtesy Potlatch Forests, Inc.)

Fig. 4-5. Inspecting finished plywood panels. (Courtesy Weyerhaeuser Company)

Cutting Hardwood Veneers

The primary methods of cutting hardwood veneers are the cathedral back cut (Fig. 4-6), plain slicing (Fig. 4-7), quarter slicing (Fig. 4-8), rift cut (Fig. 4-9A), and half-round slicing (Fig. 4-9B). The appearance of the grain structure of the wood is affected by its location on the tree and the annular rings. The color distribution is effected by the placement of the cut on the log. The sapwood tends to be lighter in color than the heartwood. In addition, the regularity or irregularity of the grain structure affects the appearance. Fir is especially irregular in grain appearance; however, some woods, such as quarter-cut walnut, are extremely regular in grain appearance.

Veneers are obtained from four areas of the tree. The four areas are the crotch,

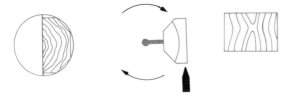

Fig. 4-6. Cathedral back cut veneer slicing. (Courtesy U.S. Plywood Corporation)

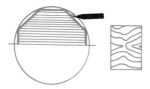

Fig. 4-7. Plain-sliced veneer. The half log or flitch is mounted with the heart side flat against the guide plate of the slicer. Slicing is done parallel to a line through the center of the log to produce a "cathedral" figure. (Courtesy U.S. Plywood Corporation)

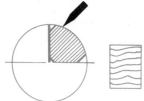

Fig. 4-8. Quarter-sliced veneer. The quarter log or flitch is mounted on the guide plate in a manner that the growth rings strike the knife at nearly a right angle, resulting in a series of straight stripes in some woods and varied stripes in others. (Courtesy U.S. Plywood Corporation)

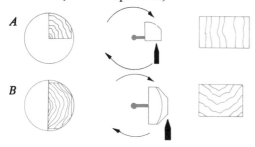

Fig. 4-9. Rift cut (A) and half-round (B) veneer slicing methods. A striped effect is obtained in rift slicing. In half-round slicing, the heart of a flitch is mounted on an off-center holder to obtain a matching symmetrical pattern with a broad grain pattern. (Courtesy U.S. Plywood Corporation)

burl, long wood or trunk, and stump (Fig. 4-10). A crotch is merely the point where the trunk forks into two or more major branches. A burl is believed to be the result of an injury to the tree at a point where the wood has grown over the injured area. The long wood part of the tree is the long straight portion of the trunk. The stump wood refers to the stump of the tree after the tree has been felled; it consists of the lower portion of the tree and the major branches of the roots.

Sawing is the oldest method of cutting and trimming veneers, but it is seldom used. Special band saws or floating-head circular saws generally are used for either plain or quarter-sawing the veneers. The sawing process is used only when the wood is extremely hard or when it splits easily.

The primary methods of matching the veneered panels are the book match, center match, balance match, running or lot match, full-flitch match, vertical butt match, random match, and slip match (Fig. 4-11). A *flitch* consists of all the veneer pieces cut from a single portion of a log.

Plywood Grades

The plywood made from fir and pine is manufactured in two classifications—interior and exterior. The classification "interior" or "exterior" depends primarily on the type of adhesives used to bond together the layers or plies. A waterproof glue is used for the exterior plywood, and the interior plywood is made with a glue that is only water-resistant. In addition, the inner plies and the back piece of veneer of interior plywood can be lower in grade than the outer or face piece of veneer.

Six plywood grades are in use; these

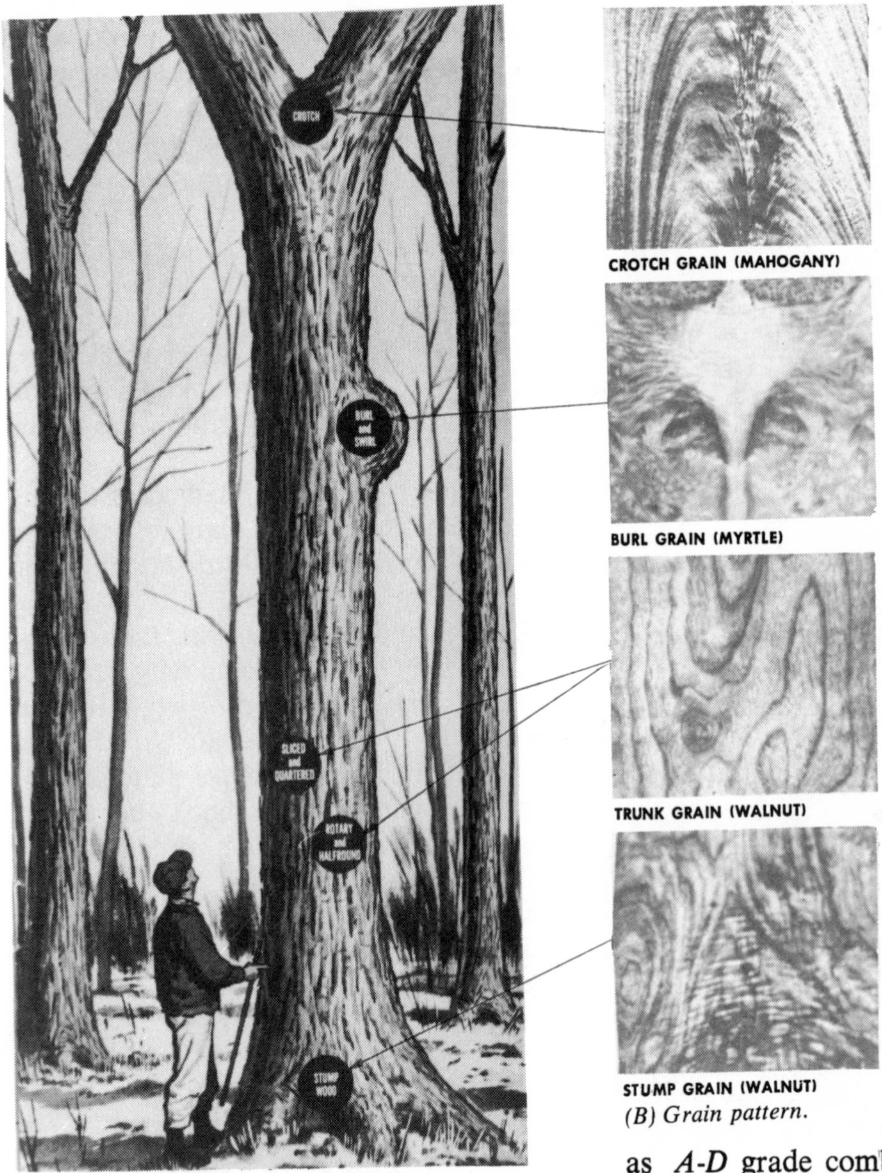

CROTCH GRAIN (MAHOGANY)

BURL GRAIN (MYRTLE)

TRUNK GRAIN (WALNUT)

STUMP GRAIN (WALNUT)

(B) Grain pattern.

(A) Locations on tree.

Fig. 4-10. Veneer patterns. (Courtesy U. S. Plywood Corporation)

grades are designated *N, A, B, C, C plugged,* and *D.* Grade *N* veneer is for special order, with a natural finish, select, all heartwood, and free from open defects. Grade *A* is the highest quality veneer that can be obtained as a standard plywood. It is smooth and even, although the veneer face can be joined or repaired. Knots are not permitted, although repaired knotholes are permitted.

Grade *B* veneer is a solid-surface veneer with circular repairs and repair plugs permitted over the knots. Knots are permitted, but they must be tight, and the knot plug must be tight.

Grade *C* veneer is the lowest grade of exterior plywood. Knotholes are permitted, if they are less than 1 inch in diameter; and minor blemishes, including splits and plugs are acceptable. A Grade *C plugged* veneer is an improved Grade *C* veneer in which the minor blemishes, with the exception of the splits, are repaired. Plywood also is available in cross grades, sometimes referred to as "good one side" (GIS) grades, such as *A-D* grade combinations (Fig. 4-12).

Grade *D* veneer is used only for the interior plies or veneers, and is sometimes called "construction" grade. It is used frequently for subdecking, walls, roof decking, and in construction areas where it will not be seen.

Veneer Paneling

Veneer paneling (Fig. 4-13) is available in hardwood or softwood decorative veneers for use in homes (Fig. 4-14), in-

VENEER MATCH

Book Match

Every other sheet of veneer is turned over, like the leaves of a book. Thus, the back of one veneer meets the front of the adjacent veneer, producing a definite matching pattern at the veneer joint. Veneer is book-matched by one of the following:

Center Match

An even number of pieces of veneer of equal width are laid up so that a veneer joint falls on the center line of the panel. This method is often used in Blueprint Matched Panels.

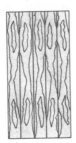

Balance Match

Any number of pieces of veneer of equal width are laid up to make the face of the panel. This method is generally used in Sequence Matched panels.

Running Match (or Lot Match)

An odd or even number of pieces of veneer may be used. Starting with the first panel, veneers are laid up in their numbered sequence, to panel edge. Any excess veneer becomes the first veneer on second panel, excess veneer becomes the first veneer on second panel, excess veneer on second panel starts the third panel and so on. All veneers are laid up in their correct, numbered sequence. All Algoma Grade Panels are Lot Matched.

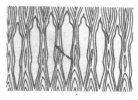

Full Flitch Match (Center Wall Match)

Balance Matched or Center Matched veneer may be further matched in this method. Veneer is selected and divided so that the final panel when installed will create a match where the grain pattern will peak in the center of the wall and taper or diminish toward the outer edges. Since the veneer is divided so that odd numbered veneers going in one direction and even numbered veneers go in the other direction there will be some grain pattern slippage. This match provides a more balanced and symmetrical appearance to the installation.

Vertical Butt Match

Where ceiling height exceeds flitch length, veneers can be specified vertical butt matched for a continuous vertical as well as horizontal pattern. In matching of face veneers every other piece of veneer is turned upside down and used to develop the top panel. For instance, odd numbered veneers will be used upside down for the top panel and even numbered veneers will be used for bottom panel. Side pattern match will not be as perfect as vertical match.

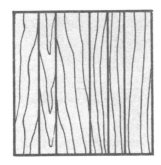

Random Match

Veneers are deliberately and carefully mismatched as to veneer, width, color and grain for the most effective appearance. Veneers from different logs are often used to make one set of panels.

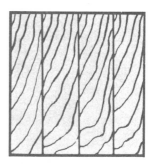

Slip Match

Veneer sheets are joined side by side, without turning. The flitch pattern is therefore repeated from sheet to sheet, and an even color is obtained. Slip match is generally used on quarter-sliced veneers and may employ Balance, Center, or Running Match (See Book Match)

Fig. 4-11. Veneer matching. (Courtesy U. S. Plywood Corporation)

Fig. 4-12. Typical grade marking for back of plywood sheet.

dustry, and offices (Fig. 4-15). It is often decorated by grooving, by routing a design, and by sand blasting or brushing with a stiff wire brush to provide the wood with a textured effect. The textured effect permits the hard grain structure to remain dominant, while the softer materials are slightly abraded or "scrubbed" away.

Various decorative effects are obtained by forming patterns with sections of veneers. *Marquetry* (Fig. 4-16) applies to the process in which an entire surface, such as a table top, is covered with a pat-

Fig. 4-13. Plywood wall paneling is attractive. (Courtesy Masonite Corporation)

terned matching of veneers. *Inlay* work is similar; however, the pattern does not cover the entire area. *Intarsia* is the term applied to "sinking" veneer pieces into a solid wood, rather than into a veneer. Usually, intarsia is done with woods of contrasting color—dark and light—and covers only a small design area. It is used for initials and small geometric patterns.

Variations of marquetry are often used for a type of flooring called *parquet* (Fig. 4-17). The parqueted pieces are formed of thin solid pieces; or they can be formed of thicker veneer pieces laminated onto a core. The pieces are laid in a geometric pattern to form small squares, like floor tiles. Then they are used in the same manner as floor tiles.

Fig. 4-14. Matched veneers increase the natural beauty of these pieces of fine furniture. (Courtesy Fine Hardwoods Association)

Laminating Wood

Lamination of wood falls into two major categories: (1) Construction, and (2) Fabrication. The processes are essentially the same; layers of wood are glued together and forced into a different shape while the glue is drying. When the glue has set, the wood pieces remain in a permanent, formed shape.

Construction Lamination

Construction lamination is used for beams, ceilings, decking, and other construction aspects. The building in Fig.

Fig. 4-15. Matched veneer paneling in a bank building. (Courtesy Fine Hardwoods Association)

4-18 features the use of laminated construction beams. Note that pieces of wood have been formed and glued together in layers to form strong, beautiful effects. The beauty of the wood enhances the interior of the building; the laminated structure is extremely strong and durable, since the grain pattern of the wood has not been cut. The diagrams in Fig. 4-19 show how laminated beams utilize this natural grain structure for additional strength. A large laminated wooden beam

Fig. 4-16. A picture formed by marquetry in which only different veneering woods and grain patterns are used.

Fig. 4-17. Parquet flooring made from various wood veneers. (Courtesy Fine Hardwoods Association)

Fig. 4-18. Laminated woods beams provide strength and natural beauty. (Courtesy Potlatch Forests, Inc.)

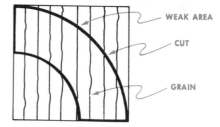

(A) Piece sawed from solid stock.

(B) Laminated piece.

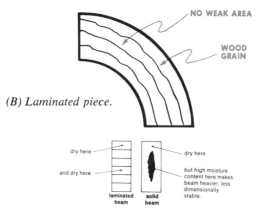

(C) Laminated beams are drier, stronger. (Courtesy Potlatch Forests, Inc.)

Fig. 4-19. Lamination utilizes the strength of the natural grain to provide a stronger piece.

Fig. 4-20. New developments in wood help to make the forests more valuable. Engineering and technology open new vistas as wood takes undreamed of shapes and forms. Soaring across great spans, beams and trusses support heavy roof loads in complete safety without a single supporting post. (Courtesy Weyerhaeuser Company)

(A) Types of laminated siding.

(B) Wall-joining detail for laminated siding.

Fig. 4-21. Laminated siding. (Courtesy Potlatch Forests, Inc.)

is being completed in Fig. 4-20. These beams are made from many pieces which are bent and glued together to retain a specific shape when dried.

Another variation of laminated material used for siding is shown in Fig. 4-21. Standard pieces of lumber are glued together to form a tongue-and-groove which permits each piece to interlock into the next piece. The tongue-and-grooved pieces provide sturdy construction with little support. The characteristics of the wood can provide excellent insulation in a small space to cut construction costs. The laminated construction is becoming more popular for use in vacation homes (Fig. 4-22).

The process used in making laminated construction pieces is similar to that used in making plywood. The glue is applied to the pieces by passing them through rollers to which glue has been applied; then the pieces are pressed together and dried either electronically or in heating units. In addition, finishes can be applied at the factory and dried in a matter of minutes (Fig. 4-23). Researchers have found that finishes last longer on certain woods and are more durable when applied at the mill to freshly surfaced wood before it has become exposed to the varying humidity and atmospheres during transportation. Careful packaging, bundling, and wrapping protects the finish on the surfaces during shipment.

Fabrication Veneers

Fabrication veneers include the same basic processes that are used in laminat-

Fig. 4-22. Vacation home featuring laminated wood construction. (Courtesy Lindal Cedar Homes)

Fig. 4-23. Factory finishing operation includes preheating the boards, spraying, and drying in ovens. Scientists have found that finishes last longer when applied at the mill to freshly surfaced wood. View shows the heating and prefinishing area with a stack of Lock-Deck® laminated roof decking in the foreground. (Courtesy Potlatch Forests, Inc.)

Fig. 4-24. Danish Modern chair designed by Finn Juhl featuring curved back and seat made of laminated pieces.

Fig. 4-25. Modern American furniture featuring formed, laminated woods.

ing, but generally on a smaller scale. One of the earliest uses of small-scale veneering was in manufacturing golf clubs. Many products are now available in laminated veneered materials. Many furniture pieces featuring curved backs, such as the Danish designs (Fig. 4-24), are made on presses where thin pieces are glued and dried in molds to produce pieces which are strong, durable, and retain the shapes provided during the drying period of the glue. A piece of modern American furniture is shown in Fig. 4-25.

Other materials can be impregnated or saturated with chemicals and cured electronically to provide flooring that resists wear and scuffing. Also, it retains the beauty of the natural wood flooring. Other plywood or wood particles can be both impregnated and compressed under heat and pressure, and sometimes radiation, to make the wood dense, hard, and impervious to most chemicals and moisture. The compression saturates the wood throughout all its fibers, thus preventing moisture from entering at any point. The radiation normally is used to harden and cure the resins used during the impregnation. Wood which has been both impregnated with chemicals and compressed normally is known as *compreg*.

Questions

1. How do veneer and plywood differ?
2. Is plywood stronger than the same thickness of wood or lumber? Why?
3. How is most plywood cut from the log?
4. What methods are used in making veneers?
5. What is a flitch?
6. How do interior and exterior grades of plywood differ?
7. Can plywood be "cross-graded"?
8. Describe lamination.

Unit 5 – Hardboard and Particle Board

Hardboard and particle board are similar products; both are made from wood fibers. Both these products can be made from small fibers, such as wood chips and sawdust, which otherwise would be wasted. Hardboard is bonded with its own lignin, which is the natural bonding in wood that holds the wood cells together. In particle board, the adhesives have been added; therefore, the natural lignin is not required to hold the various particles together.

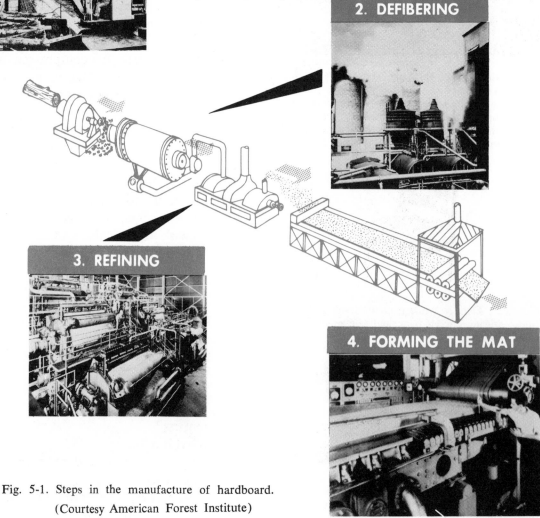

1. LOG HANDLING

1. Logs are conveyed from storage yards to huge chippers which reduce the wood to clean, uniformly sized chips.
2. The chips are then reduced to individual wood fibers by either the steam or the mechanical defibering processes.
3. Fibers are put through certain mechanical processes varying with the method of manufacture, and small amounts of chemicals may be added to enhance the resulting board properties.
4. The fibers are interlocked in the felter into a continuous mat and compressed by heavy rollers.

2. DEFIBERING

3. REFINING

4. FORMING THE MAT

Fig. 5-1. Steps in the manufacture of hardboard.
(Courtesy American Forest Institute)

42

Hardboard

Hardboard is a panel of material made from wood fibers which have been rearranged and bonded, using the natural lignin in the fibers to hold the fibers together. Hardboard has many uses, is extremely hard, and can be cured to make it relatively impervious to moisture. In addition, it can be obtained in standard widths, thicknesses, and lengths; and it can be used for a base for the bonding of veneers, plastic laminates, or other materials. The advantages of hardboard are: (1) freedom from defects; (2) patching is not required; and (3) does not

5. Lengths of mat, or "wetlap," are fed into multiple presses where heat and pressure produce the thin, hard, dry board sheets.
6. Leaving the press, moisture is added to the board in a humidifier to stabilize it to surrounding atmospheric conditions.
7. The board is trimmed to standard specified dimensions, wrapped in convenient packages, and readied for shipment.

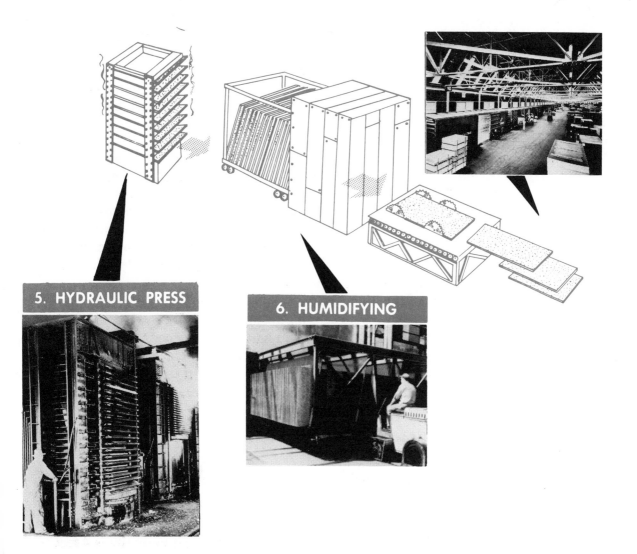

5. HYDRAULIC PRESS

6. HUMIDIFYING

warp, split, chip, or peel, since it has no grain.

In the hardboard process, the logs are conveyed from the storage yards to devices which chip the logs into small chips uniform in size. Other processes reduce the waste cuttings from the wood to small uniform pieces. The chips then are reduced to individual wood fibers, either by steam or by mechanical defibering. This process is demonstrated in Fig. 5-1. Small amounts of chemicals are added to enhance the desired properties when the chips are soaked, steamed, and cooked to produce the wood fibers. The enhanced fibers then are permitted to settle, forming a mat similar to thick paper, felt, or a thick cardboard. The lengths of mat or wetlap, as it is called, are fed into presses in which heat and pressure are applied to produce thin, hard sheets. After the wood is pressed and cured, it is humidified by adding moisture to stabilize it with its surrounding air; then it is trimmed and cut to standard dimensions, wrapped, and readied for shipment.

The first hardboard process was discovered by William H. Mason of Laurel, Mississippi in 1924. While conducting experiments to make paper and insulation board, Mason discovered the hardboard process, which resulted from a malfunction of his test equipment. The accidental development of hardboard was rapidly accepted, and the first plant was established in 1926 to produce the first hardboard under the trade name of *Masonite*.

Sizes and Grades of Hardboard

Hardboard, or *Masonite,* is available in *Standard, Tempered,* and *Service* classifications.

Standard Hardboard

The standard hardboard is produced during the basic hardboard process. It is strong, water-resistant, easy to machine, and quite useful for furniture backs and the base pieces for veneer or plastic laminates. Standard hardboard has dimensional stability—it does not shrink or warp, and is easily worked with both machine and hand tools.

Tempered Hardboard

Tempered hardboard is identical to standard hardboard, except that certain chemicals are added before the heat-treating process, causing it to become more dense, stronger, and harder with greater resistance to cuts and scratches. The tempered hardboard is often finished with various plastic surfaces, which makes it useful in bathrooms and for exterior siding. It can be obtained in uncoated sheets with a dark-brown, hard, and shiny appearance.

Service Hardboard

Service hardboard is similar to the standard hardboard, except that it is lighter in weight, can be smooth on only one side, and is available with various surface patterns. Service hardboard is not quite so strong as either the standard or the tempered hardboard.

The perforated and decorated pieces of hardboard usually are made from standard hardboard, which is available in various cut patterns. The decorative patterns are used for room dividers, screens, and paneling (Fig. 5-2). Pegboard is another well-known variation of perforated hardboard (Figs. 5-3 and 5-4). Hardboard also can be obtained prefinished, in wood-grain patterns, and in several thicknesses. The common thicknesses are generally 1/8-inch, 1/4-inch, 1/2-inch, and 3/4-inch. As with plywood, the standard width and length of a full sheet normally is 4 feet by

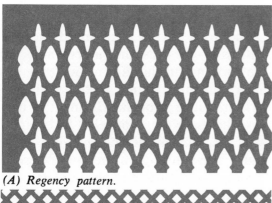

(A) Regency pattern.

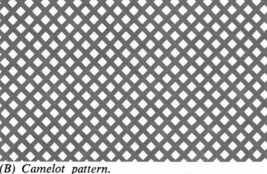

(B) Camelot pattern.

(C) Cloverleaf pattern.

Fig. 5-2. Decorative hardboard patterns. (Courtesy Masonite Corporation)

Fig. 5-3. Pegboard for garages and work areas. (Courtesy Masonite Corporation)

Fig. 5-4. Decorative pegboard conserves space in homes. (Courtesy Masonite Corporation)

8 feet. Other thicknesses and sizes are available. Some of the uses for hardboard are shown in Figs. 5-5 through 5-9.

Particle Board

Particle board is similar to hardboard, except that in addition to the added binders and bonding elements, the wood chips can be any size, and they are not necessarily uniform in size in any given piece. The particles also can be made from different woods. Any type of wood, hard or soft, can be used. There are many uses of particle board; it is sold under names such as *chipboard, chipcore, versibond,* and many others.

The two types of particle board are (1) platen-pressed or mat-formed, and (2) extruded. The platen type of particle board is made with machines and processes similar to those used to make hardboard. In the extruded type of particle board, the materials are squeezed through a set of forming rollers to emit a continuous sheet of chipboard, which is pressed, hardened, and automatically cut into lengths. The platen-pressed particle board is made in separate pieces from the beginning. The binder and chips are

Fig. 5-5. Hardboard panels for decoration. (Courtesy Masonite Corporation)

Fig. 5-6. Decorative shelves of molded hardboard. (Courtesy Masonite Corporation)

spread onto large, flat surfaces, called platens; then they are heated and squeezed to form the particle board. The platen method also is used to make the thicker types of particle board, such as ceiling tiles, insulation, and cores for the

laminated coatings.

The wood particles are mixed with the synthetic adhesives or binders and fed into forming machines in which they are made into mats similar to the wetlap in the hardboard process. During the process, the mats are controlled for weight, water, and chemical content. The chipboard is fed through a prepress where it is compressed to about one-half its original thickness, but it is not completely bonded. The mat is then trimmed on the edges and fed into steam-heated hot presses for the final curing and hardening. The hardened board is then fed to the stackers, and is cut automatically to size with sizing saws.

Fig. 5-7. Hardboard patterns for interior decoration. (Courtesy Masonite Corporation)

Particle board is a product which can be engineered and designed for specific purposes. A wide variety of products are made as standard products, but many more can be made to suit the desires of the individual customer. Particle-board products are available in a number of densities, strengths, thicknesses, and finishes. Some of the many places where particle board can be used in the home are

Fig. 5-8. Hardboard siding for a pleasing textured appearance. (Courtesy Masonite Corporation)

shown in Fig. 5-10. Particle board can be hard and dense and used like wood; it can be a core for the veneers; or it can be made into a loosely bonded material for ceiling and acoustical tiles (Figs. 5-11 through 5-14).

Particle-board production today is more than double the production of a few short years ago, when the manufacture of particle board was begun. It can be used in virtually any place where a smooth, stable panel is needed; and it is available in many textures and strengths. The major uses today are for the cores in veneered furniture, paneling, shelving, and for the interior core in sink tops and cabinets. Other uses include the laying of particle board over concrete or subfloors to provide a smooth surface for the application of carpet or floor tiles; the fireproof panels used in roof decking; and in wall structures where the panel consists of thick layers of fibrous materials and plastic binders to provide a board that is both a finished surface and an insulator (see Fig. 5-10).

Particle board can be made waterproof, it does not warp, and it requires no new methods or materials and machines to work it. It is used widely in manufacturing industrial furniture, such as school chairs and desks. Particle board also is used extensively in the furniture industries in bathroom and kitchen furniture— especially for cabinet units with the laminated plastic countertops. Particle board, in many instances, utilizes the product that normally would be discarded or wasted; thus it helps to conserve resources. Two pieces of veneer paneling, such as the paneling that might be used in making furniture, are shown in Fig. 5-15. One piece has a plywood core, while the other piece has a particle-board core.

One advantage of particle board is that it can be made in the desired width, thickness, and length; therefore, very little

Fig. 5-9. Exterior hardboard panels on commercial buildings. (Courtesy Masonite Corporation)

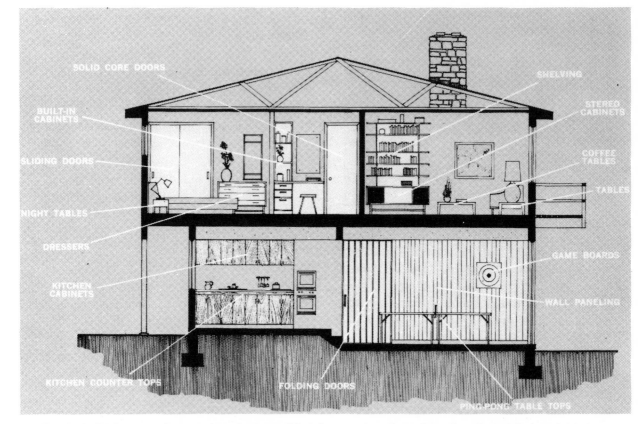

Fig. 5-10. Designers and users of products requiring flat panel surfaces have found particle board ideal for scores of uses. (Courtesy National Particleboard Association)

Furniture

tables
(dining room, coffee, end,
step, dinette, library,
game, banquet)
buffets
credenzas
book cases
headboards
office furniture
(desks, book cases,
cabinets, typewriter stands,
office machine tables,
conference tables)
school furniture
(desks, writing tables,
work tables, chairs)
church pews
chests
bureaus

Product Design

toys
pool tables
ping pong tables
game boards
portable displays
signs
pianos
organs
stereo cabinets
toy chests
coffins
dark room equipment
packaging
workbenches and cabinets
ski cores
movie sets
storage units
printing blocks

Home – Commercial Building

paneling
room dividers

wainscots
shelving
doors
(solid core, sliding, bifold)
partitions
sink tops
counter tops
cabinets
chalkboards
store fixtures
floor underlayment
mobile home floors
drawers
elevator cabs
light enclosures
vanitories
soffits
siding
concrete forms
radiator covers
flooring
mantels
valances

Fig. 5-11. Wood products include ceiling panels to enhance the appearance, light, and acoustics in a room. (Courtesy Conwed Corporation)

Fig. 5-12. Ceiling of wooden beams and ceiling tiles made from wood fibers add to the beauty and usefulness of a room. (Courtesy Conwed Corporation)

Fig. 5-13. Wood fiber ceiling materials are used widely in commercial buildings. (Courtesy Conwed Corporation)

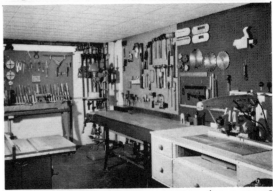

Fig. 5-14. Home craftsmen are extensive users of hardboard and particle-board products. (Courtesy Conwed Corporation)

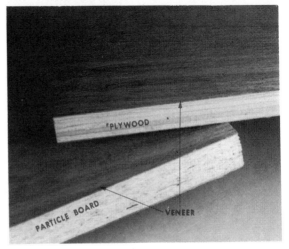

Fig. 5-15. Particle board, like plywood, can be veneered.

cutting, shaping, or waste is involved in building with the materials. Other factors which make it valuable as an industrial material are that it has no wood grain which might split, crack, or warp; it has no grain pattern that might show through a thin veneer or laminate material; and it machines easily with standard woodworking equipment. Further advantages of par-

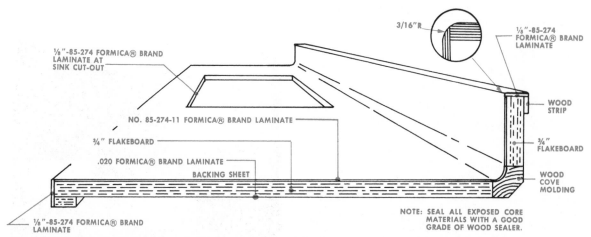

3/16"R

⅛"-85-274 FORMICA® BRAND LAMINATE

⅛"-85-274 FORMICA® BRAND LAMINATE AT SINK CUT-OUT

WOOD STRIP

NO. 85-274-11 FORMICA® BRAND LAMINATE

¾" FLAKEBOARD

.020 FORMICA® BRAND LAMINATE
BACKING SHEET

¾" FLAKEBOARD

WOOD COVE MOLDING

⅛"-85-274 FORMICA® BRAND LAMINATE

NOTE: SEAL ALL EXPOSED CORE MATERIALS WITH A GOOD GRADE OF WOOD SEALER.

Fig. 5-16. Typical construction detail for kitchen and bathroom counters with particle-board cores. (Courtesy Formica Corporation)

Fig. 5-17. Furniture and cabinets made from particle board and plastic laminates. (Courtesy Formica Corporation)

ticle board are that it can be painted or finished as desired; and it can be covered or veneered with plastics, paper, wood, or other materials (Figs. 5-16 and 5-17). Particle board is held easily with screws and fastening devices, and it is easily glued or assembled using other standard processes.

Questions

1. What is hardboard?
2. How does hardboard differ from particle board?
3. What are the advantages of using hardboard or particle board over other types of materials?
4. What type of hardboard is the strongest and hardest of the hardboards?
5. Who discovered the hardboard process?
6. Is a particle board always hard?
7. Where can particle board be used?
8. How does the use of hardboard and particle board help in conserving natural resources?

Unit 6 — Development and Manufacture of Paper

From the time man first appeared on Earth, he has sought to exchange his thoughts and to record his ideas for future use. In prehistoric times, cavemen laboriously etched pictures and symbols on stones and the walls of caves. Later, man employed other surfaces, like boards, leaves, and tablets made from stone or clay, as in ancient Babylon. The ancient Greeks used a parchment made from animal skins for writing paper. Perhaps, the first resemblance to paper was devised by the Egyptians more than four thousand years ago. The Egyptians used a reed called papyrus; it was woven together while wet, pulverized, and then pounded into a hard, thin sheet. The word "papyrus" is the origin of the modern word *paper*.

The first paper, as known today, was devised about nineteen hundred years ago by a Chinese court official, Ts'ai Lun (Fig. 6-1). Ts'ai probably mixed mulberry bark, hemp, and rags with water; mashed it all into a pulp; pressed out the liquid; and then hung the resulting mat outside to dry. This basic wood mixture set off a great revolution in communication. In early China, it became the means of communicating ideas, poetry, art, and the decrees of the emperor to the far corners of the Chinese empire.

The Chinese technique of papermaking was learned by the Moslems, who returned their concept of papermaking to the Middle East. From the Middle East, the art of papermaking was transferred throughout the Mohammedan countries and later to Spain with the invasion of the Moors from North Africa. However, the art of papermaking did not arrive in

TS'AI LUN, an official in the court of Ho Ti, emperor of Cathay, devised a writing material—see (a) Chinese symbol for paper—which replaced the bamboo strips and silk in use at that time. Shredding the bark of the mulberry tree (b), mixing it with scraps of linen and hemp, he saturated and beat it (c) and (d) to produce a pulpy mixture. He then dipped a mold (probably made of bamboo with a cloth "floor") into the pulp (e) and formed a sheet of paper on it. The paper was placed in the sun (f) and when dry was removed (g), ready for use.

Fig. 6-1. A Chinese court official, Ts ai Lun, devised the first paper. (Courtesy American Paper Institute)

Europe through Spain, until nearly one thousand years after its discovery in China. Another unique factor was that the method for making paper from wood was lost, and man has begun only in recent times to again make paper with wood and vegetable fibers—which are the most practical and plentiful of all the paper raw materials.

Oddly enough, papermaking also is believed to have crossed from China to the Americas across the Bering Straits to South America. The Mayan and Aztec Indians of Mexico made paper from the bark of the fig tree at a time when the process had been lost in Europe (Fig. 6-2).

The Mayans invented—and the Aztecs later improved—a writing material made from the fig tree. The bark (a), was softened by beating (b). It was treated with water and lime to remove the sap (c), and, finally, "felted" on flat boards (d). When dry, it was peeled off in sheets.

It seems the Mayans were the first people to produce "concertina-like" books (e) with hard covers. Paper was used by the Aztecs for some time as a form of tribute. The sketch (f) represents a tribute symbol for a large number of rolls of paper.

Fig. 6-2. The Mayan and Aztec Indians of Mexico made paper from the bark of a fig tree. (Courtesy American Paper Institute)

In Europe, during the Middle Ages, all the books were made by hand—although the Chinese had invented a form of printing. It was not until the fifteenth century, about the time of the discovery of the Americas, that Europeans developed a method of printing with a printing press. Until that time, all written work was done by hand, and there was relatively little demand for vast quantities of paper. There was little common education and only a few books.

With the invention of the printing press and the reforms in education occurring about the same time in history, more people learned to read. More people used paper to record business transactions, to write friendly messages, and to record important events in history. With this new ability came an increased demand for paper. No longer could the expensive, handmade paper be supplied in sufficient quantities.

Until the early eighteen hundreds, the Western world made paper from rags and cloth. The cloth fibers were shredded and treated, until a thin mixture of water and loose fibers resulted. Each sheet of paper was made individually by dipping a screen into the vat of water-suspended fibers and then filtering away the water. A good worker could not produce many sheets of paper in a day; therefore, paper was so expensive and the process so tedious that sufficient paper could not be produced to meet the growing demands.

During the American Revolutionary War, the colonists had little paper available. The soldiers in the Continental Army tore up old books to make wadding for their guns, and used leather was a common substitute for patches and wadding. The officers in General Washington's army sent him messages on scraps of paper; and John Adams, who later became the second President of the United States, wrote to his wife: "I send you now and then a few sheets of paper; this article is as scarce here as with you." Due to the scarcity of paper, General Washington once ordered the discharge of papermakers from the Continental Army, and sent them back to their paper mills.

In 1798, Nicholas Louis Robert, a clerk at a papermaking mill in Essenay, France, devised a plan for a machine that eventually would replace the hand-dipped screen and produce paper on a continuous roll. The machine, basically, was a long wire-screen loop which filtered the pulp as the loop turned, thereby forming a continuous mat for the pulp fibers.

Since Robert could not obtain money to produce his machine in France, he sold the patent to the Fourdrinier brothers in England. The Fourdriniers built a practical machine, but it could not provide inexpensive paper in large quantities. At this time in history, paper was made from cloth or rags, and the cloth was both expensive and scarce.

In 1719, René de Réaumur, a French scientist, had pointed to a possible solution; he had noticed wasps using tiny wood fibers to make nests which resembled paper. Réaumur suggested that paper should be made from wood fibers, but his suggestion was ignored until 1850 when a German, Friedrich Gottlob Keller, used this idea to develop a machine for grinding wood into small fibers. A few years later, Hugh Burgess, an Englishman, invented a chemical pulping process for the wood fibers; and in 1865, C. B. Pilghman, an American scientist, discovered the sulfite process for dissolving the unwanted resins in wood.

Mass-produced paper made from wood pulp provided a great increase in exchanging information. Newspapers multiplied, and less-expensive magazines appeared on the stands. The school slate vanished, giving way to notebooks and lined paper. Inexpensive paper books gushed from the presses. Paper also was used in clothing; the Boston mills produced over seventy-five million paper shirt collars during the years when detachable collars were used on shirts.

Paper was first manufactured in North America by William Rittenhouse at Roxborough, Pennsylvania (which is now a part of Philadelphia) in the early 1860's. Paper was handmade from rags at this early mill. The handmade papermaking art has grown from a village craft to one of the top ten industries in America today. The art of papermaking today is dependent on teamwork between business managers, researchers, technicians, and workers. Paper has changed from primarily a cultural product to a product adapted to use in many facets of modern life. It is used in packaging, in advertising, in building, in mass-production, in tissues and other personal products, and in many other ways.

The Papermaking Process

Most paper production begins with the men entering a forest to obtain trees, such as pine, fir, or hemlock. Nearly all the paper made today is from wood; but a small percentage is produced from rags, cotton linters, hemp, flax, and miscellaneous other fibers. In recent years, pulp mills have developed methods of making efficient use of the chips and residue from sawmill and plywood plants. One company alone uses sawmill by-products to produce more than a quarter of a million tons of paper per year; this ordinarily would have required more than one hundred million cubic feet of timber from our forests.

Millions of tons of wastepaper, including writing paper, magazines, old newspapers, boxes, and other paper and cardboard products, are collected each year and returned to the paper mills. Reclaimed paper materials are repulped and

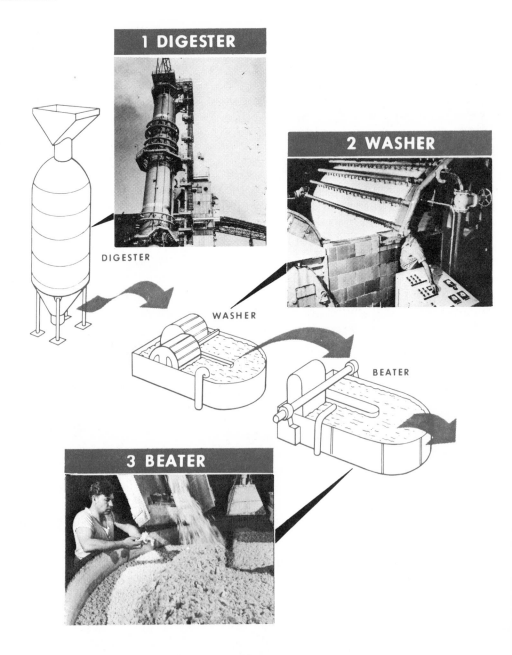

1. In the digester, sometimes known as the "pressure cooker," wood chips are cooked with chemicals under steam pressure and reduced to tiny fibers.
2. These fibers go through a washing process in which the pulp is sprayed as it revolves on large drums.
3. Moving into the beater, the fibers are separated for bonding; also sizing and coloring are accomplished in this stage.

Fig. 6-3. Papermaking by the chemical process.
(Courtesy American Forest Institute)

used in the production of large quantities of cardboard and paper. This use of wastepaper products lessens the drain on our forests.

Wood consists of millions of small cellulose fibers bound together by a gluelike natural substance or *lignin*. These cellulose fibers are the openings inside the tree through which the sap and resins flow. When the sap, resins, and lignin, as well as other materials, have been separated from the cellulose fibers by chemical means, the remaining fibers are *chemical pulp*.

When the wood is reduced to small particles by chipping or mechanical break-

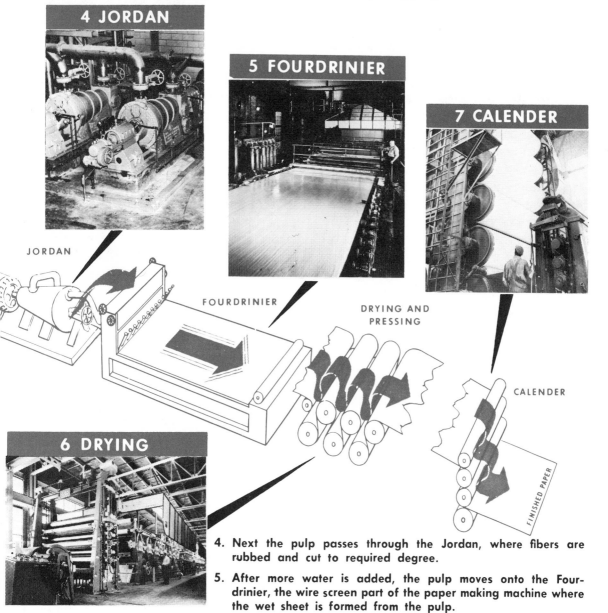

4. Next the pulp passes through the Jordan, where fibers are rubbed and cut to required degree.

5. After more water is added, the pulp moves onto the Fourdrinier, the wire screen part of the paper making machine where the wet sheet is formed from the pulp.

6. In the drying process, the sheet moves at speeds up to 2600 feet per minute.

7. Finally, the dried paper passes through calenders to give it required smoothness before it is placed on rolls.

ing, the resulting product is *groundwood pulp*. Groundwood pulp lacks the strength of most chemical pulps, but it is excellent for high-speed printing. Most of the newsprint paper from which newspapers are made is from groundwood pulp.

The mechanical and chemical methods of pulping wood are the two major processes. Other variations of pulping include the combination methods in which mechanical and chemical means are used, including the sulfate (or kraft), soda, sulfite, and cold-soda processes. Each of these processes produces a paper with the specific characteristics applicable to special uses for paper products.

The chemical process of making pulp involves cooking the wood, using one of several different methods to separate the fibers (Fig. 6-3). The method is dependent on the type of paper desired. The sulfate solution, for example, is used to make the kraft paper used in packages, corrugated board, grocery bags, and in many of the plastics used for countertops and electronic circuit boards.

The pulpwood is first sliced into thin chips about 1 inch square and ⅛ inch in thickness; then it is fed into large vats (often three or four stories tall) called digesters. The design of the digesters involves the same principle utilized by the common pressure cooker found in the home kitchen. The chips and chemicals are steamed until the mixture is reduced to a wet, pulpy mass. The cooking process dissolves the lignin and frees the wood fibers, suspending them in water.

The pulp is blown under pressure from the digesters to separate the fibers, which are then washed to remove the chemicals and other materials before the next process begins. The pulp used to produce white paper is bleached white before the next process; this is known as beating. The most common form of beating

involves passing the suspended pulp between sets of metal bars or knives to complete the separation, cut the fibers to the desired length, and fray the fiber edges, enabling them to cling together when formed into a sheet. During the beating process, color is added if desired, and size (a chemical which makes the finished paper water-resistant) can be added along with other chemicals to provide the finished paper with a specific property.

After the beating process, the pulp flows to the refiner machines where the fibers are cut to the exact size and frayed further to improve their ability to cling together in the sheet. The refined pulp, which is 99-percent water at this point and generally clear (like water), is run onto an endless meshed screen at the wet end of the papermaking machines. The papermaking machines are the Fourdrinier machines, named after the early developers of the process. The screen, which is a large loop of finely woven screen, is made to vibrate, causing the fibers to become interlaced while most of the water is drained and extracted. A sheet of paper remains, which is quickly sent through rollers for pressing the fibers together and further drying.

The newly formed wet sheet of paper travels at speeds of approximately thirty miles per hour through a long series of steam-heated rollers known as dryers. This newly formed sheet of paper, sometimes, can be 25 feet or more across. In the drying process, the water remaining is removed by heat, pressure, and suction. During the drying process, the paper receives its basic size and thickness.

After drying, the procedure again differs, depending on the type of paper desired. Many types of paper undergo a process called *calendering,* which provides a smooth finish by ironing the sheets between heavy polished rollers. Other types of paper are passed through tubs of chemicals which provide additional types of coating, such as the clay coating found on slick-surface magazines. The clay coating provides an excellent base for the printing process used to produce colored pictures. The papers are rolled into large rolls at the mills; then they are sent to various plants and factories where the paper is made into thousands of useful products (Figs. 6-4 and 6-5).

Other types of paper are made in sheets by processes quite similar to the old hand-made processes; these are known as *deckles*. The deckle papers include the special writing papers, the special parchment papers used for diplomas and similar documents, and other types of papers for which special effects and appearances are desirable.

Modern Uses of Paper

Paper finds many uses; perhaps, the most important contribution of paper to civilization today is as a medium to record knowledge. Engineering theories, technical manuals, blueprints, patents, legislation, mathematical equations, chemical formulas, and, most important of all —the ideas which drive mankind forward, are expressed on paper. In any area of endeavor, paper is vital; the more complex the undertaking, the more paper is required to combine the details of the undertaking. The building of a small rowboat or motorboat involves less than 1 pound of paper for instructions, diagrams, and materials lists. The construction of a large cargo ship, however, might require 200,000 pounds of paper, including a large boxcar load of blueprint paper.

Paper is versatile, and it represents the perfect use of a basic material. It is used constantly for other materials, since it does the job more efficiently and more

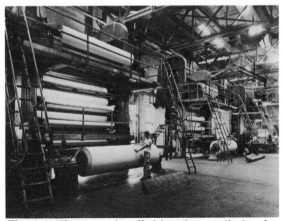

Fig. 6-4. The paper is rolled into large rolls for the users of paper. (Courtesy American Forest Institute)

Fig. 6-5. Testing the tissue on a large roll for uniform thickness prior to cutting into smaller rolls. (Courtesy Potlatch Forests, Inc.)

economically. Thick or thin, light or heavy, flexible or stiff, tough or fragile, plain or colored, large or small, the applications of paper are limited only by man's ingenuity. Paper provides lightweight cartons for eggs, as well as heavy-duty cardboard for shipping frozen meats and poultry. It is an ideal container for needles, nails, refrigerators, light bulbs, sofas, crackers, clothing, cement, and candy. In the form of layered sacks, it is used to deliver tons of food, livestock feed, and building materials.

Paper is used for many different applications in magazines, books, wrapping papers, newspapers, facial tissues, household tissues, industrial wiping tissues, construction materials, roofing, and many other items (see Fig. 6-5). Even the laminated plastics are made from layers of kraft paper which have been impregnated with plastic resins. A paper with the desired color and pattern is placed over layers of kraft paper; then the layers are placed in a large press where pressure and heat are applied to cure and harden the layers. The laminated plastics are widely used for the tops of counters, desks, and cabinet materials; also, they are used in the electronics industry for mounting circuits and electronic components.

Paper is used in making boxes and packing materials, for decorating houses, and for envelopes and food wrappers (Fig. 6-6). Other pulp products are used in making cellophane, camera film, rayon, and paint or other finishes. Paper also is used widely in science and medicine. The disposable, sterile bandages and uniforms are used in medicine; and paper is used to provide special filtering devices for separating solids from liquids in chemical laboratories. Absorbent papers are used to dry various chemicals, and special papers are used in testing. Paper can be impregnated with certain chemicals to provide a change in color when placed with acids or base materials; this type of paper is known as litmus paper.

However, the most effective use of paper is the printed word. No other method is so effective in passing information from one person to another. It is cheaper, more durable, and need not be remembered;

also, it is easily available for rereading and can store information which can be passed from person to person without confusion.

The future promises many new uses for paper. New improvements and developments provide substitutes for cloth, such as the disposable clothing now used; for heat and light reflective surfaces, such as the paper products used on space vehicles today; and for disposable containers for waste products which can be, along with the contents, reprocessed to aid man in solving the problems of pollution and depletion of his natural resources. Paper is being used for experimental shock-absorbing qualities in the manufacture of vehicles, as insulation for space vehicles, and for many other purposes. One need only to notice the paper products in the stores from month to month to be aware of the new array of paper products now available.

Questions

1. What ancient people first used a crude form of paper made from weeds?
2. Who was the developer of the first process for making real paper from pulp?
3. What product was used to make paper in the eighteen hundreds?
4. What product is used to make paper pulp today?
5. Who was the inventor of the machine used to make paper? Does the machine bear his name today?
6. Who was the inventor of the chemical pulping process?
7. What are the two main pulping processes?
8. Describe kraft paper.
9. What is meant by calendering?
10. What is a deckle?
11. List the uses for paper.

Fig. 6-6. Paper is used for a variety of packages and containers. (Courtesy Potlatch Forests, Inc.)

Unit 7—Environmental Controls

History has demonstrated that people and industry have callously disregarded their environment. Before the resources of the Earth were being used so extensively, mankind could cut the forests, and then leave the barren areas for nature to heal. Man could use these resources wastefully, with vast resources still untapped. He could discard his containers and his industrial waste carelessly without fear of depleting his sources of supplies.

Formerly, the world population was smaller and many areas were undeveloped. However, the world population has doubled since 1900, and it is expected to double again before the year 2000 (Fig. 7-1). Most of the habitable land areas of the world have been settled and developed. The natural cycles of the Earth are no longer capable of healing the world-wide ravages of man and industry.

Fig. 7-1. Pollution is a world problem. (Courtesy National Aeronautics and Space Administration)

Fig. 7-2. Urban spread reduces the land available for farms and forests. (Courtesy Westinghouse Corporation)

The resources of the earth become even more vital as the population increases; however, this is not the only problem. As the population increases, the cities spread, and the land used for houses is removed from the natural cycle (Fig. 7-2). Less land is available to supply more people.

Fig. 7-3. The increased use of resources per person is indicated by these paper products. (Courtesy American Forest Institute)

Still another factor in the problem is that the use of the various resources per person is increasing. For example, the *per capita* use of paper products in 1970 was about 80 pounds for the world population (Fig. 7-3). This is expected to increase to about 110 pounds of paper products per person by 1980.

If the resources of the world are to support the larger population, man must manage his resources carefully. In addition, his scientific and technical abilities must be utilized to improve industrial processes for preventing pollution of the environment. Techniques must be found to convert industrial wastes and the wastes from cities and communities into useful products. Thus, the environmental problems for the wood industries are centered around four areas: (1) Air, (2) Water, (3) Forests, and (4) Recycling wastes.

Conservation of the Forests

The forests of the world must be used efficiently for several reasons. These resources are important, but the trees also provide other important functions. First, the trees and the fallen leaves absorb the water from rainfall. This permits the water to be absorbed into the soil where it feeds the rivers, streams, and springs and helps to maintain the water level in the soil. The water level supplies the water for the wells which supply man with water. Secondly, a young, vigorously growing tree absorbs carbon dioxide (which is poisonous to man) from the air and, in turn, throws off oxygen (which is needed by man) into the air. This type of tree throws off a quantity of oxygen about equal to the quantity needed by one person.

A growing tree also throws off water vapor into the air. This cools the air, and the water vapor rises to form rain clouds.

The rain clouds condense, and the rain falls to continue the cycle.

When the trees are cut and removed from the land, the water rushes downhill, carrying away the rich, fertile topsoil. This *soil erosion* also permits the soil to become hard and packed; therefore, new seeds cannot take root to stop the erosion. The improper cutting of forests can cause erosion, disrupt the rainfall, deprive man of needed oxygen, and permit carbon dioxide to accumulate. The forests are said to be the lungs of the world.

The forests also provide recreational areas (Fig. 7-4). Forests, both public and private, serve as parks for outings and camping, for hunting and fishing, and for game preserves.

Private companies invite public use of nearly 62 million acres of their land.

Each person, each day, breaths oxygen production of at least one tree.

Forests are fun. Millions of Americans used commercial forests last year for recreation.

Hundreds of thousands of persons backpack on commercial forest land.

Logging increases browse for game animals.

Some of the finest fishing streams in the world are in America's commercial forests.

Fig. 7-4. The forests provide recreational areas. (Courtesy American Forest Institute)

Many forests are owned and farmed by lumber and paper industries. These industries, for the most part, have managed

their forests for several decades. Their efforts at conservation have permitted them to maintain the position that they can grow more trees then they cut (Fig. 7-5). These harvesting and conservation practices have been discussed earlier. It is important to improve these practices and to extend conservation practices to all the forests in the world.

Research also is needed to improve the various types of trees. "Super" trees can be developed which grow larger and faster and are more resistant to insects and various other factors.

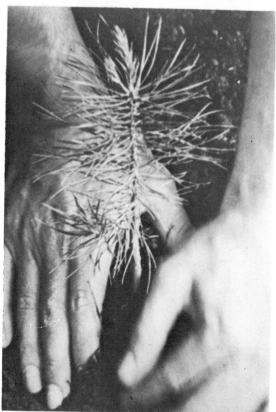

Fig. 7-5. Forest conservation aids in replenishing the forest. (Courtesy American Forest Institute)

Air Pollution and the Wood Industries

The reduction of the undesirable qualties from the smoke emitted from wood and paper factories is a serious problem. The two major problems involved in air pollution are: (1) Reducing the solid particles from the smoke, and (2) Reducing the odors.

The tiny particles or *particulates* in the smoke are removed by one of three processes. "Scrubbers" wash the particulates from the smoke by forcing the smoke through spray chambers which wash out the solids. The *precipitators* and *precipitrons* (Fig. 7-6) are electronic devices which place an electronic charge on the particles. The particles are then attracted to metal screens with unlike charges. *Filters* similar to the air and oil filters on an automobile also are used. The air is forced through porous materials in which the particulates are trapped while the air

Fig. 7-7. Special filters also are used to trap smoke particles.

Fig. 7-6. Precipitrons are installed to reduce the smoke particles. (Courtesy Weyerhaeuser Company)

escapes (Fig. 7-7). The particulates are produced primarily by the burning waste products and the fuels burned to provide the power for factories.

The more difficult problem, however, is in removing odors, since the human nose can detect odors with as little as only one part of odorous material per billion parts of air. The chief offender in producing undesirable odors is the sulfate pulp mill used in making kraft paper. Kraft paper is used in containers, construction paper, plastic laminates, etc.

In making kraft paper, the odor originates when the black liquor from which the pulp is extracted contacts the hot exhaust gases. This occurs in the boilers where the black liquor is processed; a hot gas with a high sulfur content is emitted, which causes the odor.

New boilers which keep the exhausts separate from the black liquor have been developed. The exhaust gases also are recycled back into the process in a *vaposphere* (Fig. 7-8) to reduce the sulfur content further. The present boiler and vaposphere techniques can reduce the sulfur content further. The present boiler and vaposphere techniques can reduce the

Fig. 7-8. A vaposphere condenses and recycles the vapor particles in smoke and aids in reducing odors. (Courtesy Weyerhaeuser Company)

sulfur emission from about 8000 pounds to about 400 pounds per day.

Water Pollution and the Wood Industries

The wood industries long have contributed to water pollution primarily in two ways. Formerly, the logs were soaked in the rivers to soften them for slicing into plywood. The bark chips and wood chemicals absorbed by the water contributed to pollution. Special holding ponds which are not a part of the public waterways are now used. Thus, contaminated water is no longer drained into the rivers.

The major pollutant, however, is the papermaking process. Formerly, the water used in the pulping and processing became heavily contaminated with wood fibers and chemicals. Then, this contaminated water was discharged directly into a river. Now, the water is recycled into

the process where the residues can be reclaimed. The remaining water is then drained into the clarifier tanks where chemicals are added to cause the solids to settle. Aeration basins are used to add oxygen to the water; then it is pumped to the holding ponds (Fig. 7-9). Any final

Fig. 7-9. Settling tanks and aeration basins aid in removing solid wastes from liquids.

purification to remove bacteria is done in the holding basin. Then the pure water can be discharged without harm; or it can be reused (Fig. 7-10).

Fig. 7-10. Purified water can be discharged safely.

This water purification process is identical to the process used to purify sewage. Some of the paper companies have incorporated their wastes with the raw sewage from nearby communities for mutual economy in reducing industrial and municipal pollution.

Reclaiming Wood Wastes

To promote the most efficient utilizattion of the world's forests, new techniques are being developed to reclaim and recycle the materials formerly considered to be wastes. This can be accomplished in many ways. New products can be developed from the sawdust or wood chips previously discarded as waste. Other products can be developed from reclaimed wood products, and wastes can be recycled into the original manufacturing process.

Sawdust, for example, previously was burned as waste. Now, the sawdust is used to make the chipboard used in furniture and construction. The sawdust can be compressed into fireplace "logs" (Fig. 7-11), and it also can be reduced chemically to make certain types of paper.

Where the sawdust and the chips are still burned, the heat is used to generate power to run the factory. The carbon particles in the smoke also are removed by the precipitrons; then the particles are used to make the "activated" charcoal for the filters in many devices. The carbon also can be compressed to make the familiar charcoal briquette for outdoor cooking.

A process also has been developed to reclaim the wood fibers (mostly from paper) in garbage. The *hydrapulp* process mixes the garbage with water, and through settling and centrifugal force separates the metal, glass, and other solids from the garbage. Up to 50 percent of

Fig. 7-11. This machine compresses sawdust into fireplace logs; thereby recovering useful material that formerly was wasted.

the wood fibers can be reclaimed from the remaining liquid and recycled into new paper products.

Problems in Environmental Controls

The solution to pollution is a difficult problem. There are many sources and causes of pollution. The actual solution, in most instances, must be accomplished by the industries themselves (Fig. 7-12).

Fig. 7-12. Industry and environment must learn to work together.

Although most of the industries favor these controls, they are not feasible in some instances.

First, the remedy for pollution is quite expensive. In 1971, about 750 billion dollars were spent in the entire world for antipollution controls (Fig. 7-13). This expense must be borne by the industries, which can exist only if they make a profit. Thus, the industries are faced with a terrible dilemma: If pollution is not controlled, the resources of the world ultimately will be exhausted; however, if they go deeply in debt for pollution controls, the industry might be bankrupted.

Although one might think that the simple solution is to eliminate the industry, this logic is not complete. Today, one farmer produces enough food to feed more than forty people, most of whom live in cities and work in offices, services, or industry. The farmer needs the industrial products to maintain his high rate of production. Thus, industry is vital to modern living. To eliminate industry entirely, also would eliminate in large portion of the world's population, due to hunger, disease, or war over food or resources. For the people in the world today to survive, industry and science must find ways of controlling the environment.

Fig. 7-13. Continual checking is required to prevent pollution.

Still another problem facing industry is the lack of knowledge about the environment. Since the concern for the environment is relatively recent (dating from the early nineteen hundreds in the forest industries), there is relatively little research that has been proved adequately. Therefore, a proposed remedy might accidentally prove to be harmful.

Another example is the use of nuclear reactors to generate electricity. Most of the electrical generators burn the fossil fuels (coal, natural gas, and oil) to generate the steam that turns the generators. The use of nuclear reactors conserves these fuels and also eliminates the smoke from the burning fuels. However, large quantities of water were needed to cool the reactor; then the heated water was pumped into the rivers. Investigations revealed that the heat carried to the river changed the biological balance in the river, resulting in about the same condition caused by chemical pollution.

Solutions to both these problems are being developed; however, they serve to demonstrate that little is known about this great problem. Governments, scientists, educators, and industries are all working together to solve these problems (Fig. 7-14). In the future, many more people will be needed in careers related to solving environmental problems and to continue the efforts to control the environment.

Study Activities

Woodworking provides an opportunity to study environmental problems actively. One method is to find a use for the materials that normally are classified as wastes. These materials include sawdust, small scrap pieces of wood, and pieces of wood with defects or spots. Resources can be conserved by utilizing these materials.

Fig. 7-14. Laboratory research is necessary to develop new methods of fighting pollution.

Activities which utilize these so-called waste products include making small useful objects, such as tool handles, lamps, wall brackets, picture frames, and similar projects. Another activity for utilizing products, such as sawdust, include marketing sawdust for flower beds, for the floors in animal cages, and for the raw material from which other products can be made. The wood industries are beginning to explore the latter possibility with considerable interest. Sawdust can be used for fuel, chemicals, cardboard, pulp, and other valuable items. Also, it can be reprocessed and then mixed with binding materials (similar to glue) to make molded products. The molded products include the molded decorative pieces for wood furniture and various other types of products. Products made from sawdust can be experimented with in woodworking by mixing fiber-glass resin with sawdust.

This is done by mixing a small quantity of fiber-glass resin with a catalyst, with only enough resin to bond the sawdust. The mixture should be nearly all sawdust with only a small quantity of resin; however, the mold should be prepared before beginning to prepare the mixture. Care should be taken to avoid inside edges on the mold (Fig. 7-15) which prevent the pattern being removed from the mold. The mold should be smooth, and a light coating of petroleum

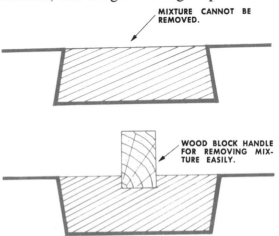

MIXTURE CANNOT BE REMOVED.

WOOD BLOCK HANDLE FOR REMOVING MIXTURE EASILY.

Fig. 7-15. Incorrect (top) and correct (bottom) methods of preparing a mold cavity for a sawdust and fiber-glass resin mixture.

jelly or paste wax should be applied before each application.

After the sawdust and fiber-glass resin have been mixed, it should be pressed firmly, but not forcefully, into the mold. Then the mixture should be permitted to cure, before it is removed from the mold. Small pieces of wood can be embedded in the back portion of the material; they should be projected slightly (see Fig. 7-15). These pieces can be used for handles to aid in removing the object from the mold; then they can be smoothed off with a chisel or sandpaper when they are no longer needed.

Another method of studying pollution is to study the effect of wood on our environment. Wood can be burned at both low and high temperatures. A piece of white cardboard can be held above the flame to collect the dust particles. The quantity of pollutants thrown into the atmosphere can be determined by collecting the soot and particles in this manner. The effects of wood on water can be studied by permitting a piece of wood to remain soaking in water for a period of two or three weeks. The acid level of the wood then can be tested with litmus paper to determine the effect of the wood on the water. The acidity of the water should be noted before the wood is placed in the water, and again after the wood has been in the water for the specified time. Also, the water should be checked for color and clearness.

Another activity for utilizing wood wastes is to redesign objects made of wood. For those interested in design, a wood project can be redesigned, to permit practice in designing products that incorporate the desirable characteristics of wood, beauty of wood, proper construction, and conservation of materials. Special products such as hardboard, fiberboard, and similar materials, as well as plastics and metal can be utilized in this manner.

Questions

1. List the various types of pollution.
2. What can be done to keep the water pure?
3. Why are the forests important to the environment?
4. How does the population affect the environment?
5. Why is "recycling" important?
6. What is a "precipitron"?
7. List the problems involved in the solution to pollution?

Unit 8 – Historical Design

The design of wood products, whether in constructing a building or a piece of furniture, affects both the appearance and durability of the products. The quality and durability of the product are affected by the strength of the material and the potential forces and loads on the object, the weatherproofing qualities of the object, and other factors such as the holding ability of nails, screws, and other fastening devices.

Factors affecting the appearance of the product include the historical aspects of the design and the quality of the designs with respect to the principles and elements of design. The surroundings also should be considered, if the object is to blend with and provide unity to the setting.

Historical design implies that a design is quite old; however, this is not entirely true, since these features are established more by influences than by inflexible patterns. In general, designs are divided into three broad categories: (1) *Traditional;* (2) *Provincial;* and (3) *Contemporary* designs.

The traditional designs derive their major influences from the various historical periods—*Early English, Gothic,* etc. (Figs. 8-1 and 8-2). The provincial designs are adapted from the traditional styles; but they were less ornamented and made from local woods. These designs include the *French Provincial* and the *American Colonial* styles. The contemporary designs include the *Scandinavian, Modern, Mission, L'Art Nouveaux,* and a style sometimes referred to as *Borax.* The *Borax* style was applied with some derision to a lower quality furniture designed generally in the modern shape, using overly elaborate veneer patterns. *Borax* furniture was produced chiefly in the nineteen twenties.

Traditional Design

Several major historical periods are included in the traditional designs. These periods usually have derived their designations from the king or queen of that period or from a leading furniture designer of that period. For typical examples, *William and Mary* and *Queen Anne* furniture (Figs. 8-3 and 8-4) have received their labels from William and Mary (1689-1702) and Queen Anne of England (1702-1714), and the *Chippendale* furniture is styled from the patterns of Thomas Chippendale, an English craftsman and designer.

The designs from France can be divided

Fig. 8-1. A chapel styled in the William and Mary period.

Fig. 8-2. A contemporary home in the Early English style.

into four major categories: (1) *Louis XIV;* (2) *Louis XV;* (3) *Louis XVI;* and (4) *French Provincial.* The latter three designs are paralleled by the so-called American traditionals, which include the *Colonial, Federal* or *Empire,* and *Victorian* designs. The chronological order of these periods can be found in Table 8-1.

Traditional designs include many phases resulting from the trade influences of various nations during the historical periods. For example, during the *Georgian-Regency* periods, the Portuguese and the English opened trading ports in the Orient—Hong Kong and Macao are two of these ports. As a result, some of the leading furniture makers during these periods, such as Thomas Chippendale, designed and made furniture which was influenced heavily by the Chinese designs.

The Chinese influence was quite popular with Europeans. In many palaces in Europe, entire rooms and extravagant pieces of furniture featured a Chinese style. The palaces Schönbrunn at Vienna, Nymphenburg in Munich, and various castles in Denmark, Scotland, and England bear pieces or entire rooms with Chinese influences. Since the Chinese styles were so popular, many cabinetmakers made furniture of lesser quality with Chinese designs. The Oriental influences slowly were absorbed into the general patterns of design to develop another de-

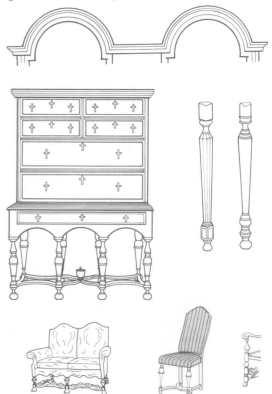

Fig. 8-3. William and Mary (1689-1702) furniture. (Courtesy The Seng Company)

Table 8-1. Chronological Tables of Period Styles

TIME	ENGLAND	FRANCE	AMERICA	OTHER COUNTRIES
Early Styles	Gothic (1100-1500)	Gothic (1100-1500)		Gothic (1100-1500) in Spain, Germany, Italy, etc.
Sixteenth Century	Renaissance Tudor (1509-1558) Elizabethan (1558-1603)	Renaissance (1500-1610)		Early Renaissance (1500-1600) in Italy, Spain, Holland, Germany.
Seventeenth Century	Jacobean (1603-1649) Commonwealth (1649-1660) Carolean (1660-1688) William & Mary (1689-1702)	Louis XIII (1610-1643) Louis XIV (1643-1715) Early French Provincial (1650-1800)	Early Colonial (1620-1700)	Late Renaissance (1600-1700) in Italy, Spain, Holland, Germany.
Eighteenth Century	Queen Anne (1702-1715) Early Georgian (1714-1754) Late Georgian (1754-1795) including: (Chippendale, 1740-1779) (Hepplewhite, 1770-1786) (Sheraton, 1780-1806) (Adam Bros., 1760-1792)	French Regency (1715-1723) Louis XV (1723-1774) Louis XVI (1774-1793) Directoire (1795-1804) Early French Provincial (1650-1800)	Late Colonial (1700-1790) (copies of English, French and Dutch styles) Duncan Phyfe (1790-1830)	European furniture of this time greatly influenced by French, Dutch, English craftsmen.
Nineteenth Century	English Regency (1793-1830) Victorian (1830-1895) Eastlake (1879-1895)	French Empire (1804-1815) Late French Provincial (1800-1900)	Federal (1795-1830) (also Duncan Phyfe) Victorian (1830-1900)	Biedermeier (1800-1850) in Germany.
Twentieth Century	Arts & Crafts (1900-1920) Modern Utility (1939-1947)	l'Art Nouveau (1890-1905) Arte Moderne (1926) Modern	Mission (1895-1910) Modern	Swedish Modern in Sweden. Modern in other countries.

NOTE: Since furniture styles have a tendency to overlap, it is almost impossible to determine the exact date when one period ends and another begins. The dates listed above are approximately correct, however, and they delineate the years of maximum popularity for each style. This table should serve as a quick reference to the leading styles in each century and as a guide to the interrelation of styles in the countries shown. (Reprinted by Courtesy Seng Co.)

sign influence based on history and trade between nations.

The traditional periods have influenced not only the furniture but also the buildings and houses made in traditional styles. The traditional styles also affected nearly everything used by the people at that time, in the way that our styles today affect the design of our furniture, homes, offices, and automobiles.

English Styles

The major design elements found in the English styles are reflected in Figs. 8-3 through 8-11. It is not unusual to find the elements from a style, such as the *Queen Anne* style (see Fig. 8-4), blended with another style, such as the *William and Mary* style (see Fig. 8-3). If the design features are blended from historical periods relatively close in time, the result usually is quite pleasing. However, blending the modern shapes with the traditional shapes can result in poor designs.

The *Early English* period includes the general period between 1550 and 1675 (see Fig. 8-2). The furniture is characterized by a shape which is straight and boxy with turned ornamentation on the legs and braces. Although the *American Early Colonial* style bears some relation to these styles, it has only a relatively minor influence today.

The *Middle English* period, in general, includes the *William and Mary* period (1689-1702) through the late *Georgian* period (1792). In this style, the growth of England as a world empire is reflected, and this style is reflected clearly in the architecture and furniture in the American colonies of that period. The *Later American Colonial* period is derived from these influences.

The *Regency* and *Victorian* periods span most of the 19th Century. These styles reflect an increasing utilization of machine methods and less-ornate ornamentation.

William and Mary—Note in the *William and Mary* style of furniture (Fig. 8-3) that marquetry and veneers were used often. The most prominent features were the flowing curves and inverted cup —a bell-shaped detail on the legs. The upholstery fabrics were tapestry, petit point, embroidery, damasks, brocades, velvets, and figured chintzes. Trumpet-shaped and octagonal legs were common, along with bun, pear, club, and hoof-shaped feet. All pieces were equipped with stretchers often set X-wise between the legs, with a finial at the conjunction. Cabriole legs were first introduced in this period. The cabinets and desks were provided with shaped skirts or aprons and drop handles on the drawers. The top rails of the cabinets were hooded with arched tops. The cabinets and highboys were made with six or eight legs, all connected with curved, flat stretchers. The upholstered settees or love seats resembled joined chairs with elaborately carved stretchers.

Queen Anne—The *Queen Anne* style of furniture (Fig. 8-4) can be recognized

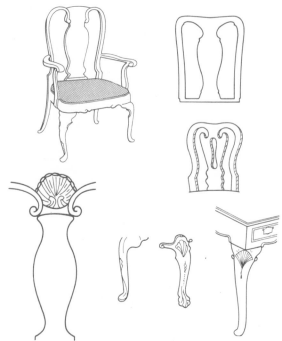

Fig. 8-4. Queen Anne (1702-1715). (Courtesy The Seng Company)

by the nearly universal cabriole leg and the undulating lines. The principal motif for decoration was the scalloped shell which appears at the knees of the cabriole legs, at the top of the chair splat, or at the center of the seat frame. Acanthus and floral motifs also were used. Favored upholstering fabrics were the brocades and embossed leather. The principal woods used were walnut, oak, and mahogany.

Chippendale—In the *Chippendale* style (Fig. 8-5) of the *Middle English* period, the chairs featured the cabriole leg. The chair feet varied, including the claw and ball, scroll, leaf-carved, hoof, and splay feet. The front rails were bowed slightly or serpentine. In the *Gothic* and *Chinese* (Fig. 8-6) styles, the back legs were slender and plain. The chair seats were upholstered and usually square with tapering sides. The chair backs were a variety of shapes, usually wider at the top than at the bottom. The splats invariably extended from the top to the rear seat frame.

Fig. 8-5. Chippendale (1740-1779). (Courtesy The Seng Company)

Fig. 8-6. Chinese Chippendale (1750-1800). (Courtesy The Seng Company)

The original modes also included "ladder backs" and ribband or ribboned backs. The divans were made with flaring arms and straight or cabriole legs. Large pieces were made with broken pediments. Fretwork decorations appeared on bookcases. Lowboys were made with cabriole legs, curved skirts, and carved decorations. Chippendale also produced beds, settees, clock cases, screens, desks, and many other pieces.

Chinese Chippendale—Open fretwork and all-over latticework of Chinese pattern are a dominant characteristic of *Chinese Chippendale* pieces (see Fig. 8-6). This characteristic appears in the chair backs and in the angles formed between the legs and seats of the chairs and

the legs and tops of the tables. The bookcases and china cabinets were made with latticed and trellised doors and with up-turned pagoda-roof tops. The legs on the chairs and small tables often were straight with decorations of raised carving in Chinese designs. Dragon feet clutching a pearl were often used. Stretchers were often used for chairs. Extensive use of carving for decoration was employed.

Hepplewhite—The *Hepplewhite* style of furniture (Fig. 8-7) was characterized by slender, fluted legs and rather low backs which give the pieces a somewhat fragile appearance. The spade feet also are characteristic. Dainty carving was used sparingly, consisting mostly of classical motifs—wheat ears, ferns, pendants,

Fig. 8-7. Hepplewhite (1770-1786). (Courtesy The Seng Company)

the back posts. The arms usually were short and serpentine or concave, curved, and carried down to the front legs. Upholstery of striped damask, silk and satin, and red and blue morocco was used with horsehair stuffing. Veneer was employed skillfully. Mahogany was the favored wood; satinwood, birch, sycamore, and imported woods also were used.

Sheraton—In the *Sheraton* style of furniture (Fig. 8-8), the secretaries were delicate and well-proportioned. The bookcases were made with shaped pediments and curved traceries on glazed doors. The

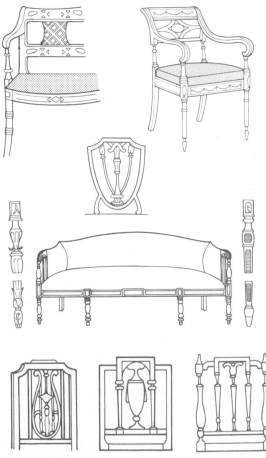

Fig. 8-8. Sheraton (1780-1806). (Courtesy The Seng Company)

husks, urns, rosettes, and the Prince of Wales feathers which he introduced. The backs of the *Hepplewhite* chairs are nearly always open and rarely upholstered. The most individual designs are the hoop, shield, and interlacing heart patterns. In the shield back, Hepplewhite kept the curve at the top unbroken. The oval backs were made with vase-shaped or lyre-shaped back splats. The *Hepplewhite* backs never reach the seat frame, always being supported above the seat by

sofas were graceful with light, slender legs. The backs of the chairs were square with delicately carved openwork in a wide variety of designs, including fretwork panels, urns, lyre or turned posts, shield, or cane. The splats rest on cross frames —never on the seat frame. The central panel often rises above the top rail. The early chairs were made with tapered legs and spade feet—the later models with spiral turning.

Adam Brothers—The *Adam Brothers* style of furniture (Fig. 8-9) featured slim, tapered legs, round or square and often fluted. The splats were a variety of designs—some square, some curved, and some open. Shield-shaped backs occa-

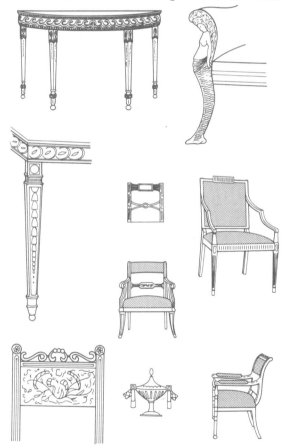

Fig. 8-9. Adam Brothers (1760-1792). (Courtesy The Seng Company)

sionally were used, even before they were popularized by Hepplewhite. The *Adam* shields usually were solid. Curved backs

and Greek legs also were used. The classical Greek and Roman patterns were used with light carvings, such as ornamental disks and ovals, spandrel fans, floral swags and pendants, drapery, acanthus, pineapples, human figures, and animal heads. The *Adam* pieces also are noted for the daintily carved moldings. Brocades, damasks, figured and striped satins, and silks were the favored upholstery fabrics. Mahogany and satinwood veneer were the favored woods, with sycamore, ebony, and other fancy woods used occasionally.

Regency—The *Regency* furniture (Fig. 8-10) featured chairs with both straight

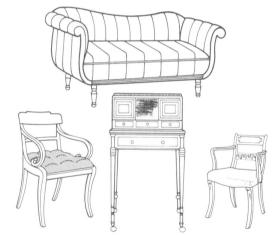

Fig. 8-10. English Regency (1793-1830). (Courtesy The Seng Company)

and concave backs, ornamented with fretwork, relief, carving, and gilding. The legs were usually straight without underbracing, sometimes slightly curved, and occasionally with classic double curves. The feet were a continuation of the legs, with straight collars or banding and an occasional use of the lion's paws. The tables often were inlaid, lacquered, and gilded, with straight legs on the larger pieces. The smaller tables were made with triangular bases. The china cabinets and bookcases were made with grillwork doors, columns, and pilasters. The sofas were of classic outline, occasionally with dog's or lion's paws feet.

Victorian—Furniture of the *Victorian* period (Fig. 8-11) is characterized by chairs with oval or horseshoe-shaped backs. The backs invariably are solid and upholstered, with some backs button-tufted in regular designs. The seats were upholstered, usually round or oval, and crowned in the center. The side rails were simple moldings with occasional carved ornaments in the center of the front rail. If used at all, the arms were curved and low, often joining the seat rail near the

Fig. 8-11. Victorian (1830-1890). (Courtesy The Seng Company)

back and serving more to brace the back than to support the arms of the sitter. Rockers were popular, with low seats and, usually, high backs. The dining chairs were made with rounded, open backs with one horizontal splat. The feet were simple scroll curves. The occasional tables usually were round, oblong, or oval with marble tops on many of them. Central pedestals were the rule, even on the larger round dining tables. Occasionally, the central pedestal was made of several carved or turned columns. The wash stand and dressers were made with marble tops.

The beds were made with high head-boards and footboards, and spool turnings were popular. Dressers often reached nearly to the ceiling with long beveled-edge mirrors. The sofas were provided sweeping curved backs with ornaments on the top rail of the back.

American Styles

The American styles were influenced heavily by the English, since the first thirteen colonies were English settlements and their influences had been brought from England. The designs brought from England were tempered by the woods available, the wealth available (remember that the colonists came to America to seek wealth, not to begin a new country), and the era in which the colony was begun. For example, the colony at Jamestown was settled in 1607. It was not until some one hundred years later that the colony of Georgia was founded and named in honor of King George of England. In the meantime, the styles in England had changed; therefore, the fashionable styles in the colonies had changed, and new furniture generally was made in the latest style. The American periods are shown in Figs. 8-12 through 8-15.

Another factor influencing design of furniture was the time available and the level of skill of the craftsmen. The craftsmen who came to America were not necessarily the best craftsmen. In many instances, they also were engaged in farming or clearing the land while attempting to build their houses and furniture; therefore, the frills, such as carved decorations and ornamental metal pieces, were omitted. Thus, the designs of the furniture and houses included designs of natural wood and a minimum of decorations. These patterns then became the *American Early Colonial* styles.

American Colonial—In the *American Colonial* period (See Fig. 8-12A), the Puritan influences resulted in simplicity of design. Some pieces were patterned after European models, but the American versions usually were simplified. Popular chairs featured the bannister backs, ladder backs, rockers, butterfly and gate-leg tables, high chests, cupboards, and settees. The seats of the chairs were solid wood, leather, and woven rushes. The upholstered pieces were scarce and usually were imported. The early legs were rough-hewn and square; the later legs were characterized by simple turning and shaping. Pine, birch, maple, walnut, and other native woods were used.

Current Early American—The currently revived or *Contemporary Early American* furniture (see Fig. 8-12B and 8-12C), has accented the utilitarian variations developed in the country or village styles of colonial American furniture which were not found in the city furniture. Decorative flourishes similar to those on the arms of the sofa and the hutch scroll were prevalent, and ornately turned legs were common. The drawer pulls and escutcheons tend toward garnished ef-

(B) Current Early American. (Courtesy The Seng Company)

(C) Contemporary Early American. (Courtesy Thomasville Furniture Industries, Inc.)

Fig. 8-12. Early American styles.

fects. Mechanical equipment is used widely to provide dual-purpose pieces, such as the sofa bed, swivel chair, and rocking chair. Maple and the fruitwoods are used extensively, with ash, hickory, and pine sometimes employed (see Fig. 8-12C). The natural finishes also prevailed.

Late Colonial or American Provincial —The *Late Colonial* period (see Fig. 8-13) reflects the transition of the colonies from the frontiers into the established communities with greater wealth and leisure. Duncan Phyfe is the only American

(A) American Colonial (1620-1790). (Courtesy The Seng Company)

(A) Late Colonial (1700-1790) or American Provincial. (Courtesy The Seng Company)

(B) Contemporary Colonial. (Courtesy Thomasville Industries Inc.)

Fig. 8-13. Colonial styling.

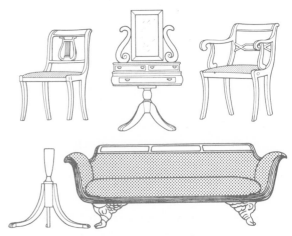

Fig. 8-14. Duncan Phyfe (1790-1830). (Courtesy The Seng Company)

craftsman during this period with a style of furniture named for him.

Duncan Phyfe—America's first great furniture designer was Duncan Phyfe (Fig. 8-14). Since he was a craftsman who conformed to prevailing preferences, this furniture was influenced by two groups: (1) The 1790-1820, 18th Century inspiration (*Sheraton, Adam, Hepplewhite*) and (2) The 1820-30, *American Empire* or *Federal* group.

Most *Duncan Phyfe* tables were made with a single-lyre or column pedestals and curule feet—sometimes three feet and sometimes four feet were used. This is a distinctive feature of modern reproductions. Other tables were made with carved molding or side rails and straight, reeded legs with turned feet. The feet were often covered with brass tips.

Mahogany was used almost exclusively. The favored upholstery fabrics were silks, satins, brocades, woolens, and later, horsehair.

Federal—The *Federal* period (Fig. 8-15) reflects the establishment of American nationalism and sense of unity. The banjo shape, American eagle, and the shield often were decorative features of this style. This period also is known as *American Empire*, since it parallels the *English Regency* or *Empire* and *French Empire* periods of time. Also during this era (1795-1830) the nations in North America were expanding westward.

In this period (see Fig. 8-15), the legs of chairs, tables, sideboards, and settees were straight. The sofas were made with rolled arms. The chests were provided with irregular fronts and mirrors. The center tables rested on heavy pedestals, and the sideboards were heavy and decorated with columns. Metal mounts were

Fig. 8-15. Federal (1795-1830). (Courtesy The Seng Company)

used extensively. Acanthus, cornucopias, glass knobs, scrolls, and patriotic themes were the favorite motifs. Mahogany was the favorite wood, with oak, ash, hickory, and the fruitwoods being used occasionally.

French Styles

The French styles of furniture include the patterns named for the kings of France and a style called *French Provincial*. The most widely known French kings are Louis XIV, Louis XV, and Louis XVI. These kings reigned from 1643 to 1792. During this time, two predominate features emerged in furniture styling—the cabriole leg (Fig. 8-16) and "rococo"

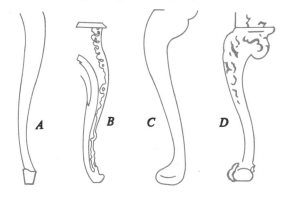

Fig. 8-16. The cabriole leg is used in various furniture styles: (A) French Provincial; (B) Louis XV; (C) Queen Anne; and (D) Chippendale. (Courtesy The Seng Company)

work. Also during this time, Louis XIV completed his famous palace at Versailles. The palace at Versailles was furnished so elegantly and extravagantly that it became the model for most of the palaces in Europe.

Until about 1675, furniture legs were made from straight-turned pieces; or they were made in a style called semicabriole. These legs were predominant in the early stages of the *Louis XIV* furniture with the full-cabriole leg becoming dominant in the later stages. The furniture made during this period was ornamented heavily with carvings and inlay work. During the reign of Louis XV (1715-1774), the furniture was similar, but the cabriole leg became longer and more graceful. The carbriole leg (see Fig. 8-16) is a graceful and flowing curved leg. Since France was the dominant world power in the early 1700s, the French influence spread throughout the other areas in Europe. Note in Table 8-1 the other styles which have been influenced by the cabriolet leg.

Louis XV—In the *Louis XV* style of furniture (Fig. 8-17), comfort, luxury, and beauty were stressed. Curves appeared where possible. Chairs were made with carbriole legs, carved knees, and scroll feet. The seats were broad and rounded, and the arm supports were carved and joined to elaborately carved seat rails which were always exposed. The tables were made with curved legs and onyx or marble tops. Furniture decorations included carving, metal inlay, ormolu mounts, painted panels, gilt, and lacquer. The upholstery fabrics used were tapestries, brocades, and velvets. The most popular woods were mahogany, walnut, oak, ebony, and chestnut.

Louis XVI—During the later years of the 18th Century, a style commonly re-

(A) Louis XV (1723-1774). (Courtesy The Seng Company)

(B) Contemporary Louis XV. (Courtesy Thomasville Furniture Industries, Inc.)

(C) Contemporary Louis XV stylings. (Courtesy Thomasville Furniture Industries, Inc.)

Fig. 8-17. Contemporary Louis XV.

ferred to as "rococo" was quite popular. This meant that every piece was decorated that could be decorated. Oyster shell or "mother of pearl" was inlaid along pieces of furniture; also, gold, silver, other ornamental metals, and even precious jewels were included. The wood itself was ornamented heavily with carving and scrollwork. Popular designs included the shapes of shells, animals, and plants.

Although the furniture of the reign of Louis XVI continued to be ornamented heavily, the cabriole leg lost its appeal, and a more clean, straight-line effect was begun (Fig. 8-18). The *Louis XVI* style

Fig. 8-18. Louis XVI (1774-1793). (Courtesy The Seng Company)

was refined, elegant in its simplicity, excellent in workmanship, and restrained in its decoration. The decoration consisted of classic motifs used chiefly to emphasize the authority and beauty of the line. A Marie Antoinette basket of flowers was a typical embellishment. The chairs were made with straight, tapered legs, carved or fluted like Greek columns. The seat rails were curved gently with square or medallion-shaped backs. Padded arm rests were common. The tables were made with straight legs like the chairs, sometimes carved or fluted, with carved aprons. Occasionally, the stretchers were curved.

French Provincial—The other major French influence, *French Provincial,* was similar to the American furniture designs in many respects (Fig. 8-19). Native woods, rather than the expensive imported woods, were used, since only the very rich could afford the expensive woods. Less ornamentation was used, since the craftsmen were required to invest more work and time in ornamentation. Note in Fig. 8-19 that the *French Provincial* furniture derives its beauty from its flowing shape, rather than from its ornamentation.

Fig. 8-19. French Provincial (1650-1900). (Courtesy The Seng Company)

The cabriole legs of the *French Provincial* furniture were simple and unornamented, and the decoration was simplified. The aprons on tables, chests, and cupboards often were shaped. Many of the chests and buffets had curved fronts. The early tables were trestle-type but the later tables were made with cabriole legs. Decoration was chiefly carved.

Recognition of Period Furniture

The leg styles and chair styles provide the most common means of recognizing furniture from the various periods. The various leg styles can be seen in Fig. 8-20A, and the various chair styles are shown in Fig. 8-20B.

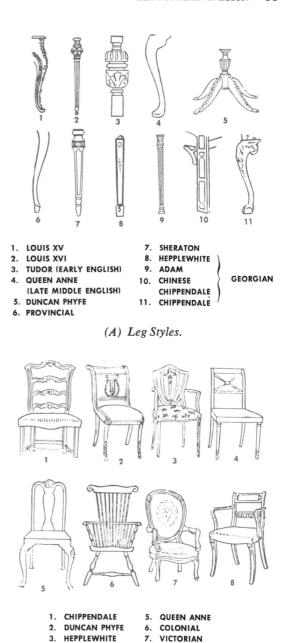

1. LOUIS XV	7. SHERATON
2. LOUIS XVI	8. HEPPLEWHITE
3. TUDOR (EARLY ENGLISH)	9. ADAM
4. QUEEN ANNE	10. CHINESE
(LATE MIDDLE ENGLISH)	CHIPPENDALE
5. DUNCAN PHYFE	11. CHIPPENDALE
6. PROVINCIAL	

GEORGIAN

(A) Leg Styles.

1. CHIPPENDALE	5. QUEEN ANNE
2. DUNCAN PHYFE	6. COLONIAL
3. HEPPLEWHITE	7. VICTORIAN
4. SHERATON	8. REGENCY

(B) Chair Styles.

Fig. 8-20. Keys of recognition for period furniture. (Courtesy The Seng Company)

The *Mediterranean* furniture (Fig. 8-21) is functional and sometimes masculine in appearance with deep carvings. The hardware is large and ornamental.

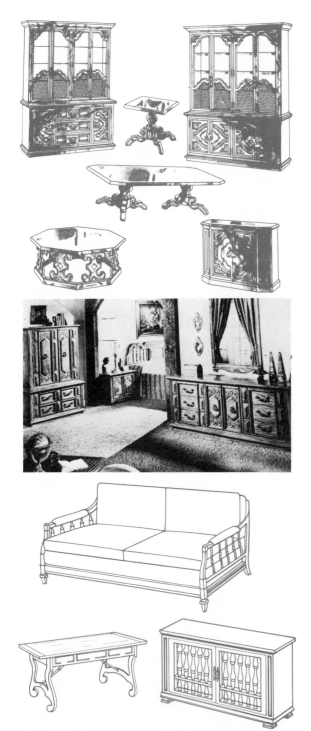

Fig. 8-21. Contemporary Mediterranean furniture. (Courtesy Thomasville Furniture Industries, Inc.)

Geometric patterns and facades of turned spindles are common. The woods are usually dark in color with red, black, or brocaded upholstery.

The *Mediterranean* influence sprang from local peasant craftsmen who used native woods and materials to build furniture for local use. The Moorish influence was effected on the decor and on the lavish use of high color and abstract geometric patterns which also were adapted by the Spanish and Italian artisans. The *Mediterranean* style prospered after the 16th Century, lost some appeal in the 19th Century, and returned to popularity in recent years as the *Spanish Modern* style.

Questions

1. What is implied by the term "historical design"?
2. List two provincial designs of furniture.
3. List two contemporary designs of furniture.
4. How have the traditional periods in history influenced our modern designs of furniture, homes, etc?
5. How and why did the Chinese influence furniture design?
6. List four of the more prominent English styles of furniture.
7. Who was America's first great furniture designer?
8. List three of the more common American styles of furniture.
9. How did Louis XIV of France influence the design of furniture?
10. Describe the French Provincial style of furniture.

Unit 9 – Design Factors

Design, whether it is a house or a small piece of furniture, presents various problems for the designer. He is required to consider the overall appearance, the structural soundness, and the final surroundings or use. A piece of *Early English* furniture is out of place in a *Danish Modern* group; even though both styles are well constructed, one style conflicts with the other. The setting is always important, since the finished piece should blend well with its surroundings to present a pleasing appearance.

Another factor in design is the materials or processes used. A project designed in a school or small shop should be appropriate for the abilities, facilities, and cost limits of the individuals who are to perform the construction.

Time is another factor in design which the beginner often fails to consider. Too many beginning workers attempt to build pieces too large or complex for the time available. A piece should be designed to be made within the facilities, time, cost, and ability limits of the builder.

Excellent design includes the function of the object. Some designers contend that design is entirely a matter of function; however, function and appearance are related, regardless of the philosophy of the designer. The function of the object should affect its shape; therefore, its function also affects its overall appearance. In designing an object or project, its intended use should be considered. The designer should contemplate methods of combining the functions and the appearance to enhance the general design pattern. Both poor design and excellent design are demonstrated in Figs. 9-1 and 9-2. In the poorly designed tray, the han-

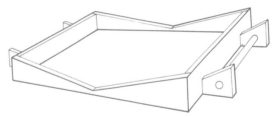

Fig. 9-1. The bulky handles on this tray indicate poor design.

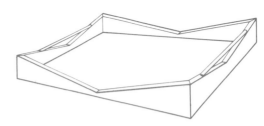

Fig. 9-2. In this improved design, the handles are incorporated into the functional design of the tray.

dles detract from the overall appearance. Although the appearance of the handles does not detract from the function of the tray, the handles do not contribute to a pleasing appearance or design. The design of the tray in Fig. 9-2 is excellent, since the function of the pieces was considered, and the handles, knobs, etc. were designed to blend with the overall appearance of the tray.

Factors in selecting a design should reflect all the considerations discussed above. Excellent design matches the materials with the purpose; also, it involves shape and ornamentation, cost and quality, and the decor. Decor refers to the appearance of the surroundings in which the object will be placed. The object should "blend—not blare."

Principles of Design

Design of wood products involves five major factors. These are:

1. Shape of the object, including the ornamentation and hardware.
2. Materials used, including fabrics and trim.
3. Proper finish, including colors and textures.
4. Construction quality and techniques.
5. Processes required to shape and fabricate the item.

If any of these factors are omitted, the resulting design may be unsatisfactory or detract from either the appearance or the utilization of the object. It is important that an object *look good* as well as *work good*.

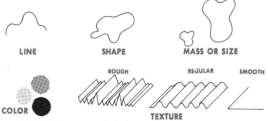

Fig. 9-3. Elements of design.

Designers utilize five basic elements of design to achieve a pleasing appearance. These elements are: (1) Line; (2) Shape; (3) Mass or size; (4) Color; and (5) Texture. The designer combines these elements in various ways to achieve certain effects, called *principles of design*. The principles of design include balance, contrast, proportion, repetition,

(A) Formal balance requires an equal shape or mass on each position.

(B) Informal balance involves balance through contrasts in texture or color, despite imbalance in size or shape.

Fig. 9-4. Balance.

direction, and many other factors. Some of these principles and elements of design are illustrated in Figs. 9-3 through 9-10.

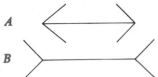

Fig. 9-5. The horizontal line (A) appears to be shorter than the horizontal line (B). This is due to the "direction" illusion provided by the slanting lines. The two lines are equal in length.

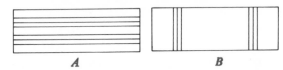

Fig. 9-6. The same basic shape can be provided a long, low appearance by use of horizontal lines (A), and it can be provided a more vertical appearance by the use of vertical lines (B), which provide the illusion of height.

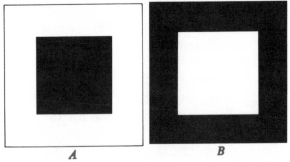

Fig. 9-7. Contrast in color can be used to provide an illusion of depth and distance in space. Note that the dark-colored inner square (A) appears to be nearer when it is bright or without color and surrounded by a dark-colored area (B).

Balance

Balance can be either formal or informal; it can be achieved by balancing two equal masses to offset each other. However, balance also can be achieved by using a bright vivid color or other element to offset a more somber dark color (Fig. 9-5).

Direction

Various lines can be used to make an object appear longer or shorter. Also,

(A) Contrasting sections of wood and ceramic tile.

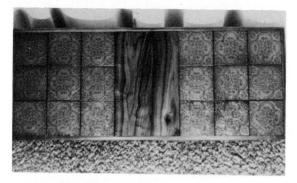

(B) Detail of top sections.

Fig. 9-8. Coffee-table top.

(A) The front and back of molded surface ornaments made from plastic and fibers.

(B) Typical ornamentation applied to a piece of furniture.

Fig. 9-9. Ornamentation can be applied after the piece of furniture has been completed.

lines can be used to make an object appear taller or wider and, in effect, present certain illusions by making one object subordinate to another (see Fig. 9-5). Horizontal lines can be used to provide a low, flat appearance to an object with a principal mass in a horizontal plane (Fig. 9-6A). However, vertical lines can be used to provide the illusion of height for a long low object which is to be placed in a given area.

Contrast

Contrast can be an aid in showing distance or nearness. Light-colored areas bordering a dark area tend to provide the illusion of depth or distance in space

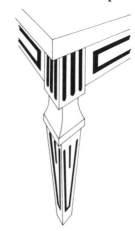

Fig. 9-10. Grooving or fluting provides both line and texture to this Italian Provincial design.

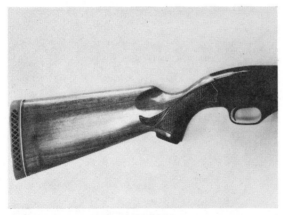

Fig. 9-11. Checkering provides texture contrast and line patterns on this gun stock.

(Fig. 9-7A). However, when these colors are reversed, the space seems to diminish and the massive light-colored object in the center appears nearer. In a larger room, an object should be made to appear closer

Fig. 9-12. Early American decor is created by combining the furniture style, wall materials, cabinet hinges and pulls, and draperies into a consistent pattern. (Courtesy Conwed Corporation)

to the viewer; however, the opposite effect is desirable in a smaller room.

Contrast can be implemented to achieve many interesting effects. A rough texture, such as coarse cloth, can be placed near a smooth metal or wood for a pleasing appearance. The cloth covers on the speakers in radios, stereos, and televisions are examples of pleasing texture contrasts. Other contrasts can be provided in color, texture, and shape. A coffee-table top with tile and wood contrasting sections is shown in Fig. 9-8. Many pleasing contrasting effects can be achieved by combining materials such as tile and wood, cloth and wood, metal and wood, or metals and plastics. Other contrasts are easily obtained, and they can either detract from or enhance the appearance of the object. The designer should be careful to make sure the contrasting materials do not detract from the object.

Ornamentation

Ornamentation applies to decoration of the object beyond the required structural necessities. Ornaments can include simple decorations; or they might include functional decorations as well—the hardware for drawers or hinges and other pieces. When used, the ornaments should be compatible with the style of the piece; they should blend with the total appearance. An ornament should not be the center of attraction; however, it should create small points of interest to enhance the total design effect. For example, an ornate Spanish-style ornament on a piece of furniture is out of place on a clean modern design. Another example of ornamentation can be found in comparing the designs of traditional pieces of furniture. The ornamentation on a piece of *Louis XIV* furniture would be completely out of place on a piece of modern furniture. When ornamentation is used poorly, the result is a displeasing total appearance, even though the piece has been constructed well.

Ornamentation can be achieved by applying a decoration to a piece of furniture after it has been completed (Fig. 9-9); or it can be achieved by enhancing its shape and contour. The slender cabriole leg of the *French Provincial* is free from an applied ornament, but its ornamentation results from its flowing, graceful shape (see Fig. 9-9B).

Surface texture or appearance also can be used for ornamental effect. The narrow grooves in *Louis XVI* and *Italian Provincial* furniture legs provide textured ornamentation (Fig. 9-10). Carvings and checkering (Fig. 9-11) are other examples of textured ornamentation.

Decorative Environment

Attractive design includes consideration of the surroundings (Fig. 9-12). A *Louis XIV* chair conflicts with a background of rough brick and ranch-style furniture. Many factors are involved in a decorative environment (Fig. 9-13). Interior designers specialize in providing the right "atmosphere" or decorative environment for a given situation (Fig. 9-14). Architects include the landscape and vegetation in the design of a building. Information relative to the decorative environment, including the best materials for walls, fabrics, floors, and colors can be found in Table 9-1.

Effects of Color

Color is known to provide definite emotional effects on people. The soft blues and green tones provide restful effects, but the vivid reds and violets used

Fig. 9-13. Modern decor is set by combining straight ornamental lines, modern furniture, and coverings. (Courtesy Conwed Corporation)

as predominant colors promote tenseness. A gray color is gloomy, and the light

Fig. 9-14. Pleasing interior contrasts can be created by utilizing different textures, such as the stone and papered surfaces in this room. (Courtesy Conwed Corporation)

Table 9-1. How to Correlate Decorative Elements

PERIOD STYLE	ASSOCIATED STYLES	WALLS & CEILINGS	FLOORS	FLOOR COVERING	DRAPERIES			UPHOLSTERY FABRICS
					FABRIC	COLORS	DESIGN	
EARLY ENGLISH TUDOR JACOBEAN CHARLES II	Italian Renaissance; Spanish Renaissance William & Mary Larger pieces of Queen Anne	Oak panels Rough plaster with oak trim Pargetry ceilings	Hardwood Stained dark, may be planks or flooring Stone, Tiles	Oriental and large pattern Domestic rugs Plain rug	Crewel embroideries, Hand blocked linen, Silk & worsted damask, Velvet, Brocade	Full bodied crimson, green and yellow	Large bold patterns: tree branch, fruits, flowers, oak leaf, animals, heraldic designs	Tapestry Leather Needlework Velvet Brocade
ANGLO-DUTCH WILLIAM & MARY QUEEN ANNE	Chippendale Early Georgian Louis XIV Smaller pieces of Jacobean such as gate leg table or windsor chair	Papered Painted (in light tones) Hung with fabrics Paneled	Hardwood flooring Parquetry	Oriental and large pattern Domestic Rugs Plain rug	Crewel embroideries, Hand blocked linen, Silk & worsted damask, Velvet, Brocade, India prints	Full bodied crimson, green and yellow	Large bold patterns: tree branch, fruits, flowers, oak leaf, animals, heraldic designs	Tapestry Leather Needlework Velvet Brocade
EARLY GEORGIAN CHIPPENDALE	Chippendale Early Georgian Louis XIV Smaller pieces of Jacobean such as gate leg table or windsor chair	Paneled Dado Painted, Paneled, or Papered in upper section in Chinese motifs.	Hardwood flooring Parquetry	Plain or small patterned rugs or carpets Oriental rugs	Crewel embroideries, Hand blocked linen, Silk & worsted damask, Velvet, Brocade, India prints	Full bodied crimson, green and yellow	Jacobean motifs Also classic medallions and garlands	Tapestry Leather Needlework Velvet Brocade
LATE GEORGIAN ADAM HEPPLEWHITE SHERATON	Chippendale (in Chinese manner) Louis XVI Duncan Phyfe Directoire	Plain plaster, Painted, Papered. Large wood panels, painted. Gesso ceilings	Hardwood flooring Parquetry	Plain or small patterned rugs or carpets Oriental rugs	Brocades, Damask, Chintz, Taffeta, Satins, Toile de Jouy	Delicate subdued, hues of rose, yellow, mauve, green and gray	Classic designs, small in scale: garlands, urns, floral, animals, etc.	Damask, Brocade, Velour, Satin, Petit Point, Leather in libraries
LOUIS XVI	All late Georgian styles 1 or 2 pieces of Louis XV and Directoire	Large wood panels, painted and decorated Wall paper in Chinese motifs	Hardwood flooring Parquetry	Plain or small patterned rugs or carpets Oriental rugs	Silks, Satin, Damask, Taffeta, Muslins, Brocade, Toile de Jouy	Delicate powder blue, oyster white, pearl, rose, pale greens, mauve, yellow	Stripes sprinkled with ribbons, flowers, medallions, lyres and other classic motifs.	Petit Point, Satin Moire, Velours, Chintz, Damask, Brocade, Tapestry

	Walls & Ceilings	Floors	Floor Coverings	Fabrics	Colors	Patterns	Upholstery
SPANISH RENAISSANCE	Italian Renaissance Early English Louis XIV	Rough plaster Painted Ceilings, same or beamed	Hardwood Tiles Linoleum in tile pattern	Spanish or Oriental rugs	Velvet, Damask, Crewel work, India prints, Printed and emb. linen	Rich vigorous colors; red, green and gold	Bold patterns in classic and heraldic designs, also arabesques	Leather Tapestry Velvet Linen Brocatelle
EARLY COLONIAL	All Early English styles William & Mary Queen Anne wing chair	Oak panels Rough plaster with oak trim Pargetry ceilings	Hardwood flooring or planks Linoleum in jaspe pattern	Braided or Hooked rugs	Crewel embroideries, Hand blocked linen, Silk & worsted damask, Velvet, Brocade	Full bodied crimson, green and yellow	Large bold patterns: tree branch, fruits, flowers, oak leaf, animals, heraldic	Tapestry Leather Needlework Velvet Brocade
LATE COLONIAL	Late Georgian Chippendale Queen Anne Duncan Phyfe French Provincial	Smooth plaster light trim Wall paper, scenic and Chinese designs Paneling Ceiling, plaster	Dark hardwood flooring Linoleum in plain or jaspe patterns	Hooked, braided, Oriental rugs. Domestic rugs or carpet, plain, two-toned or patterned.	Toile de Jouy, Damask, Chintz, Organdy, Cretonne	All colors, but more subdued than in early period	Scenic Birds Animals Floral	Haircloth Mohair Rep Linen Chintz Velours
MODERN	Swedish Modern Chinese Chippendale	Painted solid colors. Stripe, figured, plain papers. Combinations of above.	Hardwood Parquetry Linoleum in modern pattern	Carpeting Rugs in solid colors. Geometric patterns.	Textured and novelty weaves. All fabrics.	All colors. Bright to pastel.	Solid colors Modern Designs Stripes	All Fabrics Novelty weaves Plastics
FRENCH PROVINCIAL	18th Century American Colonial, Federal Biedermeier	Smooth plaster Wallpaper in scenic or Geometric designs.	Hardwood Parquetry	Aubussons Homespun carpet. Small pattern Orientals.	Chintz Cretonne Blocked linen, Velvet	Subdued colors. Pastel shades.	Screen Prints Block print	Solid colors Textured weaves Tapestry
VICTORIAN	Colonial William & Mary Queen Anne	Large pattern paper	Hardwood	Carpeting in large patterns. Orientals.	Velvet Brocades Damask	Turkey Red. Other rich colors.	Solid colors Formal Patterns	Haircloth Needlework

shades of tan are neutral. The yellow and orange colors, on the other hand, are bright cheerful colors.

The strong colors and black are not restful; therefore, these colors should be avoided in decorating bedrooms. The vivid and bright colors are desirable for kitchens and game rooms. Cheerful, but subdued, colors are preferable for dens, offices, family rooms, etc. Colors useful in decorating interiors and in selecting fabrics for interior use are provided in Table 9-2.

A basic color wheel which can be used to select colors is diagrammed in Fig. 9-15. The three primary colors from which all other colors are derived are red, yellow, and blue. Mixtures of any two of the primary colors result in the shades shown in the diagram. The *harmonizing* colors are those shades adjoining each other on the wheel. The *contrasting* colors are those colors directly opposite the first color in the diagram.

Table 9-2. Chart of Color Combinations

DOMINANT OR MAJOR COLOR	HARMONIZING COLORS	CONTRASTING COLORS	ACCENT COLOR
Pink, Rose	Red, Ruby, Orchid, Tangerine, Beige	Emerald, Olive Green, Aqua, Bottle Green	Copper
Coral	Pink, Red, Orange, Brown	Aqua, Bottle Green, Emerald, Royal Blue	Lemon
Orange, Pumpkin	Citron, Cherry, Yellow, Mustard, Copper	Bottle Green, Aqua, Royal Blue, Wedgwood	Olive Green
Yellow, Marigold	Lemon, Orange, Flame, Gold, Olive Green	Royal Blue, Aqua, Orchid	Tangerine
Lemon	Marigold, Pumpkin, Olive Green, Emerald	Lavender, Royal Blue Turquoise	Cherry
Olive Green, Chartreuse	Lemon, Marigold, Emerald Bottle Green, Wedgwood	Lavender, Orchid, Ruby, Wine	Pumpkin
Emerald, Kelly Green	Gold, Turquoise, Bottle Green, Olive Green	Cherry, Coral, Wine, Mustard	Pink
Aqua, Turquoise	Bottle Green, Emerald, Royal Blue, Lavender	Orange, Coral, Cherry, Wine	Chartreuse
Royal Blue, French Blue	Violet, All Blues, Turquoise, Raspberry	Lemon, Orange, Coral, Ruby,	Marigold
Light Blue, Cerulean	Orchid, Wedgwool Turquoise, Bottle Green	Orange, Ruby, Coral, Wine	Yellow
Lavender, Violet, Orchid	Light Blue, Royal Blue, Wine, Raspberry	Lemon, Marigold, Olive Grreen, Emerald	Chartreuse

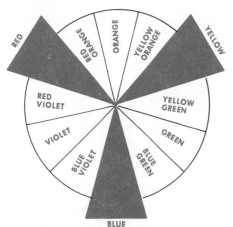

Fig. 9-15. Basic color wheel. The adjacent colors are harmonizing colors. The opposite colors on the wheel are contrasting colors.

Questions

1. What are the major factors to be considered in designing a student project?

2. How are the functions and shapes of objects related in design?

3. List the five basic elements of design.

4. List the design principles. How do they differ from the design elements?

5. What is meant by "decorative environment"?

6. Why are colors important in design?

7. How can ornamentation be achieved?

Unit 10 – Structural Design

How an object or piece of furniture is built affects its usefulness. Unless it is made to withstand the forces involved, it cannot function properly. A bookcase built in a way that it cannot support the weight of the books is not a good bookcase. The way an object is built directly affects its usefulness, and design includes a careful analysis of the structure involved.

Other design factors include the materials, the costs, and the ornamentation involved. An object which costs more than the customer can pay cannot be sold; and how it is built directly affects its final cost. If a piece of furniture is made from a solid, expensive wood, its cost is higher; however, if the same object is made from an inexpensive wood veneered with a thin coating of the more expensive wood, its final cost is less.

Other factors relating to the total cost include the wages of the workers, purchase of machines and tools required to construct the object or piece of furniture, and the time and complexity involved in the actual construction. An object which must be permitted to dry for several days

Fig. 10-2. Applied ornamentation, such as this molded panel, does not affect construction.

requires storage space; therefore, the cost of providing the storage space might be a factor in the design. Structural design, then, involves many aspects. The structural design includes every factor involved in the selection, construction, delivery, and use of the object or piece of furniture.

Ornamentation also is a factor in structural design, since the ornaments can be built into a material as an integral part; or the ornaments can be applied after the object has been constructed. Applied ornamentation has certain advantages and is sometimes used in mass-production techniques where the pieces of furniture are made by automatic machinery. An ap-

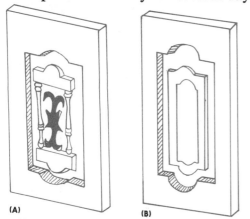

(A)   (B)

Fig. 10-1. Applied decoration can be used to change a panel from Mediterranean style (A) to Colonial style (B).

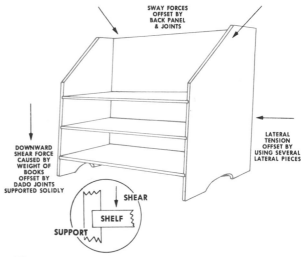

Fig. 10-3. Diagram of stresses in the design of a small bookcase.

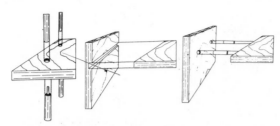

(A) Thru-pin joint. (B) Dado joint. (C) Dowel joint.

Fig. 10-4. Three methods of offsetting the vertical shear forces in a bookcase design.

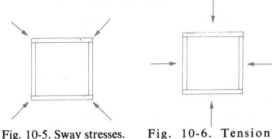

Fig. 10-5. Sway stresses.

Fig. 10-6. Tension (squeeze) stresses.

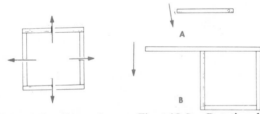

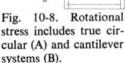

Fig. 10-7. Expansion stresses include pushing from the inside or pulling from the outside.

Fig. 10-8. Rotational stress includes true circular (A) and cantilever systems (B).

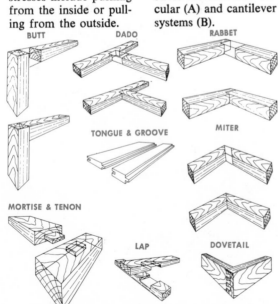

Fig. 10-9. Eight basic types of joints.

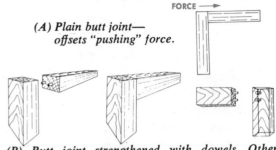

(A) Plain butt joint— offsets "pushing" force.

(B) Butt joint strengthened with dowels. Other methods of strengthening include braces, nails, screws, and splines.

Fig. 10-10. Butt joints.

plied ornament can be used to change a piece from *Mediterranean* to *Colonial* style (Fig. 10-1).

Other types of ornamentation (Fig. 10-2) can be purchased by the home craftsman, or used industrially. These ornaments can be made from plastics or wood and either stained or painted to resemble the desired wood. They can be purchased in various round and square shapes, patterns, figures, and long strips.

However, applied ornamentation has some disadvantages. It can be removed easily, must match the woods, and should be attached firmly. Ornamentation made as an integral part of the device is sturdier, blends into the wood grain, and does not show glue lines or hardware joints.

Selecting Construction Methods

A small bookcase can be used to demonstrate the factors involved in selecting the methods of construction and assembly. The stresses involved in designing a bookcase are diagrammed in Fig. 10-3. The stress is primarily in a downward direction; therefore, the sides of supports must be capable of withstanding these downward pressures. The weight of a stack of books is considerable; therefore, the joints involved must be strong. Note in the thru-pin and dado joints in Fig. 10-4 that the wood structure is used to support the weight, while small dowel

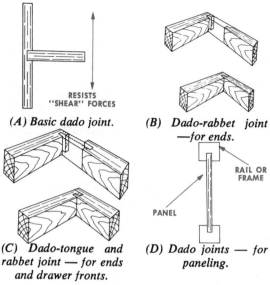

(A) Basic dado joint.

(B) Dado-rabbet joint —for ends.

(C) Dado-tongue and rabbet joint — for ends and drawer fronts.

(D) Dado joints — for paneling.

Fig. 10-11. Dado joints.

pins are used to support the weight in Fig. 10-4C. If the dowel pins are sufficiently strong to support the weight involved, they are appropriate; however, several dowels or one of the other construction methods might be needed. This type of analysis is referred to as an "analysis of shear forces," since dowels tend to shear or cut when force is applied. Other types of forces include sway (Fig. 10-5), tension (Fig. 10-6), pressure, expansion (Fig. 10-7), and rotation (Fig. 10-8).

Joint Selection

The selection of the proper joint is based on the stress analysis of the object. The stype of stress involved should be designed to offset these stresses. Eight basic types of joints (Fig. 10-9) are designed to offset certain stresses. These joints are:

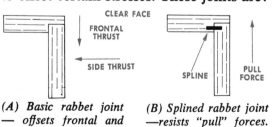

(A) Basic rabbet joint — offsets frontal and side thrusts and presents clear face.

(B) Splined rabbet joint —resists "pull" forces.

Fig. 10-12. Rabbet joints.

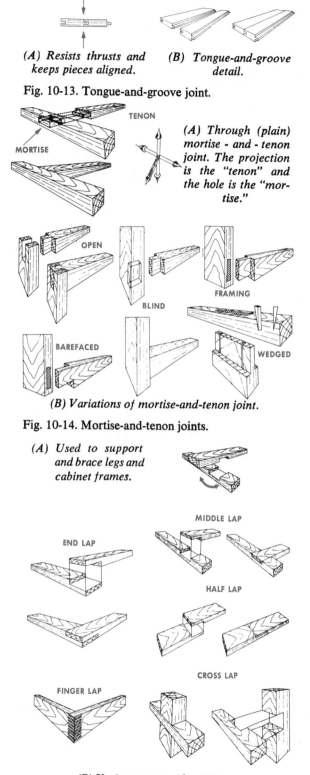

(A) Resists thrusts and keeps pieces aligned.

(B) Tongue-and-groove detail.

Fig. 10-13. Tongue-and-groove joint.

(A) Through (plain) mortise - and - tenon joint. The projection is the "tenon" and the hole is the "mortise."

(B) Variations of mortise-and-tenon joint.

Fig. 10-14. Mortise-and-tenon joints.

(A) Used to support and brace legs and cabinet frames.

(B) Various types of lap joints.

Fig. 10-15. Lap joints.

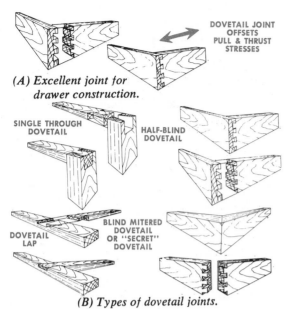

(A) Excellent joint for drawer construction.

SINGLE THROUGH DOVETAIL

HALF-BLIND DOVETAIL

DOVETAIL LAP

BLIND MITERED DOVETAIL OR "SECRET" DOVETAIL

(B) Types of dovetail joints.

Fig. 10-16. Dovetail joints.

(1) Butt; (2) Dado; (3) Rabbet; (4) Lap; (5) Tongue and groove; (6) Miter; (7) Dovetail; and (8) Mortise-and-tenon. Where possible, the strengths of the material, rather than the strength of the glue or fastening device, should be utilized to overcome the stress.

The butt joint (Fig. 10-10) offsets a "pushing" force; it can be strengthened with dowels. Other methods of adding strength to a butt joint include braces, nails, screws, and splines.

The dado joint (Fig. 10-11) is used to resist "shear" forces. The dado-rabbet joint is used for the ends (Fig. 10-11B) and the dado-tongue and rabbet joint

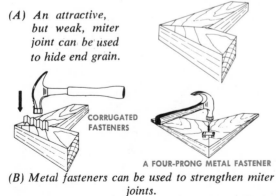

(A) An attractive, but weak, miter joint can be used to hide end grain.

CORRUGATED FASTENERS

A FOUR-PRONG METAL FASTENER

(B) Metal fasteners can be used to strengthen miter joints.

Fig. 10-17. Miter joints.

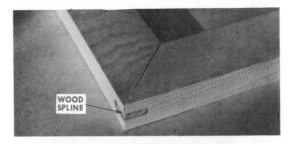

WOOD SPLINE

Fig. 10-18. Splines strengthen a miter joint.

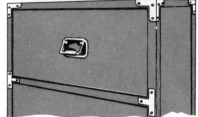

Fig. 10-19. Decorative hardware can be used to strengthen a miter joint.

(Fig. 10-11C) is used for ends and drawer fronts. Dado joints also are used for paneling (Fig. 10-11D).

Rabbet joints often are used for a smooth continuous surface. The rabbet joint (Fig. 10-12) is used to offset frontal and side thrusts, and it presents a clear face. The splined rabbet joint (Fig. 10-12B) resists "pull" forces. The tongue-and-groove joint (Fig. 10-13) resists thrust and keeps the pieces aligned.

The mortise-and-tenon joint (Fig. 10-14) can withstand forces from several directions. The projection is the "tenon" and the rectangular hole is the "mortise." The through (plain) mortise-and-tenon joint (Fig. 10-14A) and variations of the mortise-and-tenon joint (Fig. 10-14B) are used in framing and bracing. The *blind* mortise-and-tenon joint is used for framing and rails; *open* mortise-and-tenon joint for framing and bracing; *framing* mortise-and-tenon joint for rails and framing; *wedged* tenon for additional strength and *Colonial*-style decoration; and the *barefaced* tenon for thin pieces.

Lap joints (Fig. 10-15) resist the rotational stresses and are used to support

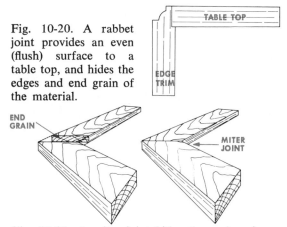

Fig. 10-20. A rabbet joint provides an even (flush) surface to a table top, and hides the edges and end grain of the material.

Fig. 10-21. A miter joint hides the end grain on this picture frame.

and brace legs and cabinet frames. The various types of lap joints are shown in Fig. 10-15B, including the middle-lap, half-lap, end-lap, cross-lap, and finger-lap joints.

Dovetail joints (Fig. 10-16) offset both pull and thrust stresses. The dovetail joints often are exposed in antique furniture, since they were considered a mark of quality achieved by painstaking layout and craftsmanship. This is one of the strongest joints used in woodworking, since it resists pulling stresses in every direction but the one from which the tenons are inserted. The single half-blind dovetail is often used in toprail and leg construction in cabinetwork; the holding ability of the joint overcomes the pulling strain. The multiple half-blind dovetail is used to attach drawer sides to the fronts, since it resists the strain when the drawer is pulled out.

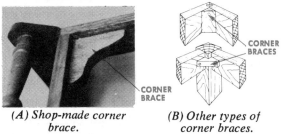

(A) Shop-made corner brace.

(B) Other types of corner braces.

Fig. 10-22. Wood braces for corners.

Miter joints (Fig. 10-17) are utilized for a smooth continuous surface, as for picture frames. The face grain of wood is more pleasing or attractive than the end grain; thus, a miter joint hides the end grain (Fig. 10-18). Since the miter joint is a weak joint, mechanical fasteners, splines (Fig. 10-18), and various types of decorative hardware (Fig. 10-19) are used to strengthen the joint.

Other jointing devices and processes are used to enhance the beauty of the lines of the material. A rabbet joint can be utilized for a smooth continuous surface. In Fig. 10-20, a rabbet joint provides an even (flush) surface to a table top, hiding the edges and ends of the material. Also, mitered joints can provide a pleasing wood-grain appearance, as for picture frames (Fig. 10-21). The miter joint hides the end grain.

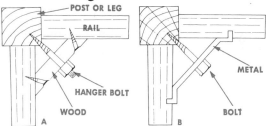

Fig. 10-23. Wood corner brace (A) and metal corner brace (B).

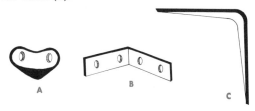

Fig. 10-24. Other metal braces, including corner brace (A), bent corner iron (B), and shelf bracket (C).

Strengthening Joints

Joints frequently are braced by the addition of small wood or metal pieces to prevent sway, shear, breaking, or a weak joint, such as the miter and butt joints (Fig. 10-22). Braces easily can be made

Fig. 10-25. A wood spline strengthens a butt joint.

Fig. 10-26. A wood spline strengthens a miter joint.

in the shop from small pieces of wood; or metal braces can be purchased.

Corner Braces

Equivalent wood or metal corner braces are shown in Figs. 10-23 and 10-24. These braces are used to prevent sway and loosening of joints. They are often used in units with legs, such as in the construction of desks and tables. The braces can be attached with special fasteners,

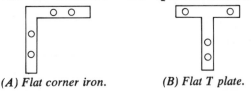

(A) Flat corner iron.   *(B) Flat T plate.*

Fig. 10-27. Flat braces are used on the edges of wood pieces.

Fig. 10-28. Decorative joint braces used in furniture construction.

such as staples; screws, glue, and nails also can be used.

Splines

Splines can be inserted in either a butt joint or a miter joint to prevent the pieces from slipping (Figs. 10-25 and 10-26).

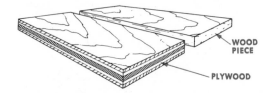

Fig. 10-29. A plywood edge can be hidden by gluing a wide, solid piece of material onto the plywood edge.

Fig. 10-30. Masking a plywood edge grain with a thin strip of wood.

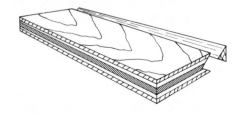

Fig. 10-31. Masking a plywood edge grain with a triangular piece of wood.

Various metal devices are used for the splines, but a thin piece of wood can be used as well. The metal splines often are used on commercial mass-production pieces, but the wood spline is the more common material used in small shops.

Edge Braces

Braces are used on the edges of wood pieces (Fig. 10-27). These braces can be hidden; or they can be exposed. Some inexpensive furniture is made with butt joints held together only by surface braces. For a pleasing contrast, the braces can be made from polished brass or copper with the wood or shelving material made from a darker material for maximum effect (Fig. 10-28).

Covering Plywood Edges

In plywood construction, exposure of the crossbands frequently is a problem. Several methods are used to cover the crossbanding. One of these methods (Fig. 10-29) involves merely gluing a piece of material onto the edge of the plywood; the plywood is the main body with a small facing material. A thin strip of wood can be applied (Fig. 10-30); or a small cut piece can be applied to mask the edge grain of plywood (Fig. 10-31).

Questions

1. Why is stress analysis important in constructing a design?
2. List the common joints and the types of forces they offset.
3. How can the joints be provided with added strength?
4. List the methods used to cover or conceal the edges of plywood.

Unit 11—Making and Reading Plans

Drawings, or plans, are essential in working with wood. Using a drawing properly is required for accuracy, proper fit of the pieces, matching the pieces, efficient use of materials, consistent quality, and materials specifications. Making a drawing carefully involves planning the details beforehand; then the work is a continuation of the planning stage. If the work is begun without plans, unforeseen details develop into problems which might prevent the work being completed. Lack of planning can cause mistakes, particularly on a complex piece. Without careful planning, the work cannot be completed with a high degree of efficiency or quality.

Using Prepared Plans

Craftsmen can obtain plans from many sources. These plans, sometimes called blueprints from the early method of making the plans, can be obtained from many sources. If the worker is part of a factory labor force, the plans or blueprints are provided him; then he works according to the details of the plan. If the craftsman is a home craftsman working as a hobbyist, he can either purchase the plans or find them in a magazine. A person working in a small shop can obtain his plans from hobby sources, books, and school plans; or he might design his own plans. Regardless of the source, planning is necessary, and it should be done carefully. In using plans made by someone else, a craftsman should always look carefully at the plans before beginning. He should visualize the steps involved, the equipment and tools needed, and the processes to be used, before beginning. Thus, he can obtain materials not on hand, special fasteners,

special glues, or hardware and finish materials for special considerations, before beginning the job.

Types of Drawings

If a person draws his own plans, the plans might be referred to as "working drawings" or plans, or simply drawings. Most of these plans feature the *orthographic projection*. This type of drawing is made with the various faces or views of the object (front, side, and top) as viewed in their respective locations. An orthographic drawing is explained in Fig. 11-1. Note that the *top view* is directly above the *front view* and that the *side view* is directly to the side; this permits the relative dimensions to be transferred easily from view to view, with each view showing the characteristics of the object when viewed from that face.

Another type of drawing used in planning is the *pictorial* drawing. In a pictorial drawing, the object is drawn in such a manner that two or more sides can be

TOP VIEW SHOWS HOW THE OBJECT WOULD APPEAR WHEN VIEWED FROM ABOVE THE OBJECT.

SIDE VIEW SHOWS HOW THE OBJECT WOULD APPEAR WHEN VIEWED FROM THE SIDE.

FRONT VIEW SHOWS HOW THE OBJECT WOULD APPEAR WHEN VIEWED FROM THE FRONT OF THE OBJECT.

(A) Book end viewed from front, side, and top.

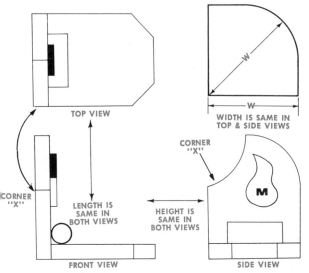

(B) The corner "X" is in the same relative position in all three views.

Fig. 11-1. Orthographic projection.

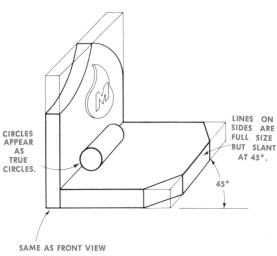

Fig. 11-2. Cabinet drawing.

seen at the same time or as the object is actually seen with the eye. The *cabinet* drawing (Fig. 11-2) and the *isometric* drawing (Fig. 11-3) are two types of pictorial drawings. Many types of pictorial drawings are used, and a knowledge of one or two of these types often can aid the craftsman in drawing his plans and in showing the details of an object.

The person who makes the plans should remember that the purpose of making the plans is to clarify the details, to plan the processes, and to establish the construction procedures. Any type of drawing which is an aid in any of these basic purposes is acceptable in planning.

Orthographic Projection

The orthographic projection is commonly based on the three views of an object. These are the top, front, and side views. The three views are aligned with the front view being the main view; the side view is placed at the side; and the top view is positioned above the front view (see Fig. 11-1B). Another feature of the

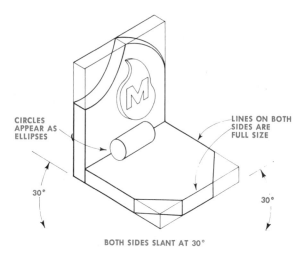

Fig. 11-3. Isometric drawing.

orthographic projection is that a given point on any view retains that identical relative position in all the views, as illustrated by the corner "X" in Fig. 11-1B. The term orthographic projection means that all the points are projected straight from the side or toward the top. This precision alignment, called *projection,* permits the dimensions to be transferred and the points to be moved to clearly define the shape and size of the details.

The purpose of an orthographic pro-

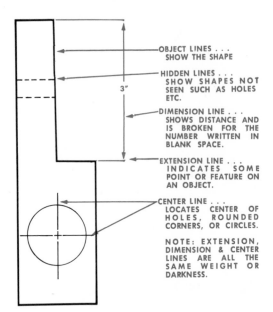

OBJECT LINES . . .
SHOW THE SHAPE

HIDDEN LINES . . .
SHOW SHAPES NOT
SEEN SUCH AS HOLES
ETC.

DIMENSION LINE . . .
SHOWS DISTANCE AND
IS BROKEN FOR THE
NUMBER WRITTEN IN
BLANK SPACE.

EXTENSION LINE . . .
INDICATES SOME
POINT OR FEATURE ON
AN OBJECT.

CENTER LINE . . .
LOCATES CENTER OF
HOLES, ROUNDED
CORNERS, OR CIRCLES.

NOTE: EXTENSION,
DIMENSION & CENTER
LINES ARE ALL THE
SAME WEIGHT OR
DARKNESS.

Fig. 11-4. Alphabet of lines.

jection is to describe the size and shape of an object. The size of an object is generally indicated by the drawing; but the drawing should not be used for a direct measurement of the size. The chief purpose of the drawing is to show the shape and to show how the shape is proportioned. Various other types of lines, called *dimension* lines, provide the exact size of the object. Measurements should never be taken directly from the drawing.

Orthographic projection is the basis for the drawings used in all industries. A working drawing made in the United States can be read by a workman in Germany, and a drawing made in Germany can be read by a workman in the United States. The processes and ideas are identical, and the methods of showing the shape of the object are identical.

Pictorial Drawings

As mentioned previously, the two types of pictorial drawings are the *cabinet* drawing, and the *isometric* drawing. Both these types of pictorial drawings use the full

dimensions, permitting the same scale to be used throughout the drawing. This is easier for the person who makes the drawing to keep the drawing free from mistakes and distortions.

Cabinet Drawing

Cabinet drawings are begun with the front view. The front view of the cabinet is identical to the front view in orthographic projection; the lines recede at 45 degrees from the front view. The full dimensions are placed on these lines, and the object is blocked in on these angles. Note in Fig. 11-2 that the cabinet drawing provides the overall shape of the object; but a disadvantage is its obvious distortion. However, the cabinet drawing remains a convenient method of showing the shape, size, and overall appearance.

Isometric Drawing

The isometric drawing is different from the cabinet drawing in that both faces slant upward from the horizontal (see Fig. 11-3). Note that the isometric views slant upward from the horizontal line at 30 degrees; the front view is on the left-hand side; the side view is on the right-hand side; and the top view, of course, is visible between them. The isometric drawing provides a more reliable presentation of the true shape of the object than does the cabinet drawing. The isometric is a relatively easy type of drawing to make, since all the lines are full size. However, an isometric drawing is sometimes avoided, since it is more difficult to show circles and arcs in an isometric drawing than in a cabinet drawing.

Using Lines

In making drawings, various types of lines are used for different purposes. An *alphabet of lines* is shown in Fig. 11-4. The *object* lines show the size and shape.

These lines are heavier and darker than the other types of lines to make the true size and shape of the object the most noticeable feature. The *hidden* lines are used to indicate the size and shape of features which cannot be seen in that view. However, since they do indicate size and shape (like the object lines), they are made the same weight as the object lines. To indicate that the features cannot be seen, the lines are drawn as dashes or "broken" lines.

Other types of lines include the *center* lines, *extension* lines and *dimension* lines. All these lines are approximately the same weight, but they are used for different effects. The center lines designate the centers of circles, arcs, ovals, and other curved surfaces. Extension lines are used in dimensioning to extend the corners of the objects away from the drawing to prevent the details and writing interfering with the view of the object. The dimension lines are used to indicate the size and length. In making these lines, care should be exercised to make these lines less prominent than the object lines. If the lines touch or are too close to the object lines, the extension lines and dimensions are confusing to read.

Construction lines and *guide* lines should be made extremely lightweight. They should be barely noticeable to the person making the drawing. When the drawing is completed, these lines should not be erased, but permitted to remain on the drawing. If they are extremely lightweight and made carefully, they are not noticeable in the completed drawing.

Detailed Drawings

Detailed drawings are made to include a small portion of an object. These drawings are made to clarify a construction detail in a blownup or larger scale. A

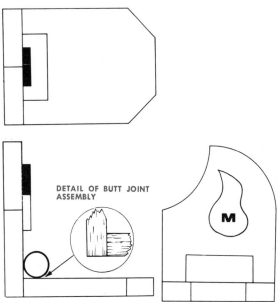

Fig. 11-5. Detail drawings enlarge and clarify small assembly features.

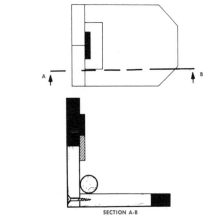

Fig. 11-6. Section drawings show the shapes of holes and details of fastening pieces.

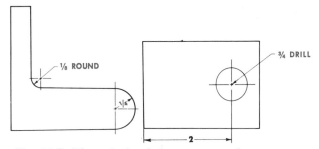

Fig. 11-7. Dimensioning holes, curves, and arcs.

joint can be shown in greater detail than on the regular drawing. Detailed drawings are used to clarify construction details

(Fig. 11-5). A drawing of a detail should be removed from the main plan, with a notation line to indicate which portion of the object is shown in the detail.

Section Drawings

Section drawings provide additional detail. In the same way that a slice of cake shows how a cake is layered, a section is used to show the interior arrangement, as though a portion of the object were cut away. Slanted lines, called *crosshatching,* indicate a view of the object with a portion cut away. Section drawings (Fig. 11-6) are used to illustrate interior shapes in counterboring techniques and special joint construction.

Dimensioning

Dimensioning is a method of placing sizes and descriptions on a plan or drawing. Extension and dimension lines indicate where the size or description is located, using numbering systems to indicate the exact size. The size should never be measured directly from a drawing, since the drawing may not be a full-size drawing; or the drawing might be distorted, since paper tends to shrink and expand with weather conditions. Measurements taken from the plans on paper might be inaccurate.

The dimensions should be placed on the object in the view which provides the best description of the size and shape of the object. Typical examples of dimensioning objects are shown in Figs. 11-7 through 11-9. The rules for dimensioning are lengthy; however, the main rules are:

1. Holes are located by their centers, not by their outer edges. Since a twist drill touches the wood first with the centered point, rather than with an outer edge, it is easier and more accurate to

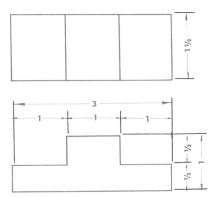

Fig. 11-8. The dimensions should be placed in the best location for indicating the size and shape (aligned method shown).

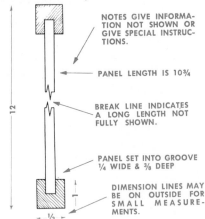

Fig. 11-9. Notes, break lines, and dimensioning of small units.

locate the centers of holes than the edges.

2. Dimensions should be placed on the view which best shows that particular feature. This avoids confusion over which feature is being described.

3. Dimensions should not touch the drawing, extension lines should not touch the object lines, and dimension and extension lines should be different from the object lines.

4. Either of two procedures can be followed in dimensioning a drawing; the *aligned* dimensioning system can be used; or the *unidirectional* system can be used. In the aligned system, the numbers are turned parallel to the lines in the view they are describing.

The numbers that rise on the paper from top to bottom are turned to be read from the right-hand side of the page.

In the unidirectional system, all the numbers are placed to be read from the bottom of the page. The same system should be used throughout the drawing to avoid confusion.

5. Dimensions should be located outside the view of the object when possible.

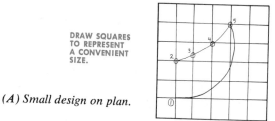

(A) Small design on plan.

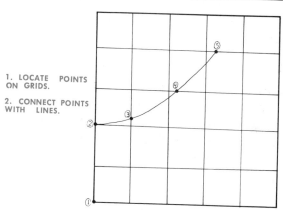

(B) Draw the grid to full size on the stock.

Fig. 11-10. A grid can be used to transfer small designs from a plan or drawing.

Transferring Designs

Sometimes, especially in drawing a curved surface, a pattern must be transferred or changed from the plan or drawing to the object. When the object is large and the plan is small, craftsmen use a grid system for a pattern transfer to aid in this process. In Fig. 11-10, a grid system is laid out to the scale on the drawing; then the same scale is applied to the actual piece. For example, if a drawing is made with 1 inch equal to 6 inches, the grids should be drawn at 1-inch intervals to represent 6-inch intervals on the object.

By using the grid system and by locating the points where the lines cross the grid lines, the points can be located on the larger grid and transferred to it. After all the points are located, the lines can be completed by connecting the points, like working a puzzle.

Questions

1. How can plans be obtained?
2. Why are plans important?
3. Why are orthographic drawings used?
4. Why are pictorial drawings used?
5. List the types of lines used in making drawings.

Unit 12 – Determining Wood Costs

The cost of a wood product is determined by the type and quality of wood, quantity of wood, glues and fastening devices, type and quality of finish, and the hardware. The labor and machine costs are dependent on the complexity of the operations involved, the time required to perform the operations, and the level of skill required of the operators. The machine costs can be considered further in the expense of the machinery required to perform the operation, the time involved in the use of the machinery, and the wear and tear (depreciation) of the machine.

These factors are considered when an architect estimates the cost of a building, when a plumber installs the pipes and water system in a house, and when a television repairman repairs a faulty television set. The final cost of products made of wood is determined by all these factors.

Board Feet

The *board foot* is the basic unit of measurement for wood. The cost of a piece of wood normally is calculated on the cost per board foot. A board foot is equal to one-twelfth of a cubic foot. A board foot can be described as a piece of wood 1 foot square and 1 inch in thickness. The formula used in calculating board feet is:

board feet = thickness (inches) ×
width (feet) × length (feet)

However, since the dimensions of most woods are in inches, the number of board feet is usually calculated by the formula:

board feet = thickness (inches) ×

$$\frac{width}{12} \ (inches) \times \frac{length}{12} \ (inches)$$

For example, a board 1″ × 12″ × 12″ contains 1 board foot of lumber. Typical diagrams and calculations of 1 board foot of lumber can be found in Fig. 12-1.

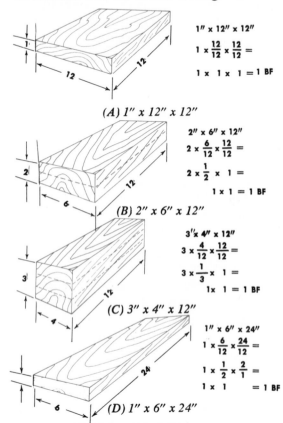

Fig. 12-1. Board-foot calculations.

Other Measuring Units for Wood

Other units also are used in measuring quantities of wood. Wood molding, trim work, and decorative materials are sold by the *linear foot* (Fig. 12-2). Molding and trim are used for decorations and are cut at special mills from select grades of lumber. A linear foot means per foot of length and does not include the volume or other dimension of wood actually used. The linear measurement is used, since special machine operations are required

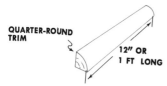

Fig. 12-2. Trim and molding are measured by the linear foot.

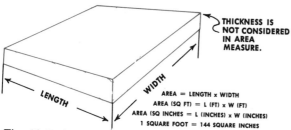

Fig. 12-3. Area measure is used on plywood, particle board, hardboard, and similar materials.

on molding, trim work, and decorative materials.

Plywood, veneer, laminated plastics, and some other materials are sold by the unit of area, rather than by the board foot or linear foot. The area of these pieces normally is calculated in square feet. Some highly complex decorative materials are sold by the square inch, but this is uncommon. A square foot of material is merely a piece 1 foot on each side (Fig. 12-3). When materials are calculated by the area measure, the thickness of the material is not considered directly in the price quoted. The price quotations for plywood and similar materials are calculated on the basis of a given material with a given thickness. One square foot of ¼-inch thickness plywood costs less than 1 square foot of ¾-inch thickness plywood. The price per square foot is quoted for each standard thickness of material; therefore, the thickness is not involved directly in calculating the cost of the material.

Bill of Materials

A bill of materials is a method of calculating the costs of the wood and other materials used in building. A bill of materials is an essential process of organizing the materials to calculate the cost of the furniture and cabinetwork, whether in a building contract cost estimate or in a small shop.

The information in a bill of materials includes the type and grade of wood used, the quantity of wood used, the unit cost, and the total cost of each piece. In his bill of materials for a construction estimate, a contractor includes labor costs, transportation charges, and other miscellaneous factors. This procedure is essentially identical to a craftsman presenting a bill for his work. Normally, a customer expects to receive an itemized bill, similar to a bill of materials, for repairing his car, constructing his house, or any job which requires a skilled craftsman.

A typical bill of materials can be found in Fig. 12-4. Note that several separate headings are listed; therefore, the total bill is easier to check and it is easier to make sure all the pieces involved are included in the work. Most bills of materials also include extra space for materials such as hardware, finishes, glues, and labor costs.

In a typical school shop, labor costs are not charged, but they should be calculated. An estimate of efficiency can be made by requiring the student to estimate the time required for the job; then this time can be checked against the actual time required in constructing the project.

The costs of the finishes can be estimated by several methods. The actual quantity of finishing material used can be either estimated or measured. However, it is more common to assess a charge per unit of area and per coat of finish applied. For most of the finishing materials, the manufacturer's specifications regarding the coverage of a finish such as paint, varnish, and lacquer can be used to estimate the cost of the square area cov-

BILL OF MATERIALS

NAME _____   PERIOD ___1ST___

PROJECT _____ **BOOK SHELF** _____

NO PIECES	SIZE OF EACH	AMOUNT OF ALL PARTS	PART	TYPE OF MATERIAL	UNIT COST	TOTAL COST
2	1" x 12" x 24"	4 BF	SHELF	PINE	30¢ PER BF	$1.20
2	1" x 12" x 12"	2 BF	SIDES	PINE	30¢ PER BF	.60
1	12" x 24"	2 Sq Ft	BACK	⅛" HARD BOARD	15¢ PER Sq Ft	.30
					SUB-TOTAL	2.10
			FINISH	LACQUER	10%	.21
						2.31

CHECKED BY _____   **TOTAL $2.31**

Fig. 12-4. A typical bill of materials.

ered; then a percentage charge based on this quantity can be assessed.

The actual cost of glues is much more difficult to estimate. It is common practice to include the cost of items, such as glue, in the overall operating cost of the shop. No direct charge is made, but a general charge can be added to cover materials such as glue, the purchase and use of paint brushes, and similar tools and materials. Usually, these overhead costs are reflected in the general labor charges and materials prices.

Sandpaper, hardware, dowels, fasteners, and the hundreds of items which can be purchased or issued by a measurable unit generally are listed by number and quantity per unit. This cost is then totaled for the miscellaneous items other than the woods or materials used. It is not uncommon for decorative hardwares to be nearly as expensive as the wood itself. Special pieces of hardware, such as concealed hinges, can be quite expensive. Generally speaking, the more ornate or more complex the unit, the greater the cost. Other pieces of useful hardware include drawer guides, electronic components, light fixtures, and similar pieces.

Consumer Costs

When a consumer purchases a piece of furniture, he pays for the raw materials, such as wood, hardware, upholstery, and fastening devices. Also, he expects to pay a reasonable price for the labor of the people who made the item. However, other factors also are included in the price of a single piece of furniture or any other item produced by a manufacturing firm. Not included in most bills of materials (but included in all manufacturing costs) are the salaries of the people of the company who do not work directly on the product, such as the secretaries, receptionists, clerks, and executives who direct, organize, and design the products. These people are vital members of any industry, but their labor costs are not calculated directly into the prices of any product or piece of material.

Taxes also are included in the consumer

costs. Every industry pays federal taxes on the shipment of goods and on the profits (income) made by the company. Many states and communities also levy taxes on the property, machines and equipment, and on the profits made. In addition, local costs include the cost of the utilities and services provided by the communities, such as water, electricity, sewage, fire protection, etc.

A company also expects to make a reasonable profit for the owners of the company to realize some profit on their investment. Also, the company must make more money than it spends, to provide money for growth and purchase of new machinery when equipment becomes obsolete and worn out. Growth is essential to remain competitive. Mass-produced goods are less expensive than goods made with small-capacity, outdated equipment.

Another factor which must be included in the mark-up for profit and for depreciation (the wearing out of machines and equipment), is the problems created by increasing inflation. Inflation means that the costs are rising and that a dollar now does not buy as much goods as in the past. Therefore, more money than is actually needed at the present time must be set aside for the purchase of new equipment and machinery at inflated prices in the future.

Another cost factor is the cost of research. New techniques and new methods constantly are on trial, since research determines the future advances in both technology and the quality of the material. During the research trials (which can be quite long and expensive) there is no income from research efforts. However, research is the key for future advancement. Researchers determine the problems and flaws in the present methods and attempt to work out improved methods and to develop new processes and new materials.

The typical products of wood research are hardboard, particle board, laminated plastics, plastic finishes, spray finishes, modern plywood and veneering processes, epoxy glues, common white glue made from polyvinyl plastics, and many other products.

Employees, or the people who make the products, also create costs not concerned directly with production. Most companies pay additional costs to provide insurance, retirement plans, sick leaves, hospitalization, and vacations for the employees. Furthermore, good employees are assets to the company. In many instances, the quality of the products produced is identical to the quality of the employees who make them. To avoid the problem of employees securing better jobs elsewhere, most companies provide regular increases in salary. Frequently, the increases in pay are yearly, but they can be more often; also they can be in the form of bonuses and extra payments. Nearly all companies and manufacturers provide some method of rewarding an employee for lengthy and reliable service.

Other costs not included directly in the cost of the product are the shipping costs (transportation and shipping charges) from the factory to the store; the cost of maintaining the factory; utilities; keeping the grass cut and the floors clean; providing restrooms, wash areas, and parking lots; keeping the roof in repair to prevent damage to machinery and goods; and many other cost factors.

Promotional costs include the advertising for a new product, the sales costs in contacting new customers and for salesmen's commissions, and the price or mark-up for the person who sells the goods. A store owner is a businessman, has money invested, and is entitled to a profit for a service performed—that of making goods available for purchasing.

Consumer costs, therefore, include many items that cannot be calculated directly in the cost of a product. These costs extend far beyond the cost of the materials and the labor.

Questions

1. List the factors included in the costs of a product.
2. List the units of measurement used in measuring quantities of wood.
3. What unit of measurement is used to measure quantities of plywood?
4. Describe a board foot. A square foot.
5. What items are included in a bill of materials?
6. How are the costs of materials, such as glue, hardware, finish, and the use of equipment, determined?

Unit 13 – Importance of Safety in Woodworking

Safety is an important factor in all types of shopwork. The formation of safe working habits prevents injuries which can cripple or disable the individual. Safe work habits protect not only the individual but also his fellow workers (Fig. 13-1). Thus, a person is responsible not only for his own safety but also for the safety of others.

The formation of safe working habits is an important part of any shopwork, whether hand tools or machine tools are involved. The machine tools extend the functions performed by the hand tools; they have been developed to increase the rate of production and the accuracy of the operation. Since the machines are faster, stronger, and quicker with heavier cuts, they usually are more dangerous to operate. Although the two most dangerous machines in the school shop are the jointer and the table saw, nearly twice as many injuries occur from the use of hand tools than from machine tools.

Safety attitudes and habits are carried over from the classroom to the job, home, and recreation. The habits acquired in a school shop can prevent injury on a job many years later. In addition, these habits and attitudes might prevent injury or death in later years. Merely learning to use a tool is not enough. An efficient

Fig. 13-1. Working safely involves the guards on the machines, safety wearing apparel, and strict attention to the work. (Courtesy Sellstrom Manufacturing Company)

worker knows the correct and safe use of the tool.

Proper safety attitudes are based on the recognition that safety is important and that accidents can happen to anyone. Safe work habits are formed by the careful, systematic development of procedures for working safely. A worker should always be aware that accidents can happen; and his mind should not wander from the operation and how he could be hurt. Then the operation should be performed in a manner that prevents the accident.

Eye Protection

Protection of the eyes presents one of the most important safety problems for

109

the woodworker (Fig. 13-2). When damaged, the eyes can rarely be replaced or repaired. For this reason, extreme care should be taken to protect them from the four industrial hazards: (1) Impact; (2) Chemical splash; (3) Dust; and (4) Light rays or glare. For woodworkers, the latter hazard (light rays and glare) is not a major factor, since these hazards are encountered chiefly in welding. However, the other hazards are common in the woodshop.

Impact

Impact protection protects the eyes from contact with flying objects; it is quite obvious that this type of protection is desirable when operating machinery that throws off chips. Many workers fail to realize that a worker at a distance also can be hurt by flying chips from machines and hand tools. Many states now require that *all* the people in a work area wear eye protection from impact.

Impact is the greatest eye hazard. Most industries even provide a visitor with this type of eye protection, and do not permit workers, supervisors, or visitors in the work areas without it.

Chemical Splash

Although there is little danger in the normal woodworking operations from this type of hazard, workers often do not realize the possible dangers from the common wood finishes. These materials include alcohol, turpentine, paint, stain, varnish, shellac, and lacquer. The liquid chemicals used for softening, preserving, bleaching, and fibering wood increase these hazards. When engaged in the finishing operations, proper protection should be worn to cover the eyes and to provide splashproof ventilation.

Dust

In some instances, lightweight impact glasses are appropriate. However, for heavy dust concentrations, the shields similar to those used with chemicals are desirable.

When wearing eye protection, two additional factors are important—fit and visibility. The protectors should be worn over prescription eyeglasses, if appropriate; in all instances, they should fit snugly without falling or sliding.

If the lenses are dirty or dusty, they should be cleaned carefully to avoid scratching. Soap and water can be used for this purpose; however, special tissues and solvents are available which are even more satisfactory. Lenses which become scratched, coated, or pitted to the point that they obscure vision should be discarded.

The safe way is the most efficient way of working, since it is usually the quickest, simplest, and easiest way. It is usually more efficient in time and effort—with less costs and loss of time, due to freedom from injury. Developing safe work habits carries over into the home and future employment, contributing to an extended and enriched way of life. In addition, safe working habits protect others by setting a standard for others to copy, by protecting other workers from careless or incom-

Fig. 13-2. Eye safety is of primary importance. (Courtesy Sellstrom Manufacturing Company)

petent use of tools and machines, and by extending the usefulness and service life of the tools and machines.

Making sure you are capable and qualified to operate a machine before beginning is important. The person best qualified in this matter is a trained person, such as a teacher or job supervisor. Being capable and qualified to operate a machine is the instructor's or supervisor's method of stating that he feels you are competent to select and utilize the best, most efficient, and safest method of doing the job. In addition, he is expressing his confidence that you can protect not only yourself but also your fellow operators by careful and practical operation of the equipment.

Reporting Accidents

All accidents resulting in an injury should be reported. This includes those accidents in which the injury is only slight or minor; however, all these accidents should be reported. A careful record of all accidents provides the individual teacher or supervisor with a valuable tool in showing where additional instruction, a safety device, or an improved procedure is required. A review of the accident reports aids an instructor in determining what safety improvements are needed in the shop. Likewise, reporting accidents occurring on the job in industry aid the management in reducing the hazards in the plant or on the job. Several methods of reporting accidents are used, including accident report forms, verbal reports, and

information blanks. The *National Safety Council* provides special forms for use in the school shop; or the individual school or teacher can devise his own forms. However, it should be emphasized that all accidents resulting in injury should be reported to aid in analyzing and providing a safer working situation.

The operations for any shop activity should include safety. A good job is done safely and correctly. Rules are sometimes helpful in teaching individuals how to use tools and equipment safely, in the same manner that learning some traffic safety rules is necessary in driving a car properly. Rules of operations promote accuracy, less spoilage or waste and expense, safer conditions for the individual and the workers near him, and quicker operations for the entire assembly, since there is less necessity of repeating the spoiled operation. Also, it is advisable to avoid talking and attempting to work at the same time. One should either stop working and talk—or he should stop talking and work.

Questions

1. Why is it important to learn safe working habits as quickly as possible?
2. How is an individual responsible for safety?
3. How are safe working habits formed?
4. How does attitude affect safety?
5. What three types of eye hazards are present in a woodshop?
6. How do accident reports help safety programs?

Unit 14 — Safety in the Shop

Safety in the shop is dependent on attitudes, work habits, and actual practices. Safety is not merely a mechanical function, depending on whether the tool is properly guarded or held properly; it is also dependent on the attitude of the individual using the tool or machine (Fig. 14-1). The proper tool must be used for the job. Using a tool for a purpose that it was not designed can result in slipping or injury and damage to the work.

General Procedures

The general procedures for machine and tool operations require the tool or machine to be sharp and in good condition, adjusted properly, and operated correctly. Failure to fulfill any of these three basic conditions can establish a chain of events which can result in an accident. Although most of the accidents in the shop do not result in injury, many of them do result in injury. When working in a shop or any other area where goods are produced, the following general procedures should be observed:

1. Do not run in the shop area. The sharp corners, hard surfaces, sharp tools, and people working can result in injury.
2. Always use the guards and required protective devices or clothing.
3. Horseplay also is dangerous for the same reason that running in the shop is dangerous.
4. Proper clothing should be worn at all times.
5. Shop aprons, smocks, or laboratory coats are desirable to protect clothing; confine loose objects to the pockets of your own clothing.
6. Protective clothing should be tight-fitting, without binding, and free from pockets or loose strings.
7. Sleeves should be rolled either all the way up or all the way down, and buttoned.
8. Never permit loose cuffs or dangling sleeve ends which can be caught in tools or machinery.
9. If safety zones are painted around the machines, be careful not to enter these zones; this can cause interference and perhaps injury to the machine operator.
10. Make sure you know the procedure involved in the operation being performed.
11. If unfamiliar with the operation of the machine or tool, check with the instructor or supervisor.
12. Never operate any equipment without the approval of the instructor and full knowledge of the operation.
13. Be neat and orderly in your work; put away all tools and equipment not being used.
14. Cluttered, messy work areas are unsafe both to the operator and to others.
15. Good housekeeping indicates good work habits and safe attitudes.
16. Be clean and neat; when the hands or materials become dirty, wash or clean them in some manner.
17. When someone needs help, be willing to help without being asked. However, do not help a student or other person, until he has been notified that he is being helped.
18. Pulling or guiding a piece of stock being cut, while the operator is un-

aware, can cause injury or accident to the operator.

General Machine Safety

When operating machinery, some factors should always be considered. Since most machines operate at high speeds, there is rarely a second chance to avoid injury:

1. All watches, rings, and other jewelry should be removed and special care should be paid to the clothing so that

Fig. 14-1. Safety is a combination of proper attitude and excellent working conditions. Proper use of guards and strict adherence to safety rules should be followed carefully.

no loose dangling objects are worn, such as sleeves, ties, or similar objects.

2. Machines should be adjusted properly for the correct cut and spacing; it is always good practice to double-check these adjustments with a second measurement of all setup operations.

3. After the machine has been properly set up, adjusted, and inspected to make sure all the cutting edges·are sharp and in good condition, any necessary protective clothing should be put on.

4. Before starting the machine, the operator should make sure no one is in the immediate area and that he is clear of the moving parts.

5. Use all safety devices on the machine; they are for the protection of the operator.

6. In using a machine, always review the operations to make sure you are familiar with the operation of the machine and the procedure to be used in the operation.

7. Read all the safety posters and notices before operating a machine.

8. If the machine is out of order, notify the instructor and place an "out-of-order" sign on the machine.

9. Never adjust a machine while it is running; always make sure it is stopped completely.

10. Stay with a machine until it stops moving; the next operator might fail to realize it is in motion.

General Hand Tool Safety

When using hand tools, one should be aware that, although they do not move with the speed of machine tools, hand tools are responsible for more accidents than machine tools. This partially results from overconfidence and failure to realize that the hand tools are dangerous. Factors to consider when using hand tools are:

1. The tools being used should be laid in neat order, with the cutting edges facing away from the operator.

2. Be sure the tool is sharp and in good condition. If the tool is not sharp or in good condition, either fix it or report to the instructor or supervisor. Always move a tool with a sharp cutting edge, such as a knife or chisel, away from the body. Never make a cutting stroke with an unguarded blade toward the body.

3. Make sure no part of the body is in front of a cutting edge. This is especially true in using a chisel or knife.

Make sure the hands or fingers are not in front of the line of movement of the cutting edge.

4. Make sure that screwdriver points are properly shaped and sized.
5. Be sure the handles are in place on all tools, especially on hammers and files.
6. Use a tool only for its intended purpose. Do not chisel with a screwdriver —or hammer with a file.
7. Do not carry sharp tools in your pockets, since the sharp points can injure you.
8. When carrying a pointed tool, always carry the tool by the blade with the point aimed downward or toward the floor.

Questions

1. What three factors comprise shop safety?
2. What three general procedures should be followed for machine or tool operation?
3. List ten general safety rules.
4. List five general safety rules for machine operation.
5. List five general safety rules for hand tool safety.

Unit 15—Working With Wood

Most of the hardwoods are purchased in the rough to avoid unnecessary waste and expense. This lumber is sold in random widths and lengths and might be *warped,* in *wind* (twisted), or *unsound* with knots and checks (Fig. 15-1). To use wood successfully, it should be selected carefully, cleared, and squared. Only then can woodworking construction be accomplished skillfully either by hand or by machine processes. Tight joints and a smooth appearance are impossible with wood which is warped, twisted, or not squared.

Selecting and Clearing Stock

"Selecting" wood refers to choosing each board for a specific purpose. The type of wood, grain pattern, and size are the more important considerations. The type of wood and the grain pattern depend on personal likes and dislikes. However, size is determined by the specified size of the completed project. Ordinarily, the boards selected are at least ⅛ inch thicker, ½ inch wider, and 1 inch longer than the final size. Also, they should be free from surface faults and structural defects. Otherwise, the effects of the knots, warps, checks, etc. should be considered.

After the stock has been selected, it should be cleared. In this operation, imperfections are removed by cutting and/or planing. The procedure in either hand or machine woodworking is:

1. *Carefully examine the stock for defects.* From either end, note where the end checks stop; then saw off that portion of the stock (Fig. 15-2). Examine the remaining portion for checks extending further into the stock. If necessary, saw again and examine again.
2. *Saw the stock about 1 inch longer than needed.* If several pieces are required, do not permit the board to remain in a single long board for cutting into smaller pieces later. It is easier to work with several short pieces than with a single long board. Also, the shorter pieces reduce the major warps, twists, etc. (Fig. 15-3).
3. *Conclude the operation by ripping the board about ½ inch wider than the required final size.* In doing this, make sure any wane in the board is located in the waste stock.

The stock then is cleared and ready for squaring, unless it is doubtful whether the correct thickness can be obtained, due to

115

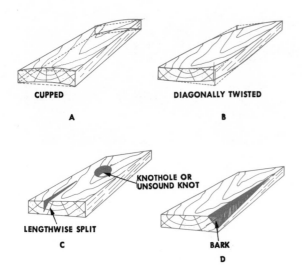

Fig. 15-1. The common faults found in rough lumber are: Warped (A); In wind (B); Unsound, with knots and checks (C); and Wane (D).

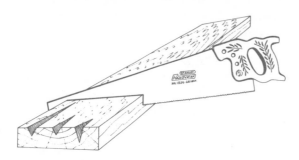

Fig. 15-2. Remove the portion of the stock with the checks.

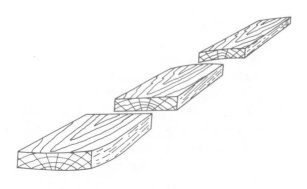

Fig. 15-3. A long board cut into shorter lengths is easier to square.

surface defects or bows. If this is doubtful, plane either face until an indication of the finished thickness can be determined. It might be necessary to plane both faces on some boards. The stock is "cleared" when all bows, winds, and other defects are eliminated.

Squaring Stock to Dimensions

Squaring involves sawing and planing the stock to the desired dimensions, forming right angles between the adjacent surfaces. This process can be accomplished either by hand or by machine and involves either a single board or several boards glued together. These parts are described by the faces, edges, and ends (Fig. 15-4). Note in the diagram that each board has two faces, two edges, and two ends. These parts are the first face, second face, first edge, etc., depending on which surface is worked first.

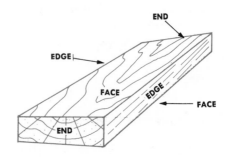

Fig. 15-4. Identification of board surfaces.

Squaring Stock by Hand Tools

Only the hand tools are used in squaring a board by hand. Among these tools are the handsaws, bench and block planes, and various measuring or layout tools. Beginning with a cleared board, hand squaring involves the following procedure:

1. *Determine the better face.* It has less warp, less twist, and/or fewer surface

defects. Its flatness can be determined quickly by placing the board face downward on a workbench and "rocking" the corners. A flat surface does not rock, but it can be warped.

2. *Secure the stock to the workbench with the first face upward.* In performing this step, note the grain direction and the clamping pressure. Avoid awkward positions in which it is difficult to plane. Guard against unnecessary pressure which can dent the stock or cause it to bow.

3. *Plane the first face.* The first face is important, since each succeeding step depends on the accuracy or trueness of the first face. Adjust the plane for a fine, even cut; then plane the first face. Begin by removing the high places. Then work the plane with the grain until the face is flat. Remember to plane with the grain. The wood will chip, or its fibers will pull upward, when planing across the grain or against the grain.

4. *Plane the first edge.* Lock the stock in the vise with the better edge upward. If needed, place a piece of soft wood between the vise jaws and the first face to prevent scratching. Plane the high spots on the edge, checking periodically for squareness with the first face (Fig. 15-5).

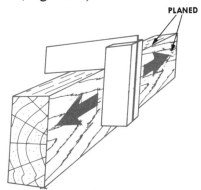

Fig. 15-5. Check the edge with a try square for squareness with the 1st face.

Fig. 15-6. Using a miter box to square an end of a board.

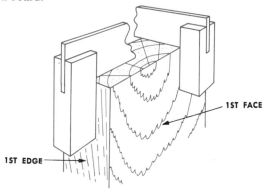

Fig. 15-7. Checking an end for squareness with both the 1st edge and the 1st face.

5. *Plane the first end.* Select the better end for the first end to be squared. This end can be worked in several ways. In one method, the end is squared with a miter box (Fig. 15-6). The wood then can be planed smooth, if desired. In another method, only a plane is used. The latter method is preferable when there is only a little extra length or waste. The first end is checked for squareness in two directions (Fig. 15-7). Note in the diagram that the first end should be square with both the first face and the first edge.

6. *Plane the second end.* Mark the required length by marking the location of the second end square with the first edge (Fig. 15-8). An extra $\frac{1}{16}$-inch allowance should be made when the end is to be sawed first and then

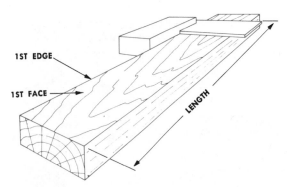

Fig. 15-8. Establish the length by marking the 2nd end parallel to the 1st end and "square" with the 1st edge. Allow an extra 1/16" for sawing first and then planing.

planed. Work this end similar to the first end, making the end square with both the first face and first edge (Fig. 15-9).

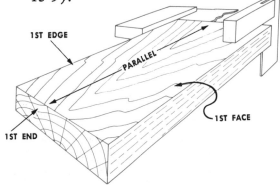

Fig. 15-9. Check the 2nd end for squareness with both the 1st edge and the 1st face.

7. *Plane the second edge.* Establish the final width by marking the location of the second edge parallel to the first

Fig. 15-10. Using a combination square to mark the width.

edge. Either a combination square (Fig. 15-10) or a marking gauge (Fig. 15-11) can be used. Allow an extra $\frac{1}{16}$ inch when the edge is to be ripped with a saw and then planed. Work this edge similar to the first edge, making it square with the ends and the first face (Fig. 15-12). If the second edge is square with the ends, it also is parallel with the first edge.

Fig. 15-11. Using a marking gauge to mark the width.

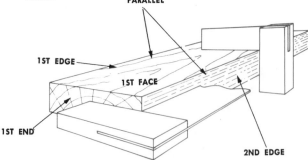

Fig. 15-12. Mark the 2nd edge square with the 1st face and both ends.

8. *Plane the second face.* Hold a marking gauge against the first face; then mark the desired thickness along the ends and edges (Fig. 15-13). While working toward these marks, plane the second face similar to the first

Fig. 15-13. The marking gauge should be held flush against the 1st face for marking the thickness.

face. Carefully check for flatness and squareness during the planing operation. When this step is finished, the board should be both the correct size and square.

The procedure for hand-squaring the stock is sometimes changed. For example, the alternate sequences in Fig. 15-14 can be used. When planing the two faces, plane equal amounts of wood from the

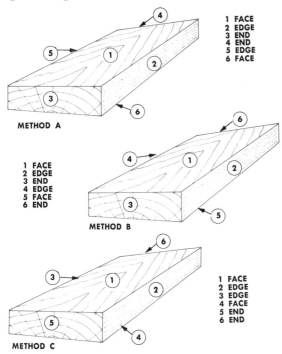

Fig. 15-14. Various methods or order of cuts can be used for squaring stock. Method A is recommended. The numbers indicate the order of cuts for squaring.

faces. Note in Fig. 15-15 that the moisture content increases toward the center of a board. When more wood is removed from one side, the stock tends to warp, due to the change in moisture content.

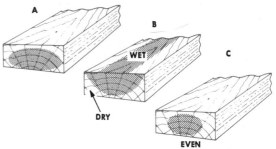

Fig. 15-15. In planing the two surfaces or faces of a board, remove equal amounts of wood from each face. The moisture content increases toward the center of a board (A); therefore, the board is more likely to warp if more wood is removed from one face than from the other face (B), since the face with more moisture dries more slowly. If the stock is removed equally (C), the two faces dry equally; therefore, warping is less likely to occur.

Squaring Stock by Machine

Stock can be machine-squared by several methods, depending on how it is to be used (Fig. 15-16). *Method A* is used to square a single board to a definite size. *Method B* is used to square several boards which have been glued together to form a larger surface.

Method A (see Fig. 15-16)

1. *Joint the first face*. If the stock is not cleared, cut to a rough length before jointing. Be sure the end checks are eliminated before attempting further machining operations. Remove as little wood as possible in jointing this face.
2. *Joint the first edge*. Hold the jointed face against the fence of the jointer. Remove all the rough spots and check the squareness with the first face. Surface this edge carefully, since it serves as a guide in ripping to width. This edge, when the jointing is com-

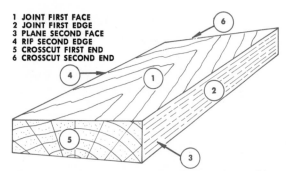

Fig. 15-16. Procedure or order of cuts for machine squaring of small stock.

pleted, is not machined again in the squaring process.

3. *Plane the second face.* The thickness of the board is established in this step. Begin by planing all the irregularities from the second face. When the second face is free from irregularities, turn the board over. Plane any rough spots remaining in the first face. Plane to the desired thickness by removing equal quantities of wood from each face. To prevent excessive planer marks, make the final cut about $\frac{1}{32}$ inch deep on each face.

4. *Rip the second edge.* The width of the board is determined by this step. Adjust the distance between the saw blade and the fence to equal the final width plus $\frac{1}{32}$ to $\frac{1}{16}$ inch. This allowance is needed to plane off the rough saw marks remaining on the second edge. After sawing, joint the edge to the exact size. This extra machining is usually omitted for edges that will not show or be finished.

Two common mistakes are often made in this step. Frequent attempts are made to joint the stock to final width without sawing first. Also, the first edge cannot be used for a guide against the fence. Avoid these practices, since they produce tapering widths which affect the squareness of the stock.

5. *Cut the first end.* Using either a circular saw or a radial-arm saw, saw as close to the rough end as possible. Check for squareness with a face and an edge. If the end is to be exposed or finished, remove the saw marks with a disk sander, hand plane, or jointer.

6. *Cut the second end.* This end is worked similar to the first end. Mark its location from the first end equal to the desired length. An extra $\frac{1}{32}$-inch or $\frac{1}{16}$-inch allowance should be made, if it is necessary to remove saw marks. Since this completes the operation, check the measurements and squareness again for possible error.

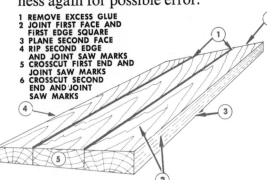

Fig. 15-17. Procedure or order of cuts for machine squaring of glued stock.

Method B (see Fig. 15-17)

1. *Remove all excess dry glue.* The excess dry glue remaining on the stock sometimes can damage or dull the sharp cutting edges on the machines. Also, it can cause the stock to be angled with the cutting edges, resulting in a tapered cut.

2. *Joint the first face.* Similar to the first method, halt the jointing when the face becomes flat.

3. *Joint the first edge.* Using the first face for a guide, joint this edge until free from rough marks and other defects.

4. *Plane the second face.* After the second face is flat, make alternate cuts

between the faces to obtain the desired thickness. Use shallow final cuts on each face to reduce the planer marks.

5. *Rip to width.* An extra ⅟₃₂-inch to ⅟₁₆-inch allowance is needed for removing the saw marks.

6. *Cut the first end.* Saw the end square, using either a table saw or a radial-arm saw. After sawing, the saw marks can be removed from the end by jointing. Do not attempt this operation on narrow stock, since it is dangerous and can result in a serious injury.

7. *Cut the second end.* Work this end similar to the first end. Since the second-end cut establishes the length, allow about ⅟₁₆-inch extra, if it is necessary to joint the saw marks away. Even though this completes the operation, check the measurements and the squareness before proceeding with the other procedures.

Certain difficulties often are encountered in *Method B.* For example, the glued surface can be too wide for the jointer. Then, omit the jointer, using the planer instead. Alternate the faces, taking light cuts until flat. Work the remaining edges and ends in the normal manner. Another solution is to divide the width into two or more parts which can be jointed. These boards, except for the ends, are squared individually. Then they are carefully glued together and cut to length. Still another method used is to hand plane the first face; then resume the normal procedure.

If the dimensions of the pieces are similar, machine them as a group. For example, two pieces with identical thickness should be planed at the same time. This is easier and saves time, since several pieces are planed at one time. Table legs also can be machined as a group. They

should not be squared individually. Use the same machine settings to save time and to lend uniformity in size.

Guidelines for Machining Stock

Guidelines or hints which can help the beginning woodworker are diagrammed in Fig. 15-18. Also, in squaring the stock, remember to inspect the wood for faults before machining it. Attempt to plan the sequence to eliminate waste. For example, in Fig. 15-19, a piece of rough stock $1'' \times 5½'' \times 25''$ is being squared to

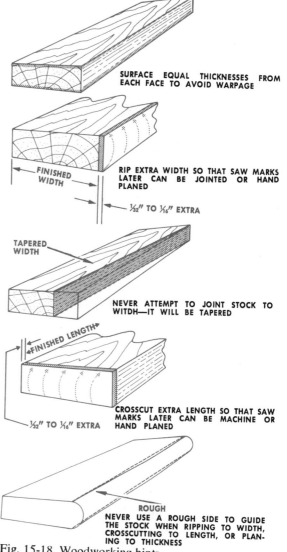

SURFACE EQUAL THICKNESSES FROM EACH FACE TO AVOID WARPAGE

FINISHED WIDTH

RIP EXTRA WIDTH SO THAT SAW MARKS LATER CAN BE JOINTED OR HAND PLANED

⅟₃₂″ TO ⅟₁₆″ EXTRA

TAPERED WIDTH

NEVER ATTEMPT TO JOINT STOCK TO WITDH—IT WILL BE TAPERED

FINISHED LENGTH

⅟₃₂″ TO ⅟₁₆″ EXTRA

CROSSCUT EXTRA LENGTH SO THAT SAW MARKS LATER CAN BE MACHINE OR HAND PLANED

ROUGH

NEVER USE A ROUGH SIDE TO GUIDE THE STOCK WHEN RIPPING TO WIDTH, CROSSCUTTING TO LENGTH, OR PLANING TO THICKNESS

Fig. 15-18. Woodworking hints.

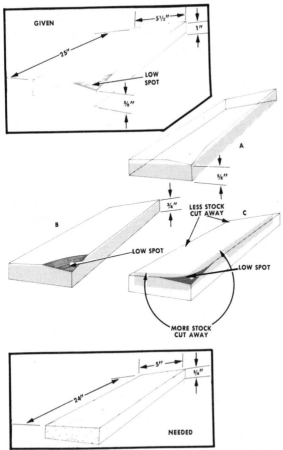

Fig. 15-19. Careful planning eliminates waste in time and material.

a final size of ¾″ × 5″ × 24″. The rough size appears to be ample; but note that one corner of the stock measures only ⅝-inch thickness. In Fig. 15-19A, the stock is machined until the low spot is eliminated. However, this sample cannot be used, since the thickness of the stock is too small. In Fig. 15-19B, the stock is machined to the required ¾-inch thickness. Although the low spot remains, the area of the low spot has been reduced. In Fig. 15-19C, the cuts along the thicker end are barely sufficient to surface and square the stock. Then, more stock is cut away along the thinner end on which the low spot is located. This eliminates the low corner and results in a board with the correct finished dimensions.

A similar example is diagrammed in Fig. 15-20. The thickness of the rough stock is 1 inch, which is sufficient thickness for a finished thickness of ⅝ inch. However, there are several unsound knots on one side of the stock. Since the knots are shallow, the stock can be used when machined properly. By removing only a little wood from the underneath side, the knots can be machined or removed from the top side (see Fig. 15-20A). Unnecessarily planing the clear side might result in a finished thickness with the knots still present.

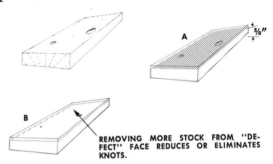

Fig. 15-20. Machine the surfaces only as needed. Unnecessary planing can result in waste.

Similar points should be remembered in joining several boards to form a larger surface. It is not always necessary to square an entire surface. For example, a hexagon-shaped table top can be made from joining three boards (Fig. 15-21). Possible ways of making the table top are shown in the diagram for making an octagon-shaped top in Fig. 15-22. The boards are sufficiently wide and long, but several boards are tapered in thickness (see Fig. 15-22A). If the boards were planed to equal thickness and then glued, the finished thickness would be too small. A more practical procedure is to clear the boards to maintain maximum thickness. Then, the boards can be glued with the tapered thickness in the waste areas (see Fig. 15-22B). Avoid the situation dia-

Fig. 15-21. Hexagon-top table.

grammed in Fig. 15-22C in which the boards were glued randomly, with the tapered thickness located within the usable area. Then, the only way to eliminate the tapered thickness is to plane the entire top to a reduced thickness, which is often less than desired.

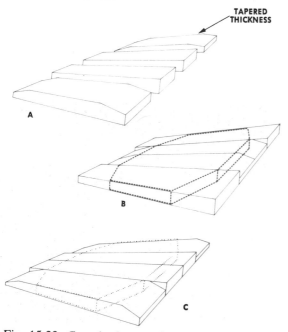

Fig. 15-22. Completely squaring an entire surface before cutting to shape is not always necessary.

Angular Cuts with Hand Tools

The common angular cuts are the chamfer, bevel, and taper (Fig. 15-23). A chamfer eliminates sharp corners and is used chiefly for decorative purposes

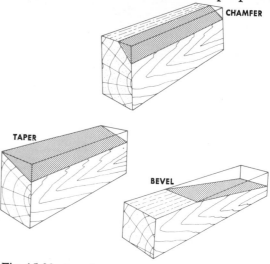

Fig. 15-23. Angular cuts.

(Fig. 15-24). A bevel, on the other hand, is not necessarily used for decorative purposes; it also is used for joining two pieces (Fig. 15-25). A taper is used for decorative purposes; for example, the legs on a

Fig. 15-24. Chamfers can be used for decorative purposes.

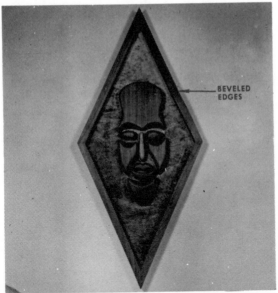

Fig. 15-25. Joints can be formed with beveled edges for a decorative effect.

Fig. 15-26. Square legs often are tapered to improve their appearance.

piece of furniture often are tapered to improve their appearance (Fig. 15-26).

Planing a Chamfer

1. *Mark the width and depth of the chamfer.* If a marking gauge is not available, use a pencil. Hold the pencil between the fingers, sliding the hand along the board while using the thumb for a guide (Fig. 15-27).
2. *Secure the stock for planing.* Several ways are suggested. Using a hand-screw clamp, the stock can be clamped to the corner of a table. Another way is to clamp the stock in a vise with the chamfered side up.
3. *Plane the corner.* Holding the plane parallel to the face of the chamfer, plane its entire length (Fig. 15-28). Work toward each of the two lines forming the boundary of the chamfer. The last stroke should produce an even shaving equal to the face and length of the chamfer. In planing the end grain, plane toward the end with shearing cuts (Fig. 15-29). Check the chamfer at intervals with a sliding

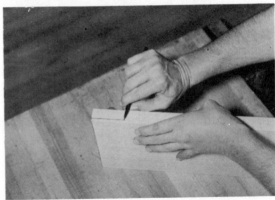

Fig. 15-27. A chamfer can be marked without using a marking gauge.

Fig. 15-28. Planing a chamfer.

Fig. 15-29. Planing a chamfer on end grain.

T bevel adjusted to the required angle (Fig. 15-30).

Planing a Bevel

A bevel is formed in a manner similar to the chamfer. First, the angle is marked on the ends, using a sliding T bevel. To complete the layout of the bevel, connect the bottom parts of the angle with a straight line (Fig. 15-31). Plane to these lines

Fig. 15-30. Checking an angle with a sliding T bevel.

Fig. 15-31. A bevel should be laid out before planing.

Fig. 15-32. A single taper laid out for planing.

while checking the angle periodically with a sliding T bevel.

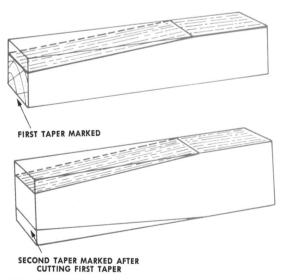

FIRST TAPER MARKED

SECOND TAPER MARKED AFTER CUTTING FIRST TAPER

Fig. 15-33. For a double taper, one side is marked and cut, before marking the stock for cutting the second taper.

Forming a Taper

1. *Mark the taper.* A single taper is shown in the diagram in Fig. 15-32. A double taper, or separate tapers on adjacent surfaces, is first marked on only one surface. After this taper is planed or cut, another taper is then marked on the following side and planed (Fig. 15-33). This is repeated as needed for stock tapered on three and four sides. When laying out identical tapers on two or more separate boards, check the depth and length on the boards. First, mark them individually; then compare their measurements (Fig. 15-34).

2. *Secure the stock in a vise.* Note in Fig. 15-35 that the stock is inclined for planing horizontally. Usually, the clamped end is the end not being tapered, especially if the stock is being tapered on several sides.

3. *Plane the taper.* Using a bench plane, work toward the lines forming the taper. Beginning at the end where the most wood is to be removed, gradually increase the length of the taper being planed (Fig. 15-36). In planing, keep the plane parallel to the desired taper (Fig. 15-37). Frequently check with a try square for flatness and squareness. For the larger tapers, the stock can be sawed first and then planed smooth.

Cutting Chamfers, Bevels, and Tapers

These cuts are made in several ways, depending on the size of cut and the machines available. Some cuts are made with a single machine; others are made with a combination of machines. The common procedures involve the band saw, circular saw, and jointer. In each instance, the stock is squared first to the overall dimensions.

Fig. 15-34. Identical tapers should be checked before cutting.

Fig. 15-35. In cutting a taper, incline the stock and plane horizontally.

Fig. 15-36. In planing a taper, gradually increase the length of the stroke.

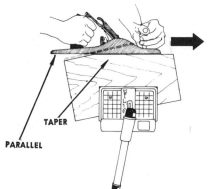

Fig. 15-37. In planing a taper, keep the plane parallel with the taper.

Cutting Chamfers and Bevels—Circular Saw (Fig. 15-38)

Chamfers and bevels can be cut in several ways. The stock can be guided with either a fence or a miter gauge, depending on the type and size of stock. Either the blade or the table can be tilted, depending on the type of table saw. Regardless of the method, the procedure is basically the same.

1. *Make necessary saw adjustments.* This includes the angle of cut and its width (see Fig. 15-38).
2. *Test the angle and the width of the cut.* To accomplish this, make a trial cut on waste stock; then check with a sliding T bevel.
3. *Make the final cut.* Before completing the cut, it may be necessary to recheck

Fig. 15-38. Tilt the blade of a circular saw for cutting a chamfer or a bevel.

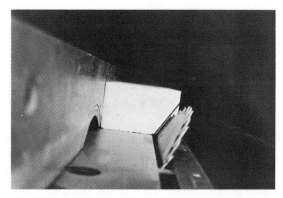

Fig. 15-39. In cutting an angle, make a short trial cut. Then make minor adjustments between the blade and the mark for the final cut.

the saw settings. In doing this, the profile of the chamfer or bevel is often drawn onto the stock. For a final check, the alignment of the blade with the marks can be noted by barely sawing into the wood (Fig. 15-39). Usually, minor adjustments, if needed, can be made without affecting the final cut.

Cutting Chamfers and Bevels—Jointer (Fig. 15-40)

1. *Draw the profile of the cut.* Use a sliding T bevel and a straightedge.
2. *Adjust the jointer.* Keeping the same setting on the sliding T bevel, adjust

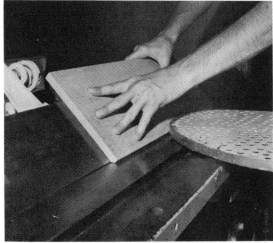

Fig. 15-40. Incline the jointer fence for an angular cut.

the fence (Fig. 15-41) to the same angle. Lower the infeed table for a series of cuts.

3. *Make several preliminary cuts.* Check the angle of the cut with the sliding T bevel, making adjustments as needed.

4. *Make the final cuts.* Joint until the outline of the angle is reached. Usually it is necessary to readjust the infeed table before making the final cut.

Cutting Chamfers and Bevels—Band Saw (Fig. 15-42)

A band saw is used for this purpose only when the stock is too small to be cut

Fig. 15-42. Chamfers and bevels can be cut on a band saw.

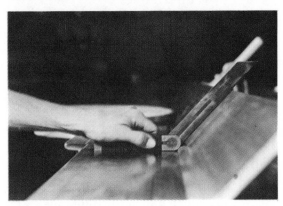

Fig. 15-41. Adjust the angle of the jointer fence with a sliding T bevel in cutting chamfers and bevels.

safely another way. The table is tilted to form the required angle (Fig. 15-43). Either the fence or the miter gauge guides the stock.

Cutting Tapers—Circular Saw Method

A jig is needed to support the stock when sawing a taper on a circular saw. Never saw "freehand" on the circular saw, since it is easy to bind the blade, causing a dangerous kickback.

Procedure for Single Tapers

1. *Mark the taper.*
2. *Adjust the jig.* The taper is deter-

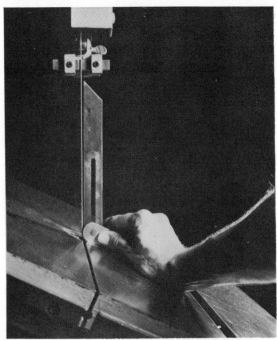

Fig. 15-43. Check the angle of the table of the band saw with a sliding T bevel.

mined by varying the clearance between the two boards (Fig. 15-44). When describing the taper per running foot, measure the clearance 12 inches from the hinged end; then set the clearance to the desired taper. Another jig is shown in Fig. 15-45. Although this jig cannot be adjusted, it is made quickly and easily.

3. *Test adjustments.* Without turning on the saw, check the layout of the taper

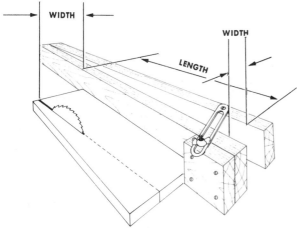

Fig. 15-44. Taper jig. Measure the length of the taper from the hinged end. The clearance between the two boards at this point is equal to the width of the taper.

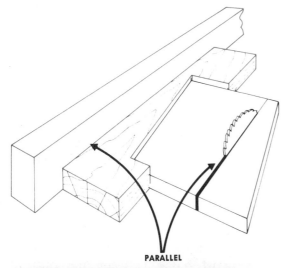

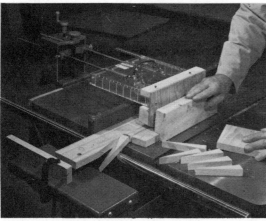

Fig. 15-45. Fixed taper jig (top) used with safety guard (bottom). (Courtesy Brett-Guard Division, The Foredom Electric Company)

with the blade. Note where the kerf should start and end when cut on the stock.

4. *Make the cut.* Be sure to keep the stock firmly against the jig and to keep the jig firmly against the fence. Apply forward pressure on the jig—not on the stock being sawed.

Procedure for Multiple Tapers

1. *Mark the stock as needed.*
2. *Design and build the jig.* The long piece slides along the fence, guiding the cut; the small block serves as a stop (Fig. 15-46). This block also helps to determine the length and width of the taper.

For an example, the jig in Fig. 15-46 is designed for a table leg 1½-inch square. This leg requires a 12-inch long taper which reduces to 1-inch square. This means that ¼ inch is

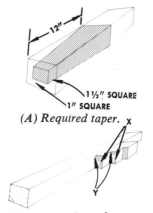

(A) Required taper.

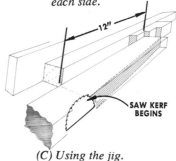

(B) The offsets (Y) are equal to the taper cut on each side.

(C) Using the jig.

Fig. 15-46. Cutting multiple tapers on the jointer.

cut from each side. Therefore, the "Y" measurements on the block are made ¼ inch. Since the "X" measurements are unimportant, they can be made any convenient size, usually 1 inch or less.

3. *Adjust for the cut.* This operation determines the length of the taper. For the example in Fig. 15-46, the fence is adjusted for the cut to begin 12 inches from the second offset of the block. The first offset is never used.

4. *Make the four cuts.* Start the jig from the same offset when making the first two adjacent cuts. Use the second offset for these cuts. The third offset is used for the final two cuts. Before making these cuts, move or adjust the fence for the cut to begin 12 inches from the third offset.

Cutting Tapers—Jointer Method

1. *Mark the taper.*
2. *Adjust the infeed table.* If the width of the taper is ¼ inch or less, adjust the infeed table for an equal amount. For greater widths, adjust for two or more cuts to provide the needed width.

Fig. 15-47. Cutting a taper on the jointer. To locate the stopblock, place the stock with the beginning point of taper resting on the lip of the outfeed table. Clamp the stopblock behind the stock. Attempt this adjustment only with the power off.

3. *Clamp a stopblock to the fence.* Determine its location by placing the stock on the jointer (Fig. 15-47). With the front of the taper resting on the lip of the outfeed table, clamp the stopblock at the end of the stock.

4. *Remove the stock from the jointer, and then start the jointer.* With the butt end of the stock firmly against stopblock, lower the stock to the knives (Fig. 15-48). Use a push stick or block when the height of the stock from the table is less than that of the fence.

5. *Finish the taper with a bench plane.* After jointing, the taper may be slightly rough. Several strokes with a plane will smooth the taper and extend it the full length marked previously.

This procedure is changed for short tapers. Marking the taper, adjusting the jointer, and positioning the stopblock are identical. The position of the operator is changed, and a second block is needed for support. Note in Fig. 15-49 that the operator stands behind the outfeed table, and pulls the stock. To position the second block, place the stock in its beginning position with the jointer turned off. Slide the support block between the outfeed table and stock, until contact is made with both the block and the table. Mark this point, tacking the support block to

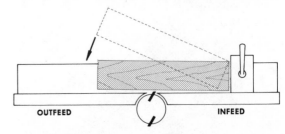

Fig. 15-48. In lowering the stock to the outfeed table, pivot against the stopblock. Lower the stock straight down, holding it against the fence. Do not apply pressure at the front end of the stock.

Fig. 15-49. In planing short tapers, the operator stands behind the outfeed table and pulls the stock.

the stock. When cutting additional tapers on adjacent sides, the location of the support block is squared to its first position.

Questions

1. What is meant by "rough" wood? Why is "rough" wood preferable to "surfaced" wood?

2. Describe the difference between cleared stock and squared stock.

3. List the recommended procedure for squaring stock by hand. How does this procedure differ from the procedure for squaring stock by machine?

4. Why is it more practical to rip a board to width, rather than to joint it to width?

5. When are chamfers, bevels, and tapers used?

6. How do the procedures differ in cutting long and short tapers on the jointer?

7. What machine should be used for cutting an edge chamfer on a board 6 inches long? Why?

8. Sketch a board demonstrating warp and end checks. Describe the difference between "in wind" and wane.

9. When sawing a board to length, why is an extra $\frac{1}{16}$ inch sometimes added?

10. Sketch a piece of stock, identifying its six main parts or surfaces.

Unit 16 – Hand Tools

Hand tools can be purchased in various shapes to perform many different operations. Most of the hand tools are relatively inexpensive and easy to maintain. A hand tool is unique, since the operator provides the power and guides the tool in performing an operation. Hand tools are used for operations which cannot be accomplished by machines, including the following:

1. Stock physically too small to be machined with portable electric equipment or the usual woodworking machines.
2. Stock with irregular shapes and thicknesses.
3. Stock constructed with cutting edges or lips which other equipment cannot reach.
4. Stock requiring additional accuracy (finishing touches) after being worked with power tools.

A person unfamiliar with the technologies of the wood industry is often lead to believe that hand tools are used only by those who do not know how to use machines. Contrary to this belief, the hand tools are vital to the superior craftsmanship performed by those who are fully acquainted with woodworking techniques and equipment. Another belief is that the hand tools are limited to small projects. Note in Fig. 16-1 and 16-2 that this is not true. Size, in these examples, had little influence in selecting hand or machine operation. The birds were cut roughly to shape and then sanded, using a band saw and a spindle sander. The bases were sawed on a band saw; then the edges were sanded with a disk sander. The holes in the base were drilled on a drill press.

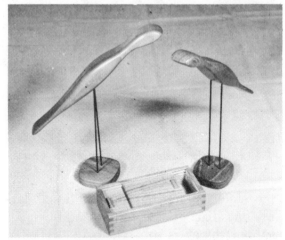

Fig. 16-1. These projects were made by machine operations, except for hand finishing.

Fig. 16-2. Hand tool operations were used predominantly in making these chairs.

Other than finish sanding by hand, only machine operations were used. The jewelry box in Fig. 16-1 also was completed by machine operations, except for the finish sanding. The individual pieces were cut with a band saw. The sides and ends are joined by box joints cut on a circular saw. An electric router was used to rabbet the bottom piece. The two pieces in the top slide back and forth in grooves cut into the sides with a circular saw.

On the other hand, the matching chairs

(see Fig. 16-2) were predominantly handmade. After rough planing, the only machine operation involved in using a band saw is to saw the individual parts to approximate size. The actual finished sizes and shapes resulted from hand operations. Due to the desired irregular shapes, the spokeshaves, surform tools, wood rasps, files, and scrapers were used in this order. All the joints were cut with hand tools, since irregular angles were formed between the mating members of each chair.

Therefore, the use of hand tools depends on the project, its material, its shape, and its operations. Hand tools should be used where the result is a better job. Likewise, machines should be used when a better job is the result.

Among the many operations involving hand tools are assembling, cutting, drilling and boring, fastening, filing, measuring and layout, planing, sawing, scraping, and shaping or forming. Many of the hand tools are discussed elsewhere, since they are associated with other operations. T' remaining hand tools are discussed here.

Safety

Working with hand tools is considered quite safe. Hand tools account for about 6 percent of all industrial accidents, compared to about 10 percent for machinery. Hand-tool accidents usually result from one of three hazards. One of these hazards lies in using tools incorrectly—for example, holding the stock in one hand while carving with a wood chisel held in the other hand. Another hazard lies in using a defective (broken) tool. Typical examples include loose or cracked handles and chipped or dull cutting edges. The third hazard lies in using the wrong tool; for example, using a screwdriver designed for slotted-head screws to remove a screw with a Phillips head.

Safe working practices aid in reducing injuries to the worker and damage to his project. The following practices are general guidlines which can result in a safer use of hand tools:

1. Follow a safe method.
2. Inspect the tool for defects or dull cutting edges before using it.
3. Select the proper tool for the job.
4. Maintain proper working conditions.
5. Discard tools which cannot be repaired.

Other safey rules which should be observed are:

1. *Hammers.* Use the correct hammer. Avoid driving a nail with a ball-peen hammer and beating a piece of metal with a claw hammer. Before using, check the handle for cracks or looseness. Never abuse a hammer by prying boards apart or by removing large nails. In driving a nail, remove the fingers from the area around the nail as soon as possible.
2. *Screwdrivers.* Use only a screwdriver with a tip that matches the screw-head slot. Never hold the work in one hand while driving a screw. Avoid using a screwdriver to pry boards apart or to remove the tops of cans.
3. *Wood chisels.* Always direct the cutting edge away from the body—never hold the work in hand while carving. Do not cut nails or pry boards apart which have been fastened together. Use only moderate force in hitting a chisel with a mallet.
4. *Files, rasps, and gouges.* Periodically, remove the wood fibers which can diminish the cutting action. When cleaning a file or rasp, do not hit it against another object to dislodge the wood fibers. Use only files with the tangs covered with handles. Never use a tang for prying.

5. *Knives.* Keep the cutting edges sharp and directed away from the body. A dull cutting edge is more dangerous than a sharp cutting edge. Never use a knife for driving screws or for prying objects apart.

6. *Wrenches.* Do not use a wrench with a cracked jaw or a wrench that is too large. Never use a pipe wrench or pliers to remove or tighten square-head and hex-head nuts. The use of extensions (or cheaters) for extra leverage generally is unsafe. Avoid using a wrench to drive a nail or to separate fastened pieces. In using an adjustable wrench, apply pressure to the fixed jaw rather than to the movable jaw. Where possible, pull a wrench rather than push it. Then, if the wrench slips, there is less likelihood of bruising a hand against another part.

Chisels and Gouges

The wood chisel is one of the most important woodworking tools. These chisels are used for trimming finished pieces, for smoothing, and for cutting joints. Several types of wood chisels are available, but the shapes are basically identical at the "working" or cutting end. One side of the chisel blade is flat; the other side is beveled to form the cutting edge (Fig. 16-3). Beginners should remember that a chisel is extremely sharp. The worker should select the proper chisel for the job and handle it correctly and carefully. At no time should any part of the body be placed immediately in front of the cutting edge of the chisel, since a slip can cause a serious injury.

Types of Chisels

Woodworking chisels are manufactured in various sizes and shapes for different

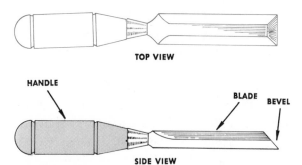

Fig. 16-3. Wood chisel with parts.

types of work. Three general categories of chisels are available, including the: (1) Tang chisel; (2) Socket chisel; and (3) Everlasting chisel. The tang chisels are made with a long steel shank extending through the handle; a cap is often found on the end of the tang (Fig. 16-4A). The force of a hammer or mallet striking the end butt of the chisel is transmitted to the chisel through the tang. A socket chisel, however, has no central tang (Fig. 16-4B). The handle fits into a socket; then the force of the blow is transmitted uniformly through the handle and to the chisel. The everlasting chisel is made in one solid piece; the handle is a flattened steel continuation of the blade (Fig. 16-4C). Sometimes, either plastic or wood inserts are placed on either side of the center tang portion to permit the chisel to be held more comfortably. The everlasting chisel was de-

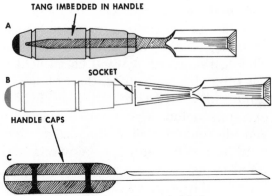

Fig. 16-4. Classification of wood chisels.

veloped specifically for use with metal hammers, making it easier and simpler for these chisels designed for roughing work to be carried in a carpenter's kit. The socket firmer and the tang chisel are made to be used with a soft-face hammer, such as a wood or plastic mallet.

Variations in the length of the chisels and in the thickness of the blades provide certain qualities and handling characteristics peculiar to the type of chisel; however, the size of the chisel is not determined by these factors. The various chisels, such as the paring, framing, pocket mortise, and glazier's chisels, are different in length and blade shape.

Chisel Sizes

The size of a chisel is determined by the width of its blade. All the various types of chisels are made with blades ranging from ⅛ inch to 1 inch in width, in ⅛-inch intervals. The chisels from 1 inch to 2 inches in width vary in ¼-inch intervals. The most common sizes are ¼, ½, ¾, 1, and 1½ inches. In general, only two or three of the more common chisel sizes are needed for most types of work.

Making Chisel Cuts

In making a chisel cut, select a chisel slightly more narrow than the cut to be made. If a 1-inch cut is to be made, the chisel should be slightly less than 1 inch —for example, ¾ or ½ inch. This permits careful and accurate work at the corners, without breaking the fibers; also, it permits the worker to move the chisel sidewise or laterally across the wood surface in chiseling out the wood, making a smoother cut possible (Fig. 16-5).

When rough work is being chiseled— work which removes most of the stock down to nearly the approximate size, but not the final size, the chisel should be

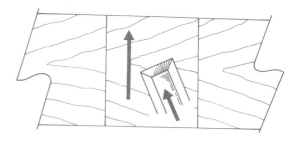

Fig. 16-5. A lateral chisel motion results in a smoother cut.

powered with a hammer or mallet. However, for the final sizing cuts and trimming, all the driving force should come from the hands of the worker. Also, it is important to remember that both hands should be on the chisel when doing work. This provides more support and more control of the chisel and keeps the hands of the worker from in front of the chisel edge, thereby avoiding injury.

The chisel should be moved *with* the grain direction. If a chisel is moved against the grain (Fig. 16-6), the chisel edge picks up the grain, causing the wood to split. A starting cut should always be made inside the marked line, leaving the portion of the material around the edges for a final light trimming.

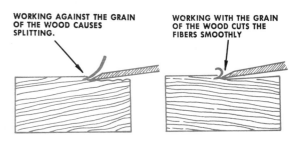

Fig. 16-6. Working "with the grain" reduces splitting.

In chiseling *across* the grain of the wood to remove the materials from a joint area (Fig. 16-7), avoid chiseling all

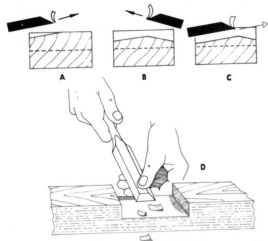

Fig. 16-7. Correct method of chiseling across the width of a board. Avoid splintered sides by working from the edges toward the center of the board (A, B, and C). Use the thumb and fingers to guide the cutting edge and to act as a stop (D).

the way across the width of the board. Chisel approximately halfway across the board; then turn the stock around and chisel from the opposite direction. This avoids splintering the corners and provides maximum accuracy with the marked guide lines.

In using the chisel to smooth a rounded surface, the area is removed as closely as possible to the surface with a handsaw. The finish trim is performed by hand with the bevel up, as indicated for rounded corners or *convex* curves (Fig. 16-8). This means that the bevel is up when the curve is on the outside of an object, to prevent the chisel digging in.

In chiseling and trimming curves into the wood, or *concave* curves, the bevel

Fig. 16-8. Chiseling a round corner.

should be down; then the natural tendency of the chisel is to move away from the wood, to prevent digging in (Fig. 16-9). When cutting a concave curve to avoid going into the grain or against the grain, the curve should be cut halfway from one direction and halfway from the opposite direction.

In cutting bevels or chamfers which extend partially across the grain (stop

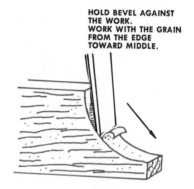

Fig. 16-9. Working a concave cut.

bevels or stop chamfers), the chisel should be moved only a portion of the distance across; then it should be reversed and moved from the opposite direction (Fig. 16-10).

In chiseling out a section surrounded entirely by wood, it is advisable first to cut small sections or notches; then remove the notches (Fig. 16-11). Remember that rough work is done at some distance from the edge of the holes and that the final

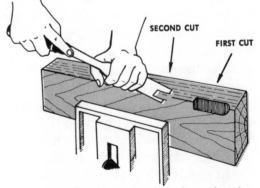

Fig. 16-10. Cutting a stop bevel or chamfer.

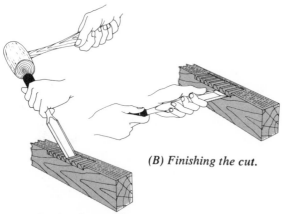

(B) Finishing the cut.

(A) Cutting the rough area.

Fig. 16-11. Chiseling out a section surrounded by wood.

trim and sizing are done carefully by hand. A setup for sharpening a wood chisel is shown in Fig. 16-12.

Gouges

A gouge is a chisel with a curved blade. The blade can be curved for rounding off the edges of the stock; then it is called a *firmer* gouge (Fig. 16-13A). A gouge with a blade curved in the opposite direction is a *paring* blade (Fig. 16-13B) and

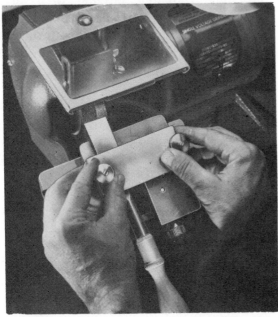

Fig. 16-12. Sharpening a wood chisel. (Courtesy Power Tool Division, Rockwell Manufacturing Company)

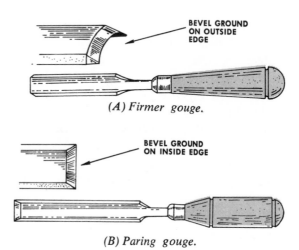

(A) Firmer gouge.

(B) Paring gouge.

Fig. 16-13. Gouges.

is used for cutting grooves and curved recesses in wood. Gouges essentially are chisels, and they are used in basically the same manner that chisels are used. The same precautions should be observed in working with gouges and chisels, with regard to trimming to size and the position of the hands for safety.

Screwdrivers (Drivers)

Screwdrivers, also known as drivers, are used with threaded fasteners or screws. The tip on all screwdrivers corresponds to either a slotted-head screw (Fig. 16-14) or a Phillips-head screw (Fig. 16-15). Depending on the need, various

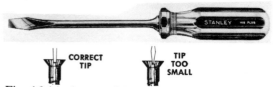

Fig. 16-14. A screwdriver for slotted-head screws. (Courtesy The Stanley Works)

Fig. 16-15. A screwdriver for Phillips-head screws. (Courtesy The Stanley Works)

screwdrivers are used in woodworking. A spiral-type screwdriver quickly drives or retracts a screw when its handle is pushed toward the screw (Fig. 16-16). Interchangeable bits are provided to accommodate different screws. An offset screwdriver is used in places where an ordinary screwdriver cannot fit into the space above the head of a screw (Fig. 16-17). The ratchet-type screwdriver is similar to the offset screwdriver, but it is speedier (Fig. 16-18). Another type of driver is the screwdriver bit, which is used with a brace (Fig. 16-19). The screwdriver bit

Fig. 16-16. A spiral-type screwdriver with interchangeable bits which turn when the handle is pushed. (Courtesy The Stanley Works)

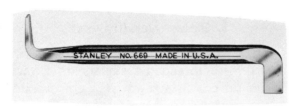

Fig. 16-17. Offset screwdriver. (Courtesy The Stanley Works)

Fig. 16-18. Ratchet screwdriver. (Courtesy The Stanley Works)

Fig. 16-19. Screwdriver bit for use in a brace. (Courtesy The Stanley Works)

is used where a large number of screws must be driven quickly.

The size of a screwdriver, other than the special types, is indicated by the tip size, blade diameter, and length. The overall length of a screwdriver should not be confused with its stated length. For example, the blade of a 6-inch screwdriver is 6 inches long. Its overall measurement, however, is 6 inches, plus the length of the handle.

Files and Rasps

Files are used to smooth edges and ends (Fig. 16-20); the rasps are used to shape the edges, ends, and faces quickly and roughly (Fig. 16-21). Neither tool should be used where other cutting tools can be used. Files should not be used to smooth joints or to square edges. Wood filings fill the pores and reduce the holding power of the glue. It is nearly impossible to file the edges square.

A file is designated by its shape, cut, and size. The shape refers to the cross-sectional area, which can be square, rectangular, triangular, circular, or a variation of these shapes (Fig. 16-22). The shape is either taper (thickness and width reduced gradually) or blunt (uniform thickness and width). The cut of a file is the pattern formed by the teeth. As shown in Fig. 16-23, the cut is single, double, rasp, or curved (Vixen). The size of a file depends on the length, which is measured from the heel to the point. (Fig. 16-24). The tang is disregarded in measuring the length. A file is classified further by the coarseness of its teeth, including the coarse, rough, bastard, second, smooth, and dead-smooth cuts.

The following points should be observed in using a file:
1. Never use a file or rasp unless a handle is placed on the tang.
2. Secure the stock firmly before filing or rasping.

3. Apply pressure firmly on the forward stroke, raising the file or rasp on the return stroke.
4. Pace the strokes at about 30 to 40 strokes per minute.
5. Using a file card, clean the file or rasp as needed (Fig. 16-25). The wire side of the card is used to dislodge difficult materials (Fig. 16-26).

Proper care lengthens the service life of a file or rasp. Files should never be stored or banged against anything that can damage their cutting edges. An excel-

Fig. 16-20. Files for smoothing edges and ends. (Courtesy Nicholson File Company)

Fig. 16-21. Rasps are used to shape stock roughly and quickly. (Courtesy Nicholson File Company)

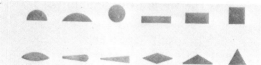

Fig. 16-22. Various shapes of files and rasps. (Courtesy Nicholson File Company)

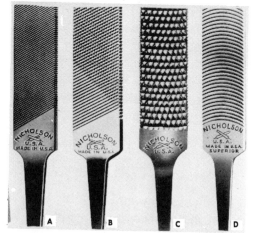

Fig. 16-23. Cuts of files, including single-cut (A), double-cut (B), rasp (C), curved or Vixen (D). (Courtesy Nicholson File Company)

lent method of storing files is shown in Fig. 16-27. Keep the teeth away from water, since rust can ruin a file. Oil and grease, if necessary, can be removed with the common chalk used with a classroom chalkboard.

Forming Tools

The forming tools are used in cutting, planing, and shaping operations. Usually known as *surform* tools, the cutting action results from diagonal rows of teeth on a thin blade. The teeth are similar to those on a file; however, the center of

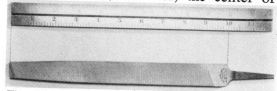

Fig. 16-24. The size of a file is indicated by its length measured from the heel to the point. (Courtesy Nicholson File Company)

Fig. 16-25. A file card is used to clean the teeth of files and rasps. (Courtesy Nicholson File Company)

Fig. 16-26. Using the wire side of the file card. (Courtesy Nicholson File Company)

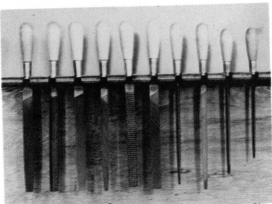

Fig. 16-27. Recommended method of storing files and rasps. (Courtesy Nicholson File Company)

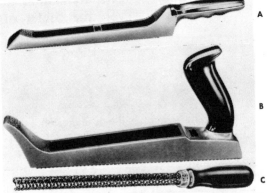

Fig. 16-28. The surform tools (A), (B), (C) are similar in use to planes, files, and rasps for planing, cutting, and shaping operations. (Courtesy The Stanley Works)

Fig. 16-29. Scallops or decorative cuts made with a surform.

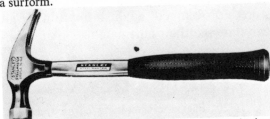

Fig. 16-30. The claw hammer is the principal hammer used in woodworking. (Courtesy The Stanley Works)

each tooth is open. Many advantages are claimed for a surform tool. Its cutting action is quick and smooth. The blade does not clog, has a long service life, and is quickly replaced.

Various surform tools are available (Fig. 16-28). Used either as a plane or as a file, a surform can be used for flat cuts, curved cuts, smooth or rough cuts, decorative cuts, and for enlarging holes. Scallops formed with the round surform tool are often used for decorative purposes (Fig. 16-29).

Hammers

A claw hammer is the principal hammer used in woodworking (Fig. 16-30).

It is used to drive nails (or similar fasteners) and to pull (retract) nails (Fig. 16-31). The size of a claw hammer is indicated by the weight of the hammer head, which is 7, 10, 13, 16, or 20 ounces. The most widely used sizes are 13 and 16 ounces. The claws are either straight or curved. A nail set and the claw hammer often are used in recessing the head of a fastener (Fig. 16-32).

Other hammers used in woodworking are the magnetic tack hammer (Fig. 16-33) and the soft-face hammer (Fig. 16-34). The ball-peen hammer is used for metalwork, but it should never be used for driving nails and other fasteners (Fig. 16-35).

Measuring and Layout Tools

The measuring and layout tools are demonstrated throughout this book. The try square (Fig. 16-36) and the steel square (Fig. 16-37) are used in checking or making square measurements. The

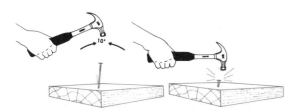

(A) Maximum force is obtained by grasping the hammer at the end of the handle.

(B) Pulling a nail.

Fig. 16-31. Using a claw hammer to drive and pull nails.

sliding T bevel is used in making and checking angular measurements. Linear measurements are made with the bench rule, folding rule, and tape rule. Bench rules normally are made from wood and are available in 1-ft and 2-ft lengths (Fig.

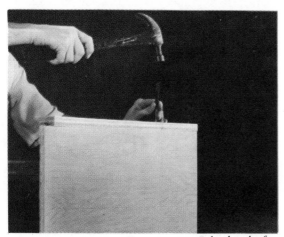

Fig. 16-32. Using a nail set to recess the head of a nail.

16-38). The folding or zigzag rules are used chiefly in carpentry (Fig. 16-39). A common length, when extended, is 6 feet. A folding rule with an end extension

Fig. 16-33. Magnetic tack hammer. (Courtesy The Stanley Works)

Fig. 16-34. Soft-face hammer. (Courtesy The Stanley Works)

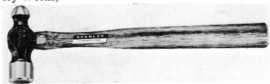

Fig. 16-35. Ball-peen hammer. (Courtesy The Stanley Works)

Fig. 16-36. Try square. (Courtesty The Stanley Works)

Fig. 16-37. Steel square. (Courtesy The Stanley Works)

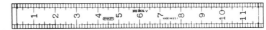

Fig. 16-38. One-foot bench rule. (Courtesy The Stanley Works)

Fig. 16-39. Folding rule (Courtesy The Stanley Works)

Fig. 16-40. Folding rule with an end extension. (Courtesy The Stanley Works)

(A) A "pocket" tape for short measurements.

(B) Tape rule for long measurements. (Courtesy The L. S. Starrett Co.)

(C) Using the tape rule for a long measurement. (Courtesy the L. S. Starrett Co.)

Fig. 16-41. Tape rules.

Fig. 16-42. Combination square. (Courtesy The Stanley Works)

Fig. 16-43. Level. (Courtesy The Stanley Works)

Fig. 16-44. Hand scraper. (Courtesy The Stanley Works)

(A) For smoothing surfaces.

(B) For smoothing surfaces and for removing old finishes.

Fig. 16-45. Cabinet scrapers. (Courtesy The Stanley Works)

for inside measurements is shown in Fig. 16-40. The tape rules are available in varying lengths (Fig. 16-41). The combination square (Fig. 16-42) is used for various purposes. It is used in measuring uniform widths and lengths, in checking squareness, in locating 45° miters and bevels, and for checking inside depth measurements. As its name implies, a level is used in leveling surfaces (Fig. 16-43).

Scrapers and Spokeshaves

Most of the scraping operations in woodworking are performed with a hand scraper (Fig. 16-44) or with one of several types of cabinet scrapers (Fig. 16-45). Although both the cabinet scrapers shown in Fig. 16-45 are used to scrape smooth surfaces, the scraper in Fig. 16-45B is used more often in removing old finishes. The hand scraper (Fig. 16-46) is used by applying pressure with the thumbs to the center of the scraper. On most

Fig. 16-46. The hand scraper is usually "pushed" away from the body.

Fig. 16-47. Burnisher. (Courtesy The Stanley Works)

work, the hand scraper is pushed away from the body; however, the cabinet scraper is usually pulled toward the body.

The cutting action of a hand scraper results from a burnished edge. Before burnishing, the edge is filed flat. After filing, the cutting edge is pressed out with a burnisher (Fig. 16-47). Note in Fig. 16-48 that the burnisher is held at a slight angle for this operation. A scraper slides over the surface, producing fine shavings when its cutting edge has been burnished properly.

A spokeshave is similar in appearance to the cabinet scraper (Fig. 16-49). Spokeshaves are used for planing and

(A) DOING THIS . . .

(B) PRODUCES A CUTTING EDGE
    LIKE THIS . . .

CUTTING EDGE TURNED
OVER BY BURNISHER

BLADE

Fig. 16-48. Pressing out the cutting edge on a hand scraper with a burnisher. The burnisher is held at a slight angle (A) to turn over the cutting edge (B).

Fig. 16-49. A spokeshave with an adjustable cutter. (Courtesy The Stanley Works)

smoothing irregular shapes (Fig. 16-50). The name is derived from the tool developed by "wheelwrights" (craftsmen who made wooden wheels) to shape and smooth the wooden spokes in wagon wheels. Spokeshaves are especially useful in working curved surfaces. The cabinet

Fig. 16-50. A spokeshave can be used to plane and smooth irregular shapes.

legs in Fig. 16-51 were shaped with a spokeshave. The cutter is similar to a plane iron; also it is sharpened with a bevel similar to the bevel on a plane iron. The cutters on most spokeshaves are ad-

Fig. 16-51. The legs on this piece of furniture were planed and shaped with a spokeshave.

justable to control the cutting depth for fine and coarse shavings. A spokeshave can be either pushed or pulled, depending on the results obtained.

Questions

1. Why are hand tools important in woodworking?
2. For what conditions should hand tools be used in woodworking? List several factors that should be considered.
3. List three hazards which lead to hand-tool accidents. How can these hazards be eliminated?
4. How should a wood chisel be held in cutting wood?
5. Why are screwdrivers made with different tips? How is the size of a screwdriver indicated?
6. List several special drivers. When should each be used.
7. Discuss the shape, cut, and size of files.
8. When should files and rasps be used in woodworking?
9. List the advantages of surform tools.
10. How is the size of a claw hammer indicated?
11. List six measuring and layout tools. Explain the use for each tool.
12. List the procedure for sharpening a hand scraper.
13. When is a spokeshave used in woodworking?
14. How is the depth of cut adjusted on a spokeshave?

Unit 17 — Handsawing

Handsaws are used to cut stock to lengths, widths, and shapes. Among the more common handsaws are the crosscut, rip, miter, coping, and keyhole saws. The parts for a typical handsaw are diagrammed in Fig. 17-1. The size of a handsaw is described by the blade length and the number of points per inch. For example, the blade of a 26-inch handsaw is 26 inches in length. This value or size often is stamped on the side of the blade along with the name of the manufacturer. The number of points also is stamped on the blade, usually in the area of the heel. Note in Fig. 17-2, that there is one point more than the number of teeth per inch. The number of points on the blade determines the fineness or coarseness of the cut. A handsaw with fewer points cuts faster, but a handsaw with more teeth cuts smoother.

The saw teeth are bent alternately left and right; this is referred to as the *set* of the saw (Fig. 17-3). The set of a saw determines the width of the cut or path (kerf), which is wider than the thickness of the blade; this prevents the saw blade from binding in the kerf.

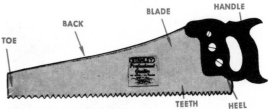
Fig. 17-1. Diagram of handsaw parts.

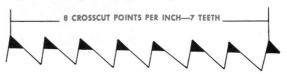

Fig. 17-2. The number of points per inch on a handsaw determines the fineness or coarseness of cut. More points produce a finer cut.

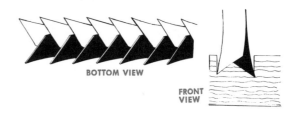
Fig. 17-3. The "set" of the saw teeth causes them to cut a path or "kerf" wider than the thickness of the blade.

Sawing Hints

1. Select the correct handsaw for the operation.
2. Support the stock firmly, but in a convenient position. Clamp with a vise (Fig. 17-4); or fasten the stock to the workbench with a hand-screw clamp (Fig. 17-5). In some instances, it is necessary merely to press the stock against the support, using either a foot or a hand for leverage (Fig. 17-6).
3. Maintain a convenient and comfortable position while sawing. Keep the body in front of or above the stock. Do not strain or stand in an awkward position.
4. Check the stock for nails, screws, or other fasteners before sawing. Never cut metal with a saw designed for cutting wood—use a hacksaw (Fig. 17-7).
5. In marking the stock, allow for the width of the saw kerf. After marking the exact cut size, always saw

Fig. 17-4. Clamp the stock in a vise before beginning the cut.

Fig. 17-6. Holding the stock with a knee while sawing.

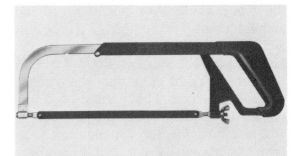

Fig. 17-7. Hacksaw. (Courtesy The Stanley Works)

on the waste side of the mark (Fig. 17-8). When cutting a long piece of stock into several shorter pieces, add an extra ⅛ inch for each saw kerf (Fig. 17-9).

6. Begin the saw kerf with slow medium-length strokes. Then increase the length of stroke and the speed. Near the end of the kerf reduce the length of stroke and the speed. Do not be haphazard by making several quick, short strokes, since the long, smooth strokes cut faster and smoother.

7. Saw along the mark, keeping the blade straight or perpendicular to the surface. A try square can be used to check the cut (Fig. 17-10).

Fig. 17-5. A parallel clamp or hand screw can be used to clamp the stock to a workbench before beginning the cut.

Fig. 17-8. Make the saw kerf on the waste side of the mark.

8. While sawing, watch the mark—not the saw blade.

9. Do not force a saw blade. If it binds, something is wrong. The wood might be too green (or wet); or the blade

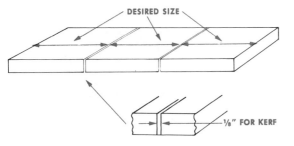

Fig. 17-9. When measuring stock for successive cuts, add ⅛ inch for each kerf.

might be covered with rust or rosin. The saw blade might have too little set. Either correct the condition or select another saw.

10. Treat a handsaw as though it were a fine, precision cutting instrument. Protect the teeth from unnecessary dulling, and keep the blade from water and other types of moisture. These agents cause rusting, which greatly reduces the efficiency of a handsaw.

Crosscut Saw

A crosscut saw is used to cut *across the grain of the wood* (Fig. 17-11). Its teeth are like small knives. In the back stroke, the outer edges of the teeth score the wood to prevent splintering (Fig. 17-12).

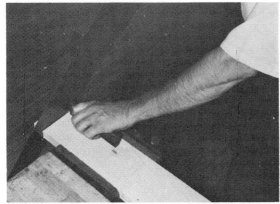

Fig. 17-10. During the cut, use a try square to check for squareness.

Fig. 17-11. A crosscut saw is used to cut "across the grain" of the wood. (Courtesy The Stanley Works)

Fig. 17-12. The outer edges of the crosscut teeth score the wood to prevent splintering (A). The teeth are shaped like small knives (B).

Then, on the forward stroke, the center portion of the teeth cuts the wood. The following steps are important in crosscutting:

1. *Mark the stock.*
2. *Secure the stock.* Use a vise, clamp, or other suitable means. Keep one end of the saw free to avoid binding the blade (Fig. 17-13).

Fig. 17-13. To prevent the kerf closing and binding the blade, support only one end of the stock while sawing.

3. *Ready the saw blade.* Position the blade about 45° to the stock with the heel resting on the waste side of the mark (Fig. 17-14).
4. *Begin the cut.* Slowly pull the saw backward while guiding the blade with the thumb of the free hand (Fig. 17-15).

Fig. 17-14. Position the blade of a crosscut saw at about 45° to the stock.

5. *Maintain squareness.* After several strokes, check for squareness or trueness. If needed, correct the error by leaning the blade toward either side.

6. *Continue the sawing.* Use long strokes and watch the mark. Twist the handle when the kerf (or blade) begins to wander from a straight line.

7. *Complete the cut.* When the cut nears the end, guard against cracking the stock. Grasp the unsupported portion of the stock; finish with slow, short strokes.

Ripsaw

A ripsaw is used to cut along, or *with,* the grain (Fig. 17-16). The teeth of the ripsaw are set similar to those on the

Fig. 17-15. Guide the saw with the thumb to start the saw kerf. Remove the thumb when the kerf is deep enough to guide the blade.

Fig. 17-16. A ripsaw is used to cut "with the grain" of the wood. (Courtesy The Stanley Works)

crosscut saw, but they are shaped similar to small chisels (Fig. 17-17). Each tooth chisels a small portion of the wood on the forward stroke. Observe the following steps in ripsawing:

1. *Mark the stock.*
2. *Secure the stock.* Use a method similar to those used for crosscutting.
3. *Ready the saw blade.* Position the saw about 60° to the stock, with the heel resting on the waste side of the mark (Fig. 17-18).
4. *Make the cut.* Begin and finish the cut, with the blade similar to the procedure outlined for crosscutting. While ripping, the kerf might attempt to close or bind the blade. Then, separate the sides of the kerf with a small wedge.

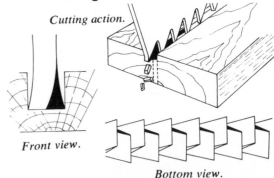

Cutting action.

Front view.

Bottom view.

Fig. 17-17. Ripsaw teeth.

Miter Saw

A miter saw produces fine cuts and is used mostly for cabinetwork and finish work. It is similar to a crosscut saw, except for its reinforced back (Fig. 17-19). For this reason, the miter saw is often called a *back* saw. It has fine crosscut teeth. Typically, the miter saws range

Fig. 17-18. The ripsaw blade is held at about 60° to the stock.

Fig. 17-19. A miter saw is used for fine cuts both across and with the grain. It is often called a backsaw, due to its reinforced back. (Courtesy The Stanley Works)

from 12 to 16 points, in comparison with about 8 points for most of the crosscut saws.

For both ripping and crosscutting, a miter saw is similar in use to a crosscut saw. However, the miter saw is lowered to a flat position as the cut progresses (Fig. 17-20). Also, the strokes should be shorter and, in some instances, slightly faster. A block is sometimes used to guide the cut (Fig. 17-21).

Fig. 17-21. Guiding the miter saw with a block of wood.

Coping Saw

A coping saw is designed for cutting *irregular shapes* in thin stock. It consists of a handle, frame, and removable blade (Fig. 17-22). The teeth on the thin blade are similar in shape to ripsaw teeth. It can be turned in the frame to various angles for sawing in places difficult to reach (Fig. 17-23). Always loosen the handle before turning the blade. Also, tighten the handle afterward. A loose blade bends and often breaks.

START

FINISH

Fig. 17-20. As the cut progresses, the miter saw is lowered to a flat position.

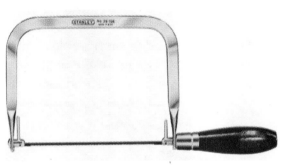

Fig. 17-22. A coping saw is used to cut a curved shape in thin material. (Courtesy The Stanley Works)

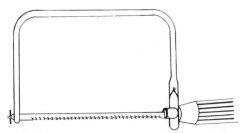

Fig. 17-23. The blade of the coping saw can be positioned in the frame at an angle for difficult-to-reach sawing.

For most sawing cuts, a coping saw blade cuts on the backward stroke. The teeth point toward the handle. The teeth are pointed away from the handle when it is desirable to cut on the forward stroke. To change a blade, loosen the handle until the blade is easily removed. Insert the pins of the new blade into the slots, and tighten the handle. The blade must be held straight. If the blade is permitted to twist, it is easily broken. Also, do not overheat a blade. Sawing too quickly heats the blade, causing it to break. In sawing with the coping saw, observe the following:

1. *Trace the pattern to be sawed.*
2. *Mount the stock in a holding device.* Since the stock is usually thin, extra support might be needed. A second board can be used for a backing, or a V block can be used (Fig. 17-24).
3. *Adjust the saw blade.* If desired, the teeth can be pointed away from the handle for the blade to cut on the forward stroke.
4. *Begin the cut.* Use short strokes and slight pressure. The frame can be

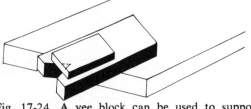

Fig. 17-24. A vee block can be used to support thin stock for sawing.

grasped with the free hand to steady the saw. Remember to saw on the waste side of the mark.

5. *Complete the cut.* Use longer strokes than in starting the saw kerf. Do not use the back portion of the blade for all the sawing. For pierced work, first cut a hole in the waste area (Fig. 17-25). Then "thread" the blade through the hole and cut the inside area.

Fig. 17-25. Cutting pierced stock with a coping saw.

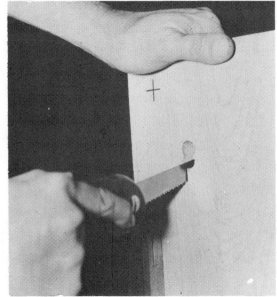

Fig. 17-26. Sawing pierced stock with a keyhole saw.

Keyhole Saw

A keyhole saw is similar in use to the coping saw when cutting *pierced* work (Fig. 17-26). The blade is narrow with ripsaw teeth (Fig. 17-27). Since a frame

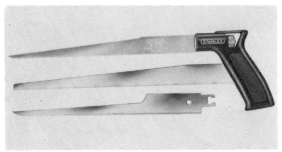

Fig. 17-27. Keyhole saw and blades. (Courtesy The Stanley Works)

is not involved, the blade is inserted quickly into the starting hole. The keyhole saw is often confused with the *com-*

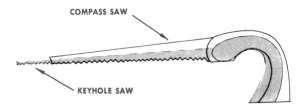

Fig. 17-28. The blades of the compass saw and the keyhole saw are different in shape.

pass saw (Fig. 17-28). Actually, there is little difference. A keyhole saw is smaller; therefore, it can be used to cut sharper curves than can be cut with the compass saw.

Questions

1. What factors should be considered in selecting the proper handsaw?
2. If a saw blade binds in the kerf, what is the probable cause?
3. Why should the strokes of the saw be slow and short near the end of the cut?
4. List the ways in which a coping saw differs from a crosscut saw.
5. Why is only one end of the stock supported in crosscutting?
6. What saw should be used to cut a 2-inch circle inside a surface? Why?
7. List the chief differences between ripsaws and crosscut saws.
8. Why are handsaws made with one point more than the number of teeth per inch?

Unit 18 — Bench Planes

Lumber mills supply both rough and surfaced stock. Coarse saw marks are found in rough lumber, while small ridges called *planer marks* or *mill marks* are found on surfaced lumber. These mill marks are removed by planing before the wood is finished. The lumber also is planed to obtain the desired sizes and to remove warps.

Lumber can be planed with either a hand plane or a machine. Hand planing is often preferred for detail and finish work, while machine planing is used for the initial smoothing of the larger rough stock. Even though machine planing is quicker, the planer marks still must be removed from the jointed and surfaced stock. Hand planing and machine planing can be combined to achieve the best and smoothest surfaces.

Types of Planes

The hand planes are divided into three classes. The *bench* planes are the general-purpose planes used to smooth a surface. Planes in this class are nearly identical, except for the difference in length. Examples include the *smooth, jack, fore,* and *jointer* planes. The *block* planes are more specialized and smaller than the bench planes. Although their appearances differ, all the block planes are designed for planing end grain. The final classification contains the *special* planes. These planes are designed for special purposes and include the *rabbet, router,* and special-purpose planes.

Smooth Plane

All the bench planes are similar, except for their length. For this reason, a bench plane often is identified by the length of its bottom. The shortest bench plain is the smooth plane, which is 8 inches or 9 inches long (Fig. 18-1). Used for light-duty work, it is an especially fine plane for level or flat surfaces which need lowering or smoothing.

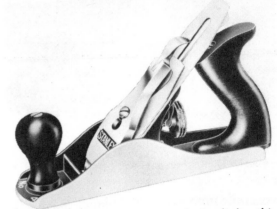

Fig. 18-1. Smooth plane (8 or 9 inches in length). (Courtesy The Stanley Works)

Jack Plane

The most popular and most useful bench plane is the jack plane (Fig. 18-2). Available in 14- or 15-inch lengths, this plane is used to smooth and true rough surfaces. Also, it can be used for a smooth plane on larger surfaces. A variation of the common jack plane is the "junior" jack plane, which is 11½ inches long.

Fig. 18-2. Jack plane (14 or 15 inches in length). (Courtesy The Stanley Works)

Fore Plane

A fore plane is 18 inches long (Fig.

18-3). It is similar in appearance and is used in a manner similar to the jack plane, but it is used for the larger rough surfaces. The longest and heaviest plane is the jointer plane (Fig. 18-4). Since it is 22 inches long, a jointer plane is used to plane extremely long surfaces. It was so named, since it could be used to produce smooth edges which could be glued together for joints. Generally speaking, the longer the plane, the flatter the surface produced.

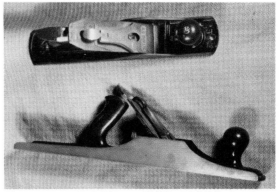

Fig. 18-4. Comparison of length of jack plane (top) with jointer plane (bottom).

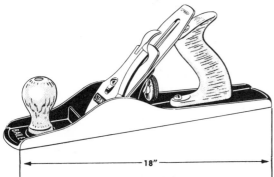

Fig. 18-3. Fore plane. It is similar in appearance to the jack plane, but its length is 18 inches. (Courtesy The Stanley Works)

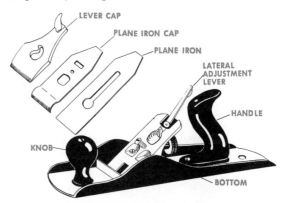

Fig. 18-5. Diagram of parts of a jack plane. (Courtesy The Stanley Works)

Assembling Bench Planes

A plane must be assembled and adjusted properly, before it can be used to produce good results. Since all the bench planes are nearly identical, correct assemblies and adjustments can be demonstrated with a single plane, such as the jack plane (Fig. 18-5). The bottom is either smooth or ribbed, with an opening for the double plane iron. A double plane iron consists of the *plane iron* and the *plane-iron cap* (Fig. 18-6). The plane iron does the actual cutting, while the cap stiffens the cutting blade. A plane-iron cap also breaks and curls the shaving and prevents the wood from splitting (Fig. 18-7). The double plane iron is supported by the *frog,* which has two adjustments. An *adjusting nut* controls the

depth of the cut, and a *lateral adjusting lever* controls the flatness or evenness of the cut.

To assemble the double plane iron, hold the plane iron in one hand and the cap in the other hand. Place the two parts together at a right angle with the

Fig. 18-6. Double plane iron.

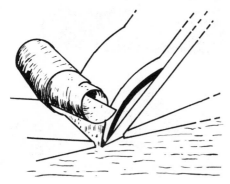

Fig. 18-7. The plane iron cap breaks and curls the shaving to prevent splitting. (Courtesy The Stanley Works)

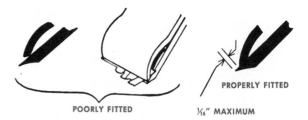

POORLY FITTED   PROPERLY FITTED   ⅟₁₆" MAXIMUM

Fig. 18-9. Poor and proper fit for a double plane iron. (Courtesy The Stanley Works)

cap located on the opposite side of the bevel of the plane iron (Fig. 18-8). Permit the cap screw to slip through the larger opening in the plane iron. Align the two parts by sliding the cap to the far end of the plane iron; then twist the two parts until they are parallel. The assembly is completed by sliding the cap forward and tightening the cap screw. The proper fit with the cap about $\frac{1}{16}$ inch from the cutting edge is shown in Fig. 18-9.

To assemble the plane, place the double plane iron with the bevel *down* onto the frog (Fig. 18-10). The slot in the plane-iron cap must fit over the upper end of the "Y" adjusting lever. Also, the slot in the plane iron must fit over the roller on the lateral adjusting lever. Next, place the *lever cap* over the *lever-cap screw* (Fig. 18-11). Secure the lever cap

in the plane by pressing down the *cam*. If this seems difficult, check several items. First, check the double plane iron to determine whether it is placed properly in the plane. Second, check the lever-cap screw. If it is too tight, loosen it slightly. When the double plane iron is loose with the cam pressed down, tighten the lever-cap screw.

Adjusting the Bench Plane

A bench plane requires two adjustments for regulating the thickness and the evenness of the cut. Begin the adjustment by turning the plane over and sighting along the bottom (Fig. 18-12). On a properly adjusted plane, the cutting edge is parallel with the bottom and extends carefully beyond the bottom. If the cutting edge is not even, adjust it by mov-

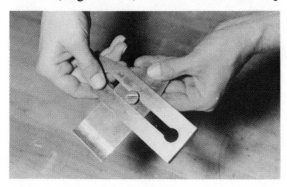

Fig. 18-8. Assembling a double plane iron.

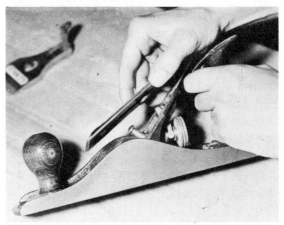

Fig. 18-10. Place the double plane iron on the frog.

Fig. 18-11. Place the lever cap over the lever cap screw.

Fig. 18-13. Even the cutting edge (center) by moving the lateral adjusting lever. (Courtesy The Stanley Works)

ing the lateral adjusting lever either to the left or to the right (Fig. 18-13). If the extension of the cutting edge is not satisfactory, change the extension by turning the adjusting nut. The depth of cut, or the extension of the plane iron, is increased when the nut is turned clockwise.

Although not often needed, the width of the mouth opening can be changed. To do this, the frog is moved by loosening the two frog screws located below the adjusting nut. The opening should be wider for planing thick shavings from open-grain wood. A narrower opening is needed for planing fine shavings from a closed-grain wood.

Using Bench Planes

1. *Secure the stock.* Stock can be secured in several ways (Figs. 18-14 and 18-15). Note how the stock is

Fig. 18-14. Clamping the stock for edge planing.

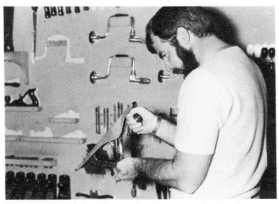

Fig. 18-12. Sight along the bottom of the plane to check for proper adjustments.

Fig. 18-15. Clamping the stock for face planing.

clamped by its ends in Fig. 18-15. Avoid clamping the edges, which can cause the wood to bow (Fig. 18-16). Even if the bow were planed until flat, the stock possibly could become bowed again after the pressure is released.

When planing the edges and the ends, the stock is usually clamped between the vise jaws. Small pieces of soft wood can be used to protect the surfaced areas (Fig. 18-17).

2. *Assume proper stance.* The proper stance is a comfortable position which permits free and easily controlled movements with the plane. This can be achieved by standing behind the work with the left foot forward, (Fig. 18-18). If left-handed, place the right foot forward, with the feet close together. When planing, "rock" the body back and forth, while slightly pushing and pulling the plane with the arms.

3. *Grasping the plane.* For planing right-handed, hold the plane by grasping the rear handle with the right hand and the front knob with the left hand (Fig. 18-19). Reverse the hands if left-handed. Although the stroke should be parallel with the body, the plane can be turned slightly toward the body for shearing cuts. Always keep the plane close to the body to make the planing motion easier.

4. *Planing.* To begin the cut, apply pressure on the front knob (Fig. 18-20). Gradually distribute the pressure evenly between the handle and the knob as the bottom of the plane contacts the stock. Toward the end of the cut, shift the pressure to the rear handle. When returning for another cut, lift the plane clear of the surface on the return stroke. Never slide the

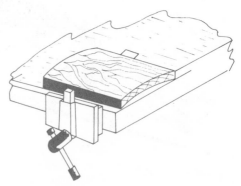

Fig. 18-16. Clamping the edges might cause the stock to bow.

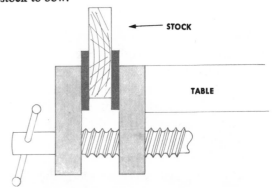

Fig. 18-17. In clamping stock, use small pieces of wood to protect the surfaced faces.

Fig. 18-18. Proper working position for planing stock.

plane backward across the stock, since this dulls the plane iron.

Always plane *with the grain* (Fig. 18-21). Attempt several slight cuts, if the direction of the grain cannot be determined. Planing against the

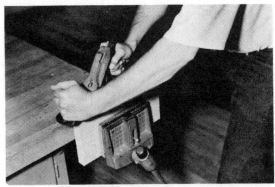

Fig. 18-19. Holding the plane.

Fig. 18-20. Shift the pressure from the front knob to the rear handle of the plane during each forward stroke.

grain pulls the wood fibers and causes chipping. If the plane "jumps," reduce the depth of the cut and/or check the plane iron for sharpness. Also, the plane can be angled slightly to produce a shearing cut, which is

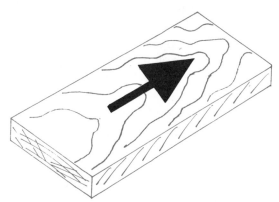

Fig. 18-21. Plane "with the grain" of the wood.

Fig. 18-22. Use a longer plane to smooth the high spots on the surface of the wood. (Courtesy The Stanley Works)

often smoother than a straight cut. When the plane rides the curves, select a longer plane. As shown in Fig. 18-22, a larger plane cuts the higher spots on a surface, while a smaller plane often follows these irregularities.

5. *Checking*. While planing a surface, check periodically for flatness and/or squareness. A *try square* or some type

Fig. 18-23. Check the flatness of the surface.

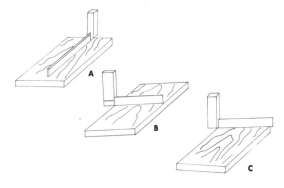

Fig. 18-24. Check the surface for flatness: (A) With the grain; (B) Across the grain; and (C) Diagonally to the grain.

Fig. 18-25. Checking the edge for high points.

Fig. 18-26. Whetting or honing a plane iron.

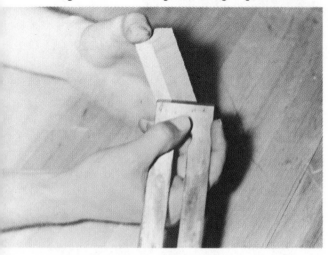

Fig. 18-27. Remove the wire edge by dragging the cutting edge over a corner of soft wood.

of straightedge is recommended for checking the flatness. As shown in Fig. 18-23, slide the straightedge across the planed surface, looking for light between the two surfaces. The higher points then can be marked and planed later. This step should be repeated until no light can be seen when the straightedge is held with the grain, across the grain, and diagonally with the grain (Fig. 18-24).

Squareness refers to the 90° angle between the adjacent surfaces, such as a face and an edge. To check the squareness, keep the handle of the try square flat against the flat surface. The high points then can be determined on the other surface by sliding the blade back and forth over the surface (Fig. 18-25).

Plane Irons

The time spent in sharpening a plane iron can be regained easily through quicker, better, and safer work. A plane iron should be sharpened when the cutting edge is nicked or when the shavings are not continuous and smooth. A dull cutting edge appears slick and reflects light when it is examined closely.

Unless damaged seriously, a dull cutting edge can be sharpened by whetting or honing. The plane iron is held 30° to 35° to an oilstone, moving it in a "figure-8" motion (Fig. 18-26). After whetting the bevel, turn the iron over; then use one or two light strokes to remove the wire edge. Hold the iron nearly flat in whetting the backside. This edge also can be removed by dragging it over the corner of a piece of soft wood (Fig. 18-27). Sharper edges can be obtained with a finer oilstone. A test for sharpness is to cut paper (Fig. 18-28).

Nicks are removed by grinding a new bevel. The grinding angle is about 25°

to 30°, which produces a bevel two and one-half times the thickness of the plane iron (Fig. 18-29). A 20° bevel is often preferred for the softer woods. Move the plane iron from side to side, quenching it often in water to prevent overheating, which softens the metal in the plane iron. After forming a new bevel, check the squareness of the edge with the sides of the plane iron (Fig. 18-30). Grinding on the bevel should be held to a minimum.

Block Planes

Block planes are small, with low-angle plane irons; they are used primarily for planing the end grain. As shown in Fig. 18-31, there is little difference in the block planes. Some block planes are made with adjustable throats and lateral-adjustment levers, while others do not have these features. The principal parts of a common block plane are shown in Fig. 18-32. Unlike the bench plane, the block plane is made with a single plane iron. The angle with the bed is less (either 12° or 20° in comparison with 25° for the bench plane), and the bevel is used "up," rather than down.

Fig. 18-29. Using a grinder with attachment to grind a plane-iron bevel. (Courtesy Power Tool Division, Rockwell Manufacturing Company)

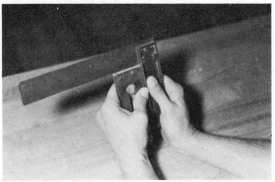

Fig. 18-30. Checking the squareness of a plane-iron bevel.

Fig. 18-28. Testing the cutting edge for sharpness.

Assembling a Block Plane

To assemble a block plane, position the single plane iron in place with the

bevel up (Fig. 18-33). Next, slide the lever cap in place; then lock it by turning the cam.

Adjusting a Block Plane

To adjust the plane iron, view the iron from the underneath side of the plane. If the iron does not protrude evenly from the bottom, adjust the lateral-adjustment lever. For planes without this adjustment, tap either side of the plane iron for proper alignment. The cam can be loosened for

Fig. 18-31. Common block planes. (Courtesy The Stanley Works)

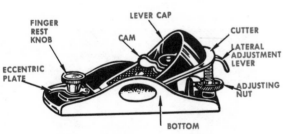

Fig. 18-32. Diagram of parts of a block plane. (Courtesy The Stanley Works)

FINGER REST KNOB
LEVER CAP
CAM
CUTTER
LATERAL ADJUSTMENT LEVER
ECCENTRIC PLATE
ADJUSTING NUT
BOTTOM

Fig. 18-33. Assembling a block plane. (Courtesy The Stanley Works)

Fig. 18-34. A block plane should be cupped in the palm of the hand while planing. (Courtesy The Stanley Works)

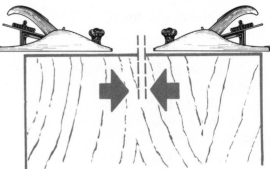

Fig. 18-35. End grain is planed from each edge toward the center.

Fig. 18-36. Planing end grain in only one direction causes chipping.

this alignment. Turn the adjustment nut to change the depth of cut, as needed.

Using a Block Plane

Besides planing the end grain, a block plane also is used for planing small pieces of wood, or for fine trimming. The plane is easy to use and is held in one hand

(A) Clamp waste stock to the edge.   *(B) Cut a bevel on the waste side.*

Fig. 18-37. Other methods of planing end grain.

Fig. 18-38. Hold the plane at an angle to plane the corners and chamfers. (Courtesy The Stanley Works)

(Fig. 18-34). Since it is used while cupped in one hand, block planes are often referred to as "palm" planes.

When planing end grain, several techniques can be used. In Fig. 18-35, the plane is moved from the ends to the center. This prevents the chipping or splitting which often results from moving the plane past the edges (Fig. 18-36). Several other methods used to avoid chipping are shown in Fig. 18-37. In Fig. 18-37A, a second board is butted flush with the board being planed. The chipping, as shown in the diagram, then occurs in the waste stock. In Fig. 18-37B, the board is beveled in a "waste" area. This method can be used only where there is ample waste or stock that will not show. Otherwise, the bevel cuts into the usable part of the stock.

Regardless of the method, a block plane usually cuts better when angled slightly sidewise. This causes a shearing cut which is usually easier to control. When cutting corners or chamfers, use the method shown in Fig. 18-38. Planing a chamfer toward the face causes the wood to chip along the face.

Special Planes

This group of planes includes the various planes designed for special jobs.

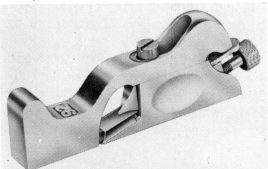

Fig. 18-39. Two types of rabbet planes. (Courtesy The Stanley Works)

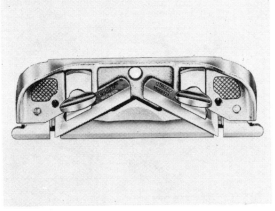

Fig. 18-40. Side rabbet plane. (Courtesy The Stanley Works)

Fig. 18-41. Duplex-rabbet plane. (Courtesy The Stanley Works)

Although there are many different types, the more common special planes are the *rabbet* or *router* planes.

The rabbet planes are used to smooth and enlarge joints (Fig. 18-39). The plane in Fig. 18-39A can be held in both hands, while the plane in Fig. 18-39B requires only one hand. This plane is

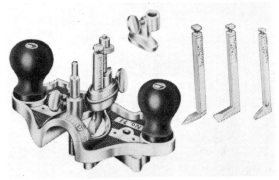

Fig. 18-42. Open-throat router plane. (Courtesy The Stanley Works)

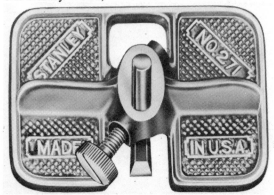

Fig. 18-43. Router plane for narrow cuts. (Courtesy The Stanley Works)

called a *bullnose* plane and can be used in closer places, such as corners, than the other type. Adjustable cutters and throat openings are found in both types. Since their sides and bottoms are machined square, rabbet planes can plane the sides and bottoms of various joints.

A *side-rabbet* plane cuts along the side of a joint (Fig. 18-40). It differs from many planes in that it is made with two cutters and a depth gauge. The side-rabbet plane is used mostly to enlarge or trim the sides of rabbets, grooves, and dadoes.

The *duplex-rabbet* plane is more versatile than most of the rabbet planes (Fig. 18-41). Equipped with two seats or frogs, the front position is used for bullnose planing and the back position is used for regular rabbet planing. A depth gauge and fence also are provided for guiding the work. The plane can be used in different ways by changing the cutters or by removing the depth gauge and/or fence.

An *open-throat router* plane is shown in Fig. 18-42. Equipped with a depth gauge and three different cutters, this plane is used mostly to smooth the bottoms of joints. Also, it can be used to form grooves and dadoes when shoulder or side kerfs are first cut, to define the sides of the joint. The cutters are marked in inches and are made with square or pointed cutting edges. Their widths are usually ¼ inch or ½ inch.

Another type of router plane is shown in Fig. 18-43. Similar to the open-throat plane, this plane is limited to narrow cuts.

Other special planes are available. Examples include a *plow* plane for cutting grooves, a *circular* plane for smoothing circular features, and a *combination* plane for shaping molding, etc. A need for quicker and cheaper planing methods has caused many of these planes to be replaced by machine operations. Therefore, few special planes are in use today.

Questions

1. Why is rough, rather than surfaced, lumber usually purchased?
2. List four bench planes and explain why each should be used.
3. Describe the procedure used for sharpening double plane irons.
4. What adjustment is wrong when the shavings from a bench plane are uneven?
5. Why is it necessary to plane with the grain of the wood?
6. When should a block plane be used?
7. What is the chief difference between a common rabbet plane and a "bull-nose" rabbet plane?
8. When should a router plane be used?
9. What is the chief difference between a flat surface and a square surface?
10. Describe how the flatness and squareness of a surface are checked.

Unit 19 — Circular Saw

A *circular* saw, or *table* saw, is used for crosscutting to lengths, for ripping to widths, and for cutting joints. Circular saws are made with either one or two blades. The circular saw with a single blade is known as a *variety* saw (Fig. 19-1). The variety saw is recommended for most general-purpose sawing and is the most common type of saw in schools. The circular saws with double blades are *universal* saws (Fig. 19-2). When one of the blades is in normal cutting position, the second blade is underneath the table. The second blade cannot cut until it is raised to the normal cutting position. The universal saws are used in sawing operations requiring different blades.

Fig. 19-1. A variety saw also is known as a tilting-arbor saw. (Courtesy Oliver Machinery Company)

Fig. 19-2. A universal saw is manufactured with a double arbor. (Courtesy Oliver Machinery Company)

Description

The size of a circular saw is usually indicated by the diameter of its blade and its arbor. For example, a 10-inch tilting-arbor saw has a 10-inch diameter blade which can be inclined for angular cuts. This does not, however, indicate that the saw can cut stock up to 10 inches in thickness. The maximum thickness of stock that can be cut depends on the height the blade extends above the top of the table. Most 10-inch saws can cut thicknesses upward to about 3⅛ inches, when the blade is perpendicular to the table. If the blade is tilted 45°, the cut is reduced to about 2⅛ inches.

Principal Parts

Although a saw has many parts, the following parts are the important parts for the operator (Fig. 19-3).

1. *Table.* The table is the working surface. It is machined accurately for true sawing; extensions can be used to increase the working area. Also, the insert plate is positioned within the table top; this permits the blade to extend above the table for sawing stock.

2. *Arbor.* The blade is fitted onto the arbor which, in turn, is connected to the motor. Most arbors are either ⅝ inch or 1 inch in diameter.

3. *Blade.* The common blades used on a circular saw are the *combination* or

164

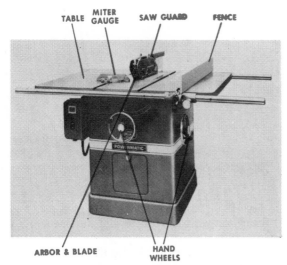

TABLE   MITER   SAW GUARD   FENCE
GAUGE

ARBOR & BLADE   HAND
                       WHEELS

Fig. 19-3. Principal parts of a circular saw. (Courtesy Powermatic, Houdaille Industries, Inc.)

planer blades, cutoff or *crosscut* blades, and *ripsaw* blades (Fig. 19-4). The choice of blade depends on the sawing operation. To avoid frequent changing of blades, the combination blade can be used for sawing both with the grain and across the grain. A cutoff blade produces a smooth cut, which is needed in joining pieces to form joints. The ripsaw blade is used for sawing with the grain to uniform widths. The hollow-ground blades are thicker at the edge and thinner near the center. This aids in preventing binding and overheating.

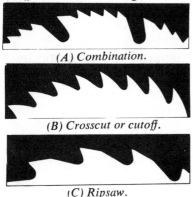

(A) *Combination.*

(B) *Crosscut or cutoff.*

(C) *Ripsaw.*

Fig. 19-4. Saw blades commonly used on circular saws. (Courtesy Powermatic, Houdaille Industries, Inc.)

4. *Handwheels.* Blade adjustments are made with two handwheels. The handwheel located in front of the saw controls the blade *height*. The other handwheel, located on the side, controls the blade *angle*. Both adjustments should be checked and adjusted before starting the saw.

5. *Saw guard.* The saw guards usually are metal, plastic, or a combination of metal and plastic. They can be either supported by the table or suspended above the table (Fig. 19-5). Most guards consist of three important parts; these are the frame, splitter, and antikickback pawls (dogs). The frame protects an operator from accidentally contacting the blade. The splitter prevents the kerf from closing to bind the blade, which can cause a kickback. If a kickback should occur, the antikickback pawls "dig-in" to prevent the stock being thrown backward (Fig. 19-6).

A guard should be adjusted for maximum protection before sawing is begun. Also, a guard should never be removed, except for making special cuts. In these instances, first obtain the permission of the instructor or supervisor; then replace the guard as soon as possible.

6. *Fence and miter gauge.* These two parts guide the stock being cut. The fence is used for parallel cuts, such as ripping; the miter gauge is used for both perpendicular and angular cuts. Located on the front end of the fence are three adjustments (Fig. 19-7). The two short levers lock the front end and back end of the fence to the extension rails. Fine adjustments are made with the vernier control knob. The miter gauge slides along slots machined in the top of the table. The angle of the miter gauge with the blade

(A) Suspended above table. (Courtesy Brett-Guard Division, The Foredom Electric Company)

(B) Conventional guard.

(C) Guard supported above table.

Fig. 19-5. Saw guards.

is set with a control knob located on the back side of the miter gauge (Fig. 19-8).

ANTI KICKBACK PAWLS

Fig. 19-6. Antikickback pawls prevent the stock being thrown backward toward the operator.

Changing the Blades

1. Turn off the power at the circular saw and at the main switch.
2. After removing the guard and the insert plate, raise the blade to its highest position.
3. Keep the arbor from turning by wedging a piece of soft wood between the blade and the table.
4. Using the special wrench, loosen the arbor nut by pulling the wrench toward the operator (Fig. 19-9).
5. Remove the nut, the outer saw collar, and the blade.
6. Replace the blade, the outer saw collar, and the nut. Be sure the teeth of the blade point *toward* the position of the operator (Fig. 19-10). Make sure the blade is free from binding against the other parts. Check this by turning the blade by hand.
7. Complete the operation by tightening the nut, lowering the blade, and replacing the insert plate. Do not forget to replace the guard.

General Safety Rules

1. Keep the guard on the circular saw adjusted properly. If it is necessary to remove the guard for a special operation, first obtain the permission of the instructor or supervisor.

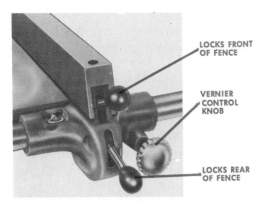

Fig. 19-7. Fence adjustments.

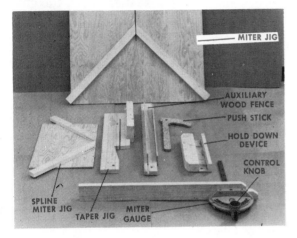

Fig. 19-8. Miter gauge and shop-made accessories.

2. Adjust the blade height to about ⅛ inch above the top surface of the stock being cut (Fig. 19-11).

3. Make any adjustments before the saw is started—never make adjustments after it is started.

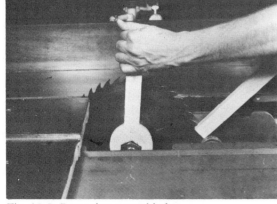

Fig. 19-9. Removing a saw blade.

Fig. 19-10. The teeth of the saw blade should point toward the operator's normal position. A plywood jig is being used to saw miters. The jig is guided by two rails which slide in the table slots for the miter gauge. (Courtesy Brett-Guard Division, The Foredom Electric Company)

Fig. 19-11. The blade height should be not more than ⅛″ above the stock. (Courtesy Brett-Guard Division, The Foredom Electric Company)

4. Do not talk to others, or glance away, while sawing.

5. Stop the saw before attempting to remove small pieces of stock from around the blade.

6. Turn off the saw and lower the blade

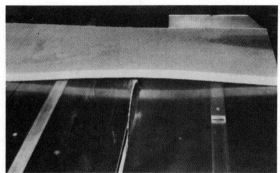

Fig. 19-12. Cut warped stock with the cupped side down.

below the top of the table when the operation is finished.

7. Obtain the approval of the instructor before using special setups and jigs.

8. Do not cut cylindrical stock.

9. Do not saw a piece of stock unless it is guided by the rip fence, miter gauge, or special jig.

10. Always wear goggles or a face shield when operating the saw.

11. Saw warped stock with the cupped surface down (Fig. 19-12).

12. When sawing, stand either to the left-hand or to the right-hand side of the blade.

13. Keep the floor area around the saw free from scraps that could trip yourself or others.

14. Maintain adequate clearance between the blade and the other parts, such as the guard, fence, and miter gauge.

Guidelines for Sawing

1. The stock can be fed fast enough to avoid overheating the blade; yet, it should be fed slow enough to avoid forcing the cut. A sharp blade cuts faster than a dull blade; therefore, the stock can be fed faster to a sharp blade.

2. Adjust the fence to position the required width between the blade and

the fence. This means that the waste portion is located on the opposite side of the blade—not between the blade and the fence.

3. Allow an extra $\frac{1}{16}$-inch width or length, if a sawed edge or end must be jointed to remove the saw marks.

4. Measure from the inside surface of the fence to the edge of the tooth set nearest the fence, when determining the position of the fence (Fig. 19-13).

5. To check a saw setting, make a trial cut on waste stock; then check the cut

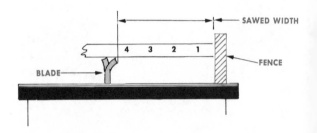

Fig. 19-13. Locate the fence position by measuring from the tooth set nearest the fence to the inside surface of the fence.

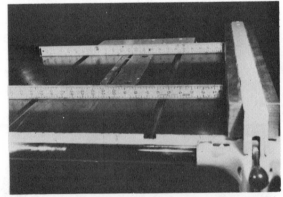

Fig. 19-14. Check the fence location for parallelism with the blade. The two measurements should be equal.

with the appropriate measuring or layout tools.

6. To prevent splitting of the wood, position masking tape along the kerf before cutting.

7. Mating parts with identical dimensions should be cut with identical saw adjustments, if possible.

Ripping Procedure

1. *Select the correct saw blade.* Either a ripsaw blade or a combination blade is suitable.
2. *Adjust the blade height.* The blade should extend not more than ⅛ inch above the top surface of the stock.
3. *Adjust the fence.* Be sure to lock the fence in position before using. Also, the fence should be parallel with the blade. If not certain, measure the front and back distances of the fence from a miter-gauge slot (Fig. 19-14). These two measurements are equal, if the blade and fence are parallel.
4. *Adjust the guard as needed.* Remove any tools, pieces of wood, etc. from the table.
5. *Make the cut.* Maintain firm contact between the stock and the fence while making the cut.

Fig. 19-15. A push stick should be used in ripping stock less than 5 inches in width.

Safety Rules for Ripping

1. Use a push stick for widths of 5 inches or less (Fig. 19-15).
2. Do not rip a piece of stock, unless its length is 6 inches or more.
3. Do not rip widths of stock less than ⅜ inch between the fence and the blade.
4. Obtain permission from the instructor before resawing a piece of stock.
5. When tailing a piece of stock, support the stock while the operator pushes (Fig. 19-16).

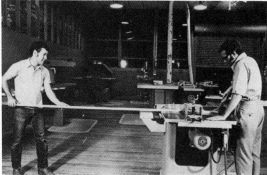

Fig. 19-16. Failure to support a long piece of stock can be dangerous and is likely to produce an irregular cut.

Crosscutting Procedure

1. *Selecting the correct blade.* Either a cutoff (crosscut) blade or a combination blade is suitable.
2. *Adjust the blade height.* It should extend not more than ⅛ inch above the top surface of the stock.
3. *Adjust the miter gauge.* When set at 90°, the cut is perpendicular to the edge resting against the miter gauge. To check this adjustment, make a trial cut; then test with a try square.
4. *Mark the stock.* Allow an extra 1/16 inch, if necessary to remove saw marks.
5. *Make the cut.* While pulling backward on the stock with one hand, use the other hand to push the miter gauge forward (Fig. 19-17).
6. *Cutting several pieces to identical lengths.* Use a fence and clearance block for this operation (Fig. 19-18). The clearance block is clamped to the rip fence. The fence and clearance block are then moved until the dis-

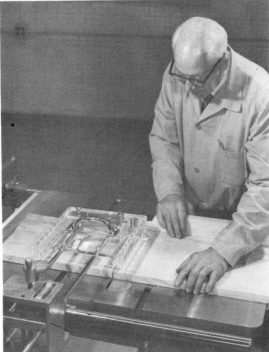

Fig. 19-17. In crosscutting, hold the stock against the miter gauge with one hand and push forward on the miter gauge with the other hand. (Courtesy Brett-Guard Division, The Foredom Electric Company)

tance between the blade and the clearance block is the desired length. To cut each piece, merely slide the stock toward the fence until it touches the clearance block. No measuring is needed. The clearance block also is needed to prevent kickbacks. Always position the clearance block on the

fence well in front of the saw blade. Make sure the stock leaves the clearance block before making contact with the blade.

Safety Rules for Crosscutting

1. Keep the fingers at least 5 inches from the saw blade.
2. Remove the fence before using the miter gauge.
3. Never cut a piece of stock with less than 6 inches contact with the miter gauge.
4. Never use the fence for a stop, unless a clearance block is used.

Fig. 19-18. Use a clearance block when cutting several pieces to identical lengths.

Cutting Rabbets

1. *Remove the splitter.* Depending on the type of guard, it might be necessary also to remove the guard.
2. *Mark the rabbet.* The profile of the rabbet is marked on the end of the stock to be cut first. Use a try square

and mark accurately, since this view serves as a guide for making the saw adjustments.

3. *Adjust for the width.* Note in Fig. 19-19 that the height of the blade is equal to the width of the rabbet. The distance between the fence and the blade

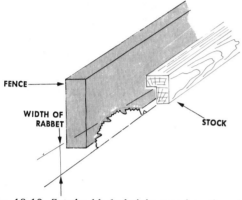

Fig. 19-19. Set the blade height equal to the width of the rabbet.

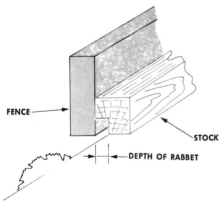

Fig. 19-20. Setting the fence at a distance from the blade equal to the depth of the rabbet.

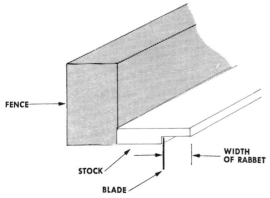

Fig. 19-21. Setting the fence for cutting the width of the rabbet.

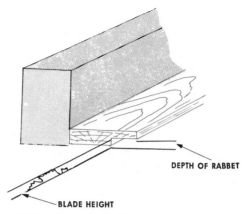

Fig. 19-22. Setting the blade height for cutting the depth of the rabbet.

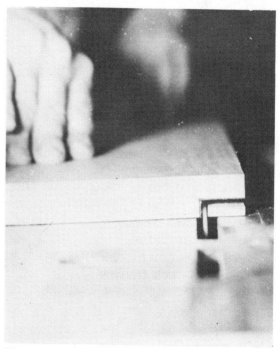

Fig. 19-23. In making the rabbet cuts, keep the blade in the waste area.

is equal to the depth of the rabbet (Fig. 19-20).

4. *Make the width cut.* Hold the stock down firmly onto the table top and firmly against the fence.

5. *Adjust for the depth.* Move the fence to a distance from the blade equal to the width of the rabbet (Fig. 19-21). The blade height is set equal to the depth of the rabbet (Fig. 19-22).

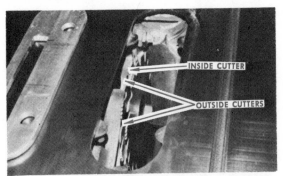

Fig. 19-24. A dado head consists of two outside cutters and one or more inside cutters, depending on the width of the cut.

When making these settings, keep the blade in the waste area of the rabbet (Fig. 19-23).

6. *Make the final cut.*

Cutting Grooves and Dadoes

1. *Remove the guard, insert the plate, and the saw blade.*
2. *Mount the dado head.* A complete dado head consists of two ouside cutters and one or more inside cutters (Fig. 19-24). The number of inside cutters depends on the width of the cut. An outside cutter cuts a ⅛-inch groove; an inside cutter cuts ¹⁄₁₆-inch to ¼-inch grooves.

3. *Position the special insert plate.* The dado head requires a special insert plate with a wider throat opening. After positioning the plate—but before turning on the power—check the clearance by rotating the dado head by hand.
4. *Adjust for location of the cut.* Use the fence to cut a groove (Fig. 19-25), which is cut with the grain. Use the miter gauge to cut a dado, which is cut across the grain.
5. *Adjust the width and depth of the cut.* Make a trial cut in waste stock. Test the accuracy of the cut with a board that is to fit into the finished groove or dado. Place paper shims between the cutters, if necessary, to increase slightly the width of the cut. If the cut is too shallow, raise the dado head with the adjusting handwheel.
6. *Make the final cut.* Push the stock slower than when sawing with a regular saw blade. Also reduce the pushing speed near the end of the cut to avoid splitting the stock.

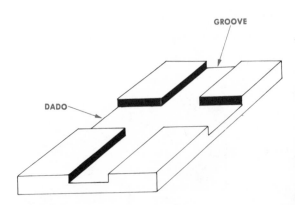

Fig. 19-25. Cutting a groove (left). A groove is cut "with the grain" and a dado is cut "across the grain" (right). (Courtesy Brett-Guard Division, The Foredom Electric Company)

Fig. 19-26. In cutting a groove or dado wider than the dado head, make the first cut; then move the stock and fence sidewise for the second cut.

Fig. 19-28. Using a dado head to cut a rabbet. (Courtesy Powermatic, Houdaille Industries, Inc.)

7. *Making the wide cuts.* If the width of the groove or dado is wider than the dado head, move the stock sidewise and make the second cut (Fig. 19-26).

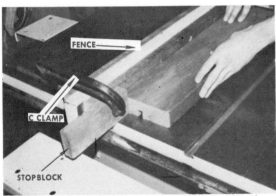

(A) Feed the stock forward to the stopblock. Then turn off the power, but do not remove the stock.

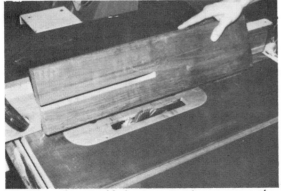

(B) When the saw blade stops turning, remove the stock.

Fig. 19-27. To cut a blind groove, clamp a stopblock to the rip fence.

8. *Making the blind cuts.* To stop the length of a cut partway through the stock, attach a stopblock to the fence (Fig. 19-27).
9. *Cutting the rabbets.* A rabbet can be cut in a single operation with a dado head (Fig. 19-28). Note that the stock is located between the blade

Fig. 19-29. Cutting a tenon with a dado head.

and the rip fence to prevent sawing into the fence.

10. *Cutting the tenons.* Tenons can be cut quickly with a dado head. Note in Fig. 19-29 that a miter gauge, fence, and clearance block are needed.

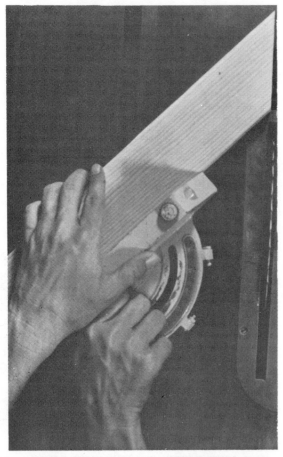

Fig. 19-30. Cutting a 45° miter with the miter gauge.

Cutting Miters

1. *Remove the guard, if necessary.*
2. *Adjust the blade height.*
3. *Set the miter gauge.* If possible, use two miter gauges adjusted to the desired angles. Two gauges, for example, can be set at 45° to form a square corner.
4. *Test settings.* Make the trial cuts, assemble the joint, and check with a try square or sliding T bevel.
5. *Make the final cuts.* Be sure to hold the stock firmly against the miter gauge when sawing (Fig. 19-30).

Questions

1. Describe the principal parts of a circular saw. What is the purpose of each part?
2. List the different types of saw blades. Name several sawing operations which can be performed with each blade.
3. What is the purpose of the saw guard?
4. Discuss the safety rules which should be followed in using a circular saw.
5. Why should the stock be cut $\frac{1}{16}$ inch longer than needed?
6. When should the following devices be used: (a) fence, (b) miter gauge, (c) clearance block, and (d) stop-block?
7. Why is a special insert plate needed for a dado head?
8. List the different operations that can be performed with a dado head.

Unit 20 – Band Saw

A band saw is used chiefly for cutting curves and irregular shapes. Crosscutting, ripping, resawing, and cutting joints also are done for certain purposes. The principal parts of a band saw are shown in Fig. 20-1.

1. *Wheels.* The band saw is mounted on two wheels; one wheel is located above the table, and the other wheel is located below the table. The lower wheel is turned by a motor, the upper wheel providing the tension for the blade. On both wheels, the rims are covered with rubber. The rubber covering prevents the blade slipping and protects the set of the teeth of the blade. The size of a band saw is determined by the diameter of the two wheels. For example, on a 30-inch band saw, the diameter of the wheels is 30 inches. The common band saws vary in size from about 14 inches to 30 inches.
2. *Guides.* Two pairs of guides are found on the band saw. One pair of guides is located above the table; the second pair is located beneath the table. The guides prevent twisting of the blade and help the blade to cut straight. The lower guide is stationary, but the height of the upper guide is adjustable. Both pairs of guides can be adjusted for the different blade thicknesses and widths.
3. *Table.* The stock being sawed is supported by a table, which usually can be tilted. The common angles with the blade are 45° to the right and about 10° to the left.
4. *Frame.* The wheels are supported by the frame. The frame also houses the motor and other internal features.

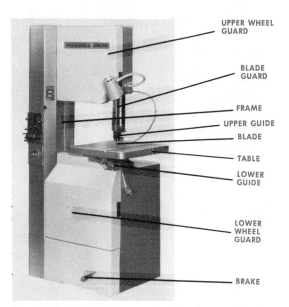

Fig. 20-1. Principal parts of a band saw. (Courtesy Power Tool Division, Rockwell Manufacturing Company)

5. *Guards.* Three guards are found on a band saw. Two of the guards protect the operator from the upper and lower band-saw wheels. The guards serve as hinged doors which can be opened when necessary. The third guard is a blade guard; it protects the operator from the teeth of the blade, which are exposed while sawing. This guard is adjustable with the height of the upper blade guide.
6. *Foot brake.* The larger band saws are equipped with a foot brake. Since a band saw continues to run for a few moments after the power is turned off, a foot brake stops the blade quicker.

Adjusting a Band Saw

Certain adjustments are necessary before a band saw can be used properly. If these adjustments are overlooked, the

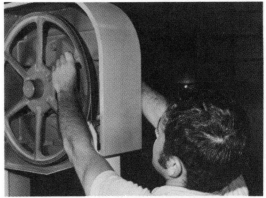

Fig. 20-2. In "tracking" a band-saw blade, open the upper wheel guard. Turn the wheel by hand during tracking.

blade might break, cut to one side, or slip from either wheel. Features requiring adjustment include maintaining the blade tension, tracking the blade, and adjusting the upper and lower guides for blade clearance. Always turn off the power before making any adjustments.

1. *Blade tension.* The tension or tightness of a blade depends on the distance between the upper and lower wheels. When these wheels are too close, the blade is loose. If the wheels are too far apart, the blade is too tight. The blade tension is adjusted with a handwheel or crank located near the top of the band saw. Some band saws are marked for the correct tension, depending on the blade width. For those not marked, check the blade tension by pushing the blade to one side and then releasing it. A correctly tensioned blade rings when it is released.

2. *Tracking the blade.* Tracking a blade refers to the saw blade running true on the rims of the wheels. To track a blade, open the upper wheel guard (Fig. 20-2). With the power turned off, turn the upper wheel by hand. Pivot the wheel, using the handwheel located on the back of the band saw,

until the blade is centered and runs true on the rim of the upper wheel. A blade improperly adjusted can jump

(A) When properly adjusted, a piece of paper barely slides between the blade and the guide.

(B) The same clearances are required on band saws with ball-bearing guides.

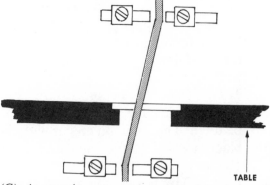

(C) An angular cut results when the upper and lower guides are not aligned properly.

Fig. 20-3. Adjusting the blade guides.

from the rim of a wheel. After adjustment, close the upper wheel guard.

3. *Aligning the upper and lower guides.* Each pair of guides consists of a blade guide located on each side of the blade and a ball-bearing support located at the back of the blade. The side guides are adjusted for minimum clearance between them and the blade. When adjusted properly, a sheet of writing paper barely slides between the blade and its guide (Fig. 20-3A and B).

Fig. 20-4. A 1/16-inch clearance between the blade and the roller is required when the blade is moving, but not sawing.

The guides usually are located on the rear one-third to rear one-half of the blade, to clear the set of the blade. Also, both the guides should be maintained in a straight line with the blade. If they are not aligned properly, the blade cuts angularly with the table (Fig. 20-3C). This also reduces the cutting life of a blade. The ball-bearing blade support is adjusted for a minimum clearance of about $\frac{1}{64}$ inch when the blade is moving, but not sawing (Fig. 20-4).

4. *Adjusting the fence.* Since the fence is used for parallel cuts, it should be located parallel with the blade. The fence is locked in place with a lever lo-

cated near the front of the table. Parallelism can be checked by measuring to the miter gauge slot from the front and rear of the table.

5. *Miter gauge.* The miter gauge is used for cuts perpendicular to and angular with the saw blade. This adjustment can be checked quickly by making a trial cut; then measure with either a hand square or a sliding T bevel.

6. *Table.* The normal position of the table is perpendicular to the blade. To check this position, use a hand square. Angular positions can be checked with a sliding T bevel.

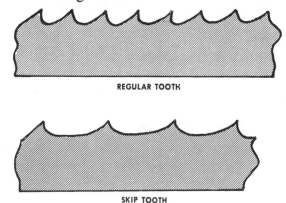

Fig. 20-5. Tooth designs on a band-saw blade.

WIDTH OF BLADE (INCH)	MINIMUM RADIUS OF CURVE (INCH)
⅛	¼
³⁄₁₆	½
¼	¾
⅜	1
½	1¼
¾	1¾

Fig. 20-6. Recommended blade widths for various curves.

Band-Saw Blades

Band-saw blades are available in either continuous rolls or precut loops. When purchased in continuous rolls, the blades must be cut to length. The length of a blade depends on the diameter of the wheel and on the distance between the upper and lower wheels. Note in Fig. 20-5 that the band-saw teeth are similar in shape to ripsaw teeth. The skip tooth is often preferred, since it cuts faster than the regular tooth.

The width of a band-saw blade depends on the cutting operation. A more narrow blade width is needed in cutting small curves (Fig. 20-6). A wider blade, however, is required for heavy-duty work, such as in resawing. If the material being sawed is too heavy for a blade or if a blade is too narrow, the blade tends to twist or cut to one side. Also, it tends to break easily.

2. Open the upper and lower wheel guards.
3. Remove the throat plate and the table aligning pin.
4. Release the tension on the blade by lowering the upper wheel.

(B) Step 2. Raising both hands, bring the far end of the loop to eye level. Then, snap the wrists, which causes the loop to fold under.

(A) Step 1. Point the teeth upward and angle the blade with the floor. Grasp the blade with the hands about shoulder-width apart—do not lap the thumbs or fingers over the blade.

(C) Step 3. As the blade folds, lower the hands while turning them inward. This coils the blade into three loops.

Fig. 20-7. Coiling a band-saw blade.

5. Remove the blade, and coil it for storage. A procedure recommended for coiling band-saw blades is shown in Fig. 20-7.

6. Replace a new blade. Point the teeth downward and toward the operator. If the teeth point upward, the blade must be twisted forward.

7. After placing the blade on the rim of the wheels, apply tension and track the blade.

8. Check the blade guides; make any necessary adjustments.

9. Close the wheel guards; replace the throat plate, and the table aligning pin.

10. Check the blade for trueness; turn on the power when set properly.

General Safety Rules

1. Make any needed adjustments before using a band saw. With the power turned off, check the upper and lower guides for proper alignment and clearance. Also, check to make sure the blade has sufficient tension and is tracking properly.

2. Keep the upper and lower wheel guards closed while sawing.

3. Adjust the upper blade guide to no more than ¼ inch above the surface of the stock to be cut (Fig. 20-8). By positioning the guide close to the surface of the stock, fewer teeth are exposed; also, the blade has less tendency to cut to one side.

4. Place the hands on either side of the blade—never in line with the blade. Hands placed at the side of the blade are less likely to contact the blade, if they should slip. Always keep the hands at least 2 inches from the blade.

5. Do not cut round stock with a band saw, unless a V block or other suit-

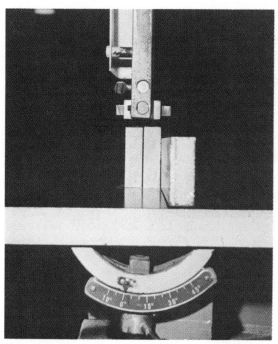

Fig. 20-8. The clearance between the upper blade guide and the stock should be not more than ¼ inch.

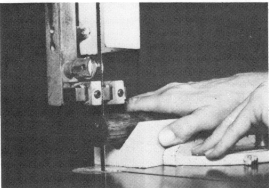

Fig. 20-9. Use a vee block to support round stock for sawing on the band saw.

able support is used (Fig. 20-9). Without this protection, round stock can slip, pulling the hands into the blade.

6. Maintain adequate contact between the stock and the table. Saw a piece of warped stock with the cup side facing downward (Fig. 20-10).

7. Turn off the power; wait for the blade to stop before backing out of the longer kerfs.

Fig. 20-10. Saw warped stock with the cupped surface down.

8. When ripping narrow widths of stock, support the stock with a featherboard, feeding the stock with a push stick (Fig. 20-11).
9. Keep the table and the work area around the saw free from wood scraps.
10. Never stand on the immediate right-hand side of a band saw. If the blade should break, it can whip in that direction.

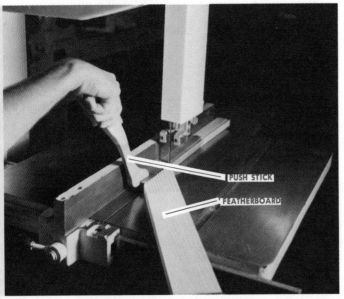

Fig. 20-11. To rip narrow widths of stock, hold the stock against the rip fence with a featherboard. Feed the stock with a push stick or scrap piece.

11. If a blade breaks, turn off the power; stand clear of the saw until both wheels have stopped turning.
12. Do not talk to others, or glance away from the work, while operating a band saw.
13. Maintain adequate clearance between the blade and the rip fence. About ⅛ inch usually is sufficient.
14. Do not jerk or twist the blade while sawing a small curve. The blade could be pulled from the guide; or it can bind and break.
15. Do not remove scraps near the blade, unless the power is turned off and the blade is stopped completely.
16. When crosscutting, at least 5 inches of stock should be in contact with the miter gauge.

Hints for Band Sawing

1. *Saw on the waste side of the mark.* If the blade begins to cut away from the mark, gradually turn the stock to return the blade to the mark. Sharp jerks or twists can break the blade or cause it to cut into the pattern.
2. *Where two cuts join, saw the shorter cut first* (Fig. 20-12). Then the blade does not have to be backed out of the longer kerfs; this requires that the power first be turned off.
3. *Make relief cuts before cutting sharp*

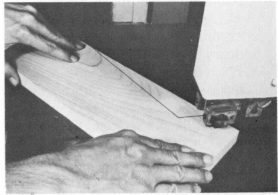

Fig. 20-12. Saw the shorter kerf first. This avoids backing the blade out of the longer kerf.

curves and small diameters (Fig. 20-13). For extremely short curves, bore a small hole for turning the blade without breaking it.

4. *In sawing freehand, guide the stock with one hand and push with the other.* Make gradual turns to avoid binding or pinching the blade.

5. *Plan the order of cuts before sawing an irregular shape.* Also, check for clearance between the stock and the frame of the band saw. It might be necessary to turn the stock over and saw from the other side.

6. *In sawing a piece of stock, support it firmly on the table.* Warped stock should be sawed with the cup side facing downward.

7. *Do not force or feed the stock faster than the blade can cut.* Excessive feed causes additional contact between the back of the blade and the blade support. This can cause the blade to break.

8. *Check the angles before making the final cuts.* Either a sliding T bevel or a hand square can be used. It is practical to make a trial cut, using a piece of scrap stock; then check the angle.

9. *Use the rip fence to saw equal widths (Fig. 20-14), and use the miter gauge to saw identical lengths.*

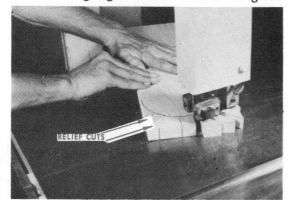

Fig. 20-13. Relief cuts should be made first for cutting sharp curves and small diameters.

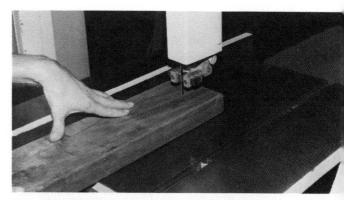

Fig. 20-14. Use the rip fence to saw equal widths.

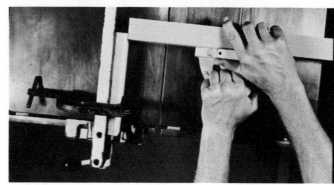

Fig. 20-15. Clamp a clearance block to the rip fence to saw identical lengths.

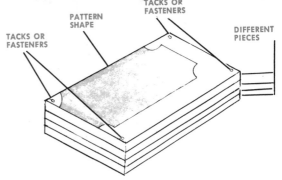

Fig. 20-16. To saw several identical shapes, tack or fasten several pieces of stock together. Locate the fasteners in the waste portion to avoid interference with the kerf.

Stopblocks and clearance blocks are used, similar to the procedures outlined for circular saws in cutting stock to identical lengths (Fig. 20-15).

10. *When cutting several pieces to identical shapes, tack the pieces together;*

then cut them all at the same cut. Nails or similar fasteners can be used; however, be sure they do not interfere with the sawing operation. The fasteners should be located in the waste area of the stock. (Fig. 20-16).

11. *When cutting a pattern which involves a series of smaller curves, first cut the pattern roughly.* Follow the larger curves; then return to cut the smaller curves (Fig. 20-17).

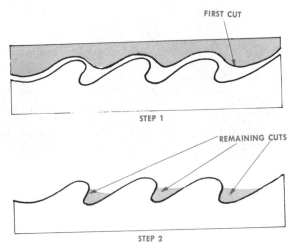

Fig. 20-17. Patterns often consist of a series of large and small curves. First cut along the larger curves. Then cut each of the smaller curves.

Making Straight Cuts

Most straight cuts on the band saw are done either freehand (Fig. 20-18) or with the aid of a rip fence or miter gauge (Fig. 20-19). Since each procedure is nearly the same, the following can be used for a guide:

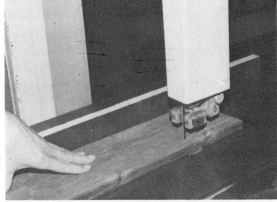

(A) Using the rip fence for a guide.

(B) Using the miter gauge for a guide.

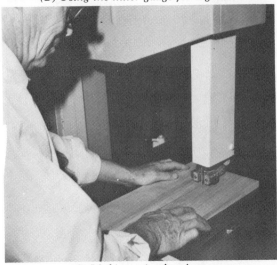

(C) Making a freehand cut.

Fig. 20-19. Making straight cuts on a band saw.

Fig. 20-18. Sawing freehand.

1. *Select a blade of the proper width.* Resawing usually requires a wider blade to avoid uneven thickness (Fig. 20-20).

2. *Mark the stock to be cut freehand or with a miter gauge.* In ripping, locate the rip fence at the required distance from the blade.

3. *Make other adjustments as needed.* Check the blade angle with the table and/or the miter-gauge with the blade. Raise the upper blade guide to about ¼ inch above the surface of the stock.

4. *Turn on the power, and wait until the blade is turning full speed.*

5. *Begin the cut.* Start the cut slowly, gradually increasing the feed. Decrease the feed near the end of the cut. If using the miter gauge or the rip fence, keep the stock firmly against it while sawing.

Fig. 20-20. Resawing reduces the thickness of a piece of stock.

Cutting Curves

1. *Draw the pattern onto the stock.* Check for sharp turns or curves, and change the band-saw blade if needed. It is sometimes helpful to bore a turning hole for cutting corners (Fig. 20-21).

2. *Remove the miter gauge and/or the rip fence from the table.* Also, remove any scrap stock which might have

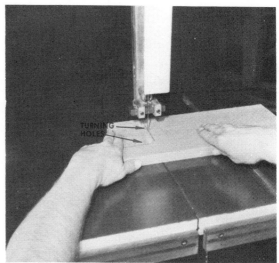

Fig. 20-21. A turning hole located at a sharp corner or small curve aids in preventing a broken blade.

been left on the table from a previous operation.

3. *Make the necessary adjustments.* Be sure to adjust the upper blade guides to the proper height.

4. *Determine the order of the cuts.* Note in Fig. 20-22 that the short kerfs are cut first.

5. *Turn on the power; wait until the saw is running full speed.*

6. *Begin the cut.* Relief cuts or rough cuts are made first.

7. *Complete the cut, turn off the power, then wait until the saw has stopped before leaving.*

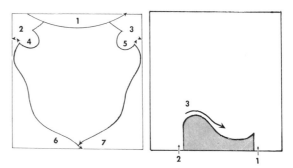

Fig. 20-22. Determine the order of cuts. Sawing the shorter kerfs first aids in avoiding dead-end cuts and in backing the blade out of long kerfs. Note the sequence of cuts on the two pieces.

Cutting Circular Patterns

1. *Make a jig similar to that shown in Fig. 20-23*. The pivot is a screw or nail placed from the bottom side of the sliding arm. Its location is square with a line extended from the front of the blade. The arm is adjusted for different radii and tightened with the wood screw and washer located in the jig.

2. *Secure the jig to the table, using C clamps.*

3. *Adjust the sliding arm until the distance of the pivot from the blade is equal to the desired radius.*

4. *Prepare for the cut.* With one end or one side of the stock positioned gently against the blade, press the stock onto the screw (Fig. 20-24).

5. *Adjust the height of the upper blade guides.*

6. *Turn on the power, with the wood in place.* After the band saw is running full speed, begin the cut. Keep the wood pressed firmly onto the screw point while turning it slowly toward the blade.

7. *After the cut is completed, turn off the power and wait for the blade to stop.* Then remove the waste and the pattern from the table.

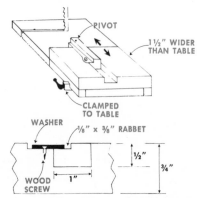

Fig. 20-23. Jig for cutting a circular pattern on the band saw. The stock is pressed onto the pivot point and turned toward the blade to cut a circular pattern.

Fig. 20-24. Using a jig to cut a circular pattern.

Questions

1. Describe the principal parts of a band saw. What is the purpose of each part?

2. List the necessary adjustments of a band saw. Explain why each adjustment is important.

3. The wheels of a 30-inch band saw are 60 inches apart. What length of blade is needed?

4. Name the three guards found on a band saw. When can they be removed safely?

5. List the general safety rules for a band saw.

6. What blade width is used when sawing 2-inch diameter circles? Why is a wider blade needed when resawing a board 6 inches wide?

7. When are rip fences and miter gauges used with the band saw?

8. Why is the skip-tooth blade often preferred to the regular-tooth blade?

9. List the procedure for changing a band-saw blade.

10. How are band-saw blades stored?

Unit 21 – Jigsaw

A *jigsaw,* also known as a *scroll* saw, is used in a manner similar to the band saw for detail sawing (Fig. 21-1). It is especially useful for pierced work, since the blade is easily removed.

The principal parts of the jigsaw include the drive mechanism, frame, table, and overarm. The drive mechanism changes the rotary motion of the motor to an up-and-down movement. The jigsaw blade is held between two chucks; whereas, only the lower chuck is needed for a *saber-saw* blade. When a regular jigsaw blade is being used, the tension on the blade is controlled by the tension sleeve located on the end of the overarm. The hold-down device presses the stock against the table to prevent it from jumping while the stock is being sawed. Most jigsaw tables can be tilted 45° to the right-hand side and 15° to the left-hand side for angular sawing.

The smaller jigsaws are known as bench jigsaws. The bench-type jigsaw is used on a workbench (Fig. 21-2). The larger jigsaws (see Fig. 21-1) are supported on their own stands or frames. Jigsaws even larger are used for production work (Fig. 21-3).

The size of a jigsaw is indicated by the distance between its blade and the base of the overarm. For example, the horizontal clearance of a 24-inch jigsaw is 24 inches between its blade and overarm (Fig. 21-4).

Most jigsaws can be varied in speed from about 600 to 1700 rpm. The variable-speed feature is needed for sawing different thicknesses and materials. This feature is most helpful in making fine cuts. The speed of the jigsaw is changed in two ways, depending on whether it has step pulleys or a variable-speed control.

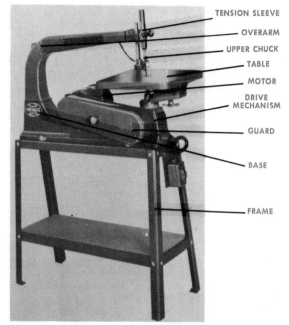

Fig. 21-1. Principal parts of a jigsaw.

TENSION SLEEVE
OVERARM
UPPER CHUCK
TABLE
MOTOR
DRIVE MECHANISM
GUARD
BASE
FRAME

Fig. 21-2. A bench-type jigsaw is used on a workbench.

For those jigsaws with step pulleys, the power must be turned off to change the speed. Then the guard is removed, and the belt is changed to a larger or smaller pulley (Fig. 21-5). A larger pulley on the motor increases the speed and a smaller pulley decreases the speed. Jigsaws with the variable-speed control are adjusted with a handwheel (Fig. 21-6). This adjustment, unlike those with step pulleys, is made only while the power is turned on.

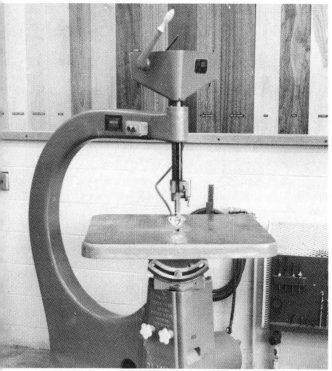

Fig. 21-3. Production sawing operations can be performed on the larger jigsaws.

Fig. 21-4. The designated size of a jigsaw is the distance between its blade and the overarm.

Jigsaw Blades

Either regular jigsaw blades or saber blades can be used with the jigsaw. The regular blade is held between the upper and lower chucks. Also called a jeweler's blade, the regular blade is used for fine detail sawing and for cutting hard materials. The saber blade is held only in the

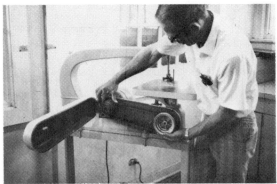

Fig. 21-5. On some jigsaws, the speed is varied by changing the belt to a larger or smaller step on the pulley. The power must be off.

Fig. 21-6. A handwheel is used to adjust the speed on a jigsaw with a variable-speed control. The power must be on while the adjustment is made.

lower chuck. It is used for fast cutting, for cutting thick stock, and for cutting simple designs.

Both the regular and the saber blades have ripsaw teeth, ranging from 7 to 32 teeth per inch (Fig. 21-7). The blades

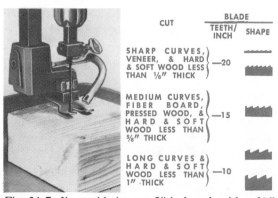

CUT	BLADE	
	TEETH/INCH	SHAPE
SHARP CURVES, VENEER, & HARD & SOFT WOOD LESS THAN 1/8" THICK	20	
MEDIUM CURVES, FIBER BOARD, PRESSED WOOD, & HARD & SOFT WOOD LESS THAN 5/8" THICK	15	
LONG CURVES & HARD & SOFT WOOD LESS THAN 1" THICK	10	

Fig. 21-7. Jigsaw blades are 5" in length with a 5/8" blank on each end. The teeth per inch and width of the blade depend on the cut.

with more teeth produce finer, but slower, cuts. Also, a blade with a higher number of teeth is thinner. A general-purpose blade has about 15 teeth per inch.

Installing a Blade

1. Turn off the power and remove the throat plate.
2. Turn the lower chuck until the flat sides of the jaws are parallel with the blade when installed. Loosen the jaws.
3. Pass the blade through the throat opening, and insert the lower ⅜ inch of the blade into the lower chuck. Point the teeth downward toward the table and forward. Straighten the blade until it is perpendicular to the table and slightly in front of the roller guide. Tighten the jaws while holding the blade in place.
4. Pull the upper chuck downward onto the upper end of the blade (about ⅜ inch) and tighten the jaws (Fig. 21-8). Check the blade for 90° angle with the table.

Fig. 21-8. The upper chuck is pulled downward until about ⅜″ of the blade fits into the chuck.

5. Adjust the tension until the blade is taut. With the power turned off, check the adjustment by turning the pulley or the drive belt by hand. If the blade buckles, move the tension sleeve upward.
6. Adjust the guide plate and the roller as needed (Fig. 21-9). Both the guide-plate slot and the blade should be aligned with each other. Also, this slot must not interfere with the set of the blade. The roller should be about 1/64 inch behind the blade when the blade is moving, but is not cutting.
7. Replace the throat plate, and adjust the height of the pressure foot. Make a trial cut; then check for squareness and drift. A drift usually occurs when the blade is too thin (Fig. 21-10). This can be corrected with a wider blade or a saber blade.

Fig. 21-9. Align the blade guide plate and roller.

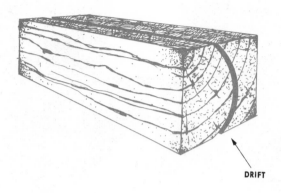

Fig. 21-10. A drift usually occurs when the blade is too thin for the stock being sawed.

Installing a Saber Blade

1. Turn off the power and remove the throat plate. If necessary, remove the regular saw blade.
2. Turn the lower chuck until the V groove in the jaws is aligned with the blade when installed (Fig. 21-11). Loosen the jaws.
3. Pass the blade through the throat opening, and insert the lower ⅜ inch of the blade into the lower chuck.

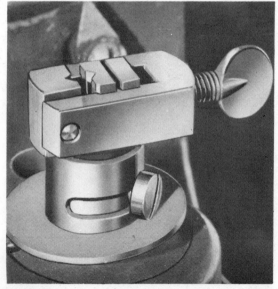

Fig. 21-11. A saber blade is inserted into the lower chuck. (Courtesy Power Tool Division, Rockwell Manufacturing Company)

Align the blade until it is perpendicular to the table; then tighten the jaws.

4. Attach the extra guide beneath the table (Fig. 21-12). This guide is needed, since a saber blade is held only by the lower chuck.
5. With the power off, replace the throat plate and check the adjustments by turning the pulley or drive belt by hand. It is not necessary to adjust the

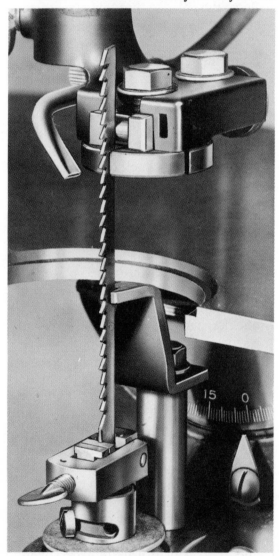

Fig. 21-12. An extra guide is required, since the saber blade is held only by the lower chuck. (Courtesy Power Tool Division, Rockwell Manufacturing Company)

tension, since the blade is held only by one chuck. Always point the teeth of the saber blade forward.

General Safety Rules

1. Turn off the power before making any adjustments.
2. Pay careful attention to each operation. Do not glance away, or talk to others, while using the jigsaw.
3. Remove the chips from around the blade only while the blade is stopped. Keep the table free from chips.
4. Check the blade tension and the height of the tension sleeve before using the jigsaw.
5. Insert the end of the blade at least ⅜ inch into each chuck.
6. Guard against drift and blade damage. Use the wider blades for the thicker stock, and use the slower speeds for the thinner blades.
7. Do not feed the stock faster than the blade is capable of cutting.
8. Point the teeth of the blade forward and toward the table. Adjust the guides to protect the set of the teeth.
9. Keep the pressure foot adjusted firmly against the stock.
10. Maintain adequate speed, depending on the blade size and the stock thickness and hardness.
11. Keep the fingers at the side of the blade—never directly in front of it.
12. Do not saw round stock, unless it is supported properly.

Operating a Jigsaw

Most of the jigsaw cuts are made freehand. The pattern is outlined on the wood; then it is sawed on the waste side of the mark (Fig. 21-13). However, a straightedge clamped to the table can serve as a guide for straight cuts (Fig. 21-

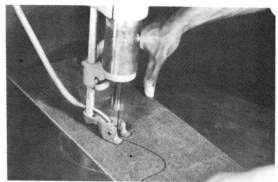
Fig. 21-13. Freehand sawing on the jigsaw.

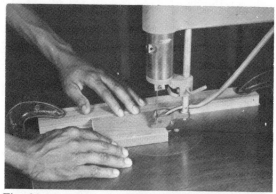
Fig. 21-14. Using a straightedge to guide the cut.

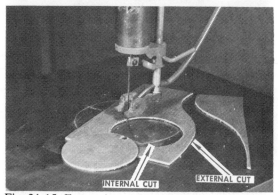
Fig. 21-15. External cuts determine the outer shape of a design.

14). The specific sawing operations often involve external and internal cuts, curved cuts, and angular cuts.

External cuts determine the outer shape of a design (Fig. 21-15). The initial kerf is begun from the edge or end of the stock and is continued until the shape is completed. Some designs first require relief cuts, similar to those made with a

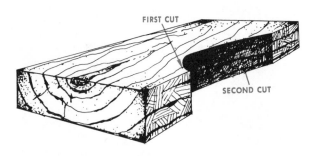

Fig. 21-16. The shorter kerfs are cut first to save time.

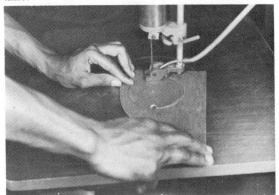

Fig. 21-17. Internal cuts determine the inside shape of a design.

Fig. 21-18. Insert the blade through a small hole in the waste area to begin the internal cut.

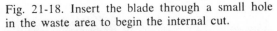

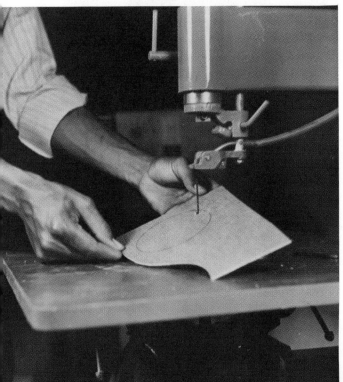

Fig. 21-19. Tilt the table for an angular cut. (Courtesy Power Tool Division, Rockwell Manufacturing Company)

band saw. Before beginning an external cut, always plan the sequence of the cuts (Fig. 21-16). The shorter kerfs are cut first to save time and to prevent the blade from binding while backing out of a long cut.

An inside shape of an object is made with internal cuts (Fig. 21-17). This type of sawing is sometimes called *pierced work*. The operation begins with drilling or boring a small hole in the waste area of the design. The jigsaw blade is then inserted through this hole (Fig. 21-18). After the shape is completely sawed, the blade must be removed from one or both chucks before the stock can be moved from the table.

Curved and angular cuts can be either external or internal. The table is tilted for angular cuts (Fig. 21-19). To check an angular cut, make a trial cut; then check the angle with a sliding T bevel.

Questions

1. List several advantages of the jigsaw over the band saw.
2. What is the clearance between the blade and the base of the overarm for a 26-inch jigsaw?

3. Describe the purpose of the drive mechanism of a jigsaw.

4. Describe two ways by which the speed of a jigsaw can be changed.

5. For what purpose is a saber blade more suitable than a regular jigsaw blade?

6. Does a jigsaw blade with 15 teeth per inch cut faster than a jigsaw blade with 22 teeth per inch? Which blade cuts finer? Why?

7. After a regular jigsaw blade is changed, why is the jigsaw turned by hand before switching on the

8. What is the cause of "drift"? How can it be corrected?

9. Why is an extra guide needed for a saber blade? Where is the guide located?

10. What is the difference between external and internal (pierced-work) sawing? Why is a hole drilled or bored before beginning an internal cut?

11. When installing a jigsaw blade, in which direction should the teeth be pointed? Why?

12. Describe the procedure for making an angular cut.

Unit 22 — Radial Saw

A radial saw is probably the most versatile piece of woodworking equipment. It is used for both rough and finish work performed by crosscutting, ripping, mitering, and beveling. Its versatility is increased further with the addition of various attachments. Dadoing, grooving, rabbeting, boring, sanding, and shaping are only a few of the additional operations that can be performed. Since the stock can be sawed without being moved, a series of simple kerfs can be used to produce intricate designs. The radial saw, in general, is both safer and easier to work with than a table saw. Another advantage of the radial saw is that it is easily transported to the work site.

Since the blade is located above the table, or stock, it can be used for many operations. However, the complete "adjustability" of the saw is equally important. The blade can be moved back and forth over the table, pivoted 360°, tilted at an angle to the table, or at an angle with the fence.

The size of a radial saw, like the table saw, depends on the diameter of its blade. A 10-inch radial saw, for example, utilizes a 10-inch diameter blade. Although radial saws range upward to 18 inches in size, the common sizes are the 8-inch and 10-inch saws.

The principal parts of a radial saw are shown in the diagram in Fig. 22-1. Basically, the saw consists of a blade attached directly to a motor supported by a yoke. "Bevel-type" angular cuts can be made by tilting the position of the motor on the yoke. The yoke either slides or can be locked in a stationary position on the turret arm. Also, it can be pivoted 360° at

its point of connection with the turret arm. In turn, the turret arm is supported by an overarm. By raising or lowering the column of the overarm, the height of the blade above the table can be changed.

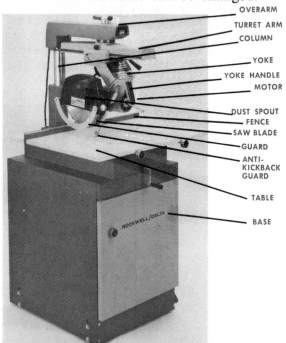

Fig. 22-1. Principal parts of a radial saw. (Courtesy Power Tool Division, Rockwell Manufacturing Company)

Adjustment

The fundamental adjustments for the radial saw are: (1) Elevating the blade; (2) Tilting the blade; (3) Angling the turret arm; and (4) Swiveling the yoke. Each adjustment involves one or several controls found on a typical radial saw (Fig. 22-2). However, some controls, or their locations, can vary slightly among the different manufacturers of saws. For example, in saws without a turret arm, the elevating crank is located toward the back of the overarm (Fig. 22-3). For another example, the fence control is not necessary on a saw with a stationary fence. The operator should acquaint himself with the manufacturer's recommendations before attempting to make adjustments on an unfamiliar saw. When the operator becomes more familiar with the saw and its various adjustments, special adjustments can be made for unusual cuts. The following procedures should serve as a guide for adjusting saws similar to the saw in Fig. 22-2 or 22-3.

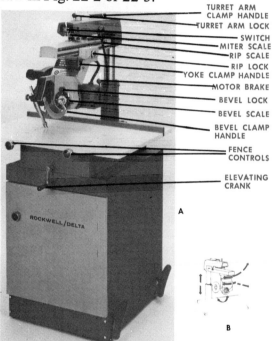

TURRET ARM
CLAMP HANDLE
TURRET ARM LOCK
SWITCH
MITER SCALE
RIP SCALE
RIP LOCK
YOKE CLAMP HANDLE
MOTOR BRAKE
BEVEL LOCK
BEVEL SCALE
BEVEL CLAMP
HANDLE
FENCE
CONTROLS
ELEVATING
CRANK

A

B

Fig. 22-2. Diagrams of controls (A) of a radial saw and adjustments (B). (Courtesy Power Tool Division, Rockwell Manufacturing Company)

1. *To raise or lower the blade.* The depth of cut is controlled by raising or lowering the blade. The procedure involves merely turning the elevating crank.

2. *To tilt the blade.* Bevels are sawed with the blade tilted at an angle to the table (Fig. 22-4). The tilt results from pivoting the motor on the yoke. To tilt the blade, first raise it clear of the

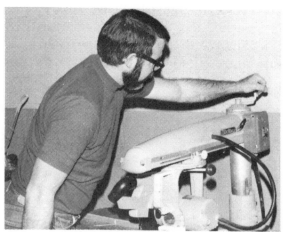

Fig. 22-3. On some radial saws, especially those without a turret arm, the elevating crank is located on the overarm.

table. Then, release the bevel clamp and pull the bevel lock forward. Next, incline the blade until the correct angle is indicated on the bevel scale. Tighten the bevel-clamp handle and lower the blade to complete the adjustment.

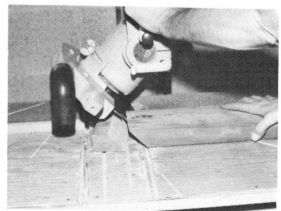

Fig. 22-4. To saw a bevel, tilt the blade at an angle with the table.

3. *To angle the turret arm.* Miters are sawed with the turret arm at an angle with the fence. As shown in Fig. 22-5, the overarm is pivoted on saws without a turret arm. Before attempting this adjustment, raise the blade clear of the table. The first step is to release the turret-arm clamp, pulling up-

ward on the turret-arm lock. Then, swing the turret arm either left or right to the desired angle. Tighten the turret-arm clamp; then lower the blade to complete the adjustment.

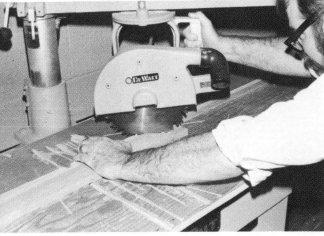

Fig. 22-5. To saw a miter, position the turret arm or overarm at an angle to the fence.

4. *To swivel the yoke.* The yoke, which holds the motor and blade, is turned for ripping (see Fig. 22-6). Similar to the preceding adjustment, the blade first is raised clear of the table. Also, pull the yoke forward until the blade is in front of the fence. To start the movement, release the yoke clamp handle. If the saw is provided with a yoke lock, pull it up. Then, swivel the yoke to the desired angle. For ripping, the blade is swiveled parallel with the fence. Tighten the yoke clamp handle; then lower the blade to complete the operation.

Blades

Five types of blades are in common use with radial saws: (1) The *combination* blade is used for sawing both with and across the grain, and it is a general-purpose blade; (2) The *crosscut* blade, often called a cutoff blade, cuts only across the grain and should never be used for rip-

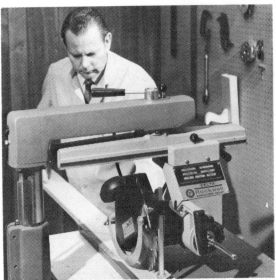

Fig. 22-6. For ripping, swivel the yoke until the blade is parallel with the fence. (Courtesy Power Tool Division, Rockwell Manufacturing Company)

ping; (3) The *ripsaw* blade is used for cuts with the grain—it is not recommended for sawing across the grain; (4) The *planer* blade is used for either ripping or crosscutting, and it produces smooth cuts; and (5) The *plywood* blade is another blade that produces smooth cuts. It is especially valuable in cutting plywood or resinous wood.

Checking the Trueness of Cut

Depending on the circumstances, the adjustment of a radial saw can be checked

Fig. 22-7. Check the squareness of the blade with the table.

in several ways. Without doubt, the best check is a trial cut; then use a measuring or layout tool to check its trueness. However, this procedure cannot be used unless there is ample extra material. Where extra stock is lacking, trueness should be checked before the cut is made. A square should be used to test the squareness of the blade with the table (Fig. 22-7); the squareness with the fence should be checked similarly (Fig. 22-8). The same procedure should be used for checking angular cuts; however, a sliding T bevel, rather than a square, should be used to check the angle.

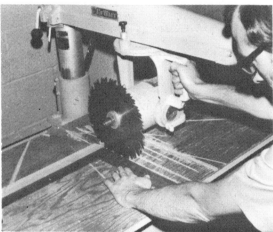

Fig. 22-8. Check the squareness of the blade with the fence.

Woodworking Hints

1. Identical lengths can be cut accurately in less time when a stopblock is clamped to the fence for a guide (Fig. 22-9).
2. The stock sometimes "crawls" in sawing miters which form less than a 30° angle with the fence. This sidewise movement can be avoided by clamping the stock to the fence or by using a stopblock.
3. Tilting the blade guard during ripping operations protects the operator and prevents the sawdust flying toward him (see Fig. 22-6).

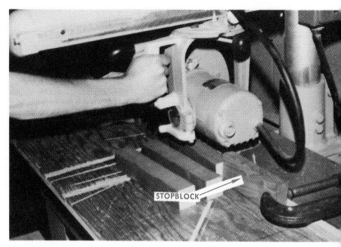

Fig. 22-9. Use a stopblock to cut identical lengths to stock.

4. Two kerfs, each made from an opposite side, are needed for stock thicker than the maximum cut of the radial saw. Since the stock is flipped over after the first cut, a stopblock is used to align both kerfs (Fig. 22-10). This technique requires adjusting the blade to a height for a cut slightly more than one-half the thickness of the stock.
5. Before crosscutting, always check the fence and table for sawdust and small chips. As shown in Fig. 22-11,

Fig. 22-10. Two kerfs are required on stock thicker than the maximum cut of the saw.

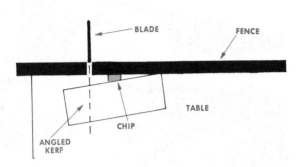

Fig. 22-11. Chips, or sawdust, between the fence and the stock can cause an untrue cut.

Fig. 22-12. Using an adjustable tool bit dado head to cut a series of dadoes. (Courtesy Power Tool Division, Rockwell Manufacturing Company)

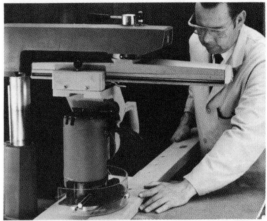

Fig. 22-13. Rabbeting with an adustable tool bit dado head. (Courtesy Power Tool Division, Rockwell Manufacturing Company)

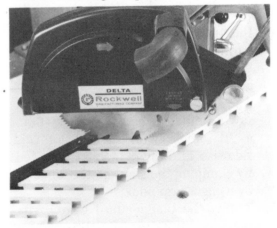

Fig. 22-14 Using a dado head to cut angular dadoes in a decorative piece. (Courtesy Power Tool Division, Rockwell Manufacturing Company)

pieces of material located between the stock and the fence or table can cause untrue kerfs.

6. Plan the sequence of cuts before starting the cuts. For a general rule, the cuts producing short lengths and widths should be sawed last.

7. When available, a dado head can "speed up" the cutting of dadoes, grooves, rabbets, and various decorative cuts. An adjustable tool bit dado head is used in Fig. 22-12 to cut a series of dadoes. A rabbet is being cut with the dado head in Fig. 22-13. In Fig. 22-14, a dado head formed with inside and outside cutters is used in cutting angular dadoes in a decorative piece.

8. Typical dado cuts also can be made with a crosscut blade. The procedure involves sawing parallel kerfs, by sliding the stock to the left or right of the preceding kerf (Fig. 22-15).

9. Decorative cuts can be made easily when the regular saw blade is replaced with a molding cutterhead (Fig. 22-16).

10. Corresponding cuts in different pieces can be paired more accurately when a stopblock is used. For example, the dadoes cut in the sides of a bookcase must be located at

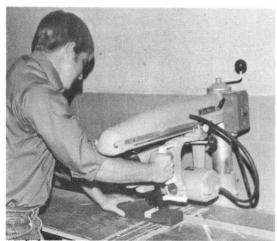

Fig. 22-15. Cutting a dado by making a series of kerfs with a crosscut blade.

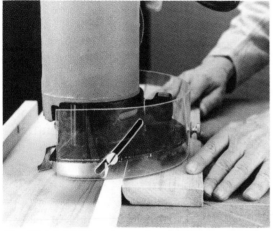

Fig. 22-16. Making decorative cuts with a molding head. (Courtesy Power Tool Division, Rockwell Manufacturing Company)

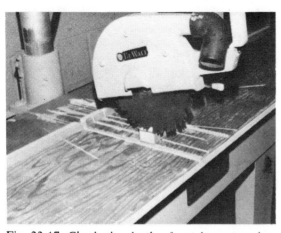

Fig. 22-17. Check the depth of cut by comparing the blade setting with an outline mark on the stock.

identical distances from the top of the bookcase, if the shelves are to be level. Therefore, a stopblock clamped to the fence serves as a guide for establishing the precise location of each dado.

11. When not sawing complete "through" cuts, establish the required depth by trial cuts. Another method is to outline the entire cut on the edge of the stock; then compare with the setting of the blade (Fig. 22-17).

12. Routine operations require cutting the kerfs through the fence. The fence should be replaced with another true edge when the stock being cut is no longer supported adequately.

13. To crosscut stock wider than the cut of the saw, cut the width partway; then turn over the piece of stock and complete the cut (Fig. 22-18). A stopblock is recommended for this operation.

General Safety Rules for a Radial Saw

1. All adjustments are made only while the blade is stopped.

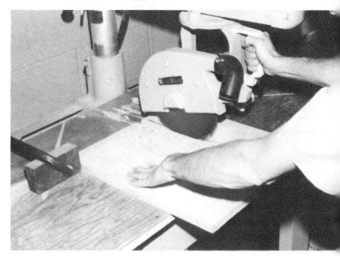

Fig. 22-18. To crosscut stock wider than the cut of the saw, use a stopblock to align the two kerfs cut from opposite edges.

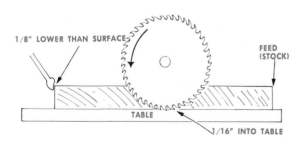

Fig. 22-19. Ripping stock with the radial saw.

2. Select the correct blade for the job. Before using, check the blade for sharpness and defects.
3. Always mount the blade with its teeth pointing in the direction of rotation of the motor.
4. For through cuts, adjust the blade height until the blade cuts about $\frac{1}{16}$ inch below the surface of the table top (Figs. 22-19 and 22-20).
5. Begin the cut only after the blade reaches its full operating speed.
6. When the cut is completed, always return the blade to the rear resting position; then lock it in place.
7. Do not remove the stock after it has been sawed, until the blade is re-turned to its rear resting position.
8. While sawing, keep the fingers at either side of the blade and never in line with the kerf being sawed.
9. For ripping, lower the antikickback guard until its fingers are about $\frac{1}{8}$ inch below the top of the surface to be ripped (see Fig. 22-19).
10. For crosscutting and similar operations, raise the antikickback guard until its fingers clear the top of the surface to be sawed (see Fig. 22-20).
11. Do not attempt to cut identical lengths by stacking the pieces on top of each other.
12. Blades without mechanical brakes should be permitted to coast to a stop. Jamming the blade into the stock to stop its turning is a dangerous practice.
13. Position the edge of the stock firmly against the fence before crosscutting.
14. Regardless of the reason, do not force the blade.
15. Keep the table top and the area surrounding the table free from wood scraps and other materials or tools.
16. Never hold the stock in a manner that requires the arms to be crossed when pulling the yoke.

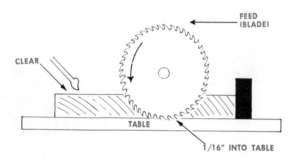

Fig. 22-20. Crosscutting stock with the radial saw.

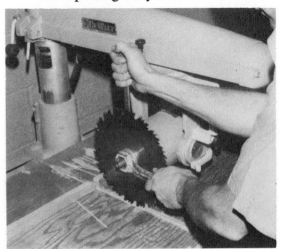

Fig. 22-21. Changing the saw blade.

Crosscutting

1. Select the proper blade. A blade is being changed in Fig. 22-21.
2. Turn the turret arm at an angle with the fence. The miter scale should read either zero for straight crosscutting or the desired angle for mitering. This adjustment is made with the overarm for those saws without turret arms.
3. Adjust the blade. The blade is 90° to the table for normal crosscutting and at an angle to the table for bevel crosscutting. In either instance, its height should be adjusted to a depth $\frac{1}{16}$ inch below the top of the table.
4. Position the yoke behind the fence and place the stock against the fence. If the yoke is not positioned behind the fence, premature contact will be made with the blade when the stock is pushed against the fence.
5. Loosen the knob of the rip clamp, and turn on the switch.
6. Make the cut while applying pressure to the stock with one hand and pulling the yoke handle forward with the other hand (Fig. 22-22). Permit the blade to cut at its own speed.
7. After completing the cut, return the yoke to the original position, turn off the switch, and tighten the knob of the rip clamp.
8. Remove the stock only after the blade has stopped turning.

Ripping

1. Select the proper blade.
2. Maintain a 90° angle between the turret arm and the fence.
3. Turn the yoke until the blade is parallel with the fence.
4. Adjust the blade. The blade should be 90° to the table for normal ripping and at an angle with the table for bevel ripping.

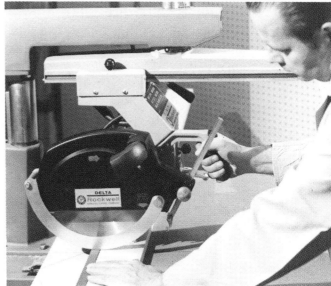

Fig. 22-22. Hold the stock with one hand and the yoke handle with the other hand while sawing. Never cross the arms to hold the stock. (Courtesy Power Tool Division, Rockwell Manufacturing Company)

5. Adjust the blade for the width of the cut, which is determined by the clearance between the fence and the blade.
6. Adjust the antikickback guard and the blade guard.
7. Turn on the power.
8. Make the cut (see Fig. 22-6). While feeding the stock, keep the piece flat on the table and firmly against the fence. The stock should not be fed faster than the blade is capable of cutting.
9. Turn off the power. Do not attempt to remove the stock from the table until the blade has stopped turning.
10. Use a push stick for ripping narrow stock.
11. Always apply the "push" to the portion of the stock next to the fence.

Questions

1. Explain why a radial saw is capable of performing many operations.

2. Discuss the difference between a radial saw with both a turret arm and and overarm and a radial saw with only an overarm.

3. When is it necessary: (1) To raise or lower the blade; (2) Tilt the blade; (3) Angle the turret arm; and (4) Swivel the yoke?

4. List five useful blades for a radial saw. When is each blade used advantageously?

5. Describe two methods of checking the adjustments on a radial saw for cutting only partway through a piece of stock.

6. Why is the antikickback guard raised when crosscutting?

7. What operations require a stopblock?

8. How can a dado be cut when a dado head cannot be used?

9. How deep should the saw blade cut into the top of the table of the radial saw when making through kerfs?

10. Describe the difference between crosscutting and ripping operations on the radial saw.

Unit 23 – Portable Electric Tools

The equipment used in woodworking is either stationary or portable. Drill presses and planers are examples of stationary equipment which cannot be moved easily. Stock machined with stationary equipment must be carried to the exact location of the machine. However, the weight of the material and the transportation costs involved often prohibit transporting the stock to a special room in which the equipment is housed; this is especially true in building construction. To overcome these difficulties, nearly all the work done with stationary pieces of equipment can be duplicated with portable electric tools. These pieces of equipment can be carried conveniently to the work, rather than carrying the work to the equipment.

It should be remembered that portable electric tools are lightweight in comparison with standard-size machinery. For this reason, the cutting actions (or depths) and sometimes the accuracy with portable tools are less satisfactory than with the stationary equipment. Also, the smaller motors on stationary equipment often cannot be used for lengthy periods of time without damage.

The portable electric tools discussed here are the routers, power planes, circular saws, jigsaws, belt sanders, and finishing sanders. The electric hand drills have been discussed earlier.

Portable Routers

The *routers* range in size from the smaller portable equipment (Fig. 23-1) to the larger production machines (Fig. 23-2). Even though their sizes differ

Fig. 23-1. Portable electric router. (Courtesy The Black & Decker Mfg. Co.)

Fig. 23-2. Stationary production router. (Courtesy Onsrud Machine Works, Inc.)

greatly, they are capable of performing nearly identical operations. Among the many operations which can be performed with either type of router are cutting joints, shaping edges, freehand cuts, and shaping patterns or designs. Since the portable routers are inexpensive in comparison with the larger machines, their acceptance is more widespread. The principal parts of a portable router are shown in Fig. 23-3.

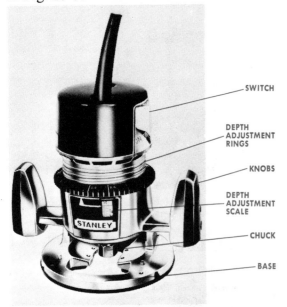

Fig. 23-3. Principal parts of a portable router. (Courtesy The Stanley Works)

1. *Motor*. A router consists, basically, of a high-speed motor turning between 18,000 and 23,000 rpm. The size of the motor, rated by horsepower, indicates the size of a router. The common router sizes range from ¼ to 3¼ horsepower.
2. *Base*. The base serves two purposes. Its flat portion supports the router; its round tube-like outer case (sleeve) encloses the motor. The depth of cut is changed by sliding the motor upward or downward inside the sleeve.
3. *Knobs*. The knobs, or handles, are connected to the base. They are held

by the operator to guide and support the router during its use.
4. *Depth-adjustment ring*. This part is connected to the outer case of the motor with threads. Depending on the direction turned, it is used to raise and lower the depth of cut.
5. *Chuck*. The shank of the router bit is held by the chuck. The common shank sizes are ⅜-inch or ¼-inch shanks. The shank size required depends on the size of the chuck.
6. *Switch*. On most routers, the switch is used to control the power and to lock the shaft of the motor. When the shaft can be locked with the switch, only one wrench is needed to tighten the chuck.
7. *Locking lever*. Located on the back side of the base, the locking lever clamps the motor to the base.

Router Bits

Many sizes and shapes of router bits are available. The various bits are described by their physical parts and by their uses (Fig. 23-4). The shanks, cutting edges, flutes, and pilots (or lack of pilots) vary widely among the router bits. A *pilot* is a shaft extending below the cutting blades; this permits the cutter to follow an edge. Internal cuts, such as grooves, cannot be made with a bit having a pilot. Also, for the internal cuts, a wooden fence or metal guide is required to guide the router. Router bits with pilots are used to produce decorative cuts or similar cuts on the edges and ends of the stock. No other guide is required, since the pilot guides the cut.

Changing a Router Bit

The procedure for changing a router bit varies slightly among the different types of routers. The chief difference is the method used to lock the shaft or bit

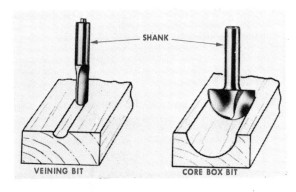

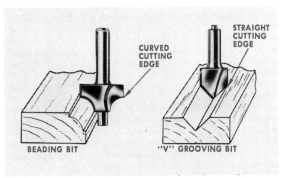

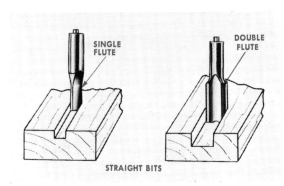

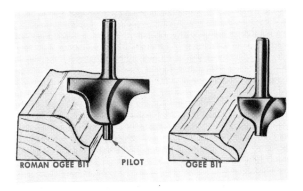

Fig. 23-4. Router bits are designated by their parts and uses. (Courtesy The Stanley Works)

before loosening the chuck. On most routers, this is accomplished either by locking the switch or by depressing a push button located on the top of the motor. On other routers, however, it is necessary to hold the shaft stationary with a wrench (Fig. 23-5). The following procedure is recommended in changing router bits:

Fig. 23-5. To change router bits, use a second wrench to hold the shaft of the router stationary.

1. Disconnect the power cord from the source.
2. Select the bit needed for the operation. Use only clean and sharp bits.
3. Lock the shaft and remove the first bit by loosening the chuck. Only the wrench furnished with the router should be used. If the bit remains tight, gently tap the chuck with the edge of the wrench until released by the collet.
4. Insert the shank of the selected bit fully into the chuck; then back it out about $\frac{1}{16}$ inch. Tighten the chuck and release the shaft locks.
5. Adjust the depth of the cut. For bits without a pilot, release the locking lever; then place the base of the router on a flat surface (Fig. 23-6). Pull the

Fig. 23-6. Adjusting the depth of cut for a cutter without a pilot.

depth-adjustment scale upward until the desired depth is indicated. Next, lower the depth-adjustment ring to the stop on the scale. To complete the operation, raise the base by its knobs. The motor slides downward until the ring and the base meet, thus establishing the depth of the cut. This position is then locked with the locking lever.

If the router bit has a pilot, the depth-adjustment scale is set relative to the lower cutting edge of the bit. Another method is to outline the profile of the cut on the edge of a board (Fig. 23-7). Then

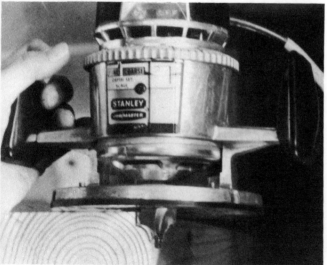

Fig. 23-7. Adjusting the depth of cut for a cutter with a pilot.

the bit is lowered with the depth-adjustment ring until the bit and the outline are even.

Operating Hints

1. A router should be moved in a direction that aids the cutting action of the bit (Fig. 23-8). In Fig. 23-8A, the feed is counterclockwise and the rotation of the bit is clockwise. Moving the router with the rotation of the bit causes the bit to skip. The router is moved from left to right in making straight cuts (see Fig. 23-8B and C). Moving in the opposite direction causes the bit to cut toward the metal guide (see Fig. 23-8B), or away from the wood fence (see Fig. 23-8C).

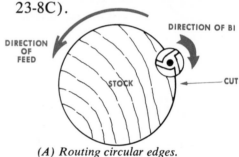

(A) Routing circular edges.

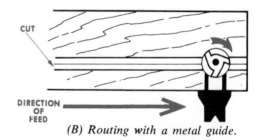

(B) Routing with a metal guide.

(C) Routing with a fence.

Fig. 23-8. The direction of feed of a router depends on the cut and on the method of guiding the router.

2. A router bit that is overheated produces poor cuts and heats or burns the wood (Fig. 23-9). Overheating

Fig. 23-9. An overheated cutter produces "burned" spots, which require sanding to avoid a poor finish.

occurs if the cutters are dull, if the bit is dirty, and if the router is moved too slowly. The "burned" spots require sanding to avoid a poor finish. Dull cutters can be sharpened with a special router attachment (Fig. 23-10); dirty router bits can be cleaned with steel wool.

Fig. 23-10. Using a router attachment to sharpen cutters.

3. The end cuts are made first on adjacent edges and ends. Then, any splitting occuring from the end routing is eliminated by the edge routing (Fig. 23-11).

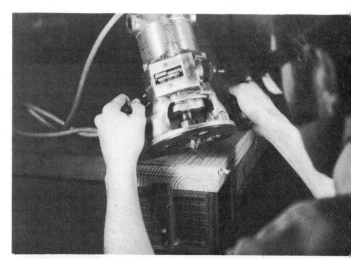

(A) First, rout the end grain.

(B) Then, edge routing eliminates splits or cracks.

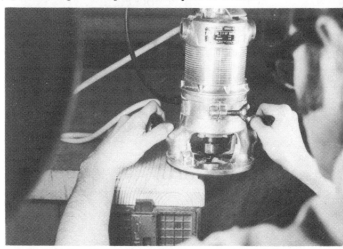

(C) Finished cut is free from defects.

Fig. 23-11. Edge routing.

4. Internal cuts, such as dadoes and grooves, usually are cut before the decorative cuts on edges and ends are cut. Otherwise, the curved edges and ends might fail to provide ample support for a metal guide; then a wood fence is necessary. Although the fence is satisfactory, it normally requires more adjustments than the guide.

5. Routing thin stock can be difficult when the edge or end is too thin to guide the pilot of a bit. The necessary thickness can be achieved by tacking a second piece to the underneath side for backing (Fig. 23-12). The second piece is cut to a shape identical to the shape being routed.

Fig. 23-12. Attach a backboard to thin stock to provide additional thickness for edge routing.

6. Extra pieces are often tacked to irregular or small shapes which are difficult to hold while routing. These pieces can be locked in a vise (Fig. 23-13).

Fig. 23-13. A scrap board can be used to hold a piece of stock for routing irregular shapes.

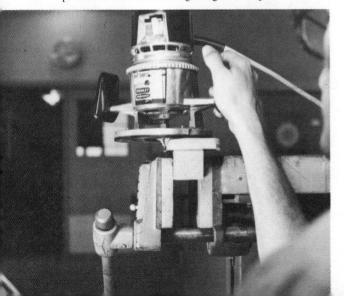

7. Router cuts are often rough. When smoother cuts are desired, make a shallow first cut. Then, increase the depth of the bit slightly and rout a second time, until the desired cut is achieved.

8. Various decorative cuts are possible by making a series of cuts with different router bits (Fig. 23-14). This design resulted from first using a concave bit (Step 1), and secondly, using a rounding over bit (Step 2).

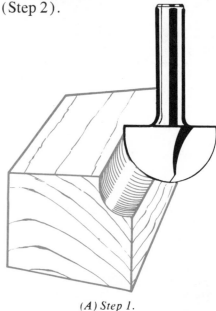

(A) Step 1.

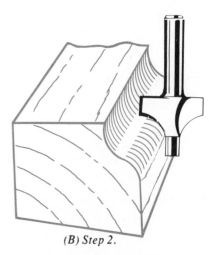

(B) Step 2.

Fig. 23-14. Several router bits might be required to make a single decorative cut.

9. Edge cuts are begun near the end and worked backward. This prevents the bit grabbing the end grain and cutting in the wrong direction.

10. For most routing operations, the stock is clamped in place; the router is then moved about the stock. Another method is to secure the router; then move the stock around the bit. This procedure requires the router to be mounted upside down on an auxiliary table (Fig. 23-15). The router then can be used in a manner similar to a shaper.

Fig. 23-16. Shaping an edge.

Cutting Grooves and Dadoes

1. Select the proper bit and fasten it into the chuck.

2. Adjust the depth of cut. If the cut is deep, use several shallow cuts.

3. Clamp the stock onto the table or workbench.

4. Mark the width of the cut on the stock and adjust the guide for the bit to cut into the waste area. This adjustment is made with the rod extensions when using the metal guide (Fig. 23-17).

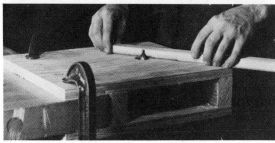

Fig. 23-15. The router can be mounted upside down to rout small shapes on an auxiliary table.

Shaping Edges

1. Select the proper bit.
2. Fasten the bit into the chuck.
3. Adjust the depth of the cut.
4. Clamp the stock to the table.
5. Check the clamps for interference with the movement of the router.
6. Place the router base on the stock, but with the bit clear of the stock.
7. Turn on the power and gradually pivot the bit into the edge.
8. Complete the cut (Fig. 23-16).
9. Turn off the power and check the cut.

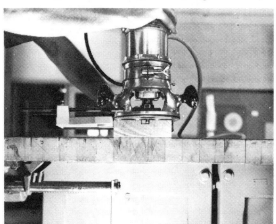

Fig. 23-17. Adjusting the metal guide.

When using the wood fence, its location is equal to the distance between the cutting edge of the bit and the edge of the base (Fig. 23-18).

5. Check for interference between the clamps and the movement of the router.

Fig. 23-18. The distance from the cut to the fence is equal to the distance from the outside edge of the cutter to the outside edge of the base.

6. Place the router base on the stock, but keep the bit clear of the stock.
7. Turn on the power and gradually begin the cut.
8. Complete the cut, turn off the power, and check the cut.

Making Freehand Cuts

1. Draw the design on the stock.
2. Fasten the proper bit into the chuck.
3. Adjust the depth of the cut.
4. Clamp the stock onto the table and check for clearance between the router and the clamps.
5. While holding the router above the design, turn on the power.

Fig. 23-19. Freehand cutting with the router.

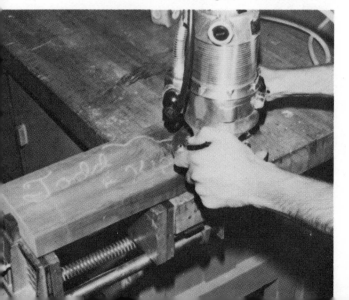

6. Gradually lower the router until the bit begins to cut (Fig. 23-19).
7. When finished, raise the router and turn off the power.

Routing with a Template

1. Design the shape to be routed.
2. Attach the template guide to the router base and insert the proper bit into the chuck.
3. Transfer the design to a piece of fiberboard with the necessary thickness. The thickness should be greater than the projection of the tip below the base (Fig. 23-20).

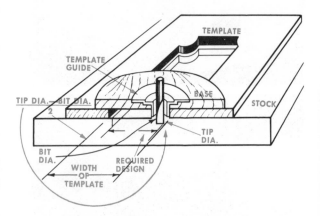

Fig. 23-20. The template size required for routing is equal to the design size plus the clearance between the diameter of the bit and the outside diameter of the guide tip.

4. Enlarge the design; then cut it out with the jigsaw. The increased size should be one-half the difference between the diameter of the bit and the outside diameter of the template guide tip. For example, a template should be ⅝ inch larger all around for a ¼-inch bit and a 1½-inch tip.
5. Adjust the depth of the cut, which is equal to the projection of the bit beneath the template (see Fig. 23-18).

6. Tack the template onto the stock and clamp the stock to the table.
7. With the bit not contacting the stock, position the router over the template.
8. Turn on the power and gradually lower the router bit into the stock. Usually, it is better practice to begin the cut near the center and work outward.
9. Complete the cut (Fig. 23-21) and turn off the power. Then remove the router from the template and check the cut.

Fig. 23-22. Using a template to cut a dovetail joint. (Courtesy The Stanley Works)

Fig. 23-21. Routing with a template.

10. Dovetail joints also are cut with a template to guide the cut (Fig. 23-22).

General Safety Rules for the Router

1. Always wear safety glasses, safety goggles, or a face shield while routing.
2. Disconnect the electric cord from the power source before changing bits or making any router adjustments.
3. Make certain the switch is off before connecting the electrical cord to the power source.
4. Do not attempt to change a bit immediately after completing the cut.

A bit becomes heated while cutting and is usually too hot to handle.
5. Securely lock the bit in the chuck before turning on the power. When routing for lengthy periods, periodically unplug the router and check the tightness of the chuck and bit.
6. Hold each handle to the router firmly while making cuts.
7. Keep the electrical cord away from the area being routed. Either place the cord over the shoulder or loop it around the wrist, holding it firmly against the handle.
8. When putting down the router, lay it on its side—never on its base and cutter. Also, do not lay down the router until the cutter has stopped turning.
9. Do not attempt to stop a bit by jamming it against another object or by grasping it with the fingers.
10. Use only sharp bits.
11. Periodically, check the screws or other parts which can be loosened by vibration.
12. Make a series of shallow cuts when a deep cut is needed.

Power Plane

Essentially, a *power plane* is considered to be either a motorized hand plane or a portable jointer. It is used to smooth and to plane the edges and ends of stock. The available power planes range from the self-contained machines (Fig. 23-23) to mere adaptations of the portable electric router (Fig. 23-24).

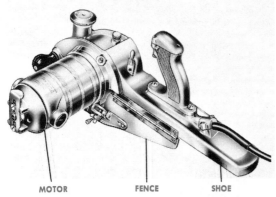

MOTOR   FENCE   SHOE

Fig. 23-23. Principal parts of a power plane. (Courtesy The Stanley Works)

Either the horsepower and speed of the motor or the width of cut can be used to describe the size of a power plane. Most of the motors are 1 or 1¼ horsepower with speeds upward to 25,000 rpm. The common widths of cut range upward to 2½ inches.

A cut with a power plane is made with a cutter similar to the cutterhead of a jointer. The depth of cut is controlled by the shoe, which is divided into two parts. The front part of the shoe governs the depth of the cut, while the back part supports the plane. Bevels up to 45° can be planed by adjusting the fence at an angle with the shoe.

Using a Power Plane

A power plane is used in a manner similar to a hand plane. The stance of the operator and the way he holds the power plane are similar to using the hand plane. The procedure below can be followed in using a power plane:

1. Determine the necessary cut.

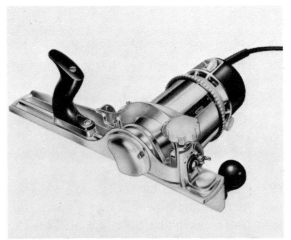

Fig. 23-24. Router adapted to a power plane. (Courtesy The Stanley Works)

2. Adjust the power plane. Its depth and squareness of cut always should be checked with the power cord disconnected.
3. Clamp the stock.
4. Hold the plane by the handle and front knob, while assuming the work position or stance alongside the stock.
5. Place the front part of the shoe on the edge of the stock and firmly press the fence against the face of the stock. In the meantime, keep the cutter free from the stock.
6. Turn on the power by squeezing the trigger switch. Begin the cut as soon as the motor reaches its full speed.
7. Maintain adequate pressure while moving the plane forward. Even though more pressure should be applied to the front of the shoe in beginning the cut, more pressure is applied to the back of the shoe near the end of the cut.
8. Smoother surfaces are planed by decreasing the final depth of the cut.

General Safety Rules

1. Disconnect the power cord before making adjustments.
2. Move the plane away from the body.

3. Keep the fingers away from the blades.
4. Wait until the blade stops turning before lowering or removing the plane.
5. Never back up with the plane in use.
6. Keep the power cord away from the work by looping it over the shoulder or around the arm.

Portable Circular Saws

Stock cannot always be sawed with a table or radial-arm circular saw, due to the location of the stock, its weight, or its attachment to other stock. A *portable circular saw,* however, can be used in these instances, since it can be carried to the work. Straight, angular, and pocket cuts are the typical kerfs which can be made with this saw. Its principal parts are diagrammed in Fig. 23-25.

HANDLE
TRIGGER SWITCH
MOTOR
BASE PLATE
BLADE
GUARD

Fig. 23-25. Principal parts of a portable circular saw. (Courtesy The Stanley Works)

1. *Base plate.* The base plate rides on the stock and supports the other parts of the saw. The depth and angle of the kerf are changed by adjusting the base plate.
2. *Guard.* An important feature of any portable saw, the swing-type guard is tension-mounted. It covers the blade when it is not in use; yet, it retracts as the kerf is cut.

3. *Blade.* The size of the saw is described by the diameter of its blade, which ranges upward to 9 inches. The type of blade depends on the operation. Four common types of blades are shown in Fig. 23-26. Although ripping and crosscutting are usually performed with a *combination* blade, a planer blade is used for the same operations if smoother cuts are desired. A *crosscut* blade produces smooth cuts across the grain. The *framing* blade is a general-purpose blade recommended for carpentry and construction sawing.

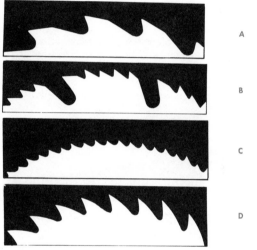

A
B
C
D

Fig. 23-26. Common blades for a portable circular saw are: (A) Combination; (B) Planer; (C) Crosscut; and (D) Framing.

4. *Handle.* The handle is used to guide the saw during cutting and to carry the saw when carrying it.
5. *Switch.* A trigger-type switch is located in the handle.
6. *Motor.* The power supplied by the motor turns the blade between 4000 and 5500 rpm. The blade and motor are directly connected.

Operating Hints

1. Since the blade cuts upward, smoother cuts are obtained when the better face is placed down (Fig. 23-27).

1/8" MAXIMUM

Fig. 23-27. The blade of a portable circular saw cuts upward, which is opposite the direction of cutting for a stationary circular saw blade. The blade should project not more than 1/8 inch below the thickness of the stock.

2. When sawing freehand, locate the base-plate guide on the waste side of the mark.
3. For ripping cuts, use either the ripping fence provided with the saw or a straightedge clamped onto the stock (Fig. 23-28).
4. For angular kerfs, tilt the base plate until the required angle is formed with the blade (Fig. 23-29).
5. Pocket cuts should be outlined completely before the first cut is made. Note in Fig. 23-30 that the guard is pulled back when starting the cut.
6. The blade is changed by loosening the arbor screw; then it is turned counterclockwise.
7. Never feed the saw faster than it can cut. If the blade loses speed, reduce the feed until the proper speed is regained.

Using the Saw

1. Determine the type of cut to be made and change the blade if necessary.

Fig. 23-28. Uniform widths can be sawed with either the ripping guide (top) or the straightedge (bottom) to guide the saw.

2. Adjust the base plate until the projection of the blade is about 1/8 inch more than the thickness of the stock.
3. Check the angle between the base plate and the blade.
4. Prepare the stock for the cut. For pocket and freehand cuts, mark the stock. A ripping guide should be adjusted or a straightedge clamped to the stock for uniform cuts.
5. Firmly support and/or clamp the stock, as needed. When clamps are

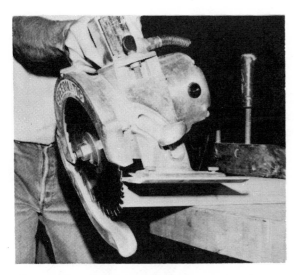

Fig. 23-29. Tilt the base plate for angular cuts.

used, always check the clearance with the saw before attempting the cut.

6. Plug in the power cord.
7. Rest the front of the base plate on the stock, but with the blade clear. Depending on the cut, align the plate guide and the mark, position the ripping guide firmly against the edge of the board, or locate the base plate squarely against the straightedge.
8. Squeeze the trigger switch and begin

Fig. 23-30. Retract the guard before beginning a pocket cut.

the cut as soon as the blade reaches full speed.
9. When the cut is completed, release the switch. Remove the saw only after the blade has stopped.

General Safety Rules

1. Always disconnect the power cord before changing a blade or making other adjustments.
2. A portable circular saw should be used only when the guard is in place and retracts properly.
3. Adjust the blade to project only about 1/8 inch below the thickness being cut (see Fig. 23-27).
4. Always feed the saw away from the body. Keep the fingers (and knees when bracing the stock) at a safe distance from the blade.
5. The saw should not be lowered or set aside until its blade has stopped turning.
6. Avoid binding the blade by keeping the kerf open.
7. In sawing old or used lumber, first check for nails or similar objects which could damage the blade.

Portable Jigsaw

A *portable jigsaw,* often called a *saber saw,* has many uses. It can be used to cut metal, plastic, and wood. Among the many operations which can be performed are straight cuts, freehand cuts, various types of rough and smooth cuts, and angular cuts. A cut unique to the portable jigsaw is the pocket cut. As shown in Fig. 23-31, the pocket cut is similar to the pierced work performed with a common jigsaw; however, the portable jigsaw can cut its own starting hole.

Most jigsaws can be used to saw stock thicknesses upward to 2¾ inches, depending on the type of saw and the blade.

Fig. 23-31. A portable jigsaw cuts its own starting hole for a pocket cut.

Greater thicknesses can be sawed with industrial jigsaws (Fig. 23-32). The size is usually indicated by the maximum cut of the saw and its "strokes-per-minute." The fixed-speed saws usually produce between 3000 and 4000 rpm, while variable-speed saws usually range between about 1000 and 3000 rpm.

The principal parts of a portable jigsaw are shown in Fig. 23-33.

1. *Handle.* The jigsaw is held and guided by its handle. To aid in guiding the

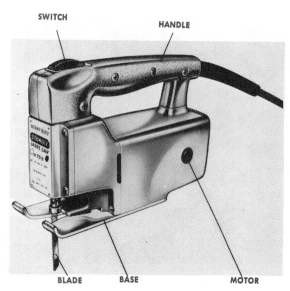

Fig. 23-33. Principal parts of a portable jigsaw. (Courtesy The Stanley Works)

cut, the free hand is often placed on the flat side of the saw.

2. *Switch.* Located near the front of the handle, a push-type switch turns the saw on and off.

3. *Base.* The base supports and/or guides the other parts while sawing. Depending on the saw, the base can be either adjustable or rigid. The adjustable bases can be tilted 45° to the left or 30° to the right for the angular kerfs (Fig. 23-34). Saws with

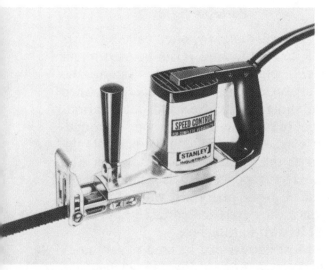

Fig. 23-32. An industrial-type portable jigsaw (Courtesy The Stanley Works)

Fig. 23-34. Tilt the adjustable base for an angular cut.

rigid bases cannot be adjusted; they are manufactured only for perpendicular cuts.

4. *Motor.* The motor is enclosed in a metal case designed as a part of the saw. The smaller saws without a handle are held by the case of the motor.

Blades

Most portable jigsaw blades are 3 or 4 inches in length with 6 to 14 teeth per inch (Fig. 23-35). The longer blades are used for the deeper cuts, while the blades with more teeth (fine teeth) are used for the smoother cuts. However, the longer blades do not necessarily have the coarser teeth. Depending on the fineness of the blade, a 4-inch blade might have more teeth per inch than a 3-inch blade.

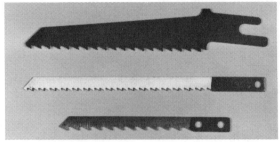

Fig. 23-35. Portable jigsaw blades are 3 or 4 inches in length with a 6 to 14 teeth per inch.

Many blades are designed specially for particular operations. Therefore, the manufacturer's recommendations should be noted before selecting a blade. If these recommendations are not available, the following principles can be used for a general guide:

1. Rough cuts usually require a 4-inch blade with 6 to 10 teeth per inch.
2. Most finish (or smooth) cuts are made with either a 3-inch or a 4-inch blade with 10 or more teeth per inch.
3. Special cuts, such as starting the holes for pocket cuts, are made by using shorter blades with about 10 teeth per inch.

Operating Hints

1. In sawing veneer or other thin material, a thicker board can be placed beneath the thin material to aid in supporting the weight of the saw (Fig. 23-36).

Fig. 23-36. To saw thin stock, support the stock and the weight of the saw with a thicker piece.

2. Portable saws with flat sides often can be clamped upside down in a vise for sawing small shapes (Fig. 23-37). The vise is tightened only sufficiently to hold the saw. Avoid excessive clamping pressure which can damage the metal case of the saw.

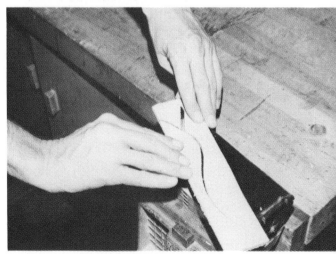

Fig. 23-37. The portable jigsaws can be mounted upside down for freehand sawing.

3. Save the broken saw blades. Frequently, they can be used in making shallow cuts.

4. If a ripping guide cannot be used, clamp a board with a true edge onto the stock. The base of the saw then can be guided along the true edge (Fig. 23-38).

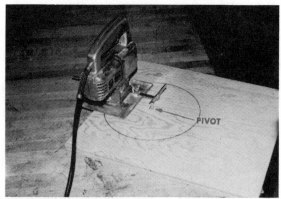

Fig. 23-39. A pivot on the saw guide can be used to cut circular holes and patterns.

Fig. 23-38. Straight cuts can be made with a straightedge for a guide.

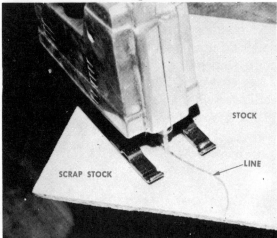

Fig. 23-40. In sawing freehand, the kerf should be made on the waste side of the mark.

5. The angle of the blade can be determined accurately by making a trial cut, then checking the cut with a sliding T bevel or square.

6. In sawing a series of curves, move the saw forward as the blade follows the curves.

7. Guide the saw with a pivot of some type in cutting circular holes and patterns (Fig. 23-39).

8. When sawing freehand, make the kerf on the waste side of the mark (Fig. 23-40).

General Safety Rules

1. Keep the base firmly against the stock being sawed. Bases which are held loosely can vibrate, breaking the blades.

2. When necessary to remove the saw from a kerf, turn off the switch while holding the saw stationary. Raise the jigsaw from the kerf only after the blade has stopped moving.

3. Do not begin any cut until the blade reaches its maximum strokes-per-minute speed.

4. Make all adjustments before turning on the power.

5. While supporting the waste areas with the fingers, make sure they will be clear of the kerf, especially when they are hidden from view.

6. Keep the power cord clear of the blade.

7. Avoid binding the blade by jerking the saw or permitting the kerf to close.

8. Disconnect the power cord from the power source before changing a blade.

Using a Portable Jigsaw

Regardless of the cut, the procedure for sawing with a portable jigsaw is about the same. Some exceptions are noted in the following suggested procedure:

1. Select the blade.
2. Mark the stock for freehand sawing or adjust the guide. When ripping to widths, the difference between the blade and the inside edge of the guide is equal to the sawed width (Fig. 23-41).

Fig. 23-42. Incline the base for beginning a pocket cut.

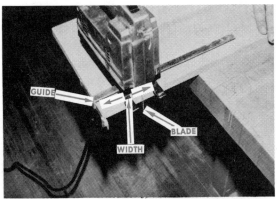

Fig. 23-41. The width of cut is equal to the difference between the blade and the inside edge of the guide.

3. Clamp the stock. When clamping the stock, it must be clamped in a manner which provides ample support; make sure the blade does not accidentally cut into the supporting device.
4. Check for clearance between the saw and any clamps which might hinder the movement of the saw.
5. Place the base on the stock, but with the blade free of the stock. Ordinarily, the base should rest flat on the stock, except when it is inclined for a pocket cut (Fig. 23-42).
6. Turn on the power and begin the cut.
7. After the cut is completed, turn off the power. Do not raise the saw from the stock until the blade has stopped moving.

Portable Belt Sanders

A *portable belt sander* is used primarily to sand flat surfaces. Its sanding ability results from an abrasive loop or belt turning on two wheels (Fig. 23-43).

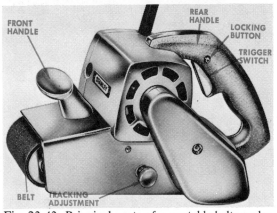

Fig. 23-43. Principal parts of a portable belt sander with open side (top) and closed side (bottom). (Courtesy The Stanley Works)

The abrasive belt is turned by a drive wheel, which is connected by a gear-tooth belt to the motor. The tension is supplied by a second wheel known as an *idler* wheel. The tracking adjustment located on the closed side of the sander prevents the abrasive belt from slipping off either wheel. Since a portable belt sander pulls itself, a trigger switch is mounted in the rear handle for a safety precaution. This switch, however, can be locked "on" by depressing the locking button, while holding the switch back. Locking the switch is necessary when the sander is turned upside down and used for a stationary sander (Fig. 23-44).

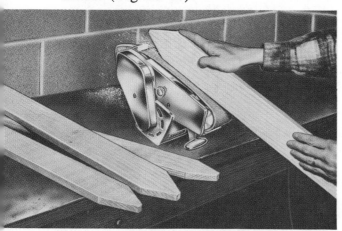

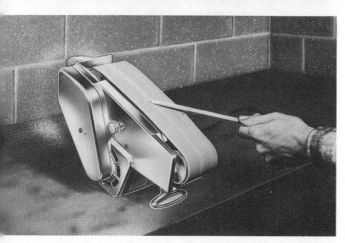

Fig. 23-44. The belt sander can be turned upside down and used in the stationary position for sanding edges (top) and sanding points (bottom). (Courtesy The Stanley Works)

The size of the sander is indicated by the size of the belt. For example, a 3 × 21 belt sander requires an abrasive belt 3 inches wide by 21 inches long. The common sizes are 3 × 21, 3 × 24, and 4 × 24.

Changing an Abrasive Belt

Although the minor details can vary among the different sanders, about the same procedure is used to change the abrasive belt on any portable belt sander. The steps listed below are suggested for a guide.

1. Select an abrasive belt with the desired grit and proper size. If the size is not known, compare the belts until the correct size is found. Another method is trial and error, with the sander turned on. On a proper-size belt, the width is slightly less than the width of either wheel, and the tension should be sufficient when pressure is applied to the idler wheel.
2. Lay the sander on the table with the open side upward. The power cord should be disconnected.
3. Release the tension lever and slide the belt upward until free from the wheels.
4. Clean the wheels and platen, if needed.
5. Slide the new abrasive belt onto both wheels until the edges of the belt are

Fig. 23-45. Placing a new belt onto the wheels of a belt sander.

even with the outer ends of each wheel (Fig. 23-45). An arrow located inside the belt must point in the direction that the drive wheel turns.

6. Apply pressure to the belt, using the tension lever.

7. Adjust the tracking adjustment knob until the belt runs evenly on the two wheels. As shown in Fig. 23-46, this adjustment should be made while the sander is tilted upside down. Also, the drive wheel must be turning during the adjustment.

Fig. 23-46. Turn the sander upside down for tracking a belt.

Woodworking Hints

1. When starting, hold the sander above the stock and engage the switch. Lower the sander only when the belt is turning at full speed.

2. Use a forward motion parallel to the work surface when lowering the sander. If lowered at an angle, the surface will be sanded unevenly (Fig. 23-47).

3. Continually move the sander parallel with the grain. The surface will be dished-out, if the sander is stopped briefly (Fig. 23-48).

4. Do not apply downward pressure while sanding. Since the weight of the sander is adequate, additional pressure serves no purpose and can cause the motor to overheat or result in uneven sanding. Only the front and rear

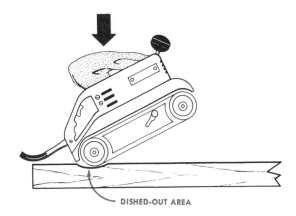

DISHED-OUT AREA

Fig. 23-47. Lowering a belt sander at an angle produces an uneven cut.

DISHED-OUT AREA RESULTS WHEN SANDER IS STOPPED BRIEFLY.

Fig. 23-48. Keep the belt sander moving to produce an evenly sanded surface.

handles are used either to guide or to lift the sander.

5. Avoid "tipping" the sander at the ends and edges of the stock (Fig. 23-49). This practice results in rounded corners and/or torn abrasive belts.

6. After a surface is sanded satisfactorily, lift the sander "straight up." The trigger switch can be released when the belt has cleared the sanded surface. Turning off a sander while its belt is touching the surface can result in an uneven surface.

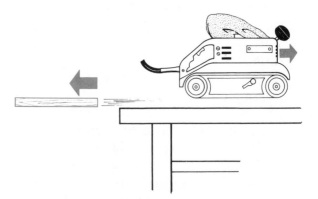

Fig. 23-50. Improperly secured stock can be thrown backward by the belt sander.

Fig. 23-49. Rounded corners and/or torn belts result from sanding too close to the edges and ends.

General Safety Rules

1. Always check the locking button and the trigger switch before plugging the power cord into an electrical outlet.
2. Disconnect the sander from the electrical outlet before replacing the belts.
3. Never lay down a sander until its belt has stopped moving. A sander should be laid on its side when it is stopped for short periods. Also, it is better practice to place a belt sander on the floor when it is temporarily not in use. A sander resting on a table can be triggered accidentally and run off the table—perhaps being damaged by the fall.
4. Hold the power cord in a manner that does not interfere with the sanding operation.
5. If the sander has a dust bag, periodically empty the contents.
6. Smaller stock must be held stationary while being sanded. A bench stop, clamp, or stopblock can be used. Unsecured stock can be grasped by the belt and thrown backward (Fig. 23-50).
7. Immediately replace a torn or badly worn belt.

8. Avoid overheating the motor; this can result from excessive pressure or from sanding for lengthy periods without stopping.

Using the Portable Belt Sander

1. Select the belt needed for the operation. If the belt has been used previously, check its condition. Replace as needed.
2. Secure the stock to hold it stationary while being sanded.
3. Place the sander above the stock and squeeze the trigger switch. Lower the sander until contact is made with the belt.
4. Using the handles to guide the sander, move it back and forth with the grain (Fig. 23-51). At the same time, grad-

Fig. 23-51. Sanding with a portable belt sander.

ually work the sander across the surface.

5. Continue until the sanding is satisfactory, but never permit the sander to sand one area more than another.
6. When finished, lift upward on the sander. Do not release the trigger until clear of the surface.
7. If the surface is not smooth, change to a finer abrasive belt and repeat the preceding steps.

Finishing Sanders

Finishing sanders are used for fine sanding. This type of sander is often called an *orbital, oscillating,* or *vibrating* sander. These terms actually refer to the motion of the abrasive pad. In an orbital sander, the motion is circular; whereas, in the oscillating and vibrating sanders, the sanding motion is "back and forth." Another popular sanding motion is the rotary motion, which is typical of the portable disk sander (Fig. 23-52).

The size of a finishing sander depends on the size of the abrasive sheet used. The common sizes are 3⅔ inches × 9 inches and 4½ inches × 9 inches. Although these sheets are usually precut to size, the regular abrasive sheets can be used when cut into thirds and halves.

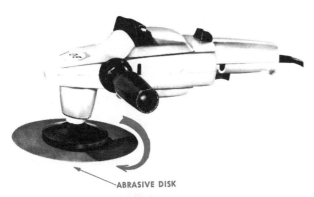

Fig. 23-52. Rotary sanding is performed with a disk sander. (Courtesy The Black & Decker Mfg. Co.)

Types of Sanders

Other than the size and the motion of the abrasive pad, most sanders are similar in construction. In comparing the two sanders in Fig. 23-53, the main differences are the switches and the ways the abrasive sheets are held. Either an "on-off" switch (see Fig. 23-53A) or a trigger switch (see Fig. 23-53B) can be used to

(A) Diagram of parts. (Courtesy The Stanley Works)

(B) Sander with trigger switch. (Courtesy The Black & Decker Mfg. Co.)

Fig. 23-53. Typical finishing sanders.

control the motor. The abrasive sheets are secured to the finishing sander with pressure clamps in Fig. 23-53A and with friction clamps in Fig. 23-53B. To use a pressure-clamp sander, move the two clamp levers until the pressure on the front and rear clamps is released. Then, the abrasive sheet is aligned with the pad of the sander, and each end of the sheet is tucked under an open clamp. Finally, the clamps are closed by returning the levers to their normal positions. In using the friction-clamp sander, feed each end of the abrasive sheet underneath a clamp while turning with a screwdriver.

Sanding with a Finishing Sander

1. Attach an abrasive sheet with the proper grit to the sander. The electrical cord should be disconnected for changing abrasive sheets and for making adjustments.
2. If necessary, clamp the stock.
3. Raise the sander above the stock and turn on the switch.
4. Gradually lower the sander until contact is made with the stock. At the same time, keep the pad parallel with the stock.
5. Sand the surface until it is finished or until another sheet is needed. While sanding, guide the sander with its handle, applying no pressure (Fig. 23-54).

Fig. 23-54. Sanding with a finishing sander.

6. Turn off the power only after lifting the sander from the stock.

Questions

1. What is the chief advantage of the portable electric tools over the stationary machines?
2. How is the depth of cut adjusted on a router?
3. List the parts of the router bit. What is the purpose of each part?
4. Describe the different methods of guiding a router.
5. What can cause a router bit to overheat?
6. How can the router be changed to a power plane?
7. Why is more pressure needed on the front shoe of the power plane when beginning the cut?
8. List the different cuts that can be made with a portable circular saw.
9. Explain several ways of guiding a portable circular saw.
10. Why is the better face of a piece of stock placed downward for sawing with a portable circular saw?
11. What should be done when a portable circular saw blade loses speed while sawing?
12. List four types of blades used with a portable circular saw. For what cuts is each type of blade used?
13. Why can the pocket cuts be made easily with a portable jigsaw?
14. What is meant by the letters "rpm" and "spm?"
15. How is the portable jigsaw adjusted for angular kerfs?
16. Discuss several methods of guiding a portable jigsaw.
17. Compare the differences in abrasives used with portable belt sanders and and finishing sanders.

18. Explain the procedure used in changing the belts on a belt sander.
19. How is an abrasive sheet tightened on a finishing sander?
20. How is the size indicated for each of the following tools:

a. Portable router.
b. Power plane.
c. Portable circular saw
d. Portable jigsaw.
e. Portable belt sander.
f. Finishing sander.

Unit 24 – Jointer

The cutting action of a jointer is similar to that of a planer. Jointers are used to plane the edges, ends, and faces of stock. Other special cuts, including bevels and rabbets, also can be performed on the jointer. The principal parts of a jointer are shown in Fig. 24-1.

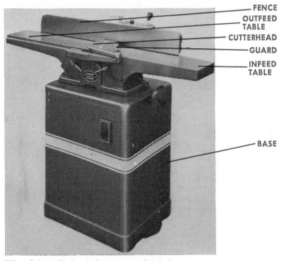

Fig. 24-1. Principle parts of a jointer.

1. *Infeed table.* The infeed table is located in front of the cutterhead, and it serves two purposes. It supports the stock being fed across the cutterhead and determines the depth of cut. The depth of cut is adjusted by the handwheel located on the front of the base.
2. *Outfeed table.* Located behind the cutterhead, the outfeed table supports the stock that has been planed. Although it serves only this purpose, the height of the outfeed table should be adjusted until it is level with the cutting circle of the cutterhead. If the outfeed table is not level with the cutterhead, the cut cannot be true.
3. *Cutterhead.* The cutterhead is a round cylinder, located underneath and between the infeed and outfeed tables. Most cutterheads are 3 inches in diameter and include three knives (Fig. 24-2). A cutterhead revolves between 3400 rpm and 5000 rpm to produce a series of short hollow cuts.

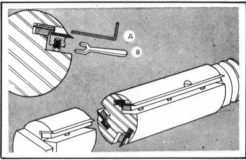

Fig. 24-2. Cutterhead of the jointer. Knife heighth is adjusted with the Allen wrench (A). The pressure which holds the knife in the cutterhead is adjusted with the wrench (B). (Courtesy Powermatic, Houdaille Industries, Inc.)

4. *Guard.* The guard on a jointer can be one of several types (Fig. 24-3). Most of the guards are designed to

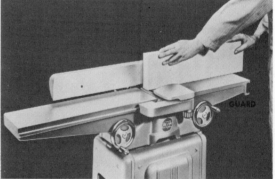

Fig. 24-3. Jointer guard. (Courtesy Power Tool Division, Rockwell Manufacturing Company)

224

protect the operator from the cutterhead, regardless of the width of the cut being made. The swinging guard keeps the cutterhead covered while planing, either by the stock or by the guard.

5. *Fence.* The fence on a jointer is similar to the rip fence on a circular saw. It guides the stock being planed. The normal position of the fence is 90° to the infeed or outfeed table. It also can be adjusted from 45° left to 45° right. This adjustment makes it possible to cut chamfers and bevels. The fence also can be adjusted across the width of the cutterhead. Its position depends on the width of the stock being jointed. A fence should be adjusted until the cutterhead exposure is about ½ inch wider than the width of the stock being jointed.

6. *Base.* The base supports the jointer. The smaller jointers which do not require a base can be placed on the top of a workbench. The larger jointers, however, require a base.

The common jointers range in size from 4 inches through 16 inches. The size is indicated by the maximum width of cut the jointer is capable of making, which depends on the length of the knives located in the cutterhead. For example, an 8-inch jointer is capable of cutting a maximum width of 8 inches. The length and width of the infeed and outfeed tables also depend on the blade size. Both the tables are slightly wider than the length of the blade, and the table lengths also increase with the length of the blade.

Adjustments

A jointer can produce smooth cuts, if it is adjusted and used properly. When not operated correctly, the cuts are rough and the operations can be hazardous. There-fore, it is extremely important that a jointer is always adjusted and used correctly. Like other machines, a jointer should not be adjusted until its power is off and the cutterhead has stopped turning.

Important adjustments include the:

1. Height of the knives in the cutterhead.
2. Height of the infeed table.
3. Height of the outfeed table.
4. Angle of the fence with either table.

Adjusting the Knives in a Cutterhead

Three knives are found on most cutterheads. Each of these knives should project the same distance for an even cut to be made. To check the height of a blade, place a straightedge on the outfeed table (Fig. 24-4). Check each knife individually by revolving the cutterhead by hand. If a knife is projecting to the correct height, it should barely touch the straightedge, without causing the straightedge to move. The straightedge should barely touch the knife while lying flat on the table. If a "crack" of light can be seen under the straightedge or if either the knife or the straightedge moves, the blade is too high and must be lowered. This

Fig. 24-4. Use a straightedge to check knife height.

procedure is begun by loosening the screws holding the knife. Then the knife can be lowered by tapping lightly with a wood block and mallet. Always check the height a second time after making this adjustment.

The knives also can be used for cutting rabbets. In this instance, make sure the end of each knife projects an identical distance from the side of the cutterhead. This projection can be checked by measuring the distance from the cutterhead, checking each knife individually.

Adjusting the Infeed Table

The vertical clearance between the infeed table and the cutting circle of a cutterhead determines the depth of cut (Fig. 24-5). This adjustment is made with a handwheel located underneath the infeed table and on the base (Fig. 24-6). Although most jointers can make cuts up to ½ inch, the recommended maximum cut is usually less than ¼ inch. However, this depth also depends on the width being planed. When cutting the greater widths, it is recommended practice to reduce the depth of cut. The stock can be fed easier, and the jointer can produce a smoother cut.

The infeed table should never be set higher than the cutterhead. If the table is higher than the cutterhead, the stock is not planed, since its surface is above the cutting circle of the cutterhead (Fig. 24-7).

Adjusting the Outfeed Table

The height of an outfeed table is extremely important. It is adjusted by a handwheel located at the back or side of the base near the outfeed table. The outfeed table should be adjusted until its height is equal to the cutting circle of the cutterhead. When the outfeed table is too high, a tapered cut results. At the

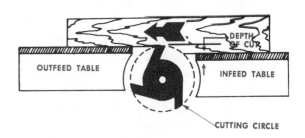

Fig. 24-5. The depth of cut is equal to the vertical clearance between the infeed table and the cutting circle.

Fig. 24-6. Depth of cut is adjusted with a handwheel located near the infeed table.

Fig. 24-7. If the infeed table is higher than the knives of the cutterhead, planing will occur only on the trailing end of the stock.

beginning of the cut, the stock also might jam against the lip of the outfeed table (Fig. 24-8). The opposite effect results

Fig. 24-8. If the outfeed table is set too high, the stock will jam against the lip of the outfeed table. If the stock is lifted onto the outfeed table, a taper results.

Fig. 24-9. Outfeed table is set too low.

Fig. 24-10. The stock is planed deeper near the end. if the outfeed table is set too low.

when the outfeed table is too low (Fig. 24-9); then the stock is higher than the outfeed table when the cut is begun (Fig. 24-10). The stock is cut deeper near the end of the cut. The outfeed table rarely should require adjusting. To adjust an outfeed table properly, however, first lower it. Then turn on the power, and begin planing the edge of a piece of stock. When the stock is cut about halfway, stop the machine, but do not remove the stock. After the cutterhead has stopped turning, raise the outfeed table until the planed edge is supported by the outfeed table; then make a trial cut. Check for jamming at the beginning of the cut or for a cut which is too deep at the end of the cut. If either condition is present, the outfeed table should be adjusted again.

Adjusting the Fence

The fence is adjusted in several ways. For ordinary planing, it is located at a 90° angle to the infeed and outfeed tables. This squareness can be checked with a hand square (Fig. 24-11). A sliding T bevel can be used to set the desired angles between the fence and the tables. The horizontal location of the fence depends on the width of the stock being planed. Adjust the fence until no more than ½ inch of the blade is exposed when planing.

Fig. 24-11. Checking the squareness of the fence.

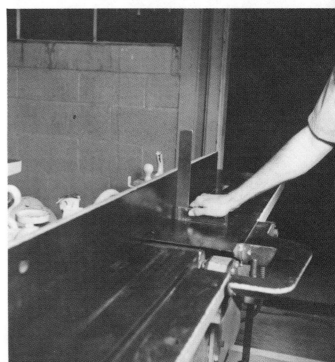

Jointing Hints

1. Joint with the direction of the grain. If the direction cannot be determined readily, make a trial cut. Planing against the grain causes small chips (or pulls the wood fibers outward) on the planed surface.
2. Protect the jointer knives from unnecessary damage. Check the stock for nails and other metal pieces before planing. Dry glue also can damage a blade, causing uneven cuts.
3. Plane a piece of warped stock with the cupped side down (Fig. 24-12). Planing with the warped side up can cause the stock to rock, producing uneven cuts.

Fig. 24-12. Plane warped stock with the cupped side down.

4. If possible, stock longer than the infeed table should be cut to smaller lengths before planing. This prevents unnecessary tapers and excessive planing.
5. When making a final cut, set the infeed table for a fine cut (about $\frac{1}{32}$ inch or $\frac{1}{16}$ inch), and feed the stock slowly. Use the same procedure for removing the saw marks on the edges of a piece of stock.

6. Two things might be wrong when the planed surface shows a series of small ridges. Either the stock is being fed too fast or the depth of cut is too deep. Dull jointer knives also can result in poor cuts.
7. Examine a piece of rough stock for uneven features before edge planing. If it is too irregular, cut to approximate evenness with a band saw before planing (Fig. 24-13).

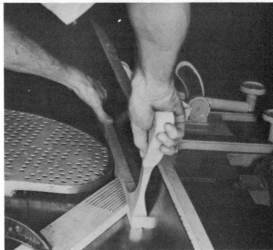

Fig. 24-13. Use a featherboard to hold thin and narrow stock against the jointer fence.

8. Use a featherboard to hold thin and narrow stock against the fence (Fig. 24-14).
9. When edge planing stock with less than $\frac{1}{8}$-inch thickness, clamp the stock between two pieces of thicker stock; then joint the three pieces at the same time (Fig. 25-15).
10. Pieces of stock requiring similar cuts should be planed simultaneously. For example, planing a taper on several boards might require a series of cuts on each board. Make the first cut on each of the boards; then make the second cut, etc.
11. Do not attempt to plane a piece of stock to an even thickness, using only the jointer. Plane one face with

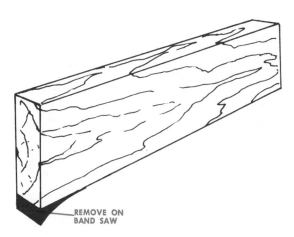

Fig. 24-14. Remove highly irregular features on the band saw before edge planing.

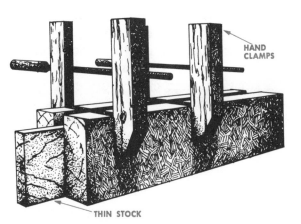

Fig. 24-15. "Sandwich" extremely thin stock between two thicker pieces for edge planing; then joint the three pieces. Be sure the clamps do not interfere with the fence.

the jointer; then finish the operation on a planer. If two faces are planed on a jointer, they usually remain nonparallel (Fig. 24-16).

12. Do not attempt to plane a piece of stock to an even width, using only the jointer. Plane one edge; then cut the stock to the desired width with a circular saw. After sawing, the saw marks can be removed with a jointer to produce the finished width.

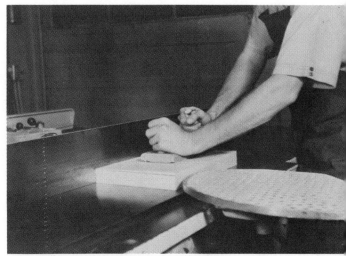

Fig. 24-16. Do not attempt to achieve uniform thickness by planing both faces on a jointer.

General Safety Rules

1. The guard should never be removed from a jointer, except for making rabbet cuts or for changing the knives in the cutterhead.
2. Adjust a jointer or any of its parts only when the cutterhead is not turning.
3. Adjust the fence for the width of the stock to be planed. The fence should be set with the exposed knives only slightly longer than the width of the stock (Fig. 24-17).

Fig. 24-17. Adjust the fence position until the exposed knives extend slightly beyond the width of the stock.

4. After turning on the power, wait until the cutterhead is turning full speed before planing the stock.

5. Maintain adequate contact between the stock and the infeed or outfeed table. Avoid planing stock which is shorter than 12 inches.

6. Use a push block in planing the faces of a piece of stock. Do not pass the hands over the cutterhead during this operation.

7. Use a push stick when edge planing stock more than 1 inch lower than the top of the fence (Fig. 24-18).

Fig. 24-19. Use a featherboard to hold down thin stock.

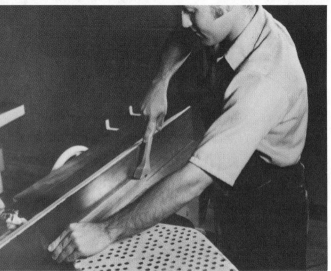

Fig. 24-18. Use a push stick in edge planing narrow widths of stock.

8. A featherboard should be used to hold stock less than 1 inch in width against the fence while edge jointing (see Fig. 24-14).

9. A featherboard should be used to hold a piece of stock thinner than ½ inch against the infeed and outfeed tables while face jointing (Fig. 24-19).

10. The maximum cut normally should not exceed ⅛ inch, depending on the width of the cut.

11. Keep the stock firmly against the table and the fence while jointing. Use a featherboard and/or special holding devices when necessary.

12. Never stand behind the infeed table. This can be dangerous, since the stock or large chips can be thrown backward.

13. Pay careful attention to the operation being performed. Do not glance away or talk to others while jointing.

14. Obtain the approval of the instructor before making special cuts on a jointer.

Face Jointing

1. Adjust the infeed table to the proper depth. Use a straightedge to determine the depth when it cannot be read from a scale located on the side of the base of the jointer (Fig. 24-20).

2. Move the fence across the tables until the exposed knives are only slightly longer than the width to be planed.

3. Check the fence for a 90° angle with both tables.

Fig. 24-20. Use a straightedge to determine the depth of cut for face jointing.

Fig. 24-21. Use a push block for face jointing. Push downward with the left hand and push forward with the right hand.

4. Check the guard to make sure it is working properly. Make sure the guard moves freely back and forth by pulling it away from the fence and then releasing it. The guard should return quickly to the fence.

5. After determining the grain pattern and the side to be planed, switch on the power; then wait until the cutterhead is turning full speed to begin planing.

6. With the flatter face down on the infeed table, position the push block on the end of the stock. Place the left hand toward the front of the stock, grasping the push block with the right hand. Assume a comfortable working position with the left foot in front of the right foot, and pointing forward.

7. Begin the cut while pressing the stock firmly against both the table and the fence. The left hand should exert only downward pressure while pushing the push block with the right hand (Fig. 24-21).

8. After the stock is supported firmly by the outfeed table, move the left hand to that portion of the stock on the outfeed table. Avoid applying downward pressure with the left hand while the hand is directly above the cutterhead.

9. Complete the cut. Do not apply downward pressure with the push block near the end of the cut. This practice can cause the jointer to cut an increased depth. This is dangerous and can cause the stock to be thrown backward.

10. Check the surface of the stock. If it is smooth and flat, proceed to the next operation. If not, plane the surface until it is smooth.

Planing Edge Grain

1. Make needed adjustments similar to those in face jointing. Remember to move the fence to the left and to check for the 90° angle.

2. Locate the stock on the infeed table. Press the stock against the fence with the left hand, placing the right hand toward the back end (Fig. 24-22). Remember to use the push stick when the stock is more than 1 inch lower than the top of the fence.

3. Begin the cut by pushing the stock with the right hand. Since some stock might have curved edges, joint the cupped or concave edge first. If the edges are extremely concave, the cupped ends sometimes are sawed flat with the band saw before edge planing (see Fig. 24-14).

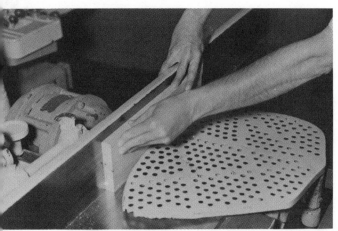

Fig. 24-22. Planing edge grain.

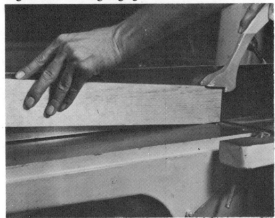

Fig. 24-23. Application of downward pressure near the end of the cut causes a deeper cut. Avoid this dangerous practice.

4. Complete the cut. Near the end of the cut, do not press downward, except on the portion of stock located on the outfeed table. When end pressure is used, the jointer makes an increased cut near the end (Fig. 24-23). This practice is extremely dangerous, and should be avoided.

5. Check the edge for smoothness and flatness. If satisfactory, proceed to the next operation. If not satisfactory, repeat until the edge is smooth and flat.

End Planing

1. Make adjustments similar to those used in edge planing. However, keep the depth of cut less than ⅛ inch. A cut between ¹⁄₃₂ inch and ¹⁄₁₆ inch is usually satisfactory.

2. Begin the cut similar to the procedure in edge jointing (Fig. 24-24).

3. Stop the cut about ½ to 1 inch from the end. Carefully pivot the board upward on its rear portion until clear of the cutterhead (Fig. 24-25). The ½- to 1-inch portion not jointed is then planed by hand. If the first cut is continued across the end, the end portion is likely to split along the edge.

Fig. 24-24. Planing end grain.

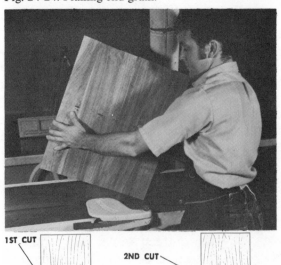

Fig. 24-25. Stop the feed on end grain about ½ inch from the edge of the stock. Pivot the stock upward until clear of the cutterhead.

4. Another procedure is to plane partway across the end, pivot the stock upward, and then feed the stock from the opposite direction. Near the end of the second cut, exert downward pressure only on the portion of the stock supported by the outfeed table.

5. Check the stock. If not satisfactory, repeat the previous step. If satisfactory, proceed to the next operation.

Planing Rabbets

1. Cut the stock until it is flat and square.
2. Outline the rabbet on the end of the stock.
3. Remove the guard.
4. Measure the width of the rabbet from the end of the knife near the rabbeting arm. Move the fence to this point; lock it perpendicular to the tables.
5. Lower the infeed table for the depth of cut. More than one cut is necessary when the depth of the rabbet is more than ⅜ inch.
6. Check the adjustments. Either compare the settings with the rabbet outlined on the stock or make a trial cut.

Fig. 24-26. Planing a rabbet.

7. Plane the rabbet (Fig. 24-26).
8. Return the jointer to its normal settings after completing the operation. Do not forget to replace the guard as soon as possible.

Questions

1. Describe the parts of the jointer.
2. What is the maximum width that can be planed with a 6-inch jointer?
3. When should a push stick and a push block be used? Why?
4. Describe the danger in planing stock when the outfeed table is too low. When the outfeed table is too high.
5. How should the depth of cut be adjusted on a jointer? What is the recommended maximum cut?
6. What causes a planed surface to be chipped?
7. List the general safety rules for a jointer.
8. Why should a person avoid standing directly behind the infeed table.
9. Where should the fence be located when face planing a 5-inch width on a 12-inch jointer? Why?
10. Why should downward pressure on the stock be reduced near the end of the cut?
11. Explain why only the jointer cannot be used to plane uniform thicknesses. Is this also true for uniform widths and lengths?
12. Why are the faces and ends of stock planed differently on a jointer?
13. List the procedure for planing the saw marks on the edge of the stock.
14. How are the width and depth cuts adjusted for planing a rabbet?
15. Why should the guard be removed before planing a rabbet? When should it be replaced?

Unit 25 – Planer

A planer is different from the other woodworking machines in several ways. Most of the machines can be used to perform various operations, but the planer is used for only one operation. It is used only to plane stock to its finished thickness. Another difference is that the stock is fed by rollers, rather than by the operator. Also, the cutting action is totally enclosed. For these reasons, the planer is one of the "safer" machines in a woodshop.

Planers vary in size from 12 inches to 24 inches. The industrial planers are often larger. The planer size depends on the largest width of stock that can be planed on the machine. A 12-inch planer, for example, can plane stock upward to 12 inches in width. If the size of the planer is unknown, the width of its table can be measured to determine its size (Fig. 25-1). Another factor limiting a planer is the maximum thickness that can be planed, which can range from 5 inches to 8 inches. The principal parts of a planer are shown in Fig. 25-2. Those parts normally hidden from view are shown in the diagram in Fig. 25-3.

1. *Table.* The table supports the stock being planed. The depth of cut is actually determined by raising or lowering the table, rather than the blades.
2. *Thickness handwheel.* Located either on the side or on the front of the planer, this handwheel is used to adjust the vertical height of the table.
3. *Thickness gauge.* The thickness gauge indicates the approximate thickness of a board after it is planed at that setting.

Fig. 25-1. The size of a planer is indicated by the width of its table.

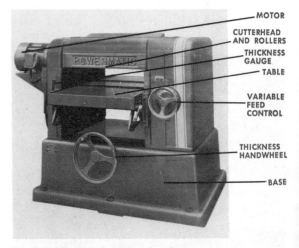

Fig. 25-2. Principle parts of a planer.

4. *Variable-feed control.* Either a handwheel or a lever can be used to adjust the power feed, which usually ranges from 15 to 50 feet per minute.

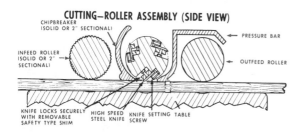

CUTTING–ROLLER ASSEMBLY (SIDE VIEW)

CHIPBREAKER (SOLID OR 2" SECTIONAL)

PRESSURE BAR

INFEED ROLLER (SOLID OR 2" SECTIONAL)

OUTFEED ROLLER

KNIFE LOCKS SECURELY WITH REMOVABLE SAFETY TYPE SHIM   HIGH SPEED STEEL KNIFE   KNIFE SETTING TABLE SCREW

Fig. 25-3. Side view of cutting and roller assembly. (Courtesy Powermatic, Houdaille Industries, Inc.)

The power should be turned on for making this adjustment. The larger planers can be adjusted up to 100 feet per minute, but the smaller planers often do not have this control. For example, a 12-inch planer usually is manufactured for a constant power feed of 15 feet per minute.

5. *Cutterhead.* The cutterhead is a 3- or 4-inch steel cylinder suspended above the table. Depending on the size of the planer, it might include three or four knives, turning at speeds ranging from 3600 to 5500 rpm.

6. *Rollers.* A planer is provided with both infeed and outfeed rollers. Corrugated edges on the infeed rollers grip the rough stock, pulling it into the cutterhead. The outfeed rollers pull the stock through the planer after it has been planed. A smooth finish on the outfeed rollers protects the planed surface.

7. *Pressure bar.* The pressure bar is located as closely as possible to and behind the cutterhead. This bar presses the stock firmly against the table, and prevents its vibrating while it is being planed.

8. *Chip breaker.* Located in front of the cutterhead, a chip breaker serves two purposes. It shields the infeed rollers from flying chips and causes the shavings to be short in length. Without the chip breaker, the shavings would peel off in long lengths, causing splits on the planed surface.

Operation

For the most part, operating a planer is relatively simple. The thickness is set, the power is switched on, the feed is adjusted, and the stock is planed. However, a check of other details can improve the quality and efficiency of the operation. Some of these are listed below:

1. Protect the knives. Check the stock for pieces of metal or other abrasive objects before planing.
2. Sharpen the knives as needed, and replace them when worn. This is usually a job for the instructor; check with him first.
3. Remove the chips and small pieces of stock from the table before turning on the planer. When the planer is equipped with an exhaust system, always turn it on before planing.
4. Keep the table top free from gum or other substances which can affect the feed of the stock. Also, protect the table top from rust and keep the rollers clean for the same reason.

Although the planer requires relatively few adjustments, they are sometimes necessary. The procedure for some adjustments depends on the planer. For this reason, the student should first check with the instructor. Irregular cuts resulting from an improperly adjusted planer are shown in Fig. 25-4. The dents in Fig. 25-4A result from too much pressure on the infeed rollers. Dents also can be caused by insufficient depth of cut. Chips occur along the planed surface or at the end of the cut when the stock is planed against the direction of the grain (Fig. 25-4B).

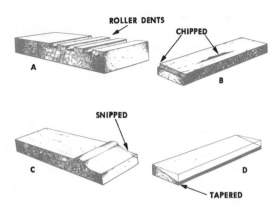

Fig. 25-4. Irregular cuts resulting from an improperly adjusted planer.

Note in Fig. 25-4C that the last portion of the stock is cut deeper. Either the table or the pressure bar is too loose. The stock in Fig. 25-4D is tapered in thickness. Probably, the cutterhead and the table are not parallel; however, a second reason is possible. The knives might be worn unevenly; or they might have been fitted into the cutterhead at an angle.

Operating Hints

1. In planing two or more boards to identical thickness, plane both boards at the same time, if possible. Since their rough thickness usually varies, it might be necessary to plane them separately at first. For example, three boards with thicknesses of 1⅛ inch, 1 inch, and ⅞ inch are to be planed to ¾ inch. Begin with the 1⅛-inch board; plane it until it is approximately equal in thickness to the 1-inch board. Then plane these two boards at the same time until their thickness is approximately equal to the thickness of the remaining board. The three boards then can be planed together to the desired ¾-inch thickness.
2. Measure the finished thickness. Do not rely on the depth gauge of the planer, since it indicates approximate dimensions which might be inaccurate.
3. When necessary to match the thickness of one board with another, plane the board with the greater thickness. Periodically, compare their thickness by placing both boards on a flat surface (Fig. 25-5). This is usually a more reliable practice than comparing the two thicknesses with a square or tape measure.

Fig. 25-5. Comparing the thicknesses of two boards.

4. For boards requiring identical thickness, make the final cut on each board with the same machine setting.
5. Stock less than ¼ inch in thickness can be planed, if it is held by a support block (Fig. 25-6).

Fig. 25-6. A support block is essential for planing stock less than ¼-inch thickness.

6. A piece of stock several inches less than 14 inches in length can be planed, if it is followed by a second piece longer than 14 inches (Fig. 25-7). The second piece, however, must be butted firmly against the trailing end of the first piece. Although a number of pieces can be planed in this manner, the final piece to be planed should be at least 14 inches in length.

7. Stock that is too wide to be planed first on a jointer can be planed only with the planer. Begin the planing operation with a series of light cuts. When nearly flat, turn the stock over; then plane the other side. After the second side is nearly flat, alternate each side until the desired thickness is obtained. Do not attempt this operation with stock that is warped severely or in wind.

8. Periodically, check the planed surfaces for chips and/or mill marks. Chips are often caused by planing against the direction of the grain (Fig. 25-8). These can be eliminated by turning the board around; then feed from the opposite end. Mill marks are a series of parallel ridges extending across the width of the stock. These marks, which are rarely noticed by the unskilled eye, detract greatly from a finished surface (Fig. 25-9). Caused by dull knives, improperly sharpened knives, or poor depth adjustments, mill marks can be removed by sanding and/or scraping. Smoother surfaces are often achieved by reducing the depth of cut and/or the rate of feed.

9. A piece of stock can be edge-planed safely to the desired width when, and only when, the stock does not tend to flip over (Fig. 25-10). This de-

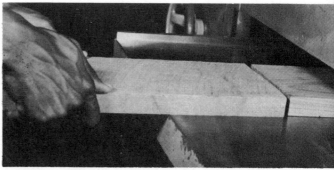

Fig. 25-7. A length of stock less than 14 inches can be planed, if followed by a second piece longer than 14 inches. Firmly butt the longer piece against the end of the shorter stock.

Fig. 25-8. Planing against the grain often causes chips.

Fig. 25-9. Mill marks mar the appearance of a planed surface.

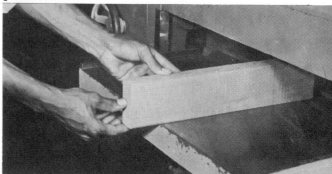

Fig. 25-10. Planing an edge of the stock to width.

pends on both the width and the thickness of the stock. Stock between ¾ inch and 1 inch in thickness can be edge-planed safely when less than 3 inches in width. On the other hand, stock 5 inches or 6 inches in width should be at least 2 inches in thickness to be edge-planed safely.

10. Do not feed stock through the planer at the same place each time. The knives wear evenly only when the stock is fed evenly from left to right, or vice versa. The infeed rollers sometimes have difficulty in grasping the stock. To remedy this problem, raise the trailing portion of the board slightly above the table, until the rollers catch the stock (Fig. 25-11).

Fig. 25-11. Slightly raise the trailing end of the stock, if it is difficult for the infeed roller to grasp the stock.

General Safety Rules

1. Adjust the table height for a cut not more than ¹⁄₁₆ inch, before turning on the power. If the stock tapers, use its thicker portion in determining the table height (Fig. 25-12).
2. Plane only stock which is at least 2 inches longer than the distance between the infeed and outfeed rollers. About 14-inch lengths can be planed on most planers.
3. Maintain adequate contact between the table and the stock. The portion

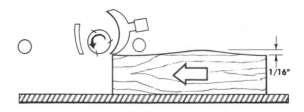

Fig. 25-12. Adjusting the depth of cut. Use the thicker portion of the stock to adjust the table height.

of the stock contacting the table must be planed flat first, using a jointer.

4. Avoid planing stock with a thickness less than ¼ inch, unless a special device is used (see Operating Hints).
5. Stand on the switch side of the planer. Also, do not stand directly in line with the table to observe the cutting action. Chips are sometimes thrown backward from the planer to cause serious injury.
6. Keep the fingers at a safe distance from the rollers. When feeding short pieces, keep the hands above the stock and release the stock as soon as the rollers grasp it (Fig. 25-13). Fingers placed on the lower face can be caught between the stock and the table.
7. If the stock stops feeding, turn off the planer; wait until the cutterhead and the rollers have stopped turning. Then lower the table and remove

Fig. 25-13. In feeding a short piece of stock, place the hands on the top face. Release when the infeed roller grasps the stock.

the stock. Never force a jammed board by beating its end with another board.

8. Boards with different thicknesses should not be planed at the same time. Since the planer should be adjusted for the larger thickness, a board with a smaller thickness might be kicked backward.

9. Always support a piece of long stock while it is being planed. If an auxiliary table (or rollers) is not available, have a second person tail the stock (Fig. 25-14).

Fig. 25-14. Support a piece of long stock while it is being planed.

10. Remove the planed stock from the table as quickly as possible. Guard against mishaps similar to that in Fig. 25-15.

11. Avoid planing stock with large unsound knots or bad cracks. These faults should first be removed with a band saw, if possible.

Fig. 25-15. This mishap is the result of failure to remove the planed stock from the table.

12. Do not wear loose clothing while using a planer.

13. Avoid planing "top-heavy" stock which could become jammed in the planer (Fig. 25-16).

(A). When the tapered trailing end is pressed down, the front end rises and jams.

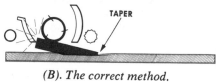

(B). The correct method.

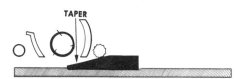

(C). Avoids jamming.

Fig. 25-16. Avoid planing "top-heavy" stock.

Planing to Thickness

1. Using the jointer, plane either face until it is flat and true.

2. Measure the thickness at the thickest portion of the stock; adjust the table height for the desired cut. The depth of cut should be about $\frac{1}{16}$ inch less than the measured thickness.

3. Turn on the power; wait until the cutterhead and the rollers have reached full operating speed. If necessary, adjust the rate of feed.

4. Place the stock flat on the table with its length perpendicular to the cutterhead (Fig. 25-17). The stock should be positioned with the "jointed" side down and with the cut to be made with the direction of the grain.

5. Push the stock forward until it is grasped by the infeed rollers. Immediately release the stock and step toward the switch side of the planer.

Fig. 25-17. Feed the stock perpendicularly to the cutterhead. If the stock begins to feed at an angle and if a quick jerk fails to straighten the feed, stop the planer, remove the stock, and begin to feed the stock again.

6. As the stock clears the outfeed rollers, step toward the rear of the planer and remove the stock from the table.
7. Check the planed area for chips or other faults. Correct as needed.
8. Readjust the depth and plane the stock to the required thickness.

Questions

1. Why is the planer considered one of the "safer" machines in a wood shop?
2. How is the size of a planer determined?
3. The planed surfaces might be chipped. Why? How can this condition be corrected?
4. How is the depth of cut adjusted? What should the thickness gauge read when planing a thickness that varys from 1½ inches to 1⅜ inches?
5. The stock being planed should rest flat with the table. List two conditions which might result if the stock is not flat.
6. Describe several ways of eliminating mill marks from a planed surface.
7. Why is it dangerous to feed pieces of stock of different thickness into a planer at the same time?
8. A surface planer is used chiefly to plane finished thicknesses. Can it also be used to plane finished widths? Fully explain your answer.
9. List the safety rules for a planer.
10. Why should planed stock be removed from the table as quickly as possible?
11. Describe the procedure used in planing short pieces of stock.
12. Explain why a support block is needed in planing stock with a thickness less than ¼ inch.

Unit 26 – Shaper

A shaper is used for cutting molding, shaping decorative edges, and making certain types of joints. Among the common joints which can be cut on the shaper are the rabbets, grooves, dadoes, and special joints, such as the tongue-and-groove joints and the rule joints used for folding table tops. Stock can be machined with a shaper for either straight or curved edges, and it can be fed either freehand or guided. The typical guiding devices include the fences, miter gauges, and jigs. The principal shaper parts are shown in Fig. 26-1.

1. *Table.* The table supports the stock. It includes a groove, a throat opening, and several holes. The miter gauge slides along the groove, and the spindle projects upward through the throat opening. The fence, ring guard, and starting pin can be fastened to the table, using different holes.
2. *Fence.* The two halves of the fence are independently adjustable. However, both halves can be locked together and adjusted at the same time. Another adjustment is the fence opening or clearance between the two halves of the fence. This distance depends on the diameter of the cutter. The distance is increased for the larger cutters and decreased for the smaller cutters.
3. *Spindle.* This part is a vertical shaft connected to the motor by a belt. Either a three-lip cutter slipped over the spindle (Fig. 26-2) or two knives held between collars on the spindle are used to do the cutting. The spindle speed usually varies from 7000 to 10,000 rpm.

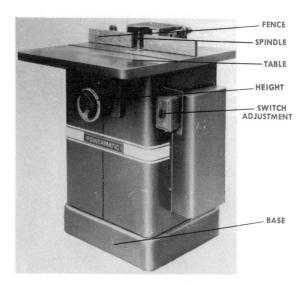

Fig. 26-1. Principal parts of a shaper.

4. *Height adjustment.* The height of the spindle above the table is controlled by turning a handwheel located under the table.
5. *Base.* The base supports the table and encloses the motor and the other working parts. The smaller shapers usually are built with a frame, rather than a base.

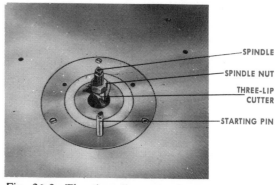

Fig. 26-2. The three-lip cutter is secured on the spindle by the spindle nut. The starting pin is used to guide the initial cuts in freehand shaping. (Courtesy Powermatic, Houdaille Industries, Inc.)

6. *Motor.* A motor provides the power for the spindle, and it can be controlled by a reversing switch. A reversing switch changes the direction of the motor which, in turn, changes the direction of the spindle.

7. *Guards.* Other than the ring guard (Fig. 26-3), a shaper usually is not provided with a separate guard. The table and fence, for the most part, shield as much of the spindle and cutter as possible.

8. *Hold-down devices.* For straight shaping, steel spring clamps hold the stock firmly against the fence and the table (Fig. 26-4). A featherboard can be used to hold the stock against the fence (Fig. 26-5).

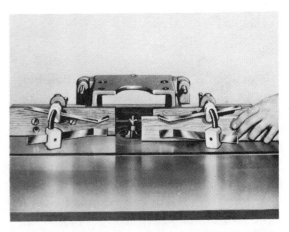

Fig. 26-4. Hold-down guides aid in holding the stock firmly against the fence and the table while feeding freehand.

Fig. 26-5. Use a featherboard to keep the stock firmly against the fence.

STARTING PIN | RING GUARD

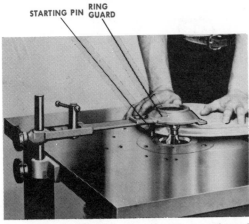

Fig. 26-3. Position the ring guard over the spindle for freehand shaping. Note how the work is steadied against the starting pin.

9. *Starting pin.* This part is a small metal rod mounted into one of several holes located near the throat opening of the table. Serving as a guide in freehand shaping, the starting pin is used to pivot the stock into the cutter. *The starting pin is never used with the fence.*

The size of a shaper is indicated by the size of its spindle and table. On most shapers, several sizes of interchangeable spindles are available. Extensions are often added to the table to increase its size and stability for working long pieces of stock.

Cutters

A cutter is described by its size, cut, and physical shape. Note in Fig. 26-6 that various sizes and shapes of cutters are available. The physical shape of the cutter refers to the way it is made and the way it is fitted onto the spindle. Most of the cutters are either three-lip cutters or individual knives.

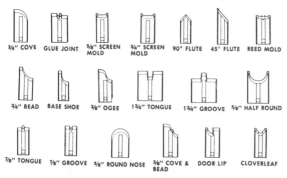

(A) Three-lip cutters. (Courtesy Power Tool Division, Rockwell Manufacturing Company)

¾" COVE GLUE JOINT ⅝" SCREEN MOLD ¾" SCREEN MOLD 90° FLUTE 45° FLUTE REED MOLD

¾" BEAD BASE SHOE ⅜" OGEE 1¾" TONGUE 1¾" GROOVE ⅝" HALF ROUND

⅞" TONGUE ⅞" GROOVE ⅝" ROUND NOSE ⅜" COVE & BEAD DOOR LIP CLOVERLEAF

(B) Individual cutters or knives. (Courtesy Powermatic, Houdaille Industries, Inc.)

Fig. 26-6. Various sizes and shapes of shaper cutters are available.

The three-lip cutters are of solid construction, with a hole for the spindle matching the diameter of the spindle (Fig. 26-7). The cutters can be changed by locking the spindle and removing the spindle nut (see Fig. 26-2). The spindle is locked with a steel pin or locking lever located underneath the table. Some shapers, however, require the spindle to be held with a special wrench. The three-lip cutters are preferable to individual knives, since they can be changed easily. Also, they are safer, since it is impossible for them to become loosened during the shaping operation.

The individual-knife type of cutter is

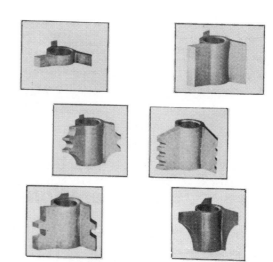

Fig. 26-7. Three-lip shaper cutters.

formed by two flat knives fitted in mating slots between the collars (Fig. 26-8). Changing these knives is a critical procedure, since both knives must be *equal in width* and *project equally in length* from the collars. Knives with uneven widths cannot be tightened sufficiently, and they can be thrown loose when the shaper is turned on. On the other hand, uneven cuts are made when the knives do not project equally from the collars. Since one of the knives does most of the cutting, excessive vibration is produced. Also, this vibration can lead to the knives being thrown from the spindle.

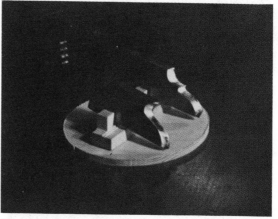

Fig. 26-8. The cutter can be made up of two flat knives.

To change the flat knives, lock the spindle; then the spindle nut and top collar are removed. The new knives should be positioned in the slots of the bottom collar (Fig. 26-9). Next, the top collar and the spindle nut are replaced. Final tightening of the spindle nut is not attempted until the projection of each knife is checked. The check involves positioning the stock to barely contact the cutting lips of one of the knives (Fig. 26-10). This length is then compared to the length of the second knife.

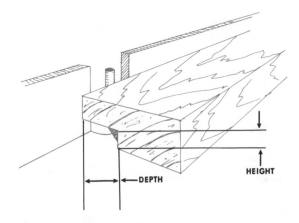

Fig. 26-11. Both height and depth are important factors in a shaper cut.

Fig. 26-9. The flat knives are held between slotted collars.

Fig. 26-10. In checking the projection of the knives, both knives should barely contact the stock.

Adjusting the Cut

A cut made with a shaper involves both *height* and *depth* (Fig. 26-11). The height is determined by the projection of a cutter above the table; it is controlled with the height-adjustment handwheel. This dimension can be measured directly or compared to the profile of the cut outlined on the end of the stock (Fig. 26-12).

The depth is determined by the distance a cutter length "bites" into the wood. This distance is adjusted with the fence or guide collars. For the collars, the depth is equal to the greatest perpendicu-

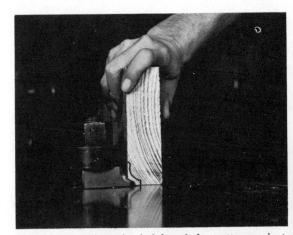

Fig. 26-12. Adjust the height of the cutter against the outlined profile of the cut.

lar distance between the collar and the cutting lips of the cutter (Fig. 26-13). Also, it is equal to the radius of the cutting circle of the cutter minus the radius of the collar. The depth of cut can be changed by selecting a collar with a different outside diameter (Fig. 26-14). The collars serve as "stops," limiting the distance the stock can be fed into the cutters. When using the fence, the depth is equal to the greatest distance the cutting lips project beyond the fence (Fig. 26-15). This adjustment can be made by sliding the fence toward the front or back side of the spindle.

Operation Hints

1. In replacing a cutter, point its cutting lips in the direction of rotation of the spindle. Cutters pointed opposite the direction of rotation of the spindle are dangerous and cannot cut (Fig. 26-16).

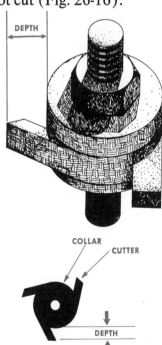

Fig. 26-13. The depth of cut is equal to the greatest perpendicular distance between the collar and the cutting lips of the cutter.

Fig. 26-14. When a collar is used to guide the stock, the depth of cut is changed by a collar of different diameter. The common diameters of collars are $\frac{7}{8}''$, $\frac{15}{16}''$, $1''$, $1\frac{1}{16}''$, $1\frac{1}{8}''$, and $1\frac{1}{4}''$. (Courtesy Powermatic, Houdaille Industries, Inc.)

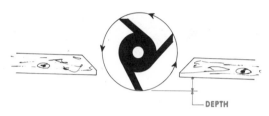

Fig. 26-15. When the stock is guided by the fence, the depth of cut is determined by the projection of the cutter beyond the fence.

2. A series of shallow cuts is more practical and safer than a single deep cut.
3. The intricate or more complicated designs can be cut by shaping the stock several times, using different machine settings or cutters (Fig. 26-17).
4. For heights of cut less than the thickness of the stock, both halves of the fence should be aligned with each other (Fig. 26-18).
5. The halves of the fence should be offset when the height of the cut is equal to the thickness being shaped (Fig. 26-19). This offset, which is adjusted with the trailing half of the fence, is equal to the depth being removed from the stock.
6. When edge-shaping an entire surface, begin with either end and continue in the same direction until finished (Fig. 26-20).

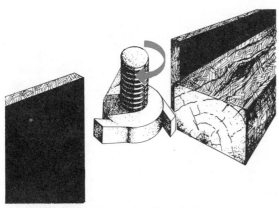

Fig. 26-16. Point the cutting lips of the cutter toward the direction of rotation of the spindle.

Fig. 26-17. Intricate designs often can be made by a series of cuts with different cutters or machine settings.

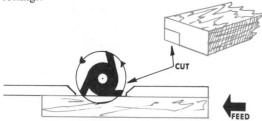

Fig. 26-18. Both halves of the fence should be aligned for height of the cut is equal to the thickness of the stock.

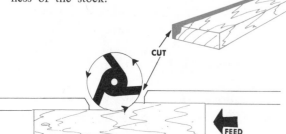

Fig. 26-19. The two halves of the fence are offset if the height of the cut is equal to the thickness of the stock.

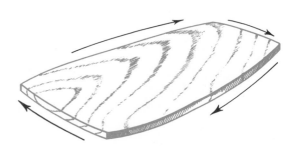

Fig. 26-20. In edge shaping, begin at one end and continue in the same direction until all the edges are shaped.

7. If the stock is roughly cut, reduce the rate of feed and/or the depth of the cut. Also, check the direction of the grain, since shaping against the grain can produce splitting.

8. In attempting to reproduce a particular shape, use the shape as a guide for the adjustments (Fig. 26-21).

9. If the stock heats or burns, increase the rate of feed. The stock also can heat or burn from the friction created by a collar needing cleaning.

10. In shaping identical, straight pieces, continuously feed the pieces with their ends butted together.

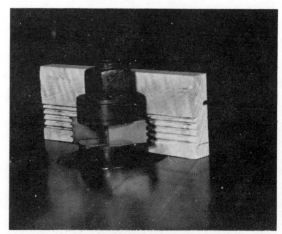

Fig. 26-21. To reproduce a given shape, use that shape for a pattern in adjusting the shaper.

General Safety Rules

1. Make adjustments only while the power is off and the spindle is not turning.

2. Before turning on the power, check the clearance of the cutter with the table, fence, or other items that could obstruct its rotation.

3. Make sure the spindle nut, fence, ring guard, or hold-down devices are tightened securely before using the shaper.

4. Remove tools or extra material from the table before turning on the power.

5. Position the cutter on the spindle in a way that the front of its cutting lips do the cutting (Fig. 26-22). The direction of the spindle can be changed when the shaper is equipped with a reversing switch.

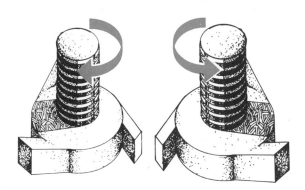

Fig. 26-22. If the direction of rotation of the spindle is reversed, turn the cutter upside down.

6. If individual knives are used on the spindle, they must project equally in distance from the collar and must be identical in width.

7. Never begin shaping until the spindle has reached its full speed.

8. Avoid edge shaping on short lengths, unless a miter gauge is used.

9. Feed the stock against the direction of the spindle rotation (see Figs. 26-18 and 26-19).

10. Shaping, regardless of the type, cannot be performed safely without using either the fence, the miter gauge, or the collar to guide the work.

11. A board should not be backed-up after it has been shaped, because of the "kickback" hazard.

12. Keep the fingers clear of the cutter. Use a push stick for close work.

13. Neither rough stock nor stock which does not rest flatwise on the table should be shaped.

14. When possible, shield the cutter by making cuts on the bottom portion of the stock, rather than on its top portion (Fig. 26-23).

Fig. 26-23. It is a safer practice to make shaper cuts on the bottom portion of the stock than on the top portion.

15. Adjust the cutter until the unused portions of its cutting lips are below the top of the table (Fig. 26-24).

16. Adjust the fence opening to a minimum, using the cutter for a guide.

Shaping Straight Edges

1. Prepare the stock for shaping. It is safer to shape only stock with uniform width and thickness. Stock which does not rest flatwise on the table should not be machined with a shaper.

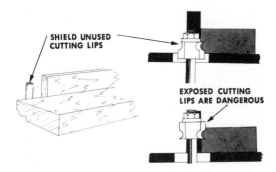

Fig. 26-24. Adjust the cutter until the unused portions of the cutting lips are below the top of the table.

2. Mount the cutter onto the spindle. If a cutter which is already mounted is to be used, check the tightness of the spindle nut.

3. Adjust the fence for the depth of cut. In making this adjustment, raise the cutter above the table. Then the projection of the cutting lips beyond the fence can be measured or compared to the profile of the cut outlined on the stock.

4. Adjust the height of the cut. The spindle should be raised or lowered until the cutter produces the desired cut.

5. Clamp the hold-down device in place. The stock should be used for a guide in positioning the steel spring clamps or featherboard. Be careful in making these adjustments, since it is difficult to feed the stock if these devices are too tight. If they are too loose, poor cuts or kickbacks can occur.

6. Test the adjustments. Make a trial cut, using a board with a thickness identical to the thickness of the stock to be shaped. Make adjustments as needed.

7. Make the final cuts.

Shaping Curved Edges

1. Remove the fence and the hold-down devices from the table.

2. Prepare the stock for shaping. It should rest flatwise and firmly on the table. Also, minor irregularities on the edges should be removed.

3. Determine the cut. For a guide in adjusting the cutter, outline the profile of the cut on the end of the stock.

4. Mount the cutter and the collar on the spindle. Use the profile of the cut in selecting the type of cutter and the diameter of the collar.

5. Fasten the starting pin to the table. Since the pin can be located in one of several holes on the table, its exact location should be selected with regard to the rotation of the cutter and to the shape of the stock.

6. Attach the ring guard to the shaper.

7. Check the adjustments. Using a piece of scrap stock, make a trial cut. Change the adjustments as needed.

8. Make the final cuts. When starting a cut, firmly position the stock against

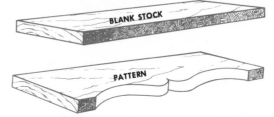

(A) Attach the blank stock to the pattern.

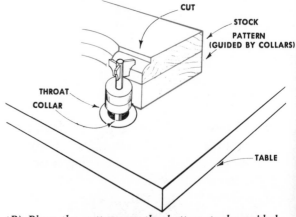

(B) Place the pattern on the bottom to be guided by the collar.

Fig. 26-25. Using a pattern to shape thin stock.

the starting pin. Then pivot the stock until the contact is made with the spindle. At this point, the stock is guided gradually from the pin, while maintaining contact with the cutter.

Shaping Thin Stock With a Pattern

While shaping, the uncut edge of the stock might be too thin to support the collar. In this instance, a second piece (or pattern) can be used to provide the necessary edge. As shown in Fig. 26-25, the pattern can be tacked to the first piece; then both pieces are identical in shape.

Questions

1. Explain the different adjustments for the fence of the shaper.
2. List two ways of guiding the stock during the different shaping operations.
3. Why is a three-lip cutter usually preferable to a cutter with individual knives?
4. Why is the starting pin not used with the fence?
5. How is the height and depth of a cut adjusted?
6. What procedure should be followed in edge shaping a surface, such as a table top?
7. If the cut is rough, what can be done to produce a smoother cut?
8. If the edge being shaped is heated or burned, what can be done to eliminate the problem?
9. Why should the knives of a cutter project identical distances from the collar?
10. Discuss why it is usually safer to make cuts on the lower portion of the stock.
11. Compare the differences between shaping the straight edges and shaping the curved edges.
12. Why is a pattern used?

Unit 27 – Cutting Holes

A *bit* is used to bore holes in wood and some types of plastics, and a *drill* is used to cut holes in metals. Among the more common bit types are the auger, *Foerstner,* and expansive bits. Although usually turned with a tool called a *brace,* some bits with special shanks can be used in hand drills and drill presses.

Auger Bit

The principal parts of an auger bit are the head, twist, and shank (Fig. 27-1). In the head can be found the cutters, spurs, screw, and throat (Fig. 27-2). The *screw* pulls the bit through the wood and the more threads found on the screw, the finer and slower the cut produced (Fig. 27-3). The two *spurs* score the outer edges of the hole and prevent chipping. The actual boring is done by the *cutting lips,* which serve as small planes. After the shavings are cut, the throat conveys them to the *twist.* The twist then moves the shavings out of the hole to prevent the chips binding the bit. The *shank* is that part of the bit which fits into the turning tool. The shank can have four tapered sides for use in a brace; or it can be straight for use in a hand drill and drill press. The end of the shank is called the *tang,* when the shank is square in shape.

Auger bits are sized in sixteenths of an inch, ranging in size from $\frac{4}{16}$ inch to $2\frac{4}{16}$ inch. The sizes are indicated by a whole number stamped on the tang—the whole number representing the number of fractional sixteenths (Fig. 27-4). For example, a number *4* indicates the $\frac{4}{16}$-inch size, a number *9* indicates the $\frac{9}{16}$-inch size,

Fig. 27-1. Auger bit parts. (Courtesy the Irwin Auger Bit Company)

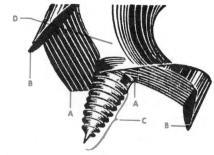

Fig. 27-2. Parts of the head of an auger bit. (A) Cutters, (B) Spurs, (C) Screw, and (D) Throat. (Courtesy The Irwin Auger Bit Company)

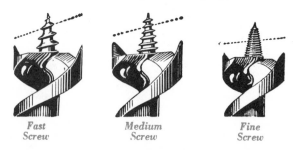

Fast Screw   Medium Screw   Fine Screw

Fig. 27-3. Threads on the screw. (Courtesy The Irwin Auger Bit Company)

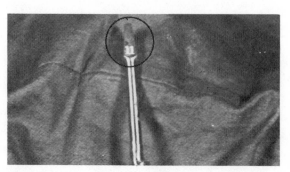

Fig. 27-4. The size of an auger bit is stamped on the tang.

etc. All the auger bits, except the dowel bits, are made about $\frac{1}{64}$ inch over size. If the bit were not slightly larger, the fit between two parts of the same "size" probably would be too tight. The wood, in these instances, might crack when forcing the part into the hole.

Several types of auger bits are available, depending on the need or purpose. The different types of boring heads are shown in Fig. 27-5. The bit in Fig. 27-5A is used chiefly by electricians and electric linemen for making quick cuts in most woods. The bit in Fig. 27-5B is designed for heavy boring in railroad, shipyard, and bridge construction. The boring head in Fig. 27-5C is for general-purpose work, and is used widely in furniture, cabinet and frame construction. This boring head produces a fast and smooth cut. The bit in Fig. 27-5D is recommended for hard woods or for dense grain structures. It is especially recommended for boring holes in the end grain.

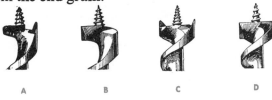

Fig. 27-5. Various boring heads including (A) Electrician's bit; (B) Railroad bit; and (C) General purpose. (Courtesy The Irwin Auger Bit Company)

Caring for an Auger Bit

The bits in Fig. 27-6 are cared for (or sharpened) in similar ways. All bits should be protected from rust by wiping occasionally with an oily rag. Also, their cutting edges should be protected. Banging the bits against other tools easily can damage the boring heads. A twist sometimes becomes bent, which can be detected by rolling the bit over a flat surface. To correct this damage, place the

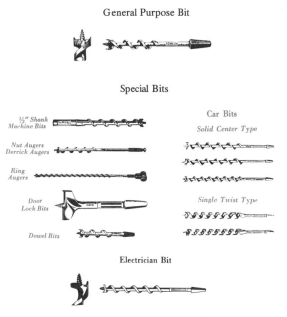

Fig. 27-6. Auger bits. (Courtesy The Irwin Auger Bit Company)

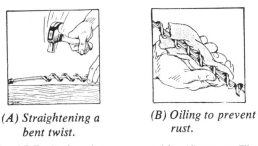

(A) Straightening a bent twist.　　*(B) Oiling to prevent rust.*

Fig. 27-7. Caring for an auger bit. (Courtesy The Irwin Auger Bit Company)

high spot upward and tap lightly with a hammer (Fig. 27-7).

A bit should be sharpened when its cutting edges become dull or uneven. Both these conditions are noticeable when boring holes. Shavings without uniform thickness result from the cutting lips cutting unequally. One of the lips might be dull; or it might have been sharpened incorrectly. When both lips are dull, they slide over the wood. To sharpen a cutting lip, support the bit on its screw (Fig. 27-8). File only the upper edge; remove the metal equally from each lip. Maintain the original angle in filing.

If the edges of the shavings are rough, sharpen the spurs. Support the bit against a board with the screw pointed upward (Fig. 27-9). Gently file the inside portion of the spur. Do not file the outside portion.

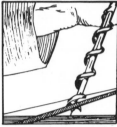

Fig. 27-8. Sharpening a cutting lip. (Courtesy The Irwin Auger Bit Company)

Fig. 27-9. Sharpening a spur. (Courtesy The Irwin Auger Bit Company)

Foerstner Bits

Blind holes, or holes which do not extend entirely through the stock, are often bored with a *Foerstner* bit. Since the bit

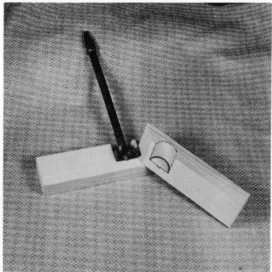

Fig. 27-10. A Foerstner bit can be used to cut a blind hole with a flat bottom.

has no screw, a blind hole bored with the bit has a flat bottom (Fig. 27-10). For this reason, a *Foerstner* bit is preferable for boring blind holes in thin stock. Also, it is sometimes used to enlarge a hole.

The method of indicating the size of a *Foerstner* bit is similar to the method used for auger bits. *Foerstner* bits usually are available in sizes from ¼ inch to 2 inches, but can be obtained in larger sizes. Their shanks are either straight for machine chucks or tapered for braces (Fig. 27-11).

Fig. 27-11. Foerstner bit.

Expansive Bits

An expansive bit is similar to a common auger bit, except for a movable cutter (Fig. 27-12). By adjusting the cutter, the boring range of the bit can be increased (Fig. 27-13). The common diameters range from ⅝ inch to 1¾ inch and from ⅞ inch to 3 inches. Also, other cutters are available for diameters upward to 5 inches.

To adjust the cutter, loosen the screw; then slide the cutter in or out. Be sure to tighten the screw after making the necessary adjustment. The size, or the hole

Fig. 27-12. Expansive bit. (Courtesy The Irwin Auger Bit Company)

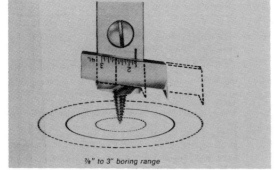

Fig. 27-13. The boring range for common expansive bits is upward to 3 inches in diameter. (Courtesy The Irwin Auger Bit Company)

diameter, is read by aligning the marks on the cutter with the single mark on the bit. These marks refer to the *diameter* of a hole and should never be confused with its radius. If it is necessary to bore a hole without determining its size in inches, begin by drawing the outline of the hole. Using the center of the hole for a guide for the screw of the bit, adjust the spur of the cutter to the outer edge of the hole.

Drilling Tools

A *drill* is used to cut holes in wood, plastic, and metal. The drills are made from either carbon steel or high-speed steel. The carbon-steel drills are recommended for the softer materials, such as wood. The high-speed drills are needed for the harder materials. For example, high-speed drills are recommended for most metals and some wood products, such as particle board. High-speed drills are indicated by the letters *HS,* meaning "high speed," marked on their shanks. Most of the drilling tools are used in drill presses and electric hand drills; therefore, they have straight shanks.

Twist Drills

The principal parts of a twist drill are the *cutting lips, flute,* and *shank* (Fig.

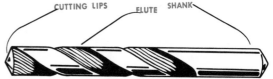

Fig. 27-14. Principal parts of a twist drill.

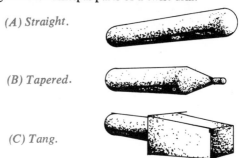

(A) Straight.

(B) Tapered.

(C) Tang.

Fig. 27-15. Three types of shanks found on twist drills.

27-14). The cutting lips cut the material, and the flute removes the material from the hole. The shank, which fits into the chuck, can be *straight, tapered,* or *tang* (Fig. 27-15). The straight and tapered shanks are used in drill presses; the tang shanks are used with a brace.

Size

The size of a twist drill is stamped on its shank. An exact size is indicated by numbers, letters, or fractions. See Table 27-1 for comparison of designations. The fractional method of indicating size is more common in woodworking.

Sharpening

Twist drills are sharpened with a grinding wheel. A properly sharpened twist drill is shown in Fig. 27-16. Note that the cutting lips form an angle of 118° and that the clearance angle is 12° to 15°.

Fig. 27-16. Correct angles for the cutting lips of a twist drill.

Table 27-1. Number, Fractional, and Letter Sizes for Twist Drills

Drill No.	Frac.	Deci.	Drill No.	Frac.	Deci.	Drill No.	Frac.	Deci.	Drill No.	Frac.	Deci.
80	—	.0135	42	—	.0935	7	—	.201	X	—	.397
79	—	.0145	—	3/32	.0938	—	13/64	.203	Y	—	.404
—	1/64	.0156	41	—	.0960	6	—	.204			
78	—	.0160	40	—	.0980	5	—	.206	—	13/32	.406
77	—	.0180	39	—	.0995	4	—	.209	Z	—	.413
									—	27/64	.422
76	—	.0200	38	—	.1015	3	—	.213	—	7/16	.438
75	—	.0210	37	—	.1040	—	7/32	.219	—	29/64	.453
74	—	.0225				2	—	.221			
73	—	.0240	36	—	.1065	1	—	.228	—	15/32	.469
72	—	.0250	—	7/64	.1094	A	—	.234	—	31/64	.484
			35	—	.1100				—	1/2	.500
71	—	.0260	34	—	.1110	—	15/64	.234	—	33/64	.516
70	—	.0280	33	—	.1130	B	—	.238	—	17/32	.531
69	—	.0292				C	—	.242			
68	—	.0310	32	—	.116	D	—	.246	—	35/64	.547
—	1/32	.0313	31	—	.120	—	1/4	.250	—	9/16	.562
			—	1/8	.125				—	37/64	.578
67	—	.0320	30	—	.129	E	—	.250	—	19/32	.594
66	—	.0330	29	—	.136	F	—	.257	—	39/64	.609
65	—	.0350				G	—	.261			
64	—	.0360	—	9/64	.140	—	17/64	.266	—	5/8	.625
63	—	.0370	28	—	.141	H	—	.266	—	41/64	.641
			27	—	.144				—	21/32	.656
62	—	.0380	26	—	.147	I	—	.272	—	43/64	.672
61	—	.0390	25	—	.150	J	—	.277	—	11/16	.688
60	—	.0400				—	9/32	.281			
59	—	.0410	24	—	.152	K	—	.281	—	45/64	.703
58	—	.0420	23	—	.154	L	—	.290	—	23/32	.719
			—	5/32	.156				—	47/64	.734
57	—	.0430	22	—	.157	M	—	.295	—	3/4	.750
56	—	.0465	21	—	.159	—	19/64	.297	—	49/64	.766
—	3/64	.0469				N	—	.302			
55	—	.0520	20	—	.161	—	5/16	.313	—	25/32	.781
54	—	.0550	19	—	.166	O	—	.316	—	51/64	.797
			18	—	.170				—	13/16	.813
53	—	.0595	—	11/64	.172	P	—	.323	—	53/64	.828
—	1/16	.0625	17	—	.173	—	21/64	.328	—	27/32	.844
52	—	.0635				Q	—	.332			
51	—	.0670				R	—	.339	—	55/64	.859
50	—	.0700	16	—	.177	—	11/32	.344	—	7/8	.875
			15	—	.180						
49	—	.0730	14	—	.182	S	—	.348	—	57/64	.891
48	—	.0760	13	—	.185	T	—	.358	—	29/32	.906
—	5/64	.0781	—	3/16	.188	—	23/64	.359	—	59/64	.922
47	—	.0785				U	—	.368			
46	—	.0810	12	—	.189	—	3/8	.375	—	15/16	.938
			11	—	.191				—	61/64	.953
45	—	.0820	10	—	.194	V	—	.377	—	31/32	.969
44	—	.0860	9	—	.196	W	—	.386	—	63/64	.981
43	—	.0890	8	—	.199	—	25/64	.391	—	1	1.000

Special Boring and Drilling Tools

This group of tools includes the boring and drilling tools used for special purposes. Most of them are available with either straight or tang shanks.

Countersinks and Plug Cutters

Holes are usually countersunk or counterbored to accommodate flathead screws. The countersink enlarges the mouth of the hole for the screw head to fit flush with the surface. Two types of countersinks are shown in Fig. 27-17. Countersinks are not sized, except for 82° angles. To increase the size of a hole with a countersink, the countersunk portion is made deeper. This depth can be estimater, rather than measured. Countersunk holes which are too deep or too shallow should be avoided (Fig. 27-18).

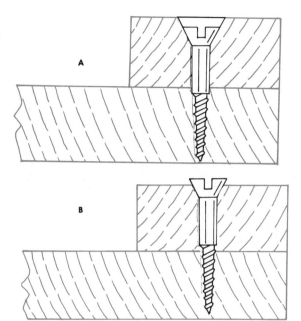

Fig. 27-18. The screw head should be flush with the surface. Avoid countersunk holes which are too deep (A) or too shallow (B).

Fig. 27-17. These countersinks are used with a brace (top) and an electric hand drill or drill press (bottom). (Courtesy The Stanley Works)

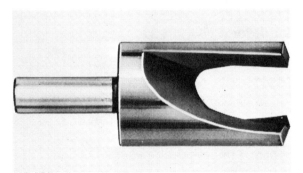

Fig. 27-19. Plug cutter. (Courtesy The Stanley Works)

A hole is *counterbored* to permit the entire screw head to be located beneath the surface. To hide the screw head, a plug is then fitted into the counterbored portion. The plugs are cut with plug cutters which match the diameter of the counterbore (Fig. 27-19). The plugs should be cut from the grain of wood similar to the surface they are to be glued into. For example, do not cut the plugs from end grain, if they are to be used in face grain. Since the end grain and face grain do not match, they detract from the finished appearance of a surface.

Screw-Mate Drill

A *screw-mate drill* is designed for drilling holes for wood screws (Fig. 27-20). It produces the pilot hole, shank clearance, and correct depth in a single drilling operation. Depending on the type of drill, it also can be used to countersink or counterbore the hole. The size of the

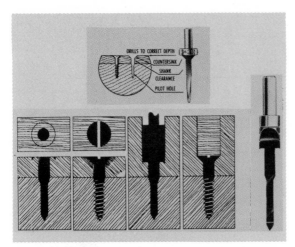

Fig. 27-20. Screw-mate drills provide the pilot hole, shank clearance, and countersink or counterbore in a single operation. (Courtesy The Stanley Works)

Fig. 27-21. The dowel bit is shorter than the auger bit. (Courtesy The Irwin Auger Bit Company)

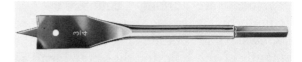

Fig. 27-22. Speed bit. (Courtesy The Stanley Works)

special drills is indicated by the screw size. In selecting a screw-mate drill, obtain a size identical to the size of the screw. For example, the correct size of drill for a NO. 8 F.H. $\times$ 1½-inch screw is: $8 \times 1½$.

Dowel Bit

A *dowel* bit is used to bore holes for dowels (Fig. 27-21). Although it is nearly identical to the common auger bit, there are some differences. A dowel bit is shorter and its twist is usually greater than the twist of a common bit. The chief difference is in size. Where a common bit is ⅟₆₄ inch oversize, the dowel bit is nearer the actual size.

Speed Bit

A *speed bit* is a wood-boring tool designed for electric hand drills and drill presses (Fig. 27-22). It is used to produce a quick, clean hole and is especially advantageous for boring angled holes. The size is indicated by the fractions of an inch stamped on the flat part of the bit. The common sizes are in 16ths of an inch, ranging from ¼ inch to 1½ inch.

Boring and Drilling Holes

Regardless of the method used, the preliminary steps in boring and drilling are nearly identical to cutting holes. First, the center of the hole is located with short, intersecting dashes (Fig. 27-23). Second, a scratch awl or center punch is used to mark the exact center of the hole (Fig. 27-24). The center of a drill or the screw of a bit fits into this mark. Third, the stock is secured to a vise, workbench, or suitable support and then drilled or bored.

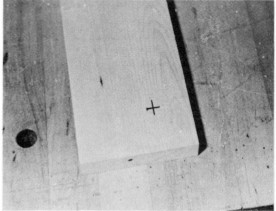

Fig. 27-23. The location of a hole is usually indicated by short intersecting dashes.

Boring With a Bit and Brace

A common auger bit is held in a brace (sometimes called a bit brace). The principal parts are shown in Fig. 27-25. The

Fig. 27-24. Marking the exact center point for drilling or boring a hole.

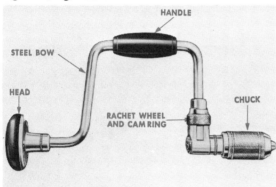

Fig. 27-25. Principal parts of a bit brace. (Courtesy The Stanley Works)

chuck until the jaws are slightly larger than the tang of the bit. Insert the corners of the tang into the V grooves of the jaws and tighten the chuck (Fig. 27-26).

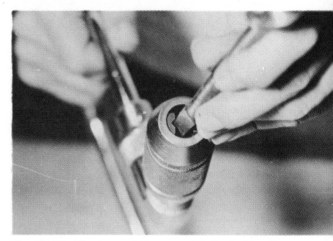

Fig. 27-26. The tang of the auger bit fits inside the chuck jaws of the brace.

A *through hole* is bored from one side of a board to its opposite side. The operation is begun by placing the screw of the bit against the wood. While applying slight pressure on the head, turn the handle slowly to begin the cut (Fig. 27-27). After the cutting lips make contact, the brace is turned slightly faster while apply-

boring angle and the pressure on the bit are controlled through the head of the brace. The steel bow and handle transfer the power from the operator to the bit. The cam ring and ratchet wheel determine the boring direction. When the cam ring is in its center position, the bit turns with the brace. If the cam ring is set toward the right-hand side, the bit turns to the right with the brace, but it does not turn when the brace is turned in the opposite direction. The opposite is true when the left-hand position is used. This adjustment permits boring holes in tight places, such as in corners. The jaws in the chuck hold the tang of a bit. To install a bit, turn the

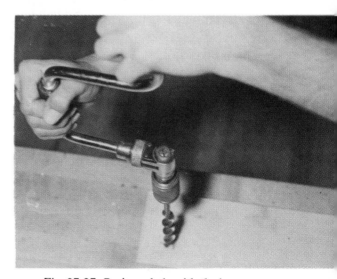

Fig. 27-27. Boring a hole with the brace.

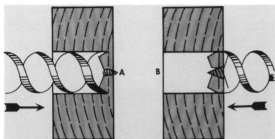

Fig. 27-28. Completing the cut. When the screw breaks through the bottom surface, the boring is stopped (A). Then the cut is completed from the opposite direction (B).

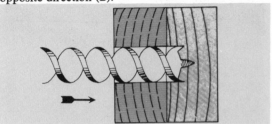

Fig. 27-29. Another method of completing the cut. A second piece butted against the bottom surface of the stock prevents splitting when the hole is bored from only one direction.

Fig. 27-30. A bit gauge attached to the bit can be used to control the depth of a blind hole. (Courtesy The Stanley Works)

Fig. 27-31. A try square can be used to check the squareness of the hole.

ing moderate pressure. Both the pressure and the speed are reduced near the end of the cut. Several methods can be used to avoid splitting the bottom side of the board. One method is to change the bit to the bottom side as soon as screw extends through that side of the board (Fig. 27-28). In another method, a piece of waste stock is attached firmly against the bottom side (Fig. 27-29). If neither method can be used, complete the cut while exerting only slight pressure and reducing the boring speed as much as possible.

A *blind hole* can be bored similarly to a through hole, except that a blind hole does not pass completely through the stock. Several methods can be used to stop the hole before it reaches the bottom side. A bit gauge, a block of wood, or a piece of tape can be used to control the depth (Fig. 27-30).

Holes are bored either *perpendicular* or *inclined* to a surface. For perpendicular holes, check the angle with a try square while boring (Fig. 27-31). Inclined hole angles can be checked with a sliding T bevel (Fig. 27-32). Be careful in starting the bit for an inclined hole. If the brace is turned too quickly or if too much pressure is applied, the bit can slip. A jig is sometimes used to guide the boring of inclined holes (Fig. 27-33). Also, a speed

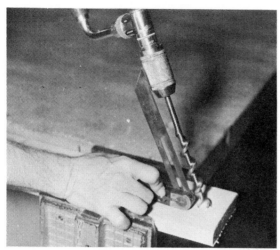

Fig. 27-32. A sliding T bevel can be used to check the angle of inclined holes.

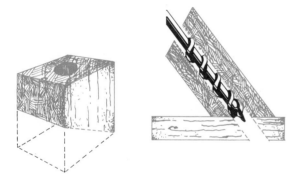

Fig. 27-33. A wooden jig can be used to guide the angle of a bit.

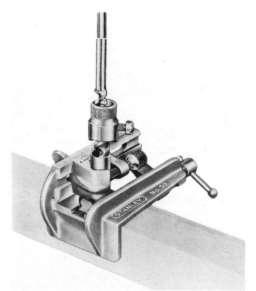

Fig. 27-34. A dowel jig establishes the exact locations of mating holes. (Courtesy The Stanley Works)

Fig. 27-35. Hand drill. (Courtesy The Stanley Works)

bit, rather than a common auger bit, might be advantageous.

Dowel holes are blind holes paired to accommodate dowel pins. Since the two holes must be aligned, their locations are especially important. Dowel jigs are used to assure the precise locations of the mating holes (Fig. 27-34).

Drilling Holes

Holes are drilled in much the same way they are bored. The chief difference is in the tools needed.

1. *Hand Drill.* A hand drill requires a straight-shank drill for cutting holes ¼ inch, or less, in diameter (Fig. 27-35). The hole is drilled by applying pressure on the handle while turning the crank.
2. *Automatic Drill.* The automatic drill is often substituted for a hand drill (Fig. 27-36). It is especially advantageous for small-diameter holes, and it drills as the handle is moved up and down.

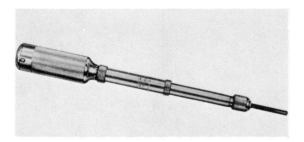

Fig. 27-36. Automatic drill. (Courtesy The Stanley Works)

3. *Electric hand drill.* The common sizes of electric hand drills are ¼ inch, ⅜ inch (Fig. 27-37), and ½ inch (Fig. 27-38). These sizes indicate the largest hole diameter that can be drilled and they also indicate the size of the chuck. However, a high-quality hand drill is capable of drilling diameters in metal equal to its rated size and about twice that size in hardwoods. For example, most ¼-inch hand drills can drill ¼-inch diameters in metal and ½-inch diameters in hardwoods by using special ½-inch drills with ¼-inch shanks.

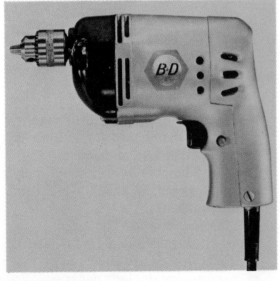

Fig. 27-37. A ¼" electric hand drill. The ⅜" electric hand drill is similar in appearance. (Courtesy Black & Decker Mfg. Co.)

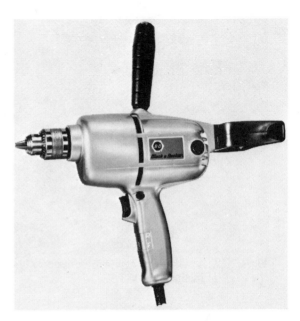

Fig. 27-38. A ½" electric hand drill. (Courtesy Black & Decker Mfg. Co.)

Electric hand drills might have only a single speed; or they can be variable-speed drills. The variable-speed drills are recommended for drilling materials with varying degrees of hardness. Soft materials can be drilled at faster speeds than hard materials. Some drills also have reversing switches, which change the direction of the drill.

As with any electrical device, an electric hand drill should never be used unless it is grounded properly. Also, it should never be used when a person's clothing or parts of his body are wet. Never stand in water or on wet ground while drilling.

To use an electric hand drill, open the jaws of the chuck with a chuck wrench. Slide the shank of the drill into the chuck and tighten. Be sure to remove the chuck wrench before drilling. When starting the hole, place the drill or bit in the center mark. Then squeeze the trigger switch while applying slight pressure. Increase the pressure while drilling, but decrease the pressure near the end of the cut.

Several attachments can be used with an electric hand drill. Drivers can be used for driving screws (Fig. 27-39). Sanding disks and drums also are available. For shaping, round forming tools are used frequently (Fig. 27-40).

Fig. 27-40. Circular edges can be shaped with round forming tools used with electric hand drills and drill presses. (Courtesy The Stanley Works)

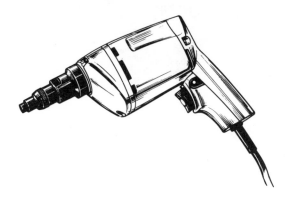

Fig. 27-39. Electric drill with driver attachment for driving screws. (Courtesy The Stanley Works)

Questions

1. List the principal parts of an auger bit. How is the size of an auger bit indicated?
2. When is a *Foerstner* bit used? What type of shank does it have?
3. What is the advantage of using an expansive bit?
4. Describe the difference between a carbon-steel drill and a high-speed drill? Which type of drill is usually used for drilling holes in wood?
5. List the different methods of indicating the size of a twist drill.
6. Sketch a countersunk hole and a counterbored hole.
7. Why is the screw-mate drill preferred for drilling holes for screws?
8. What is the chief difference between a dowel bit and an auger bit?
9. Compare a through hole with a blind hole.
10. How is the size of an electric hand drill indicated?

Unit 28 – Drill Press

A *drill press* is a machine used to drill and bore holes in either wood or metal. It also can be used for routing, sanding, shaping, and mortising of wood. Drill presses are available in either floor or bench models (Fig. 28-1). The size of a drill press is stated in terms of the largest diameter of stock that can be drilled on the machine. For example, a 15-inch drill press can drill a hole in the center of a piece of stock 15 inches in diameter.

Most of the drill presses are manufactured with variable speeds. This means that the speed can be changed from slow to fast, depending on the operation. The common ranges of drill presses are from 475 to 4800 rpm. On some drill presses, the speed is changed by shifting the belt on the cone pulleys (Fig. 28-2). This is done only with the power off. On other drill presses, variable-speed drives permit dialing the correct speed (Fig. 28-3).

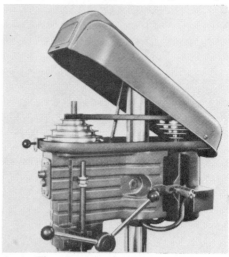

Fig. 28-2. The speed is changed on this drill press by shifting the belt on the cone pulleys. This can be done only when the power is turned off. (Courtesy Powermatic, Houdaille Industries, Inc.)

Fig. 28-3. The speed is changed on this variable-speed drill press by dialing the desired speed. This can be done only when the power is turned on. (Courtesy Powermatic, Houdaille Industries, Inc.)

Principal Parts

The principal parts of a drill press are shown in Fig. 28-4. The *table* is used to support the work; it slides up and down

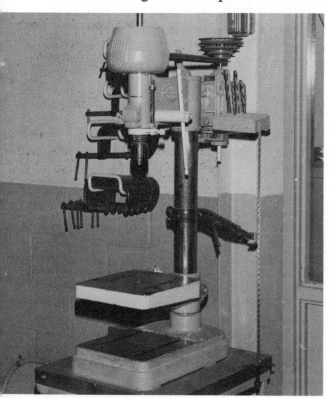

Fig. 28-1. Bench-type drill press.

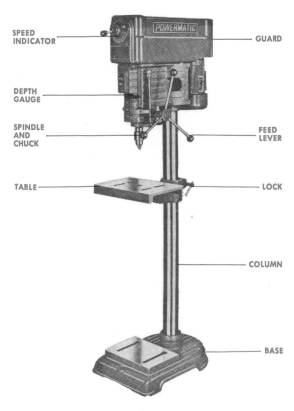

SPEED INDICATOR

DEPTH GAUGE

SPINDLE AND CHUCK

TABLE

GUARD

FEED LEVER

LOCK

COLUMN

BASE

Fig. 28-4. Principal parts of a drill press. (Courtesy Powermatic, Houdaille Industries, Inc.)

on the *column,* and is locked in place with the *table lock.* An index pin can be loosened to incline the table relative to the twist drill. The *feed lever* is used to raise and lower the twist drill, which is held in the *chuck.* A *depth gauge,* located on the side of the drill press, indicates the depth of the hole being drilled. The *guard* located on the top of the drill press protects the operator from the belts, pulleys, and motor.

Boring and Drilling

Both boring and drilling operations can be performed on a drill press if the cutting tool has the proper type of shank. The common boring or drilling tools usually include the auger bits, speed bits, and straight-shank drills. To insert a cut-

ting tool into the chuck, first open the jaws of the chuck, using a *chuck wrench* (Fig. 28-5). Place the cutting tool into the chuck and tighten it with the chuck wrench. Make sure the drill is fitted properly into the chuck and is centered properly. After checking for wobble, turn off the drill press and tighten the chuck again. Remember to remove the chuck wrench from the chuck before turning on the power.

When drilling, it is advisable to clamp the stock to the table. The stock can be clamped with a C clamp, a hand clamp, or a special drill press clamp (Fig. 28-6).

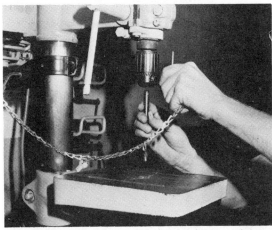

Fig. 28-5. A chuck wrench is required to tighten any cutting tool in the chuck. Be sure to remove the chuck wrench before turning on the power.

SPECIAL CLAMP

Fig. 28-6. Most stock should be clamped to the table with a C clamp, a hand clamp, or a special drill press clamp.

General Safety Rules

1. Always make adjustments with the power switch off.
2. Be sure to remove the key from the chuck before switching on the power.
3. Keep loose clothing away from the turning parts of a drill press.
4. After turning off the power, do not attempt to stop the drill by grasping the chuck.
5. Maintain sufficient clearance between the fingers and the drill. Clamp small pieces of stock to the table; or use a drill press vise.
6. Hold the stock firmly against the table while drilling. Be especially careful with long, thin stock. Brace one end of the stock against the column to prevent its being caught and swung by the twist drill (Fig. 28-7).

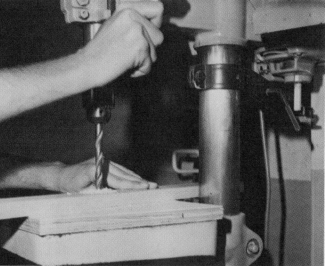

Fig. 28-7. Unclamped lengthy pieces of stock can be braced against the column; this prevents the stock being caught and swung by the cutting tool.

7. Avoid overheating a twist drill by feeding it either too fast or too slow.
8. Select the correct cutter, drill, or bit for the operation. Never use an auger bit in the drill press unless the feed screw has been filed smooth.
9. Before using, make sure the cutter, drill, or bit is fitted properly into the chuck. The shank should be inserted at least ⅜ inch into the chuck. Do not attempt to center a square or tang bit into a chuck.
10. Periodically check the cutter or the tightness of the drill in the chuck when performing high-speed operations.
11. Select and maintain a safe speed, depending on the drill, operation, and material.
12. Reduce the feed near the end of the cut to prevent binding the drill with the stock.
13. Keep the guard in place, except when it is necessary to remove for changing speeds and when the power is turned off.
14. If needed, use an auxiliary table made of wood to protect the table and the drill or cutter.

Drilling Perpendicular Holes

1. *Protect the table.* Place a board on the table to prevent drilling holes in the metal table. This board should be square and should have uniform thickness.
2. *Mark the center of the hole.*
3. *Adjust the table height.* Position the table with the point of the drill about ½ inch above the stock.
4. *Check the depth and squareness.* If the depth gauge is preset, release the locking nuts and lower the drill to the desired depth. As shown in Fig. 28-8, lower the drill to the desired depth for checking squareness with a try square.
5. *Clamp the stock.* When clamping, keep the clamping devices away from the feed lever or other moving parts.
6. *Drill the hole.* Use only enough pres-

Fig. 28-8. A try square can be used to check the squareness of the twist drill with the stock.

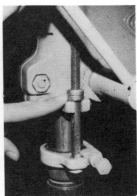

Fig. 28-9. To set the depth gauge for a blind hole, lower the twist drill to the desired depth marked on the stock (left). Hold the drill steady and tighten the locking nuts (right).

sure to keep the drill or bit cutting. Avoid excessive pressure which could break the twist drill or cause it to drill off center. If the wood smokes, the drill is too hot. Raise the drill and permit it to cool before continuing the cut. When completing the cut, reduce the feed to keep the stock from splitting.

Cutting Blind Holes

To cut a blind hole, first mark the center of the hole. Then mark the desired depth on the edge of the stock. Using the feed lever, lower the twist drill to the desired depth (Fig. 28-9). While holding the twist drill at this depth, tighten the locking nuts on the depth gauge and then check the adjustments by drilling a trial hole in a scrap of wood. Measure the depth and readjust if necessary. When drilling a series of blind holes, periodically check the depth gauge. Excessive vibration sometimes can loosen the locking nuts, resulting in a hole either deeper or more shallow than needed.

Inclined Holes

An inclined hole is drilled similarly to a perpendicular hole, except that the table is changed from its square position with the drill. To drill an inclined hole, tilt the table and check the angle with a sliding T bevel (Fig. 28-10). A support is usually needed for angled drilling. Also clamp either a straightedge or the stock to the table (Fig. 28-11). When starting the twist drill, use only slight pressure on the feed lever and move it slowly. If the drill tends to move off center, mark a small starting hole, using a sharp instrument.

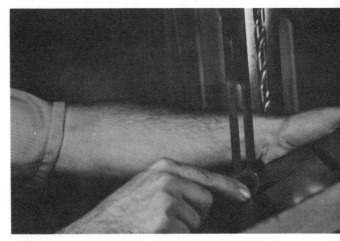

Fig. 28-10. Use a sliding T bevel to check the angle with the stock for an inclined hole.

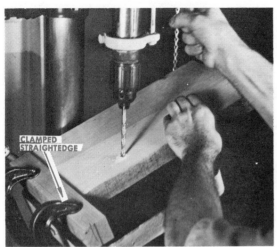

Fig. 28-11. A straightedge clamped to the table is an aid in drilling unclamped stock supported by a tilting table.

Evenly Spaced Holes

Evenly spaced holes are located at equal distances. When drilling these holes, particularly in similar pieces, a jig is often used to eliminate repeating the measurements (Fig. 28-12). A similar jig can be used for drilling holes at equal distances from the edges and ends. This type of jig often involves only a straightedge clamped to the table.

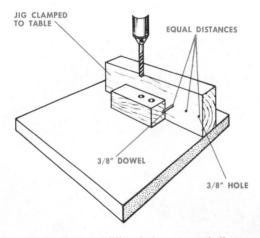

Fig. 28-12. Jig for drilling holes at equal distances. After drilling the first hole, the dowel is moved forward for the next hole. The distance between holes is identical to the distance between holes in the jig.

Cutting Holes in Round Stock

To cut holes in round stock, always support the stock in a V block (Fig. 28-13). Stock not supported in a V block tends to turn while drilling. Also, it can be necessary not only to mark the location of the hole but also to make a small beginning hole with a punch or awl.

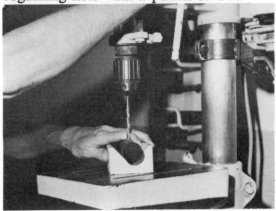

Fig. 28-13. Use a vee block to support round stock for drilling.

Cutting Holes in End of Stock

The table is usually turned to a perpendicular position for drilling holes in the ends of stock. As shown in Fig. 28-14, the stock is supported by the top of the table and, if needed, can be butted against the lower table located on the base. Avoid excessive pressure which can cause a bow in long pieces when drilling holes in the end of a piece of stock.

Sanding With a Drill Press

A drill press is often used for sanding the edges of irregular cuts and interior curves. As shown in Fig. 28-15, a sanding drum is mounted similarly to a twist drill. These drums, including abrasive sleeves, range upward to 3 inches in diameter. The sleeve is changed by loosening a nut and sliding the sleeve on or off.

The edge being sanded is supported by an auxiliary table, which is usually

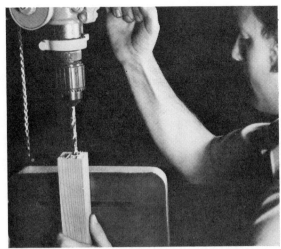

Fig. 28-14. To drill a hole in the end grain of a long piece of stock, support the opposite end on the base of the drill press. Turn the table perpendicular to its normal position.

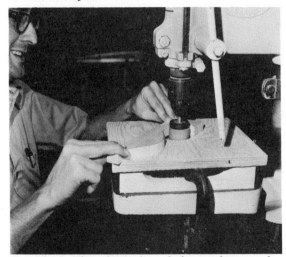

Fig. 28-15. The edges of workpieces often can be sanded with a sanding drum on the drill press.

raised above the table of the drill press. Located in the auxiliary table is a hole slightly larger than the drum. A drum is capable of sanding an entire thickness of of an edge when it is lowered partially through the hole. Also, the drum can be adjusted for even wear of the abrasive sleeve.

Sanding drums sometimes can be made by turning wooden cylinders to desired diameters (Fig. 28-16). In these instances, the drum is held in the chuck by

a bolt which is tightened through the center of the drum. If an abrasive sleeve is not available, a common abrasive paper can be glued to the cylinder. The procedure below should be followed in edge sanding on a drill press.

1. Saw the stock to shape. Remove the highly irregular features by planing or filing.
2. Choose the correct size of sanding drum and abrasive grit. The diameter of the drum should be nearly equal to the diameter to be sanded.
3. Place the drum into the chuck and tighten. Set the drill press speed between 1000 and 1500 rpm. Avoid the faster speeds, which can cause overheating of the sleeve.
4. Attach the auxiliary table to the table and adjust its height. The height also can be adjusted by lowering the quill and locking it in place.
5. Check the adjustments. If no further adjustments are needed, turn on the power.
6. Begin sanding only after the drum has reached its operating speed. Always move the stock against the direction of the drum. While sanding, avoid excessive pressure and never hold the stock in one place too long.

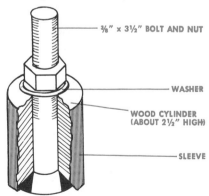

Fig. 28-16. Cutaway view of a sanding drum. A wood cylinder can be turned to the required diameter and, if a sleeve is not available, a sheet of abrasive paper can be glued to the cylinder.

Mortising With a Drill Press

A mortise-and-tenon joint can be used to join an end of a board to the face or side of another board (Fig. 28-17). Although the tenon can be cut on various machines, a mortise can be cut only by hand or with a mortiser (Fig. 28-18). In many woodshops, a mortiser is not available, since it is limited to a single operation. Instead, a drill press equipped with a mortising attachment is used (Fig. 28-19).

The attachment consists of a casting, a fence, several hooked rods, and a hold-down device. To mount the attachment, the casting is secured to the quill of the drill press, and the fence is clamped to the table. The cutting is performed by a hollow chisel and a bit (Fig. 28-20). The chisel is held in the casting of the mortising attachment, and the bit is secured either in the chuck of the drill press or in a ½-inch spindle chuck. Two hooked rods on the fence hold the stock against the fence. An adjustable hold-down device also is attached to the fence. Its purpose is to prevent the stock being raised when the chisel is raised. The following procedure can be used for a guide when mortising with a drill press.

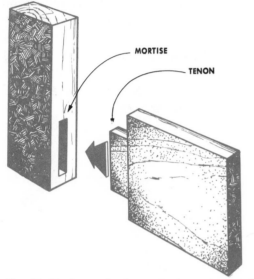

Fig. 28-17. A mortise for a mortise-and-tenon joint can be cut on the drill press.

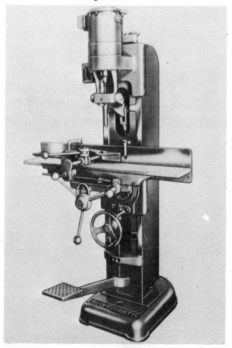

Fig. 28-18. A mortiser. (Courtesy Powermatic, Houdaille Industries, Inc.)

1. Mount the mortise attachment on the drill press.
2. Insert the hollow chisel into the casting; rotate it until one side is parallel with the fence. Tighten the chisel in place with the setscrew.
3. Pass the bit upward through the chisel from the bottom end, and place the shank in the chuck. Adjust the bit for a ⅟₃₂-inch to ⅟₁₆-inch clearance between its spurs and the chisel. Tighten the chuck or setscrew as needed.
4. Draw or outline the location and depth of the mortise onto the stock.
5. Adjust the table until the stock is about 1 inch lower than the end of the chisel.
6. Adjust the depth of the cut and tighten the locknuts on the depth gauge of the drill press.

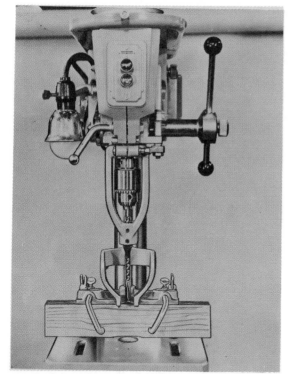

Fig. 28-19. Drill press equipped with a mortising attachment. (Courtesy Power Tool Division, Rockwell Manufacturing Company)

Fig. 28-20. Hollow chisel and bit. (Courtesy Powermatic, Houdaille Industries, Inc.)

RABBET

Fig. 28-21. Rabbeting on the drill press.

7. Secure the stock to the fence with the hooked rods; move the fence until the mortise is aligned with the chisel. Tighten the hold-down device onto the top of the stock.

8. Test the adjustments with the machine turned off. Lower the chisel and check the position where the cut is to begin. Make the adjustments, if needed.

9. Turn on the power and make the initial cut. Slide the stock over and continue the cuts until the mortise is completed.

Protect the chisel and the bit from damage while cutting the mortises. If either the chisel or bit overheats, stop cutting until it is cool. Feeding the chisel too fast or too slow can cause the extra heat. Also, jamming the chisel too hard against the stock can break the chisel and/or the bit. The last cut should be a full-width cut. A smaller cut can cause the bit to bend and break.

Routing With a Drill Press

Most of the routing operations which can be performed with a portable electric router also can be performed on the drill press. As shown in Fig. 28-21, the stock is moved around the cutter, rather than being clamped to the table. This feature is especially helpful in routing small pieces or in routing stock which is difficult to clamp.

To change a drill press from the drilling to the routing operations, tighten the router bit in the chuck similarly to tightening a drill in the chuck. At least ½ inch of the shank of the bit should make contact with the jaws of the chuck. Next, increase the speed of the drill press to its maximum (about 4800 rpm). The lower speeds produce rough cuts and splintering of the edges. After changing the cutter and the speed, turn on the power for about 15 seconds. Then, stop the cutter and recheck its tightness in the chuck. Also, it is good practice to periodically recheck this adjustment when routing for lengthy periods.

The stock should be fed toward the rotation of the bit. Routing in the same direction is dangerous, since the stock easily can be pulled from the hands of the operator. Also, it is difficult to control the feed, which is important. Feeding the stock too fast produces rough cuts, while feeding it too slowly heats or burns the stock and the bit.

Adjusting the drill press depends on the bit and the type of cut. For example, only the depth of cut is adjusted in cutting a rabbet with a rabbet bit (see Fig. 28-21). This also is true when edge routing with a bit having a pilot (Fig. 28-22). In cutting grooves and dadoes, however, the additional fence adjustment is required (Fig. 28-23.) Similar adjustments also are required for veining and fluting (Fig. 28-24). The following procedure can serve for a guide when routing with a drill press:

Fig. 28-23. Use a fence to support the stock for routing grooves and dadoes.

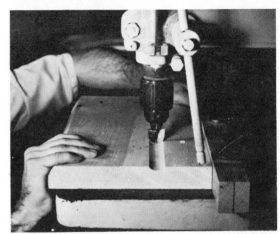

Fig. 28-24. Veining and fluting operation on the drill press.

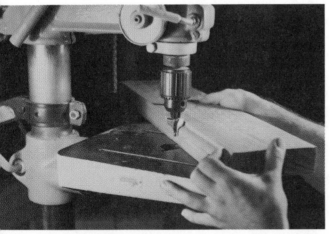

Fig. 28-22. Edge routing for decorative cuts on the drill press.

1. Select a sharp, clean cutter; then tighten in the chuck.
2. Change the speed of the drill press to about 4800 rpm; recheck the tightness of the cutter in the chuck.
3. Adjust for the depth of the cut. Either raise the table or lower the quill, and lock in place.
4. If needed, position the fence and clamp it to the table.
5. Check the adjustments and the direction of rotation of the cutter.
6. Hold the stock flat on the table and begin the cut by feeding the stock against the direction of rotation of the cutter. When routing the outside edges, reduce splintering by making the end cuts first.
7. Continue routing until finished.

Shaping With a Drill Press

Several adjustments and special attachments are needed for shaping with a drill press. The drill press speed should be set at its maximum speed, or about 4800 rpm. Also, for most operations, a wooden table is clamped to the metal table of the drill press. Since the cutters cannot be held by the chuck, a special spindle is required. This spindle (Fig. 28-25) is held by the chuck. Three-lip cutters are then attached to the spindle.

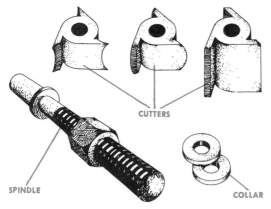

Fig. 28-25. Shaper attachment with cutters for the drill press.

Other adjustments are needed to determine the height and depth of a cut, as well as in deciding how the cut is to be guided. The height of a cut is changed by lowering or raising the table. Also, it can be changed by lowering the quill to a locked position. The depth of cut is adjusted with the fence or collars, which also guide the cut. The larger cuts result from using the smaller collars or from moving the fence toward the center of the spindle. Never guide the cut with a collar when the height of the cut is equal to, or nearly equal to, the thickness of the stock, unless a pattern is attached. Most of the shaping operations can be performed by the following procedure:

1. *Prepare the stock for shaping.* Do not attempt to shape stock which cannot be laid flat on the table.
2. *Select the required spindle, three-lip cutter, and collars.* Fasten the spindle to the drill press and assemble the cutter and collars onto the spindle.
3. *Attach the wooden table to the drill press table.* Make sure the hole in the wooden table is aligned with the spindle.
4. *Adjust the height and depth of cut.* Check the adjustments by making a trial cut on scrap stock. Be sure to feed the stock in the direction opposite the rotation of the spindle.
5. *Make the finished cut.* When shaping the center edges, always perform the end cuts first. Also, keep the stock firmly against the table and the collars or fence.

Questions

1. List the operations that can be performed on a drill press.
2. How is the speed of a drill press changed?
3. When should the stock be clamped to a drill press table? Why?
4. List the general safety rules for a drill press.
5. Describe how the depth is adjusted for drilling blind holes. How can this adjustment be checked?
6. Drilling inclined holes can be a problem. Identify this problem and explain how it can be solved.
7. Why should round stock be supported by a V block for drilling holes in the stock?
8. What size of sanding drum should be used for sanding irregular curves with a series of ½-inch and 1-inch radiuses? Why?
9. Why is the drill press speed reduced when sanding, as compared to the speed when routing?
10. What can be done to eliminate rough router cuts on a drill press?

11. When mortising on a drill press, what can be done to prevent overheating of the hollow chisel?

12. Describe how a drill press is adjusted for correct depth when cutting mortises.

13. When is routing with the drill press preferred to routing with a portable electric router?

14. How is the height and depth of a cut controlled when shaping with a drill press?

Unit 29 – Stationary Sanding Machines

The stationary sanders are used widely in woodworking. These machines include the disk sander, spindle sander, and belt sander.

Disk Sander

The disk sander is used to sand the edges and ends of the stock, rather than the broad faces. Chamfers, bevels, and tapers also can be sanded. The parts of a typical disk sander are shown in Fig. 29-1.

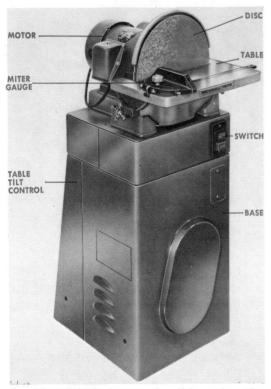

Fig. 29-1. Principal parts of a disk sander. (Courtesy Power Tool Division, Rockwell Manufacturing Company)

1. *Disk*. The disk consists of a metal plate covered by an abrasive sheet. Although the two parts are held together with a special cement, screws are used on some models to aid in holding the abrasive sheet.

2. *Motor*. Sanding occurs when the disk is turned by the motor. The disk and motor usually are connected directly, but they can be connected by a belt on the larger models. Normal speed is about 1725 rpm.

3. *Table*. The stock being sanded is supported by the table, which can be tilted for angular sanding. Angles up to 45° can be formed by tilting the table up or down.

4. *Controls*. The tilt of a table is adjusted with a control located near the table. Some models have another control, usually found under the table, which is used to adjust the clearance between the table and the disk. Not all models have this adjustment.

5. *Miter gauge*. The miter gauge is used to guide the stock for sanding angles.

The size of a disk sander is indicated by the diameter of its disk. The common sizes range from 8 inches to 18 inches. The smaller sanders, without stands, are used on workbenches (Fig. 29-2). A disk sander is sometimes combined with a belt sander (Fig. 29-3).

273

Fig. 29-2. Bench-type disk sander. (Courtesy Power Tool Division, Rockwell Manufacturing Company)

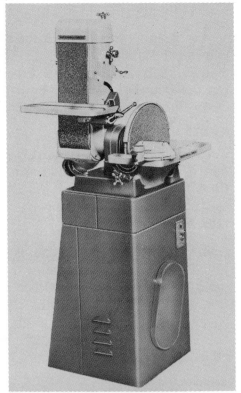

Fig. 29-3. Combination belt-disk sander. (Courtesy Power Tool Division, Rockwell Manufacturing Company)

Replacing an Abrasive Sheet

A worn abrasive sheet (or disk) is slick. Its sanding action is slower, and the wood is more easily "burned" from excessive friction. Worn sheets and those with torn edges should be replaced imme-

diately. The procedure listed below can be followed for most disk sanders:

1. Remove the worn or torn abrasive sheet from the metal disk (Fig. 29-4). If screws are used, remove them before peeling off the abrasive sheet.
2. Clean the metal disk thoroughly. While the disk is turning, use a piece of hardwood to scrape away any remaining cement from the disk (Fig. 29-5A).
3. Apply the new cement evenly to the surface of the disk (Fig. 29-5B). To do this, begin in the center and work toward the edge while the disk is turning.

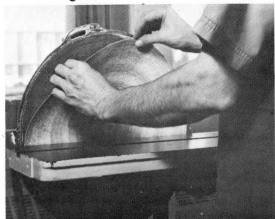

Fig. 29-4. Peeling a worn or torn abrasive sheet from the metal disk.

4. Select the correct abrasive sheet. Both the diameter and the grit size should be considered in selecting an abrasive sheet.
5. Position the new sheet. The sheet should be centered on the metal disk; then press it against the disk, using the palm of the hand. If necessary, replace the screws at this point.
6. Smooth out the abrasive sheet. Any irregularities can be eliminated by sanding from the center toward the edge with a piece of narrow stock about 2 inches wide.

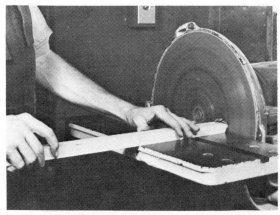

(A) Removing the cement with a piece of hardwood.

(B) Applying cement to the disk.

Fig. 29-5. The power is turned on for removing and applying cement to the metal disk.

(A) Sanding on the right-hand side of the disk.

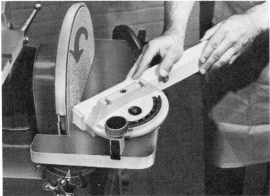

(B) Sanding on the left-hand side of the disk.

Fig. 29-6. All sanding operations should be done on the down-turning side of the disk. Since the disk can be reversed, the correct side for sanding can be reversed. (Courtesy Power Tool Division, Rockwell Manufacturing Company)

General Safety Rules

1. While using the disk sander, stand directly in front of the disk—never at the side.
2. Make adjustments only when the switch is off and the disk is not turning.
3. Avoid using abrasive sheets which are worn, torn, or adhere loosely to the metal disk.
4. Check the clearance between the disk and the table by turning the disk by hand.
5. Perform all sanding with the stock firmly on the table and on the "down" turning side of the disk (Fig. 29-6).
6. Wait until the disk is turning at full speed before beginning to sand.
7. Keep the fingers at a safe distance from the abrasive.
8. Permit the disk to coast to a stop. Do not attempt to stop a disk by jamming the stock against it.

Sanding Operations

All sanding, regardless of the operation, should be done on the down turning side of the disk (see Fig. 29-6). The stock should be moved back and forth across the down turning side of the disk. Failing to move the stock causes uneven wearing of the abrasive and causes the stock to overheat and burn. When beginning the

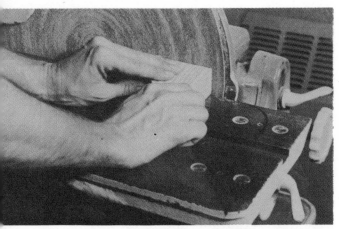

(A) Sanding perpendicularly.

(B) Sanding an angle.

Fig. 29-7. An angle or bevel can be sanded by tilting the table.

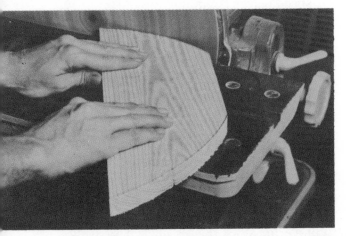

Fig. 29-8. Outline the desired shape on the surface of the stock for freehand sanding. Then sand to the mark.

sanding, the stock should be moved carefully toward the disk until contact is made. Jamming the stock against the disk can rip the abrasive sheet or result in its being thrown from the hands of the operator. Apply only enough pressure while sanding to maintain contact between the disk and the stock. Excessive pressure can result in overheating the stock and tearing the abrasive sheet.

Either freehand or straight sanding can be performed with a disk sander. Both types can be angular or perpendicular, depending on the angle formed between the table and the disk (Fig. 29-7). A common procedure for freehand sanding is to mark or outline the shape, and then sand to the mark (Fig. 29-8). Straight sanding involves using a miter gauge for a guide. As shown in Fig. 29-9, the table can be either perpendicular or inclined to the disk while using the miter gauge.

Spindle Sander

A spindle-type sander can be used to sand regular and irregular curves. All the sanding is done freehand, without the benefit of a miter gauge or a straightedge. The principal parts are a spindle, sanding drum, table, motor, and frame (Fig. 29-10). The sanding drum is attached to the spindle which, in turn, is connected to a motor. The spindle speed varies from 1800 to 3600 rpm for most sanders. On many spindle sanders, the spindles also move up and down while turning. A spindle sander is often referred to as an oscillating-spindle sander, because of the "up-and-down" characteristic. The table supports the stock, and it can be tilted as needed.

The size of a spindle sander is indicated by the diameter of the spindle or sanding drum. Several drum diameters upward to 3 inches are available on most sanders, but

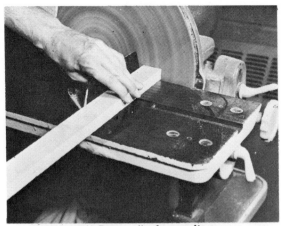

(A) Perpendicular sanding

(B) Angular or inclined sanding.
Fig. 29-9. Sanding with a miter gauge.

Fig. 29-10. Spindle sander. (Courtesy Boice Crane, A Division of Wilton Corp.)

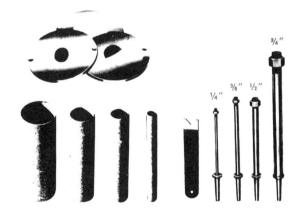

Fig. 29-11. Typical abrasive sleeves and spindles for a spindle sander. (Courtesy Boice Crane, A Division of Wilton Corp.)

the drums can range upward to 6 inches in diameter on the large industrial-type models. The width or height of a drum usually is about 6 inches.

An abrasive sleeve (Fig. 29-11) fitted around the sanding drum should be changed when it becomes worn or torn. The exact procedure for changing the abrasive depends on how the drum is made. Most of the sanding drums are made of rubber; however, metal and wood also are used. Pressure is used to hold an abrasive sleeve on the rubber drums. This pressure is created by tightening the spindle nut or by blowing air into the center of the drum (much like an innertube). To change this type of abrasive sleeve, re-

duce the pressure; then the sleeve can be slipped off. A sheet of abrasive, rather than a sleeve, is wrapped around a wooden drum. The abrasive, in these instances, is replaced by removing the tacks or staples which hold it in place. Special cement, similar to the type of cement used with a disk sander, is used for a metal drum. To replace the abrasive sleeve, first peel the sleeve from the drum. Then clean the drum, apply more cement, and slide the new sleeve over the drum.

General Safety Rules

A spindle sander is relatively safe to use. Perhaps, the most dangerous feature is the possibility of the fingers and/or stock being caught between the sanding drum and the opening in the table. Minor injuries also can occur when the fingers are brushed carelessly against the abrasive. Holding the stock haphazardly can result in the stock being pulled from the hands of the operator. Always hold the stock firmly while resting it flatwise on the table. Also, care should be taken to avoid wearing loose clothing while working around the revolving spindle.

Operation

The first rule to remember in sanding is to feed the stock *against* the rotation of the spindle (Fig. 29-12). Stock fed with the rotation of the spindle tends to "skip" or "jump." Also, move the stock continually to avoid overheating. If the spindle does not oscillate, the height of the table should be changed periodically for the

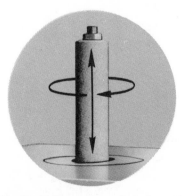

Fig. 29-12. Feed the stock against the rotation of the spindle. (Courtesy Boice Crane, A Division of Wilton Corp.)

abrasive to wear evenly. The diameter of the sanding drum should correspond to the curves being sanded, if possible. Using the incorrect drum size produces poor results (Fig. 29-13).

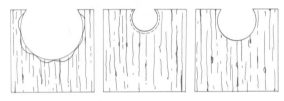

SANDING DRUM TOO SMALL | SANDING DRUM TOO LARGE | CORRECT SIZE

Fig. 29-13. Irregular sanding results when curves are sanded with sanding drums that are either too small or too large.

At the beginning, the stock should be pivoted into the drum. Only enough pressure should be applied to maintain contact between the stock and the drum. Sanding should not begin until the spindle has reached its full operating speed. The common sanding procedures are diagrammed in Fig. 29-14.

(A) Table and spindle at 90°.

(B) Table inclined for angular sanding.
Fig. 29-14. Sanding on the spindle sander.

Belt Sander

The belt sander in Fig. 29-15 is used to sand flat surfaces. On this sander, the stock is placed on the table and underneath the abrasive belt. Contact is made between the stock and the belt by pressing downward on the belt from its inside surface with a sanding block (Fig. 29-16). The area is sanded by working the block over that part of the belt above the stock and by pushing back and forth. While sanding, the block should be kept moving. If the block is stopped momentarily, the surface is sanded unevenly at that point (Fig. 29-17). The chief advantage of this type of sander is that large flat surfaces can be sanded. However, a disadvantage is that the machine is limited to a single special operation. For this reason, a smaller belt sander is often preferable.

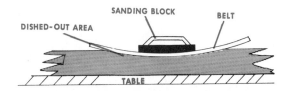

Fig. 29-17. Momentarily stopping the movement of the sanding block results in a surface sanded unevenly.

The smaller belt sanders are used widely to sand the surfaces, edges, and ends of small stock (Fig. 29-18). Contour sanding also is possible, if the upper belt guard is removed (Fig. 29-19). A typical belt sander can be operated with the belt in either a vertical or a horizontal position. Another unique feature is the table, which can be tilted for sanding angles; or it can be removed for horizontal sanding.

Fig. 29-15. Belt sander. (Courtesy Boice Crane, A Division of Wilton Corp.)

Fig. 29-16. Press down on the stock with a sanding block.

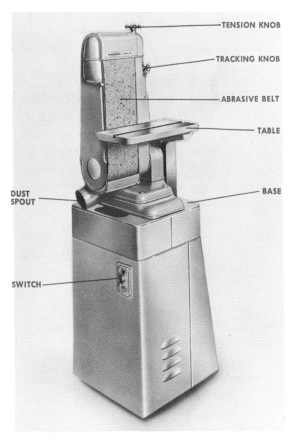

Fig. 29-18. Belt sander. (Courtesy Power Tool Division, Rockwell Manufacturing Company)

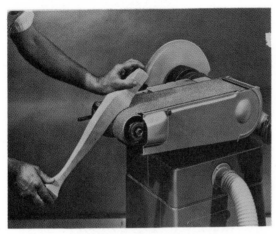

Fig. 29-19. The upper belt guard is removed for contour sanding. (Courtesy Power Tool Division, Rockwell Manufacturing Company)

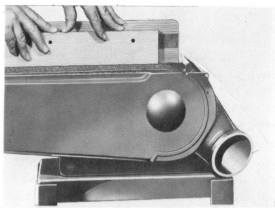

Fig. 29-20. Edge sanding with the belt in a horizontal position. (Courtesy Power Tool Division, Rockwell Manufacturing Company)

Replacing an Abrasive Belt

The first step in changing an abrasive belt involves removing the belt guard and/or the outside portion of the metal base. Next, the tension knob is turned until the tension is released on the idler pulley. The used belt is then pulled outward from both pulleys. This procedure is reversed when installing another belt. After the belt is replaced, it must be tracked properly before sanding. This adjustment is made with a tracking knob located near the upper belt guard.

Fig. 29-21. Belt in an inclined position for angular sanding. (Courtesy Power Tool Diviscion, Rockwell Manufacturing Company)

General Safety Rules

1. Make adjustments only while the switch is off and the abrasive belt is not turning.
2. When the table is moved, check the clearance with the belt before turning on the power.
3. Do not begin sanding, unless the belt is running at full speed.
4. Avoid wearing loose clothing around the sander.
5. If possible, position the back of the stock firmly against the backstop while sanding.

Fig. 29-22. Belt in horizontal position for sanding flat surfaces. (Courtesy Power Tool Division, Rockwell Manufacturing Company)

6. Stand in front of the belt—never directly behind it.
7. Use a holding device or jig in sanding small pieces difficult to hold.
8. Lower the stock evenly onto the belt to prevent it being jerked backward.

Operation

Sanding with a belt sander is quite simple. The stock is brought gradually into contact with the belt. Then, while maintaining adequate pressure, it is moved about until the sanding is completed. The various procedures depend on the type of sanding being performed. For example, a fence serves as a guide for edge sanding with the belt in a horizontal position (see Fig. 29-20). A piece of stock supported by the table is sanded at an angle when the belt is inclined (Fig. 29-21). If the belt is used vertically, the sanding should be perpendicular to the face supported by the table. Surfaces, or faces, should be sanded with the belt in a horizontal position (Fig. 29-22). For this operation, the table should be replaced by a backstop.

Questions

1. What type of sanding is performed with a disk sander?

2. A disk sander is often combined with another type of sander. Name the other machine. What is the advantage of using this combination?
3. How is the abrasive sheet or belt attached to a: (1) Disk sander; (2) Spindle sander; and (3) Belt sander?
4. Why is all sanding performed on the downward turning side of a disk?
5. What is meant by "burning" the wood? How can burning be prevented?
6. When should a spindle sander be used?
7. How is the size indicated for a: (1) Disk sander; (2) Spindle sander; and (3) Belt sander?
8. Explain why the stock is fed opposite the rotation of a spindle sander.
9. What does "oscillating" mean?
10. List the advantages of a small belt sander, as compared to a large belt sander.
11. How is contour sanding performed on a small belt sander?
12. What do the letters "fpm" indicate?
13. Why is a backstop needed for sanding flat surfaces (or faces)?
14. Describe several ways in which angles can be sanded with a small belt sander.

Unit 30 — Selecting and Using Glues

The selection and application of glue is an important factor in determining the quality of a finished wood product. A piece of furniture that falls apart is useless; a building made with construction plywood that peels is poor in quality; and wooden structural beams and rafters that deteriorate are dangerous. The proper glue should be selected for the job.

Factors to be considered in selecting the type of glue to be used include whether the object is to be clamped, the strength required, whether the glue must be waterproof or water-resistant, the heat involved, and the types of material to be fastened. A boat obviously should be glued with waterproof glue, and an object to be used in a damp, humid climate should be glued with a water-resistant glue at least. Furniture to be used in the desert countries does not need the water-resistive qualities. The glue needed to fasten wood to wood is different from the glue needed for glass or plastics. Another factor in selecting glues includes the length of time required for the glue to set and harden. A fast-drying, or "fast-setting," glue is advantageous when only a few clamps are needed and the assembly is simple; but this is a disadvantage when many pieces are to be assembled at the same time. A fast-setting glue might be well dried or set before a large piece of furniture can be assembled. Therefore, a slower drying glue might be preferred in assembling a large unit.

Two general classifications of glue are available: (1) Natural, and (2) Synthetic. The natural glues are made from products found in nature, such as milk products, animal hides and hooves, and fluids from trees. The synthetic glues are chiefly the result of the chemical plastics products developed over several years. With the manufacture of synthetic chemicals which resembled plant and animal (organic) chemicals, the ability of the plastics industries to make glues and adhesives has increased tremendously. Glues are available that can hold metal, are extremely strong, require no clamping, and ad-

283

here in difficult conditions, such as cold or damp surfaces. However, many of the synthetic glues are extremely expensive and do not lend themselves for use in a small shop. The selection of the glues to be used on any activity should be based on several factors (Table 30-1).

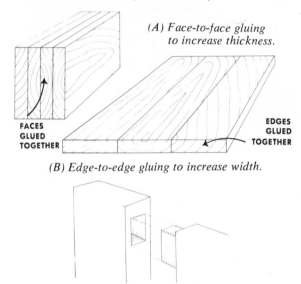

(A) Face-to-face gluing to increase thickness.

FACES GLUED TOGETHER

EDGES GLUED TOGETHER

(B) Edge-to-edge gluing to increase width.

(C) Permanent glue joint.

Fig. 30-1. Types of gluing.

In gluing, do not fail to read the manufacturer's specifications on the container before beginning the operation. This provides information on what to expect, the length of time involved for hardening or setting, and the types of pressure required on the pieces being joined.

Natural Glues

The two most common natural glues are the animal or hide glues and casein glue, which is made chiefly from milk products. Animal glue, commonly referred to as hide glue, is made from the hooves, bones, sinews, and skin linings of animals. The better grades of animal glues are strong and extremely durable. The two types of these glues available are the melted or heated glue and the water-soluable glue. Both these glues are similar, but the hot glue sets quicker than the cold glue. Both these glues require the workroom and the objects to be glued to be reasonably warm and clean.

Table 30-1. Adhesive Characteristics

TYPE OF ADHESIVE x—indicates can be used xx—indicates best for this purpose	TYPE OF USE							CONDITION OF USE							
	Wood to Wood	Wood to Plastic	Wood to Plastic Laminates	Wood to Metal	Paper or Cloth to Wood	Metal to Metal	China or Ceramics	Plastic Tops (counters, etc.)	Wood Paneling	Veneers	Boats—Marine	Interior	Outdoor	Tiles—Horizontal	Tiles—Vertical
Animal (Hide)	x				x					x		x			
Casein	x		x					x	x			x			
Urea Resin	xx		x					x		x		xx			
Resorcinol	x										xx				
Polyvinyl (White)	xx	x	x		xx			x	x	x		x		xx	
Epoxy				xx		xx	x					xx	xx		
Household Cement (clear, with vinyl base)		x			x		xx							x	
Contact Cement	x	x	xx	x	x			xx	xx	xx				xx	x
Mastics	x		x							x		x		x	xx

The casein glues used in homes and schools generally are in the form of a dry powder. The powder is mixed with water at the time of use and in the desired quantity. Then the glue is blended and permitted to stand for a few minutes to become smooth and even-textured. The glue is relatively slow in drying, but it is extremely hard and resistant to moisture. Certain stains are caused by the glue, resulting from its alkaline chemical composition. Oak and mahogany, which are slightly acid woods, stain quite easily when casein glue is applied. Normally, the shelf life of casein glue is approximately one year. It can be tested to determine whether it is fit to use, merely by moistening the fingers. Dip one finger into the powder; then briskly rub two fingers together. If the fingers seem sticky, the glue can be used; however, if the fingers do not seem sticky, the glue should be discarded.

Another type of natural glue is made from the sap of trees. Rubber cement and mastic cement are natural glues from tree sap. The rubber cement is used extensively in joining paper to paper. The mastic cements are made from the sap of the mastic tree, which grows in southern Europe. It is an excellent cement for tiles, paneling, and flooring. Both the mastic and the rubber cements have been displaced by superior synthetic products.

Synthetic Resin Glues

The synthetic glues generally are made from the plastic compounds developed through research to resemble organic compounds. These include several hundred types of special glues, and it is impossible to list them here. However, some of the major types are the urea formaldehyde-resin glues, the polyvinyl resins, the resorcinol resins, and epoxies.

The synthetic resins generally are classified into two areas: (1) Thermoplastic resins, and (2) Thermosetting resins. The thermoplastic resins are glues which become soft when heated. The thermosetting glues are not affected by heat after they have set. In addition, they usually either require heat in setting or generate small quantities of heat during the setting process. The heat required can be merely the heat in a warm room.

Urea Formaldehyde Resin Glues

Urea formaldehyde resin glues (often called "urea" glues) normally are supplied for the home, school, and shop in a powder form similar to the casein glues. They are tested in much the same manner, have much the same appearance, and many of them have the same characteristics. The urea resin glues found in industrial situations in liquid form have a storage life of one year or more when stored properly in cool dry areas. The glue is relatively slow in drying, which permits several minutes for assembly. At least 20 to 30 minutes can be used in clamping or assembling. Therefore, the glue should be used in an area where the temperature is not lower than about 70°. In addition, the clamping time required for this glue is approximately four hours with some curing time required after removal of the clamps before the wood can be worked.

Polyvinyl Glues

The polyvinyl glues are perhaps the best known and most widely used glues under various names. They are often called "white glue." This glue is often supplied in the plastic squeeze-bottle type of container, and it is quite handy. The white glue is supplied in liquid form, and it is ready to use when squeezed from the bottle. The glue can be used in a location in which the temperature is approximately 60° or higher, and it is transparent when completely dry or set. The polyvinyl resins, however, cure or set quickly, usually in approximately 30 minutes. Only 4 or 5 minutes can be permitted before the assembly is complete. A longer assembly time affects the curing and the strength of the glue. The chief disadvantages of the polyvinyl resins are: (1) Lack water-resistance, and (2) Affected by high temperatures. They can be used on many materials, such as wood, paper, leather, some ceramics, and for many household uses. Again, the disadvantages are low resistance to water, low resistance to temperature, and generally unsuitable on non-porous surfaces. These glues should not be used on materials used outdoors or where the temperature is higher than 160°F.

Resorcinol Resin Glues

The resorcinol glues are recommended for a product which is to be exposed to weather or continuous water soaking. It is an excellent glue for outdoor furniture or boats. Normally, the glue is supplied in liquid form with a catalyst, which can be either a powder or a liquid. The two elements, the glue and the catalyst, are mixed at the time of use. Both the wood and the glue should be at a temperature of 70°F or higher when the resorcinol resins are used, or the full strength and water-resistive capabilities will not be achieved. The curing time of the glue is relatively short, and it should be worked quickly. The setting of this glue can be speeded, if a means of heating the glue line or work area can be accomplished.

Rubber-Resin Glues

The rubber-resin glues are quite helpful in assembling countertops, tabletops, ceramics to wood—such as ceramic tile —and for assembling the laminated plastics to other materials. Examples of this type of glue are a contact cement and a rubber cement. Although they are not identical, they do exhibit similar characteristics. The glue normally is applied to both surfaces to be joined; then both surfaces are permitted to dry. The two pieces are aligned carefully and pressed together with a roller or with the hands. Neither clamping pressure nor special curing devices are required. The glue does not possess great strength, but flat surfaces do not require great strength. After the glue is applied, the pieces to be joined should be aligned carefully, since the glue bonds on contact and should not be moved. One method of aligning counters and the larger pieces of laminated plastics is to place a sheet of waxed paper between the objects; then, when the two pieces are aligned, the waxed paper is removed and the pieces are bonded.

Epoxy Glue

Another type of artificial resin glue is the epoxy glue. The epoxies require both a resin and a catalyst hardener; these substances are mixed at the time the glue is prepared for use. The amount of catalyst can be varied to harden the mixture either rapidly or slowly, and the glue can be used to bond nearly any substance. The epoxies are extremely tough, strong, and durable. Their setting time can vary from a few minutes to several hours. Generally, the epoxies are quite expensive for extensive use, but they are extremely practical for gluing small objects, especially decorative items. These epoxy resins also are used in fiber-glass work.

Gluing and Assembly

Three broad classifications of gluing and assembly are used; these include: (1)

Face-to-face gluing in which the thickness of the stock is built up or increased; (2) Edge-to-edge gluing in which the width of the object is extended or increased, as in making a wider surface; and (3) Permanent joint gluing. All these types of gluing are diagrammed in Fig. 30-1. Joint gluing normally requires clamps after the joint areas have received a thin coating of glue.

When clamping or assembling the pieces of work, a test assembly should be made, without the glue. Thus, the difficult

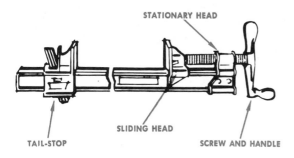

(A) Parts diagram.

(B) Correct clamping with bar clamps.

Fig. 30-2. Bar clamp. (Courtesy Adjustable Clamp Co.)

or time-consuming operations can be emphasized and adequate preparation can be made. Also, the basic adjustments for the clamps can be made before beginning the assembly. Therefore, less assembly

time is needed. This can be quite important when fast-setting glues are being used.

In gluing, the type of clamp used depends chiefly on the shape of the work to be glued. The most common types of clamps are the bar clamp (Fig. 30-2), the hand-screw or parallel clamp (Fig. 30-3), and the C clamp (Fig. 30-4). To glue and hold irregular shapes while gluing, the band or strap clamp (Fig. 30-5) is often used. The band can be made from cloth webbing; or it can be made of steel. The strap clamp is quite useful for gluing round and curved objects, as well as in gluing hexagonal and octagonal pieces.

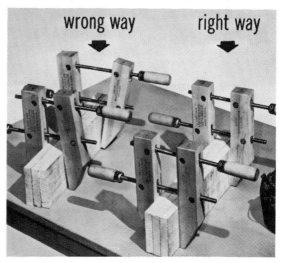

Fig. 30-3. Wrong and right ways to use the hand screw or parallel clamp. (Courtesy Adjustable Clamp Co.)

Picture frames can be glued with the clamp setup in Fig. 30-6. Cabinet doors and paneled areas also can be clamped in these devices. These frames aid in holding the miter joints square, while pressure is applied with a clamp in the middle section.

When the material is glued, electronic gluing machines are employed frequently to speed up the drying process. These machines use radiation similar to radar to heat a small area around the glue line; the

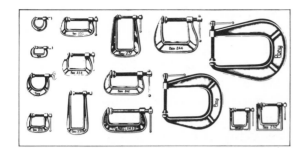

Fig. 30-4. C clamps. (Courtesy Adjustable Clamp Co.)

(A) Band clamp.

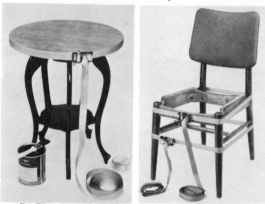

(B) Clamping a round shape.   (C) Band clamp for assembly.

(D) Clamping a rectangular shape.

Fig. 30-5. Band or strap clamp for irregular shapes. (Courtesy Adjustable Clamp Co.)

heat causes the glue to set quicker. Care should be taken in using electronic glue machines to keep the fingers or other parts of the body away from the electrodes.

Fig. 30-6. Setup for clamping a picture frame. (Courtesy Adjustable Clamp Co.)

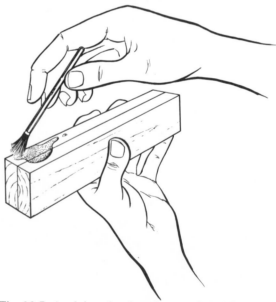

Fig. 30-7. Applying glue for edge-to-edge gluing.

Edge-to-Edge Gluing

In edge-to-edge gluing, the glue is spread on each of the edges to be joined. The glue can be applied with a brush, with an applicator, or with the fingers (Fig. 30-7). The glue is spread lightly over the entire surface to be joined; then the pieces are clamped (Fig. 30-8). In gluing stock edge-to-edge, the annular rings (grain of the wood) should be alternated (Fig. 30-9) to prevent warping of the material. Warpage can be reduced further by using boards narrow in width. A board wider than 5 or 6 inches often warps; thus it should be ripped to a smaller width. As the pressure is applied, a small quantity of glue should be squeezed from the glue line. The time allotted for clamping and drying depends on the type of glue and the gluing arrangement.

Fig. 30-8. Edge-to-edge clamping. (Courtesy Adjustable Clamp Co.)

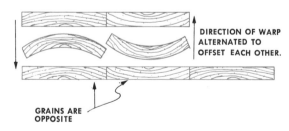

Fig. 30-9. Alternating the grain in pieces of stock to prevent warping.

Face-to-Face Gluing

Face-to-face gluing is employed when the thickness of an object is to be increased or built up. Occasions for building up the thickness include making a pedestal lamp, building up the thickness

for turning a bowl on a lathe, and similar pieces of work. Face-to-face gluing is similar to edge-to-edge gluing in the method of application of the glue and in the thickness of the coating applied. The coating should be thin, and any suitable method can be employed to spread the glue evenly. When the material is clamped (Fig. 30-10), care must be taken to spread the pressure equally to avoid uneven adhesion of the faces. When contact cement is used, the pressure should be applied in the central area (Fig. 30-11) and then moved toward the edges. A veneer press (Fig. 30-12) can be used in assembling wide, flat areas.

Fig. 30-10. Face-to-face gluing and clamping.

Gluing Joints

Joints are cut into the wood to provide strength and rigidity to the object. The chief objective of gluing is to hold the joint in place, rather than to provide strength to the joint. Normally, the joint is strong; the glue prevents the joint from slipping or moving out of place. The type of joint used determines the type of glue and the clamping procedures. When using dowels, the glue should be applied to the dowel, rather than to the hole. If the glue is placed in the hole and the dowel is driven in or forced in with pressure (Fig. 30-13), the condition is much like using a hydraulic jack, causing the wood to

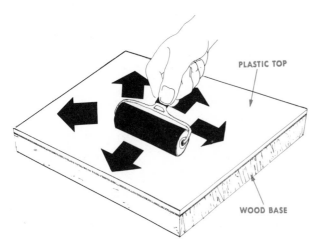

Fig. 30-11. Applying pressure to a laminated table or countertop.

split and break. Generally, in gluing joints, only enough glue should be used to thinly coat the areas to be joined. Then

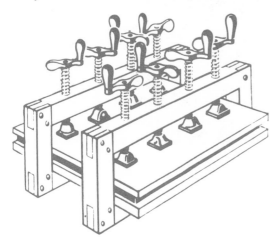

Fig. 30-12. A veneer press for assembling wide, flat areas. (Courtesy Adjustable Clamp Co.)

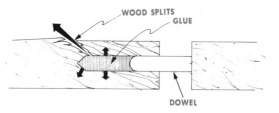

Fig. 30-13. Do not fill the dowel hole with glue.

the joint should be clamped or held with mechanical fasteners to complete the joining process.

Questions

1. What factors should be considered in selecting the type of glue?
2. List the chief types of natural glues used in woodworking.
3. What glue should be used if a waterproof joint is desired?
4. What type of glue should be used for water-resistant gluing?
5. What type of glue should be used to attach a plastic countertop?
6. List the three broad classifications of gluing.
7. What type of clamp is commonly used for edge-to-edge gluing?
8. What type of gluing is often done with a hand-screw clamp for pressure?
9. Why are the dowels coated with glue, rather than placing the glue in the hole and then inserting the dowel?

Unit 31 – Metal Fasteners

Although joints and dowels are in common use in furniture construction, many other types of fasteners also are used, particularly in building construction. Mechanical fasteners made of metal are used extensively to fasten wood to metal; to attach special hardware, such as hinges, locks, and handles; and in joints in which dowel or cut joints are difficult.

Probably the most common fastener, other than nails, is the wood screw. Screws can be used to fasten pieces together without glue, thereby permitting them to be disassembled. Also, screws are used in situations requiring the boards to be held together more firmly than with nails. Since screws hold more permanently, they are less likely to loosen than boards held with nails.

The types of screws used most frequently in woodworking are the flathead (FH), oval-head (OH) and round-head (RH) wood screws (Fig. 31-1). The oval-head and the round-head screws usually are used in situations where the screw head will be visible. The flathead wood screw is commonly used where the screw head will be exposed, but not seen, or where the screw head is to be counterbored and covered with a decorative plug or filler (Fig. 31-2). All the basic shapes —flathead, round head, or oval head— can be obtained in the standard slotted head or the special Phillips-head screw.

Wood screws vary in length from ¼ inch to 6 inches and are designated by gauge or diameter and length. The gauge sizes range from No. 0 to No. 24, accord-

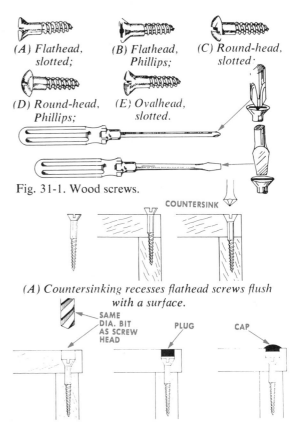

(A) Flathead, slotted; *(B) Flathead, Phillips;* *(C) Round-head, slotted;*

(D) Round-head, Phillips; *(E) Ovalhead, slotted.*

Fig. 31-1. Wood screws.

COUNTERSINK

(A) Countersinking recesses flathead screws flush with a surface.

SAME DIA. BIT AS SCREW HEAD PLUG CAP

(B) Counterboring recesses the screw head below the surface. Then the holes can be plugged or capped to improve the appearance of the surface.
Fig. 31-2. Countersinking and counterboring.

ing to the diameter of the straight portion of the shank. The smaller screws are designated by the smaller number—the diameter of a No. 1 screw is smaller than the diameter of a No. 10 screw. The details for screw sizes can be found in Fig. 31-3. The screws are described in the following manner:

$$1 \times 10 - FH$$

This indicates that the screw is 1 inch long, a No. 10 in diameter, and a flathead (FH) screw. Normally, the screws are

NUMBER GUAGE	APPROXIMATE SHANK DIAMETER	SHANK HOLE		PILOT HOLE
		Twist-drill size	Auger-bit number	Twist drill size
1	5/64	5/64	—	—
2	3/32	3/32	—	1/16
3	3/32	7/64	—	1/16
4	7/64	7/64	—	5/64
5	1/8	1/8	—	5/64
6	9/64	9/64	—	3/32
7	5/32	5/32	—	7/64
8	11/64	11/64	—	7/64
9	11/64	3/16	—	1/8
10	3/16	3/16	—	1/8
12	7/32	7/32	4	9/64
14	15/64	1/4	4	5/32

(AUGER BIT NOT USED)

Fig. 31-3. Correct size of holes and bits for wood screws.

sold either in boxes of 100 screws or in boxes of 1 gross, which is 12 dozen, or 144 screws. In comparing the prices of screws, it is important to note whether the box of screws contains a gross (144) or only 100 screws. Screws also can be purchased in smaller quanties at various stores. Usually, they are much more expensive in the smaller packages.

Fastening with Wood Screws

The first step in using wood screws to fasten two pieces of wood together is to prepare the hole for the shank. The center of the hole is located; then a sharp dent is made in the wood with an awl. The hole should be drilled in the top piece of wood (Fig. 31-4) with the diameter approximately the same as the diameter of the shank of the screw. The relative sizes for the twist drills to be used with the numbered screws can be found in Fig. 31-3. The pilot hole for the threaded portion of the screw then can be located (Fig. 31-5). Since the pilot hole is smaller than the shank hole, the threads of the screw

dig into the surrounding wood to provide the firm, strong fastening action. Special combination wood drills are available with two or more sizes on the same drill —one size for the pilot hole, a slightly larger size for the shank hole, and a third size for automatically countersinking or counterboring the screw. (Fig. 31-6).

The proper size of screwdriver should be used in turning the screw to prevent damage to the slot of the screw. The tip of the blade should fit the slot snugly, without movement.

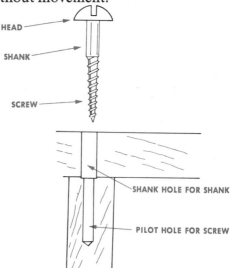

Fig. 31-4. Shank and pilot holes for screws

Machine Screws

Machine screws differ from wood screws in that the machine screw is similar to a small bolt. It is not made with a tapered thread to bite into the wood. Instead, a special nut is required on the opposite side of the wood (Fig. 31-7), and it is tightened to hold firmly. The chief difference between a machine screw and a bolt is that the bolts are ¼ inch in diameter, or larger, and the machine screws are smaller than ¼ inch in diameter. Machine screws are available in the same basic head styles found in wood screws and in both slotted and Phillips heads; they are described in a manner similar to

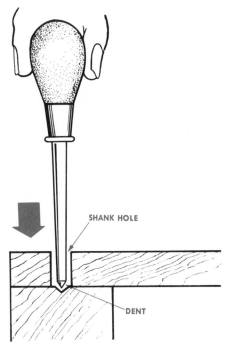

Fig. 31-5. Locating the pilot hole.

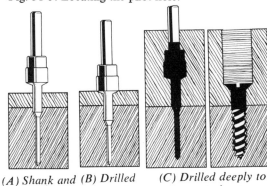

(A) Shank and pilot hole.   *(B) Drilled deeper to countersink.*   *(C) Drilled deeply to counterbore.*

Fig. 31-6. Combination drill. Drilling for the pilot hole, shank hole, and countersinking or counterboring is performed or combined in a single operation.

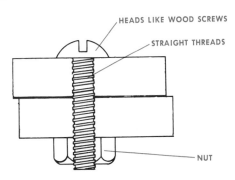

Fig. 31-7. Machine screw.

wood screws relative to the size or diameter of the screw and the head shape. However, machine screws also are designated by the number of threads per inch. For example, a machine screw is designated:

$$6 - 32 \times 1 \, RH$$

This indicates that the screw is a No. 6 in diameter, with 32 threads per inch, and that it is 1 inch long with a round head (RH). Typical machine screws are shown in Fig. 31-8.

In drilling the holes for machine screws, drill the hole the same size or equal to the largest diameter of the screw.

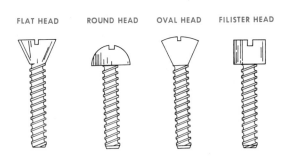

Fig. 31-8. Types of machine screws.

Nails

The various types of nails commonly used in woodworking are shown in Fig. 31-9. The *common* nails are made with heavy, flat heads. The *box* nails have thinner, flatter heads and are slightly smaller in diameter than the common nails. The *finishing* nails have small heads and often are set with a nail set and covered with putty or plastic wood. A *brad* is a small finishing nail, which varies in length from ¼ to 1¼ inches. It is used for nailing thin stock. A *casing* nail is made with a cone-shaped head. Since this type of head provides excellent holding power, the casing nail is used for cabinetwork and interior trim.

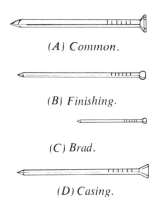

(A) Common.

(B) Finishing.

(C) Brad.

(D) Casing.

Fig. 31-9. Types of nails.

The size of nail is indicated by the term *penny* or the symbol *d*. A *2d*, or 2-penny, nail is 1 inch in length. For each additional penny, add ¼ inch in length upward to 3 inches. For example, a 3-penny nail is 1¼ inch and a 10-penny nail is 3 inches in length. Some important principles to remember in using nails are:

1. The length of a nail should be three times the thickness of the board being nailed.
2. The *6d* and *8d* nails are used to nail 1-inch siding, sheathing, etc.
3. The *16d* and *20d* nails are used to nail 2-inch framing.
4. Galvanized nails increase weather resistance.

Other Fasteners

Special screws include the lag screws, which are larger in diameter—like bolts, but their threads are similar to those on a wood screw (Fig. 31-10). Lag screws are commonly used to attach a heavy object to a wall, to fasten heavy wood pieces together, and to bolt machinery or workbenches to wood floors. Lag shields can be used with the lag screws to attach an object to a masonry or metal wall.

Stove bolts are identical to the machine screws, except that the diameters are larger than ¼ inch. They are avail-

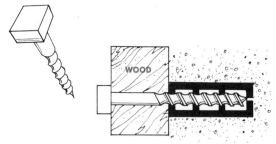

Fig. 31-10. Lag bolt.

able with round heads, oval heads, flat heads, etc.; also, they are available in standard slotted or Phillips-head styles.

Machine bolts are unlike the machine screws. The machine bolts (Fig. 31-11) do not have slotted heads for use with a screwdriver. The heads of the machine bolts are generally square or hexagonal-shaped for turning with a wrench. The various turning tools are shown in Fig. 31-12.

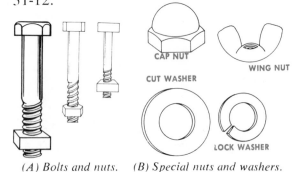

(A) Bolts and nuts.   *(B) Special nuts and washers.*

Fig. 31-11. Machine bolts.

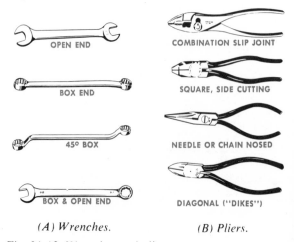

(A) Wrenches.   *(B) Pliers.*

Fig. 31-12. Wrenches and pliers.

Carriage bolts are designed specifically to attach wooden pieces to metal. The carriage bolts originally were designed to bolt the wood sides of wagons, carriages, and stagecoaches to a metal frame (Fig. 31-13). The special head on the carriage bolt is round and smooth on the outside; however, immediately beneath the head a square section prevents the bolt turning in

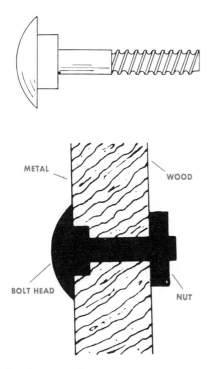

Fig. 31-13. A carriage bolt is used to fasten wood to metal.

the wood. In use, the square head is driven downward into the round hole when the bolt is inserted. The square portion of the upper shank thus is jammed into the round hole firmly, permitting the bolt to be tightened with a wrench at the threaded end.

Special fastening devices, such as corrugated fasteners and straddle staples, also are used. These two devices are shown in Fig. 31-14. They are especially helpful in joining the corners of objects, such as screen doors, together.

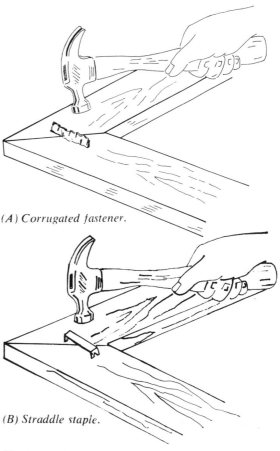

(A) Corrugated fastener.

(B) Straddle staple.

Fig. 31-14. Metal fasteners for a miter joint.

Questions

1. What is the chief difference between a bolt and a machine screw?
2. How is the size of a wood screw determined?
3. Which is larger in diameter, a No. 6 or a No. 8 wood screw?
4. Which machine screw is larger in diameter, a No. 6 or a No. 10?
5. How does a carriage bolt differ from a machine bolt?
6. How does a machine screw differ from a stove bolt?
7. Why is a pilot hole made smaller than the shank hole?
8. What is the chief difference between countersinking and counterboring?
9. How can a screw head be hidden?

Unit 32 – Lamination in Shop and Industry

Laminated articles can be manufactured and fabricated in a school shop or mass-produced in industrial factories. The laminated pieces can be made from layers of wood, plastics, or metals pressed into various shapes. The shapes retained result from the combination of the adhesives and the natural properties of the materials. When the layers are from different materials, such as wood and metal, great care should be exercised in selecting the proper glues and adhesives.

This type of molding is often used to bend solid wood pieces. The thicker pieces of wood can be bent and formed when they have been softened properly by the use of steam or hot and cold water. In some instances, relief cuts are made in a thick piece of wood to permit the pieces to bend more easily (Fig. 32-1). Small veneers are often placed in the relief cuts to maintain a solid thickness. When the piece is dried, the glues, veneers, and original piece are formed into a single solid mass. Other veneering and relief-cut techniques are used to form curved countertop edges and walls. This technique is shown in Fig. 32-2.

As the adhesives and the laminating techniques became more refined and as the various types of wood became more scarce and more costly, the laminating process was developed, using thin veneers and other laminating materials. These materials were laminated and molded to obtain strength, pleasing shapes and appearances, and contrasting materials.

The advantages of the molded laminates include a minimum of shaping and

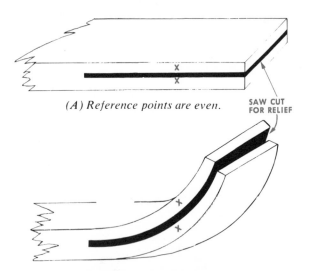

(A) Reference points are even.

SAW CUT FOR RELIEF

(B) Reference points are uneven.

Fig. 32-1. Relief cuts in molding solid pieces.

(A) Make relief cuts nearly through the board.

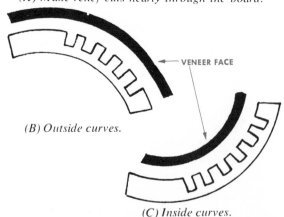

VENEER FACE

(B) Outside curves.

(C) Inside curves.

Fig. 32-2. Relief cuts and laminated facings on curved surfaces.

forming operations, less cutting and machine tooling, maximum use of material with the least waste, increase in strength for the weight by utilizing the natural strength of grain structures, and the abil-

Fig. 32-3. The unusual shape and springiness of this chair results from its laminated structure; these characteristics are virtually impossible with solid wood. (Courtesy Fine Hardwoods Association)

ity to create unusual designs. The chair in Fig. 32-3 is an example of a laminated piece of furniture.

Laminating Molds

The key to producing the molded laminates is the mold. Two types of molds are used—fixed and adjustable. Adjustable molds are used principally in industy to form structural laminates, such as the beams and rafters in Figs. 32-4 to 32-7. Fixed molds are used primarily in the fabrication of the smaller products and are

Fig. 32-4. A laminated wood framing and decking system are incorporated in this building, which is the first structure of its type built in Florida. (Courtesy Potlatch Forests, Inc.)

Fig. 32-5. A laminated beam. (Courtesy Potlach Forests, Inc.)

Fig. 32-6. Lock Deck® siding (ceiling). (Courtesy Potlach Forests, Inc.)

Fig. 32-7. This hidden connector system makes possible the solid, full-strength joints between the beams and laminated uprights (left) and the upright-foundation pier tie-ins (right), without exposing the metal connectors. (Courtesy Potlach Forests, Inc.)

adaptable to the small shop. Some examples of fixed molds are shown in Figs. 32-8 through 32-11.

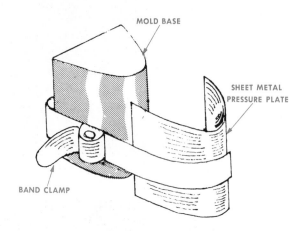

Fig. 32-8. Form for laminating sharp angles.

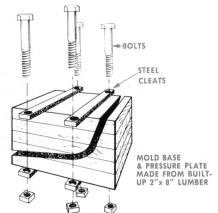

Fig. 32-9. Form for laminating the ends of water skis.

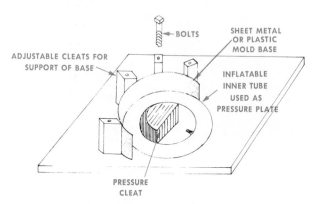

Fig. 32-10. Adjustable mold for larger curves.

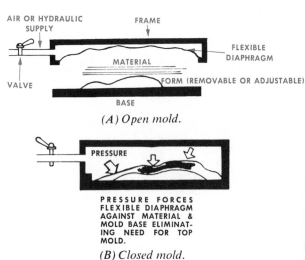

(A) Open mold.

PRESSURE FORCES FLEXIBLE DIAPHRAGM AGAINST MATERIAL & MOLD BASE ELIMINATING NEED FOR TOP MOLD.

(B) Closed mold.

Fig. 32-11. Mold for smaller shapes.

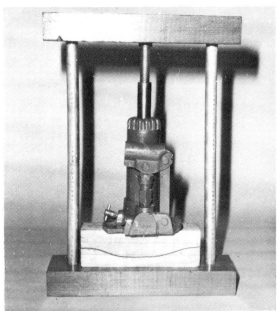

Fig. 32-12. Clamping form.

All the fixed molds feature a firm base support with a smooth surface made from metal, polished wood, or laminated plastics, such as those used on countertops. The molding surface should be smooth, and it can be made from the same materials used in the base support. It is not necessary for the molding surface to be as solid as the base, if a means of applying pressure evenly is provided (see Figs. 32-8, 32-9, and 32-11). The third requirement is a means of applying pressure. For extremely small molds, this pressure can be applied with simple devices, such as a rubber band. However, for the larger pieces, the pressure can be applied with bolts, clamps, jacks, or inflatable diaphragms, which can be made from the inner tubes from automobile tires. All these methods are used industrially; however, in those industrial applications in which speed of assembly is an important factor, either a fast-setting adhesive or some type of heating process is used to speed the setting and hardening time of the adhesives. A mold made and used in a small shop is shown in Fig. 32-12. Typical projects made with this type of mold are shown in Fig. 32-13.

Fig. 32-13. Formed objects.

Forming and Working the Laminate Materials

Laminating can be done easily by using the thin wood veneers; the sheet metals, such as brass, copper, and aluminum; or the various sheet plastics. In using different types of materials, great care should be exercised to select the proper adhesive. Most of the thin layers can be worked with wood tools; but many metal

tools, such as tin snips and squaring shears, can be used effectively on metals, plastics, and the thin wood veneers. Only a few special tools are required; however, some special tools, such as the rollers (Fig. 32-14) used for spreading pressures, are desirable. Contact cement also is the desirable adhesive in many instances. See Table 30-1 for the proper glues to use.

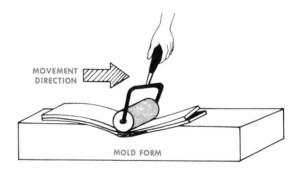

Fig. 32-14. A roller can be used to mold small pieces made with contact cement.

If the radius of the bend is quite small, it is good practice to soak the veneer in hot water or steam until it softens. The wet wood, however, tends to weaken the glue joint. Therefore, it is more satisfactory to clamp the soaked material in the form; then permit it to dry to provide maximum glue strength and some preforming of the material. When the material is dry, the glue is applied and the material attains the final molded shapes.

When using pressure molds which utilize either air pressure or hydraulic pressure, low-pressure systems are more satisfactory. A suitable low air pressure source in many shops is the compressed-air supply for spray-gun equipment. Excessive air pressure can cause the diaphragms to explode with considerable force. Hydraulic fluid, such as the low pressure in most water systems or the low air pressure from spray equipment, can be used effectively. Other types of pressure systems include the use of weights and wedges. If contact cements are used and if the shape is not an extreme radius, the form can be obtained merely by applying pressure in the center portion, working toward the edges with a roller.

When the laminating layers are different types of materials, such as plastics and metals, used with contact cement, it is advisable to roughen the surfaces of the metals or plastics, since the glue sticks better to a rough surface than to a smooth surface. The porous structure of the wood permits the cement to adhere to the wood easily. The extremely flat, smooth surfaces of metals and plastics make binding difficult with certain types of cements. The surface is scored or roughened to provide a smooth surface, such as a metal or a plastic, with a rough texture for the cement to bond (Fig. 32-15).

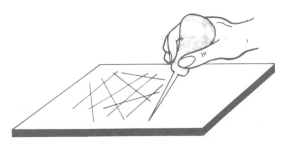

Fig. 32-15. Scoring a smooth surface improves adhesion.

Adhesives, such as the epoxy resins, adhere to nearly any type of surface and can be used effectively with smooth metals and plastics. When the epoxy resins are used, care should be exercised to make sure the resins do not bind the object to the mold. One method of preventing this is to line the mold with a sheet of waxed paper.

In industrial situations where high production rates are important and where wax paper is quite cumbersome, certain chemical compounds are used to prevent the materials sticking to the mold. If the material sticks to the mold, lumps which, in turn, cause faulty spots in the finished product are formed. Agents or chemicals known as mold-release agents are sprayed onto the molds after each operation. These chemicals (waxes, silicon compounds, or oils) keep the materials from sticking to the sides of the molds.

The workers usually brush the surface of the molds with a brush, glove, or similar material to break loose any particles which might adhere to the surface. Then the surface is coated with the release agent, and the succeeding unit is assembled. The type of release agent required depends on the type of bonding agent, cement, or plastic resin used and on the type of material being assembled. Waxes and oils are not desirable for laminating wood, since the wood can absorb the wax or oil, thereby marring the finish on the wood product. Materials should be used which do not react with the material being molded; or materials should be used which do not interfere with the sticking capability of the bonding cement.

The molds should be protected during the storage process. A smooth mold provides a smooth product; however, a roughened mold or a damaged mold does not permit the product to retain its smooth surface. Therefore, the molds must be protected carefully during storage and moving. This can be done by padding the surface of the mold; or if the mold is a two-piece mold, it can be clamped together to make sure the smooth inside portions of the mold are connected. Expandable molds and combination molds do not need this careful protection. However, when a mold is not in use, it should be stored in a place where other tools and materials are not thrown against it to damage or mar the surface of the mold.

Laying Laminated Plastics

Plastic laminates are used widely for countertops, tables, wall coverings, desks, and furniture. The plastic laminates are extremely popular, since they can be provided with any pattern, appearance, and to some extent, texture desired. The laminates also can be molded and shaped into various articles other than those with a flat surface (Fig. 32-16). The plastic laminates are available under trade names, such as *Formica, Micarta, Nevamar,* etc. The plastic laminates also are popular, because they are quick to apply, require no finishing, blend with nearly any design, and are highly resistant to scuffs, impact, heat and cold, stains, and liquids. They are ideal for use in areas where liquids are used frequently, as for the walls and cabinets in kitchens, bathrooms, and laundry areas. Some of these uses, as well as other uses, are shown in Figs. 32-17 through 32-23.

The plastic laminates were developed in the early nineteen hundreds by Emil Haefely of Basle, Switzerland. He had discovered a method of bonding kraft paper into layers, using shellac for the bond-

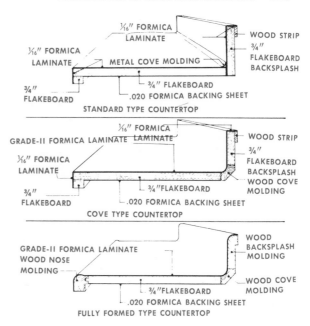

Fig. 32-17. Laminated countertop construction detail. (Courtesy Formica Corporation)

Fig. 32-18. The plastic laminates combine beauty and practicality in a modern kitchen. (Courtesy Formica Corporation)

ing glue and then pressing the materials together in a heated press to dry and cure the shellac. George Westinghouse, the founder of Westinghouse Corporation, saw this process and brought it to the United States in 1909, where the product was to be used primarily for an insulating

Fig. 32-16. Factory-made laminated chair.

Fig. 32-19. Sturdy and easily cleaned counters and walls for commercial use are made from plastic laminates. (Courtesy Formica Corporation)

Fig. 32-21. Reinforced plastic laminated desktops are extremely sturdy. (Courtesy Lyon Metal Products, Inc.)

Fig. 32-20. Sturdy and decorative interiors are formed from plastic laminates. (Courtesy Formica Corporation)

Fig. 32-22. The plastic laminates permit great beauty and combine the plastics and metals. (Courtesy Lyon Metal Products, Inc.)

material. As the ability to produce synthetic materials increased, the plastic materials, such as phenol and formaldehyde, were used for bonding agents in place of shellac. The plastic laminates can be made with paper, cloth, wood, or nearly any other material (Fig. 32-24). They are re-sistant to heat, moisture, and corrosive materials; are impervious to oil and water; and are excellent insulators for electricity (Fig. 32-25). Also, they are smooth enough to use as bearings for some materials and machines.

The uses of these materials include pul-

Fig. 32-23. This attractive unit utilizes wood-pattern plastic laminates to provide beauty, strength, and durability. (Courtesy Murphy-Miller, Inc.)

Fig. 32-25. Plastic laminates are bonded and cured in huge steam-heated presses. (Courtesy Micarta Division, Westinghouse Electric Corporation)

Fig. 32-24. This laminating material (paper, cloth, etc. is being impregnated with phenolic resin before it is stacked and cured. (Courtesy Micarta Division, Westinghouse Electric Corporation)

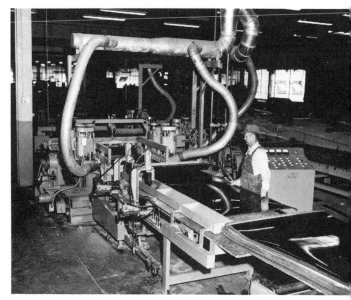

Fig. 32-26. These finished sheets of plastic laminate are run through double trim saws to remove the rough edges. (Courtesy Micarta Division, Westinghouse Electric Corporation)

leys, propeller shafts for seagoing boats, cases for electrical equipment, parts for generators, small gears for automobiles, and the boards used to make printed circuits for radio and television units. Perhaps the best known plastic laminate product, however, is found in nearly any

color or pattern and used for counters, cabinet tops, wall coverings, and cabinet faces in kitchens and homes (Fig. 32-26).

When working with the plastic laminates, one should remember that these materials are quite flexible and strong and that they are both harder and more brittle than wood. Woodworking tools can be used to cut the plastic laminates, but the teeth of the cutting tools should be very fine and very sharp. Coarse-toothed tools usually chip the surfaces of the plastics and ruin their entire appearance. In addition, when working with this material, a small allowance (⅛ inch or less) of extra material should be permitted to hang over the edges; then the edges can be filed or trimmed smooth to the exact fit. This slight overlap also helps to compensate for small alignment errors when the material is laid. When filing or sanding the extra material off the edges, be sure the stroke is applied in a downward motion (Fig. 32-27). This avoids chipping of the plastic laminate by the tool.

The plastic laminate material is flexible, but it can break and chip when handled. The plastic laminates are made from layers of kraft paper soaked with phenolic resins; these layers are hardened and cured under great heat and pressure. Since the last layer of paper is the desired pattern, anything that can be printed on paper can be made into a plastic laminate. The plastic laminates should be handled carefully to protect the edges and the corners from chipping. When laying them flat, the surfaces should be supported firmly; then an object dropped on the surface does not cause a shearing action to break the plastic.

To assemble a plastic laminate to a surface, the laminate is first cut to an exact size. The size of the laminate should be identical to the size and shape of the surface to be covered, plus an extra ⅛ inch or less for the final finishing and assembly. Next, a trial assembly should be made to be sure the laminate is the correct shape and size and that too much extra material does not remain on the edges. Any adjustments should be made after the trial assembly; if any adjustments

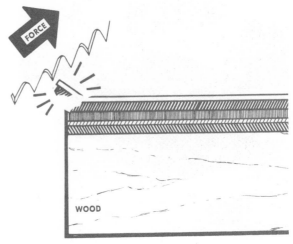

(A) A backward stroke chips the edges.

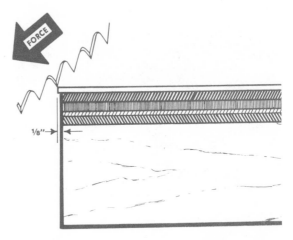

(B) On the forward stroke, the edges are supported and worked properly.

Fig. 32-27. Filing or sawing the plastic laminates.

are made, a second trial assembly also is required. Also, it is an excellent practice in laying large surfaces with plastic laminates to practice the slipsheet method of laying. The slipsheet is a large sheet of waxed paper or hard-surfaced paper which is placed between the two glued surfaces to prevent the two surfaces from sticking, until the laminate has been positioned properly.

After the piece has been cut to size and the slipsheet prepared, contact cement should be applied to both surfaces (the surface to be covered and the back of the plastic laminate); the cement then should be permitted to dry thoroughly. Then place the slipsheet on the surface to be covered, and place the laminate on the slipsheet. Lift one edge of the laminate slightly; then pull the slipsheet outward slightly. Press the exposed areas with the hands to hold the laminate and the surface firmly together (Fig. 32-28). This serves as an anchoring system to hold the laminate in alignment while the remainder of the slipsheet is removed. Then remove the remainder of the slipsheet, complete the pressure application, and trim the edges. On a large surface area, it is sometimes better practice to move the pressure from the center toward the edges. Rollers or large rags held in the hand are used to apply the pressures which force the two adhesives surfaces together. The slipsheet prepared for this type of operation should be prepared in sections; then the pressure can be applied in the center first, while the slipsheets are removed slightly in sections.

In many instances, as in the installation of a sink or a lavatory in a large counter-

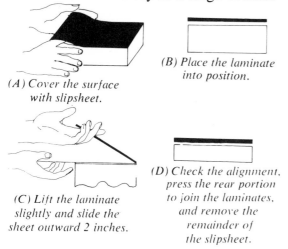

(A) Cover the surface with slipsheet.

(B) Place the laminate into position.

(C) Lift the laminate slightly and slide the sheet outward 2 inches.

(D) Check the alignment, press the rear portion to join the laminates, and remove the remainder of the slipsheet.

Fig. 32-28. Slipsheet method of plastic laminating.

top area, the hole in the laminate is cut after the laminate has been attached to the countertop. This makes assembly and alignment easier and helps to prevent breaking the plastic while working on a large surface. When cutting out these sections, a keyhole saw or saber saw normally is used. Holes can be drilled near the corners of the area to be cut out, and the saw blades can be inserted into the holes to begin cutting (Fig. 32-29). It should be remembered that an extremely fine-

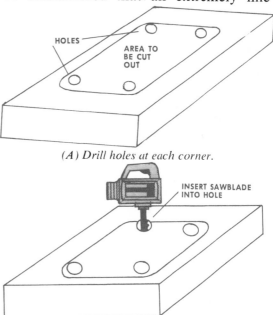

(A) Drill holes at each corner.

(B) Insert the saw blade into a hole to begin the cut.
Fig. 32-29. Cutting the plastic laminates.

toothed saw blade should be used for this operation to prevent chipping of the plastic surface. The edges of the plastic surface also should be trimmed, using sandpaper or a smooth file, as discussed previously.

When assembling the plastic laminates to countertops which also are to have the edges covered with the laminate, the edges should be covered first. The edges are glued on and then dressed to fit evenly with the top surface. Then the top is applied and finished evenly with the laminate sides. The ⅛-inch extra material on

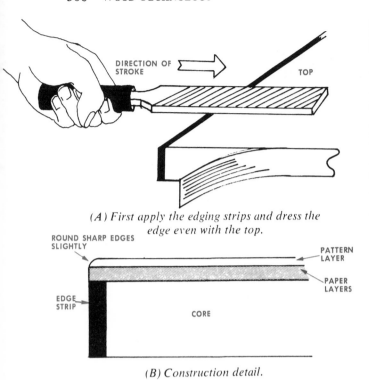

DIRECTION OF STROKE

TOP

(A) First apply the edging strips and dress the edge even with the top.

ROUND SHARP EDGES SLIGHTLY

PATTERN LAYER

PAPER LAYERS

EDGE STRIP

CORE

(B) Construction detail.

Fig. 32-30. Edging with the plastic laminates.

Fig. 32-31. Display of patterns available in the plastic laminates.

the top also helps to provide an overlap for the edges. When sanding or finishing the edges of a plastic laminate which has been placed on top of laminated edges (Fig. 32-30), the edging should be trimmed at a slight angle. This prevents an extremely sharp corner and also helps to hide minor irregularities or chips on the edges. A typical display of the variety of patterns available in the plastic laminates is shown in Fig. 32-31.

Questions

1. What types of materials can be used in making the laminated articles?
2. Can wood and other materials be combined in lamination?
3. What technique is used to help in bending a solid piece which is to be curved and rounded?
4. What are the advantages of using the molded laminates?
5. Are the laminated materials used only on small items, such as furniture and decorations?
6. What two types of pressure systems can be used for the force in pushing the lamination molds together?
7. What is a mold release?
8. When and where was the plastic laminate process developed?
9. What are the qualities or advantages of using the plastic laminates?
10. Where are the plastic laminates used?
11. What type of cement is used most commonly to assemble the plastic laminates to countertops and other units?
12. Why should one be careful in cutting the plastic laminates?
13. What materials can be used to make the plastic laminates?

IDEAS FOR LAMINATED PROJECTS

CANDLE HOLDER

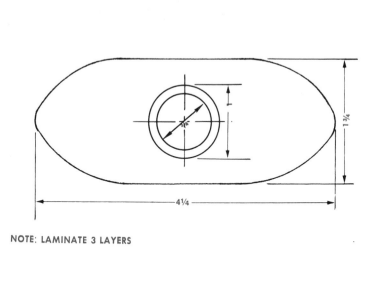

NOTE: LAMINATE 3 LAYERS

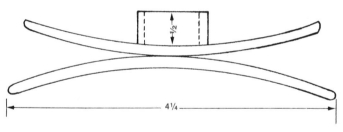

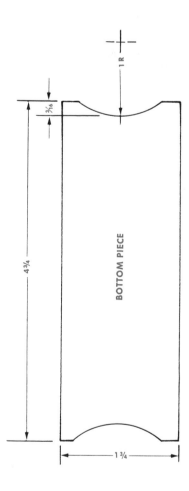

CANDLE HOLDER

Materials:
    Veneer: 6 pieces, each 1¾″ × 4¾″
Procedure:
1. Select & cut stock
2. Glue & clamp sections in forms until dry
3. Cut & finish to shape
4. Assemble pieces
5. Hand sand
6. Apply finish as desired.

Photo Courtesy Eldred Adams

SHOE HORN

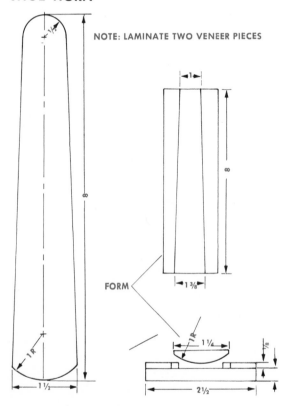

SHOE HORN

Materials:
    Veneer: Cut 2 pieces 1¾ × 8½
Procedure:
1. Cut stock
2. Glue and clamp in form until dry
3. Cut to finish shape
4. Hand sand
5. Apply finish (wax works very well)

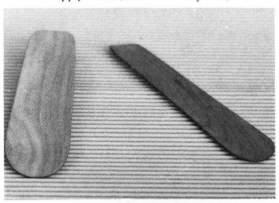

Photo Courtesy Eldred Adams

LETTER OPENER WITH
COPPER OR ALUMINUM BLADE AND WOODEN HANDLE

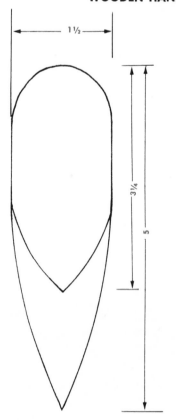

LETTER OPENER

Vaterials:
   Veneer: 2 pieces wood 1½ × 3¼
           1 piece metal 1½ × 5

Procedure:
   1. Select materials & cut stock to size & shape
   2. Glue & clamp pieces together using epoxy glue
   3. Finish sanding & polishing
   4. Finish as desired

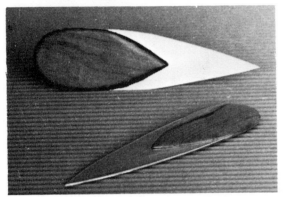

Photo Courtesy Eldred Adams

JEWELRY TREE

JEWELRY TREE

Materials:
   5 pcs. veneer 3″ × 8″ for tree body
   3 pcs. veneer ⅝″ × 3″ for lower branch
   3 pcs. veneer ⅝″ × 2½″ for second branch
   3 pcs. veneer ⅝″ × 2″ for third branch
   3 pcs. veneer ⅝″ × 1½″ for top branch
   1—⅜″ dowel × 1½″ long
   1—¾″ × 3″ round wooden base

Procedure:
   1. Select and cut veneers to size for tree body
   2. Glue and clamp tree body
   3. Select and cut veneer for branches
   4. Glue and mold to shape
   5. Shape and form tree, branches and joints
   6. Cut and shape base and dowel
   7. Hand sand all parts
   8. Assemble all pieces
   9. Final sanding and finish as desired

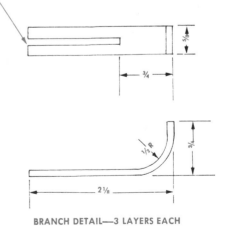

Courtesy Eldred Adams

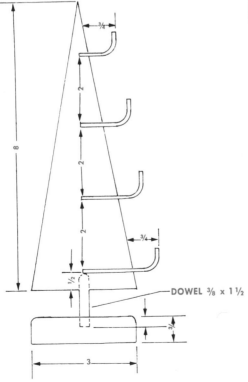

CUT SLOT THICKNESS OF TREE

BRANCH DETAIL—3 LAYERS EACH

NOTE: 5 LAYERS OF VENEER FORM TREE
3 FOR BRANCHES   BASE IS ROUND ¾ x 3

DOWEL ⅜ x 1½

LAMINATED NAPKIN HOLDER

Materials:
BODY—3 or 4 pcs. laminate material 5″ × 14″
BASE—3 or 4 pcs. laminate material 4″ × 4″
SCREWS—2—¼″ × 6/32 machine screws

LAMINATED BOOK END

Materials:
BASE: 2 or 3 pcs. laminate 3″ × 6″
BRACE: 2 or 3 pcs. laminate 2″ × 4″

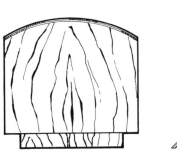

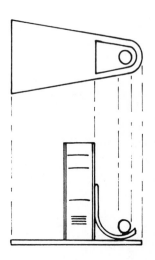

SALAD SPOON OR FORK

Materials:
3 or 4 pcs.
Laminate—3″ × 12″

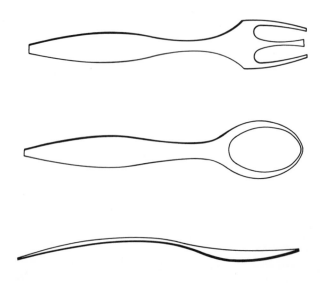

Unit 33 – Sandpaper

Sandpaper is sold in many grades and sizes, and it is made from various abrasive materials. The abrasives in sandpaper are small particles from very hard materials. Each tiny particle has small, sharp edges which make smooth cuts. Sandpaper is used to smooth and prepare the surfaces of the wood for the application of the finishes. Sanding removes the defects and improves the appearance of the finished wood products.

Abrasive Materials

Abrasive materials can be divided into two general categories—natural abrasives and synthetic or man-made abrasives. The natural abrasives are made from materials which occur in nature, such as emery, garnet, and flint. These abrasives are rocks which can be reduced to extremely tiny fragments. The tiny fragments are bonded or glued to a backing material. The backing material can be either cloth or paper, depending on the particular use desired. For example, the belts for power sanders are made from cloth, whereas the sandpaper for hand-sanding applications is backed with paper. Special waterproof paper is used for the so-called "wet or dry" types of sandpaper. The glue used to make "wet or dry" sandpaper also is a special glue.

The synthetic or man-made abrasives used for sandpaper are silicon carbide and aluminum oxide. These abrasives provide certain special characteristics; in general, they are less expensive for the quality received, and the tiny fragments which make up the sanding surfaces are easier to control, in regard to size, than the natural abrasive materials.

Abrasive materials also are used in the loose, unbonded form. Materials, such as rottenstone (a form of shale rock), are treated with acid to produce a fine polishing powder. Pumice, which is a pulverized volcanic lava, also is used in a similar manner. Both these products are used with water or oil to produce a fine, polished, hand-rubbed surface. Pumice is usually the coarser of the two materials and is frequently used with water. Rottenstone is much finer in texture and is generally rubbed with oil.

The comparative qualities, sizes, and costs of these abrasive materials can be found in Table 33-1. Note in Table 33-2 that the materials are obtainable in sizes ranging from coarse to extremely fine. The coarse materials generally are used for the rougher work and for removing old paint. The fine materials are used for finish sanding, and the extremely fine materials are

Table 33-1. Comparison of Abrasives

SOURCE	TYPE	RELATIVE COST	USEFUL LIFE	COLOR
NATURAL	FLINT	LOW	SHORT	TAN
	GARNET	MEDIUM-LOW	MEDIUM-SHORT	TAN TO ORANGE
	EMERY	HIGH	LONG	GRAY TO BLACK
MAN-MADE	ALUMINUM OXIDE	MEDIUM	MEDIUM-LONG	TAN TO BROWN
	SILICON CARBIDE	MEDIUM-HIGH	MEDIUM TO LONG	GRAY

Table 33-2. Sizes and Uses of Sandpaper

Class	Grit Size		Use	Available In
	Screen	Number		
Extra Coarse	24 30 36	3 2½ 2	Sanding texture, paint removal, etc.	Flint, garnet, emery, silicon carbide, and aluminum oxide
Coarse	40 50	1½ 1	Final texture sanding, Removing defects, removing old finishes	All the above
Medium	60 80 100	½ 0 2/0	Removing rough spots, sanding to size	All the above
Fine	120 150 180	3/0 4/0 5/0	1st pre-finish sanding	All the above
Extra Fine	220 240 280	6/0 7/0 8/0	Final prefinish sanding	Not available in emery
Ultra Fine	320 400 500 600	9/0 10/0 — —	Sanding between coats	1. Not available in flint 2. Garnet no finer than #400 3. 500 and 600 only in silicon carbide and aluminum oxide

used for removing minor imperfections and dust motes from varnished and lacquered finishes.

Abrasive Size

The abrasive size is determined through a process called *screening*. This is merely a process in which wire screen, similar to that used on windows, is placed in successive layers. Each layer or screen is slightly finer, or smaller in size, than the layer above it. The abrasive materials are dumped into the top frame, and the entire stack of screen frames is vibrated. The larger pieces of abrasive are trapped in the larger screens, and the smaller pieces of abrasive material fall through the holes until they are trapped by the openings of a particular size. Note in Table 33-2 that two numbering systems are used to de-

termine the coarse or fine size. The first system is based on the number of openings per inch in the screen that collects the material. For example, if a screen with 220 openings per inch collects the material, the material is called 220-grit; the back of the sandpaper bears the number 220. However, this identical size also can be classified 6/0. This designation is derived from a different numbering system, but the sizes are identical.

The factors which should be considered in selecting both the abrasive size and the abrasive material fall into two primary categories. The first consideration is whether the surface is to be smooth or rough. If the surface being sanded is rough in places, a relatively rough sandpaper should be used first. If the surface of the material is relatively smooth, a smooth sandpaper of fine grit should be used. Generally, the first sanding operations are performed with a rougher grit. Common cabinetmaking operations usually begin with 120-grit or a 150-grit sandpaper. This is the first step in sanding before finishing. A 220-grit or a 280-grit abrasive usually is used for sanding immediately before applying the finish. Sanding between the finish coats is done with an ultrafine-grit size, such as a 400-grit or a 600-grit sandpaper.

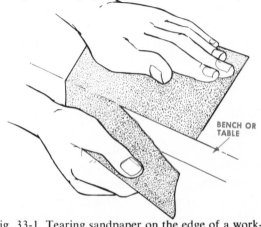

Fig. 33-1. Tearing sandpaper on the edge of a workbench or table.

Selection

The second consideration in selecting the correct sandpaper is the grade or quality of the abrasive. If a piece of sandpaper is to be used extensively, an abrasive material, such as emery, silicon carbide, or aluminum oxide, should be used. These abrasive materials do not clog, and they generally can withstand severe use longer than the other abrasive materials. However, their expense is medium to high in comparison with the other abrasive materials.

If the sandpaper is to be subjected to moderate use for a limited period of time, a medium grade of sandpaper, such as garnet, is quite satisfactory. However, if the sandpaper is to be used only once under limited conditions or on materials that clog the grit particles quickly—as in removing old paint—the cheapest type of abrasive material should be used. Flint is the proper abrasive for these conditions.

Using Sandpaper

The first step in using sandpaper is to prepare the paper for use with either a block or by hand. Generally, the sandpa-

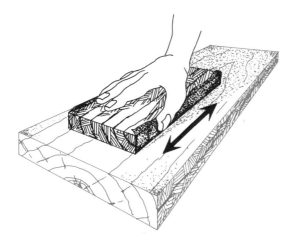

Fig. 33-2. Wrap the sandpaper around a block of wood and sand with the grain of the wood.

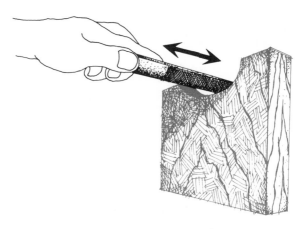

Fig. 33-3. Wrap the sandpaper around a dowel for sanding inside curves.

per sheet should be torn into four equal pieces by tearing the sandpaper into quarters of a sheet across the sharp edge of a workbench or table (Fig. 33-1). The smaller pieces are then wrapped around a block, either a commercial block or a small piece of scrap wood. The sandpaper is stroked with the grain and across the surface of the wood in smooth, even strokes (Fig. 33-2). Be sure the strokes are across the entire length of the surface and that they are applied evenly and firmly. After the preliminary sanding, successive sanding is done with the finer abrasive sizes. The end and edge grains are sanded, except that the end grain is not sanded with the grain of the wood.

To sand the curved surfaces, hold the sandpaper in the hand, rather than with a sanding block. To sandpaper a round hole in wood, the sandpaper can be wrapped around a dowel or round piece (Fig. 33-3). To sand a convex surface or an outside curve, a flat block can be used (Fig. 33-4). For specific abrasive uses after the first finish coat has been applied, refer to the discussion of wood finishes.

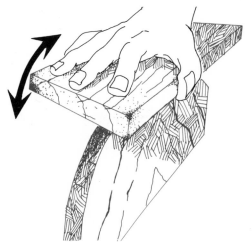

Fig. 33-4. Wrap the sandpaper around a wood block for sanding outside curves.

Questions

1. What size and type of abrasive paper is most suitable for removing old paint from the outside of a house?

2. Which abrasive material is the most expensive?

3. Which abrasive size, 100-grit or 200-grit, indicates the finest abrasive material?

4. Which abrasive size, 6/0 or 4/0, indicates the finer abrasive?

5. Which abrasives are man-made?

6. Which abrasives are natural abrasives?

7. List the advantages of man-made abrasives.

8. In which direction, with the grain or across the grain, should one move the sandpaper?

9. What type of sanding block should be used to sand the inside surface of a hole?

10. What type of sanding block should be used to sand an outside curve?

Unit 34 — Wood Finishing

A *finish* is the coating applied to a surface. Its purpose is to seal, beautify, and protect the wood surface. Each of these purposes is equally important for a quality finish. The finishes can be opaque, hiding the wood grain; or they can be transparent, accenting the wood grain. The less expensive woods, such as pine and fir, are often finished with an opaque finish. The more expensive woods (walnut and maple) are finished with a transparent finish to accent their beautiful grain patterns.

An excellent finish requires an orderly procedure. Most of the finishes are applied by: (1) Preparing the surface; (2) Staining; (3) Filling and/or sealing; and (4) Applying the top coats of finish. Depending on the specified finish, this schedule can be changed slightly. The common methods of applying the finishes are rubbing, rolling, dipping, brushing, and spraying.

Safety Rules

1. Before using an unfamilar finishing material, read the directions and note all the precautions and hazards.
2. Keep each container clearly marked with a permanent, legible label.
3. Apply (or remove) finishes only in well-ventilated areas. Avoid inhaling the fumes and wear a respirator as needed.
4. Avoid excessive contact of the skin and the finishing materials. As quickly as possible, thoroughly wash the hands and other parts of the body which have been in contact with the finishes.
5. Do not eat or drink anything while applying the finishes.
6. Wear gloves when handling paint removers and solvents which irritate the skin. However, do not wear rubber gloves or other items made from rubber when handling the rubber-base paints.
7. Keep the finishing materials and their fumes away from open flames and other ignition sources.
8. Avoid spontaneous ignition. Immediately dispose of rags saturated with paint, thinner, solvent, or other combustible material. When necessary, store these rags in airtight metal containers.
9. Do not store the finishes, especially the highly inflammable thinners and solvents in glass containers. Regardless of the type of container, avoid storage in direct sunlight.
10. Remove wax with a nonflammable solvent.
11. Do not use gasoline for a solvent or thinner; it is extremely volatile and explosive. When favorable conditions exist, gasoline can explode more forcefully than either dynamite or TNT.
12. Immediately wipe up any finishing material that has been spilled.

Preparing a Surface

To achieve a quality finish, first prepare the surface. This preparation depends on the finishing material. Most of the paints and enamels do not require the thorough preparation required by the varnishes and lacquers. Minor scratches and similar surface defects are often deemphasized by the opaque finishes; whereas, the transparent finishes tend to

315

magnify these defects. Also, stained surfaces (as compared to unstained surfaces) emphasize the defects and require more sanding (Fig. 34-1). In general, a finish is never used to hide a defect which can be removed practically.

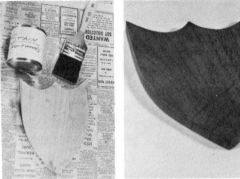

(A) Before staining. (B) After staining.

Fig. 34-1. Staining magnifies surface defects and scratches.

Removing or eliminating the surface defects and blemishes is the first step. Since glue neither stains nor accepts a finish, it should be removed completely from the surface. A glue affected by moisture can be softened with water; then it can be lifted with a chisel (Fig. 34-2). A water-resistant glue can be removed by careful cutting or scraping. Attempting to remove glue by sanding is not recommended, since the glue particles then are forced into the pores, causing light-colored spots.

Fig. 34-2. A glue affected by moisture can be softened with water and then lifted with a wood chisel.

Minor surface dents frequently can be raised by wetting the dent and the surrounding area with water. If the dent is severe, applying heat to a damp cloth covering the dent should raise the wood sufficiently (Fig. 34-3). This method is not satisfactory if the wood fibers are broken or cut.

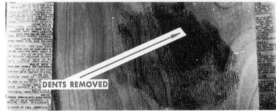

Fig. 34-3. Removing dents.

Holes, cracks, and similar imperfections can be patched. The commercial patching materials available include wood dough, wood putty, plastic wood, and stick shellac. The defect is filled with the patching material, permitted to set, and then sanded flush with the surface. Since most of the patching materials cannot be stained after they are set, each is selected for a particular wood color. Similar results can be obtained by mixing glue or lacquer with sawdust. The desired color can be achieved by using sawdust from wood identical to the surface being patched or by adding several drops of oil color. Where possible, the wood strips, rather than patching materials can be used to produce more favorable results.

Surface blemishes created by dirt or grease normally can be removed with benzene or naphtha. Dark-colored spots are formed naturally in various woods. These spots can be eliminated by bleaching. Oxalic acid, hydrogen peroxide, or a commercial bleach can be used in bleaching.

The next step in preparing for a finish is smoothing the surface. Mill marks should be removed first. Although these marks appear unimportant on unfinished surfaces, they can become quite pronounced after they are stained and finished (Fig. 34-4). Mill marks can be removed by several methods. These marks can be hand planed and then scraped; or they can be sanded off. Removing the mill marks also eliminates the surface scratches. The remaining scratches require additional sanding. In sanding a scratch, proceed to sand an area larger than the scratch; otherwise, the immediate area stains differently from the total surface.

Fig. 34-4. Mill marks which might be barely noticeable on an unfinished surface (left) can be extremely distracting on the finished surface (right).

As shown in Fig. 34-5, these areas usually are lighter in color. Also, limiting the sanding to a small area creates low spots.

The preparation for a finish should be concluded with a finish sanding. The purpose of this step is to produce a smooth, flat surface. Finish sanding is accomplished in two steps; first with a fine (120-180 grit) abrasive wrapped around a sanding block; then, follow with a very fine (220-grit) sanding. Prior to this step, the surface can be moistened with water

(A) Before staining.

(B) After staining.

Fig. 34-5. Uneven sanding can cause a light or a dark spot on a stained surface.

to raise the grain. However, since the stain might raise the grain, wetting a surface at this point is sometimes omitted. Sanding should be *with the grain*—never across the grain.

Staining

Staining, unless omitted from the finishing schedule, is the second step. A stain is used to develop color on a surface by accenting its grain pattern. Stains also are used on the less expensive woods to imitate the more expensive woods and to create special shading effects. Although some stains can be mixed with fillers and applied in combination, these methods are not recommended for quality finishes. The various stains are water, oil (a "non-grain-raising" stain), and spirit.

Water and a water-soluble dye can be mixed to produce a water stain. The color can be varied by adding more, or less, powdered dye (usually aniline dye) to hot water to obtain the desired color. The water stains produce an excellent transparent color, rarely fade or bleed, and penetrate well. They are especially recommended for darkening sapwood. The water stains, however, raise the grain and are slow in drying. Alcohol is sometimes added to minimize raising of the grain. A water stain is usually applied by spraying, since brushing tends to produce streaks where the brush strokes overlap. Wood filler and water stains cannot be mixed satisfactorily.

An oil stain is produced by combining an oil-soluble dye with benzol naphtha, or turpentine. These stains are easy to apply, can be combined with a filler, and do not raise the grain. However, they tend to fade or bleed and do not penetrate deeply. The color of an oil stain is not so sharp, or bright, as the color of a water stain. Most of the oil stains can be purchased in premixed colors.

A "non-grain-raising" stain which does not raise the grain can be produced from an acid-base dye dissolved in a solvent, such as alcohol or acetone. These stains produce a color quality similar to the water stains, but they do not raise the grain. Compared to the water stains, the NGR (non-grain-raising) stains dry rapidly, bleed, and penetrate poorly. Special safety precautions are required for these stains, because of the solvents involved.

The spirit stains are produced from aniline dyes dissolved in alcohol. Their characteristics are similar to the water stains (both are similar in content). The spirit stains are difficult to apply and will bleed. Also, they fade easily when exposed to direct sunlight. These stains usually are recommended for touchup work, since they can penetrate the common finishes.

Stains, or color pigments, also are combined with the varnishes and sanding sealers. This is a method of quickly applying the color and finish in a single operation; but this method should be limited to the less-expensive woods. The stained finishes should be sprayed, since brushing tends to produce streaks where the brush strokes overlap. Since only slight penetration is achieved, minor scratches in the finish are exaggerated greatly.

A similar procedure is used in applying the different stains. After the stain is mixed thoroughly, it should be tested. The most practical method of determining the effect of a stain on a certain type or piece of wood is to prepare a sample piece. Two pieces of wood, even though they appear to be identical, can stain differently.

The stains can be brushed, wiped, or sprayed. Regardless of the method, the stain should be spread uniformly over a surface (Fig. 34-6). The surplus stain should be wiped from the surface when the desired color is achieved. Final wiping

Fig. 34-6. Applying stain with a brush.

should be "with the grain," using a clean, lint-free cloth (Fig. 34-7). When staining the parts separately, permit the stain to penetrate for an equal period of time

Fig. 34-7. Use a cloth to wipe the surplus stain from a surface. Final wiping should be with the grain.

on each part. Failing to do this can result in light- and dark-colored spots. If the excess stain is not removed at this time, dull, opaque streaks which distract from the finish might be produced (Fig. 34-8). If the stain dries for too long a period, it can be softened with an appropriate solvent. A second coat of stain also might help. After it is sufficiently dry, a stained surface (if necessary) can be sanded lightly with a fine abrasive.

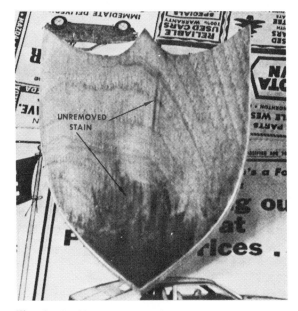

Fig. 34-8. Unremoved stain causes dull, opaque streaks when the finish is applied.

Filling and/or Sealing

Filling a wood surface involves using a wood filler to fill the porous woods. This is done after staining, if a stain is used. sealing accomplishes about the same purpose, but with a different material. This step seals the wood and creates a smoother surface for finishing (Fig. 34-9). In Fig. 34-9A, no wood filler is used; therefore, the finish is rough and uneven, since it has penetrated the wood pores. Since the pores of the wood are filled in Fig. 34-9B, the finish is smooth and level.

Fig. 34-9. A wood filler fills the pores in the wood. On an unfilled surface (left) the finish is uneven, because the finish has penetrated the pores in the wood. The finish is smooth on the filled surface (right) because the filler has sealed the pores in the wood.

The open-grain woods (ash, oak, walnut, etc.) require a paste filler, which consists chiefly of finely ground silicon (silex). Other ingredients can be added to cause a paste filler to be either a slow-dry or a quick-dry filler. The slow-dry fillers contain silex, linseed oil, drier, and turpentine. The drying time ranges from 12 to 24 hours. The finishes might blush (bleed), if they are applied before the filler is completely dry (Fig. 34-10). The quick-dry fillers dry in about one hour.

Fig. 34-10. If applied before the filler is completely dry, a finish may blush (turn white).

For this type of filler, a synthetic-resin vehicle replaces the linseed oil, which causes the lengthy drying period of the slow-dry filler. The synthetic resin, however, dries too quickly; naphtha can be added to prolong the drying time.

The close-grain woods (birch, maple, pine, poplar, etc.) require a liquid filler. Either a commercial filler, varnish, or shellac is suitable. An excellent varnish filler can be made from 1 gallon of rubbing varnish mixed with about 2 or 2½ pounds silex, 1 pint of drier, and 1 quart of turpentine.

Paste filler usually is applied by brushing a generous quantity of filler with the grain and then across the grain (Fig. 34-11). After the filler begins to dry, a coarse-textured cloth is rubbed across the

Fig. 34-11. Brush the wood filler first "with the grain" and then "across the grain."

grain. This cloth is sometimes moved in a circular motion while crossing the grain (Fig. 34-12). This rubbing action not only removes the surplus filler but also forces the filler into the pores. Finally, the surface is wiped lightly with the grain, using a clean, lint-free cloth. Excess filler remaining on a surface too long hardens and is difficult to remove. Wiping the surface with a cloth soaked in solvent can be a help in removing the excess dried filler. Otherwise, the area must be re-sanded and refilled.

Fig. 34-12. After the filler begins to dry, rub across the grain with a coarse-textured cloth to force the filler into the pores and to remove the surplus.

In applying the filler, limit the area being filled. If applied to a large area, the filler can harden before the surplus can be removed. Do not overlook the surplus filler near the inside corners. A sharp or pointed dowel rod covered with cloth can be used to remove the filler from these areas (Fig. 34-13). Before proceeding to a final finish, remember to check for any filler that might have been overlooked. Similar to the stain, the excess filler remaining on a surface produces dull, opaque streaks (see Fig. 34-8).

Fig. 34-13. The filler can be removed from tight areas with a cloth wrapped around a pointed dowel.

Shellac

Since shellac is one of the oldest finishes still in use, it is the only finish with an animal origin. Shellac is produced by dissolving a resinous material in denatured alcohol. This material is derived from the lac bug found in India and Siam. The quality of the shellac depends largely on its cut. The standard cut is a 4-pound cut, which consists of 4 pounds of shellac dissolved in 1 gallon of denatured alcohol.

Shellac is available in either a natural or a bleached condition. The natural color, called orange shellac, usually is applied only to the darker woods. The bleached color, known as white shellac, can be applied to all woods; but it is especially appropriate for those woods light in color. Most of the shellacs, unless highly refined, appear cloudy in the container. This condition disappears after drying, leaving a clear, transparent coating. The cloudy condition results from the natural wax in the shellac.

Shellac penetrates well, is easy to apply, and dries to produce a hard, durable surface. Depending on the thickness of each application, the first coat dries in 3 to 6 hours. Each additional coat, however, requires a drying time of 12 to 24 hours.

Shellac can be sprayed or brushed. When brushed, a soft varnish brush should be used. An area should be coated in two strokes (Fig. 34-14). The forward stroke

Fig. 34-14. Apply shellac in two strokes. The forward stroke (left) spreads the shellac, and the return stroke (right) smooths it.

spreads the shellac, and the return stroke smooths it. Excessive brushing (brushing back and forth over the same area) creates a rough finish. A shellac finish usually requires two or three coats. Two thin coats, rather than a single heavy coat, provide a better finish.

Varnish

Varnish is a resin material mixed with linseed oil and turpentine. A drying agent sometimes is added to speed up the drying process. The varnish resins originally were made from fossil gums, but these resins generally have been replaced by the synthetic resins. Although most of the varnishes dry in 24 to 48 hours, the newer synthetics dry in 6 hours or less. Various types of varnish finishes can be used. Each finish is made for a particular purpose.

1. *Rubbing and polishing varnish.* Used for finishing furniture, this varnish contains less oil than most of the varnishes. It rubs well, but tends to be brittle. The usual drying time is 24 to 48 hours.
2. *Spar varnish.* Containing more oil than most of the varnishes, spar varnish is used for exterior surfaces which have not been filled. Spar varnish is resistant to alcohol, water, and various environmental elements. The drying time varies from 12 to 48 hours.
3. *Floor varnish.* Floor varnish, with a "medium" oil content, is more or less a general-purpose varnish. It is elastic, extremely durable, and used on surfaces subjected to excessive wear. Floor varnish is used chiefly for floors and interior trims. Drying in about 12 hours, it is harder than spar varnish and dries quicker.

4. *Polyurethane varnish.* This varnish is a plastic-type finishing material. It provides an extremely durable finish for both interior and exterior applications. Its resistance to water, alcohol and other solvents, acids, and the environmental elements is outstanding. Polyurethane varnish normally dries in 4 to 5 hours.

5. *Varnish stain.* A varnish stain is used for interior work not requiring a quality finish. Its only advantage results from its color, or stain, being mixed with a general-purpose varnish. This permits a quick finish, which eliminates applying the stain and varnish separately. Varnish stain dries quickly, but shows surface scratches; and it streaks when applied unevenly.

Most of the varnishes are applied with about the same procedure. Best results can be achieved when the room temperature is 70° to 80°F and when excessive humidity can be avoided. The immediate surroundings should be free from dust, since the drying time can range upward to 48 hours. Also, never mix the different varnishes to complete a job. Each varnish is distinctive in its composition. The different compositions cannot blend when they are mixed; therefore, an unsatisfactory finish results. The following procedure is recommended for applying the varnishes.

1. After the surface has been prepared properly, remove all the dust by wiping with a clean, lint-free cloth.

2. Select a varnish suitable for the purpose. As needed. stir the varnish until it is mixed thoroughly. Do not shake; shaking the varnish creates bubbles which are harmful to the final appearance of the finish.

3. Estimate the quantity of varnish needed; then pour that quantity into another container. This protects the unneeded varnish (for later use) from dust and other particles which might be transferred by the brush.

4. Thin the varnish with turpentine, as needed. Usually, the first coat is thinned. Other coats, especially the final coat, should not be thinned.

5. Select a quality varnish brush about 2 or 3 inches in width.

6. Prepare the brush. Dip it into the varnish until the bottom one-third to one-fourth of the bristles are coated. Then work the brush until the varnish is distributed evenly throughout the bristles.

7. Apply a thick, even coat of varnish over a small area (Fig. 34-15).

Fig. 34-15. Apply varnish in a thick, even coat.

Quickly brush this area, first across the grain and then with the grain. To smooth the area, remove the surplus varnish from the brush and brush lightly lengthwise.

8. After the surface has dried sufficiently, sand lightly with a fine abrasive. Wipe clean and apply a second coat. Additional coats can be applied in the same manner until a satisfactory finish is obtained.

Lacquer

Lacquer is one of the most popular wood finishes, especially in the furniture industry. Depending on the type of lacquer, it can be applied hot or cold and either sprayed or brushed. Using a lacquer for a wood finish provides many advantages. A short drying time of 30 minutes to 1 hour permits the finish to dry dust free. Lacquer is easy to apply and produces a smooth surface, which can be gloss, semigloss, or flat. When applied properly, a lacquer finish is durable, hard, and resists water and alcohol stains. A lacquer finish retains its original appearance with minimum upkeep.

Lacquer is a synthetic finish produced from nitrocellulose. Although nitrocellulose is obtained from both cotton and wood fibers, most of the lacquers currently are made from cotton fibers. The nitrocellulose results from treating the cotton fibers with nitric and sulfuric acids. The various resins and solvents then are combined with the nitrocellulose to form the lacquer.

One unique feature of lacquer is that it requires a special thinner (or solvent). The thinner is made by blending the various solvents used in manufacturing the lacquer. Therefore, a lacquer actually is used to dissolve the lacquer. Also, each brand of lacquer might require its own particular thinner. A thinner for one of the lacquers does not necessarily work with another lacquer, unless the ingredients in the two lacquers are nearly identical.

Evaporation causes a lacquer to dry into a hard, protective film. The steps preceding its application are stain, fill, and seal. The sealing can be accomplished with a thin coat of shellac or with a lacquer sealer, called sanding sealer. A sealer reduces the number of coats needed to obtain a quality finish. The staining and filling depend on the wood and on the type of finish desired.

A brushing lacquer is thin, with a consistency similar to water. The lacquer is applied with a fairly wide brush which should not be too soft. In brushing, the brush should be filled generously and moved quickly lengthwise of the stock (Fig. 34-16). Each stroke should slightly overlap the preceding stroke.

Fig. 34-16. When brushing lacquer, overlap the brush strokes.

Small quantities of thinner can be added to the lacquer if it does not spread satisfactorily. After the lacquer has begun to dry, do not attempt additional brushing until the surface is completely dry. Brushing too soon results in a rough finish. Although sanding between the coats is unnecessary, rough surfaces can be sanded lightly with a very fine abrasive. The key to brushing lacquer successfully is rapid strokes, using generous quantities of lacquer.

Lacquer can be sprayed either hot (Fig. 34-17) or cold (Fig. 34-18). When sprayed cold, a thinner should be added to reduce the lacquer to spraying consistency. A typical mixture is half lacquer and half thinner; but this proportion can vary with the type of lacquer. Normally, the thinner is added to the lacquer until it is thin enough to be sprayed evenly. Hot lacquer is "thinned" by the heat, rather

Fig. 34-17. Spraying hot lacquer. (Courtesy The DeVilbiss Company)

Fig. 34-18. Spraying cold lacquer.

than by the thinner. The normal spraying temperature ranges between 140° and 160°F. Hot lacquer, compared to cold lacquer, usually dries quicker, can be applied thicker, and sets smoother. The spraying pressure for hot lacquer is much higher.

The procedure for spraying is quite simple. First, the surface is sealed; then it is sanded smooth. Next, several top coats of lacquer finish the operation. Although two coats normally are sufficient, additional coats can be applied if desired. Sanding between applications of the lacquer coats is unnecessary, unless the surface is rough.

If necessary to sand, wait until the lacquer is thoroughly dry. Although most coats dry in 30 minutes to 1 hour, heavier coats require a longer drying time.

Hand-Rubbed Finishes

The hand-rubbed finishes are a tradition in fine cabinetmaking. No smoother, more lustrous finish is possible or superior to the hand-rubbed finish. The hand-rubbing can be done with shellac, varnish, or lacquer products. The basic procedure is identical for all the finishes.

1. Steel wool should be rubbed over the finish after each coat has dried. A fine steel wool should be used for this process; then remove the white powder.

2. After three to five successive coats, each of which has been steel wooled, the rubbing process begins with sanding the surface with extremely fine "wet or dry" sandpaper (600-grit) and a few drops of water.

3. A small quantity of pumice powder should be mixed with water to a thin, paste-like consistency; then this mixture should be rubbed in a circular motion across the surface with a soft rag. This should be continued only until the resulting surface is smooth and free of the tiny raised dust motes.

4. A rottenstone compound should be made by mixing rottenstone with oil and rubbing in a circular motion across the finished surface. This process is similar to that for the pumice stone. Since rottenstone is a much finer abrasive compound, it leaves a much smoother surface. Rottenstone should be rubbed on the surface with a hard cloth pad or with an old felt chalkboard eraser. This should be continued until a definite sheen is obtained.

5. Remove all the compounds from the surface; then rub with a soft cloth. For additional luster, a wax polish or a lemon-oil polish can be used.

Oil Finish

The oil finishes have been made more popular by the various contemporary designs featuring the "sculptured" and/or natural appearances. These finishes also are excellent for achieving the antique appearances typical of the colonial, hand-rubbed finishes. An oil finish consists of linseed oil combined with turpentine. Linseed oil is produced from flaxseed, and turpentine is derived from the resin of pine trees. A typical mixture is 1 part raw linseed oil and 1 part turpentine, or 2 parts boiled linseed oil and 1 part turpentine. One ounce of beeswax per quart can be added to increase the luster of the finish.

An oil finish is recommended for the darker woods (cherry, teak, walnut, etc.). The light-colored woods (ash, birch, maple, etc.) tend to become dull when an oil finish is applied. An oil finish penetrates the wood and does not crack, chip, or peel. A properly applied finish is resistant to water, most stains, and heat. It is especially desirable for furniture exposed to scratches and spots. Portions of an oil finish can be reworked, without refinishing the entire surface.

Application

An oil finish can be used for a wipe-on finish. It is easy to apply, since errors can be corrected merely by applying more oil. However, a quality oil finish requires much rubbing and effort. Contrary to most thinking, an oil finish is not a quick finish. The process basically involves applying oil, and then rubbing and working it into the pores of the wood. A glossy surface is achieved only by continuous rubbing. For example, a single application

results in a darker, duller surface. A surface becomes less dull with additional applications and rubbing. The following procedure is recommended for oil finishes:

1. After preparing for the finish, remove the dust from the surface.
2. Apply generous quantities of oil, using either a brush or a cloth (Fig. 34-19).

Fig. 34-19. Linseed oil finish. Brush on and allow the oil to penetrate (top); then wipe off the surplus (bottom).

3. Using a cloth, thoroughly rub the oil into the surface until uniform color appears.
4. As the oil soaks into the wood, apply more oil to the dull spots which appear, and continue the rubbing.
5. Repeat the preceding step until the surface is saturated fully or becomes sticky. The appearance of the dull spots should halt at this point.

6. If the surface is sticky, apply additional oil, and immediately wipe the excess oil from the surface, The oil not removed becomes gummy, does not dry, and the surface must be refinished.

7. After the first coat has dried at least 24 hours, apply a second coat in a manner similar to the first coat.

8. If needed, additional coats can be applied at 12-hour intervals. The final coat can be smoothed by wet/dry sanding. Two coats are sufficient for some surfaces, while other surfaces might require four, five, or even more coats.

9. After the final coat has dried at least 6 hours, polish and/or wax until a satisfactory gloss is achieved.

The oil finishes can be applied either hot or cold. The hot oil is often preferable, since it penetrates the wood more quickly. However, the cold oil is preferable for a carved surface where a hot oil might become sticky too quickly. In heating, never heat the oil directly. Place the oil container in a container of water, then apply heat to the water.

Paint

Paint provides an opaque, protective film used chiefly for the less-expensive woods (Fig. 34-20). Precise descriptions

Fig. 34-20. Applying a paint finish.

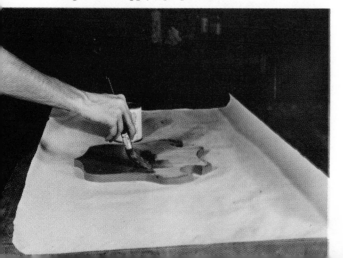

of the paints and their characteristics are difficult, since there are many different types and brands. The term "paint" is used chiefly in referring to oil-base, water-base, and enamel paints. The oil-base paints should be thinned with turpentine or mineral spirits. The water-base paints, often called "latex" paints, should be thinned with water. Enamel, a mixture of varnish and paint pigment, should be thinned with turpentine. Another type of paint is the acrylic (rubber-base) paint. Although the brushes used with this paint can be cleaned in water, the paint is resistant to water after a 30-minute to 2-hour drying period.

Most of the paints can be rolled, sprayed, and/or brushed. The drying times range from 30 minutes to 48 hours, depending on the type of paint and its application. The finish provided by a paint can range from flat to glossy; it is suitable for either inside or outside work, but not for both inside and outside work. Since the paints and their uses vary considerably, the instructions provided with the paint should be read before using it.

Commercial Finishes

Numerous finishing materials are formulated specially and sold under various commercial names and brands. These finishes have gained much popularity, chiefly as a result of their overcoming certain disadvantages demonstrated by the conventional finishes. Typically, most of the commercial finishes are easy to apply, require a short drying time, and are resistant to wear, water, and most of the staining materials.

Deft

A *Deft* finish is similar to a lacquer finish and is easily applied by rubbing, rolling, brushing, or spraying. It produces a durable finish which dries to the touch in 30 minutes, but it should not be re-coated for 2 hours. This short drying time causes the finish to be nearly dust free. The interior finish (Fig. 34-21) is semi-gloss, but the exterior finish (Fig. 34-22) is gloss. *Deft* does not raise the grain, and

Fig. 34-21. Interior semigloss finish. (Courtesy Deft, Inc.)

Fig. 34-22. Exterior gloss clear finish. (Courtesy Deft, Inc.)

it does not darken or yellow with age. After three or more coats, *Deft* is resis-tant to alcohol and water, is its own sealer, and ordinarily requires no thin-ning. The finish also is available in aero-sol spray cans (Fig. 34-23). Since this fin-ish dissolves itself, the *Deft* finishes are easily touched up with *Deft*. When com-binded with a quick-drying stain, projects can be finished easily in only one day. The following procedure is recommended in applying *Deft*:

1. After the surface is prepared prop-erly, remove the dust from the surface by wiping with a clean, lint-free cloth.
2. If desired, stain the wood. A vinyl wood stain, designed for a *Deft* fin-ish, or other quick-drying stains can

Fig. 34-23. Finishes also are available in aerosol spray cans. (Courtesy Deft, Inc.)

be used. The vinyl stain dries in 1 hour, and the cleanup can be made with water (Fig. 34-24).

Fig. 34-24. Vinyl stains dry quickly and water can be used for cleanup. (Courtesy Deft, Inc.)

3. Apply a liberal quantity of *Deft* un-til the surface is coated fully and evenly.
4. Wait 2 hours to apply the second coat. If the surface is rough, it should be sanded lightly with a fine abrasive. The second coat should be applied in a manner similar to the first coat.
5. Repeat the preceding steps for addi-tional coats. The exact number of coats depends on the wood and on the type of finish desired.
6. For a hand-rubbed effect, rub the final coat with 4/0 steel wool or a rubbing compound. Brushes and other items should be cleaned with lacquer thin-ner.

Minwax

Minwax is a combination stain-wax finish which can be rubbed or brushed to produce a natural-appearing finish (Fig. 34-25). Its penetration is excellent, and it requires no previous operations, such as staining and sealing. A filler can be used, but this is not necessary. Since *Minwax* actually becomes a part of the wood, the finish cannot crack or scratch. Worn or damaged spots in the wood can be retouched without refinishing the entire surface.

Fig. 34-25. A combination stain-wax produces a natural-appearing finish. (Courtesy The Minwax Co., Inc.)

Minwax is recommended for floors, trim, paneling, and furniture. It is available in transparent and masking (opaque-type) colors. The transparent colors are used for woods with even tones and colors. The masking colors tend to produce uniform color on woods without an even color.

The finishing operation usually can be completed in two coats. A liberal first coat should be permitted to stand for 5 to 15 minutes, or until the wood is penetrated sufficiently. Then a clean lint-free cloth can be used to remove any excess finish. Using the same procedure, a second coat should be applied 12 to 24 hours later. Even though *Minwax* does not raise the grain, the wood can be wet/dry sanded between coats. After the final coat has dried, Minwax paste wax can be used to obtain a soft wax finish (Fig. 34-26).

Fig. 34-26. Paste wax. (Courtesy The Minwax Co., Inc.)

Watco Danish Oil

A *Watco Danish Oil* finish is similar to a linseed oil finish, but it is quicker to apply and and requires less rubbing. The finish is a polymerizing liquid which penetrates and becomes a part of the wood. It does not scratch, crack, or peel. When applied properly, it resists most stains, water, and heat.

Watco Danish Oil can be applied directly to the wood; or it can be applied over surfaces treated with stain or oil paste fillers. Also, it is available in natural and dark colors. Retouch work is possible without refinishing an entire surface.

The finishing schedule is similar to that for linseed oil. On the first coat, the wood is saturated fully and then wiped clean (Fig. 34-27). The wood is saturated again

Fig. 34-27. Applying a Danish oil finish.

in at least 24 hours. Near the end of the saturation period, all the surfaces are wet/dry sanded for smoother finishes. Any surplus finish should be wiped clean and never left on a surface to dry. After the second coat has dried for 6 hours or more, apply a wax with a high carnauba content, and polish until the desired luster is obtained. Normal wear and periodical polishing increase the beauty of the finish.

Antiquing

Antiquing is a method of finishing which has become quite popular. It is used to: (1) Quickly restore the appearance of old, worn furniture; or (2) Provide new and unfinished furniture with the beauty typical of the older, period designs. Antique finishing supplies are available commercially in kits. These finishes also can be duplicated by combining the various common finishing materials.

Quality antiquing begins with preparing all surfaces for the finishing schedule. Any surface finished previously should be sanded with a fine abrasive. Any loose pieces of a finish coat should be scraped and sanded until smooth. Special aging effects, such as scratches, dents, and worm holes, can be added where desired. Scratches can be made with any fairly sharp tool, while dents can be produced with hammers, chains, etc. (Fig. 34-28).

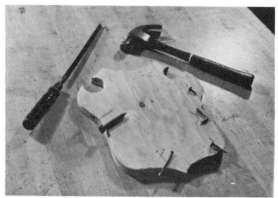

Fig. 34-29. Various types of fasteners can be used for producing antiquing patterns.

Fig. 34-30. Bookcase finished with an opaque antique finish.

Fig. 34-28. Making dents for antiquing.

Interesting patterns also can be formed, using various fasteners and the profiles of odd and thin shapes (Fig. 34-29). Opaque and transparent antique finishes are demonstrated in Figs. 34-30 and 34-31.

After a surface is prepared adequately, a base coat should be added. The base coats used most often are a latex paint, an enamel, or a clear finish used as a sealer. Wood which has not been finished previously usually is sealed before apply-

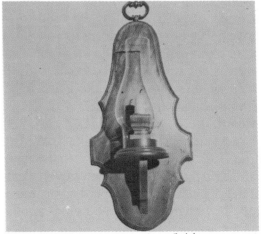

Fig. 34-31. Transparent antique finish.

ing an opaque base coat. Raw wood also may require two applications of a base coat. The first coat should be sanded lightly when thoroughly dry, before a second coat is added.

The glaze is applied only after the final base coat has dried at least 24 hours. If the glaze is applied too soon, the base coat can be dissolved; then it is lifted when the glaze is wiped (Fig. 34-32).

Fig. 34-32. If the glaze is applied too soon, the base coat will be dissolved.

The glaze can be applied with a brush in a thin, even coat; or it can be sprayed. It is often necessary to work the glaze into a hole, dent, or similar recess, using a fairly stiff brush. The glaze is then permitted to dry partially before it is wiped. Since the antique effect is achieved by wiping the glaze, various techniques can be used. A soft cloth can be used to remove most of the glaze; or a rough-textured cloth can be used to streak it. Generally, light strokes can be made with the grain to remove most of the glaze. Highlighted areas can be formed with heavier strokes.

A glaze is nearly mistake free. If it dries for too long a period, more glaze can be applied and then wiped immediately. Unsatisfactory final appearances can be reworked by applying another glaze coat and rewiping.

Certain techniques can be utilized to improve the appearance of an antiqued surface. For example, dry brushing produces an attractive grain pattern (Fig. 34-33). In this method a dry brush is moved with the grain after removing the

Fig. 34-33. The glaze can be dry brushed to produce an attractive grain pattern.

surplus glaze. Worm holes can be imitated with an old toothbrush filled with a small quantity of glaze. Small dots of glaze, resembling worm holes, can be thrown onto the surface by bending the bristles and then releasing them (Fig. 34-34). Mottled surfaces can be produced

Fig. 34-34. Small dots of glaze can be thrown onto a surface with a toothbrush by bending the bristles and releasing them to produce a worm-hole finish.

with "plastic kitchen wrap" pressed onto the glazed surface and then removed gently (Fig. 34-35). Special tones and colors can be sprayed onto the decorative cuts to develop shadowing and to increase the surface depth (Fig. 34-36).

A glazed surface, when completely dry, can be rubbed to increase the luster of the finish. Where subjected to excessive wear, glazed effects can be protected with another coat. Any clear finishing material compatible with the base coat can

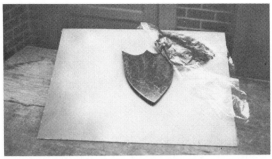

Fig. 34-35. A mottled surface can be produced by pressing plastic kitchen wrap onto a glazed surface.

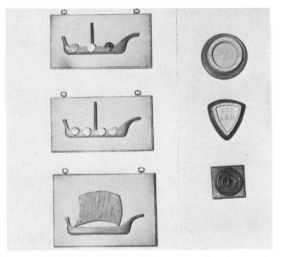

Fig. 34-36. Spraying special tones and colors onto decorative cuts develops shadow effects.

be sprayed or brushed after the glaze has dried 24 hours or more.

Applying Finishes

Finishes can be applied by rubbing, rolling, brushing, and spraying. The exact method depends on several factors, including the peculiar characteristics of the finishing material, method of application, size or shape of the object, or the number of objects requiring a finish. A general rule is to select a method which can do the best job with the least effort.

Rubbing and Rolling

A folded cloth should be used to apply the finish by rubbing. The finish should be rubbed continually while adding fin-

ish until the desired results are obtained. This method is usually limited to the smaller projects, since considerable time and effort are needed to produce a quality finish.

Rolling a finish involves a roller used to spread the finishing material (Fig. 34-37). This method is used widely for interior wall finishes and other large areas. It is not recommended for small finishing operations, since a roller cannot reach the tight areas (Fig. 34-38).

Fig. 34-37. Spreading the finish with a roller.

Fig. 34-38. Since a roller cannot be used in tight areas, it is not recommended for small finishing operations.

Brushing

Applying a finish with a brush is one of the oldest finishing methods. Most brushes are made with either animal or nylon bristles. The common sources for animal bristle are various types of squirrel, skunk, badger, mink, and swine. The swine source, especially the wild and domesticated boar, was the most popular source until a shortage forced the use of a synthetic (man-made) bristle known as nylon. The nylon bristles last longer than the hog bristles, resist the plain solvents and water, do not become moldy, and produce smoother applications.

The principal parts of a brush are diagrammed in Fig. 34-39. The handle is either wood or plastic. Most of the wood handles are made from hardwoods, but the softwoods are used for the larger brushes to reduce their weight. The bristles are the most important feature of any brush. They should hold (soak up) the finish and then spread it uniformly onto the surface. At the same time, the bristles should retain their shape without tangling. The ferrule is the metal band which holds the bristles to the handle. A wood or rubber divider separates the bristles. This enables the brush or its bristles to hold more finish. The less-expensive brushes are often made with oversize dividers.

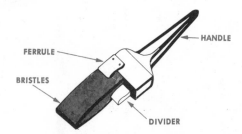

Fig. 34-39. Principal parts of a brush.

Brushes are often discarded before they are worn out as a result of poor care and upkeep. The service life of a brush can be lengthened by observing the following points:

1. Avoid using the brush edgewise. This causes the bristles to split (Fig. 34-40).

Fig. 34-40. Using a brush edgewise (top) causes the bristles to split (bottom).

Fig. 34-41. Storing a brush on its bristles causes the bristles to be bent out of shape.

2. Do not permit a brush to stand or be stored on its bristles; this causes them to be bent out of shape (Fig. 34-41).

3. When dipping a brush into a can of finish, use only the lower one-third or one-half of the bristles.

4. Avoid forcing the bristles into corners and holes.
5. Never interchange brushes and finishes. For example, a brush used for varnish should not be used for paint. The various types of brushes are shown in Fig. 34-42.

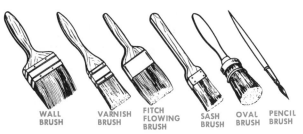

WALL BRUSH   VARNISH BRUSH   FITCH FLOWING BRUSH   SASH BRUSH   OVAL BRUSH   PENCIL BRUSH

Fig. 34-42. Various types of brushes.

When a job is completed, the brush should be cleaned immediately with the proper solvent. To clean a brush, use water for water-base (latex) and acrylic paints and use denatured alcohol for shellac; use lacquer thinner for lacquer, sanding sealer, and *Deft*. Turpentine should be used to clean a brush used for linseed oil, oil-base paints, enamels, and most of the varnishes. Mineral spirits, rather than turpentine, usually can be used. The following procedure is recommended for cleaning a brush:

1. Remove the surplus finish by wiping the flat side of the bristles.
2. Wash the bristles in solvent until thoroughly clean.
3. Squeeze the flat side of the bristles to remove the solvent. Any remaining solvent then can be removed by turning the handle quickly.
4. Gently wash with soap and water until a sudsy lather is produced. This indicates the brush is free from both finish and solvent.
5. Rinse and dry the bristles.
6. If the bristles tend to separate, wrap the brush in paper to return the bristles to shape (Fig. 34-43).

Fig. 34-43. Wrapping a brush in paper (top) aids in holding the bristles together for storage (bottom).

Brushing Hints

1. Brush from the center of the surface area to eliminate any surplus finish "running-down" an edge or end (Fig. 34-44).

Fig. 34-44. Brush from the center outward. If brushed from an edge or end, the finish "runs down."

2. When brushing a panel, brush the corners first (Fig. 34-45). Then, working from the corners and toward the centers, brush across the grain and finally with the grain.

Fig. 34-45. Brushing panels. Begin at the corners (top) then finish the inside area (bottom)

3. Where possible, use long strokes and brush with the grain. Apply only enough pressure to spread the finish.
4. If the brush pulls or drags, thin the finish until it can be applied easily. Be careful not to thin the finish too much.
5. Where the brush strokes overlap, gradually raise the brush until it is clear of the coated area (Fig. 34-46).
6. On a vertical surface, begin at the top and work downward (Fig. 34-47).
7. On a horizontal surface, begin at the far side and work forward (Fig. 34-48). Avoid reaching over a finished area with a brush.

Fig. 34-46. Where the brush strokes overlap, lift the brush until clear of the coated area.

Fig. 34-47. When brushing vertical surfaces, begin at the top and work downward.

Fig. 34-48. When brushing horizontal surfaces, begin at the far side.

Spraying

The spray finishes can be applied quickly and easily only after a person is familiar with the technique. Most furniture spraying, unless it is highly industrialized, is performed with a suction-feed spray gun. The industrial type is a pressure-feed spray gun. Another type is the electrostatic spray gun which utilizes unlike electrical charges (Fig. 34-49).

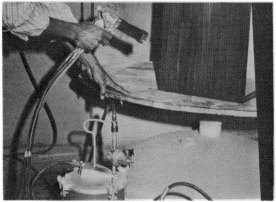

Fig. 34-49. Spraying with an electrostatic spray gun.

Even quicker and smoother finishes result from this method. The equipment for suction-feed spraying includes an air compressor, various hoses and connections, an air filter and regulator (transformer), and a spray booth or exhaust fan. The suction-feed spray gun is a nonbleeder-type which requires a paint cup and cup attachment.

A spray gun utilizes compressed air to atomize sprayable material for applying to a surface. The source is an air compressor (Fig. 34-50). The spraying pressure is determined by the hose size, consistency of a finish, and temperature. The air filter removes oil, dirt, and water from the compressed air; the regulator controls the air pressure (Fig. 34-51). The particles of finish suspended in the atmosphere are drawn off with a spray booth (Fig. 34-52) or exhaust fan. Finish not removed can settle on a surface to form an

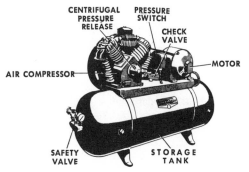

Fig. 34-50. Air compressor. (Courtesy The DeVilbiss Company)

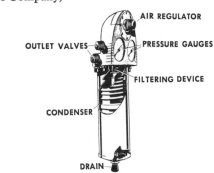

Fig. 34-51. Air transformer with principal parts. (Courtesy The DeVilbiss Company)

Fig. 34-52. Spray booth. (Courtesy The DeVilbiss Company)

overcoat. An overcoat, sometimes called a mist coat, results in a rough finish.

The principal parts of a spray gun are shown in Fig. 34-53. The air cap directs the compressed air into the finish, which then atomizes into a spray. This part also controls the direction of the spray pattern. Turning the horns of the

Fig. 34-53. Principal parts of a spray gun. The principal components are the Air Cap (A), Fluid Tip (B), Fluid Needle (C), Trigger (D), Fluid Adjustment Screw (E), Air Valve (F), Spreader Adjustment valve (G) and Gun Body (H). (Courtesy The DeVilbiss Company)

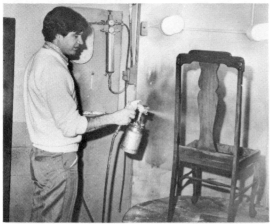

Fig. 34-54. The horns of the air cap are changed for vertical (top) and horizontal (bottom) spraying.

air cap changes the pattern from vertical to horizontal, or vice versa (Fig. 34-54). The fluid tip, along with the fluid needle, governs the quantity of finish directed into the airstream. Either more finish or less finish can be applied by adjusting the fluid needle adjustment. The size of a spray pattern can be changed by the spreader

adjustment valve, which actually controls the airflow. The cup holds the finish to be sprayed. A small vent hole located on the lid must remain open while spraying.

Spraying Procedure

The procedure for using a spray gun is:

1. Start the compressor; then it can compress the air sufficiently before it is needed.
2. Prepare the finishing material. The thinner normally is added until the spraying consistency of the finish is reached. The actual quantity of thinner required depends on the finish. Some of the finishes require little thinning, but other finishes require considerable thinning.
3. Fill the cup to about two-thirds full. If the mixture contains foreign particles, or particles which cannot be atomized, strain before filling.
4. Assemble the spray gun, connect the hoses, and adjust the pressure. The pressure varies for the various setups and types of finishes. A suitable pressure should atomize the finish completely, without fog or overspray.
5. Test the spray pattern and adjust as needed. An acceptable pattern should be about 10 inches wide when sprayed from a distance of 6 or 8 inches (Fig. 34-55). If the pattern is

Fig. 34-55. The spray pattern should be about 10 inches wide when a properly adjusted spray gun is held 6 to 8 inches from the surface.

too wet, either increase the air flow or decrease the material flow. For a dry pattern, increase the material flow, thin the finish, or decrease the airflow.

6. Spray the finish. While spraying a surface, keep the spray gun in motion. The slightest hesitation can result in a build-up of material which can "run" or "sag" (Fig. 34-56).

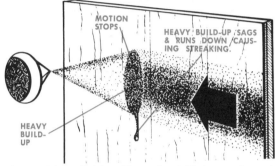

Fig. 34-56. A finish will sag (run) if the motion of the spray gun is too slow or stopped momentarily.

7. After spraying, pour any surplus finish in the cup into a secondary container. Never return the surplus finish to the original container of unthinned finish.

8. Clean the spray gun and the cup. Unscrew the air cap several turns and loosen the cup, but keep the fluid tube in the cup. Activating the trigger while covering the air cap with a cloth forces any material remaining in the gun backward into the cup (Fig. 37-57). Next, empty the cup and add a small quantity of thinner. The thinner must be identical to that used to reduce the consistency of the finish. Spray the thinner through the spray gun. If necessary, wipe the finish from the outside of the spray gun and cup, using a cloth containing the appropriate thinner.

Spraying Hints

1. Keep the spray gun 6 to 8 inches from the surface being sprayed (Fig. 34-

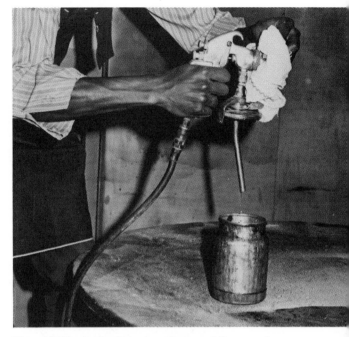

Fig. 34-57. Activating the trigger while covering the air cap forces the finish from the gun.

58). Holding the gun too close to the surface can cause sags; but holding the gun too far from the surface can cause excessive overcoating (Fig. 34-59). Also, tilting a spray gun produces an uneven spray pattern.

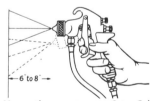

Fig. 34-58. Keep the spray gun 6 to 8 inches from and perpendicular to the surface. Tilting (note the hidden lines) the gun causes an uneven coating. (Courtesy The DeVilbiss Company)

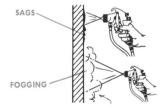

Fig. 34-59. Holding the spray gun too close to the surface causes sags, and holding the gun too far from the surface causes fogging. (Courtesy The DeVilbiss Company)

2. While spraying, watch the surface being coated—do not watch the spray gun.

3. Move the spray gun parallel with the surface being sprayed, keeping the wrist flexible (Fig. 34-60).

4. To produce an even coat, aim the spray gun with the spray pattern overlapping one half of the previous pattern (Fig. 34-61).

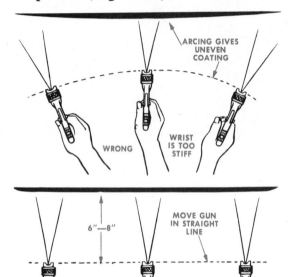

Fig. 34-60. Move the spray gun parallel with the surface. (Courtesy The DeVilbiss Company)

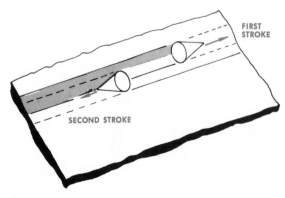

Fig. 34-61. Overlap the spray patterns to produce even coats.

5. Adjust the horns of the air cap for a convenient spray pattern (see Fig. 34-54). Position the horns horizontally for vertical strokes and vertically for horizontal strokes.

6. Reduce overcoating by spraying the edges and/or ends before spraying the adjacent areas (Fig. 34-62).

Fig. 34-62. Spray the edges and ends to reduce overcoats. (Courtesy The DeVilbiss Company)

7. When spraying a flat surface in a horizontal position, beginning with the nearer edge minimizes overcoating (Fig. 34-63).

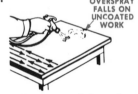

Fig. 34-63. Avoid overspray on flat surfaces by beginning at the near edge. (Courtesy The DeVilbiss Company)

8. If possible, move the spray gun either back and forth or up and down (Fig. 34-64). Never limit the movement of the gun to a single direction.

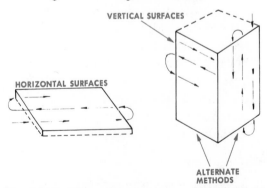

Fig. 34-64. Move the spray gun either back and forth or up and down—never in only one direction.

General Wood Finishing Hints

1. When pouring from a container with an offset spout, position the spout on the upward side (Fig. 34-65).

Fig. 34-65. In pouring from a container with an offset spout, pour with the spout at the top.

2. Nail holes located in the lid groove of a can of finish permit the surplus finish to drain back into the can, rather than down the outside of the can (Fig. 34-66).

Fig. 34-66. Nail holes in the lid groove permit the surplus finish to drain into the container.

3. When replacing the lid of a container, position the lid in the lid groove; then firmly apply pressure with the heel of a shoe. Do not attempt to "hammer" a lid.

4. After using an aerosol spray can, turn the can upside down and spray until the pattern is clear. This prevents clogging the nozzle.

5. A brush can be stored for short periods without cleaning by tightly wrapping its bristles in plastic kitchen wrap.

6. Save the thinners or solvents used for cleaning the brushes. They can be used again for the same purpose.

7. Do not use compressed air to remove dust from an unfinished surface. Harmful moisture can be deposited, and the filler can be forced from the pores.

8. Since colors tend to fade, do not expect two surfaces finished with identical stains to match, unless they are stained and finished at approximately the same time.

9. Do not apply paint or enamel to a varnished surface, because it will crack. Generally, quick-drying finishes cannot be used over the quicker drying finishes.

10. If a skin forms over the surface of a stored finish, remove the skin before mixing (Fig. 34-67). Turpentine can be added to an oil-base paint before sealing its container to prevent the skin forming on the surface.

Fig. 34-67. Remove the skin from the surface before mixing the paint.

11. If a finish requires straining, a discarded nylon stocking is useful for this purpose.
12. Avoid staining the light-colored woods with a dark stain. Even the smallest scratch can be magnified by a darker color.
13. Do not use opaque finishes on the expensive woods, unless absolutely necessary.
14. When finishing an object, do not overlook the back, bottom, etc. For a finish to be effective, the wood must be sealed completely.

Care of a Finish

It is often necessary to repair scratches and stains occurring from the routine use. Since there are so many finishes, a universal recommendation is difficult to describe; however, one or a combination of the following practices might be helpful:

1. Remove minor scratches, using paste wax and fine steel wool. For the oil finishes, wet/dry sanding with oil removes the scratches.
2. For a deep scratch, conceal the scratch, using iodine for the red-colored woods and brown shoe polish for the brown-colored woods.
3. Furniture polish and several drops of alcohol can be used to minimize the scratches on a shellac finish.
4. A mixture of cigar ash and castor oil, or rottenstone and linseed oil, rubbed over an alcohol stain might eliminate the stain.
5. A clouded area resulting from excessive heat on a varnished surface can be cleared, using spirits of camphor.
6. Water marks usually can be removed either with thinned shellac and linseed oil or with olive oil and white vinegar (Fig. 34-68).

Fig. 34-68. A water mark.

Questions

1. Discuss the purpose of a finish.
2. Define a schedule, as related to a finish. List the steps of the finishing schedule.
3. List the steps required in preparing a surface for finishing.
4. Why is a wood stained? List four wood stains and their advantages.
5. What is the purpose of a wood filler? What might result from applying a lacquer or another finish before the filler is dry?
6. List the advantages, the thinners or solvents, and the drying times for shellac, varnish, lacquer, and paint.
7. List the advantages of an oil finish, as compared to either a varnish finish or a lacquer finish.
8. How should shellac, varnish, lacquer, and paint be applied? Is it necessary to sand between coats for each of these finishes? Why?
9. Why is a wood antiqued? List a step-by-step procedure for antiquing.
10. List and describe the principal parts of a paint brush.
11. List five rules for taking care of a paint brush.
12. Describe how the spray pattern should be adjusted for a suction-feed spray gun.
13. Discuss the techniques which should be followed in spraying.
14. How should a finish be cared for after it has dried?

Unit 35 — Planning Lathework

Lathework involves material which has been rounded by turning the workpiece against a stationary cutting tool (Fig. 35-1). The turning operation is an old

Fig. 35-1. Basic turning process.

method of making round pieces and segments. The turnings, or the round pieces made on a lathe, are used extensively in industry in both woods and in metals. Wood turnings are used for the legs of furniture, stretchers in bracing the chair legs, decorative pieces in wall supports, room-divider screens, stair railings, and many other places. In a bed, for example, the corner posts—especially in the colonial furniture stylings—are often ornately turned pieces. Metal turnings are used to form the axles for wheels, the tools to cut other materials to shape, and the shafts and cams in various types of machinery.

Planning the Shape

The shape of the turning is extremely important, since it determines not only the shape, grain, and color of the wood but also how well it blends into the other design environmental factors. The shape is the primary consideration.

Several basic shapes are used—the *Colonial* style involves beads and grooves; the *Scandinavian* style employs the ogive, or reverse curve; the *Spanish* and *Mediterranean* stylings feature the "jug" shape; and some of the modern stylings utilize a straight taper. All these shapes are diagrammed in Fig. 35-2. The basic shapes rarely are made from a single solid piece of wood. The pieces usually are made by building up a single larger piece from several smaller pieces. This can be done in several ways.

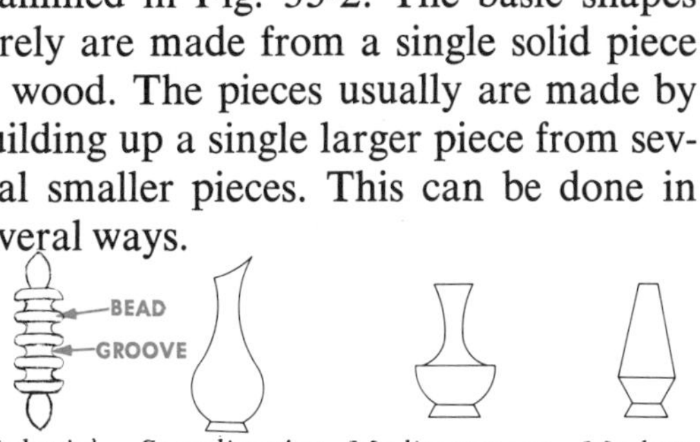

Colonial. Scandinavian Mediterranean. Modern.
Fig. 35-2. Basic turned shapes.

In the core method, a solid piece of wood is used for the center portion, with additional faces glued on and built up to provide special grain appearances (Fig. 35-3). The layered effect, used extensively

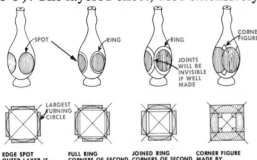

Fig. 35-3. Core layering for special effects.

for bowls and lamp bases, is made from pieces glued face-to-face and stacked (like a stack of plates) to form the desired height and width (Fig. 35-4). The

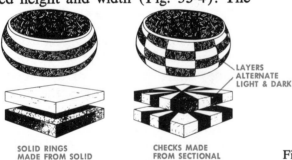

Fig. 35-4. Stack layering for special effects.

other basic layering process used to obtain a straight, longitudinal line for the grain is shown in Fig. 35-5. This method is commonly used when the face graining is undesirable, as in making furniture

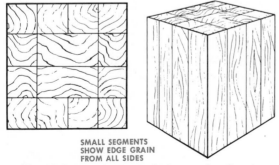

Fig. 35-5. Layering to avoid face-grain effects.

legs, bed posts, lamp columns, and other long straight pieces.

Special Lathe Effects

Other special effects can be obtained with the lathe by special techniques. These special effects include polka dots made from contrasting wood colors; special grain effects; combinations of texture involving different types of wood, such as cork and walnut; stripes; checks; diamond shapes; and many other effects. Some of the techniques for obtaining these patterns are shown in Figs. 35-6 and 35-7.

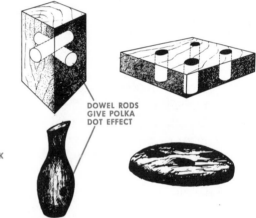

Fig. 35-6. Dowel rods can be used to provide a polka-dot effect.

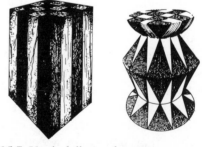

Fig. 35-7. Vertical diamond patterns.

Special effects should be used sparingly; they should be used only to provide the decoration required for the object to blend with its surroundings. A brightly colored, brightly patterned, heavily figured piece only attracts attention. However, if the piece blends with its surroundings, it improves the surroundings. If the piece clashes with its surroundings, as many heavily decorated pieces do, it detracts from the appearance of the remainder of the room by becoming the focal point, which is only different——rather than well designed.

Questions

1. How can solid rings of wood be built into a bowl?
2. How can a polka-dot design be achieved on a lamp?
3. What type of turning characterizes the *Colonial*-style furniture?
4. What is the chief problem in obtaining special effects on lathework?
5. What construction problems are conceivable in making special effects?
6. Make several sketches which combine style features, such as straight tapers with curves.

Unit 36 – Turning Techniques

In making lathe turnings, several different methods are used. The competent woodworker should be aware of all these methods. The same principles and tools are used throughout all the operations; however, the mountings and applications are different.

The wood turnings used in industry are produced on wood lathes; the metal turnings used in industry are produced on metal lathes—called engine lathes. The metal lathes, or engine lathes, are used to produce bearings, axles, shafts, knobs, handles, and countless other pieces. The basic turning principle is nearly the same in both metalworking and woodworking. A piece of metal can be turned on a wood lathe, but the wood lathes generally turn too rapidly for most of the metalworking processes. Also, the metal turnings require a lathe which is structurally stronger and sturdier (bearings, etc.) than most of the wood lathes. The metals that can be cut safely on wood lathes are the softer metals, such as copper and aluminum. Generally, when a piece of metal is cut on a wood lathe, a special cutting tool is required. It is inadvisable to attempt to cut metal on a wood lathe until one has acquired considerable experience.

Turning Between Centers

The most common method of turning wood on a lathe is "between centers" turning. The piece of stock is mounted between the two holders or "centers." The *live center* is attached to the headstock spindle which provides the turning force for the workpiece. The opposite end of the stock is supported by the *dead center*, which does not turn. Sometimes a *cup center* is used for this purpose. The stock is rotated against the cutting tool to form the basic shape desired. The cutting tool is supported on a tool rest during the cutting operation.

Generally, long pieces of stock are turned between lathe centers. If the stock is basically long and square in shape, the center of the stock is found by drawing diagonals on each end; then shallow cuts are made in one end for the insertion of the spurs, which provide the driving force (Fig. 36-1). The cup center is placed on the center point formed by the crossing diagonal lines; then it is driven into the end of the stock by the force of the tailstock handwheel.

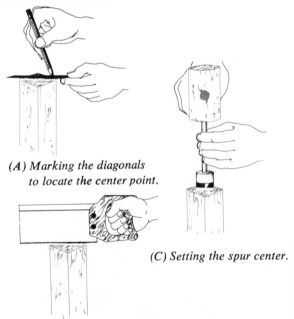

(A) Marking the diagonals to locate the center point.

(C) Setting the spur center.

(B) Slotting one end for the spur center.

Fig. 36-1. Preparing stock for turning between centers.

When a piece of larger stock is to be turned between centers, it is often advisable to cut off the corners with a saw. If the material is large, the corners should be faced with a plane or a jointer. This reduces the sharp edges, making the roughing work easier and quicker. Between-centers turning is used for making the long and straight pieces, such as baseball bats, table legs, bed posts, and lamp columns.

Faceplate Turning

When bowls, bases for lamps, and similar objects are to be turned, the stock should be mounted on a *faceplate*. The stock is attached to the faceplate with screws or bolts. Then the faceplate is screwed onto the spindle of the headstock. This permits the stock to be rotated against the cutting tool without being supported by the tailstock center. Also, it permits the operator to work across the face of the stock. To mount faceplate stock, cut the stock to size and cut off the corners and edges (Fig. 36-2). Locate

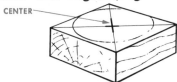

(A) Square stock is cut and centered for faceplate turning.

(B) Trim the corners for the turning.

Fig. 36-2. Preparing stock for faceplate turning.

the center point of the stock and attach the faceplate, using the hole on the back side for a guide in centering the faceplate onto the stock. The pilot holes for the screws are drilled and the faceplace is attached, using short, heavy wood screws (Fig. 36-3).

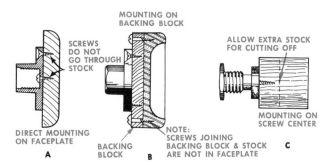

Fig. 36-3. Methods of attaching a faceplate to the stock. (A) Direct mounting of the stock onto a faceplate. (B) Mounting the stock onto a backing block. (C) Mounting the stock onto a screw center.

When delicate or thin sections are to be made in the stock, it is advisable to use a scrap piece for a mounting plate. To prepare a mounting plate, an extra piece of material of lesser grade or quality, or a piece of scrap, can be glued on (Fig. 36-4). To make the mounting plate easier to separate from the stock, place

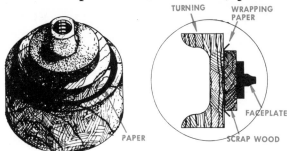

Fig. 36-4. Scrap wood can be used for a mounting plate in faceplate turning of thin sections of stock.

a layer of newspaper or wrapping paper in the glue joint. This weakens the joint slightly; then the materials can be separated after the turning has been completed, using a chisel and a sharp blow from a mallet. It is advisable to use not more than one layer of newspaper, since the material might separate too easily. There is danger from the material being thrown off, due to the centrifugal force and the pressure from the cutting tool, if more paper is used.

Outboard Turning

Outboard turning is a type of faceplate turning in which the faceplate is mounted on the outside portion of the headstock of the lathe (Fig. 36-5), when the stock is

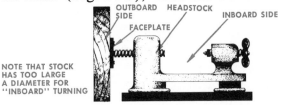

NOTE THAT STOCK HAS TOO LARGE A DIAMETER FOR "INBOARD" TURNING

OUTBOARD SIDE   HEADSTOCK   INBOARD SIDE
FACEPLATE

Fig. 36-5. Outboard turning of large-diameter stock is performed on the faceplate on the outboard side of the headstock.

too large in diameter to be turned on the inboard side of the headstock spindle. This technique is used for turning the larger bowls and flat pieces, for forming the rounded areas on chair seats, and for similar operations. When performing outboard turning, a floor stand can be used to support a toolholder. Care should be exercised on the heavier pieces to make sure the stock is turned at the slowest possible speed. A large piece has a high peripheral speed, despite the fact its rate of rotation might be slow; therefore, at the outer edges, the tool might be cutting at the same speed that a smaller piece rotated at a high rpm is cutting. In addition, higher speeds on the heavier objects might cause them to be separated from the faceplate and fly through the shop, causing injury to the operator or workers in other areas.

Lathe Tools

Several types of lathe tools are used in basic turning. Each lathe tool is designed for a special use and application, and it cannot be used effectively for other jobs. A special tool is used to turn a long straight cut. A different type of tool is used to turn an inside curve, called a groove. Different turning tools are used

for roughing and reducing the stock to general size, finish cuts, beads, grooves, and long paper cuts. Special turning tools are used for cutting deep grooves in the stock and for cutting off the stock from the remaining material when the turning is completed. Although the number of tools which might be used is quite large, the most common turning tools are:

1. Roundnose gouges, ¾-inch and ½-inch.
2. Square-nose chisel.
3. Roundnose chisel.
4. Spear- or diamond-point chisel.
5. Two skew chisels, ½-inch and ¾-inch.
6. Parting tool.

In general, the procedure for cutting stock to shape and size on a lathe is as follows:

1. Adjust the tool rest to approximately 5° above center with ⅛ inch or less clearance between the stock and the tool rest (Fig. 36-6).

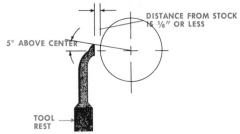

DISTANCE FROM STOCK IS ⅛" OR LESS

5° ABOVE CENTER

TOOL REST

Fig. 36-6. Correct adjustment for turning the stock.

2. Check for adequate clearance between the stock and the tool rest by rotating the stock by hand.
3. Set the lathe for the slowest speed.
4. Hold the gouge firmly in place on the tool rest; then turn the stock to a round shape.
5. When using the gouge, cut from each end toward the middle to prevent splintering.
6. Set the calipers to the diameter desired.

7. Cut the stock with the gouge, or chisel, until the desired diameter is reached on the end; then continue to reduce the stock in successive stages to this diameter. Mark the locations of prominences, such as beads, grooves, and papered sections, with a pencil; then turn the stock to the desired shape, using the skew chisels and other chisels (Figs. 36-7 and 36-8).

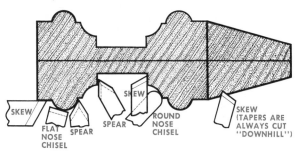

Fig. 36-7. Types of turning tools.

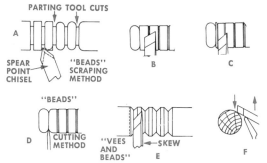

Fig. 36-8. Sequence of cuts for turning beads and grooves.

8. Trim the ends of stock to be separated to approximately ½ inch in diameter. Do not attempt to cut off the stock completely with a parting tool, since this is dangerous and prevents the material being sanded on the lathe. To cut off the ends, remove the stock from the lathe; then cut off the scrap pieces by hand.

In general, the roughing cuts are made with the gouges. The finished cuts are made to reduce the stock to the proper shape and size, and are made with scrap-

ing tools, such as a chisel. The chisels are available in various shapes, such as the skew, roundnose, and square-point chisels. These chisels take smaller cuts, but they shear the wood cleaner with smoother cuts. In addition, higher speeds can be used with the scraping tools. The deep grooves should be made with parting tools, and the ends are often trimmed with skew chisels.

The larger pieces of stock should be rotated at the slowest possible speed. Smaller pieces of stock should be turned at the higher speeds. The highest possible lathe speed should never be used, unless the stock is quite small. The higher speeds are used effectively for sanding, but the finishes should always be applied at the slower speeds. The use of slow speeds for the finishing operations prevents the finishing material being thrown from the surfaces of the material. When applying the metallic materials to an object—for example, in applying plastic aluminum to provide a metallic, banded effect—the material should be applied in layers and it should be applied to a groove which has been undercut (Fig. 36-9).

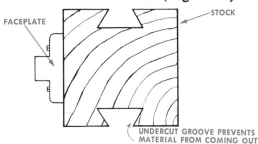

Fig. 36-9. Undercut any grooves which are to be filled with a decorative metallic material, such as plastic aluminum.

Special Lathe Operations

Several additional operations can be performed on the lathe. Sanding, finishing, polishing, and various types of chucking operations also can be done easily on a lathe.

Sanding

To sand on the lathe, hold the sandpaper in both hands underneath the work (Fig. 36-10). After the material has been turned to the approximate diameter with a gouge and finished to the desired size, the material then should be sanded. Sand-

STOCK   ROTATION

FOLDED
SANDPAPER
HELD UNDERNEATH
WORK

Fig. 36-10. Sanding on the lathe.

ing on the lathe is quicker and, in many instances, smoother than sanding by hand. The following procedures should be observed in sanding on the lathe:

1. Move the tool rest completely away from the work. Set the lathe for a slow speed and fold the sandpaper to be used. It is not necessary to begin with coarse, rough sandpaper. The medium grades are generally sufficient, with the fine grades being used for extremely fine sanding.
2. Hold the sandpaper underneath the the work; carefully move the sandpaper back and forth across the areas to be sanded until they are smooth (see Fig. 36-10). Be careful not to round off edges that should remain square.
3. Stop the lathe; use fine sandpaper to sand slightly with the grain to remove any cross-grain sanding marks.

Special safety precautions are:

1. Remove the tool rest for sanding.
2. Sand on the bottom side of the turning piece.

Finishing on the Lathe

The finish is often applied to lathework before the stock is removed from the lathe. Several types of finishing materials can be used, such as the French polish or the Danish Oil finish. The French polish method combines shellac and oil and is applied with a pad of soft cloth. The pad is first moistened with thin shellac; then a few drops of linseed oil are placed on the pad. The pad is held on the underneath side of the material to be polished in the same manner as in sanding. To apply an oil finish, merely soak the pad in the oil and wax combination; again, hold the pad on the underneath side of the stock. To apply materials, such as stain and wood filler, special precautions might be necessary. Stain is easy to apply; however, a wood filler tends to stick and should be removed quickly with a coarse cloth.

Chucking

Chucking can be performed on a lathe by turning a standard Jacobs chuck onto the spindle. The chuck can be used to hold small pieces of round stock, such as dowels and other small pieces, for special forming.

A temporary chucking device easily can be made for lathework by turning a larger piece, boring a hole (Fig. 36-11), and sawing two cuts to form four split jaws. A metal ring then can be used to

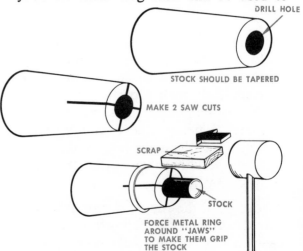

DRILL HOLE

STOCK SHOULD BE TAPERED

MAKE 2 SAW CUTS

SCRAP

STOCK

FORCE METAL RING
AROUND "JAWS"
TO MAKE THEM GRIP
THE STOCK

Fig. 36-11. Making a lathe chuck.

tighten the jaws for holding small objects for sanding, polishing, and light-duty cutting operations. Always make sure the tool rest is adjusted properly for both height and spacing. The spacing should be approximately ⅛ inch, or less, and

DRILL 1/16"

DRILL ½"

(A) Salt and pepper shakers.

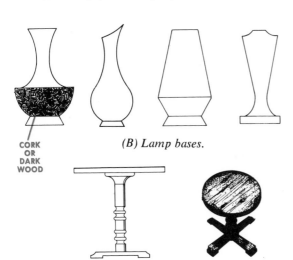

CORK OR DARK WOOD

(B) Lamp bases.

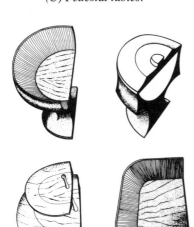

(C) Pedestal tables.

(D) Bowls and dishes.

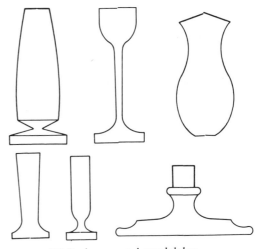

(E) Bud vases and candelabra.

Fig. 36-12. Lathework projects.

never more than ¼ inch from the stock. The height of the tool rest should be adjusted to slightly above center. Various lathework projects are shown in Fig. 36-12.

Safety Precautions

The special safety precautions for the lathe also apply to general machine operations. However, these additional factors should be observed:

1. Do not wear loose clothing and do not permit apron strings or loose pockets to dangle.
2. Fasten the sleeves all the way down —or roll them all the way up. Do not permit loose sleeve corners to dangle partially rolled up.
3. Remove all rings, watches, jewelry, and similar items which might be caught by moving parts.
4. If long hair is worn, wear a cap, net, headband, or similar device to hold the hair tightly and away from the work area.
5. Wear goggles, face shields, or similar eye protection devices.
6. Make sure all the adjustments are made on the machine before turning

on the machine. Never adjust the machine while it is moving. Always turn off the machine and permit it to stop completely before making adjustments.

7. Make sure all the jigs, clamps, rests, and attachments are tightened.

8. Never stand directly in front of the stock when turning on the lathe switch.

9. Never take extremely large cuts with the gouge during the roughing operation. This can loosen the material from its mountings or cause large chips to fly off, endangering the operator and those working near him.

10. Never touch the stock with the fingers while it is turning.

11. Maintain good housekeeping while working.

12. Maintain a healthy attitude toward safety.

Questions

1. What is the chief difference in "faceplate" and "between-centers" turning?

2. When is "outboard" turning necessary?

3. What is the recommended distance between the tool rest and the stock?

4. List two special safety precautions necessary in sanding on the lathe.

5. What lathe speed is recommended for applying a finish?

6. Sketch a skew chisel. List two occasions for its use.

7. When should the roundnose chisel be used?

8. When should a gouge be used?

9. What lathe speed is recommended for "roughing" cuts?

10. Why is a piece of paper sometimes used in mounting a piece of stock onto a faceplate?

Mass Production

Mass production refers to the manufacture of goods on a large scale through specialized operations. In general, the work is moved toward the worker, and each worker performs only one or two operations of the many operations required to make the product.

There should be no doubt that the North American nations are industrial leaders. The United States enjoys the highest standard of living of any nation in the world, a status achieved largely by its ability to mass-produce high-quality products. The remainder of the world regards the United States as the expert in mass-production techniques. However, to the general public, a modern manufacturing system usually is taken for granted and quite often misunderstood. Many persons feel that the huge organization, vast machinery, and complex financial structure are too difficult to understand. Yet, it is this vast operation which provides the homes, jobs, and our means of good health, personal freedoms, entertainment, and high standard of living conditions. ..

It is generally understood that nearly eighty percent of our high-school graduates will be making their livelihood within the industrial system. Fulfilling the training needs of the youth of today certainly has become a major concern of our modern educational system. If education draws its content from the demands of the society, the various segments or processes of industry must be surveyed and analyzed to derive the basic ideas of our industrial society. One of the most dominant aspects of modern industry is mass production.

This unit, which is concerned with the industrial process of mass production, is a simplified method of depicting the role of manufacturing in a technical society. "On-the-job" training is often said to be the best teacher; therefore, actual experience in a project should create a tremendous insight into how an industry operates. The various concepts of production should become apparent and should help to understand industry, by the experience of coordinating the knowledge of the machine and tool operations into a practical and meaningful experience. At this point, the vocational advantages must not be overlooked. The experience in mass production is a definite taste of industry, and it enables the student to formulate opinions as to whether he would like to consider a career in any of the aspects of industry. In the mass-production experience, the student is provided the opportunity to experience jobs in business administration, personnel management, clerical, labor, labor relations, and other organizational features.

The student is placed in a situation which requires him to think in a deductive manner. Up to this point, the materials and ideas have been given to him. He has been taught the safety rules and the manipulative skills, but he has not been placed in a true problem-solving situation. A mass-production project problem does not necessarily provide him with an end or a clear path to a solution; but the student should be able to draw on his past experiences, and through application and fact arrive at a logical solution to the mass-production problem. He should soon begin to realize what "organization" is and how critical the planning processes are in an industry.

Unit 37 – Manufacturing in the United States

From his earliest appearance on earth, the efforts of man to satisfy his needs and desires has led to the development of the vast industrial complex of today. The development of the modern industrial system has evolved from the one-man process which produced goods for the family and, in time, to the production of surplus items which could be bartered or sold outside the home. From his hunting and nomadic wanderings to the development of communities, man's manufacturing system also has changed. Specialization of effort began to emerge. Men who possessed unusual skills in the trades, such as weaving, carving, metalworking, and other handicrafts, began to devote full time to these occupations. The weaver furnished cloth in exchange for food from the farmer who needed cloth. With the growth and development of the specialized occupations came the formation of groups of workers who regulated wages, training methods, etc. Each occupation was characterized by its own group, the trade guild. The basic idea of the guilds still exists in our country in the form of organized labor unions.

Mass-Production Concept

The mass-production concept was a natural development in the United States. The perfect climate for development was established in the freedom of thought, liberty of personal action, and man's respect for education, accompanied by a mixture of thinking, doing, and inventive people. The abundance of raw materials, high labor costs, readily available markets, and a shortage of trained labor provided the incentive for a sequence of inventors and manufacturing geniuses to develop a method of production characterized by duplication, interchangeability, and large quantities of parts.

Historically, mass production can be traced to 1798 when Eli Whitney was commissioned by Congress to produce 10,000 muskets in a two-year period of time. At that time, muskets—as well as all other machines—were made by hand and each musket was different in size. At the end of the two-year period, Eli Whitney had produced only a few muskets. To say the least, the government was quite upset until Eli Whitney journeyed to the capital to explain and demonstrate why he had not fulfilled the terms of his contract. He entered the room with a large box, laid its contents into neat piles, and requested those present to assemble the ten parts into finished muskets without machining or filing.

Eli Whitney had spent most of the two-year period in devising methods of making identical parts. Once his factory was "tooled up," the actual construction of a musket required only a short time. Eli Whitney's ideas were the foundation of mass production, which is dependent on the accurate interchangeability of parts. Mass production requires standardized and precision-made parts, division of labor, and trained workers with narrow and specialized skills. The journeyman or the apprentice no longer produced the entire product.

Development of Mass Production

In the ensuing years, the development of mass-production techniques paralleled the growth of the United States. With a steady influx of people from Europe, the Orient, and the opening of the American West, there was an urgent and constant demand for more products. The relatively simple needs of the early settlers soon gave way to the more complex requirements of both people on the move and those of rapidly growing communities.

Throughout the 19th Century, industry was geared to meet the immediate needs of the consumer. In the early 20th Century, this emphasis was shifted to the production of goods for filling the needs and desires that people thought were unattainable and to create new markets. This great stride forward came through the organization and enthusiasm of Henry Ford, who brought many innovations and contributions together in the production of the automobile. Through his ingenuity, each job was broken down into its simplest operation, special tools and machines were developed to perform the op-

Fig. 37-1. The automobile body begins here where precision-stamped body panels are set carefully into fixtures. (Courtesy Chevrolet Motor Division, General Motors Corporation)

Fig. 37-2. Automatic welding equipment performs 95 percent of the 3900 welds on each automobile body. (Courtesy Chevrolet Motor Division, General Motors Corporation)

erations (Figs. 37-1 and 37-2), and everything in the plant moved toward the final product. This change in production concepts made it possible to produce 1 car every 6 seconds and to cut the cost of the car nearly in half. By eliminating labor costs, the products were cheaper and the worker made more money. The concept of parts moving to the man (Fig. 37-3)

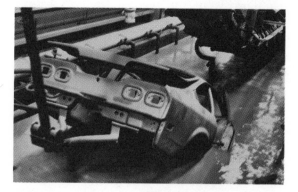

Fig. 37-3. The work is moved to the station where the operation is completed by the simplest, most efficient means. (Courtesy Chevrolet Motor Division, General Motors Corporation)

and the sequences and coordination of all the movements of the parts toward the whole product is the basis of the mass-production concept as we know it today (Figs. 37-4 and 37-5).

The development and refinement of mass-production techniques has been a

Fig. 37-4. The engine and rear-axle assembly are positioned by hydraulic lifts, to prevent workers wasting time in positioning heavy parts. (Courtesy Chevrolet Motor Division, General Motors Corporation)

Fig. 37-5. The aluminum-block engine is guided into position while the "dolly" and body are synchronized to move along the assembly line at 30 feet per minute. (Courtesy Chevrolet Motor Division, General Motors Corporation)

Fig. 37-6. An air wrench tightens all the interchangeable nuts on the wheel at the same time. (Courtesy Chevrolet Motor Division, General Motors Corporation)

continuous process throughout the years. However, the essential ingredients of the

process: (1) Ability to interchange parts (Fig. 37-6); (2) Movement of materials to and from the worker, rather than from the worker to the materials; (3) Specialized role of the worker; and (4) Efficiency are still the backbone of the system. These concepts are illustrated further in Figs. 37-7 and 37-8.

The effects of mass production on society are quite significant. Higher wages, improved working conditions, quality products at a minimum cost, a wider range of job opportunities, the continual development of new and better products, and standardization of products through-

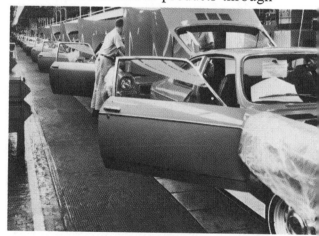

Fig. 37-7. With the hatchbacks up and the doors open, the body moves down the final line while the seats and carpet are installed. (Courtesy Chevrolet Motor Division, General Motors Corporation)

Fig. 37-8. Running on its own power, the automobile heads for another inspection area. (Courtesy Chevrolet Motor Division, General Motors Corporation)

out the country have contributed greatly to the higher standard of living enjoyed by the people of this country.

Organization of Industry

Mass production is only one phase of the industrial enterprise employed by the manufacturing complex to produce large quantities of goods quickly and at the lowest cost. The relationship of mass production to the other activities within this complex structure is as important as the production process itself.

The goods produced must be sold to a consumer; otherwise, there would be no profit. To sell the goods, they must be transported to the customer (Fig. 37-9).

Fig. 37-9. In this new shipping technique, 30 vehicles are carried nose down in completely enclosed railway cars which protect against damage. Packaging ideas are effective on large and small objects. Efficient packaging means lower cost. (Courtesy Chevrolet Motor Division, General Motors Corporation)

In addition, some care must be taken to produce the type of product the customer really wants, and care must be taken to produce goods of high quality to make sure the customer will buy again when he needs more goods. Without the customers returning to buy again, an industry could remain working only a short time.

Whatever the product, certain functions or activities of the various manufacturing industries are common to each industry.

Usually, the only differences are in their basic organizational patterns or in certain patterns or processes of production methods. Within industry, there exists a basic sequential pattern of those activities which occur *prior* to actual production, *during* the production run, and *after* the production run has been completed.

Organizing a Company

The initial activities are those involving the basic organization of the company. There are three basic forms of organization which satisfy the needs of nearly any new enterprise. These three types of organization are: (1) Individual proprietorship or one-person ownership; (2) Partnership; and (3) Corporation. These organizations are discussed later in more detail. After the organizational pattern has been established, it is necessary to determine the source of funds (or capital) needed to set up the firm, since large sums of money are needed to set up the production methods.

After the capital is obtained, the next step is to set up the personnel organizational structure; then a market study is necessary to indicate the kind and type of products needed, availability of materials, cost and profit factors, and the engineering requirements necessary to bring the product from the drawing board to the production stage.

Production Planning

Once the process of manufacturing has been developed, production planning begins. Facilities, process flow, plant layout, and scheduling systems are analyzed and organized to make sure all the production requirements are met. Materials must be obtained and the machines and equipment must be identified before the tooling-up process can begin. Once the making of the individual parts of the product commences, quality controls are used continually throughout the process to insure production of a quality product. Efficient final assembly is the ultimate outcome. Packaging and shipping are the next steps in the mass-production process.

The final stage involves activities, such as advertising, marketing, and distribution of the goods to the customers. The final activity entails the final accounting of the financial structure of the firm. Included in this phase is the payment of all bills, invoicing, and the payment of dividends to the stockholders or owners.

Introduction to Business Organization

Manufacturing firms in the United States vary in their characteristics. One can find small one-man businesses operating in basements, one-room shops, and garages. In contrast, there also exists throughout the country the large corporate manufacturing complexes consisting of one or more large buildings and headed by a board of directors.

Single Proprietorship

Undoubtedly, the oldest form of business is the one-owner or single-proprie-

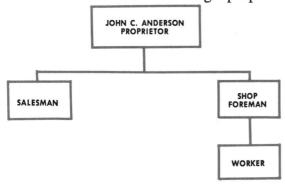

Fig. 37-10. Single proprietorship.

torship type of firm (Fig. 37-10). Evidence exists that this type of business organization was commonplace to the ancient Egyptians, Greeks, and Romans.

There are certain advantages in the individual proprietorship, if the individual is willing to work long and hard. When he works hard and there is a substantial return or profit, he is not required to share with others. In addition, he is free to make decisions and to do many things in his business without consulting or being directed by others. On the other hand, the single owner is required to suffer all losses which might occur during the operation of the enterprise. The most important characteristics of the single proprietorship are:

1. Anyone possessing the legal right to act for himself can start a business. He has only to secure the facilities, equipment, supplies, and in some states a license to do business. Then, he can open his doors to his customers.
2. Other than the costs of the business itself and a license, no other costs are usually incurred in starting a business of this type.
3. The single owner receives all the benefits of his business, but he also must assume all the responsibility for its losses.
4. Unless the single owner has large resources of his own, it is often difficult to obtain the unlimited credit needed to expand the business. Inability to expand is often a cause for failure of the individual proprietorship or the reason for the formation of a partnership or corporation.
5. Since uncertainties are associated with a single owner, this type of organization is not conducive to a business requiring long-run commitments.

General Partnership

This type of organization is a contractual business agreement between two or more persons who have the right to enter into a contract (Fig. 37-11). From the

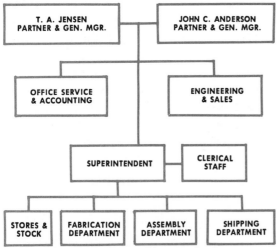

Fig. 37-11. Partnership organization.

business standpoint, a partnership conducts business in much the same manner that the single proprietorship conducts business. Legally, it also is like the single proprietorship in that the partners must share the obligation of debts. One of the partners can bind the others, and the assets of all the partners can be taken to pay any or all the debts of the partnership. Additional characteristics of a partnership type of business organization are:

1. The rights of each partner can be defined clearly through a written partnership agreement.
2. The rights and responsibilities of the partners are clearly governed by common law and statutory requirements.
3. Unless specified otherwise, the profits are shared equally, even though the original investment of each partner might be different.
4. Unless specified otherwise, the power of control or management is shared equally.
5. An individual partner cannot transfer his interest in the general partnership without permission from the other partners.

6. The unlimited liability of this type of business arrangement gives it a high credit rating.

The Corporation

The corporation is a legally created "artificial" person (Fig. 37-12). This

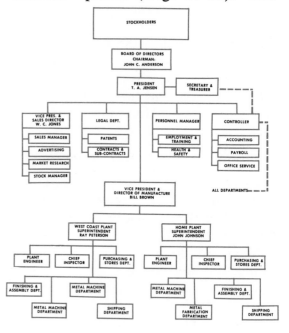

Fig. 37-12. Corporation organizational structure.

means that the corporation itself possesses an identity separate from the people who own stocks or securities in it. The chief advantage of this type of structure is that the liability of each stockholder is limited to the possible loss of his investment; but his personal belongings cannot be affected by the debts of the corporation. This business format also provides a means of securing funds from many sources, according to the financial abilities of the investors. Utilizing the individual unit or stock process for investing, the prospective investor can purchase a unit or stock process for investing; also, the prospective investor can purchase shares of stock for very little or for very much, depending on the likelihood of success of the new company and its ability to pay its stockholders a profit.

Other characteristics of the corporation are:

1. They can be chartered for a definite period of time, or forever. This feature lends stability to the business in that its business life is not dependent on the life or service of any one person.
2. The activities of the corporation are limited to those set forth in its charter. Because of this feature, charters usually are quite broad in nature to permit the corporation to engage in nearly any activity.
3. By its very nature, that of an artificial person, the corporation cannot act in its own behalf, but it must operate solely through delegated power and authority.

Establishing a Business

The entire class should be divided into groups to investigate the types of business organization appropriate for school operations. The corporation generally is the best type of business; but a class should explore all the factors and decide this matter for themselves. The corporate type of structure provides the widest range of experiences and opportunities for each member of the class.

The class then should be organized into a model company. An appropriate organizational chart identifying the structure and the personnel necessary to make the model industry function should be prepared.

Chartering a Corporation

The first act of business, from the legal standpoint, is to obtain a state charter (Fig. 37-13) or a contract for partnerships. This action is required by law in all

Fig. 37-13. Sample corporation charter.

states. The initial steps of incorporation involve: (1) Securing the necessary application forms (Fig. 37-14) from the

ARTICLES OF INCORPORATION
OF

We, the undersigned natural persons of legal age or more, acting as incorporators of a corporation under the State Business Corporation Act, adopt the following Articles of Incorporation for such corporation:

FIRST: The name of the corporation is _____

SECOND: The period of its duration is _____
THIRD: The purpose or purposes for which the corporation is organized are:
FOURTH: The aggregate number of shares which the corporation shall have authority to issue is: (Note 1)
FIFTH: The corporation shall not commence business until at least the minimum allowable dollars has been received by it as consideration for the issuance of shares.
SIXTH: Provisions limiting or denying to shareholders the preemptive right to acquire additional or treasury shares of the corporation are: (Note 2)
SEVENTH: Provisions for the regulation of the internal affairs of the corporation are: (Note 3)
EIGHTH: The address of the initial registered office of the corporation is _____
and the name of its initial registered agent at such address is _____

NINTH: The number of directors constituting the initial board of directors of the corporation is _____, and the names and addresses of the persons who are to serve as directors until the first annual meeting of shareholders or until their successors are elected and shall qualify are:
Name   Address

TENTH: The name and address of each incorporator is:
Name   Address

DATED _____, 19_____

_____

STATE OF _____)
) ss
COUNTY OF _____)
I, _____, a notary public, hereby certify that on the _____ day of 19 _____, personally appeared before me, _____
and _____, who being by me first duly sworn, severally declared that they are the persons who signed the foregoing document as incorporators and that the statements therein contained are true.
In witness whereof I have hereunto set my hand and seal this day of _____, A.D. 19_____.

_____
NOTARY PUBLIC

Fig. 37-14. Charter application.

state; (2) Complete and file the forms; and (3) Pay the required fees to the state authority. On payment of the fees, the corporation charter is issued. A typical charter contains the following:

1. Title of corporation.
2. Name of state granting charter.
3. Purpose of the corporation.
4. Location of the corporation.
5. Number of years for which the firm is incorporated.
6. Number of directors.
7. Name and addresses of directors.
8. Capital stock subscribed for and paid up.
9. Notarization seal.

The corporation then is in business and the first meeting of the stockholders should be called. The members first vote on the proposed by-laws. The by-laws provide the general rules for operating the business; they also list the various officers needed for the corporation and the duties of these officers.

Corporation Officers

The corporation officers perform the active management of the company for and in place of the stockholders. The by-laws usually specify that the officers are to be chosen by the board of directors. The highest ranking officer is the president or chairman of the board. The company president is elected by the board of directors and is responsible for all the activities of the company; therefore, he directs the overall program of the company. The other officers are the vice-president, secretary, treasurer, and sometimes a comptroller. Often, it is the practice in some companies to name several vice-presidents, each with responsibilities for specified operations in the company. These responsibilities might include pro-duction, sales, personnel, and similar operations.

The secretary keeps the corporation seal, signs the documents, and records the minutes of the meetings held by the directors and stockholders. The treasurer is usually the chief financial officer; he is often responsible for the entire accounting operation. It should be remembered that some companies might have more or fewer executives or officers, depending on the size of the company and the type of business.

The class now should be organized at two levels—management and labor. Each student should perform or serve in at least two capacities—one in management, the other in labor.

The president of the firm shall be elected by vote of the group. The vice-presidents can be either elected or appointed by the president, as determined by the charter. Other managerial positions can be filled by appointment, by volunteers, or by an application, interview, and appointment method patterned after modern industrial practices. When the activity reaches the manufacturing stage, all the positions should be staffed by students, each making a written application for the job and submitting to a personal interview.

Preproduction Planning

With the class organized on the management level (Fig. 37-15), efforts should be directed toward raising capital, identification of a salable product, design, market potential and survey, pilot-model development, and other preproduction planning.

Financing the Enterprise

Under the system of private enterprise, as known in the United States, a new busi-

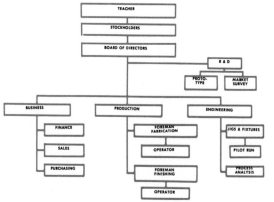

Fig. 37-15. Typical classroom organization chart for production.

ness must secure funds with which to operate. These funds can be obtained from the investment of money by the corporation members or from the sale of stock or shares. Once the business venture is in operation, capital is obtained from the sale of the product manufactured.

To provide authenticity, each member of the class should invest a sum of money in the firm. For his investment, he will be given shares of stock. (Fig. 37-16)

CERTIFICATE
NO. _____

School Manufacturing Inc.

Authorized Capital Stock _____ Shares   Par Value $_____ Per Share

THIS CERTIFIES THAT

_____ IS THE OWNER OF

_____ SHARES OF THE CAPITAL STOCK OF

School Manufacturing Inc.

TRANSFERABLE ONLY ON THE BOOKS OF THE CORPORATION BY THE HOLDER THEREOF IN PERSON OR BY REPRESENTATIVE UPON SURRENDER OF THE CERTIFICATE PROPERLY ENDORSED.

IN WITNESS HEREOF, THE SAID CORPORATION HAS CAUSED THIS CERTIFICATE TO BE SIGNED BY ITS DULY AUTHORIZED OFFICERS.

THIS _____ DAY OF _____ AD 1968

_____   _____
TREASURER   PRESIDENT

Fig. 37-16. Typical school stock certificate.

The number of shares will be determined by the size of his investment in relation to the value of each share of stock. The stock value will be determined by the action of the board of directors. The value of each share should be quite small in a school situation. If additional capital is needed, the corporation members might sell stock to other members of the student body.

Shares can be issued as either common or preferred stock. Common stock is the least complicated and the most frequently issued stock. The holders of common stock are in about the same position as the partners in a partnership. They participate in the management of the business, and they share in the profits and losses, if any.

As the name implies, preferred stock guarantees its owners certain priorities or preferences not available to the holders of common stock. These priorities might include granting of dividends, distribution of assets after the dissolution of the firm, or voting rights. However, there should be no guarantee that dividends will be paid, unless they are earned and declared by the board of directors. Usually, there is no right to vote extended.

Product Identification and Selection

After the birth of a new business venture and the development of the preliminary financial structure, the members of the firm next must turn to the identification of a product to sell. Questions which will need to be answered concern items such as: What will be the demand for this product? What is the competitive situation? Is the product a style item which might attract additional investors? Can the product selected be produced in the existing school laboratory facilities?

Each student should identify and design a potential product. The articles should be presented to the group by the designer. This can be accomplished either by an actual model of the product or by a presentation sketch. Each item should be accompanied by a cost estimate, suggested retail price, material list, and the various steps needed to construct it.

In addition to the marketability of each item, consideration should be given to utility. The product should have some usefulness, as well as eye appeal. Many fortunes have resulted from an enterprising manufacturer producing a novelty item combining both these characteristics and features.

Other considerations in product selection are: Can all the parts be constructed in the shop or will some of them have to be purchased? Does it lend itself to realistic mass-production methods? Does the product interest other class members? Does it infringe on existing patent rights?

The product ideas should be presented to the class for close scrutiny. The merits and drawbacks of each product should be discussed thoroughly by the students and the instructor. After all the ideas have been presented, a vote should be taken and at least two possible products should be selected and subjected to further consumer research study.

Market Research

Preproduction planning begins in earnest when the organizational plan is completed and the product decision has been made. The product designs should be prepared and reproduced; then they can be presented to the consumer market. Market research should be conducted to determine product preference. Each member of the company should interview several prospective customers to determine and record their degree of acceptance of each of the product designs.

The results of the interviews should be tabulated and used to assist in identification of the product to be manufactured. The class then can take steps to set up the departments in the various areas, such as Research and Development, Engineering, Finance, Sales, Production, and Inspection. Once the first departments are set up, class members can volunteer or be assigned to work in a department. The feasibility of the various items from the initial research should be presented to the board of directors. The merits of cost, design, and appropriate production procedures are considered in reaching the decision on the single item to be placed in production.

Questions

1. Why is "standardization" vital to mass production?
2. How do mass-produced goods differ from those made by a craftsman?
3. Who first devised the idea of interchangeable parts?
4. Why is the movement of parts to the worker important?
5. Do goods which are mass produced cost more or less than handmade items?
6. What is meant by *capital*?
7. How do the three types of business organization differ?
8. What is "market research"?
9. List the functions of the four chief corporation officers.

Unit 38 – Production Planning

During this phase of the operation, the various departments listed in Figs. 38-1 and 38-2 begin to coordinate their efforts for the production stage. A pilot model or *prototype* is made and displayed for further market surveys, to aid financing, and

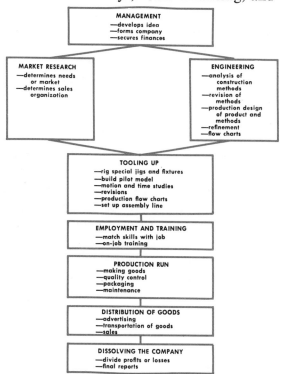

Fig. 38-1. Typical production sequence for a school project.

to refine production details. These details include making the jigs and fixtures and include the analyses and charting of the flow of materials during production. A time schedule is devised; the number of items to be produced is determined (limited in schools, so that production does not become time consuming and de-

tract from the ideas involved); redesign of jigs and fixtures; and analysis of the operations is continued until the production "run" becomes feasible. It is common practice for a product design and the "tooling" for it to be revised several times before it is ready for production. Production planning encompasses all the activities necessary to ready the facilities for the actual production run.

Factors which must be considered are: (1) The particular design to be used, (2) The best method of producing the item, and (3) The production and marketing deadlines that must be met. The importance of these planning factors is reflected in the final success or failure of the company.

Activity in the production-planning operation begins by division of the class into various functioning departments. These departments are: Finance, Marketing, Engineering, Tooling, Personnel, and Quality Control.

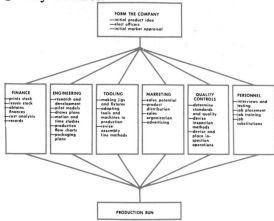

Fig. 38-2. Divisions of simultaneous departmental activity in product planning.

Finance Department

It will be the function of this group to determine the cost of the item to be produced. This operation is commonly termed "cost analysis" in industry (Fig. 38-3). It will be necessary to consider the various costs, such as material, machine, labor, packaging, and transportation, in determining the total cost of the product.

This group also will be involved in the establishment of policy on stock, the value of the stock, who may buy stock, the financing needed to operate the business, securing the finances, and keeping the records related to these matters. It also shall be the duty of the group to oversee the design and printing of the stock certificates.

Recordkeeping is an important obligation of the finance department. Records must be kept on stock issuance and sales, material purchases, working time on the job, inventories of supplies, and records of product sales. It is essential to the operation of the company that complete and accurate records be maintained.

Fig. 38-3. Students performing a cost analysis on a prototype to determine all the cost factors.

Marketing Department

One of the prime functions of the marketing department is to conduct the market survey. The department members will use a model or product fascimile (usually a pilot model made by another department) for this purpose. They may use illustrations and plans prepared for this purpose. In any case, the survey will explore the potential market.

Factors influencing the potential market include three primary considerations: (1) Whether the product is vital to the population served—food, clothing, and so forth—or the degree of necessity; (2) The extent to which the population is already served—or, the number of other companies which also market your item; and (3) Whether the projected price range is within the purchasing power of the population. The marketing department finds the information through surveys of the potential market. Usually, a questionnaire is carefully devised beforehand to include these factors. Then the questionnaire is sent (or taken by personal interview) to portions of the potential "market." In this manner, the department learns what the buyers want in their product, what they dislike about the present products, and the price ranges desired.

At this point, the company should be flexible enough to revise its production goals either upward or downward. If the market survey indicates a receptive populace, an advertising campaign will be conducted to stimulate the sales potential. The campaign might be limited to the class or school community; or extend beyond the school to the local community.

Engineering Department

The engineering department normally consists of both the engineering and tooling functions. However, for organization of school manufacturing study units, the two functions—engineering and tooling—are divided into separate categories. The engineering department is responsible for planning the production line or assembly line. In addition, consideration is given to the packaging of the product, to research and development into the problems and processes, and to improvement of the product.

The research and development group will be primarily responsible for the development of a working model or prototype of the item to be constructed. This model is used to test the entire manufacturing setup. Through this item, the "bugs" or problems will be found. As the prototype is developed, tests will be made to correct errors and to improve the design. All changes, once accepted, are to be made on the plans or working drawings of the item. The relationships between form, function, and construction are emphasized. The importance of testing parts and materials before they are put into service also become obvious. Failure in service results in costly replacement, great financial loss, and loss of prestige and good will toward the corporation.

Several types of analyses are used in planning the sequence and scheduling of the assembly-line process. These analyses include motion studies, time studies, job analyses, and production flow charts.

Fig. 38-4. An engine completed on a subassembly line is lowered into place. (Courtesy Ford Motor Company)

Time studies are used to determine the length of time required for each individual operation. Motion studies are analyses in which the engineers break down the operation into the smallest possible movements and determine the most efficient means of moving. By combining motion and time studies, the length of time and the necessary work station equipment can be devised. Once these are devised, the times developed in the studies are combined to form a plan for assembly and for the sequencing and scheduling of the assembly of small pieces onto the main parts.

For example, in Fig. 38-4 a smaller subassembly is attached to a larger subassembly in the making of an automobile. It is quite common in industry for several assembly lines to be working at the same time; then all the parts produced by the smaller assembly lines are combined to produce the major product on the primary assembly line of the plant (Fig. 38-5). Another example of this type of op-

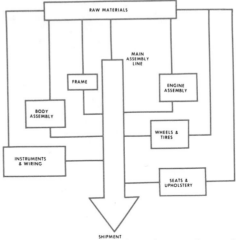

Fig. 38-5. Sequence flowchart for a subassembly. Several subassembly lines are combined for the final product.

eration would be the assembly of the drawers on one line and the assembly of the chest frames on another line. The proper sequencing requires that the drawers be made and inserted into the chest when the chests are properly completed (Figs. 38-6 and 38-7).

Fig. 38-6. The drawer frames only are made on this assembly line. (Courtesy I-XL Division, Westinghouse Electric Corporation)

Motion Studies

For a motion study, the engineer or technician investigates and analyzes the operation being performed by breaking it down into the basic motions. These ba-

Fig. 38-7. The drawers and doors are made on different assembly lines and combined with the frame at a later stage. (Courtesy I-XL Division, Westinghouse Electric Corporation)

sic motions can include reaching, grasping, picking up, twisting, striking with a hammer, etc. The industrial engineers use a very complex system of symbols to signify these motions. Each motion or basic movement is called a "therblig" which is

the name of one of the early-day engineers, Gilbreth, spelled backward. Gilbreth might be known more widely as the father in the book *Cheaper by the Dozen.*

Motion studies also consider the types of motions and the need for motions made by the assemblers and operators. The parts used during the operation should be arranged in a way that the natural motion of the operator doing the assembling job is not interrupted to pick up each new part or tool. How the simple positioning of parts affects worker efficiency is shown in Fig. 38-8. The motion analyses include

Fig. 38-8. Physical factors in motion studies.

all these factors in the movements of the operator performing the job. The motion study also is one of the primary studies in devising the jigs and fixtures utilized on the machines in the production run. Various holding devices, known as *jigs* or *fixtures,* can be devised to eliminate the time-consuming motions for the operator. An example is the use of a special holding device for a cutting operation to be done without measuring or by screwing and unscrewing a vise. However, the jigs and fixtures are discussed elsewhere.

Time Studies

When the motions required to perform the operation are determined, it is a simple matter to time each of these motions within each individual operation. By taking an "average" time for each operation, an average production time can be estimated. By timing and analyzing the fundamental operations, such as drilling holes, cutting stock to length, etc., the major processes for constructing the object can be determined by collecting and combining the analyses for each of the operations. Time studies permit the engineers to change and improve the setups and schedulings for the assembly process. If one machine can drill holes faster than another machine, the first machine is generally preferred. However, even though a drill press can be adapted to drill certain types of holes in small stock, it might be more practical to permit a second worker to drill the same holes with an electric hand drill while the stock is clamped in a vise where the first job—such as cutting to length—was done. This eliminates the time involved in removing the work from the vise and the setup time on the drill press. Although these operations might seem trivial at first glance, it should be remembered that only a half

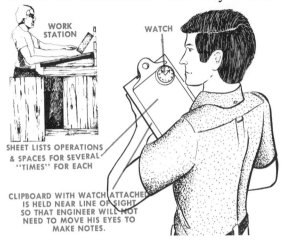

Fig. 38-9. Setup for performing a time study.

cent saved in any type of cost (labor, materials, or wear and tear on the machinery) in producing 10,000 units results in saving a considerable sum of money. This money can be used by the company for increased profits to its shareholders; can be passed on to the customer by reducing the cost of the item; can be used to undersell competitors; can be used to acquire more production—thus, more profits; or can be used to compromise and reduce the cost slightly, thereby increasing the profits slightly.

The continual use of time and motion studies during the actual production run in industry is a means of determining the efficiency of operations and the practicality of the methods used. Motion and time studies also are used to determine the efficiency of individual workers; to fix their rates of pay; to determine the basic production rates for the average worker; and to establish incentive pay plans.

Incentive pay systems operate essentially on the principle that an average worker can produce an average number of workpieces each day. If he exceeds this average number of workpieces, he is paid more. Before the average number of pieces completed by a worker per day can be determined, the workers must be timed to determine the number of pieces they can produce. This, of course, also is helpful in the establishment af a labor cost per item; then adequate cost analysis can be made to make sure the product is sold at a profit, rather than at a loss.

Although time studies are made in industrial situations with a stop watch, a wrist watch with a seconds hand is satisfactory for most school uses. The watch should be strapped onto a clipboard or a notebook; then it can be seen easily by the person making the time study (Fig. 38-9). One or more motion and time study people can be used to time the various operations in making the object. For the initial runs, the pilot models often are timed during the first phases of construction. Each operation should be timed by two or more people, or during several operations. This provides an excellent "average" time for the operation.

Flow Charts

Motion and time studies are tools used by industrial engineers in making flow charts. Flow charts are literally the "road maps" for planning the routes and sequence of delivery on the assembly line developed to mass-produce a product. To move all the materials to the proper stations in the correct sequence, it is necessary to know the time required to complete each operation.

The use of motion and time studies to make flow charts helps to eliminate "bottlenecks." A bottleneck is created when more pieces are brought to a station than the station can produce. An excellent demonstration of this principle is provided by turning a water tumbler upside down, as compared to turning a soda pop bottle upside down. With the water tumbler, the water rushes out because the opening is large. With the soda pop bottle, however, the soda leaves the bottle in small dribbles, because the opening is too small to permit free passage of the liquid. This is the derivation of the term "bottleneck." Placing the times required for the various operations on the flow chart permits the engineers to plan the number of stations required for each operation; and they can pattern the flow to provide a smooth and continuous operation on the assembly line.

Flow charts, then, are assembled collections of the operations, including the moving, storage, inspection, and packaging stations which are involved in making

the entire product. The places where each operation, such as drilling the holes or cutting to length, are performed are called "stations." A typical operational flow chart is shown in Figs. 38-10 and 38-11. The operational flow chart is the basis for planning the layout and the number of individual stations for each operation of

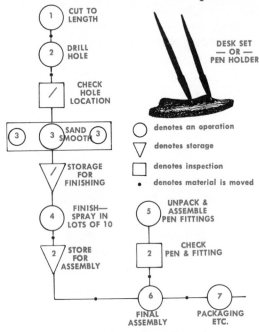

Fig. 38-10. Operational flow chart.

FLOW CHART

SYMBOL	DESCRIPTION	COMMENTS
1	Remove stock from racks and cut to length	
•	Cut stock is moved to drilling stations	
2	Hole is drilled in stock	
•	Stock is picked up by inspector #1	Inspector also routes material to sanding stations to prevent bottlenecks
1	Inspection done as stock is moved	
•	To sanding stations	
3	Parts are sanded	
▽	Sanders stack finished pieces in bins for movement	
•	Bins are moved to finish area	
4	Sanded stock is spray finished in lots of 10 pieces	
•	Lots of 10 units are moved from finish area for drying and assembly	
5	Pen and fittings are unpacked and assembled as units	
2	Inspector picks up, checks pen units and carries them to final assembly area	
6	Pen units are assembled to base	
•	Assembled units are conveyed to packaging area	
7	Finished desk sets are packaged for delivery	

Fig. 38-11. Detailed flow chart description.

the assembly line itself. Some typical classroom layout and flow charts combined are shown in Figs. 38-12 and 38-13.

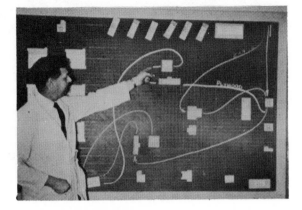

Fig. 38-12. Facilities chart.

Packaging

Packaging is the process of devising a holder and carrier and a protective covering for a marketed product. The packaging of a product is included in the assembly line. The packaging of the automobile into the boxcar (see Fig. 37-9) is an excellent example of large-scale packaging.

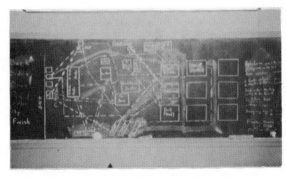

Fig. 38-13. A layout chart combines the operational flow chart with the actual shape and location of facilities.

A trip to the supermarket can provide many examples of smaller-scale packaging with all types of plastics and paper products used in the packaging. For packaging in a school shop situation, cardboard often can be trimmed and cut to form a small box with support pads for the product itself. The techniques used in industrial packing to prevent the pieces slipping or jarring together include the use of small pieces of plastic foam, shredded paper, corrugated cardboard pieces or spacers, as well as rigid bracing made from wood, plastic, or other types of materials. Some of the more expensive products, such as typewriters, cameras, and some household appliances, are packaged with formed styrofoam cases inside the outside covering. Regardless of the product, however, some means of carrying or shipping the product to the customer—either wholesale or retail—should be considered in the production planning.

Tooling Department

Tooling is an extremely important part of the production process, since it is the process which determines how the product will be made. The engineering department and the tooling department are the two primary departments involved in the efficient manufacture of the product. The other departments are involved primarily with the people, the financing, and the clerical processes. The mechanical problems are dealt with almost entirely in the tooling and engineering processes. Tooling involves making or adapting the tools and machinery for high-speed, repetitive, production output. It must be remembered that each operation in the mass-production sequence will be repeated over and over by one person. Tooling permits even the simpler hand tools to be adjusted to perform only one operation in one stroke or motion and no other. In addition, tooling permits the tools or machines to be adapted for production work; then the operator is not required to perform measuring or operations other than the direct application of his machine.

Jigs and Fixtures

Jigs and fixtures are devices which permit the machine and tool operators to position the stock and to perform operations without measuring and holding. The set-up time for the operation in the tool or machine is held to an absolute minimum. A *jig* is a device which holds or supports the work while an operation is performed on it. A *fixture,* however, not only supports or holds the work in place but also guides a cutting tool of some type during its cutting operation. Generally, in industrial setups, the jigs and fixtures are treated as a single general class of tooling. Both devices are the primary methods of adapting general tools and machines for production work. The use of jigs and fixtures permits an operator to spend all his time in operating or using his major skill. He is not required to spend considerable time in setting up, in making precise measurements, or in positioning the tools. This permits the operator to work on a greater number of workpieces during his working day. His work output is greater, the labor cost per item is less, each piece is exact, and no mistakes result from failure to read a rule properly, from slipping with a tool, or from other human mistakes. All this minimizes production costs; therefore, the ultimate cost to the consumer is minimized. This is one of the reasons that mass-produced goods usually are better and cheaper than handmade goods. The students are using a shop-made fixture to locate and guide the drilling operation on a project in Fig. 38-14.

Other tooling factors include the use of movers, baskets, trays, conveyors, and similar devices to move the materials from one station to another. Also, special carrying devices which position the workpiece for the worker at the next station are used. Dull tools also slow the produc-

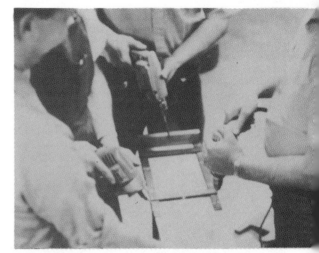

Fig. 38-14. A shop-made fixture can be used to eliminate measuring, marking, and center punching for the drilling operation.

tion lines. Special crews are on hand at all times to readjust the machines; to sharpen the tools; to insert new knives, blades, or other cutting edges; and, in general, to make the necessary repairs and maintenance to keep the production line at its full operational level.

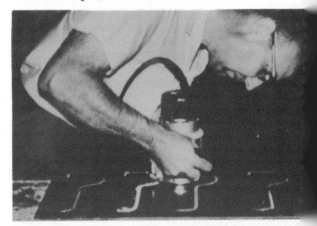

Fig. 38-15. A template reduces setup time.

The "setup" men who work on these maintenance and setup crews are often the most highly skilled and highly paid workers in the factory. They must know the correct function and performance and the correct setup and tooling for each and every machine they work on. This, of course, can be acquired only after many years of training and experience (Figs. 38-15 and 38-16).

Fig. 38-16. A jig is used on this assembly line to hold the parts in place for nailing.

Revisions

Constant revisions in tooling and engineering planning are necessary to make sure the final product is manufactured

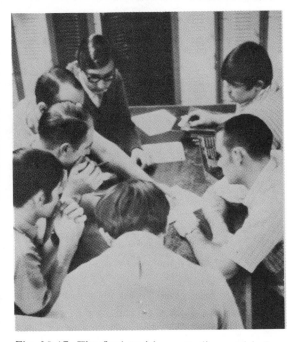

Fig. 38-17. The final revisions are discussed before beginning production.

with the greatest efficiency (Fig. 38-17). It is not unusual to make two or three pilot models and to revise the charts several times.

Quality Control

Quality controls are the necessary operations in the assembly line where the inspectors use special tools and devices to make sure the goods being produced meet the required standards. The various inspection stations in the subassembly lines make sure all the pieces going to the main assembly line will fit when they reach the main line (Fig. 38-18). The attainment of necesssary quality controls for the assembly line requires three basic processes. These are: (1) Determining standards; (2) Inspection methods; and (3) Placing the inspection stations.

Determining Standards

Quality is not automatic. Quality is achieved, first, by establishing a standard; and, secondly, by making sure the standard is achieved. For example, if $\frac{1}{4}$-inch bolts are being produced, it is necessary that all the bolts are the same thread style, if they are to fit, and that all the bolts are the proper size. Two methods of insuring this are by checking each piece and by statistical control methods, whereby a sample of each production run is tested. In statistical methods, each piece is not tested—only a small percentage is tested on the assumption that if the pieces tested are satisfactory, the remaining pieces also are satisfactory.

With quality controls, it must be realized that even though the machines can be made to produce duplicate parts, the parts will not be duplicated perfectly. A small variation will occur. The important objective in quality controls is to determine how much variation can occur be-

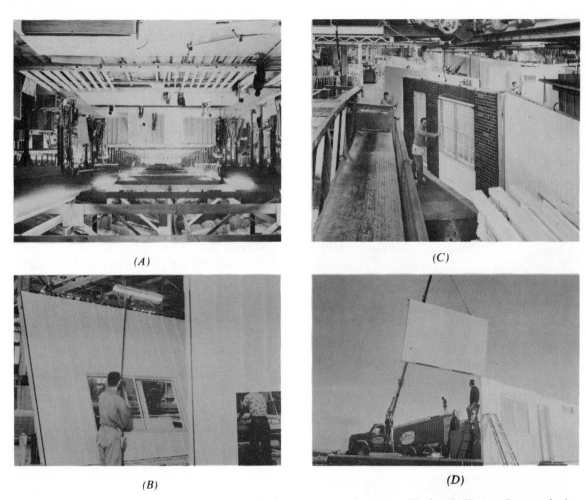

(A)

(C)

(B)

(D)

Fig. 38-18. Production line sequence for producing a home. (Courtesy National Home Corporation)

fore the part is not suitable for use. In other words, a part will not be exactly the correct size—it will be slightly too large or slightly too small; then the quality control experts must determine the point at which the part is too small or too large to be usable in the assembly of the product. Once these standards or limits are set, some method of measuring the pieces can be devised for use by the inspectors on the assembly line (Fig. 38-19).

Inspection Methods

Many types of inspection methods are used (Fig. 38-20). Special templates are used to check the curvatures and involved

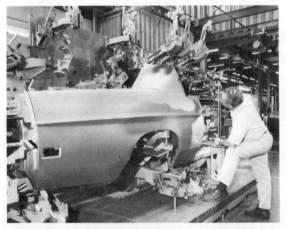

Fig. 38-19. A quality control inspector using a height gauge to make sure this body side meets engineering specifications. (Courtesy Ford Motor Company)

shapes of objects. Various types of devices are used for measuring thickness, roundness, and many other features. These devices can include direct measuring of objects, such as with micrometers, rulers, and other caliper-type devices. Special gauges called "feeler gauges" involve the use of levers and gears to move a pointer on a dial or scale. These devices are especially useful for determining surface thickness, surface irregularity, and roundness. The optical measuring methods also are used widely. The optical methods cast a shadow of the object—much like an overhead projector—against predetermined marks on the screen. Since the shadow is projected on a large scale, an operator measuring small parts easily can determine whether the part is adequate.

Fig. 38-20. Testing cabinet doors with a heavy weight for strength and function. (Courtesy I-XL Division, Westinghouse Electric Corporation)

Other types of gauges, called "go–no-go" gauges, also are used. Instead of requiring an inspector to make a measurement with a micrometer—which involves time as well as the risk of reading the micrometer setting incorrectly—a hardened-steel set of "go–no-go" gauges is used. One of the holes is too large, and the other hole is too small. The part should not "go" or fit into the gauge which is too small; but it should "go" into the gauge which is too large. Thus, the part is inserted into the too-large hole or "go" hole. If acceptable there, the part is then tried on the "no-go" gauge; if it does not fit, the part is accepted. However, if the part also goes into the too small (no-go) gauge, the part is rejected.

Not all the operations are critical in the size involved. In producing an automobile, for example, some portions of the body need not be aligned with great precision. The machine parts require greater precision; the alignment of the wheels and axles and the placement of other factors also is critical. However, the placing of an electrical wire might vary several inches and still be quite functional and safe. The engineers devising the assembly process also must determine what placements and dimensions are critical for satisfactory standards. Once the critical standards of quality are identified, the placement of the quality control stations in the assembly line can occur.

Locating the Inspection Stations

After the engineers and technicians have identified the operations which must be performed to maintain standards, the inspection stations along with the devised inspection methods are placed in the assembly line. In placing the inspection stations, certain factors must be considered. The inspection station should not slow the production rate. Instead, the inspections must occur at the same rate or faster than the movement of the objects on the assembly line. The method of inspection must be simplified to prevent this pace being interrupted. If the production pace is faster than the inspection, several inspection stations must be inserted. Usually, however, a different method of inspection can be devised. The inspectors often are the same people who must move the parts from one station to the next station, the inspection of parts occurring in the movement process. In any event, the inspection should be an integral part of the assembly line; and it should support, rather than slow, the production rate.

When a part is rejected, the rejected part should be removed from the assembly line with a minimum of disruption. The flow of parts should permit the inspector to remove the part physically or through some mechanical means, without disrupting the flow of materials on the assembly line. In many industrial situations, the inspectors make few movements; also, they are expected to reject a certain number of pieces per day.

Personnel

The personnel department, although small in many instances, has several important functions. The personnel department must supply the manufacturing areas with people who are qualified to perform their jobs. Although the personnel department may or may not be actually in charge of job training, it certainly is greatly concerned with it. In addition, personnel departments frequently are assigned the additional duties of plant relations, in which they handle worker grievances and many worker social functions, such as picnics, company newspapers, press releases to the local newspapers, and many other items.

Testing and Interviewing

The first step in employee selection is an interview and testing process. This may be formal, requiring lengthy interviews and many types of tests, both manipulative and written; or it can be an informal conversation. In either instance, some attention is given to the employee qualifications which are advantageous to the company. The jobs available must be matched with the people available. The color-blind person should not be placed in a job in which he must distinguish between two similar colors. Likewise, a small and frail employee should not be placed on a job which requires great physical strength. The purpose of the interview and the testing is to determine the quality and characteristics of the employee, including factors, such as intelligence, special mechanical or manipulative abilities, special physical characteristics or personality traits, and to compare the characteristics of the person with the requirements for the job.

Personality traits are often as important as physical ability. For example, salesmen should be congenial, confident, and like people. A shy, bashful person may not be well suited for saleswork, even though his ability may be extremely high.

Job Analysis

Job analysis includes an investigation and analysis of the job in regard to the working conditions and the physical characteristics required of the worker. It includes factors such as heat, dampness,

PHYSICAL DEMANDS FORM

Job Title ______ Occupational Code ______

Dictionary Title ______

Firm Name and Address ______

Industry ______ Industrial Code ______

Branch ______ Department ______

Company Officer ______ Analyst ______ Date ______

PHYSICAL ACTIVITIES		WORKING CONDITIONS	
___ 1 Walking	___ 16 Throwing	___ 51 Inside	___ 66 Mechanical Hazards
___ 2 Jumping	___ 17 Pushing	___ 52 Outside	___ 67 Moving Objects
___ 3 Running	___ 18 Pulling	___ 53 Hot	___ 68 Cramped Quarters
___ 4 Balancing	___ 19 Handling	___ 54 Cold	___ 69 High Places
___ 5 Climbing	___ 20 Fingering	___ 55 Sudden Temp. Changes	___ 70 Exposure to Burns
___ 6 Crawling	___ 21 Feeling	___ 56 Humid	___ 71 Electrical Hazards
___ 7 Standing	___ 22 Talking	___ 57 Dry	___ 72 Explosives
___ 8 Turning	___ 23 Hearing	___ 58 Wet	___ 73 Radiant Energy
___ 9 Stooping	___ 24 Seeing	___ 59 Dusty	___ 74 Toxic Conditions
___ 10 Crouching	___ 25 Color Vision	___ 60 Dirty	___ 75 Working with Others
___ 11 Kneeling	___ 26 Depth Perception	___ 61 Odors	___ 76 Working Around Others
___ 12 Sitting	___ 27 Working Speed	___ 62 Noisy	___ 77 Working Alone
___ 13 Reaching	___ 28	___ 63 Adequate Lighting	___ 78
___ 14 Lifting	___ 29	___ 64 Adequate Ventilation	___ 79
___ 15 Carrying	___ 30	___ 65 Vibration	___ 80

DETAILS OF PHYSICAL ACTIVITIES:

DETAILS OF WORKING CONDITIONS:

DETAILS OF HAZARDS:

Fig. 38-21. Check the activity and condition required in performance of the job.

noise, and whether the workers should have a high sense of smell, touch, or taste. Can you visualize a cook, who cannot tell the difference between salt and sweet, preparing your food? Sample job analysis forms are shown in Figs. 38-21 and 38-22. These forms are used by the industrial engineers and personnel men to determine the characteristics of the jobs involved. The job analysis is the chief tool used by personnel men to match an employee to a job.

WORKER CHARACTERISTICS FORM

Job Title _____ Schedule No. _____

Indicate the amount of each characteristic required of the worker in order to do the job satisfactorily by putting an X in the appropriate column. Following are the definitions of each level:

O—The characteristic is not required for satisfactory performance of the job.
C—A medium to very low degree of the characteristic is required in some element or elements of the job.
B—An above-average degree of the characteristic is required, either in numerous elements of the job or in the major or most skilled element.
A—A very high degree of the characteristic is required in some element of the job.
When in doubt between A and B, rate B; when in doubt between B and C, rate B; when in doubt between C and O, rate C. If some characteristic not on this list is required, write it in, rate it, and define it briefly at the bottom of the form.

Amount				Characteristics Required	Amount				Characteristics Required
O	C	B	A		O	C	B	A	
				1. Work rapidly for long periods					26. Arithmetic computation
				2. Strength of hands					27. Intelligence
				3. Strength of arms					28. Adaptability
				4. Strength of back					29. Ability to make decisions
				5. Strength of legs					30. Ability to plan
				6. Dexterity of fingers					31. Initiative
				7. Dexterity of hands and arms					32. Understanding mechanical devices
				8. Dexterity of foot and leg					33. Attention to many items
				9. Eye-hand coordination					34. Oral expression
				10. Foot-hand-eye coordination					35. Skill in written expression
				11. Coordination of both hands					36. Tact in dealing with people
				12. Estimate size of objects					37. Memory of names and persons
				13. Estimate quantity of objects					38. Personal appearance
				14. Perceive form of objects					39. Concentration amidst distractions
				15. Estimate speed of moving objects					40. Emotional stability
				16. Keenness of vision					41. Work under hazardous conditions
				17. Keenness of hearing					42. Estimate quality of objects
				18. Sense of smell					43. Unpleasant physical conditions
				19. Sense of taste					44. Color discrimination
				20. Tough discrimination					45. Ability to meet and deal with public
				21. Muscular discrimination					46. Height
				22. Memory for details (things)					47. Weight
				23. Memory for ideas (abstracts)					48. _____
				24. Memory for oral directions					49. _____
				25. Memory for written directions					50. _____

Fig. 38-22. Job analysis—Worker characteristics form.

Job Training and Placement

Job analyses, motion and time studies, and operational charts are all used in personnel work to help train employees. It is quite common for a plant to maintain a training program in which the employees are provided some training before they are permitted to enter the production line for their on-the-job training. To train the individuals to perform, someone other than the machine operators should know what is involved in the job. The personnel man—who also might be the training director for the factory—may merely withdraw the job descriptions from a file to determine what operations the employee is required to learn to do. Later training normally is done on the job under the supervision of a section or plant foreman who is responsible for the production rates within that department.

Activities

1. Visit an assembly line; report on one department of production planning.
2. Form class departments for planning a production run.
3. Make weekly departmental reports to the class on the factors being considered and the progress made.

Questions

1. What departments are involved in production planning?
2. What departments are most concerned with efficient production?
3. Why is job analysis important to job placement?
4. How is a "motion study" different from a "time study"?
5. Describe a "flow chart."
6. How does a pilot model aid in planning production?
7. Why is job efficiency important?
8. What is the purpose of a market survey?
9. What information should be recorded by a finance department?
10. Why are quality controls necessary?

Unit 39 – Production Run

The production run in the school shop begins with cutting the stock. Accuracy is achieved more readily when a large number of pieces are cut in a single setup on the table saw (Fig. 39-1). Special fixtures are used to shape the parts (Fig. 39-2). Jigs aid in the assembly of parts (Fig. 39-3), and rows of dowels aid in the alignment of the stock as it moves from station to station (Fig. 39-4). In Fig. 39-5, a

Fig. 39-1. The production run begins with cutting the stock.

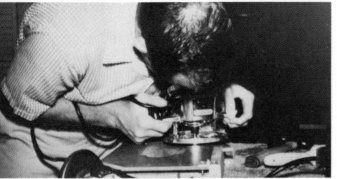
Fig. 39-2. Special fixtures are used to shape the parts.

vise-powered form is used to shape the handles from strips of flat steel. Several parts can be mounted for finishing in a single spraying operation (Fig. 39-6). In-

Fig. 39-3. Jigs are an aid in assembly.

spection of the finished pieces is an important operation before packaging (Fig. 39-7).

Industrial mass production, of course, usually involves larger pieces and much larger quantities than the school shop operation. Some of the operations involved in the production of kitchen cabinets can be seen in Figs. 39-8 through 39-13.

Fig. 39-4. Special rows of dowels aid in keeping the stock aligned as it moves from station to station.

The output on the industrial assembly line is nearly constant. Interruptions occur from breakdowns of machinery, labor strikes, or stopping to retool the line. Retooling occurs frequently in the automo-

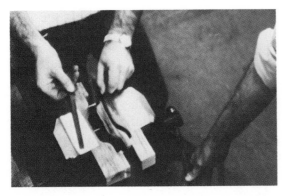

Fig. 39-5. This special vise-powered form is used to make handles from flat steel strips.

tive industries, toymaking industries, and many other industries. However, retooling is not so frequent in some industries, especially in the machine tool and heavy-equipment industries.

The actual production run for a school class might require only a short time. Only one or two class periods is usually the time required for the production run. However, the overall smoothness and efficiency of the production run depends directly on the planning and organization, as well as on the work done on the assembly line. The effects of planning are similar, whether the situation is an industrial production line or a school production line.

The production run in the school stresses safety, efficiency, accuracy, assembly, and the finishing and packaging of

Fig. 39-6. Parts are mounted for speedy finishing.

the product. Appropriate announcements should be made to the school staff and the student body for the production and sales through a publicity campaign. This is generally handled by the marketing department through their advertising activities. During the actual run, proper controls should be exercised to maintain both the quality and the quantity at the desired levels. The product must be maintained

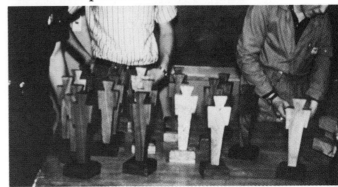

Fig. 39-7. The finished pieces are inspected before packaging.

as an acceptable market item, and maximum learning also should take place during the run. However, only the needed number of items should be produced.

Preparation for the Production Run

When the various departments have perfected their plans for the production experience, preparation should be made for the actual production run. The departments make their final reports; then the production officers, such as the foremen, are designated by either the personnel department or by the officers of the company. Sufficient materials must be on hand and in storage to manufacture all the pieces to be made during the production run, plus an estimated number of pieces for faulty parts. The material and the production sequence should be arranged for continuous production, once the run has started. Equipment which has been borrowed from other departments of the

Fig. 39-8. The incoming lumber from storage begins its journey through the plant to be made into kitchen cabinets. (Courtesy I-XL Division, Westinghouse Electric Corporation)

school or shop facilities should be obtained for a specified length of time and returned promptly.

Job Training

One of the preparations which must be made for the run is the actual instruction of the class members to perform each of the specific jobs on the production line. Each class member will not perform every job. However, each job must be per-

Fig. 39-9. A finishing mill assembles the door and drawer frames. Note the excellent houskeeping. (Courtesy I-XL Division, Westinghouse Electric Corporation)

formed by a trained operator. Some jobs will require a small period of training; however, some jobs might require considerable preparation. Some time might be required to instruct the operators in the use of the special tooling or the procedures developed for mass producing the product. It is an excellent practice to re-

quire each operator to demonstrate his job to the class during one class period. This serves two purposes: (1) The ability of the operator to demonstrate his job indicates whether he is ready and has been trained properly for the production run; and (2) The class is informed on the jobs performed and the special equipment and machinery involved; also, it is a review of the entire production line.

During the Production Run

During the production run and prior to the run, class attitudes must be developed to maintain a safe and clean environment. Some study of industrial safety procedures might be relevant here, as well as inviting speakers or visitors from industry to visit the class and share their ideas and their experience. Special safety instruction also might be necessary.

Preparations for Ending the Production Run

Before the production run is begun, preparations should be made to end the run. Since school production runs are, of necessity, very short, something must be done for some special problems which might be incurred. The first problem encountered is that when the run is first

Fig. 39-10. The cabinet "cases" are assembled in this area. Since each cabinet is identified with the man who made it, pride in workmanship is high. On the way, the cabinet receives the doors and drawers. (Courtesy I-XL Division, Westinghouse Electric Corporation)

started, the operators at the latter stages of the assembly line are idle until the work reaches their stations. Conversely, when the last pieces to be made enter the production line, the first operators are idle after the last piece has passed their work stations. Special problems with idle workers, therefore, exist in the classroom both at the beginning and at the end of the production run. These workers might be utilized at the various packaging stations or in carrying materials. Also, they might be moved from work station to work station in the assembly line to aid in preventing bottleneck situations. The parts might be prepared in a manner which simulates pieces acquired from contractors, rather than performing the entire operation on the assembly line.

Quantity Controls

Some discussion has been made previously in regard to quality controls—or to *how good* the items must be. An additional control during the production run must be enforced; this is the *quantity* control. The number of items made is important not only in industry but also in the schooly situation as well. In industry, it is quite wasteful and costly to produce an extra piece or two—for example, a few hundred extra engines for automobiles, etc. The labor and material cost in

Fig. 39-12. The front frames for corner cabinets form a cathedral-like setting for a craftsman assembling shelves for a revolving base cabinet. The skilled cabinetmaker is fitting the "spinner" section to the case before applying the outer shell. (Courtesy I-XL Division, Westinghouse Electric Corporation)

extra parts represents money invested by the company for which it can receive no return. Likewise, if a class or student company purchases materials which are not used or sold, this material represents lost profits and wasted effort. Some means must, therefore, be devised to make sure only the required number of units is built during the production run.

Fig. 39-11. The workman applies toner to the kitchen cabinet. This is the first step in the finishing process. The various hoses channel a variety of materials piped into the booth; therefore, various finishes can be applied at the same location. (Courtesy I-XL Division, Westinghouse Electric Corporation)

Fig. 39-13. A heavy weight is applied to test the rigidity of the doors; this is one of the steps taken to achieve the standard of quality desired. (Courtesy I-XL Division, Westinghouse Electric Corporation)

Personnel Problems

Personnel problems exist during production runs, due to the "humanness" of the employees. These problems also might exist during the production run in the school manufacturing experiment. These problems include properly trained personnel and absence through sickness or from moving to another city. Some provision should be made during the production run to substitute for absent class members and for refresher training for employees who falter or lag in production rates.

The foreman or production supervisors should make some provision for this problem. In industry, the foremen often fill in for employees who are sick or on vacation. Many factories also utilize small groups of employees whose regular job is to "fill in" for absent employees.

Questions

1. What problems might be experienced during a production run, resulting from the "humanness" of the operators and assemblers?

2. What is meant by "quality control"? Why is it important?

3. What special factors should be considered for ending a production run?

4. What problems can cause an interruption in an assembly line?

5. How does the job of an operator differ from the role of the craftsman who makes the product from start to finish?

6. What are the advantages of production tooling—such as the use of jigs and fixtures?

7. What are the disadvantages of production tooling?

8. What problems are encountered by the personnel employed by a company which are caused by the interruption of a production line?

9. What problems result for production tooling by a model change?

10. What factors might necessitate a model change?

Unit 40 – Terminal Reports

The final phase of the mass-production experience consists of a series of reports to the class by the various departments of the corporation. The production run is evaluated by the production foreman or by the officers of the company. A production report can be used for this purpose (Fig. 40-1). Factors which must be eval-

---

PRODUCTION REPORT

Number of items produced   _____

Time required for run   _____

Average time to make each item   _____

Number of persons on assembly line _____

Number of man-hours
   required for run   _____

Number of man-hours per item   _____

Were personnel well-trained?   _____

Were items produced to satisfactory
   quality and quantity?   _____
Special problems encountered:

Comments and suggestions for improvement:

Attach a list that gives the names and jobs of
   each person involved in the production run.

Fig. 40-1

uated in the production report include the number of people and the time involved in the actual production run, the number of items produced, the time required to make each item, comments as to quantity and quality controls, training of per-

sonnel, suitability of the plant layout, and the tooling involved.

Engineering

The Engineering department should report on the effectiveness of the layout of the assembly line and on the bottlenecks which were avoided successfully and those that developed unexpectedly. The product design also should be considered, and recommendations should be made for future improvements. Some attention should be paid to both the types of and the effectiveness of the analyses made by the department during the planning stage.

ENGINEERING REPORT

Time required in planning   _____

Department members   _____

Man-hours for planning   _____

Special planning problems experienced:

Bottlenecks, breakdowns or interruptions that oc-
   cured unexpectedly:

Evaluation of plant layout:

Evaluation of analyses made:

Evaluation of product design and efficiency in
   production:

Recommended improvements:

Fig. 40-2

Some comment should be made as to the overall efficiency of production and planning. A typical engineering department report form is shown in Fig. 40-2.

Finance

The reports include a fiscal report by the Finance department as the corporation is liquidated and the profits or losses are distributed or assessed. A form suitable for use in making a finance report is shown in Fig. 40-3. Note that the profit remains after the expenses have been deducted from the total income. No real provisions are made for the labor costs in school shops. However, these costs could be included in a report on the assumption that each member of the class who performs a function for the company receives some compensation for his labor.

The Marketing department report should include the recommendations which were made as a result of the market

surveys, the number of orders placed or the number of sales made as a result of the advertising, and the type of sales promotion, publicity, and advertising during the sales period. A suitable report form is shown in Fig. 40-4.

MARKETING REPORT

Time required for activities   —————

Department members   —————

Man-hours required   —————

Results of market surveys:

Number of orders taken or sales made:

Delivery or sales problems:

Type of sales promotion and publicity:

Recommendations and comments:

Fig. 40-4

Quality Control

The Quality Control department should report on items such as the number of items made, the number of items sold, and the number of items which remained unsold. By comparing the number of items unsold with those which were sold, some idea of the product acceptance by the public might be derived. The quality control report should include the total number of items rejected and the number of those rejected items which were redone and used. The report also should include the total stock wasted by the rejected parts. The cost of the rejected parts easily can be calculated, once this is known. A typi-

FINANCE REPORT

Time required in activities   —————

Department members   —————

Man-hours required   —————

Total man-hours in all departments ————

Number of shares of stock   made ————

and sold ————
(attach a list of shareholders)

Income derived from:
  capital investment   —————
  sales of goods   —————
  Total   —————

Expenses incurred:
  advertising   —————
  labor costs   —————
  material costs   —————
  Total   —————

Profits or Losses: per share   —————
                              Total ————

Dividends or assessments
  per share   —————

Comments and suggestions:

Fig. 40-3

cal quality control report is shown in Fig. 40-5.

```
QUALITY CONTROL REPORT

Time required in planning          _____

Department members                 _____

Man-hours used in planning         _____

Number of items made               _____

Number of items sold               _____

Number of items unsold             _____

Number of items rejected           _____

Number of rejected items that
    could be re-done                _____

Amount of waste by reject parts    _____

Cost of rejected parts             _____

Special problems found during inspection:

Comments and suggestions for improvement:
```

Fig. 40-5

Tooling

The Tooling department report should list the special tools and devices that were developed for use on the production run. The report should include the time required for the development and construction of these devices, as well as the time saved by the use of each device. Some evaluation should be made of the special tooling devices with regard to the efficiency and the usability of these devices. This includes their durability, their ease of changing for retooling processes, and the expense as opposed to the production rate of these devices. A tooling report is shown in Fig. 40-6.

Personnel

The Personnel department also should report on its activities (Fig. 40-7). The

```
TOOLING REPORT

Time required in preparation      _____

Department members                _____

Man-hours required                _____

List special tools and devices designed for the
    production run:

Estimate the time saved by each device:

Comments on efficiency of tooling:

Comments on durability of these devices:

Special problems encountered:

Comments and suggestions:
```

Fig. 40-6

```
PERSONNEL REPORT

Time required for activities       _____

Department members                 _____

Man-hours required                 _____

Number of jobs analyzed            _____

Number of jobs filled              _____

Comments on worker efficiency:

Special problems encountered:

Suggestions for worker training or selection:

Compare the total number of man-hours for "Blue
    Collar" workers with "white collar" workers.
```

Fig. 40-7

personnel report should include the number of jobs analyzed for the worker characteristics required, the number of jobs filled, comments on observed worker efficiency during the production run, and the processes used by the personnel department to match the proper employee with the proper job.

In addition, the personnel report should compare the total number of man-hours involving "blue-collar" workers in the production run with the "white-collar" workers involved in planning. The "blue-collar" workers are those workers who make and repair various items, who are operators and assemblers, and, in general, who are directly involved in the actual production of the goods. The "white-collars" are the planners, executives, sales and advertising personnel, and clerical staffs. The term "white" or "blue" collar actually is derived from the white shirts traditionally worn by management and the blue workshirts traditionally worn by production workers while at work.

Other factors which can be included in the evaluation of the production run are the evaluation of the management personnel by the workers, and the evaluation of the workers by the management. The interest in the production run, and the special problems and interests found during these studies also are of interest. Methods of manufacture are always a matter of consideration, along with suggestions for their improvement. The processes of product selection and develop-

ment also are factors for evaluation, as well as the quality and popularity of the finished product. The safety factors and controls are factors to be considered and evaluated during the entire study. Evaluation of these factors and controls are factors to be considered and evaluated during the entire study. Evaluation of these factors can be accomplished through assignments of various departments or to general class discussions.

Corporations normally are ended by formal petition through a department of the state government. However, the school corporation normally is discontinued with the conclusion of the reports and the completion of the financial obligations.

Questions

1. Check the values of some stocks listed in the financial section of the newspaper. What factors influence the "values" of these stocks?
2. List the factors entering into the final "cost" of a product.
3. Which takes more time—the planning or the producing?
4. List the advantages to an industry of long production runs with little retooling.
5. What is meant by a "blue-collar" worker?
6. What is meant by a "white-collar" worker?

SKETCHBOOK OF IDEAS FOR MASS-PRODUCTION PROJECTS

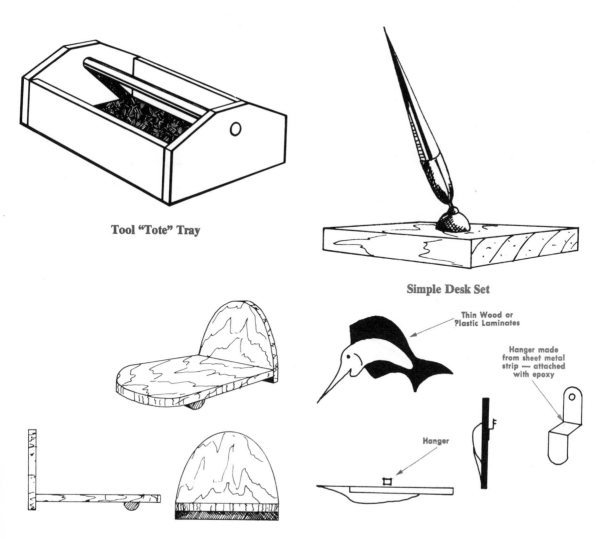

Tool "Tote" Tray

Simple Desk Set

Book Rack

Thin Wood or Plastic Laminates

Hanger made from sheet metal strip — attached with epoxy

Hanger

Decorative Wall Plaques

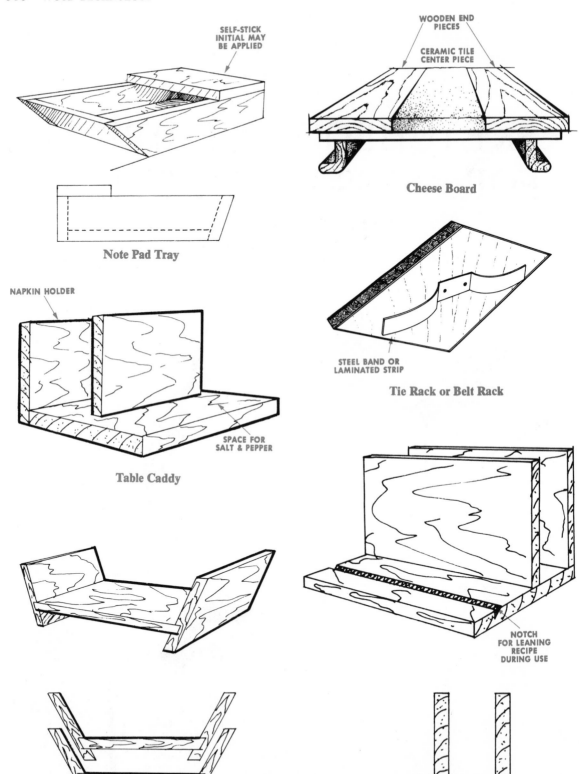

SELF-STICK INITIAL MAY BE APPLIED

Note Pad Tray

WOODEN END PIECES

CERAMIC TILE CENTER PIECE

Cheese Board

NAPKIN HOLDER

SPACE FOR SALT & PEPPER

Table Caddy

STEEL BAND OR LAMINATED STRIP

Tie Rack or Belt Rack

NOTCH FOR LEANING RECIPE DURING USE

Stacking Snack Trays

Recipe File & Rack

Unit 41 – Planning a Building

The success and efficiency in utilizing a building are due largely to planning before the building is constructed. If the building is to perform the functions it is designed to perform with a minimum of inconvenience and expense, many factors should be considered before the building is constructed. Modifications to a new building are not wise, since they increase the building cost through poor and inefficient use of materials and funds. Modifications of older building are often wise, but these also should be planned before beginning to remodel the buildings.

Factors which should be included in planning a building are selection of the site, location of the building on the site, and specific building functions—whether the building is a dwelling for a family or a small business. Factors affecting construction of the building include quiet areas for office work, study, or resting; plumbing, heating, and cooling; electrical requirements; flow of traffic to the building; pedestrian or people traffic within the building; building costs; growth of the family or business; keeping valuables or confidential materials safe; and contracting and estimating.

Site Selection

Planning and selecting the site for a building include several important considerations. When planning to build, one should consider the primary use of the building; for example, a house which is to shelter only one family should be located in an area zoned or restricted for one-family dwellings. However, if an individual wishes to build a building, such as an apartment building, which is to house two or more families, he must be careful to select a zone which permits multiple-family dwellings. It would be a costly mistake to begin construction on a two-family dwelling if the city permits only one family per dwelling. It is a common practice in most cities and towns to zone certain areas within the city for stores and businesses, industrial areas for large factories, multiple-unit residential areas which have greater requirements for parking and util-

(A) Industrial. (Courtesy Chevrolet Motor Division, General Motors Corrporation)

(B) Single-family residential. (Courtesy National Homes Corporation)

(C) Apartment houses.

Fig. 41-1. Utilities, parking, and street requirements vary with building zones.

ities, and some areas for single-family dwellings (Fig. 41-1). The latter areas are designed to provide quiet restful areas for people to live in, free from the heavy traffic and business functions which are both noisy and dangerous to children playing in the area. Zoning also aids a city in planning its needs.

The site should be selected after considering the various zoning regulations and the particular function of the building —whether it is a business, industry, apartment, or home. Other factors to be considered include property adjacent to the proposed site, buildings or structures which must be cleared from the land before the new building can be constructed, ease of access from streets or highways, and availability of adequate utility services, such as electricity, water, and gas. Additional services include sewage and garbage removal.

Building Location

After the site has been selected, it is important to place the building in the proper position on the plot of land. An example of poor location of a building is a store located so close to the street that neither parking space nor sidewalks are possible; therefore, potential customers find it inconvenient to do business. Factors influencing the location of a building include drainage of the water from rain and snow, type of soil for supporting the foundation of the building, woods and trees on the plot of land, needs for parking and entrance of utility services, and use of other natural resources. Some of these factors are considered in Fig. 41-2. Other factors to consider include placement of the building for obtaining the best view, to prevent damage to the wildlife and natural areas, to provide playground space, to provide adequate en-

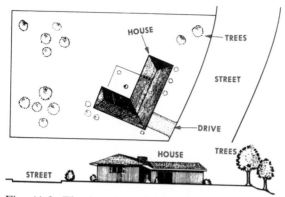

Fig. 41-2. The location of a building is important with regard to easy access to the street and to trees and landscaping.

Fig. 41-4. The building site usually requires the use of heavy machines. (A) Holes must be dug for water and sewage pipes. (B) Large areas are leveled for roads, shopping centers, etc. (C) Power shovels are used to dig basements.

trance to business areas, and to provide parking areas for employees and customers.

Another factor in locating the building is the landscaping required. The lower areas can be filled in, using heavy equipment. The higher areas can be cleared, basements dug, and utilities such as water and sewage and electricity obtained for the building. To accomplish all this, an initial survey of the lot is required. A surveyor uses a transit and a level to lay out the various locations and to mark the land to be cleared, leveled, or filled (Fig. 41-3). Surveying is the process of mapping

Fig. 41-3. Surveyors locate the utility lines and building sites.

the plot of land and measuring the necessary angles and distances both horizontally and vertically for the people who operate the machines (Fig. 41-4). The survey involves the use of stakes and guidelines to make sure the building is placed in the proper direction and that

the landscaping is done properly on the site.

General Planning

The plans for the building usually are made by an architect. The architect draws the designs for the shape and decoration of the building and specifies the construction techniques. The contractor or builder actually constructs the building (Fig. 41-5). A building contractor often can construct a small building from standard plans, without the direct aid of an architect.

However, when an individual wants a building constructed to fit his particular needs, several functions must be considered. If there are to be separate study or rest areas, the building should be planned to prevent interference from other activities within the building. Quiet areas, such as bedrooms, offices, or libraries, should be located at a distance from the activity areas, such as recreation rooms, gymnasiums, kitchens, and other areas which generate noise.

Access should be provided to the various areas to permit greatest efficiency.

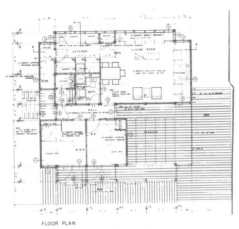
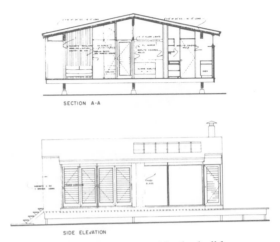

Fig. 41-5. The building plans include the floor plans and elevations to guide the builder.
(Courtesy Masonite Corporation)

For example, if a small shop building were being constructed for the repair of automobiles, a wide door should be constructed through which automobiles can be driven easily into the shop with a minimum of turning or changing directions.

In a private home, it is more convenient for the inhabitants to be able to carry bundles, groceries, or other materials directly from their car to the area in which these articles are to be stored, such as a kitchen or a pantry. Easy access is important to the other areas of the building as well. Hallways require space and increase the cost of the building. They should be avoided and the rooms should be arranged to provide for maximum use and access without complicated hallway arrangements. When hallways are used, care should be taken to construct them wide enough for the movement of furniture and equipment. Many homeowners have been trapped in undesirable situations where the basements were remodeled to include narrow hallways and doorways; therefore, when new appliances, such as washers or dryers, were purchased, they were found to be wider than the doors. This necessitated the removal of doors and walls to move in the appliances. This results in repairs and additions which are indeed expensive.

Commercial buildings should be planned for maximum use and for the access of the supplies used in the business. The customer and visitor areas should be separated from the living and work areas. For example, the guests in a private home should be brought directly into a living room or similar area, rather than through the bedroom areas. The customers in a commercial building should enter an office or reception area, rather than directly into the work area where the production of the goods or services might be interrupted.

Heating and Cooling

Utilities include plumbing, water, heating, cooling, ventilation, and electrical use. All these usually are installed by tradesmen skilled in each of the areas. Heating, cooling, and ventilating systems require ducts to convey cool, heated, or fresh air to the various parts of the building through sheet metal "pipes." These ducts are prepared by sheet metalworkers and are fitted together in large sections during the construction phases of the building (Fig. 41-6).

Fig. 41-6. A gas furnace and ductwork installation in a small home.

Humidity, which is the water vapor present in the air, can cause discomfort; also, it can cause expansion and contraction of the furniture and various parts of the house. The humidity, as well as the basic heating and cooling period, is often controlled. Humidifying - dehumidifying units are used to maintain water vapor at a relatively constant level throughout the house during the heating and cooling cycles. In the colder climates, the winter cold removes the water vapor from the air and dries out the furniture and wooden areas, often causing splits and warping. The addition of water vapor to the air prevents this condition and makes the heat more comfortable. During the summer months, however, the vapor content or humidity increases, causing additional periodic changes.

When air-moving ducts are used, two systems must be employed; the conditioning ducts provide a path for the air to be carried to the individual locations. Return ducts are provided to return the air to the heating or cooling unit where it can be recycled for additional use. Fresh air can be added as required.

Heating or cooling by moving the air is called *convection* heating or cooling.

These "forced-air" systems are quite common. However, other systems also are used. *Radiant* heat is the heat emitted directly from a hot object. The heat from stoves and steam radiators are examples of radiant heat (Fig. 41-7).

Fig. 41-7. Radiant heat is radiated from a hot object.

Plumbing

Plumbing refers to the pipes used for water supply, sewage, and drainage in a building. Water is brought into the house or building where it is distributed as needed for cooking, washing, and sanitary facilities. Most homes and commercial buildings are provided with hot-water heaters which are supplied by the same water intake that supplies the cold-water systems. However, the hot-water heater is provided with a separate piping system to furnish hot water to the various bathrooms, lavatories, or cleaning areas as required.

At each sink, lavatory, shower, etc., provision must be made to drain away the used water. These drains also form systems of pipe which also are installed by the plumber (Fig. 41-8).

Two types of plumbing materials are used—metal and plastic. Much of the water pipe used in homes is made of copper; however, in industrial uses, high-pressure liquids, steam, and chemicals usually are conveyed by steel pipes. Glass piping is used for corrosive chemicals to withstand chemical action and extreme heat

Fig. 41-8. A plumber is installing drains and water pipes in this home. (Courtesy National Homes Corporation)

Fig. 41-9. The drains carry the wastes to the sewer lines or cesspools. Note the drain trap at the upper end of the pipe.

and cold. Many homes now utilize plastic plumbing for the cold water and drainage systems. Special plastics must be used for the hot-water systems, since the common plastic pipe becomes softened from the heat.

The drains usually are larger than the supply pipes and are designed with a slope. The slope simply means that the drains always point downward. The reason for this requirement is that the water is usually delivered to the building from a pressurized water supply, such as a pump or water tower. However, since the drain has no pump, it depends on gravity to remove the waste water and materials from the building to the main drainage systems. Cesspools are used where these drainage systems are unavailable (Fig. 41-9). Considerations for the drain include the fact that the low drainage pressures will not force the solid materials along the drainage routes. The slope of the drain must be gradual; then the water can drain slowly enough to carry any solid materials along with it. However, if the drain is not sloping, none of the materials will drain away. In addition, the drains must be vented. The venting permits air to enter the pipes; this prevents the water from forming vacuum pockets which prevent the water from

draining. The drains also utilize a *trap*. The trap is a bent section of tubing which always contains some water. The water in the trap prevents odors from entering the building (Fig. 41-10).

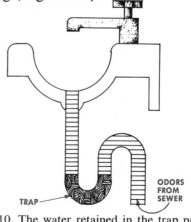

Fig. 41-10. The water retained in the trap prevents sewer gas odors from entering the building.

Electrical Considerations

The electricity for the building is provided by an electric service company. In rural areas, this can be a rural electrification agency, commonly called *REA*. In the cities, this service is usually provided by a city or area electrical service company. The service is brought to the building on utility lines which can be either on poles or underground (Fig. 41-11). The electricity is brought into the house; then it is distributed according to load requirements. The wiring of a building or house should be spread about; then all the various machines or appliances are not operated from a single circuit, since this could overload and heat the wire. The heated wires could, in turn, cause fires which would destroy the building. It is customary to protect the various circuit of wires with *fuses* or *circuit breakers*. These devices shut off the wire electrically when too much load is placed on a particular circuit.

Electrical wiring and materials are installed by an electrician before the in-

Fig. 41-11. The electrical service lines bring the electrical power to the building.

terior of the building is finished. In buildings used for dwellings, much of the wiring is done with a cable covered with a plastic or cloth covering called "romex." However, in most industries and commercial situations, the wiring is run through special metal tubing called *conduit*. This protects the wiring from damage by a puncture or from being scraped or hit.

Two types of electrical systems are commonly used in homes and businesses. These are 120-volt and 240-volt systems. The 120-volt systems are used for most of the common appliances, such as refrigerators, radios, televisions, etc. The 240-volt systems are used for electric ranges, electric furnaces, hot-water heaters and similar heavy-duty appliances. Larger voltage systems are used for the large motors and machines.

The installation of wiring for these systems is, of course, less expensive at the time of construction than at a later time. The building designer should carefully

plan the locations for outlets, lights, switches, thermostats, special control devices, and the outlets for appliances, such as stoves, hot-water heaters, washers and dryers, or special machines and equipment.

The electrical requirements should be evenly distributed from the main switchbox and fused with the proper protective fusing devices. It is sometimes wise to leave space for additional circuits, if future growth is anticipated. Compare, for example, the period of time between 1930 and 1950 and the period from 1950 to 1970. During these two twenty-year spans, the use of electricity differed tremendously. From 1930 until 1950, considerable growth and the use of appliances was experienced. However, since 1950 the growth and the use of electrical appliances have been greater and should continue to grow.

Traffic Flow

Traffic flow in a building consists of two basic types: (1) Movement of the people within the building; and (2) Movement of people and vehicles outside the building. The outside movement of people includes traffic from the access streets and highways into the motor parking areas, as well as the movement in the outdoor areas for recreation or work.

Interior traffic flow includes an analysis of movement inside the building. For example, visitors to a business should enter through an attractive entrance. This arrangement permits secretary-receptionists to direct the visitor to the person he wishes to visit. This conserves the working time of many other workers and also protects the special production methods or confidential material from being copied by competing companies through simple visitation.

In a home, the visitors should be brought into an area designed and used for either casual living or formal entertaining, rather than into areas of the home designed for sleeping, washing, or other purposes (Fig. 41-12). Therefore, the layout of the home or business also depends on the traffic flow of individuals

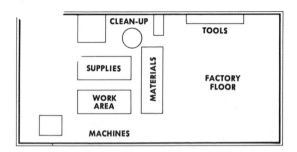

Fig. 41-13. Poor traffic planning hampers the necessary traffic flow inside a building.

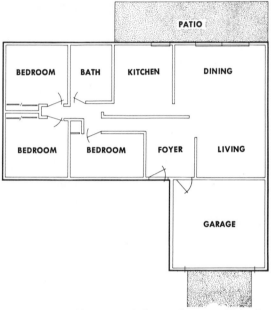

Fig. 41-12. This type of floor plan provides the occupants with privacy and the guests with comfort by separating the entry, guests, quiet, and activity areas.

within that building and the activities performed during the day.

A housewife, for example, should work in a kitchen in which the stove and refrigerator are located conveniently. Requiring the housewife to walk from the stove location in one area to a refrigerator located two rooms away would be both inefficient and tiring. Similarly, in a business, if a worker is required to stop work, walk the entire length of a long building to obtain the tools he needs, and then return to his work station only to use the tools briefly and return them, involves more time in walking than in working. This type of interior traffic (Fig. 41-13)

is costly for the employer and reduces the production rate; therefore, the purpose for being in business is handicapped. Where machinery moves within a building, the aisles should be wide and well lighted. Safe movement is as important as the ease of movement.

Cost Factors in Building

Cost factors vary with the location and with the type of building. A building in a cold climate should be insulated more heavily than a building in a more moderate climate (Fig. 41-14). A building in a

Fig. 41-14. The quality and type of insulation and other materials affect the total costs of the building.

wet climate requires more protection from moisture than a building in a dry climate or desert. Thus, the type of building varies with the climate and temperature considerations and these, in turn, affect the overall cost and construction of the building. Other considerations include whether the building is to be sheathed on the outside with brick, stone, wood, composition sheathing, or other material. A metal building might require only a painted surface, an insulation layer, and a thin interior wall. Whereas, the standard wood-frame construction involves considerably more assembling processes. Floor-finishing methods also affect the cost factors. Floors laid with terrazzo tile are more expensive than floors laid with plywood and covered with carpeting. The floors laid with plywood and then decked with hardwood also are more expensive than the simple plywood decking. A floor might be subfloored with individual boards laid diagonally and then covered with hardwood flooring running in a different direction. This provides additional strength and sturdiness and also adds to the building costs.

Other factors which influence building costs are types of windows, door types and sizes, porches, balconies, two-story or one-story houses, and interrupted-wall shapes. The most economical process is merely to build a rectangular building. However, this type of building is less artistic in style and is less pleasing in appearance; in many buildings, the wall sections are basically rectangular, but some breakup in the long lines is provided. When this is done, additional costs are incurred from the extra construction techniques involved (Fig. 41-15).

Factors such as insulation, special wiring for machinery, air conditioning, humidity controls, larger garages, fireplaces, and other additions to a home can increase its costs measurably. The decoration of the interior through carpeting,

Fig. 41-15. Folding doors increase the cost, but add to the utility and convenience of the building. (Courtesy Pella Rolscreen Company)

special draperies, and special paint or wallpapering processes utilizing special trim and finish work with woods or pre-finished hardwood sections increase the costs of the home. Built-in appliances, such as stoves, exhaust hoods, dishwashers, garbage-disposal units, refrigerators, special ovens, and other units of this type, add to the total building costs above the actual construction.

Future Considerations

When contracting or constructing a building, consideration should be provided to potential growth. Small families with small houses should not fail to consider the fact that their families might grow. Family growth can require the addition of more rooms as the family grows and desires privacy. This necessitates either moving or adding to the present building. It is wise to consider designing and constructing the house in a way that it can be enlarged conveniently at a later date.

In commercial buildings, such as those used for small industries and businesses, it should be remembered that periodic interior remodeling is often necessary to attract customers (Fig. 41-16). Therefore, the interior arrangements should be designed and constructed in a manner which

Fig. 41-16. Folding doors and partitions are used in all types of buildings. (Courtesy Pella Rolscreen Company)

facilitates future remodeling. Businesses and small industries also tend to grow; therefore, constructing a building which can be enlarged is a wise measure for the small commercial and industrial firms as well.

When planning for future considerations, careful attention should be provided utilities, plumbing, and the electrical wiring; then as the building grows, completely new wiring and plumbing installations are unnecessary in the older part of the building. Some attention also should be provided the future patterns for traffic flow and access from the older part of the building to the newer part without the disruption of the normal activities within these areas.

Contracting and Estimating

In making an agreement with the contractor to begin the process of construction and in estimating to secure bids for the construction, specifications must be made. These specifications describe the building and its contents in detail. A contractor needs detailed specifications to make an accurate and reasonable estimate on the building. He must know what the building is required to do, how large it must be, and generally what types of utilities will be required before he can make

his estimate. Details of the outside appearance and basic construction materials desired also should be specified, since they also affect the costs of making the building. The quality of the materials used should be specified, particularly the quality of carpeting, size of electrical wiring, sanitary conveniences, special plumbing needs, etc.

The first step in preparing estimates and contract specifications is to prepare the documents which provide the written descriptions of the work to be done, the types of materials to be used, the loads and weights to be carried or supported, colors and types of paint, carpets, and other construction features. The building should be described fully in the specifications and all the details of construction and finishing should be provided, including the number of rooms, how they are heated, how they are cooled, the types of ducting and ventilation, types of windows and doors, as well as all other details. These descriptions are known as the *construction specifications.*

The specifications normally are prepared by an architect, a contractor, or other person familiar with building details. The specifications then become a part of the written building contract, after they have been analyzed carefully by all the parties concerned. The building specifications include the general conditions and the specific conditions. General conditions concern matters, such as insurance of employees, which party (the builder or the owner) pays for the materials used in construction, who is to furnish the utilities (electricity and water) during the construction, what types of tools are used, and who is to furnish the labor and materials.

Specific conditions detail the types and qualities of materials used in each step of the building construction. Also, the specific conditions cover the size of the electrical wiring, number and location of the electrical outlets, shape and size of the sheet metal ducting to carry heat and ventilation to the various rooms, types of windows, thickness of the walls, composition of the sheathing, type of roof, doors, locks, doorknobs, window screens, plaster or concrete details, and similar matters pertaining to construction.

Specifications, such as the general and specific conditions, are necessary to estimate the total cost of a building. Contractors and builders can total the costs for the specific types of material and labor from the specifications. The estimator uses each section of the specifications to prepare a detailed list of materials and their cost. He then totals each section, such as plastering, ductwork for ventilation, installation of doors and windows, etc., and then uses these subheads for the preparation of the work estimated. For each section he computes the average installation speed of one worker for each type of job; then the labor cost is added to the material cost.

For example, a plasterer might complete 10 square feet of walls in 1 hour. If 500 square feet of walls are to be plastered, 50 hours of labor cost are required to plaster the walls. The estimate for plastering then includes the cost of the plastering materials, plus 50 hours of labor cost. Even though the contractor hires five men for 10 hours work, the estimate is still valid.

The operating expenses are the other expenses incurred by the contractor. This category includes the insurance workers (workman's compensation) to pay their medical costs in the event they are injured; transportation cost of the materials to the construction site; cost of special tools or machines; storage cost of the materials while they are being used; costs of fuel, electricity, and water at the construction site; and maintenance of buildings and offices. In addition, the contractor must make a reasonable profit in his business. This profit is usually calculated and includes a small percentage of all the costs involved in building. The finished estimate consists of four major parts—the cost of materials, the cost of labor and subcontractors, operating costs, and profit.

When the final arrangements are made to construct the building, a contract is made. The contract specifies all building conditions and materials. The contract also may specify the time the builder or contractor is permitted to construct the building. The contract, when complete, will include the specifications, plans, and various conditions; normally, is is signed by both the owner and the contractors.

Questions

1. List the general factors which should be considered in planning a building.
2. List the specific factors which should be considered in planning the interior of a single-family dwelling.
3. List the factors which should be considered in planning the site location of a small store.
4. List the services included in "utilities."
5. What two classes of heating are commonly used for homes?
6. What is a duct?
7. What is the purpose of a drain trap?
8. What supplies the pressure for drainage flow?
9. Into which room should a door between a house and a garage open?
10. Why do building costs vary?
11. What are "general" contract specifications?

Unit 42 – Structural Classification and Preparation

Building construction is broadly considered to be one of two types—*substructures* and *superstructures*. The substructure of a building includes its foundation and basement (if it has a basement); it supports the weight of the remaining portion of the building (Fig. 42-1). The superstructure of a building is the portion supported by the substructure; generally,

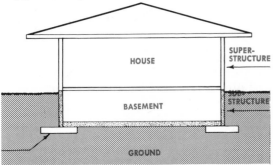

Fig. 42-1. The underground substructures support the superstructure or remainder of the building.

it includes the walls, roofs, flooring, and other features. The substructure rarely is seen or noticed by most people; however, the superstructure is readily noticeable. The type of superstructure is classified in accordance with several basic types of structural processes. If the building is constructed entirely of stone or brick, is is a *masonry* building. However, if the building is constructed of wood or metal framework and the outside is coated with stone or brick which does not support the weight of the roof, it is a *frame* building with a stone or brick *veneer*. A building built with certain types of wood or metal framework also is a frame building. Other buildings can be built from cast concrete with veneer sections of brick, decorative castings, or stonework decoration.

Tall buildings, such as the skyscrapers in New York and other large cities, are built by constructing the steel frameworks which support the weight of the floors and all other parts of the building. The walls and decorative portions are attached to this steel framework; therefore, they are not a portion of the structural or *loadbearing* materials. Various types of materials can be used to face or veneer a building. The masonry work includes all the types of bricks, concrete blocks, tiles, and terracotta clay tile, as well as stone or stone products. The sheathing is wood or sheets of fiberboard sections used in building the exterior walls. In the large commercial buildings, the exterior walls can be glass, metal, plastic, and many other materials.

The walls are either mass-wall or frame-wall types. The mass-wall superstructure is a solid wall of stone, concrete, or other stone-like material. The frame-wall superstructure can be wood, as in most houses today (Fig. 42-2); of

Fig. 42-2. Wooden frame house.

398

metal, as in many commercial buildings (Fig. 42-3); or of heavier metal and con-

Fig. 42-3. Metal frame building with metal exterior siding applied onto a steel frame. (Courtesy Chevrolet Motor Division, General Motors Corporation)

crete frameworks (Fig. 42-4). However, in some newer developments in building construction practices, aluminum frames

Fig. 42-4. These large buildings are constructed of concrete and steel framework.

can be made easily to replace the wood frames now used in the construction of private dwellings. The aluminum frames (Fig. 42-5) are lightweight, rigid, and

Fig. 42-5. Constructing an aluminum framework for a house. (Courtesy Aluminum Company of America)

easily assembled; also, they can be made for common nails to be driven into them. Normally, however, they are constructed with screws and bolts or with special bonding cements.

Building Foundations

One of the most important considerations in constructing a building is the ground on which the building is to be placed. The soil can be hard or soft, wet or dry, dense and firm, or loose and shaky. The ground can expand when it is wet and shrink when it dries. Ground containing moisture can freeze and expand even more; then it becomes soft, shrinks, and settles when it thaws (Fig. 42-6). De-

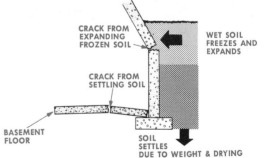

CRACK FROM EXPANDING FROZEN SOIL

WET SOIL FREEZES AND EXPANDS

CRACK FROM SETTLING SOIL

BASEMENT FLOOR

SOIL SETTLES DUE TO WEIGHT & DRYING

Fig. 42-6. Determine the soil conditions in selecting the site for a building.

spite all these factors, buildings are located on nearly any and all types of soils. Obviously, different methods of making the foundations are used with the different types of soils. One fact always remains—the buildings begin with the foundation.

The foundation distributes the weight of the building over the surface of the ground to prevent the building sinking, settling, or tilting from uneven support. Cracks in the walls or floors of buildings usually result from the stresses caused by the building settling unevenly into the soil when the weather or soil conditions change.

A spectacular example of uneven soil density is in the Italian city of Pisa. Ap-proximately five hundred years ago, a cathedral was built and, in the custom of those days, the bells for the church were installed in a separate tower. The cathedral was built on a more solid foundation than the bell tower and remains relatively level today. The bell tower was built accidentally in a location with a hard soil on one side and a softer soil on the other side; then it began to settle. The bell tower, now known as the famous leaning tower of Pisa (Fig. 42-7), actually leans at an angle of approximately 16 or 17 degrees from the vertical axis. It has been a scenic attraction for approximately two hundred years, and leans slightly more each year. The Italian government is, of course, attempting to halt the leaning of the tower, but has had comparatively little success to date. Some day, if the leaning continues, the building will fall to the ground.

Foundations generally include three parts. The *bearing surface* is the portion of the ground that the foundation is built on. The bearing surface can be prepared to aid in draining water, to minimize the effects of heat or cold, and to aid in absorbing vibration and various other conditions. The *footing* is the lower portion of the foundation; it rests on the bearing surface (the ground which supports the building), and is the portion of the foundation that distributes the weight of the entire building (Fig. 42-8).

(A) The famous leaning tower of Pisa is a result of uneven settling of the soil.

(B) The cathedral was built about the same time on firmer soil and does not lean.
Fig. 42-7. Soil conditions can affect a building with a poor foundation.

BEARING
SUPPORT
FOOTING
BEARING
SURFACE
Fig. 42-8. The foundation of a building generally includes the bearing surface, footing, and bearing support.

Three types of footings are used on the bearing surface. The *spread footing* (Fig. 42-9) is the simplest type of footing and is used in the harder more closely packed

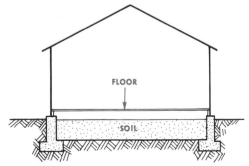

Fig. 42-9. A spread footing.

soils. The *raft* or *slab footing* (Fig. 42-10) is used in either the harder or looser

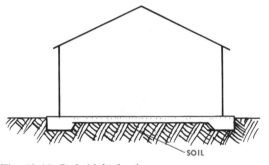

Fig. 42-10. Raft (slab) footing.

soils; it functions as a boat on which the building is "floated." When a building is to be built on a very soft, damp soil (marsh or a loosely packed earth of uneven hardness) and where bridges and other structures are built in rivers and in open bays, the *pile footing* is used. The pile footing is a long column driven deep into the soil to a firmer area. Pile caps are placed on the pilings to provide a bearing area for the remainder of the structure (Fig. 42-11). Houses can be built on pile footings, which can be steel, concrete, wood, or stone. Special augers can be used to bore into the soil. When they reach a desired depth, a special attachment is extended to drill a larger hole, as indicated

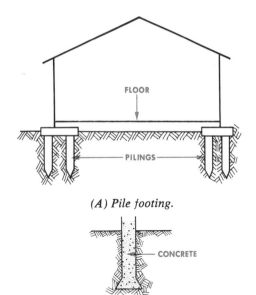

(A) Pile footing.

(B) Footed concrete pilings support extra weight.

(C) Special augers are used to bore holes in the soil for concrete pilings.

(D) The hole is filled with concrete for a supporting pile.

Fig. 42-11. Concrete pilings and piers.

in Figs. 42-11C and 42-11D. Then the hole is filled with reinforced concrete and it functions as a supporting pile.

Another famous place with foundation problems is the Italian city of Venice. A typical "street" or canal in Venice is shown in Fig. 42-12. This city was built hundreds of years ago over a shallow bay in the Adriatic Sea. Now, poor techniques, age, rising sea levels, and settling of the soil frequently combine to flood this historic old city.

(A) "Main street" in Venice is a wide canal.

(B) Water surrounds the city.
Fig. 42-12. Settling of the soil and rising sea levels threaten the historic city of Venice.

Concrete Formwork

In most modern small buildings, the foundations are concrete. Concrete is a mixture of portland cement, sand, and gravel or *aggregate*. The portland cement is the binder or glue for holding the other materials in a firm, solid mass. Portland cement is made from limestone which has been crushed and treated with heat and water to provide it with its hardening characteristics. Concrete can be compared to man-made stone, since it exhibits many of the qualities of stone. However, in addition to being a "moldable" substance, concrete can be made with many of the qualities lacking in stone by the use of additives, gravel, aggregates (types of gravel and stone), and reinforcing steel.

Some buildings are made from specially treated forms of concrete, known as prestressed concrete. This type of concrete is more expensive, but it supports far heavier loads, and can be used for longer spans than the common types of concrete. Prestressed concrete is made by stretching (or stressing) steel rods or cables in a mold and then filling the mold with concrete. As the concrete hardens, the tension on the steel is reduced gradually, creating forces which "squeeze" the concrete particles together to make the concrete stronger. The prestressing principle is demonstrated in Fig. 42-13. How-

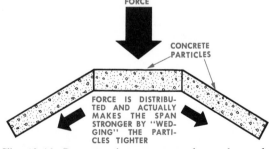

Fig. 42-13. Prestressed concrete can be made much stronger than ordinary concrete.

ever, prestressing is used rarely in small buildings, such as private dwellings or the smaller stores. Most contractors do not prepare the prestressed concrete themselves; but they purchase it from special plants where the *stressing* can be done, since the stressing process requires special equipment and forms.

Most buildings are constructed with ordinary concrete which has been reinforced with aggregate, reinforcing steel rods, and mesh. Since the concrete is mixed and

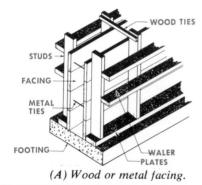

(A) Wood or metal facing.

(B) Forms ready for pouring the concrete.

(C) After the forms are removed.

(D) Forms being positioned and filled
with sand for concrete steps.

Fig. 42-14. Form construction.

then poured into the molds, the first construction step is to prepare the bearing surfaces and to construct the forms to serve as molds for the concrete mixture. When the concrete hardens, the forms should be removed and the concrete permitted to finish curing. Concrete cures for approximately twenty-eight days, and it does not "dry" in the usual sense of the word. In fact, during the initial hardening processes, concrete should be kept moistened to prevent the surface scaling and pitting.

The concrete forms are built from various types of dimension lumber and from plywood. Some special applications for buildings, such as the round supporting piers or columns, also might require special forms for their construction. The construction of a typical concrete form is detailed in Fig. 42-14. The form is built at the construction site after the ground has been prepared for a bearing surface. Spacers are used within the concrete forms to keep the walls of the forms at the proper width; therefore, the thickness of the poured concrete wall will not vary

(Fig. 42-15). Without spacers (Fig. 42-16), the weight of the concrete could cause the forms to bend. If the wall of the form is warped inward, the wall section is too thin and is weakened. If the form wall bulges, too much concrete is used.

The concrete forms can be treated to prevent the concrete sticking to the form. This permits the form to be reused. The

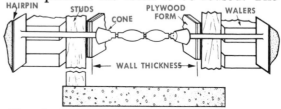

Fig. 42-15. Spacers are needed in concrete forms to maintain the correct thickness of the concrete walls. If the form wall is warped inward, the wall section is too thin and the wall is weakened. If the form wall bulges outward, too much concrete is used.

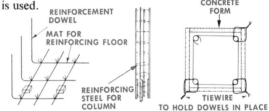

Fig. 42-16. In forms without spacers, the weight of the concrete could cause the form to bend.

Fig. 42-17. Steel reinforcement for a round concrete column (top). A cardboard mold is placed around the steel reinforcement (bottom). The mold is unwrapped after the concrete has set.

forms can be given a special shape; then the concrete comes from the mold with the special lines or decorative effects provided by the face of the molds (Fig. 42-17). In the multistory buildings, the concrete floors usually are made with cavities in the bottom to reduce the weight. The molds are placed on steel scaffolding and the boxes, called "pans," as shown in Fig. 42-18, are placed on large flat panels (Fig. 42-19A). Then the concrete slab is poured and the scaffolding and forms are removed when the concrete has set

(Fig. 42-19B). The spaces between the concrete and steel frame are walled in with various types of masonry, panels, or glass. Concrete is used in many types of buildings, ranging from homes to athletic stadiums (Fig. 42-20).

Special machines are used to make the concrete slabs for highways and for some types of irrigation and drainage ditches. These machines (Fig. 42-21) make a smooth, shaped surface while the form is actually moving. The form supports the surface of the concrete and provides it with the shape and smoothness desired. This is called *slip-form* concrete work.

Where two or more sections of concrete are joined, such as a wall to a footing, special anchoring devices are re-

(A) Stacks of steel pans.

(B) Pans are removed after the concrete has set.

Fig. 42-18. Steel pans are used to form cavities in the upper concrete floors to reduce weight.

(A) The pans are placed on flat decking.

(B) A special coating permits the pans to be removed easily after the concrete has hardened.

Fig. 42-19. Molds for concrete floors in multistory buildings.

quired to hold the two sections together securely (Fig. 42-22). Reinforcement rods or dowels in the first section are extended outward several inches. The extended portions of the dowels are formed into hooks and project into the form for the next section. As the next section is poured, the concrete settles around the anchoring hooks of the dowels anchored in the previous section, providing a firm,

solid joint, due to the holding action of the concrete around the anchoring pieces. The reinforcement steel used in concrete formwork is not smooth. Ridges on its surface provide added holding power in the concrete.

Steel mesh or "matting" is used to reinforce large flat surfaces to add strength to the concrete and to help in preventing cracking. Concrete, although it is very strong, has a high expansion and contraction rate; therefore, when it is cooled or heated, it shrinks or expands. This causes cracks in many concrete surfaces. Therefore, when concrete is expected to expand in heat and contract with cold, joints are placed in the concrete and filled

Fig. 42-20. Concrete is used in many types of buildings from homes to athletic stadiums.

(A) Pouring and molding the concrete as the machine moves.

(B) Hopper of a slip-forming machine.

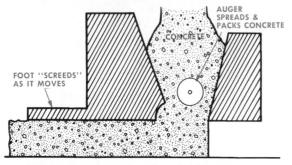

AUGER SPREADS & PACKS CONCRETE

CONCRETE

FOOT "SCREEDS" AS IT MOVES

(C) An auger spreads and packs the concrete.
Fig. 42-21. Slip-forming machines.

with a waterproof, fibrous material. These *expansion joints* aid in preventing cracks in the concrete. In addition, the reinforcement within the concrete prevents the concrete from breaking, even though cracks may occur.

Concrete is made by mixing one portion of cement with two portions of sand and three portions of aggregate. The mixing of concrete which can be used for most purposes is then as easy as "one, two, three." Special additives, called *admixtures,* can be added to the concrete to provide special characteristics, such as quick hardening, hardening in cold or

Fig. 42-22. Hooked reinforcement dowels are used to join two concrete sections.

damp areas, special colors, waterproofing, and other effects. The basic "one, two, three" mixture also can be changed to provide the concrete with special strength or smoothness qualities, as desired.

Most of the building contractors, however, do not mix their own concrete. They specify the particular quality or mixture they desire; then a concrete company mixes and delivers the concrete to the building site in special trucks with mixers on the truck beds. These trucks can drive to the construction site and pour the concrete through a pouring spout in nearly any direction (Fig. 42-23). This is a con-

Fig. 42-23. A concrete truck mixes the concrete and pours it where it is needed on the building site.

siderable savings for the contractor in equipment and time. As the concrete is being poured, it must be forced into the forms evenly to prevent the formation of large air pockets. When pouring extremely large areas, the workers actually enter the forms and walk in the freshly poured concrete, using vibrators, hoses, and shovels to make sure the concrete is packed properly.

After the concrete has been poured, it is surfaced. A *screed* is used to level the surface. This can be done by hand or by several different types of machines. However, the screeding is a leveling process which makes the surface straight, flat, and level or at the desired angle. A screed can be merely a piece of lumber or steel worked on a form; for small sections, it can be done by hand.

After screeding, the concrete is permitted to stiffen; but immediately before the concrete hardens, the surface is *floated*. To "float" a concrete surface merely means that the surface is smoothed after the screeding to make it smooth or to provide a desired surface texture. Sidewalks, for example, can be floated, to remain slightly rough for firm footing. However, a basement can be floated smooth for ease in cleaning and general appearance. The floating can be done by hand, using a push stick similar to a janitor's broom, except that the "broom" has a flat board on the end. Floating also can be done with a steel trowel or with a finishing machine similar in appearance to a power lawnmower. The blades, however, do not cut; they are driven in a circular motion to smooth the surface of the concrete.

After floating the surface, the concrete is permitted to harden, and it is cured properly for the first few days by keeping it wet. Although the concrete will harden in approximately one day's time, it continues to harden for nearly a month. Concrete which has been in place for the proper length of time for complete hardening is referred to as "cured" concrete. The forms are stripped from the concrete

after the concrete has set, but while it is still green. The forms can be stripped from the concrete after twelve to twenty-four hours.

Finishing Concrete

After the forms have been stripped from the "set" concrete, patching and plastering might be required. The formed concrete often contains minor holes and air pockets which do not affect the structural qualities or strengths of the concrete building. However, these minor defects can mar the finished appearance. In addition, concrete forms sometimes do not join evenly and small ridges made while in the forms can be smoothed. Holes and cavities in the concrete forms can be filled by using a smooth mixture of concrete and sand without gravel in a process called *patching*. However, to provide a smooth, white surface on the concrete, it should be plastered with a special plaster for concrete use (Fig. 42-24). The plaster

Fig. 42-24. Concrete framework is smoothed with plaster.

then is a coating over the concrete to cover the minor bumps and cavities and to provide the concrete with a smooth, gleaming appearance.

The concrete also can be veneered with brick (Fig. 42-25) or with various

Fig. 42-25. Concrete can be veneered with brick for the sake of beauty.

panels made of nearly any material, including cast concrete panels with decorative stones embedded in it (Fig. 42-26). These panels are attached to *furring strips* placed in the concrete forms before the concrete was poured. The furring strips permit the areas to be bolted or nailed to the concrete wall. It is important to place all the holes and attaching devices in the concrete walls and foundations before the concrete is poured into the form. Concrete is rarely broken or cut after it is poured. This requires extra labor and material costs. It is simpler, quicker, and less expensive to place the objects in the forms initially.

When plumbing pipes and electrical conduit work are to be set into the concrete, they also are placed before the concrete is poured. Electrical conduits, plumbing, water pipes, drains, or anchor

(A) Concrete veneer panels used for decoration and to close walls.

(B) Close-up view of stones imbedded in concrete for decoration.

Fig. 42-26. Concrete can be veneered with decorative panels of stones imbedded in cast concrete.

bolts (Fig. 42-27) for attaching the stud walls are placed into the concrete forms before the concrete is poured. The con-

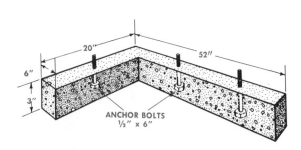

Fig. 42-27. Anchor bolts are placed in the concrete forms before the concrete is poured.

crete is poured around them; then they are anchored firmly and bedded. Some architects also have been experimenting with hot-water pipes which weave back and forth underneath the surface of the concrete to keep it at a constant temperature the year round. This prevents cracks, expansion, or breaks from expansion due to temperature change; also it serves as a heating and cooling element for the building to maintain a constant temperature.

Concrete also is molded into special forms. Molded concrete bannisters are used for porch railings on a large building in Fig. 42-28. This type of concrete

Fig. 42-28. Cast concrete pieces are decorative.

decoration is considerably more economical than the carved stone pieces of similar size and shape.

Molded concrete also has its more practical aspects. Sewer pipes made of cast concrete are shown in Fig. 42-29. These

Fig. 42-29. Cast concrete pipe.

pipes are available in sizes taller than a man. They are strong, do not rust or corrode, and can be assembled quickly without welding or special joining procedures.

Questions

1. Name the two broad types of structures.
2. What class of building is constructed entirely of stone or brick?
3. What type of building is constructed on a framework?
4. List the three types of basic foundation methods. Where are they used properly?
5. What is the name of the special molds in which the concrete used in buildings is molded?
6. Why are steel rod and mesh embedded in concrete?
7. What is meant by slip-forming concrete?
8. What is an admixture?
9. What is meant by screeding of concrete?
10. How can concrete be finished or decorated?

Unit 43 – Basic Wood Building Construction

Buildings with wood frames play an important role in the everyday lives of people today. Throughout the world, wood is the most common material for constructing dwellings. In the United States, more wooden buildings exist than any other type. Although new methods, processes, and techniques are being developed, the basic wooden (or frame) building process continues to be the most widely used type of building.

Reasons for the popularity of wood-frame buildings include the sturdiness and lightweight characteristics of the wooden frame building (in comparison with the solid stone or brick buildings), the natural sound and thermal insulation qualities, ease of construction, and ease of modification. This type of building also is less expensive to construct and more comfortable to live in than most other types of buildings (Fig. 43-1).

Flooring

After the foundation has been laid, the flooring process is begun. While the foundation was being poured, long heavy bolts were placed in the soft concrete with the threaded ends protruding. After the foundation has hardened, the bolts are imbedded firmly to serve as *anchor bolts* to hold the wooden framework in place. Holes bored in the *sill plate* permit it to be attached to the foundation by sliding over the anchor bolts; this attaches the sill plate firmly to the foundation (Fig. 43-2).

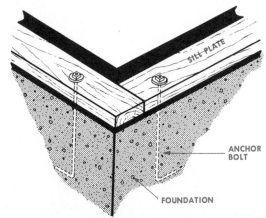

(A) Sill plate is bolted in place after the concrete has hardened.

(B) Finished foundation with anchor bolts and reinforcement dowels.

Fig. 43-2. Anchor bolts are imbedded in the foundation when the concrete is poured.

Fig. 43-1. Frame construction. (Courtesy Lindal Cedar Homes, Inc.)

If the foundation includes a wide area, girders might be needed to provide additional support for the flooring. Girders are long support beams of steel, aluminum (Fig. 43-3), or several strong pieces of lumber fastened together. In areas such as basements, where the span (distance between the walls) is great, girder supports are used to support the floor joists.

Fig. 43-3. Positioning a metal girder to support the floor joists. (Courtesy Aluminum Company of America.)

In Fig. 43-4, a girder is supported by adjustable jacks which are removed after a *load-bearing* wall has been constructed in their place.

Fig. 43-4. Adjustable jacks support the girder until permanent supports are installed.

After the sill plate and the girders have been installed to form solid supports, the *floor joists* are positioned. Floor joists (Fig. 43-5) are made from various sizes of strong lumber. In areas where base-

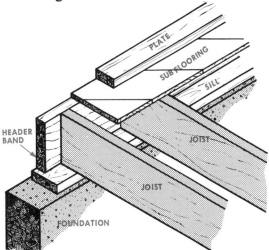

Fig. 43-5. Floor joists support the flooring.

ments are common, 2″ × 12″ lumber normally is used for the floor joists. The joists are spaced to comply with local building standards which usually require either 16 inches or 24 inches between centers. Carpenters designate this spacing as 16 inches *on centers* (abbreviated "O. C."). This means that the joists are placed with the center of one joist 16 inches from the center of the next joist. Basic units of 16 inches or 24 inches are used, since they are easy multiples of the standard 4-foot (48 inches) width of most decking and sheathing materials. These sizes eliminate costly cutting of materials; this also makes construction easier and quicker.

After the floor joists are placed, a side piece called a *header band* is nailed across the ends. This band provides a weather barrier for the ends of the joists and aids in keeping them spaced and aligned properly. To keep the floor joists spaced evenly, additional pieces are often used between the joists. A diagonal brace, or *bridging,* is used along with separate pieces of 24-inch thickness lumber between the joints (Fig. 43-6). The thicker lumber braces also serve as fire stops to prevent flames spreading between the floors.

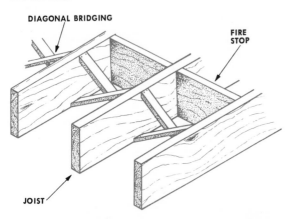

Fig. 43-6. Bridging prevents the joists twisting or bending out of their position.

After the floor joists have been placed and braced properly, the *subflooring* is installed over the joists (Fig. 43-7). The subflooring can be individual boards placed diagonally across the joists. This

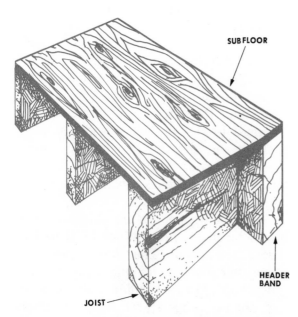

Fig. 43-7. Subflooring is laid over the joists. Either diagonal boards or plywood can be used.

type of subflooring is extremely strong, but the labor cost for this type of installation is quite expensive. The finish flooring is not installed until the walls are placed. Buildings constructed in recent years often have plywood subflooring which, because of its crossbanded construction, is extremely strong. Standard sections of plywood (4 ft × 8 ft) are nailed directly to the joists, without cutting or trimming. Although this appears to be less sturdy than solid wood, it should be remembered that plywood is stronger pound-for-pound than steel. Surprisingly, one layer of ¾-inch thickness plywood is as strong or stronger than the traditional diagonal flooring processes. Also, it is quicker and easier to install.

In many areas, building codes permit the use of subflooring without additional finished floor layers. The subfloor is merely carpeted or covered with vinyl linoleum tiles. This method is inexpensive, strong, and quite durable. Its chief disadvantage is that subflooring without additional decking does not provide the soundproofing effect for the floors beneath it; also, it can sag in later years.

Although hardwood is a high-quality finished flooring material, it is expensive —particularly when carpeting is to be used. For carpeted floors, a finished floor is often made from standard 4′ × 8′ sheets of particle board in thicknesses of ⅜ inch or more. This provides additional soundproofing and strength easily and quickly. In addition, the wide, flat surfaces provide smooth surfaces for carpeting.

Framing the Walls

Several methods are used for framing the walls. The pieces for each wall section can be cut individually and assembled on the construction site; they can be assembled at the building site from pieces cut at another place; or they can be built at a factory or lumberyard in sections, and then erected on the site. The basic construction, in all instances, is essentially the same (Fig. 43-8).

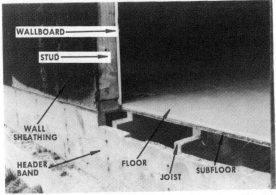

Fig. 43-8. Cutaway view at doorway of wall and floor section.

Some advantages of the preassembled sectional wall frames are that special equipment can be adjusted and set up at the factory to produce large quantities of materials cut to precisely the same length. This permits quicker assembly and construction time, and the waste of lumber is less than when each piece is hand-cut on the construction site. The use of pre-assembled units is discussed later.

Sectional walls also can be prebuilt and finished at the factory. They are shipped directly to the site as completed walls. The exterior wall siding, sheathing, and framing are assembled at the factory, and the building is assembled quickly on the subflooring.

The basic parts of a frame wall (Fig. 43-9) are the *sole plate, studs, headers,* and *top plates.* The sole plate is attached directly to the floor joists through the subflooring. The studs are the vertical braces for the wall and are attached to the sole plate. Usually, the studs are placed on 16-inch or 24-inch centers for use with the standard 4' × 8' materials. The studs are spaced by using fire blocks, which are

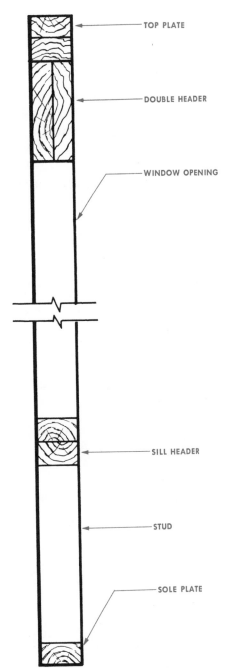

Fig. 43-9. Typical wall cross section.

normally staggered at different heights between studs. This makes them easier to nail to the studs. The fire blocks serve as barriers to prevent flames from a fire which might start in another part of the house from spreading through the hollow spaces between the floors and walls.

Another temporary method of bracing the wall section is to nail a diagonal piece across the corners to form a strong triangular section (Fig. 43-10). This triangular brace usually is removed before the sheathing is applied. Then the sheathing replaces the brace and supplies the necessary sturdiness. The wall studs are topped with one or two 2″ × 4″ pieces or top plates. The top plates form the support on which the roofing system is laid.

Fig. 43-10. Temporary diagonal braces hold the walls in place until the other walls are installed.

The windows and door sections are positioned in the walls before the exterior sheathing is applied. In the precut and preassembled units, the wall sections are made with the units framed out (Fig. 43-11). The windows and doors normally are not cut into the preassembled wall sections on the site; they are built into them at the factory.

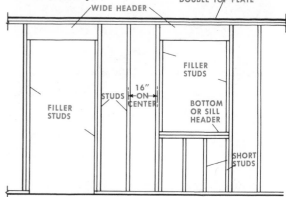

Fig. 43-11. Typical wall construction.

Window and Door Framing

Windows normally are made in a way that the preassembled window units (Fig. 43-12) can be inserted into a framed opening in the wall sections made specifically for the window. Many sizes and types of windows are available. The *double-hung* windows move up and down; the *sliding* windows move back and forth horizontally, and usually are made of steel or aluminum; and the *casement* windows normally are made of steel or aluminum with sliding or opening segments. The contractor normally uses preassembled window units, which are inserted into the framed opening. The opening is framed (see Fig. 43-11) with the sill plates on the top and bottom of the opening area. Shortened studs are used at the regular spacing to provide maximum support for the wall coverings.

The door units also are commonly sold with precut frames and trim work for

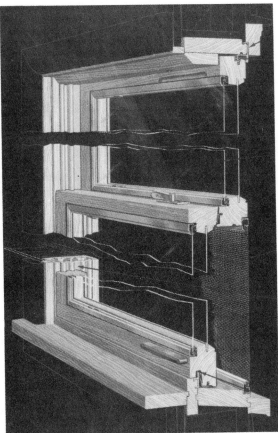

Fig. 43-12. Cross section of a preassembled double-hung window unit, including the exterior trim. (Courtesy Pella Rolscreen Company)

(A) Double headers on garage doors.

(B) Double header on an interior door.

easy installation. The door normally is framed out with a large header made of solid wood (Fig. 43-13). This header not only serves as a brace but also is the top anchor for the finished door frame and trim work. The door frame and window-units, like the doors in Fig. 43-13, normally are installed after the exterior sheathing is applied. Interior doors for the inside rooms are rarely installed before the inside walls have been finished.

Sheathing and Weatherproofing

The walls of most frame buildings are first covered with a composition material or *sheathing* to aid in forming insulation and weather barriers (Fig. 43-14). The composition sheathing is available in large

(C) Door unit including door, frame, and trim.

Fig. 43-13. Door framing.

(A) Sheathing strengthens and weatherproofs a building.

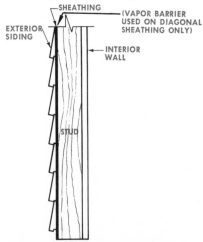

(B) Cross section of wall construction.
Fig. 43-14. Insulation and weatherproofing.

panels which are nailed directly onto the outside edges of the studs. The panels are treated to be moisture-resistant, are good insulator pieces, and also form a moisture

barrier to prevent the water or water vapor reaching the interior of the house. The sheathing panels also strengthen the house and prevent the wall sections from losing their alignment.

An older method of sheathing features diagonal wood or board sheathing similar to the diagonal subflooring. This layer of diagonal boards is stronger than normal composition sheathing; but the material costs, labor, waste, and installation costs are considerably more than for the composition sheathing. A separate moisture barrier also must be applied over the diagonal sheathing. The separate moisture barrier usually is composed of layers of waterproof paper.

Sheathing is applied to all the exterior walls of the house with the exception of the door and window units. It can be either nailed or stapled with special devices. Where the wall sections are pre-assembled at another location and brought to the site, the wall sheathing can be already installed.

Roof Construction

After the walls have been assembled and sheathed, the roof structure can be constructed. The building then is roofed, decked, and sealed to be weatherproof; the remainder of the operations inside the building can be completed, regardless of the weather.

Several types of roof construction are used. The most common types used in homes today are the gable roof, the hip or ranch roof, and the shed roof. Other common types of roofs include the mansard and the gambrel roof (Fig. 43-15). The gable roof and the hip roof are very popular, and they are among the most economical of the roof types.

The roof must slope at an angle for the water to run off. This angle is the *pitch*

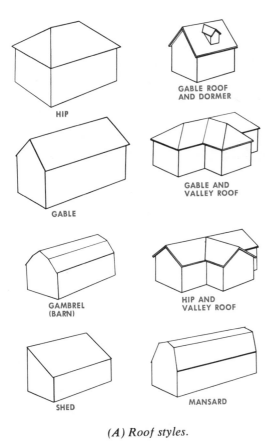

(A) Roof styles.

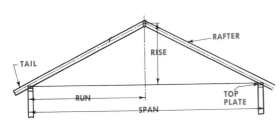

(B) Slope description (pitch).
Fig. 43-15. Roof construction.

Although the shed roof is the simplest type of roof to construct, a disadvantage is that insulation and air circulation space are more difficult to provide with the shed roof than with the other types. Air space between the roof and ceiling provides additional insulation which helps to keep the building warm in winter and cool in summer.

Most contractors now use preassembled roof trusses; therefore, the hip roof and gable roof (which are nearly identical) can be made easily from the standard factory-made roof trusses. The trusses are lifted into place and spaced, using lightweight stringers of 1-inch wood. When the decking and stripping of the roof is completed, the bracing stringers are removed. The roof trusses also are tied to the top plates of the wall sections, using steel straps, toenailing, and spacer boards. Most of the roofs today are decked solidly (Fig. 43-16), rather than stripped. The solid decking is easier to work with, and provides a footing for the workmen as they work on the remainder of the roof. Roof strips are used frequently, however, when wood shingles are to be used. The clay or terra-cotta roof tiles require stripped roofing.

and is described by the length of the *rise* for the distance the roof *runs* (Fig. 43-15B). Steep roofs are desirable in regions where heavy snows are common; this causes the snow to slide off the roof, and the roof is not required to support the weight of the snow. The high-pitched roofs also provide more insulating air space between the roof and the ceiling than the roofs with less slope.

Fig. 43-16. Solid roof decking installed over the rafters. (Courtesy Signode Corporation.)

After the roof is decked, *roofing felt* is used to make the roof waterproof. The first step is to lay down a moisture barrier, which is thick waterproof paper. The roofing felt is laid in long strips (Fig. 43-17), beginning with the bottom strip.

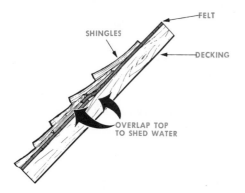

Fig. 43-17. Cross section of roof construction.

All roofing material is applied from the bottom upward. Then each top piece can overlap the piece below, permitting the water to run off the roof, rather than seep between the roof pieces and leak into the house.

After the roof deck has been covered with a felt, the installation of the final roofing material is begun. Composition shingles can be made from paper felt, impregnated with tar, and coated with gravel to prevent damage and scraping of the roof pieces. Wood shingles and asbestos shingles can be used, as well as tiles or other materials.

When a shed-type roof is used, many buildings are now made from a very thick fibrous panel which combines the insulation and decking material. This material is placed directly onto the roof supports, and a *built-up* roof is placed above the insulation. A built-up roof consists of successive layers of roofing felt, tar, and gravel. The gravel aids in protecting the tar and felt segments from being punctured by limbs, rocks, or other objects which might fall onto the roof. Nearly all

the flat roofs for stores, offices, and many homes are built in this manner, since shingles do not shed water well on low-pitched roofs. A built-up roof can be seen in Fig. 43-18.

Fig. 43-18. Cross section of a built-up roof used for a low-pitch roof.

This roofing material is especially economical in situations where exposed wood beams are used. The material is available with a textured ceiling surface on the bottom. This type of roof construction is discussed later in more detail.

Exterior Siding

After the wall sheathing and framing have been installed and the roof made weatherproof, the exterior siding is applied. Although board siding is traditional on frame houses, many other products are now available. Both aluminum and plastic are used, and they are weatherproof and resistant to rot and decay. Plywood panels also are used to provide the effects of the traditional wood siding. The panels provide the advantages of being quicker and easier to install and are often treated chemically to retard rot and decay and to repel insects such as termites.

Particle board and other wood by-products also are used to make the panels. Prefinished siding is available which is painted or provided with a natural wood finish at the factory. Composition or asbestos siding is available, and the frame house also can be veneered with brick or stone (Fig. 43-19). Different types of siding can be combined for a pleasing appearance or special weathering characteristics.

Fig. 43-19. Brick veneer combined with the traditional wood siding.

The appearance of the exterior of the house should provide both pride and satisfaction to the owner, as well as to provide shelter. The color is important, but the appearance of the sections also should lend decoration to the exterior (Fig. 43-20). Panels or siding can be made to run either vertically or horizontally. Special shapes can be provided either the vertical or horizontal siding pieces, permitting

Fig. 43-20. Painting the eaves with a long-handled roller.

them to retain their ability to drain water properly. Also, it is important that any procedure used for the exterior siding be windproof to prevent the wind seeping through cracks and crevices into the house.

Most of the siding is nailed onto the walls at the intervals of the wall studs. Where the masonry veneers (brick or stone) are used, the foundation is extended outward slightly to support the weight of the veneer; however, the bricks are laid up with a small air space between the sheathing and the barrier for vapor and the masonry veneer. To anchor the veneer to prevent its falling away from the side, small strips of steel are used at close intervals; those strips extend into the wet mortar of the bricks or stone as it is laid and are nailed or bolted to the wall studs (Fig. 43-21).

Brick and masonry are often used as siding for the frame homes. These sidings provide an appearance of a more solid substance, but they are, of course, more expensive. The expense of brick siding is greater, since the bricks cost more; and

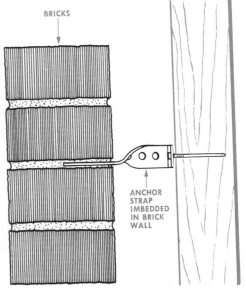

Fig. 43-21. Anchor straps provide space and hold the brick veneer to the frame wall.

the expense of laying each brick individually is much more than nailing on long boards or panels.

Installation of Utilities and Services

Temporary electrical service during construction is installed with the service head and meter connected as shown in Fig. 43-22. However, the electrical service must be connected permanently.

After the basic exterior weatherproofing of the structure is completed, work on the inside can continue without interruption from rain, snow, or high winds. The next procedure is to install the wiring, gas lines, heating and ventilating ducting, as well as the drains and water pipes, before the interior walls are closed.

The electrical wiring is distributed as desired from a service panel throughout

(B) Temporary service drop.

Fig. 43-22. Temporary electrical service for construction.

(A) Electricity is brought to the building site from service lines and transformers.

the house. For most frame buildings, a nonmetallic cable called *romex* is sufficient. This cable is run through holes drilled in the wall studs to the outlet boxes, switch boxes, and junction boxes (Figs. 43-23, 43-24, and 43-25). The electricians install the wiring, switches, outlets, and light fixtures after the wall and ceiling panels have been erected. Other utilities which can be installed include telephones, water softeners, laundry facilities, and special electrical considerations, such as well pumps, air conditioners, etc.

The pipes and drains are installed through the walls and between the floor joists in a manner similar to the electrical wiring (Figs. 43-26 and 43-27). Two

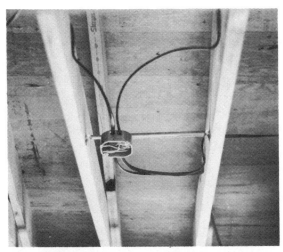

Fig. 43-23. Junction box positioned to support a ceiling light.

Fig. 43-24. Electric wires can be connected safely at a junction box.

Fig. 43-25. Switches and electric outlets are installled in an outlet box.

Fig. 43-26. Plastic drain pipes and copper water pipes are strapped to the floor joists.

Fig. 43-27. A drain pipe installed in a wall is hidden when the wall is covered.

basic types of metallic pipe systems are used for the plumbing and drains. Steel pipe is used, but it is not so highly recommended as the copper pipe, since water tends to rust the steel pipes in a few years, causing expensive repairs. Copper pipe, on the other hand, does not corrode nearly so quickly and can last as long as the house itself. Plastic pipe also is being used for the plumbing and drains. The plastic pipe, especially since the recent technical advances in plastics, has several advantages—it is lightweight, easily carried, and strong; does not corrode nor react with water or other chemicals normally used in the home; and is easily worked and shaped without special tools or heat.

Copper pipe must be soldered carefully. Steel pipe must be threaded and screwed together with sufficient pressure to make it waterproof. Plastic pipe is welded together merely by the application of special solvents which soften the plastic. The two pieces are coated with solvent and joined; as the plastic sets to a hardened state, it fuses both pieces together into a single watertight piece. Plastic is the quickest, cheapest, and easiest type of plumbing to install. It has two disadvantages—plastic pipe is not so strong as metal pipe and it is cut easily by sharp objects, including the teeth of rodents.

When installing drains, *traps* are necessary. The traps prevent the entry of air into the drainage pipes, insuring better drainage. Also, they help to prevent odors and germs from the sewers entering into the living areas. Cleanout plugs should be included in the drains; then if a stoppage occurs, the tools used to clean drains and pipes can be inserted easily. Cleanout plugs are installed between the trap and the drain; they can be unscrewed to provide easy access to the drainage systems (Fig. 43-28).

The drain systems also must be ventilated with long *vents* extending upward through the roof sections. The vents permit the air to escape as the water drains,

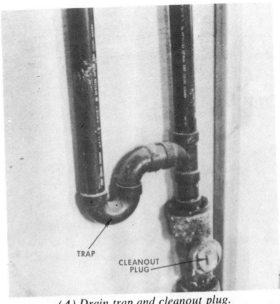

(A) Drain trap and cleanout plug.

(B) Ducting for heating and cooling.

(C) Insulation and heat duct.
Fig. 43-28. Plumbing and heating and ventilating ducts are installed before the interior walls are closed.

preventing the "gurgling" effect which often accompanies the emptying water.

Where the drain vents and chimneys extend through the roof, special pieces called *flashing* are used to make the area around these holes watertight. The flashing is applied in the same manner that the shingles are laid, with the top of the flashing resting underneath the top shingles and the lower portion of the flashing resting above the shingles below. In this manner, the water drains off the roof, rather than into the roof. Special flashing sleeves are available for most of the standard sizes of vents and drains. The sleeves are made of soft lead which easily can be cut, shaped, and fashioned to fit the roof slope and needs; also, they are easily nailed and fastened to the roof. Chimney flashing consisting of soft metal pieces which extend upward and around the chimney to prevent water seeping between the chimney and the roof is shown in Fig. 43-29.

Fig. 43-29. Flashing is installed between the chimney and the roof to prevent leaking at the chimney.

Insulation

Insulation has been mentioned several times. It is made from several substances which have certain qualities. The insulation must have a "dead" air space; this means that the air is trapped and cannot move within the substance. An insulation material should be noncombustible to prevent burning or aiding fires. Insulation should be installed easily. For this reason, it is available in three forms: (1) Solid sheets of foamy plastics or wood fibers treated to be fireproof; (2) *Blown* insulation, consisting of small individual pieces which can be blown into place with air pumps and hoses; and (3) *Rolled* insulation. In Fig. 43-30A, workmen are installing rolled insulation in widths that fit

(A) A workman cuts the rolls to length while a second workman staples the pieces in position.

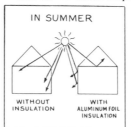

(B) Reflected heat make the house cooler in summer and warmer in winter.

Fig. 43-30. Insulation. (Courtesy Gypsum Association)

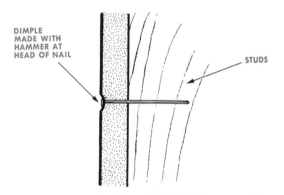

(A) Dimple formed by hammer.

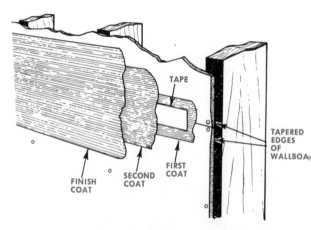

(B) Wallboard is nailed to the studs. (Courtesy Gypsum Association)

(C) Plastering and taping the corners of the wallboard.

(D) Wall after finish taping.
Fig. 43-31. Installing wallboard.

between the wall studs without cutting. Note the shiny, aluminized surface of the insulation. This makes the insulation more efficient by reflecting heat. The reflected heat makes the house cooler in summer and warmer in winter. The shiny side should be installed facing the interior (Fig. 43-30B).

Interior Walls and Ceilings

The interior walls and ceilings for the basic wooden buildings fall into three major categories — plaster, wallboard (sometimes called *Sheetrock* or drywall), and paneling. Plaster requires nailing lath strips across the inside of the stud sections. Wire mesh is then attached to the lath and the plaster is applied. Plaster, however, is not used extensively, since it is costly to install and difficult to repair. The modern substitute for plaster is wallboard. Wallboard is made from gypsum, which is a chalky substance. The gypsum is placed between two layers of heavy paper, making each board fairly strong and easy to handle. Wallboard is available in standard 4′ × 8′ sizes and is easily cut or punctured with a hammer, making installation extremely quick and economical. The wallboard must be trimmed slightly with plaster to hide the joints.

Wallboard is nailed to the studs; a slight dimple formed with the hammer around each nailhead enables the plaster to cover the nailhead. A paper tape is then placed over the joint with a mixture of plaster to cover the joint and nail holes (Fig. 43-31). When dry, this leaves a smooth, even "one-piece" effect which is easily painted for the final touches.

The third type of wall construction common today is the use of prefinished paneling. The paneling can be a wood product, such as those discussed earlier in Chapter 2; it can be thin plywood; or it can be a plastic material. The panels frequently are applied directly to the studs; but the better construction practices require the installation of wallboard and then the installation of the paneling. The paneling can be either nailed or glued to the wallboard. The development of new types of cements has made the gluing of paneling easier and quicker, in many instances, than nailing.

A special type of half-paneled effect also is used. This is called *wainscoting* and means that the top portion of the wall is plaster (or wallboard which looks like plaster) and the bottom portion is paneling—usually wood. Wainscoting has the advantage of placing a durable panel at the bottom to prevent scruffs, mars, and hand prints showing easily, but the top portion of the wall is painted in a lighter color for contrast, design, and reflection of light to provide the room with a spacious and airy effect. A room trimmed with the wainscot effect is shown in Fig. 43-32.

Fig. 43-32. Wainscot walls. The top portion is wallboard or plaster with wood paneling at the bottom of the wall.

Ceilings are installed in a manner similar to the walls. Plaster is commonly used and, when completed, it is normally provided with a texture (Fig. 43-33). Plaster ceilings are highly desirable in effect and appearance, but they are as expensive and costly to install as the plaster walls.

Wallboard, instead of plaster, is commonly used on ceilings—with much the same effect. When wallboard is used on the ceilings, it is often painted with a special paint, called texture paint. Texture paint is similar to plaster and provides the appearance of textured plaster. A third type of ceiling also is used; this is the suspended ceiling. The materials used in

Fig. 43-33. Plaster ceilings can be textured for a pleasing effect.

(A) Acoustical tile applied directly (Courtesy Conwed Corporation)

(B) Frame for a suspended ceiling.

suspended ceilings are called ceiling tiles or soundboard. Both materials are made from wood fiber products, but the acoustical ceiling tile has been textured to deaden sound.

A ceiling made from soundboard or ceiling tile can be either a suspended ceiling or applied directly. In Fig. 43-34A, the ceiling tiles are applied directly to the support units. The suspended ceiling is not applied directly to the support, but is installed by resting the ceiling on metal or wooden racks. The racks have been hung or suspended below the ceiling joists (see Fig. 43-34B.)

Installation of Doors and Windows

Doors and windows can be cut individually; however, that is a very expensive and time-consuming process. As mentioned previously, the most common method of installing doors and windows is

(C) Installing panels for a suspended ceiling.

Fig. 43-34. Installing ceiling tile.

by using preassembled units (Fig. 43-35). These units are installed in the rough framed opening and nailed into place. The door units are installed to include the door framing, hinges, doors, handles, and locks. In many instances, they are even painted and finished as desired. The door units are leveled by using thin tapered

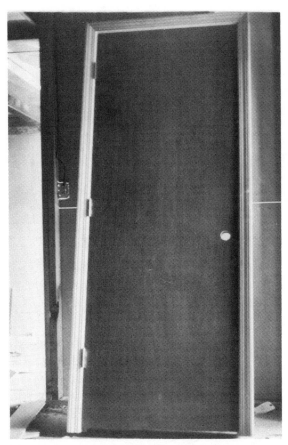

Fig. 43-35. Preassembled door unit immediately prior to installation. Note the complete jamb (finish frame), hinges, trim work, and precut hole for the latch and doorknob.

pieces of wood, such as shingle, to *shim* the finished door frame to make the door hang straight and square.

The doors and windows are available in two basic types—*interior* and *exterior*. Interior windows are rarely used, except for special decoration effects. The exterior doors, however, are built to withstand heat and moisture. Interior doors are not weatherproof. The doors can be either finished or unfinished and purchased separately to fit special openings. Special installation devices are available for use with sliding doors and folding doors. After the door is installed, the edges of the opening remain visible. These edges are covered later with trim work.

Trim Work

Trim work is used to mask the edges of the window and door openings to improve appearance. *Trim* is made from special lumber planed to certain shapes. This lumber is called *millwork*. Examples of interior and exterior trim are shown in Figs. 43-36 and 43-37. The trim not only

(A) "Casement" trim for an interior door frame.

(B) Door trim includes casement and stop pieces.
Fig. 43-36. Interior trim work.

(A) Exterior trim improves the "weathertight" quality of the house and adds beauty.

(B) Some trim work is applied after the opening is framed and the exterior siding is applied.

(C) "Ready-built" window units installed complete with trim before siding is applied.

(D) The flanges on aluminum units cover the edges of the opening.

Fig. 43-37. Trim work.

beautifies by hiding the rough edges of the opening but also increases the weather resistance of the door or window by closing the small gaps through which wind and moisture enter (Fig. 43-38).

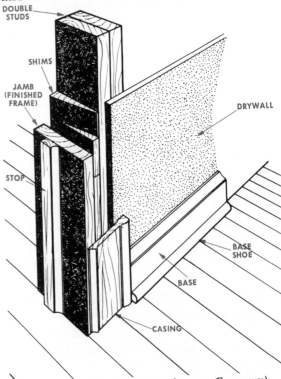

(A) Door. (Courtesy Weyerhaeuser Company)

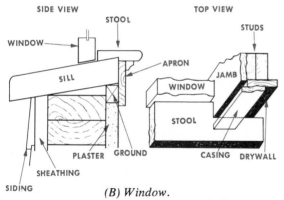

(B) Window.

Fig. 43-38. Typical interior door and window framing and trim.

The trim also is applied to floors and ceilings to hide the edges of the materials, to mask uneven panels, and to cover small irregularities at the joints. Trim is used to form weather blocks for windows and for a "stop" to prevent the doors swinging too far when they are being shut. Places where trim is commonly used are shown in Fig. 43-39; several common trim

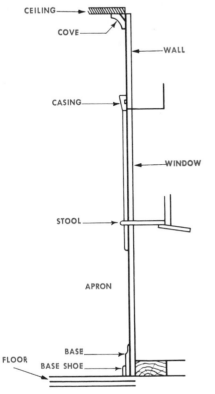

Fig. 43-39. Places where trim is commonly used.

shapes are shown in Fig. 43-40. Trim or millwork is available in several types of

Fig. 43-40. Types of trim (millwork).

wood and in metal and plastic shapes for use with laminated plastic paneling.

When preassembled door or window units are used, they are often finished before the walls are painted. However, the chief factor in determining whether the trim or walls is to be finished first depends on which is easier to remove from the other. Carpeting can be installed after the trim work is completed (Fig. 43-41).

Fig. 43-41. Workman installing carpeting after the finished trim work, painting, and doors are installed.

Activities

1. Using the wall section in Fig. 43-42, draw plans for a small (2' wide × 4' high) wall and roof model to include:
   1 ceiling light
   1 light switch
   1 electrical wall outlet
   1 exterior water faucet
   1 window unit
2. Draw specifications for the materials needed for:
   wall studs, rafters, sole plates, etc.

floor and ceiling joists
sheathing
exterior siding
roofing material
subflooring
flooring
interior walls (construction material and finish)
window unit
type of water pipe
roof pitch
electrical wiring, outlets, and fixtures
trim work
types of nails

3. On a suitable foundation, construct a wall section following the previously determined specifications.

Questions

1. List the advantages of wood in constructing buildings.
2. List the major construction steps in building a frame house.
3. Draw a diagram of a wall cross section. Label the parts.
4. What does "O. C." mean?
5. Why are "standard" sizes economical?
6. What is sheathing?
7. What is siding?
8. On which side (outside or inside) should the shiny side of aluminized insulation be installed?
9. What is a "fire stop"?
10. Which part of a roof is installed first, the top or bottom?
11. Sketch three roof styles.
12. Can a frame house be built with brick walls?
13. What is the purpose of insulation?
14. List the advantages of plastic plumbing.
15. What is "flashing"?
16. What is "dry wall"?
17. What is "trim"?

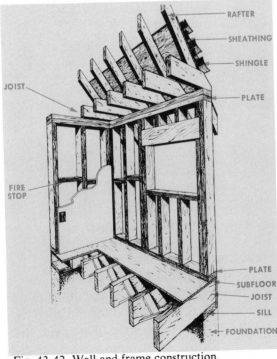

Fig. 43-42. Wall and frame construction.

Unit 44 – Trends in Building Construction

A number of factors are important in the required development of new building methods and building materials. The population in this country and in the world is increasing rapidly. With this increase in population, the costs of labor and materials also are increasing. In the face of these increasing populations and increasing costs, people with lower incomes are able to buy less; yet, their needs are increasing, and they have difficulty in finding housing within their income ranges. "The rich get richer and the poor get poorer," is sometimes appropriate in the face of rising costs. New methods and techniques must be developed to enable buildings to be constructed at a low cost for people with lower incomes to be able to purchase adequate housing. Several factors can be important in these developments: (1) Research is important to develop new products and test them to make sure of their quality and durability;

(B) One man could lift this wall safely.

(C) Wall is held erect firmly by safety stop—5 minutes elapsed time.
Fig. 44-1. Special jacks and devices are used to raise and position an entire wall section. (Courtesy Proctor Products Company)

and (2) New techniques in constructing and assembling these new products must be developed (Fig. 44-1).

The construction time for a typical one-family frame home is approximately six weeks. The costs of building this type of home are considerable when con-

(A) Jacks are in position against the top plate.

structed with typical "on-site" methods. Several things can be done to speed construction time and, therefore, decrease the cost of the labor involved. This is, of course, considerable savings to the consumer. The use of faster construction methods saves on labor; also, the use of new multipurpose materials reduces the cost of materials.

New Building Methods

Several new developments in construction have decreased the construction time, thereby reducing the overall labor costs. Typical of these developments are the use of special jacks and devices to raise and position wall sections (see Fig. 44-1). One or two men now can accomplish as much work as six or seven men could accomplish only a few years ago. Construction methods which require large numbers of men at certain times is wasteful of manpower and, therefore, increases the expense. An entire wall now can be raised with special holding devices. To align and position these large wall sections, much force is needed; this must be provided either through mechanical advantage, such as levers, or through using large numbers of men. A small mechanical device can provide the mechanical advantage necessary for only one man to apply the force (Fig. 44-2).

(A) Straightens and holds the sill plate for nailing.

(B) Pulls partitions together for nailing.
Fig. 44-2. A "Little Pee-Vee" provides the mechanical advantage, requiring only one man to apply the force. (Courtesy Proctor Products Company)

Other developments include special devices for driving nails or staples. If the construction process can remain the same with only the time required for assembly reduced, labor costs are reduced to result in substantial savings. With a special tool, such as the gun-type nailer (Fig. 44-3), a carpenter can drive nails merely by pulling the trigger to drive the nail in one quick motion. One man can load and drive the nails much quicker and easier at several times the rate that a carpenter can reach into a sack for each nail and then drive it with several strokes of a hammer. An automatic gun-type nailer that uses car-

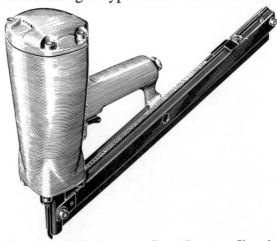

Fig. 44-3. Paslode gun nailer. (Courtesy Signode Steel Strapping Company)

tridge-belt nail packs is shown in Fig. 44-4. The nail packs load into the machine and are fed through the driving mechanism of the nailer. Both these nailers are

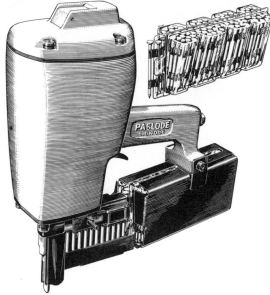

Fig. 44-4. Special nail packages speed loading of the gun nailer. (Courtesy Signode Corporation)

operated by compressed air. In Figs. 44-5 through 44-7, gun nailers are being used to assemble wall studs, to make girders from $2'' \times 12''$ lumber, and for on-site construction of wall stud sections to be raised into position later.

Fig. 44-6. Using a gun nailer to make a girder from smaller pieces. (Courtesy Signode Corporation)

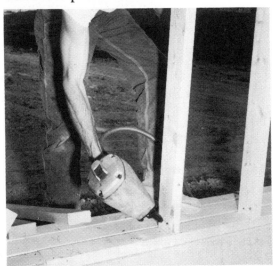

Fig. 44-5. Toenailing a stud to the sill plate with a gun nailer. (Courtesy Signode Corporation)

Fig. 44-7. Assembling wall sections with a gun nailer. (Courtesy Signode Corporation)

Another development in the construction of wood frame-type buildings is the use of aluminum and metal frames (Fig. 44-8). Aluminum frames are lightweight,

Fig. 44-8. This subflooring is screwed to aluminum floor joists. (Courtesy Aluminum Company of America)

sturdy, and quickly assembled (Fig. 44-9). Also, they can be nailed; the common construction materials can be applied over

Fig. 44-9. Erecting an aluminum frame wall section without jacks or heavy equipment. (Courtesy Aluminum Company of America)

the aluminum framework in the same manner that the materials are applied over a wood framework (Fig. 44-10). This

Fig. 44-10. Aluminum frame for a house made with wood. (Courtesy Aluminum Company of America)

means that no special materials or metal-working tools are required for finishing and constructing the house. The aluminum frames are precut and preformed at the factory; then they can be assembled quickly with screws and bolts. The electrical and plumbing installations can be made quickly and easily, since it is not necessary to drill holes for the passage of conduit, electrical wiring, or plumbing pipes (Fig. 44-11). The holes and spaces

Fig. 44-11. Pipes, plumbing, and wiring require no drilling in aluminum studs. (Courtesy Aluminum Company of America)

already exist in the metal frames. Thus, easy construction and quick assembly through technical innovations reduce the overall costs substantially.

Ready-Built Housing

A recent development is the so-called "ready-built" housing unit. These houses are not constructed—they are manufactured. They are built on production lines in the same manner that an automobile or a kitchen cabinet is produced. The chief advantage of the manufacturing process is that large numbers of units can be produced; there is no time lost by the workmen in moving from one building site to another; workmen are not required to carry new materials to their work site; individual cuts and measurements are not required, since all the parts are cut on special measuring jigs and fixtures; and there is no lost time from movement of materials or workers. All the various sections of the house, including the walls, floors, roofs, ceilings, and even the plumbing and electrical installation, are completed in the factory (Fig. 44-12 through 44-17).

Fig. 44-13. The interior walls are installed while other workers install the wiring and plumbing. (Courtesy National Homes Corporation)

Fig. 44-12. The assembly line for these houses begins with the wall section. (Courtesy National Homes Corporation)

Fig. 44-14. Worker installing the plumbing while the interior wall is being placed. (Courtesy National Homes Corporation)

Fig. 44-15. The interior walls can be painted or paneled, as desired. (Courtesy National Homes Corporation)

Fig. 44-16. Worker touching up the finished exterior siding. (Courtesy National Homes Corporation)

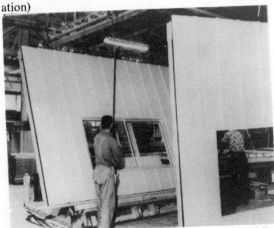

Fig. 44-17. The window units are installed while on the assembly line. (Courtesy National Homes Corporation)

Note in Fig. 44-18 that the wall sections are quickly and easily moved into storage position and can be transported quickly to a building site. Instead of re-

Fig. 44-18. Finished wall sections are moved by conveyor to the storage areas. (Courtesy National Homes Corporation)

quiring large numbers of construction workers, only a small number of workers is needed to assemble the home (Fig. 44-19).

Fig. 44-19. Wall sections are assembled quickly on the site with a crane. (Courtesy National Homes Corporation)

Two processes are used in making "ready-built" housing (Fig. 44-20). The first process features on-site assembly of the individual wall sections. The second process also begins with the preparation

Fig. 44-20. The entire finished home was built at the factory. (Courtesy National Homes Corporation)

of a basement or foundation as does the first (Fig. 44-21). In the second method, the walls are *assembled* into room-like segments at the factory. The preassembled house module is then shipped to the site

Fig. 44-21. On-site preparation for a factory-built home. (Courtesy Kingsberry Homes, Boise Cascade Corporation)

on trucks (Fig. 44-22). The building segments are then positioned, as shown in Figs. 44-23, 44-24, and 44-25. Several segments can be combined for a larger building.

The workers position and combine the "boxes" as desired. The building is completed with the necessary roofing, decking,

and interior work (Figs. 44-26 and 44-27).

Fig. 44-22. The assembled house sections are trucked to the building site. (Courtesy Kingsberry Homes, Boise Cascade Corporation)

Fig. 44-23. The preassembled sections are positioned on the foundation. (Courtesy Kingsberry Homes, Boise Cascade Corporation)

Fig. 44-24. Sections are added to make larger buildings. (Courtesy Kingsberry Homes, Boise Cascade Corporation)

Modular Construction

Modular construction is a term applied to the small, completed buildings made

Fig. 44-25. These sections are in place and joined together. (Courtesy Kingsberry Homes, Boise Cascade Corporation)

Fig. 44-27. The roof decking is nailed onto the roof trusses. (Courtesy Kingsberry Homes, Boise Cascade Corporation)

at a factory site and transported to the construction site, where they are merely connected together to provide the larger building. Modular construction differs from "manufactured" housing in that the modules are complete with interior and utility details. The modular units permit more flexibility, provide all the advantages of mass-produced goods, and can be used on buildings of nearly any size.

Fig. 44-26. Preassembled roof trusses are used on the house sections. (Courtesy Kingsberry Homes, Boise Cascade Corporation)

Fig. 44-28. This building module can be used either separately or as an addition to a building. (Courtesy Intramodular Structures, Inc.

As shown in Figs. 44-28 and 44-29, this method is applied to construction of a small building. A smaller unit can be used for a small building, as shown in Fig. 44-28. The same module also can be used for an addition to a building (see Fig. 44-29).

The modular technique has been used successfully on construction of large apartment-type dwelling units and hospi-

Fig. 44-29. Modular addition to a building. (Courtesy Intermodular Structures, Inc.)

tals, hotels, and other buildings. The modernistic apartment dwelling displayed in Montreal, Canada at Expo-67 is an example of modular construction.

In addition, modular techniques can be used on the exterior and on the interior of buildings. Mass-produced kitchens (Fig. 44-30) and bathrooms (Fig. 44-31) are combined and preassembled to interior wall units. During the construction process, these preassembled kitchen and bathroom modules are often positioned before the exterior pieces (Fig. 44-32). These units are very adaptable, striking in appearance, and quite functional. The service units can be installed either on-site or factory-built into the entire unit.

Fig. 44-32. Placing modular wall units. (Courtesy Republic Steel Corporation)

Preassembled doors, windows, roof trusses, kitchen cabinets, and other parts are available. Kitchens made with preassembled pieces are shown in Figs. 44-33 and 44-34.

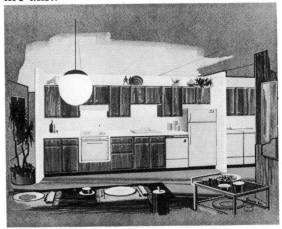

Fig. 44-30. Modular kitchen and laundry system. (Courtesy Republic Steel Corporation)

Fig. 44-31. Modular bathroom system. (Courtesy Republic Steel Corporation)

Even when modular techniques are not used, construction time can be reduced measurably by using preassembled pieces.

Fig. 44-33. Inexpensive ready-built kitchen cabinet system. (Courtesy Formica Corporation)

Fig. 44-34. Custom-made kitchen using ready-built units. (Courtesy Formica Corporation)

Preassembled roof trusses, as mentioned previously, provide several advantages for the builder. The trusses can be used on modular and factory-built buildings, as well as on buildings made on the building site. These pieces are available in a variety of sizes and in a variety of roof styles.

These features are combined with lower construction cost to provide a distinct advantage for the builder. The trusses can be made on the site, but this requires carpenters to cut and measure each board individually. By utilizing special equipment to make the cuts (Fig. 44-35), individual measurements and material handling are eliminated.

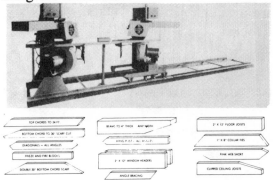

Fig. 44-35. Only one operator is required to make a variety of cuts on this automatic saw. (Courtesy Idaco Engineering & Equipment Co.)

The cut pieces are placed in position on special hydraulic presses (Fig. 44-36). Metal pieces called *gussets* are used to "nail" the various pieces together into the completed truss. The hydraulic presses simultaneously force all the gussets into place. Two workers are using this type of machine to assemble the trusses from previously cut parts in Fig. 44-37. Note the precut pieces in front of the machine and the stack of completed trusses behind the machine.

Three men—one man to operate the saw and two men to operate the assembler—can assemble seventy-five to one

Fig. 44-36. Hydraulic presses or assemblers join the roof trusses in one operation. All the gussets are attached simoultaneously. (Courtesy Idaco Engineering & Equipment Co.)

Fig. 44-37. Workers can assemble the roof trusses quickly with the assembler. (Courtesy Idaco Engineering & Equipment Co.)

hundred trusses per day. This high rate of production reduces labor costs considerably.

Wood and Construction of Larger Buildings

Wood products also are used in the construction of large buildings. The typical construction process used in building a small home cannot be used effectively in constructing large buildings. Developments since 1945 have included the development of wood products, such as hardboard, chipboard, and laminated girders. The wood girders can be used to span long distances, maintain the natural beauty of the wood, and can be adapted easily to large-scale commercial building processes. The use of laminated beams has permitted the use of wood in large buildings, such as gymnasiums (Figs. 44-38 and 44-39). The mass production of laminated timber structures has resulted in reduced cost; therefore, these beams are used on the more common structures and buildings, such as barns, sheds, warehouses, and even in factories (Fig. 44-40). The natural beauty of wood is still desirable; therefore, wood is used in some places to enhance the appearance, as in the church under construction in Fig. 44-41.

Fig. 44-40. Wood-beam construction is used in factory buildings. (Courtesy Timber Structures, Inc.)

Fig. 44-41. The laminated wood beams in this church combine excellent design, natural wood beauty, and strength. (Courtesy Timber Structures, Inc.)

Fig. 44-38. Laminated wood beams can span great distances. (Courtesy Timber Structures, Inc.)

Fig. 44-39. Laminated wood beams add beauty as well as strength. (Courtesy Timber Structures, Inc.)

Wood structural units are made to a specified size from the specifications of the architect and contractor at the factory, thereby eliminating waste, error through improper measurements, and la-

bor costs from cutting, sizing, and joining each piece. The individual pieces are prepared at the factories, wrapped to protect them from weather and from scratching and marring during shipment, and shipped directly to the builder. The builder places them in position without removing the paper wrapping. The paper wrapping (Fig. 44-42) remains in place until the building is nearly completed inside and out. The wrapping paper protects the building pieces from marring and damage during the construction process. Buildings made from the precut pieces are assembled easily, require less construction time, and thereby reduce the costs to the consumer.

Fig. 44-42. Wood beams are protected by treated wrapping paper during construction. (Courtesy Timber Structures, Inc.)

Another wood product used on large-scale commercial buildings is shown in Fig. 44-43. This material combines insulation and roof decking into a single product. Since it is easily worked and installed, its construction cost is low. Similar products are now used for both interior and exterior walls.

(A) Combine roof decking and insulation.

(B) Exterior siding on commercial buildings.
Fig. 44-43. Wood fiber products are used in both the interior and exterior of buildings. (Courtesy Gypsum Association)

Activities

1. Visit a construction site. Make a list of the new products and methods seen.
2. Review Units 4 and 5. List the products used in building construction.

Questions

1. List the advantages of mass-produced housing.
2. Name the two construction methods used for factory-built houses. How do they differ?
3. Describe a "modular" building.
4. How is a modular building different from a factory-built building?
5. How can wood be used in the construction of a large building?
6. How important are technical developments in improving quality or in reducing costs?

IDEAS FOR DESIGN PROJECTS

The project ideas are presented here to challenge the student by presenting problem-solving situations. The situations can range from simple, quick projects to more complex and difficult operations.

The students are encouraged to use their creative abilities to modify these projects and to apply their technical knowledge to the details of construction.

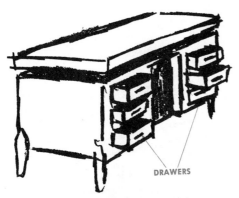

Walnut Desk (Solid or Veneer)

Double Picture Frames
(Shaped on a Drill Press)

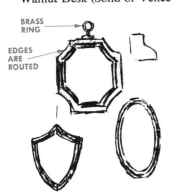

Antiquated Wall Decoration

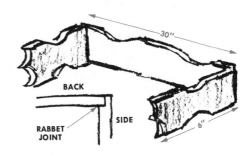

Alternate Designs

Cutting Board

Bow or Gun Rack

Table and Bar Stool

Salt Shaker and Pepper Mill

Stereo Cabinet

Table (Cane for Contrast)

DOWELS

RUBBER WEBBING

BRACE

BUCKET SEAT IS RE-
MOVABLE, COFFEE TA-
BLE ELEMENT IS MOV-
ABLE

CUSHIONS OF 2" FOAM

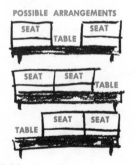

POSSIBLE ARRANGEMENTS

SEAT TABLE SEAT

SEAT SEAT TABLE

TABLE SEAT SEAT

Combination Seat and Coffee Table

Section IX

Upholstery

In furniture design, the appearance or "customer appeal" is a primary consideration. The covering of upholstered furniture should be attractive in design, color, and texture, and it should provide serviceability.

Furniture and automobile upholstery represent a large portion of industry, and provide fine opportunities for careers. Most consumers probably will select three or more sets of upholstered furniture in their lifetime, and will choose from several automobile upholstery fabrics.

The knowledge of simple upholstery methods can be the basis for an understanding of furniture design and fabrics. These simple experiences with upholstery can be extremely rewarding when one becomes a user and purchaser of upholstered furniture and automobile upholstered accessories.

Upholstery can be quite complicated; however, the beginner can practice several simple types of upholstery. These can be classified as:

1. Overstuffed seat and back.
2. Springs (tied or tight-spring).
3. Padded (or slip) seat and back.
4. Zigzag or no-sag wire springs in seats and backs.
5. Webbing.

The overstuffed, springs, and padded-seat upholstery have been practiced for many years; however, the more modern no-sag springs with foam rubber or rubberized hair is a relatively new procedure, and is being used more and more in automotive upholstery and in furniture.

Unit 45 – Upholstery Tools and Equipment

Certain tools and equipment have been designed for upholstering and the construction (or repair) of the frames of furniture. Various other tools and equipment are useful in both upholstering and woodworking.

Hammers

Professional upholsterers use a *magnetic upholstering hammer* (Fig. 45-1) for numerous tacking jobs in upholstering. Therefore, the hammer should be lightweight, without a wide or broad head. The hammer usually ranges between 6 and 9 ounces with an 11- to 12-inch handle and a curved 5½-inch head.

Hickory is used for the best wood handles.

The surface diameter of the hammerhead used for tacking is approximately ½ inch. The opposite end is smaller ($\frac{5}{16}$ inch in diameter), is usually split and magnetized. The smaller end is used to hold and start small tacks. Attempting to work without this convenient upholstering tool can be quite frustrating. The stapling guns (both manual and automatic) are gaining in popularity for some tacking operations, both temporary and permanent (Fig. 45-2). The automatic staplers, air and elec-

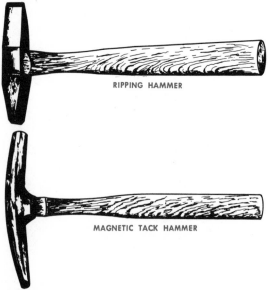

RIPPING HAMMER

MAGNETIC TACK HAMMER

Fig. 45-1. Upholstering hammers. (Courtesy C. S. Osborne & Co.)

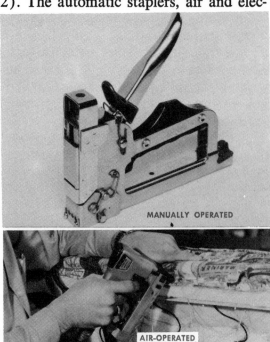

MANUALLY OPERATED

AIR-OPERATED

Fig. 45-2. Typical stapling guns. (Courtesy Fastener Corp.)

trically operated, are made for high-volume work.

Upholstering Shears

The *upholstering shears* should be strong enough to cut heavy or coarse materials; consequently, shears 10 to 12 inches in length are desirable to provide a cutting edge of about 7 inches. Shears with a bent handle are more satisfactory, since they do not raise and distort the fabric during a cutting operation (Fig. 45-3).

(A) Inlaid blades—tailors' enameled handles.

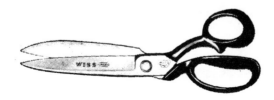

(B) Raised blade—heavy duty.
Fig. 45-3. Upholstering shears. (Courtesy C. S. Osborne & Co.)

Webbing Stretchers

A *webbing stretcher* is a hard block of wood shaped for grasping in the center by the upholsterer (Fig. 45-4). The end which rests against the frame usually is padded with rubber to prevent damage to the wood surface and to prevent slippage when the webbing is pulled taut. Steel points on the opposite end of the webbing stretcher pierce the webbing (Fig. 45-5).

PLAIN END

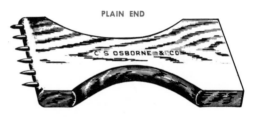

RUBBER END

NONSKID

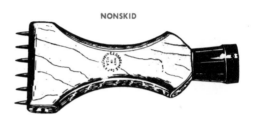

Fig. 45-4. Webbing stretchers. (Courtesy C. S. Osborne & Co.)

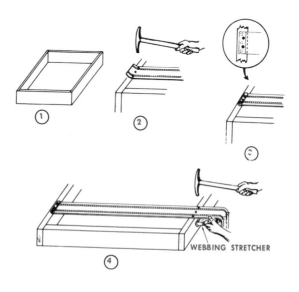

Fig. 45-5. Steps in using the webbing stretcher.

Steel webbing stretchers are used when steel webbing, or steel bands, are part of the construction (Fig. 45-6).

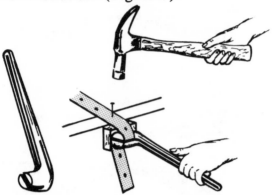

Fig. 45-6. Using the steel webbing stretcher. (Courtesy C. S. Osborne & Co.)

Pliers in Upholstering

Webbing pliers (Fig. 45-7) are designed to grasp the material between wide, grooved jaws. A knob beneath the jaws provides greater pulling pressure when used as a fulcrum. Some protection, such as a wooden block, is advisable to protect the wood surface of the frame. However, the *webbing stretchers* are prefer-

Fig. 45-7. Webbing (or leather) stretcher pliers.

able to webbing pliers, since the stretchers are less limited in their use. The pliers are more suitable for working with the shorter lengths of webbing for prestretching webbing that has come loose, and for stretching leather.

A number of other pliers are designed for specific operations in upholstering. The *spring-clip pliers* (Fig. 45-8) are designed specifically for setting spring or edge wire clips. The *hog-ring pliers* (see Fig. 45-8) are used to set the standard

hog-ring clips (upholstery fasteners which resemble hog rings). The *nail pliers* (see Fig. 45-8) are available for removing upholstery tacks and nails.

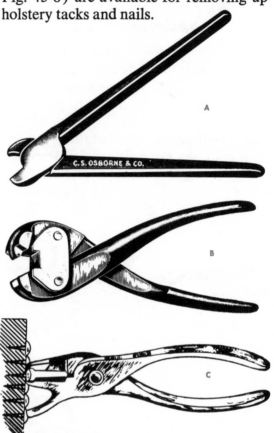

Fig. 45-8. Hog-ring (A), spring-clip (B), and nail-removal (C) pliers. (Courtesy C. S. Osborne & Co.)

The *ripping tool* and *claw tool* (Fig. 45-9) are not pliers, but they are used to perform similar functions. They can be used to remove upholstery tacks when replacing old covers. The chief distinguishing feature is that the claw tool is provided with a notch for gripping the tack.

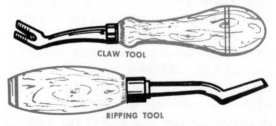

Fig. 45-9. Claw and ripping tools. (Courtesy C. S. Osborne & Co.)

This notch is not provided on the ripping tool. The beginning upholsterer often prefers the claw tool, since the notched blade grips the tack. However, as experience improves, this proves to be a disadvantage, since a tack tends to stick in the notch, thereby reducing the efficiency of the removal operation. Most experienced upholsterers prefer the ripping tool. A combination tool has been developed to combine both the ripping and tack-pulling functions into a single tool.

Mallets

A *rubber mallet* (either 16 or 32 ounces) is recommended for driving the ripping tool (or claw tool) when stripping fabric from the frame (Fig. 45-10). Mallets made of rolled rawhide also are available. Both rubber and rolled-rawhide mallets are helpful in avoiding a scarred wood surface.

Fig. 45-10. Rubber mallet.

Upholstering Needles

Several types of needles are used in upholstering. Each type is designed for a specific function. The three basic types of needles are the straight, curved, and packing needles.

The *straight needles* (Fig. 45-11) range from 4 to 20 inches in length, and are either single- or double-pointed. The double-pointed needles are preferable, since they can be pushed back through the material without the need for reversing the needle.

The *curved needles* (Fig. 45-12) can be purchased 2 to 10 inches in length (a circumference measurement) and in ex-

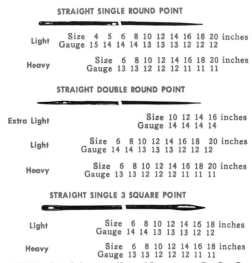

Fig. 45-11. Straight needles. (Courtesy C. S. Osborne & Co.)

tra-lightweight, lightweight, and heavyweight needles. The lightweight curved needle is preferable for the thinner cover fabrics. The curved needle is advantageous in that the upholsterer is not required to reach behind the work to push the needle through—as with a straight needle. The curved needles are available in either round or triangular points.

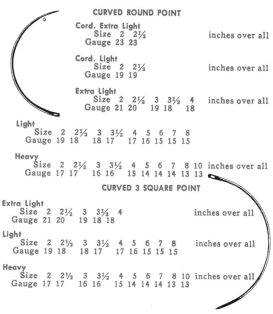

Fig. 45-12. Curved needles. (Courtesy C. S. Osborne & Co.)

The *packing needles* (Fig. 45-13) are used in sewing upholstery material that requires a needle heavier in gauge than the heaviest gauges of straight or curved needles. The packing needle is characterized by a thicker shaft near the point. These needles range from 3 to 10 inches in length, and can be purchased with either a bent shaft or a straight shaft.

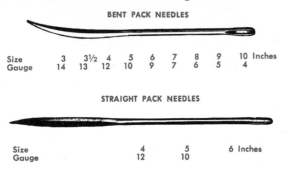

BENT PACK NEEDLES

Size	3	3½	4	5	6	7	8	9	10 Inches
Gauge	14	13	12	10	9	7	6	5	4

STRAIGHT PACK NEEDLES

Size	4	5	6 Inches
Gauge	12	10	

Fig. 45-13. Packing (pack) needles. (Courtesy C. S. Osborne & Co.)

Tufting tools can be used to simplify the tufting process. One type of tool eliminates the use of twine (Fig. 45-14). A pronged tufting button is inserted in a hollow needle. The needle pierces the material; then it is removed. A special washer is placed on the prongs which are,

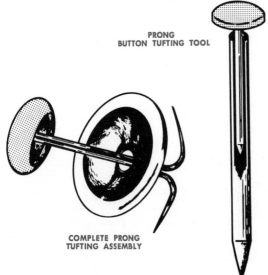

PRONG
BUTTON TUFTING TOOL

COMPLETE PRONG
TUFTING ASSEMBLY

Fig. 45-14. Tufting without twine. (Courtesy Handy Button Machine Co.)

in turn, bent to secure the button. Tufting needles, used with twine, also are available for the tufting process.

Stuffing Regulators

A stuffing regulator is used to remove irregularities in the stuffing materials—a process best performed beneath a sublayer muslin cover. The *stuffing regulators* (Fig. 45-15) are similar in appearance to upholsterers' needles, but they are constructed from a heavier gauge of steel. Their length ranges from 6 to 12 inches. A stuffing regulator is used only when working on the interior of a piece of furniture, since its larger size leaves an unsightly puncture hole in the cover fabric.

UPHOLSTERERS' REGULATOR WITH EYE

Length	6	8	10	12 Inches
Light	9	9	8	7 Gauge
Heavy	6	5	5	5 Gauge
Extra Light	11	10	10	Gauge

Fig. 45-15. Stuffing regulator. (Courtesy C. S. Osborne & Co.)

Stuffing Rod

A *stuffing rod* (or stuffing iron) is a length of steel (usually about 18 inches) used for pushing the stuffing into difficult-to-reach corners. A toothed edge on one end of the rod aids in gripping the stuffing (Fig. 45-16).

Fig. 45-16. Stuffing iron.

Upholsterers' Pin (Skewer)

The *upholsterers' pin* (or skewer) is a short length of steel wire used for positioning the stuffing before the tacking or sewing operations. Usually, the pin is about 3 or 4 inches in length and is pointed on one end. A loop on the opposite end is used for grasping the pin (Fig. 45-17).

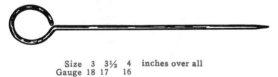

Size   3   3½   4   inches over all
Gauge   18   17   16

Fig. 45-17. Upholsterers' pin. (Courtesy C. S. Osborne & Co.)

Cushion Iron

The *cushion irons* (Fig. 45-18) are used in pairs to compress a cushion, which eases the application of the final cover.

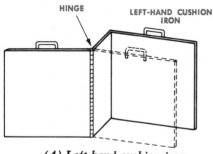

(A) Left-hand cushion iron.

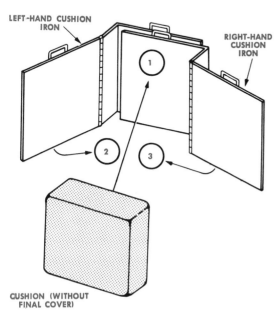

(B) Nesting cushion irons and cushion. Perform in sequence.

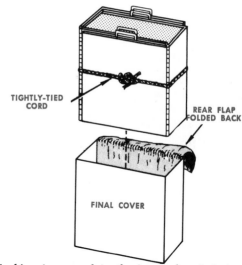

(C) Cushion is secured in the irons; then it is inserted into the final cover.

Fig. 45-18. Cushion irons and their use.

Before applying the final cover, the cushion irons are placed over the opposite sides of the cushion stuffing and pulled together tightly with a piece of cord. After the covering has been installed on the cushion, the cushion irons are removed. The cushion irons are far less expensive than the cushion-filling machines found in the professional upholstery shops. Cushion irons can be purchased (see Fig. 45-18); or homemade cushion irons can be constructed from corrugated cardboard (Fig. 45-19).

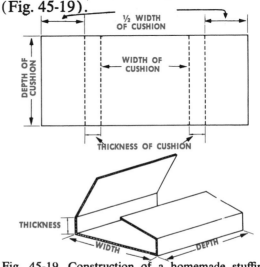

Fig. 45-19. Construction of a homemade stuffing box.

Other Equipment

A heavy-duty *sewing machine* is another piece of equipment that makes upholstering easier. A sewing machine found in most homes is not rugged enough for many of the heavier fabrics used in upholstering.

The *trestles* used by upholsterers essentially are benches with padded tops which are used to elevate a piece of furniture to a convenient height for the upholsterer to be comfortable while working. Trestles normally are used in pairs, and closely resemble a carpenter's sawhorse.

Another convenient piece of equipment is the *cutting table,* which is quite useful in laying out and cutting the fabric. A cutting table can be constructed inexpensively from two-by-fours and ¾-inch plywood.

A *button-covering machine* (Fig. 45-20) is a valuable piece of equipment for production or semiproduction upholstering. These machines are manufactured for both hand operation and power (electric and air) operation.

In addition to the tools mentioned, the various types of saws, planes, drills, etc. usually utilized in woodworking for furni- by the upholsterer in his trade. Excellent upholstery can be performed with a relatively small number of tools. However, the upholsterer, depending on the volume

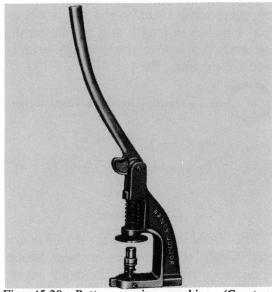

Fig. 45-20. Button-covering machine. (Courtesy Handy Button Machine Co.)

of work, must decide whether it would be advantageous to acquire the individual tools.

Questions

1. List five simple types of upholstery.
2. List the tools commonly used in furniture upholstery.
3. Describe the *webbing stretcher* commonly used in upholstery.
4. Describe the needles commonly used in upholstery.
5. Why is the sewing machine commonly found in most homes not satisfactory for use in upholstering?

Unit 46 – Webbing in Coil-Spring Upholstery

The upholstery materials in the seats of open-frame furniture are supported by webbing. Since this type of support plays the most important role in the construction of the seat, it is extremely important to select a high-quality webbing and to attach it properly to the seat frame. Either a low-quality webbing or an incorrectly attached webbing (or both) results in an uncomfortable piece of furniture at best and is an invitation to trouble later. The service life of low-quality webbing is short, and other complications, such as a sagging seat, are likely to develop.

The four types of webbing used in upholstering are: (1) jute, (2) steel, (3) decorative, and (4) rubber. The jute webbing is used most frequently for supporting upholstery materials in the seats of various pieces of furniture. Steel webbing is used for the same purpose in the less expensive grades of furniture. The decorative webbing includes cotton and plastic webbing where the webbing is exposed to view, as in lawn and patio furniture. Rubber webbing is used in place of jute webbing in the less-expensive modern or contemporary styles of furniture.

Installing the Webbing

Regardless of the shape of the seat frame (square, rectangular, round, or semiround), it is viewed from four sides with the boundaries determined by the four leg posts. The four sides are referred to as the front rail, back rail, and the two side rails (Fig. 46-1).

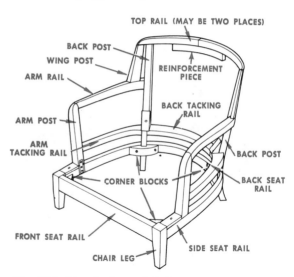

Fig. 46-1. Terminology of chair parts.

Webbing is required across the opening of the frame for padded seats and those seats which use coil-spring units. The webbing strips for the padded seats are tacked to the top of the seat rails. On seats with the coil-spring units, the strips are tacked to the bottom of the seat rails. Since it is necessary to place the coil springs with an allowance of approximately 2½ inches of spring extending above the top edge of the seat rails, it is necessary to nail the webbing strips to the bottom of the seat rails (Fig. 46-2).

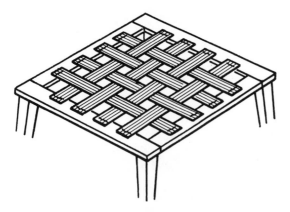

WEBBING ATTACHED TO THE TOP OF THE FRAME. NO SPRINGS ARE USED IN THIS TYPE OF CONSTRUCTION

(A) Nonspring construction for padded seats.

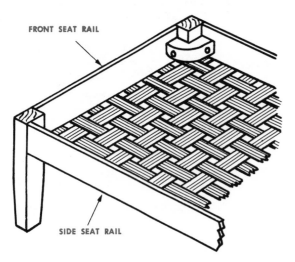

WEBBING ATTACHED TO BOTTOM OF THE FRAME. THE COIL SPRINGS ARE SEWED TO THE WEBBING AND EXTEND APPROXIMATELY 2½ INCHES ABOVE THE FRAME SEAT RAILS

(B) Construction for coil-spring units.

Fig. 46-2. Two methods of webbing placement.

The following steps in installation of the webbing are used with either padded seats or coil-spring units.

1. First attach the webbing to the front rail; then stretch it to the back rail. Thus, the webbing stretcher does not contact the front rail of the frame to damage the wood surface.

2. Measure and locate the midpoint of the width of the frame. Mark this point on the inside surface of both the front and back rails (Fig. 46-3).

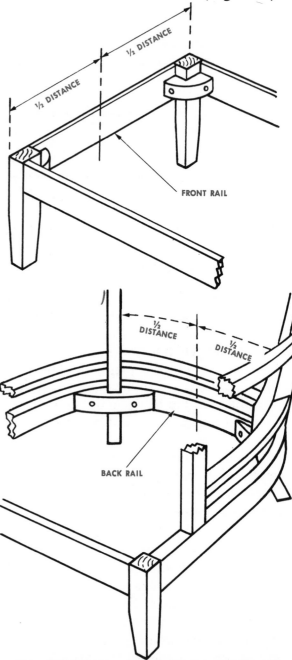

Fig. 46-3. Marking the frame for centering the webbing strips.

3. Ideally, a strip of webbing should be centered on the midpoint with the remaining webbing divided equally on each side (Fig. 46-4). To deter-

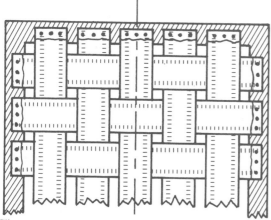

Fig. 46-4. Spacing of webbing strips, with one strip used for a center strip.

mine whether this is possible, temporarily secure a strip of webbing in position and space out the remaining strips. In a seat opening, the strips should be spaced ½ inch to 1½ inches apart. Mark the position of these strips on the inside surface of the front rail. Do not cut a strip of of the frame opening is impossible, arrange the strips evenly on either side of the midpoint. Then the midpoint is in the center of the spacing between the two center strips of webbing (Fig. 46-5).

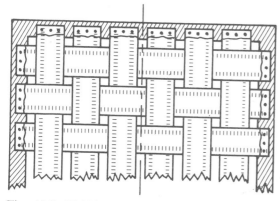

Fig. 46-5. Webbing strips spaced equally on both sides of center mark.

4. Tack the webbing strip to the front rail with No. 12 upholstery webbing tacks. The barbs on the shanks of the webbing tacks grip the wood

more securely than the smooth-shanked upholstery tacks (Fig. 46-6).

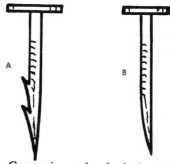

Fig. 46-6. Comparison of a barbed webbing tack (A) and a common upholstery tack (B).

5. Position the webbing; then tack it to the front rail with three webbing tacks (Fig. 46-7). Make sure the tacks enter the exact midpoint of the rail. The nearer they are placed to either the front or the back edge of the rail, the greater the possibility of splitting the wood, which must be avoided.

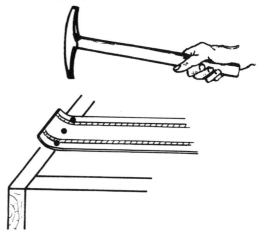

Fig. 46-7. Attach the webbing strip to the bottom of the front frame with three tacks.

6. Cut the webbing strips with only about 1½ inches of webbing extending beyond the front rail. Fold back the end of the webbing until it is recessed from the outer edge. Then tack the folded end to the seat rail

with two more webbing tacks (Fig. 46-8), but *do not* place them in a line parallel with the three tacks under the fold of the webbing. Staggering the tacks reduces the danger of splitting the wood frame. The last two tacks should be placed ⅛ inch toward the inside of the front rail. Since most furniture rails are at least 1 inch in width, these tacks are far enough from the inner edge to avoid splitting the wood.

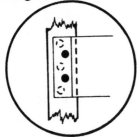

FIRST THREE TACKS
BENEATH FOLD

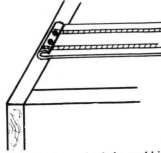

Fig. 46-8. Fold back the end of the webbing strip and fasten with two more tacks. Do not place these tacks in line with the three tacks under the webbing fold.

The three-and-two tack arrangement can be reversed to a two-and-three tack arrangement if desired (Fig. 46-9). Some upholsterers prefer a four-and-three arrangement. Recessing the end of the webbing strip hides it, and avoids unsightly bulges when the cambric and upholstery covering are attached.

7. Stretch the webbing strips across the frame opening. Place the rubber end

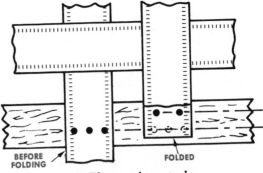

(A) Three-and-two tacks.

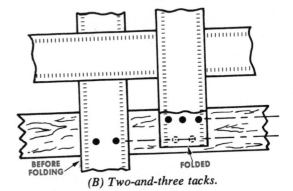

(B) Two-and-three tacks.

(C) Four-and-three tacks.

Fig. 46-9. Tacking patterns for attaching webbing strips.

of the webbing stretcher against the wood frame, with the opposite end slightly higher. Pull the webbing strip taut and downward over the other end of the webbing stretcher, inserting the nails through the webbing. If additional protection is required for the frame surface, place a block of wood, heavy cloth, or piece of old carpet between the frame and the webbing stretcher.

8. Keeping the rubber edge of the webbing stretcher against the wood frame, force the nail end (the nearest end) downward until the webbing is taut. Then, the problem is to determine how taut the webbing should be. Some "give" to the pressure of the hand is desirable. The webbing must "give" under the weight of the person sitting in the chair. The "give" is related directly to the natural resilience of the jute fiber. If the webbing is pulled too taut, the tacks might be pulled loose; or the jute fibers in the webbing might begin to weaken under the strain. On the other hand, if the webbing is too loose, a secure seat foundation is not provided. Eventually, the springs will slip out of place, and the stuffing will begin to fall through.

9. Tack the webbing strip to the back rail of the frame with No. 12 upholstery webbing tacks. Make sure the webbing strip is parallel to the side rails. The webbing strips should be spaced evenly and in a row. Cut off the webbing strip at about 1½ inches beyond the frame, and fold back. The edge of the fold should be adjacent to the parallel line of tacks. The fold then is recessed from the outside edge of the back rail of the frame. Tack the folded webbing in place, staggering the tacks in relation to the tacks beneath the fold (Fig. 46-10).

10. Following the same procedure, tack the remaining webbing strips in place between the front and back rails

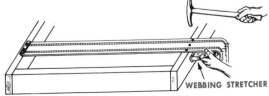

Fig. 46-10. Stretching a webbing strip.

(Fig. 46-11). Keep the strips straight and spaced evenly. The webbing later will be used as a guide for attaching the springs.

Fig. 46-11. Completed webbing on front-to-back rails.

11. The webbing strips parallel to the back and front seat rails must be interlaced with those already tacked in place (Fig. 46-12). If spring edge

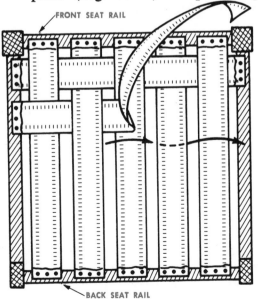

Fig. 46-12. Interlacing the webbing strips (side-to-side rails).

construction is required in the seat, the first strip of webbing must be placed as near the front rail as possible (Fig. 46-13). This provides additional support to the front row of springs.

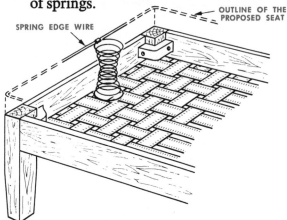

Fig. 46-13. The first strip of webbing should be placed as close to the front rail as possible in spring edge construction.

12. Selecting either side rail, tack the end of the webbing strip in place. Then complete the webbing, using the procedure outlined above in Steps 5 through 11. Remember to interlace each strip to provide greater strength and proper weight dispersement.

Webbing the Backs

The backs of furniture, especially the padded backs, do not need the strength of webbing required for the seats. Most of the pressure or weight is exerted downward or toward the floor. The direction of the pressure or weight is exerted primarily through the opening of the seat frame; however, some pressure is exerted against the back. Since the strength of the webbing required in the back is less than that needed in the seat, the webbing can be stretched by hand; thus, a webbing stretcher is not needed. In addition, cotton webbing or a lightweight grade of jute webbing can be used.

The procedures used to attach the webbing to the seat rails can be used on the backs. However, the horizontal interlaced strips are used only when marshall-spring units are involved in the construction of the back. When the back is an unusually high back, one or two horizontal webbing strips are used to provide additional support. When the curve in a back is an especially strong curve (as in a barrel-back chair), the horizontal webbing should be avoided, since it tends to distort the form (Fig. 46-14).

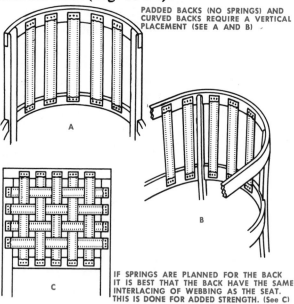

Fig. 46-14. Attachment of webbing on various types of chair backs. The strips of webbing are placed vertically on padded and curved backs (A and B) in nonspring construction. Interlacement of webbing strips is required for construction that utilizes spring units to increase strength.

Rubber webbing usually is purchased in 1¾-inch widths. It is used in the less expensive modern or contemporary styles of furniture in place of jute webbing. The attachment of rubber webbing is far more simple than for jute webbing, but it is subject to relatively rapid deterioration. Several methods of attachment are used. A metal clip can be attached to the frame, with the webbing inserted through an opening in the clip. The teeth on the edge of the clip hold the webbing in place. (Fig. 46-15). A problem with this type of construction is that the edge of the metal clip wears against the rubber webbing, causing it to rip.

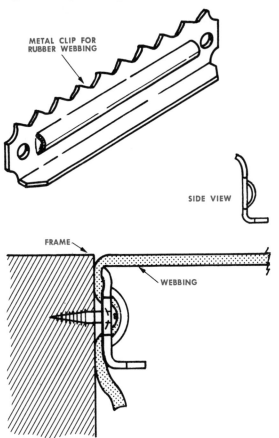

Fig. 46-15. Metal clips for attaching rubber webbing.

be inserted and tacked or stapled to the bottom (Fig. 46-17).

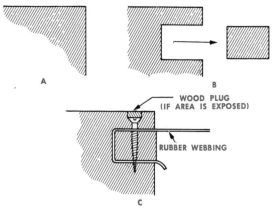

Fig. 46-16. Steps in alternate method for attaching rubber webbing strips.

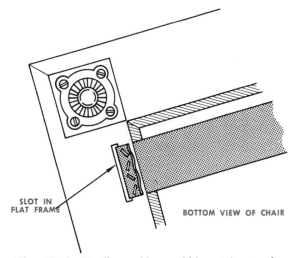

Fig. 46-17. Stapling rubber webbing strips to the bottom of a flat frame.

Tacks also can be used to hold the rubber webbing in place. Precautions are necessary, since the pressure against the webbing tends to rip the rubber where the tacks have been inserted. If the wood frame permits, cut a groove deep enough for the webbing and a narrow strip of wood to lock the webbing in place (Fig. 46-16).

If the frame is constructed for the rails to lie flatwise, holes or slots can be cut through the wood. Then the webbing can

Sagless Springs and Bar-Spring Units

Two methods of avoiding the use of webbing in open-frame construction are available. Sagless springs or bar-spring units can be used. The sagless springs are strips of spring wire bent to form a zigzag pattern and coiled; then, when straightened, the wire attempts to return to its coiled position. Thus, the zigzag-coiled spring provides the spring action for the seat. Sagless springs are attached to the frame with special metal clips (Fig.

46-18). The bar-spring units consist of rows of springs attached to a metal bar which is then attached to the frame (Fig. 46-19). Both sagless springs and bar-spring units are discussed later.

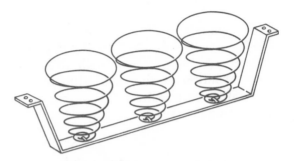

Fig. 46-19. Bar springs (spring bar unit).

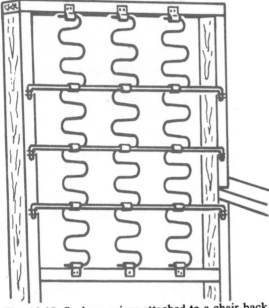

Fig. 46-18. Sagless springs attached to a chair back.

Questions

1. List the four types of webbing used in upholstery.
2. What is the purpose of webbing in furniture upholstery?
3. What are the four sides of the seat frame called?
4. How do the webbing requirements for the backs of furniture differ from the requirements for the seats?
5. What two methods are used to avoid the use of webbing in open-frame construction of furniture?

Unit 47 – Springs

Springs are designed to "give" under pressure and to regain their shape when the pressure is removed; therefore, springs are the primary method of providing seating comfort in upholstered furniture, and seating comfort is related directly to the quality of spring construction.

Upholstery springs are made from highly tempered steel wire and are coated with a substance to prevent corrosion; they are manufactured in various gauges and sizes. The three types of springs discussed here are: (1) Coil springs; (2) Innerspring units, or marshall springs; and (3) Sagless-wire, or sinuous coil springs.

Coil Springs

The *coil springs* can be purchased with either a single coil or a double coil (Fig. 47-1). The single-coil springs are cone-shaped, and they are used in the bar spring units (see Fig. 46-19). Normally, they are found in the less-expensive furniture. The double-coil springs are found in high-quality furniture, and each spring is attached separately, rather than in units.

Double-coil springs can be used in the seat, back, arms, cushion, or in any cushioned area. The method of attachment depends on the base provided (wood board, jute webbing, or steel webbing). The double-coil springs are preferable to the single-coil springs in furniture construction, since they provide superior seating comfort. Even among the double-coil springs, varying degrees of seating comfort are provided. The seating comfort of a spring is related to the degree of firmness the spring can provide. The firmness is based on the gauge of the wire and the width of the coil at the center of the spring. The spring wire remains open at both ends. The upper end of the spring is bent to prevent tearing the fabric (Fig. 47-2).

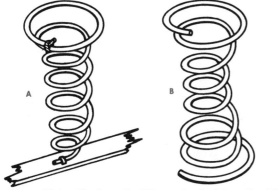

Fig. 47-1. Single-coil (A) and double-coil (B) springs.

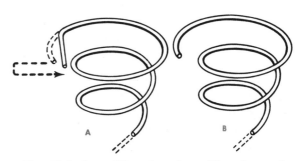

Fig. 47-2. Bent (A) and nonbent (B) spring ends.

Each spring height indicates a different spring size. Each size is available in three different grades of firmness—hard, medium, and soft. These grades are determined by the width of the center portion of the double coil (Fig. 47-3). The hardest grade of firmness is provided by springs with the narrowest center width, and the softest grade of firmness is provided by the widest center width. A medium grade of firmness is provided by springs ranging in height from 7 to 10½ inches. These are the springs used most commonly.

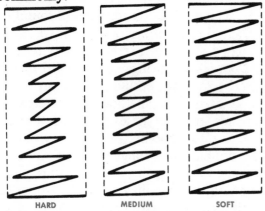

HARD   MEDIUM   SOFT

Fig. 47-3. Three degrees of spring softness.

Seat Coil Springs

The heavy-gauge (9- to 11-gauge wire) double-coil springs are used in the seats, since they can withstand the most punishment and produce the most comfort. The upper wire is bent to prevent ripping the fabric; this is not necessary with the lower wire, since it is attached to the webbing.

The seat springs are sold in hard, medium, and soft sizes. As mentioned previously, a hard spring has a narrower center width, and a soft spring has a wider center width. Therefore, the "size" of a spring is determined by the width of the center portion of the coil—not by the actual height of the spring. The size is the degree of compression each spring is subjected to when pressure is placed on it.

This is an important consideration in tieing down the springs.

Pillow Springs

Pillow springs are not used in pillows: therefore, the name can be misleading. Since they are lightweight, pillow springs are used in the backs and arms— never in the seats (Fig. 47-4). These springs are made from a lightweight wire. They usually can be obtained in heights ranging from 4 inches (14-gauge wire) to 10 inches (12-gauge wire). Both ends of the spring wire are attached to the coil. This precaution protects the fabric from being ripped by the exposed end of the wire.

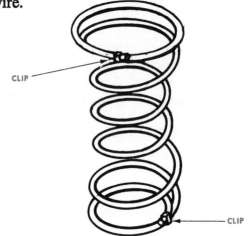

CLIP

CLIP

Fig. 47-4. Pillow spring.

Cushion Springs

The *cushion springs* are used in automobile, truck, and bus seats. They can be purchased in either 4-inch (11-gauge) or 6-inch (10-gauge) heights with either or both ends tied. The gauge of the wire in cushion springs is slightly heavier than the gauge of the wire used in the pillow springs. Note that a 4-inch pillow spring is made from 14-gauge wire and that a 4-inch cushion spring is made from 11-gauge wire. This is not inconsistent, since the height of a spring is not necessarily related to the gauge of the wire used in the spring.

Innerspring Units

Innerspring, or marshall-spring, units are used in the backs, cushions, seats, and sometimes the arms of overstuffed furniture. The springs are 3 inches in diameter and are sewed individually into burlap or muslin pockets. The marshall-spring units are used in backs containing springs 6 inches in height. Those in the cushions are smaller, usually only 3½ inches.

The innerspring units can be purchased either in ready-made units or in strips. If they are purchased in strips, it is necessary to sew them together to form the desired size or shape of the unit. The strips consist of groups of springs (usually six springs in a group) sewed into a burlap or muslin casing. The groups are separated by a 2½- to 3-inch space, and they are the bending sections of the strip. A strip can be bent or folded back on itself at these points to form a square or rectangular spring unit. The successive strips are sewed together with stitching twine (Fig. 47-5). Sew along both the top and the bottom of the springs.

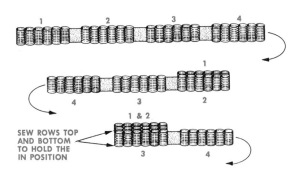

Fig. 47-5. Construction of an innerspring unit.

Attaching Coil Springs

The method used to attach the coil springs depends on the type of base. The four most common bases are: (1) Web-bed; (2) Web-panel; (3) Slat; and (4) Solid-wood.

The *webbed base* (Fig. 47-6) consists of parallel, interwoven rows of webbing stretched from side to side and from the back to the front. The springs usually are sewed to the webbing.

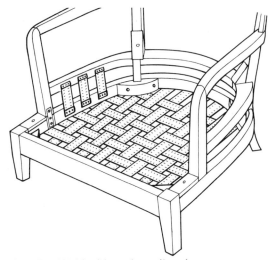

Fig. 47-6. Webbed base for coil springs.

After the webbing is attached, the number of springs needed for the seat can be estimated. Usually, three rows of three springs, or nine springs, are required. However, the total number of springs, in the long run, is determined by the size of the frame opening. The springs should be spaced in a manner that they are:

1. Evenly distributed (the same distance apart, for a comfortable seat).
2. Not spaced too closely (a hard uncomfortable seat).
3. Not spaced too far apart (a loose, lumpy seat).

The type of spring selected (height of the spring and gauge of the wire) is determined by the resiliency desired in the seat. To increase the resiliency, increase the height or distance the spring is tied above the top of the seat rail. The lower the spring is tied, the lower the resiliency provided in the seat. Generally, the top of the spring should be at least 3 inches above the top of the seat rail (Fig. 47-7).

Thread a double-pointed straight needle (or a comparable curved needle, if preferred) with stitching twine. Take four stitches for each spring. The final stitch on each spring should be directly opposite

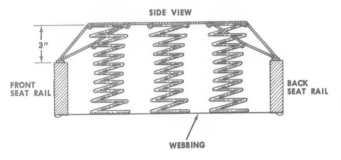

Fig. 47-7. Method of tying down coil springs.

the next spring to be stitched (Fig. 47-8). Be sure to align the springs carefully in rows before making the final attachment. Springs to which the spring edges are attached generally are placed against the seat rails of the frame.

Spring edge wire can be purchased in 9- or 10-gauge wire for the seats of furniture. Its primary purpose is to strengthen the edge of the seats and to create the desired contour. The spring edge wire is

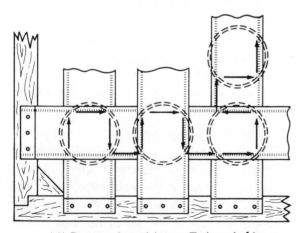

(A) Bottom view of frame. Twine stitching springs to webbing is exposed.

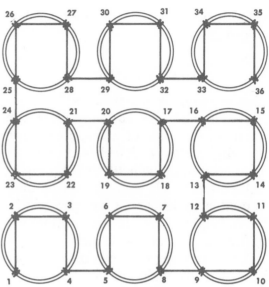

(B) Stitching pattern.

Fig. 47-8. Method of stitching the coil springs to the webbing strips.

sewed with heavy cord to the tops of the double-coil springs (Fig. 47-9).

Double-coil springs also can be attached to the webbing with staples. The *Klinch-It* tool is a laborsaving device used to fasten

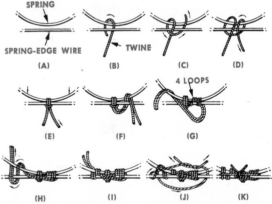

Fig. 47-9. Various steps in tying the clove-hitch knot which is used to tie the spring edge wire to the coil spring.

the springs to webbed bases (Fig. 47-10). It is available in either a hand-operated or an air-operated tool. Advantages of stapling the springs to a webbed-panel base (Fig. 47-11) include: (1) Time saved, in that it is unnecessary to stitch

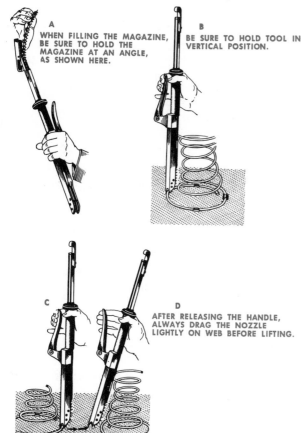

Fig. 47-10. Various steps involved in using the hand-operated "Klinch-It" tool. (Courtesy the Seng Co.)

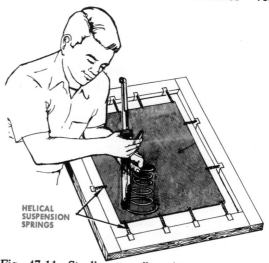

Fig. 47-11. Stapling a coil spring to a webbed-panel base.

each spring to the webbing; and (2) The stitching twine is replaced with the more durable steel staples.

The *webbed-panel bases* are made from a single piece of webbing material (burlap is sometimes used) large enough to fit inside the furniture frame with a 2½- to 4-inch gap between the panel end and the frame on all sides. Helical springs are attached to the frame with metal clips and to a wire imbedded in the edge of the webbed seat panel. The springs are sewed or stapled to the panel (see Fig. 47-11).

A *slat base* is used in the less-expensive lines of furniture. This base does not possess the natural resiliency of a webbed base. The springs can be attached to a slat base with staples, tacks, or folded strips of material (Fig. 47-12). They are attached to a solid-wood base in the same manner. However, with the solid-wood bases, it is necessary to install a cloth "silencer" to reduce the noise made by the metal striking the wood (Fig. 47-13).

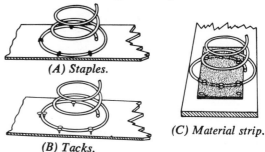

(A) Staples.

(B) Tacks.

(C) Material strip.

Fig. 47-12. Three methods of attaching coil springs to a slat base.

Fig. 47-13. A piece of cloth functions as a "silencer" to reduce the noise made by the metal spring striking the wood.

Sagless Wire Springs

The sagless wire springs are easier and quicker to install than the coil springs. Unlike coil-spring construction, webbing is not used, and it is not necessary to tie the springs at a given height.

The lengths of sagless spring wire are attached to the front and back seat rails (and to the top and bottom rails on the back) with special metal clips. Metal connectors or links sometimes are used, instead of helicals, on the interior rows (Fig. 47-14).

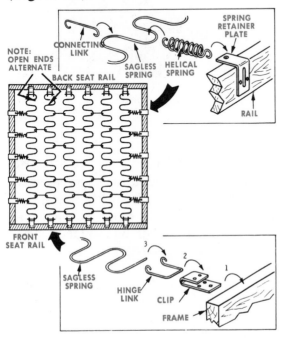

Fig. 47-14. Sagless wire spring construction.

Sagless springs are made from a continuous length of spring wire which has been bent into a zigzag shape and rolled into a coil. When a length of this spring wire is removed from the coil, cut to size, and attached to the frame, an example of sagless (sinuous) wire-spring construction is presented. The resilience is produced by the steady pull of the spring wire in its attempt to regain its former coiled shape.

The sagless springs normally are sold in bundles of 10 coils or in boxes of cut lengths (standard radii). Precut lengths with special radii also can be ordered. These special radii are used for pieces of furniture that require a lower crown. Generally, the larger the radii, the lower the

crown. However, an increase in the radius requires an adjustment in the wire gauge (the gauge must be increased correspondingly) and another adjustment in the spring length (the length must be shortened). If these adjustments are not made, the support characteristics will be reduced substantially.

Generally, a 7- to 8-gauge wire is recommended for chair seats and a 10- to 12-gauge wire is recommended for the backs. A well-known brand name of sagless springs "No-Sag" is sold in three different types: (1) Original "No-Sag" (Table 47-1); (2) "XL" (Table 47-2); and (3) "Supr-Loop" (Table 47-3). The tables provide the size requirements for a variety of seat and back dimensions. These springs also can be purchased in custom configurations that can be adapted to special furniture designs.

Sagless wire springs are attached to the frame with metal clips. *No-Sag* offers a variety of these clips. Some clips are designed specifically for back frames (Fig. 47-15), while other clips are designed

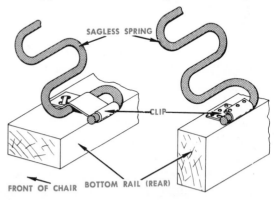

Fig. 47-15. Back clips used with "No-Sag" springs. (Courtesy No-Sag Co.)

for the seats (Fig. 47-16). A number of miscellaneous clips are available for use in various furniture construction (Fig. 47-17).

As mentioned earlier, the rows of sagless wire springs can be tied together

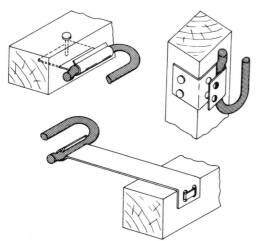

Fig. 47-16. Seat clips used with "No-Sag" springs. (Courtesy No-Sag Co.)

with either *metal connecting links* or *helical springs*. The helical springs always are used to tie the side of the spring rows nearest the frame edge, regardless of the method of tying the inner rows. The metal connecting links are a less-expensive method of tying the inner spring rows (see

Table 47-2. "XL" Spring Sizes for Seat and Back Applications.

Seats				Backs			
Inside Seat Dimension (inches)	Standard Crown (inches)	Gauge XL	Length (inches)	Inside Back Dimension (inches)	Standard Crown (inches)	Gauge XL	Length (inches)
12	1⅞	11½	11¼	16	1⅛	12	15½
13	1	11	12¼	17	1⅜	12	16½
14	1⅛	10½	13¼				
15	1⅛	10½	14¼	18	1½	12	17¾
16	1³⁄₁₆	10½	15¼	19	1⅝	12	18¾
17	1⅜	10	16¼				
18	1¼	9½	17¼	20	1⅞	12	19¾
19	1¼	9½	18¼	21	1⅝	12	20¾
20	1½	9½	19½				
21	1⁹⁄₁₆	9½	20½	22	1⅝	12	21¾
22	1¾	9	21½	23	1¾	12	23
23	1¹³⁄₁₆	9	22½				
24	2	9	23½	24	1¾	12	24
25	1½	8½	24⅜	25	1⅞	11½	25
26	1⁹⁄₁₆	8½	25¼				
27	1¾	8½	26¼	26	2	11½	26

Table 47-1. "Original No-Sag" Spring Sizes for Seat and Back Applications.

Seats				Backs			
Inside Rail Dimension (inches)	Standard Crown (inches)	Gauge No Sag	Length (inches)	Inside Rail Dimension (inches)	Standard Crown (inches)	Gauge No Sag	Length (inches)
12	1¼	11	11¾	16	1½	12 or 13	16
13	1¼	10½	12¾	17	1⅝	12 or 13	17
14	1⅜	10	13¾				
15	1½	10	14¾	18	1¾	12 or 13	18¼
16	1⅝	10	15¾	19	1⅞	12	19¼
17	1⅝	9½	16¾				
18	1¾	9	17¾	20	2	12	20¼
19	1¾	9	18¾	21	2	12	21¼
20	1⅞	9	20				
21	1⅞	9	21	22	2	12	22¼
22	1⅞	8½	22	23	2¼	11½ or 12	23½
23	2	8½	23				
24	2	8½	24	24	2¼	11½	24½
25	2	8	24⅞	25	2½	11	25½
26	2	8	25¾				
27	2	8	26¾	26	2½	11	26½

Table 47-3. "SuprLoop" Spring Sizes for Seat and Back Applications.

Seats				Backs			
Inside Seat Dimension (inches)	Standard Crown (inches)	Gauge Supr-Loop	Length (inches)	Inside Back Dimension (inches)	Standard Crown (inches)	Gauge	Length (inches)
12	1¼	10	11½	16	1⅜	11½	15½
13	1¼	10	12½	17	1½	11½	16½
14	1¼	9½	13½				
15	1½	9½	14½	18	1¾	11½	17¾
16	1¾	9	15⅝	19	2	11½	19
17	1¾	9	16⅝				
18	1¾	9	17⅝	20	2	11½	20
19	1⅞	9	18½	21	2	11	20⅞
20	1⅞	9	19½				
21	1⅞	9-8½	20½	22	2	11	21⅞
22	1⅞	8½	21½	23	2¼	11	22¾
23	1⅞	8½-8	22¼				
24	2	8	23½	24	2¼	11	23¾
25	1¾	8	24½	25	2¼	11	24¾
26	1¾	8	25⅛				
27	1¾	8	26⅛	26	2¼	10½	25⅞

Fig. 47-17). They can be purchased in standard sizes 1 inch to 6 inches, with ⅛-inch increments. It is recommended that each link should be 1⅜ inches shorter than the spacing of the metal clips holding the ends of the rows of sagless wire springs. This reduces noise to a minimum and provides a taut, firm seat.

Hinged links (see Fig. 47-17) can be inserted between the clips on the back seat rail and the sagless wire spring to create movable pivots that increase the arc of the spring upward to 2½ inches. These links are sold in three lengths: (1) Regular (1¹⁄₁₆-inch); (2) Medium (1⁷⁄₁₆-inch); and (3) Long (1¹³⁄₁₆-inch).

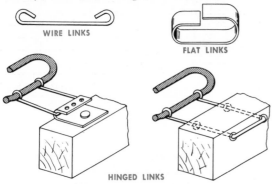

Fig. 47-17. Links used with "No-Sag" springs. (Courtesy No-Sag Co.)

Flat links (see Fig. 47-17) are used to fasten sagless wire springs to each other or to a border wire. These links are available in four sizes, depending on the gauge of the wires to be connected. Pliers are used to close the open ends.

Border wire (Fig. 47-18), the equivalent of spring-edge wire in coil-spring construction, is available in No. 6 to No. 12 gauges and in any specified length. It is used to shape and to add support to edges or corners.

Torsion springs (Fig. 47-19) are available in 10- and 11-gauge wire. These springs are used to support border wire in the construction of spring-edge seats and backs with sagless springs.

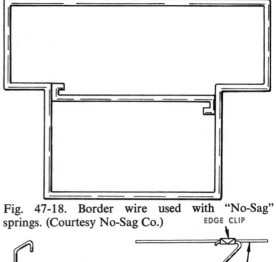

Fig. 47-18. Border wire used with "No-Sag" springs. (Courtesy No-Sag Co.)

Fig. 47-19. Torsion springs. (Courtesy No-Sag Co.)

Although it is not necessary to purchase special tools for working with sagless wire springs, some suggestions should be made here to make the work easier. Two types of tools which can be used to stretch the springs and which can be quite valuable are the spring stretchers in Fig. 47-20.

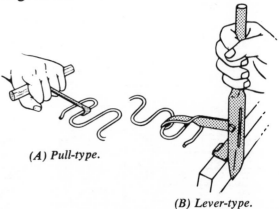

(A) Pull-type.

(B) Lever-type.

Fig. 47-20. Two types of spring stretchers used with sagless springs. (Courtesy No-Sag Co.)

The ends of the springs should be bent to prevent their slipping from the clips. A vise and hammer can be used; or a tool designed specifically for the job can be used (Fig. 47-21).

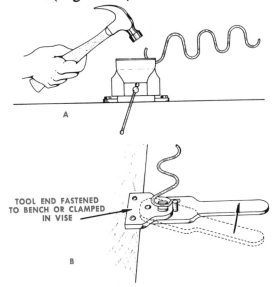

Fig. 47-21. Two methods (A) and (B) of bending the ends of sagless wire springs.

The helical springs are short (1⅜ to 6 inches), lightweight springs used to connect the outside rows of sagless wire springs to the side rails and sometimes to interconnect the spring rows. They contribute to an even distribution of the seating load, and provide more comfort than the metal connecting links. Two-inch lengths are recommended for 4-inch spacings; 3-inch lengths for 5-inch spacings; and 4-inch lengths for 6-inch spacings of the rows of sagless wire springs.

The *No-Sag* manufacturer produces several types of helical springs for furniture construction (Fig. 47-22). Note that all the springs are open-wound, except for the seat springs. The standard sizes for the more common helical springs can be found in Table 47-4. The retainer clips for helical springs are shown in Fig. 47-23.

The close-wound seat helical springs (see Fig. 47-22A) are used for securing

Table 47-4. Helical Spring Sizes (Other sizes available on special order).

Seat Helical Springs (inches)	Back Helical Springs (inches)	Snap-End Helical Springs (inches)
1⅜	2-0	1-½
1-½	2-½	1-¾
1-⅝	3-0	2-0
1-¾	3-½	2-¼
2-0	4-0	2-½
2-½	5-0	2-¾
3-0		3-0
3-½		3-¼
4-0		3-½
		3-¾
		4-0
		4-¼
		4-½
		4-¾
		5-0
		5-¼
		5-½
		5-¾
		6-0

the outside rows of sinuous wire to the side rails of wood seat frames. Also, they can be used for spring interties to improve filling support and more even distribution of loads. The back helical springs (see Fig. 47-22B) are used to unitize sinuous wire back springs and for an improved base for filling. Also, they can be used to provide softer seats. The snap-end helical springs (see Fig. 47-22C) are used to

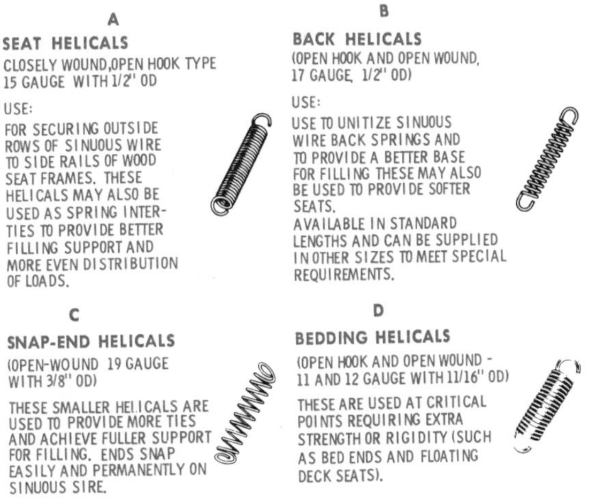

A
SEAT HELICALS
CLOSELY WOUND,OPEN HOOK TYPE 15 GAUGE WITH 1/2' OD

USE:
FOR SECURING OUTSIDE ROWS OF SINUOUS WIRE TO SIDE RAILS OF WOOD SEAT FRAMES. THESE HELICALS MAY ALSO BE USED AS SPRING INTERTIES TO PROVIDE BETTER FILLING SUPPORT AND MORE EVEN DISTRIBUTION OF LOADS.

B
BACK HELICALS
(OPEN HOOK AND OPEN WOUND, 17 GAUGE, 1/2' OD)

USE:
USE TO UNITIZE SINUOUS WIRE BACK SPRINGS AND TO PROVIDE A BETTER BASE FOR FILLING THESE MAY ALSO BE USED TO PROVIDE SOFTER SEATS.
AVAILABLE IN STANDARD LENGTHS AND CAN BE SUPPLIED IN OTHER SIZES TO MEET SPECIAL REQUIREMENTS.

C
SNAP-END HELICALS
(OPEN-WOUND 19 GAUGE WITH 3/8' OD)

THESE SMALLER HELICALS ARE USED TO PROVIDE MORE TIES AND ACHIEVE FULLER SUPPORT FOR FILLING. ENDS SNAP EASILY AND PERMANENTLY ON SINUOUS SIRE.

D
BEDDING HELICALS
(OPEN HOOK AND OPEN WOUND - 11 AND 12 GAUGE WITH 11/16' OD)

THESE ARE USED AT CRITICAL POINTS REQUIRING EXTRA STRENGTH OR RIGIDITY (SUCH AS BED ENDS AND FLOATING DECK SEATS).

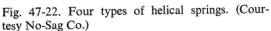

Fig. 47-22. Four types of helical springs. (Courtesy No-Sag Co.)

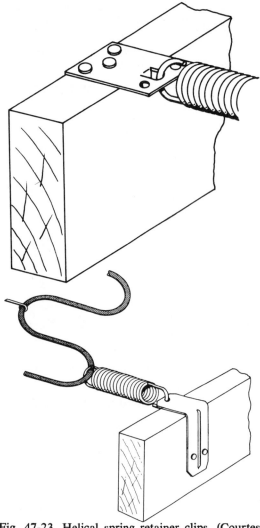

Fig. 47-23. Helical spring retainer clips. (Courtesy No-Sag Co.)

provide more ties to achieve fuller support for filling. The ends snap easily and permanently onto sinuous wire. The bedding helical springs (see Fig. 47-22D) are used at critical points which require extra strength or rigidity, such as bed ends and floating deck seats.

Before installing sagless wire springs, it is a wise practice to check the condition of the frame. A weak frame cannot withstand the steady pull of the sagless wire springs. It might be necessary to strengthen the frame before the springs can be used.

Corner blocks should be used for reinforcement, especially if there is no overlap of seat rails. If possible, the front seat rails should overlap the side rails. The pulling force of the springs naturally lies between the two rails to which they are attached (Fig. 47-24). The wood used in

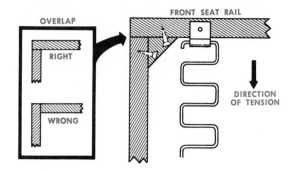

Fig. 47-24. Frame overlap detail.

constructing these rails should be ¾ inch in thickness. Long frames (sofas, love seats, etc.) should have one or two center braces (Fig. 47-25).

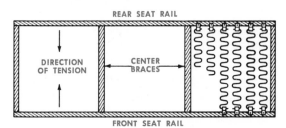

Fig. 47-25. Center braces are used to reinforce a long frame.

Sagless wire springs normally are installed from the back to the front rails on the seats, from the bottom on the seats, and from the bottom to the top rails on the backs. However, side-to-side attachment is possible and produces satisfactory results. For explanation purposes, the conventional method is described here. The step-by-step procedure for installing sagless wire springs is:

1. Measure the frame for the length of spring required. The measurements should be taken from the inside of

the seat rails (Fig. 47-26). These measurements aid in determining the correct arc (crown) to be used, the length of the wire, and the gauge of the wire. After measuring the distance between seat rails, enter Tables 47-1 to 47-3 with these dimensions to determine the crown (arc of the spring), the wire gauge, and the length of the spring.

Fig. 47-26. The measurements required are the inside dimensions of the frame rails. (Courtesy No-Sag Co.)

2. To determine the number of rows of sagless wire springs needed, measure the distance between the arms; then refer to Table 47-5.
3. A "standard" crown (one with the arc of the spring extending above the seat rail) normally is 1¼ to 2 inches. The total deflection should be about twice the dimension of the crown. Therefore, if the crown is 2 inches, the total deflection should be 4 inches.

The height of the crown can be increased by adding ¼ to ½ inch to

Table 47-5. Seat Dimensions for Sagless Springs

Distance Between Arms Along Front Seat Rail (inches)	Number of No-Sag springs	Center-to-Center Spacing of Clips (inches)	Center Spacing of Two Outside Clips From Inside-Arm Posts (inches)	Size of Connecting Links (inches)
21 Chair	5	4¼	2	2⅝
22 Chair	5	4½	2	2⅞
23 Chair	5	4¾	2	3⅛
24 Chair	5	5	2	3⅜
25 Chair	6	4¼	1⅞	2⅝
40 Sectional	9	4½	2	2⅞
50 Love Seat	11	4½	2½	2⅞
52 Love Seat	11	4¾	2¼	3⅛
58 Sofa	12	5	1½	3⅜
59 Sofa	12	5	2	3⅜
60 Sofa	13	4¾	1½	3⅛
61 Sofa	13	4¾	2	3⅛
62 Sofa	13	4¾	2½	3⅛
63 Sofa	14	4½	2¼	2⅞
64 Sofa	14	4½	2¾	2⅞
65 Sofa	14	4¾	1⅝	3⅛
66 Sofa	14	4¾	2⅛	3⅛

the length of the spring. A lower crown can be created by subtracting the same length. Generally, each ½-inch change in spring length results in a similar ¼-inch change in the crown measurement. Thus, reducing the length ½ inch will reduce the crown measurement ¼ inch.

4. Unwind the length of sagless wire spring; then press it flatwise onto the work area and onto the top of a yardstick. Be especially careful, since sagless wire springs snap back into the coiled position when they are released to cause possible injury. The distance between each of the outside edges (Fig. 47-27) is the true length of the spring required, as indicated in Tables 47-1 to 47-3.

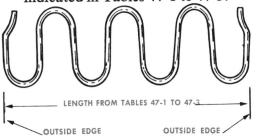

Fig. 47-27. Dimensions of sagless wire springs.

5. Cut the spring one-half loop longer than the measured length of the spring. This additional length can be removed when the exact height of the crown is determined. Since this is spring steel, the surface of the sagless wire spring can be notched with a file or hacksaw, and snapped off at the desired point.

6. File the cut end of the spring to remove any burr, and then bend it (see Fig. 47-21). The end is bent to prevent slipping out of the clips or hinge links.

7. Cut as many lengths of sagless wire springs as the measurements in Step 2 indicate.

8. Locate and mark the positions for the metal clips. Nail the clips in place with webbing tacks or barbed nails.

9. Attach the lengths of sagless wire springs to the metal clips on the frame with alternating open ends (see Fig. 47-14).

10. Locate and mark the positions for the helical springs on each side rail of the frame. The number and location is arbitrary, depending on the weight loads anticipated and the size of the frame.

11. Tie the inner rows together with either helical springs or metal connecting links.

12. In Steps 10 and 11, locate the helical springs (or metal connecting links) in alternate positions in each row (see Fig. 47-14). Turn the open end of the helical spring downward to prevent loose wire snagging in the padding and materials placed over it.

In attaching sagless wire springs to the back, follow the procedure in Steps 1 through 12. Remember that the wire gauge usually is different. Border wire, flat links, and torsion springs can be used to construct a square edge.

Questions

1. What is the primary purpose of springs in furniture upholstery?
2. List three types of upholstery springs.
3. What are the two types of coil springs?
4. What are *pillow* springs?
5. List the four most common bases on which coil springs are attached.
6. Why are sagless wire springs quicker and easier to install than coil springs?

Unit 48 – Burlap, Muslin, and Stuffing Materials

Burlap, muslin, stuffing, and padding are combined in upholstery work to form the central core of an upholstered piece of furniture. Each layer performs a practical function essential to the strength and comfort of the piece of furniture. Burlap is utilized as the base for the stuffing. The principal function of the stuffing and padding is to provide softness for the seating comfort. The muslin cover is an optional layer of material that provides a protective barrier for the outer upholstery fabric, preventing the stuffing (especially down, feathers, and animal hair) from working through to the surface.

Burlap

Three important functions in upholstery are served by *burlap*. These functions are: (1) Used to cover the springs in furniture with spring construction; (2) Covers the webbing and serves as a foundation base for furniture without springs (open-frame construction); and (3) Used to make edge rolls.

Burlap is a strong, coarse fiber of plain design and woven primarily from jute fibers (Fig. 48-1). Its grade is indicated by its weight in ounces per yard. The grades begin at 5 ounces per yard, and range upward to 14 ounces per yard. The widths range from 35 inches to 100 inches; the most common width in upholstery is 40 inches. The weights commonly

Fig. 48-1. Burlap.

used range from 8 ounces per yard to 14 ounces per yard, depending on their function. For example, the inside portion of a wing requires a burlap weighing only 8 to 10 ounces, whereas the frame opening in a piece of furniture of nonspring construction requires a 12- to 14-ounce heavy-duty grade of burlap.

Muslin

Muslin is a lightweight to medium-weight, plain fabric which sometimes is used between the stuffing and the outer upholstery cover for additional protection. The most common width of muslin sold for upholstery. purposes is 36 inches. When a pile fabric is used, the muslin protects the pile from the constant rubbing action of the stuffing against it (Fig. 48-2).

Stuffing

The quality of a stuffing is determined by its resilience, which is its ability to spring back to its original shape after being compressed by a pressure of some

Fig. 48-2. Muslin.

type. The higher the quality of the stuffing, the more quickly it resumes its original shape. The inferior grades of stuffing will pack when they are pressed downward.

Tow is a stuffing material made from the stems of flax plants. The stems are crushed and processed until a hairlike fiber is produced. Tow is inexpensive and easy to work with. Unfortunately, it packs (compresses into lumps) easily, and its resiliency probably is lower than any of the stuffing materials. For this reason, it frequently is used as a base for a higher-quality stuffing. The tow is spread evenly across the burlap and stitched into place, using a 4-inch curved needle for the stitching. A higher-quality stuffing is spread across the tow base.

Tow also is used an a solid base (seat or arm top). It is spread evenly across the surface to be covered; then it is secured in position with a piece of burlap. The burlap is stretched across the tow and tacked in place. Tow also is used frequently in making edge rolls. Since it packs easily, it is more practical to err on the side of "too much" tow, rather than "too little." Tow can be purchased in three grades, and is sold by the pound.

Sisal is even less expensive than tow; therefore, it often is used as a substitute for tow. Whereas tow is derived from the fibrous stem of the flax plant, sisal is taken from the large leaves of the sisal hemp plant. Like tow, sisal is easy to work with. Unfortunately, it also tends to pack, and is used as a base for the more resilient stuffing materials. The sisal fibers are white, long, and coarse. Sisal can be rubberized (fibers receive a thin coating of rubber) and manufactured in pad form or sold in loose form as a filler. The seats, arms, and backs of furniture utilize sisal.

Palm-leaf fiber is processed from palm leaves, and is only slightly more resilient than either sisal or tow. Best results are obtained when the palm-leaf fibers are used as a base for a stuffing of higher quality. Like sisal and tow, the palm-leaf fibers tend to pack and form lumps.

Coconut-shell fiber or coco fiber possesses the same characteristics found in palm-leaf fiber. It is processed from the coir, which is the coarse fiber found in the outer coconut husk.

Rubberized coconut fiber is produced by impregnating the coir with a synthetic rubber latex. The result is a mildew and odor-resistant pad of uniform density. Rubberized coconut fiber pads are manufactured under the trade name *Coirtex*. It is used for insulators in mattresses, automobile seats, and airplane seats. The pads are available in ¼-inch and ½-inch thicknesses, and can be purchased by the roll or in the specific sizes required for the furniture.

Excelsior is a stuffing from woods such as the cottonwood and black willow. The wood is shredded in the same manner that the palm leaves are processed. The excelsior will pack when it is new, and it will crumble into small pieces after a period of time.

Kapok is a seed fiber which resembles cotton. It is derived from the seed pods of the kapok tree. Kapok is quite soft and is used frequently as a stuffing in cushions and life preservers. Also, it can be used either alone or mixed with other stuffing materials in pillows. Unfortunately, kapok tends to separate and pack into uncomfortable lumps. Usually, it can be purchased by the pound.

Cotton is another seed fiber, but it finds much more use in upholstery than does the kapok fiber. It is used both as a stuffing for cushions and pillows and as a protective layer between the outer upholstery cover and the stuffing material. Also, it is used to stuff arms, channels (pipes), tufts, and corners. Cotton definitely is inferior as a stuffing for cushions and pillows; it tends to pack and form uncomfortable lumps. The cotton used in upholstery is derived from the linters—short fibers remaining on the cotton seeds after the ginning process. These short fibers are removed and woven into pads. Cotton is purchased by the roll (27-inch width) in several weights.

Moss commonly known as *Spanish Moss*, is not a true moss. It hangs in long strands from trees, taking both moisture and nourishment from the air. Moss is second only to animal hair as a stuffing for upholstered furniture, and it is quite easy to work with. Since it is somewhat less resilient than hair, it should be built up to a higher level than required, when used as a stuffing, to allow for the slight packing that will occur.

The moss gathered from trees is processed before it can be used commercially. This not only cleans the moss (removes dirt, twigs, etc.) but also removes the outer bark of the moss, leaving the fine hairlike inner fiber. A higher grade of moss is produced each time it is processed. The number of times the moss has been processed is indicated by the symbol X. The processing also changes the color of the moss; consequently, the grades can be recognized easily by their color. Moss can be purchased by the pound.

Several types of animal hair are used, but *horsehair* (from both the mane and tail) is the best type of hair for stuffing. Only the hair from the tails of cattle is as long as horsehair (from the tail). The XXXX grade of moss often is used for a substitute. Horsehair is purchased by the pound.

Rubberized hair is produced by a process in which each hair (any type of hair) is covered with rubber. It is lightweight and available in three grades—soft, medium, and firm. Generally, only the "firm" grade is recommended for upholstery (Fig. 48-3).

Fig. 48-3. Rubberized hair.

Paratex consists of 20-percent horsehair and 80-percent hog hair impregnated with rubber (Fig. 48-4). It is equal to foam rubber and plastic polyurethane in resilience. Also, it is mothproof, non-

Fig. 48-4. "Paratex" installed beneath cotton padding. (Courtesy Blocksom & Co.)

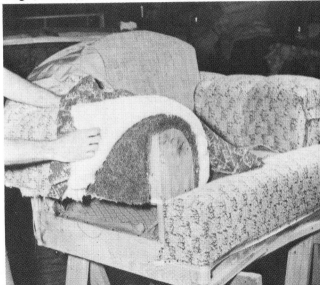

allergenic, and resistant to mildew. It can be laminated in any thickness, and it conforms to all contours, including sharp bends around corners and edges, without separating. It can be attached to the frame without difficulty, and it can be tacked, stapled, sewed, hog-ringed, or button-tufted.

Down is the short, fluffy feather found in young birds or near the skin of adult birds. It is lightweight and is an excellent insulator. Down can be purchased by the pound; and it often is used in a mixture (55-60 percent) with feathers.

Attaching the Burlap (Spring Construction)

The burlap cover serves two functions in spring construction. Primarily, burlap provides a foundation for the stuffing above it—a surface over which the stuffing can be spread evenly and sewed. Also, perhaps equally important, the burlap prevents the stuffing from spilling downward into the springs. The following details are important steps in the application of burlap over the seat springs:

1. Measure across the frame opening; allow for ¾- to 1-inch overlap for tacking to the frame. Do not permit the measuring tape to depress the springs when taking the measurements. Apply the burlap in a manner that does not depress the springs. Depressing the springs causes continuous pressure against the burlap. In time, this pressure causes the burlap to tear, weakening the upholstery (Fig. 48-5).

2. Using the seat measurements and a ½-inch allowance along the edges, cut a heavy-grade burlap. The ½-inch allowance will be turned under to provide a nonfraying hem for tacking. A lighter grade of burlap can be used on the backs, arms, and side panels. Be sure to cut along the weave.

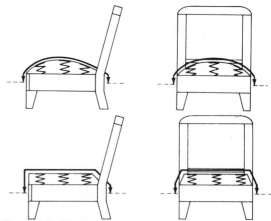

Fig. 48-5. Measurements for a burlap cover over seat springs.

3. Center the burlap over the seat springs and the frame opening. Make sure an equal portion of burlap overlaps on each side.

4. Fold about ½ inch of burlap under, and place a temporary tack in the midpoint of the burlap at the center of the back seat rail (Fig. 48-6).

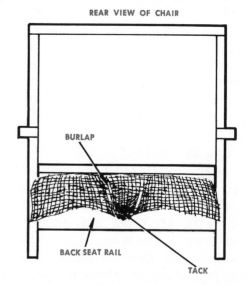

Fig. 48-6. Temporarily tack the burlap to the back seat rail.

5. Pull the burlap as tightly as possible, without depressing the springs; then place a tack through the midpoint of the burlap at the center of the front seat rail. Again fold the burlap under

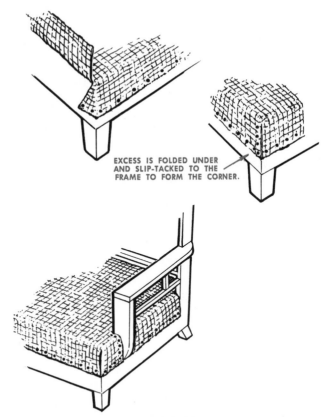

EXCESS IS FOLDED UNDER AND SLIP-TACKED TO THE FRAME TO FORM THE CORNER.

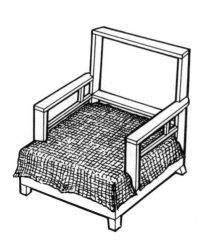

Fig. 48-7. Temporarily tack the burlap to the front seat rail.

about ½ inch before tacking (Fig. 48-7).

6. Cut back each corner of the burlap to a point equal to the overlap on the sides. Cut and fit the burlap for the arm and back posts. Pull the burlap tight on the sides, and place a tack through the midpoint of the burlap at the center of each side rail. Fold under ½ inch before tacking. Begin tacking toward the corners and posts, moving away from the center tack on each seat rail (Fig. 48-8). This is temporary slip-tacking.

7. When the slip-tacking of the burlap around the four sides of the frame has been completed, check the surface above the tops of the springs. If the burlap is smooth and tight, the burlap is ready to be stitched to the top coils of the springs. Use a curved needle with stitching twine, following the pattern diagrammed in Fig. 48-9.

8. Permanently tack the burlap in position. Beginning at the center of each frame rail, move toward the corners and posts. Smooth out all wrinkles in the burlap as the tacking proceeds.

Fig. 48-8. Method of slip-tacking the burlap to the side seat rails and forming the corners.

Remember to keep ½ inch of burlap turned under at the bottom.

9. Fold under the excess burlap at the corners, and tack them. Be sure the folded-under material is smooth and flat before the burlap is tacked. If the material is bunched, unsightly bulges

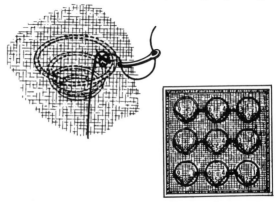

Fig. 48-9. Stitching pattern used for sewing burlap to the coil springs.

and wrinkles can occur. It might be desirable to sew the corner seams.

Sewing burlap to sagless wire springs does not present a great problem. The knots should be spaced and sewed to the spring in a manner that they will not slip along the spring wire.

Attaching the Burlap (Nonspring Construction)

Nonspring construction is divided into two types, including those pieces with a/an: (1) Open frame, and (2) Wood base or closed frame. In either type of nonspring construction, a padded seat should be constructed to provide comfort for the sitter. A variation of the open-frame, nonspring construction is the removable, or slip, seat.

Open frames in which springs are not used still require the attachment of crisscrossed lengths of webbing. Burlap (usually a heavy grade) then is placed over the webbing, covering the frame opening to provide a stronger base and a surface to which the stuffing can be attached (Fig. 48-10). To construct this type of furniture, follow the procedure:

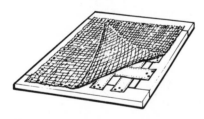

Fig. 48-10. Method of attaching burlap over an open frame, without springs.

1. Center the burlap above the frame opening. Cut off enough burlap to permit some overlap. The size of the overlap depends on whether an edge roll is to be used. This can be determined by fashioning a mock-up of

an edge roll. Construct the edge roll from heavy paper, staple the edges, and stuff with cotton. Lay the piece of burlap across the opening, and slip-tack into position. Now, place the paper edge roll on its final location, slip-tack it in position, and pull the burlap over it. This provides a rough idea of the allowance needed (Fig. 48-11). If an edge roll is not used on

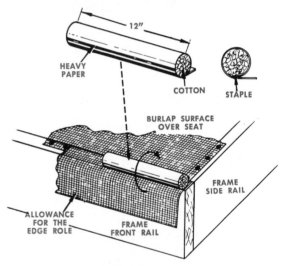

Fig. 48-11. Using a paper edge roll to determine allowance.

a frame rail, an overlap of only 1 or 2 inches is necessary. These areas are at the back of the frame and sometimes along the sides nearest the back.

2. Cut the burlap to rough measurements, and slip-tack to the frame. Is it centered properly? If so, remove the slip tacks from the front, pull the burlap taut, and tack permanently in position. A tacking strip, usually a thin strip of cardboard, placed along the surface of the frame is advisable. This prevents the tacks slipping through the wide weave of the burlap. Tack from the center outward toward both sides, pulling the burlap tightly and smoothing out the wrinkles as the tacking proceeds.

3. Repeat the procedure for the back of the frame.

4. Follow the same procedure for each side of the frame. Where an edge roll is not to be used, fold back the excess burlap, and tack it to the frame. Be careful to stagger these tacks (as in tacking webbing), since the tacks are being placed over another row of tacks.

5. Measuring, cutting, and attaching the burlap to the other portions of the frame (wings, arms, or side panels and backs with no springs) is identical to the procedure for covering the seat portion (Figs. 48-12 and 48-13).

Fig. 48-12. Burlap cover on an inside arm.

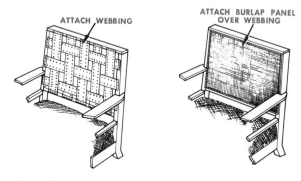

Fig. 48-13. Burlap cover on an inside back.

Attaching Edge Rolls

Rolls of burlap filled with stuffing are tacked along the edges of the wood frame or stitched to the burlap at the point where the springs exert the most pressure. Thus, the edge rolls function as buffers between the edge of the frame or springs (in a spring-edge seat) and the outer up-

holstery cover. A second, but equally important, function is that the edge roll prevents the stuffing from working its way downward over the edge to the frame. Finally, the edge roll contributes to the contour of the chair.

Ready-made edge rolls can be purchased or built from burlap and stuffing. These are sold by the foot or in large rolls. The edge rolls are made in several sizes, ranging from ½ inch to 1½ inches in height. A number of different shapes can be purchased; the shape depends on how it is to be used. The edge rolls used to close the gap between the seat foundation and the cushion in the front of chairs and sofas usually are larger than those tacked to frame edges (Fig. 48-14). The

Fig. 48-14. Roll attached to chair frame. (Courtesy Sackner Products, Inc.)

former edge rolls are attached to the burlap above the spring unit (and directly above the spring edge wire, if used). For this reason, they are often referred to as *spring edge* rolls or *stitch edge* rolls (Fig. 48-15).

All the edge rolls should be well packed with stuffing to provide a continuous, firm surface. This is assured

Fig. 48-15. Ready-made, stitched edge roll. (Courtesy Sackner Products, Inc.)

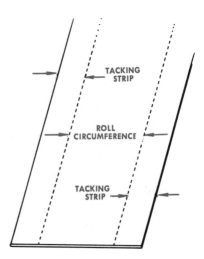

Fig. 48-16. Measurements for an edge roll.

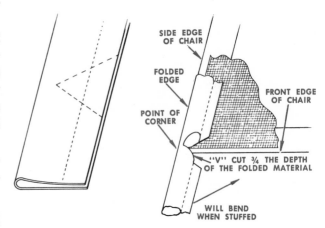

Fig. 48-17. Folding and cutting for a corner.

when ready-made edge rolls are purchased.

The larger edge rolls tend to break down after a period of time. Tow produces the firmest stuffing, but other fillers often are used. The edge roll is either tacked to the frame or, in spring-edge seats or unusually large edge rolls, sewed to the burlap.

If a ready-made edge roll is not utilized, the procedure for forming a handmade edge roll is as follows:

1. Estimate the diameter of the edge roll required for the seat. This will depend on the projected height of the finished seat from the floor. For example, if the projected height of the finished seat from the floor is 18 inches and the top of the seat rails is 16 inches, the diameter of the edge roll should be 1½ inches.

2. Measure and cut a piece of burlap wide enough to create the diameter required with sufficient excess for at least one 1-inch tacking strip and long enough to extend around the circumference of the seat (Fig. 48-16).

3. Determine the location of the corners. Fold the roll-edge strip, and make a vee cut at the correct point for the corner (Fig. 48-17). Cut through not more than three-fourths of the folded, flat material. After the roll is stuffed, the vee cut can be made slightly deeper to eliminate unevenness.

4. Attach the bottom edge of the burlap to the frame with No. 6 upholstery tacks.

5. Begin forming the roll. Starting with a small quantity of stuffing, fold the burlap around it, pack the stuffing firmly in place, and tack the first sections of the edge roll. This will be the shorter section on the side. Sew the corner seam before beginning the next section of the edge roll. Continue to proceed in this fashion around the

edges of the frame until the entire edge roll is completed (Fig. 48-18).

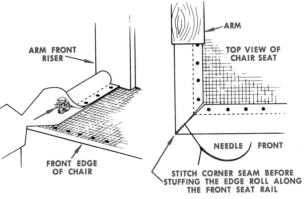

Fig. 48-18. Forming and stuffing the edge roll.

A slightly different procedure is used in forming an edge roll that is stitched in place. The stuffing inside the edge roll should be stitched to prevent its moving about. This can be a problem with the larger edge rolls (1¾ to 2 inches in diameter). A suggested stitching pattern is diagrammed in Fig. 48-19.

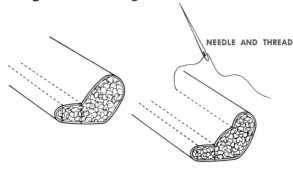

Fig. 48-19. Stitching pattern for an edge roll.

The corners of ready-made edge rolls are formed with a vee cut (Fig. 48-20). Several shapes of ready-made edge rolls that can be purchased are diagrammed in Fig. 48-21.

Attaching Loose Stuffing and Padding

The properties of the various stuffings and padding materials have been dis-

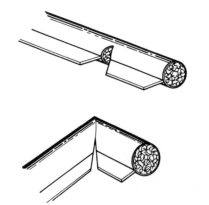

Fig. 48-20. A vee is cut in a ready-made edge roll to form a corner.

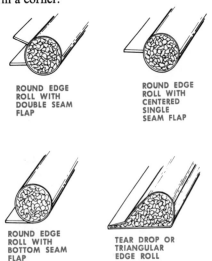

Fig. 48-21. Various shapes of ready-made edge rolls.

cussed previously. The method of attaching the burlap cover has been described. Also, the use of the roll edge has been explained. A procedure for spreading and attaching loose stuffing is:

1. Determine the depth of the stuffing. Some upholsterers suggest at least 1 inch. Other upholsterers advise using sufficient stuffing to prevent the hand feeling the spring when the stuffing is pressed down.
2. Make sure there are no lumps in the stuffing when it is spread. All lumps should be torn apart.
3. Spread the stuffing evenly over the surface to be covered.

4. Stitch the stuffing to the burlap, using 2- to 3-inch stitches. Stitching patterns are suggested in Fig. 48-22.

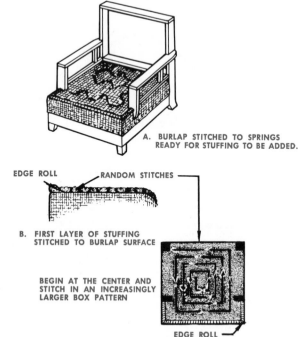

Fig. 48-22. Stitching the first layer of stuffing over the burlap.

5. Distribute at least 25 percent additional stuffing over the surface, than has been sewed down. This additional stuffing should be a higher-quality stuffing—curled animal hair, for example. DO NOT cover the edge roll Fig. 48-23).

6. Cover the stuffing with a layer of cotton padding (Fig. 48-24). This layer does not cover a roll edge, if used.

For a variation of the above procedure, cover the stuffing with a layer of lightweight burlap which, in turn, is attached to the stuffing with several random stitches, before placing the cotton padding (Fig. 48-25). Do not pull the stitches too tightly. The next step is to cover the stuffing and cotton padding with a muslin cover.

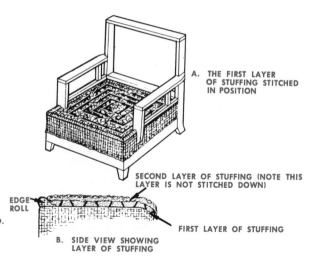

Fig. 48-23. Applying the second layer of stuffing.

Muslin Cover

A layer of muslin is optional, but it provides an excellent base for the final cover. Usually, it is easier to position the stuffing with a regulator beneath a muslin cover than through the outer upholstery fabric. Also, cutting and sewing the pieces of muslin in place provides practice in handling a more expensive surface fabric later.

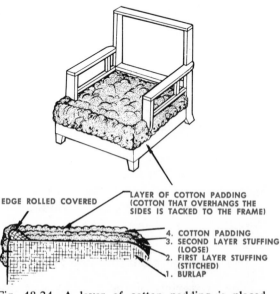

Fig. 48-24. A layer of cotton padding is placed over the stuffing.

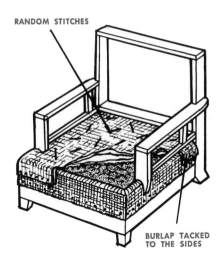

Fig. 48-25. A cover of lightweight burlap is placed over the stuffing.

In the less-expensive grades and in the higher-quality mass-produced furniture, the muslin cover often is omitted entirely. When a muslin cover is used (Fig. 48-26), it forms the upper layer in three types

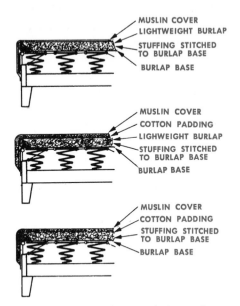

Fig. 48-26. Various furniture upholstery layers.

of construction: (1) Muslin, lightweight burlap, and stuffing; (2) Muslin, cotton padding, lightweight burlap, and stuffing; and (3) Muslin, cotton padding, and stuffing.

Measuring and Cutting for the Seat

Select sufficient muslin for covering the piece of furniture being upholstered. Only a rough estimate can be made until the measuring and cutting is completed. The procedure for measuring is:

1. Measure across the seat and downward over to the sides to slightly beyond the center of the side rail. This is approximately the line along which the muslin will be tacked; however, an additional 1 inch of fabric is needed on each side to be folded double for tacking. The fold protects the muslin from ripping when tension is placed on it. If the entire side of the chair is to be upholstered, the measurement should be extended to the bottom of the side rail, plus a tacking allowance for the material to extend underneath the chair to permit tacking to the bottom edge of the side rails. This provides additional protection to the outer cover at the sharp edge of the side rail.

2. Measure the front-to-back depth of the seat, with the same 1-inch allowance for tacking and folding. Remember to make the width and depth measurements across the center of the seat (Fig. 48-27).

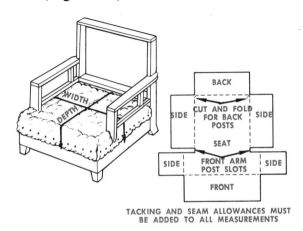

TACKING AND SEAM ALLOWANCES MUST BE ADDED TO ALL MEASUREMENTS

Fig. 48-27. Measuring for the muslin cover.

3. Mark the measurements on the muslin, and cut the piece to cover the seat. Be sure to add the tacking and seam allowances to all measurements.

4. Slip-tack the muslin cover to the back seat rail. Place the first tack in the center and space the other tacks on either side, smoothing out the wrinkles as the tacking proceeds.

5. Pull the muslin tight against the seat, but do not pull it tight enough to depress the springs; then slip-tack it to the front seat rail. Again, tack from the center outward, smoothing the wrinkles in the material as the tacking proceeds.

6. Pull the muslin tight against any corner posts, and cut the material to fit the post (Fig. 48-28).

7. Pull the muslin cover downward to the side rails, and slip-tack into place. Follow the same tacking procedure outlined in Steps 4 and 5.

8. If satisfied with the appearance of the muslin cover, permanently tack the muslin in place. Fold the muslin for tacking in the same manner that the burlap was folded.

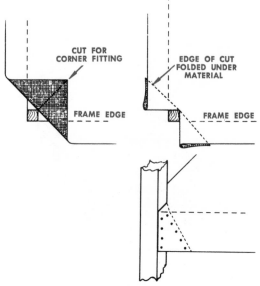

Fig. 48-28. Cutting and forming a corner.

Questions

1. List three functions of burlap in furniture upholstery.
2. What determines the quality of a stuffing in upholstery?
3. List five common stuffing materials.
4. What is the primary purpose of the burlap cover in spring construction for upholstery?
5. What are the two types of nonspring construction in upholstery?
6. What is an edge roll?

Unit 49 – Cushions

A variety of cushions are used in upholstery. They are best classified by their inner construction. The two chief categories are: (1) Stuffed cushions, with springs; and (2) Stuffed cushions, without springs. The latter category includes cushions with side strips and without side strips (top sewed directly to the bottom with a single strip of welting all around the cushion to conceal the seam). Cushions are made in various shapes and sizes. The basic shapes are square and rectangular; but round, triangular, and, of course, the familiar T-shaped cushions are used frequently in overstuffed furniture.

Measurements

The measurements for a cushion should be taken over the widest and deepest portions of the seat area. The depth measurement should be made from the farthest edge in the inside back to a corresponding point on the front. Of course, the tape measure should be kept parallel to the side rail of the frame. Generally, a measurement between the insides of the two arms provides the width measurement for the cushion (Fig. 49-1). However, in T-shaped cushions, a second measurement is required between the two outside edges (Fig. 49-2) and across the front of the frame. For al types of cushions, an additional ½- to ¾-inch allowance is needed for the seams when the pattern is cut.

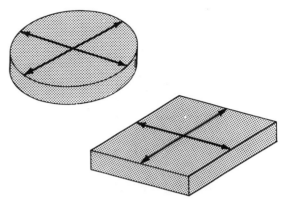

Fig. 49-1. Measurements for the top and bottom of a round and square or rectangular cushion.

The vertical width of the sides depends on the thickness of the cushion. Then, placing the end of the tape in the middle of the back, find the required length for a side strip all around the four sides of the cushion (Fig. 49-3). As with the tops and bottoms, an additional ½- to ¾-inch allowance is needed when the pattern is cut for seams along the top and bottom edges of the side strip.

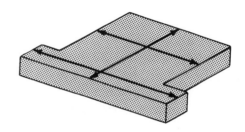

Fig. 49-2. Measurements for the top and bottom of a T-shaped cushion.

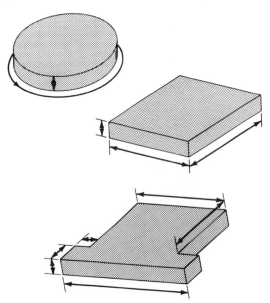

Fig. 49-3. Measurements for the side boxing of a cushion.

Making the Pattern

After obtaining the depth and width measurements, cut a paper pattern with at least a 4-inch allowance around each edge for final adjustment. Place the paper pattern on the seat and, with a marking pencil, draw a line coresponding to the upholstered curve of the inner arms and back around the edges of the pattern. Then, with a ruler, straighten the lines of the pattern until the cushion sides are straight from corner to corner. Provide an additional ½- to ¾-inch allowance around the edges for seams. This is the finished pattern for both the casing and the upholstery cover. Trim away any excess paper on the outside edge of the seam allowance; then the pattern is ready for pinning to the material. If a muslin pattern is preferable to a paper pattern, cut the pattern from a piece of muslin (for a cushion casing) or from a piece of the final cover fabric. Be sure to include a 4-inch allowance around each side for adjustments. Place the pattern over the seat, mark the edges, and cut out both a top and a bottom for the cushion (Fig. 49-4).

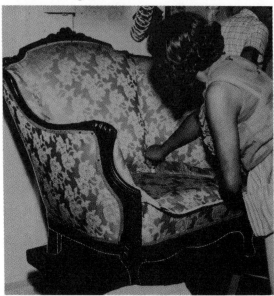

Fig. 49-4. Marking the outline of the cushion and cutting the cushion top.

Only slight adjustment of the measurements for the side strip is required. Do not forget to add an additional ½- to ¾-inch allowance along the top and bottom edges for seams, and a like allowance at the end of the side strip for a vertical seam on the back of the cushion, before cutting the pattern.

Stuffed Cushions (No Springs)

An inner lining is needed in cushions stuffed with feathers, down, or animal hair to prevent the stuffing working its way outward through the outer upholstery fabric; that is, it contains the stuffing. It is a wise practice to provide several compartments for the stuffing, to prevent the stuffing from sliding from one end of the cushion to the other end.

Stuffed cushions can be made either with a side strip on all four sides or with the top sewed directly to the bottom. In the latter method, a single seam is sewed around the entire cushion and concealed with a welting strip (Fig. 49-5).

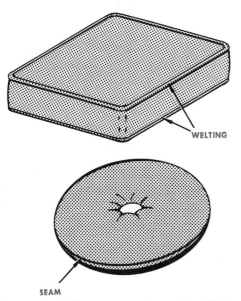

Fig. 49-5. Cushion construction with side boxing and without side boxing.

The steps in constructing a stuffed cushion with no springs are:

1. Place a paper pattern for the top and bottom on a heavy grade of muslin. Either pin the pattern to the material or carefully mark the edges of the pattern with a soft lead pencil. If the material is dark in color, chalk can be used for marking. Cut out the top and bottom; then lay them aside for a moment.

2. Place the pattern for the side strips on the muslin. Pin or mark the pattern on the material; then cut out the side strip.

3. Sew the bottom of the casing to the front and sides of the side strip, leaving the back open.

4. Insert the stuffing firmly into the casing, but do not pack it. The farthest corners (the front corners) should be filled first, filling outward from these corners. If animal hair, down, or kapok are used, separate the stuffing to prevent lumps when they are inserted into the casing.

5. In the cushion construction described above, it is a problem to prevent the stuffing sliding from end to end, especially when down or feathers are used. This results in packing or the formation of uncomfortable lumps. Prevent sliding of the stuffing by securing it in place with several stitches through the top of the casing (Fig. 49-6). Do not pull the

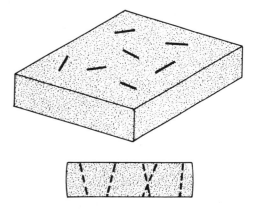

Fig. 49-6. Random stitches through the casing keep the stuffing in position.

stitches tightly enough to depress the cushion. The stitches merely hold the stuffing in position inside the casing.

6. Another method of preventing sliding of the stuffing is to divide the casing into several compartments. Divide the bottom cover into three equal sections. Using a soft-lead pencil, mark the two lines dividing the three sections on the inside of the bottom cover (Fig. 49-7). Sew

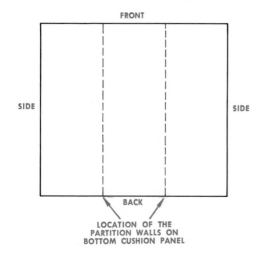

Fig. 49-7. Method of marking the location of the partition walls.

the side strips to the bottom all around the cushion, including the back.

7. The measurements of the two inner partition walls should be identical to the side strip (except for length). For example, if the side strip is 4 inches wide, with a ½-inch seam allowance on each edge, the partitioning walls should be the same width. The length of each inner partition should extend across the interior of the casing, with an allowance for sewing to the inside at the front and

back of the side walls of the cushion (Fig. 49-8).

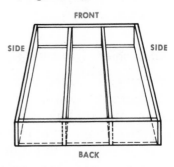

Fig. 49-8. Interior construction of a partitioned casing.

8. Sew the top covering of the casing in position, leaving a gap at the back for filling each compartment (Fig. 49-9).

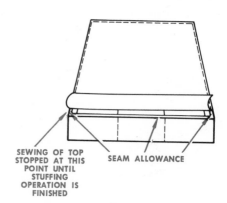

Fig. 49-9. Stuffing a partitioned casing.

9. Fill the casing with stuffing (see Step 4); then sew the remainder of the top closed.

10. The outer upholstery cover then can be constructed. The pattern used to cut the casing can be used to cut the outer upholstery cover. Exercise caution in centering the design (stripes, checks, etc.). For example, the stripes should be cut vertically with the bottom edge of the cushion (on the side strips) or parallel to

the side edge (on the top and bottom cover)—not diagonally to them (Fig. 49-10). Stripes extending

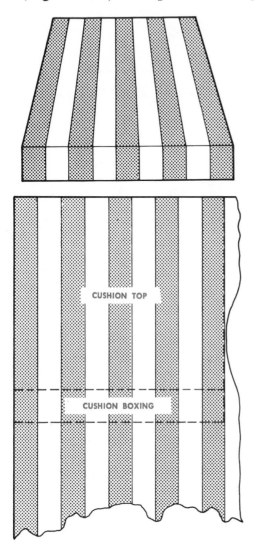

Fig. 49-10. Cutting a striped pattern.

from front to back on a cushion should be aligned to match the stripes on the inside back and bottom front of the chair or sofa. Failure to align the stripes detracts from the appearance of the job. Another chief difference in constructing the outer upholstery cover is that the edges of the material are not sewed together directly. Instead, welting is

inserted to conceal the seam. The seam itself is blind sewed (Fig. 49-11). The only place welting is not

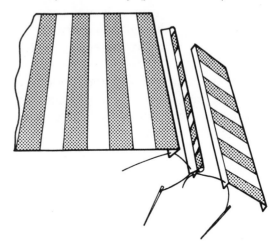

Fig. 49-11. Welting on the edge of a cushion conceals the seam.

used is on the vertical seam on the side strip at the back of the cushion. The material pattern on the welting, especially where stripes are involved, is positioned with the stripes placed diagonally when assembling the welting.

Stuffed Cushions (With Springs)

The springs used in cushions usually are less than 4 inches in both height and diameter, which is smaller than the springs used in general upholstery. The springs used in cushions should be sturdy, but compact, to fit between the layers of stuffing and cotton on the inside.

Each row of inner springs in the cushion is encased in muslin. First determine the number of rows required to fit the cushion. Then sew the rows together to build a section of springs of the required size.

The steps involved in constructing a stuffed cushion containing a section of springs are:

1. Measure and cut the pattern in the same manner described at the beginning of this unit. Using the pattern, cut a casing from a heavy grade of muslin. Use the same pattern to cut the pieces for the outer upholstery cover.

2. Sew the side strip to the bottom of the casing. Position the seam that joins the two ends of the side strip on the back of the casing, and sew it closed. This might be considered a trial or dry run, since the seam on the casing does not show. However, the seam on the outer upholstery cover is always located on the back of the cushion.

3. With the innerspring units, a layer of lightweight burlap provides additional protection against the stuffing slipping outward and working downward through the springs (Fig. 49-12).

Fig. 49-12. Innerspring unit covered with lightweight burlap.

4. Cover the bottom of the casing with a layer of cotton (Fig. 49-13).

5. Cover the layer of cotton with a 1½- to 2-inch layer of stuffing. Spread the stuffing and distribute it evenly. Place the innerspring unit on the layer of stuffing (see Fig. 49-13).

6. Spread a layer of stuffing across the top of the spring unit; then cover the stuffing with a layer of cotton. Cut a strip of cotton for the side strip, and sew the strip in position (Fig. 49-14).

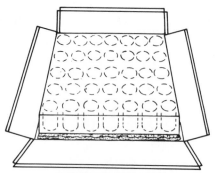

PLACING THE SPRING UNIT

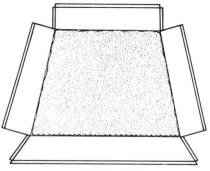

COTTON LAYER

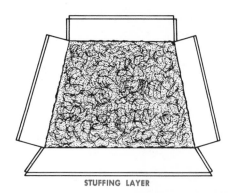

STUFFING LAYER

Fig. 49-13. Positioning the cotton and stuffing base inside a casing.

7. Sew the top of the casing to the side strips. Then the casing is ready for the upholstery cover. The patterns used to cut the casing can be used to make the cover. The seams should be blind sewed and concealed by lengths of welting (see Fig. 49-11).

8. Although Steps 1 through 7 describe the construction of a cushion with a

muslin cover, a cushion can be constructed without the casing. Also, the layer of lightweight burlap around the springs is optional (Fig. 49-15).

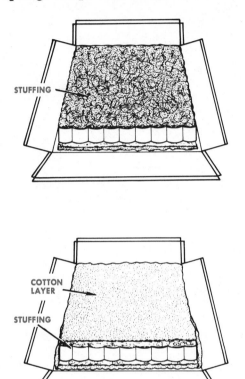

Fig. 49-14. Positioning the cotton and stuffing top layer inside the casing.

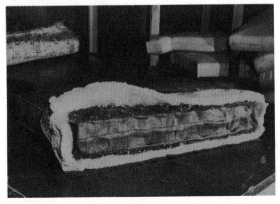

Fig. 49-15. Spring cushion constructed without a casing.

Zippers

A zipper, rather than sewing, sometimes is used to close the back of the outer upholstery cover. The zipper is placed in the center of the side strip extending across the back of the cushion. If the side strip is 3 inches in width (on the finished cushion), cut two strips 1½ inches wide, with a ⅝-inch allowance (to be turned under along the center edge), plus ½ to ¾ inches on each outer edge for the seam allowance (Fig. 49-16). First, sew the

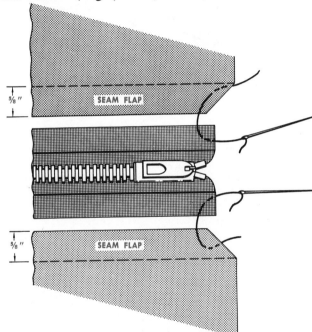

Fig. 49-16. Method of installing a zipper.

center edges and the zipper together. Note that the ⅝-inch allowance turned under along the center edge is sewed to the zipper material with a single stitch carried through the outer upholstery cover. The side strip with a zipper then is sewed to the top and bottom covers with a welting strip to conceal the seam (see Fig. 49-11). Since the back strip is a separate piece of material, vertical seams are used to connect it to the side strips at each corner. It is not necessary to use welting to conceal these seams.

It is recommended that the zipper be extended entirely across the back; therefore, the casing can be inserted or removed with less difficulty. The zipper openings on cushions vary from only a partial opening on the back (perhaps, 2 inches from each corner) to an opening extending around the back for several inches (Fig. 49-17). Zippers can be purchased in units

Fig. 49-17. Various zipper styles for cushions.

varying in length, along with instructions for installing them.

Installing Final Cover

Cushion irons usually are required to install the assembled spring cushion in the final cover. The cushion irons are used to compress the cushion for placing the cushion inside the outer cover (see Fig. 45-18).

A commercial machine is shown in Fig. 49-18. When the top is lowered, the sides move toward each other. This action compresses the inner cushion to a size smaller than the outer cover. The outer cover is then placed over the compressing plates of the machine (see Fig. 49-18). A foot control then moves a back plate toward the operator, pushing the inner cushion from the compressing plates and pulling the outer cover off the machine. When the stuffed cushion has cleared the machine, the rear zipper is closed and the

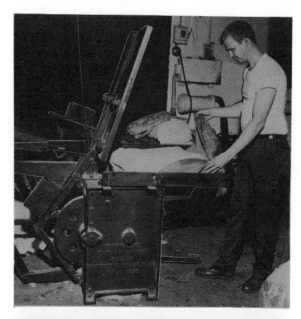

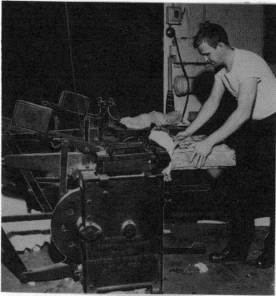

Fig. 49-18. Using a commercial cushion machine. (Courtesy Kwick-Bed Sofa Corp.)

cushion is completed. Prior to inserting the innerspring unit on a "Tee" cushion, the "Tee" ends are stuffed by hand.

Construction Pointers

In addition to making sure the design on the outer upholstery cover is centered properly, it is necessary to extend the same precaution to the pile fabric. The pile fabrics (velvet, velveteen, corduroy, mohair, etc.) have received their names from the short hairlike filaments that cover the surface. When a hand is moved over the surface of a pile fabric, the pile smooths or stands (like the fur on an animal), depending on the direction the hand is moved. Cut the outer upholstery cover in a way that the pile is smooth when the hand is moved toward the floor on the side strips and toward the front on the top of the cushion. If a piece of material is cut with the pile in the opposite direction—for example, contrasting pieces on the joined ends, the two slightly different colors produce a less attractive piece of upholstery or furniture.

The cushions can be made reversible or nonreversible. The reversible cushions require equal attention in centering the design of both the top and bottom covers. A plain good-quality material can be used for the bottom cover on a nonreversible cushion. The material on the sides overlaps the bottom to conceal the plain fabric from view.

Rather than cut separate top and bottom covers, a single piece of material can be used. This piece of material should be cut long enough to extend from the back bottom edge of the cushion around the front to the back top edge. The interior construction is the same; but a tightly rolled section of cotton can be used in place of a flat piece of cotton over the stuffing in front, to prove a slightly rounded appearance on the front of the cushion. The welting is extended around the top and bottom edges of the sides and back.

Questions

1. What are the two types of inner construction used in cushions for upholstery?
2. Describe briefly the method of making the pattern for a cushion.
3. What materials are used to stuff cushions which have no springs?
4. What two methods are used to close the backs of the outer covers on cushions?
5. What two methods are used to install the final cover on an assembled spring cushion?

Unit 50 – Padded Seats and Slip Seats

Overstuffed upholstery in furniture usually involves two sets of springs (seat and back) and several layers of stuffing and upholstery material, resulting in a piece of furniture with far more seating comfort than the other types of furniture. Also, it is usually much heavier and more expensive. On the other hand, tight-spring upholstery involves only one set of springs (in the seat) and a padded back, resulting in furniture lighter in weight and usually less expensive than the overstuffed furniture.

A third type of furniture upholstery involves the padded seats or slip seats, in which no springs are used. The bases of the padded seats are either a closed base (solid piece of wood) or an open base. Both the open and the closed seat bases can be attached permanently; or they can be removable. The removable seat base, also called "slip seats," can be removed by loosening the screws or fasteners holding it to the frame. The chairs with padded seats also can be constructed with padded backs which might be removable. The opening in an open-frame seat base is covered with webbing and burlap.

The upper outside edge of the wood is chamfered in both the closed (solid wood base) and the open bases on slip seats. The chamfered edge provides a smoother surface against the pull of the fabric (Fig. 50-1). Also, the chamfered edges are found frequently on the outside edges

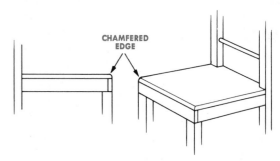

Fig. 50-1. Upper outside edge of seat base should be chamfered.

of closed seats on padded chairs. These seat bases are nonremovable.

Closed Seat Base (Nonremovable)

Upholstering a chair with a nonremovable closed seat base requires the following procedure:

1. If the seat is to be reupholstered, remove all the old upholstery. Examine the outside edges of the seat base. If necessary, round or chamfer these edges (Fig. 50-2). Round or chamfer

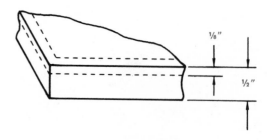

Fig. 50-2. Chamfer dimensions.

494

the edges to approximately one-quarter the thickness of the seat base. The rounding should be done on the front and both sides.

2. Since the closed seat construction consists of a solid wood base, there is no need for springs, webbing, or an initial layer of heavy burlap.

3. The seat can be padded with three types of stuffing: (1) loose (animal hair, moss, etc.), (2) cotton, or (3) foam padding.

4. If a loose stuffing is chosen, an edge roll must be attached around the seat base. The primary purpose of the edge roll is to prevent the stuffing slipping downward over the edges of the seat frame (Fig. 50-3). Read the instruc-

Fig. 50-4. Apply the first layer of loose stuffing.

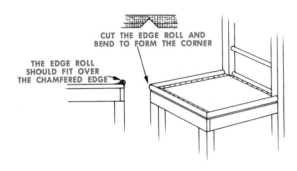

Fig. 50-3. Method of attaching the edge roll.

tions for attaching an edge roll in Unit 49.

5. Loose stuffing can be added in two layers. The first or lower layer is distributed level with the top of the edge roll. Spread the stuffing evenly, removing all the lumps as it is spread. Do not pack it down (Fig. 50-4).

6. Distribute the upper layer of stuffing in a manner that the edges of the seat will be firm (without lumps or depressions) and there will be a crown in the middle, when the layer of stuffing is compressed by the stuffing material (Fig. 50-5).

Fig. 50-5. Apply second layer of loose stuffing.

7. Cover the stuffing with a cotton pad, extending it over the edge roll (Fig. 50-6).

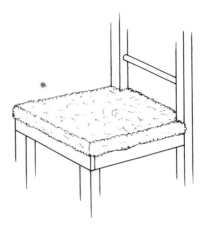

Fig. 50-6. Place the cotton padding over the layer of stuffing.

8. Measure and cut a piece of muslin to fit over the cotton pad, extending to the underneath edges of the side rails by at least ¾ inch. Tack the muslin to the frame (Fig. 50-7).

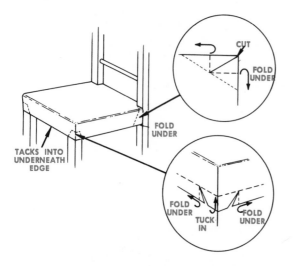

Fig. 50-7. Method of attaching the muslin.

a. For another method, place the muslin over the loose stuffing, extending it to the bottom and tack it. Place the cotton over the muslin cover; this is held in place by the outer cover (Fig. 50-8).

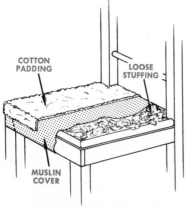

Fig. 50-8. Cutaway view of layers of muslin and cotton over loose stuffing.

b. For a third method, measure and cut a piece of lightweight burlap, extending it around the bottom for

tacking. Place the cotton over the burlap; then measure and cut a piece of muslin to fit over the cotton and around the bottom of the seat. Tack the muslin to the frame bottom (Fig. 50-9). The muslin is covered by the final cover.

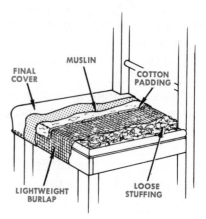

Fig. 50-9. Cutaway view of layers of burlap, cotton padding, and muslin over loose stuffing.

c. In still another method, the use of loose stuffing is avoided entirely. The lower layer is cut smaller than the upper layer and extends to (but does not overlap) the chamfered edge (Fig. 50-10). Foam

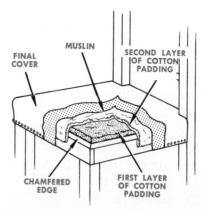

Fig. 50-10. A layer of cotton padding can replace the loose stuffing.

padding is used to replace the loose stuffing. This method is described in more detail in Unit 51

9. It is not necessary to extend the burlap and muslin layers around to the bottom of the frame. Since the side rails are wide enough, both layers of material can be tacked at midpoint (Fig. 50-11).

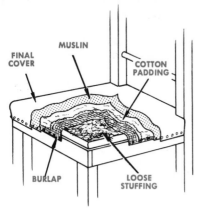

Fig. 50-11. Place tacks at midpoint on the seat rail.

Closed Seat Base (Removable)

1. Remove the seat from the chair. Usually, the seat is attached with screws through the bottom of the frame. Remove the old upholstery, if the seat is to be reupholstered (Fig. 50-12).

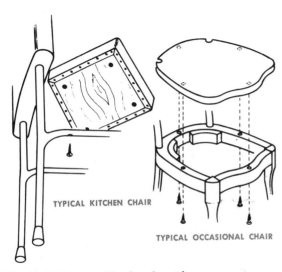

Fig. 50-12. Removable closed seat bases.

2. Since the arrangement of the layers of upholstery stuffing and material is a matter of personal choice, one of the methods described for the nonremovable closed seat base can be used. The chief factor is the degree of softness desired (Fig. 50-13).

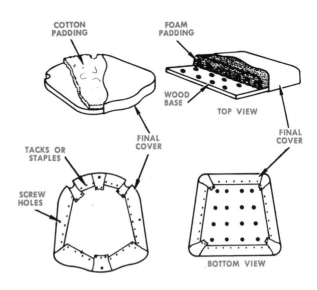

Fig. 50-13. Upholstery for removable closed seat bases.

Open Seat Base (Nonremovable)

The lightweight frame construction of this type of chair is similar to the tight-spring construction. The former does not use a spring base, which is the principal difference in the two types of construction (Fig. 50-14). The nonspring, padded chairs are used in bedrooms, dining rooms (in the more expensive dining room chairs), and in various locations in the home. Since they are light in weight, they can be moved easily. The padding also is quite comfortable.

It should be remembered that the webbing is attached to the top of the seat rail in the nonremovable open seat-base construction. The various steps in upholstering this type of furniture are shown in

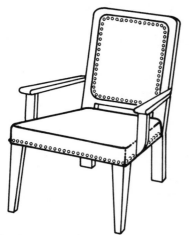

Fig. 50-14. Padded chair with nonremovable open seat base.

Fig. 50-15. Also, the various layers of material are shown in the diagram. Various layers of material can be added to increase the comfort. For example, a layer of foam rubber can be inserted to enhance the comfort.

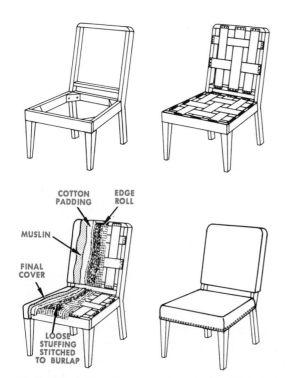

COTTON PADDING   EDGE ROLL
MUSLIN
FINAL COVER
LOOSE STUFFING STITCHED TO BURLAP

Fig. 50-15. Upholstery for nonremovable open seat base.

Open Seat Base (Removable)

A removable seat (slip seat) also can be provided on an open seat base. The opening is covered with webbing before the burlap is attached. The procedure for constructing a removable seat with an open seat base is:

1. Attach the webbing to the top of the seat base (Fig. 50-16). See Unit 46

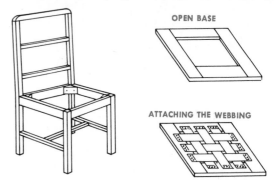

OPEN BASE

ATTACHING THE WEBBING

Fig. 50-16. Method of attaching the webbing on a removable open seat base.

for more detail in attaching the webbing.
2. Measure and cut a piece of heavy-weight burlap to fit over the webbing. Do not extend the burlap to overlap the edges of the open seat base. Fold back the burlap and tack down on the upper surface. A tacking strip can be used to provide additional tacking strength (Fig. 50-17). This strip can

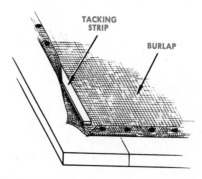

TACKING STRIP
BURLAP

Fig. 50-17. Tacking strips can be used to attach a burlap panel to webbing.

be either open-tacked or blind-tacked —the latter is stronger.

3. The remaining procedure is diagrammed in Fig. 50-18. Basically, it is identical to the construction described for construction of a removable closed seat base. Note that the second layer of cotton (Fig. 50-18C) extends around to the bottom outside edge of the seat base; however, it does not extend underneath the bottom of the seat base. Only the muslin (Figs. 50-18D and 50-18E) and the final cover extend underneath—where they are tacked in place. The muslin and the final cover are attached in the same manner, except that more care is required in making the corners.

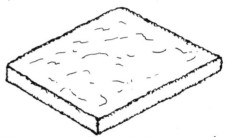

(C) Extend a second layer of cotton over and around to the bottom outside edge of the seat base.

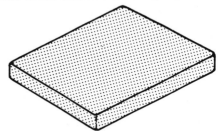

(D) Install the muslin cover.

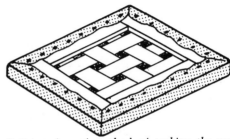

(E) Bottom view of method of tacking the muslin cover.

Fig. 50-18. Upholstery procedure for a removable open seat base.

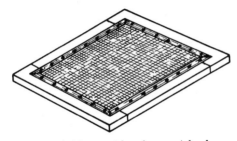

(A) Cover the webbing with a layer of burlap.

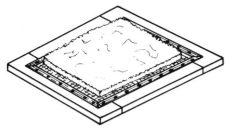

(B) Place a layer of cotton over the burlap.

Questions

1. List the three types of construction used in upholstery of overstuffed furniture.
2. What is meant by a "slip seat"?
3. What is meant by padded seat construction?
4. What is meant by a closed seat base?
5. Where are the nonspring, padded chairs usually found in the home?

Unit 51 – Foam Padding

Foam padding is a product made from either natural rubber or plastic, which is synthetic. Its density varies from very soft to very firm, depending on the air content. The degree of softness or firmness is determined by the weight required to produce a depression of 25 percent. Therefore, an extra-soft density requires 5-10 pound pressure, whereas a firm density needs 40 pounds or more pressure.

Foam rubber produced from natural rubber is produced by whipping the latex mixture, which is composed of latex, gelling agents, and other ingredients, until a mixture of approximately 85-percent air to 15-percent rubber is obtained. Flexible polyurethane foam, which is the plastic derivative, is produced by introducing a chemical activator into the plastic base materials. Polyurethane foam is cheaper than foam rubber. Also, it is lighter in weight. A 22-inch square piece of polyurethane foam that is 4 inches in thickness weighs 1 lb 4 oz. On the other hand, a piece of foam rubber identical in size weighs 5 lb 3 oz. Foam rubber also is considerably more expensive than polyurethane foam. Thus, the weight and price factors have resulted in the replacement of foam rubber for upholstery and cushioning material by the polyurethane foam.

Manufactured Product

The foam rubber is manufactured in four types of stock. These are: (1) slab stock, (2) core stock, (3) molded cushion units, and (4) molded pillow units.

Slab stock (Fig. 51-1) is a thin pad ranging in thickness from ¼ to 2 inches

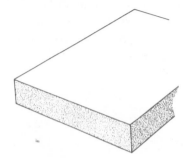

Fig. 51-1. Slab stock.

in ¼-inch graduations. It can be purchased in various widths and lengths, depending on the manufacturer. Foam rubber slab stock is available in four densities: (1) very soft (5-10 lb), (2) soft (10-25 lb), (3) medium (25-50 lb), and 4) firm (40-60 lb).

Cored stock or cored utility stock (Fig. 51-2) contains numerous cores of

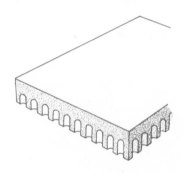

Fig. 51-2. Cored stock.

uniform size, shape, and distribution. The cores produce greater resiliency in the material, which results in greater seating comfort. Its thickness ranges from ¾ inch to 4½ inches. The widths and lengths depend on the manufacturer. Cored stock is available in the same densities as slab stock, and in an additional grade of extra-firm (60-85 lb).

The molded cushion units (Fig. 51-3) are completely molded pieces of foam padding used in making cushions or bolsters. Square and rectangular cushion units are available in the following sizes:

12 × 12	18 × 22	22 × 22
16 × 16	20 × 20	22 × 24
16 × 18	20 × 22	22 × 32
18 × 20	20 × 24	22 × 36

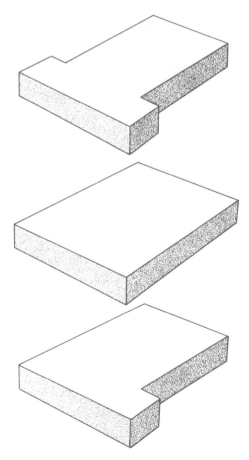

Fig. 51-3. Types of molded cushion units.

T-shaped and L-shaped cushion units also are available. Bolster units can be found in wedge or round shapes. The molded pillow units (Fig. 51-4) are man-

Fig. 51-4. Molded pillow units.

ufactured in round or square shapes, and are available in 12 × 12, 14 × 14, and 16 × 16 sizes. Both the cushion and pillow units are available in a variety of thicknesses.

Flexible polyurethane foam can be purchased in three forms: (1) slab stock or pad form, (2) molded cushion units, and (3) molded pillow units. The sizes offered are similar to the sizes available in foam rubber. However, cored stock cannot be purchased in polyurethane foam.

Advantages of Foam Padding

Neither foam rubber nor flexible polyurethane foam will mildew, which is not true with other types of foam padding, and they are nonallergenic. Although foam padding is slightly more expensive than other padding, it is much easier to work with. Also, it is lightweight, resilient, and washable. Foam padding provides a comfortable, uniform support by equalizing the pressure at the point of contact. When the pressure is removed, the foam padding immediately resumes its shape.

Tools and Supplies

A pair of heavy shears (at least 6 inches long) is recommended for cutting foam padding. The padding can be marked for cuts on the smooth side with a marking pen and straightedge. Soapstone, a powdery stone which feels soapy, is sprinkled across the surface of the working area to prevent sticking or gripping of the foam pad. Also, it is used to absorb the excess bonding cement along the edges of the seams; or it can be dusted into the holes in cored stock to prevent sticking together of the core walls.

The manufacturer of foam padding usually sells a bonding cement for use with his product. The bonding cement can be used on both foam rubber and flexible polyurethane foam. It is used not only to bond the seams together but also to fasten the tacking or reinforcement tape to cement the padding to the base. The tapes can be purchased in various widths, depending on the requirements of the piece of work.

Laying Out and Cutting Foam Padding

Foam padding is quite resilient; it gives quite easily under pressure, but immediately springs back when the pressure is released. Therefore, if the upholstery covers are to fit smoothly and snugly, the foam padding must be cut slightly larger than the measurements designated for the pattern. The excess, or allowance, is determined by the size of the padding and by its firmness. However, this practice does not hold true for fully molded reversible cushions, pillows, or bolsters, since an allowance is included in their measurements before they are cut.

A firm padding requires a smaller allowance than the softer padding. The larger pieces of padding require larger al-

lowances than the smaller pieces. A padding less than 6 inches in width should receive an allowance of ¼ inch. Up to 12 inches in width, the allowance should be ½ inch, and above a 12-inch width, the allowance increases ¼ inch to ½ inch for each 12 inches of width (Table 51-1).

Table 51-1. Allowances for Measurements in Excess of 1 Foot

Measurement	Allowance
12-23"	1"
24-35"	1¼"
36-47"	1½"
48-59"	1¾"
60-71"	2"
72-83"	2¼"

All the various thicknesses of slab stock can be cut with heavy shears. This is also true for cored stock up to 2 inches thickness. The thicker cored stock should be cut twice—once along the top and once along the bottom. The top cut is made first across the smooth (closed) surface. The cut must be deep enough to separate each core at the top. The second cut is made from the bottom (the open cores) for the purpose of separating the core walls. Either heavy shears or a sharp knife can be used to make the two cuts (Fig. 51-5).

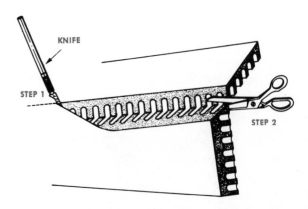

Fig. 51-5. Cutting cored stock.

Reversible or Loose Cushions

Both foam rubber (cored stock) and polyurethane foam can be purchased in T-shaped, L-shaped, square, and rectangular cushions on a piece of furniture. These cushions are manufactured in various sizes, and it is not difficult to find the desired size. A slight crown is sometimes found on the cushions. A higher crown can be formed by gluing together two pieces of crowned cored foam rubber. The procedure is as follows:

1. After selecting two crowned and cored sections of equal measurements, position them with the core openings together. After making sure the dimensions of the two pieces match, apply the bonding cement to their surfaces (Fig. 51-6). Place the two pieces on

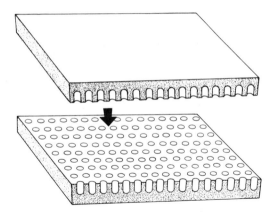

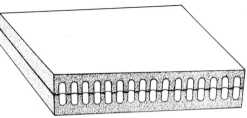

Fig. 51-7. Glue the two pieces of foam padding together and let dry.

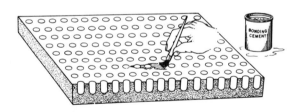

Fig. 51-6. Applying the bonding cement.

a flat surface with the core openings facing upward. Brush the bonding cement onto the surface; permit it to dry until the surface is tacky.

2. When the cement has become tacky, place the two halves together. Make sure they are both aligned correctly. Hold them in this position for 1 or 2 minutes. Let them dry for 2 hours (Fig. 51-7).

The crown can be increased by beveling the open core bottoms and inserting a few glued layers of thin slab stock before cementing the two halves together (Fig. 51-8). The total material removed

from the top and bottom by beveling should be less than the total thickness of the slab insert—the greater the difference, the greater the arch.

The edges of the cushion can be given a rounded contour by cementing a piece of slab foam padding onto each side of the cushion. This padding should be 1½ to 2 inches less than the center crown of the cushion. Its length should be identical to the length of the cushion side to which

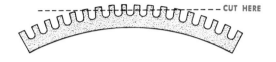

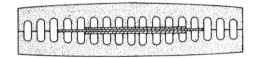

Fig. 51-8. Insert thin slab stock to form a crown.

it is glued. Cement the slab to the edge of the cushion, using tape for additional joint strength (Fig. 51-9). The tape can

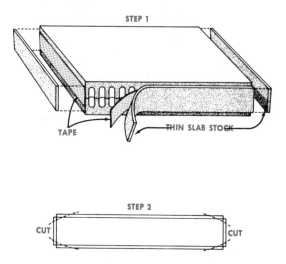

STEP 1

TAPE

THIN SLAB STOCK

STEP 2

CUT   CUT

Fig. 51-9. Cement foam slabs to the sides of the cushion.

be purchased with the bonding cement. The combined unit can be cut for the desired contour.

Attaching Foam Padding

Foam padding can be attached to either an open or a closed base. Springs, webbing, or both springs and webbing can be used on an open base. The very nature of open construction provides ample ventilation when using foam padding. However, a closed base made of metal, wood, or plastic should have holes drilled through it at evenly spaced intervals to provide the necessary ventilation (Fig. 51-10). Tape can be glued to the sides and folded under the bottom for tacking to hold the foam securely in place.

If springs are used for a base, they should be covered with burlap which is stitched to the coil tops. The foam padding then is placed over the burlap, and can be covered with a layer of muslin (Fig. 51-11).

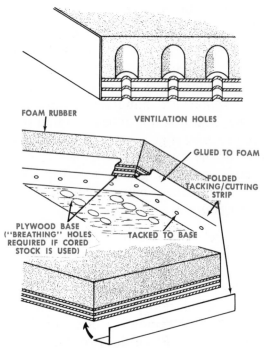

FOAM RUBBER

VENTILATION HOLES

GLUED TO FOAM

FOLDED TACKING/CUTTING STRIP

PLYWOOD BASE ("BREATHING" HOLES REQUIRED IF CORED STOCK IS USED)

TACKED TO BASE

Fig. 51-10. Method of placing foam padding over a closed or solid seat base.

Forming Edges

The chief advantage of working with foam padding is the ease with which the edges can be made. Three of the more common edges are: (1) square or

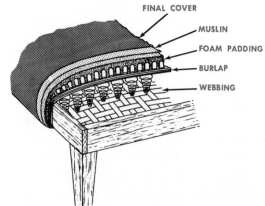

FINAL COVER

MUSLIN

FOAM PADDING

BURLAP

WEBBING

Fig. 51-11. Cutaway view of foam padding used with spring construction.

straight, (2) cushion, and (3) feather or contour edge (Fig. 51-12).

The square or straight edge is cut with a ¼- to ½-inch overhang around the

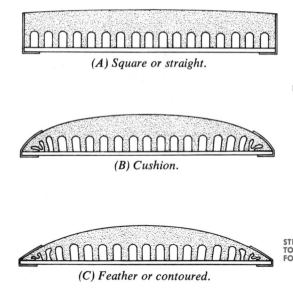

(A) Square or straight.

(B) Cushion.

(C) Feather or contoured.

Fig. 51-12. Three types of edges for foam padding.

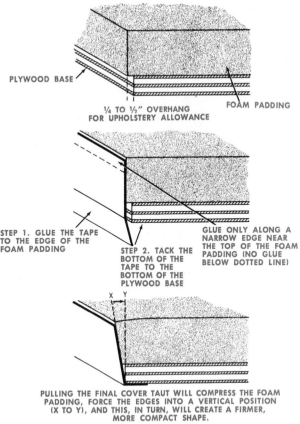

PLYWOOD BASE

¼ TO ½" OVERHANG FOR UPHOLSTERY ALLOWANCE

FOAM PADDING

STEP 1. GLUE THE TAPE TO THE EDGE OF THE FOAM PADDING

STEP 2. TACK THE BOTTOM OF THE TAPE TO THE BOTTOM OF THE PLYWOOD BASE

GLUE ONLY ALONG A NARROW EDGE NEAR THE TOP OF THE FOAM PADDING (NO GLUE BELOW DOTTED LINE)

X Y

PULLING THE FINAL COVER TAUT WILL COMPRESS THE FOAM PADDING, FORCE THE EDGES INTO A VERTICAL POSITION (X TO Y), AND THIS, IN TURN, WILL CREATE A FIRMER, MORE COMPACT SHAPE.

Fig. 51-13. Forming a square edge.

edges of the base. This overhang is the upholstery allowance. Attach the tape to the sides of the foam padding and bend the excess tape around to the bottom of the base. *Do not* pull it taut—or the contour of the square edge will be distorted. Tack the tape to the bottom of the base. The edge will not be truly vertical, because the upholstery allowance (the top of the pad) still extends beyond the base. When the cover is placed over the padding, the overhang will be eliminated (Fig. 51-13).

To form the cushion edge, cut the foam for a ⅞-inch overhang. The tape is cemented 1 inch inward on the upper edge of the foam padding and allowed to dry. Then it is pulled downward, until the upper outside edge is even with the top of the base. Extend the excess tape around to the bottom of the base, and tack it in place. This causes the core walls near the outside edge of the padding to collapse and be forced inward toward the center of the padding. This is important in formation of the cushion edge; therefore, do not cement the bottom of the padding to the base (Fig. 51-14).

The feather or contour edge is distinguished from the cushion edge in that the curvature of the edge is more gradual. The feather edge is formed by compressing (tucking under) the cores. The overhang allowance for the foam pad is identical to that for the cushion edge; however, the lower outside edge is beveled. The beveling determines the degree of curvature for the feather edge. The tape is applied as described for the feather edge in (Fig. 51-15).

Crowns, Saddle Seats, and Slip Seats

Both the feather and the cushion edges produce slight crowns. However, the higher crowns, especially near the center of the seat, can be constructed by inserting sections of slab stock beneath the

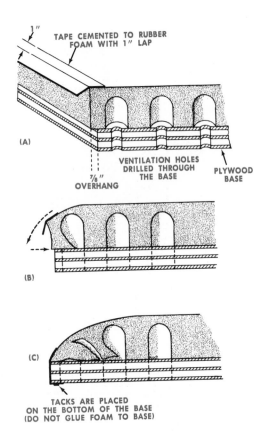

Fig. 51-14. Forming a cushion edge.

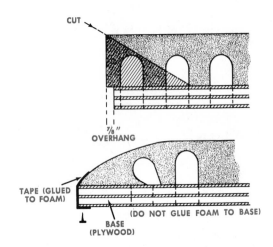

Fig. 51-15. Forming a feather or contoured edge.

main padding. The height of the crown depends on the number and thickness of the slab stock sections inserted.

The opposite condition of the crown is the contoured depression found in saddle seats or seats molded to fit the shape of the human body. The wood base should be cut to the desired shape and then covered with a thin layer of slab foam padding.

Slab stock also is used in constructing the slip seats. The padding is approximately ¾ to 1 inch in thickness, and is cut to include an upholstery allowance of ¼ to ½ inch. (Fig. 51-16).

Backs

The backs can be cut from either solid slab or cored stock. The base for the back can be either closed or open. Again, remember to provide the necessary ventilation holes in a closed base. Since the backs receive less pressure than the seats, foam padding which is softer in density usually is used in their construction. The methods used in construction of the backs are identical to those used in constructing the seats.

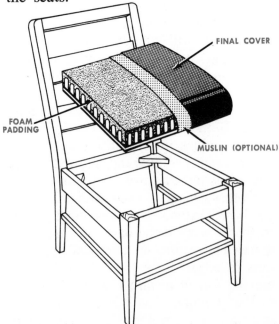

Fig. 51-16. Cutaway view of a foam-padded slip seat.

Arms

Either solid slab or cored stock is used on the arms, especially on the inside arm sections of overstuffed furniture. Again, a softer-density padding usually is used, since the pressure is not so great against this surface (Fig. 51-17). Also, note that

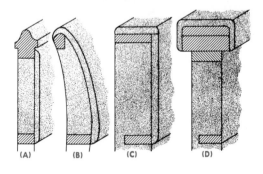

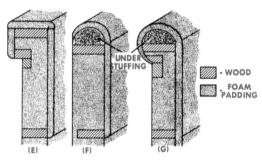

Fig. 51-17. Steps in construction of an arm using foam padding.

stuffing can be placed between the foam padding and the top of the arm rail for greater resiliency.

Pipes and Tufts

Foam padding makes the construction of pipes (channels) and tufts much easier than construction with loose stuffing, because the foam padding can be cut to the desired shape. Then each section is of uniform size and in a single piece. Note the steps in using foam padding to construct channels (pipes) in Fig. 51-18 and tufts in Fig. 51-19. The formed channel slabs are inserted into pockets in the final cover.

Upholstery Cover

The upholstery cover is attached over foam padding in the same way it is attached over loose stuffing. Usually, a muslin cover is not needed over foam padding, although it can be used to reduce possible friction between the padding and the outer cover.

Bolsters

The long pillows used to extend the width of a couch or bed are called bolsters. They are loose (not permanently attached to the furniture) and are covered with an upholstery fabric. The fabric of the bolster can be either sewed permanently or made removable by placing a zipper along one side. Bolsters are found

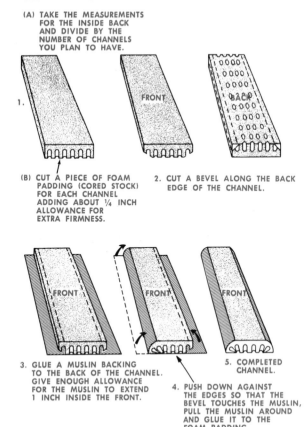

Fig. 51-18. Channels constructed from foam padding.

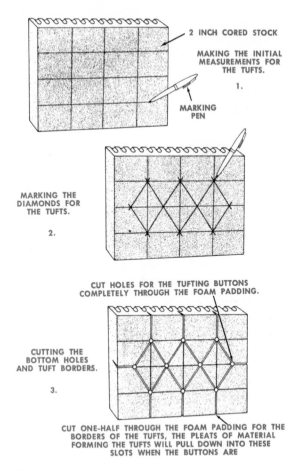

2 INCH CORED STOCK

MAKING THE INITIAL MEASUREMENTS FOR THE TUFTS.

1.

MARKING PEN

MARKING THE DIAMONDS FOR THE TUFTS.

2.

CUT HOLES FOR THE TUFTING BUTTONS COMPLETELY THROUGH THE FOAM PADDING.

CUTTING THE BOTTOM HOLES AND TUFT BORDERS.

3.

CUT ONE-HALF THROUGH THE FOAM PADDING FOR THE BORDERS OF THE TUFTS, THE PLEATS OF MATERIAL FORMING THE TUFTS WILL PULL DOWN INTO THESE SLOTS WHEN THE BUTTONS ARE

Fig. 51-19. Method of constructing tufts with foam padding.

in various sizes and shapes, including wedge, round, and square shapes (Fig. 51-20. The shape can be changed by cementing pieces of foam padding to the bolster or by cutting away unwanted material.

Foam padding can be purchased in premolded shapes for constructing bolsters. Generally, these are either wedge-shaped or roll-shaped. As with the reversible (or loose) cushions and pillows, the uphol-

stery allowance is already included in their measurements. A muslin cover is not needed between the upholstery cover and the foam padding in a bolster.

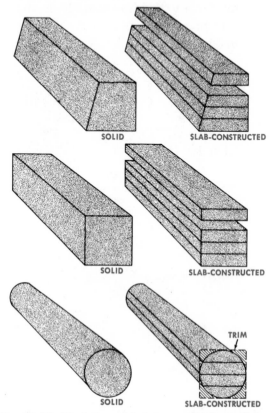

SOLID   SLAB-CONSTRUCTED

SOLID   SLAB-CONSTRUCTED

TRIM

SOLID   SLAB-CONSTRUCTED

Fig. 51-20. Varieties of bolsters made from foam padding.

Questions

1. How is foam padding produced?
2. List the four types of stock in which foam rubber is manufactured.
3. List the advantages of foam padding.
4. In what shapes can foam rubber cushions for furniture be purchased?
5. What is the chief advantage in working with foam padding?

Index